THE ANCIENT WORLD

800 B.C.—A.D. 800

Western Society: Institutions and Ideals

THE SERIES VOLUMES AND THEIR EDITORS:

Volume I THE ANCIENT WORLD: 800 B.C.-A.D. 800
Richard J. Burke, Jr., Oakland University

Volume II THE MEDIEVAL WORLD AND ITS TRANSFORMATIONS 800-1650
Gerald M. Straka, University of Delaware

Volume III THE MODERN WORLD: 1650-1850
Peter H. Amann, State University of New York at Binghamton

Volume IV THE CONTEMPORARY WORLD: Since 1850
Melvin Cherno, Oakland University

McGRAW-HILL BOOK COMPANY *New York St. Louis San Francisco Toronto London Sydney*

Richard J. Burke, Jr.
Associate Professor of Philosophy, Oakland University

VOLUME I

THE ANCIENT WORLD

800 B.C. — A.D. 800

THE ANCIENT WORLD 800 B.C.—A.D. 800, Volume I

Library of Congress Catalog Card Number 67-10882

1 2 3 4 5 6 7 8 9 0 H D 7 4 3 2 1 0 6 9 8 7

The following articles or selections have been reprinted in this volume with the permission of the publishers:

Selection from THE ILIAD, translated from Homer by Alston Hurd Chase and William G. Perry, Jr. Copyright 1950, by A. H. Chase and W. G. Perry, Jr. Reprinted by permission of Atlantic—Little, Brown & Co.

"Antigone," from THE THEBAN PLAYS of Sophocles, translated by E. F. Watling. Penguin Books, 1947.

Selection from Aristotle, PARTS OF ANIMALS, translated by A. L. Peck. Loeb Classical Library, Harvard University Press, 1961.

Selection from Sextus Empiricus, OUTLINES OF PYRRHONISM, translated by R. B. Bury. Loeb Classical Library, Harvard University Press, 1933.

Selection from THE NATURE OF THE UNIVERSE by Lucretius, translated by R. E. Latham. Penguin Books, 1951.

Selection from THE MISHNAH, translated by H. Danby. The Clarendon Press, Oxford, 1933.

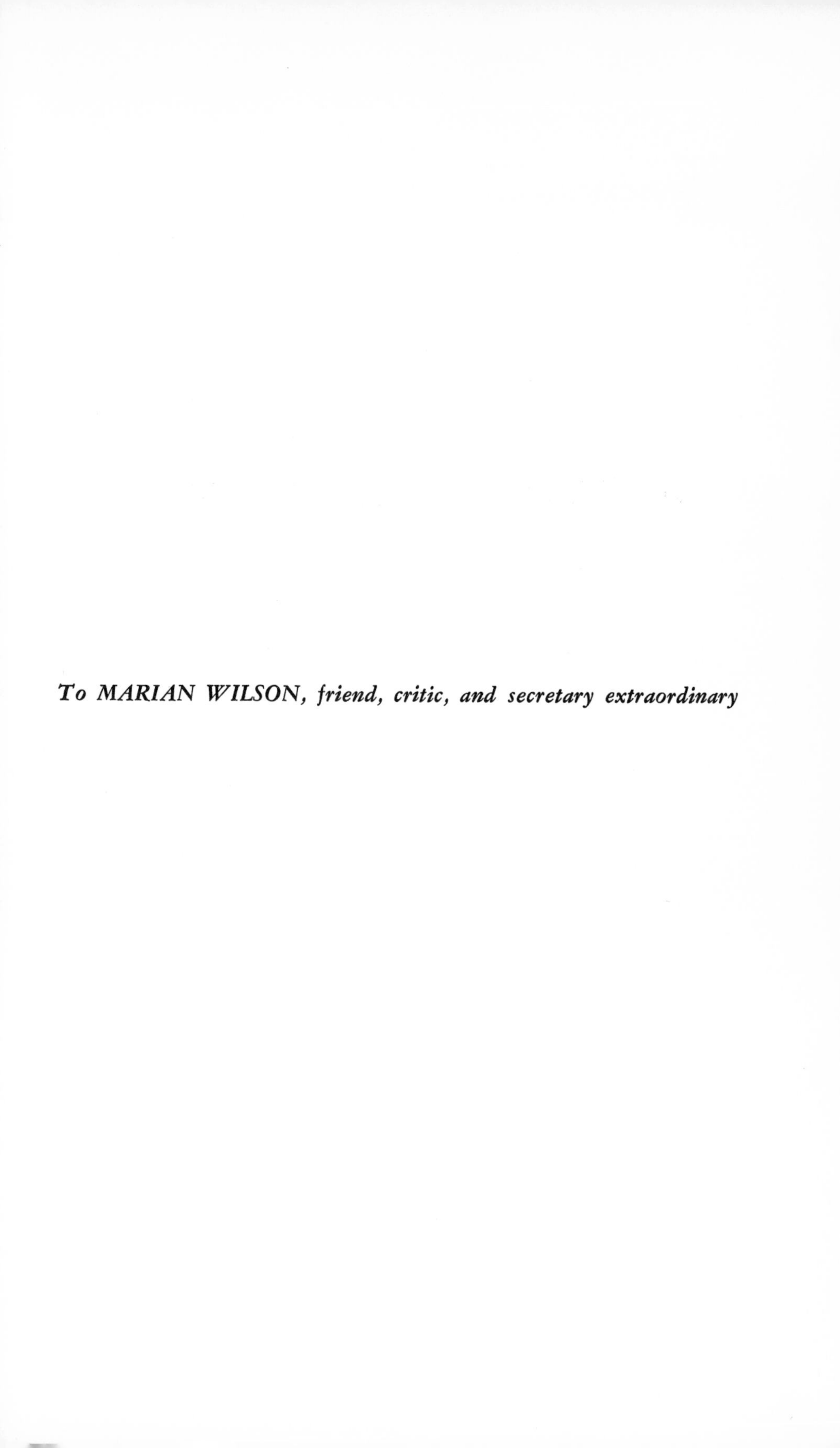

To MARIAN WILSON, friend, critic, and secretary extraordinary

Preface

This anthology grew out of a college freshman course in Western Institutions and Social Ideas taught by a staff that used original sources as materials for discussion and analysis. To keep a discussion course stimulating and exciting to teacher and student alike, we found ourselves supplementing existing anthologies with new documents. This anthology is the logical end product of these efforts. On the basis of our experience in discussing original documents in an introductory course, we determined that three principles should characterize our anthology.

First, we asked that an anthology have a range sufficient to allow real flexibility. A useful anthology should permit the revamping of a course from year to year, if only to prevent the instructors from going stale. In theory, our four volumes at well over one million words could include enough selections to supply a two-year discussion course meeting four days a week. Attractive as some of us might find such a prospect most Western civilization courses meet for a single academic year and, at that, for one or two weekly discussion sessions. We would expect most courses to use less than half of the anthologized documents in any one year. Consequently, this anthology should provide every instructor (or staff) with ample leeway to assign material to fit his particular students.

Our arrangement of the readings within each of the four volumes is topical as well as chronological. Although we have grouped together documents that are likely to be discussed together (or that provide a common pool from which to choose one reading) and have put them in what seems to us a sensible sequence, our organization in no way impinges upon the freedom of the instructor to rearrange as he sees fit.

Second, we felt that a useful anthology should have definite limits and a point of view; otherwise flexibility might dissolve into chaos. Our limits are explicit: we selected documents either to portray ideas about Western society or to illustrate Western political, economic, religious, or other institutions. We did not seek to present historical events as such, leaving this task to a text or to the discretion of the instructor. By focusing on institutions and social ideas, we excluded "pure" philosophy (such as linguistic analysis) and "pure" science (such as the Quantum Theory) on the one hand, and literature and art for their own sakes on the other. Selections from Chaucer's *Canterbury Tales* and Dostoevski's *The Brothers Karamazov* appear in this collection because in our judgment they illustrate certain values and institutions better than other available documents. It is in any case obvious that with the availability of primary works in paperback, an instructor who so wishes can easily pick supplementary literary works. By focusing on the

West, we have deliberately excluded documents from cultures like the Byzantine or Islamic that are related, yet raise complex questions of affiliations best handled in text or lecture.

Third, we relied on our classroom experience for selecting documents that by their content and format lend themselves to fruitful and interesting discussion. By choosing selections of from ten to twenty pages, we have been able to include many documents in full and others in excerpts substantial enough to permit the author's line of argument and point of view to emerge. Although almost every conceivable type of document—from philosophical treatise to personal diary—is represented, we have been sparing in the use of legal and constitutional texts that tend to appeal to professional historians, but are too technical for undergraduate discussion. In making our selections, we have tried neither to draw up a catalogue of familiar names nor to stock a museum of esoterica. We have tried to find and edit the most interesting and significant documents that illustrate major ideological and institutional trends. Some two dozen documents have been especially translated into English for this anthology. Our guidelines throughout have been significance, intrinsic interest, and discussability.

Our introductions preceding the documents attempt to provide just enough background to permit intelligent reading, without prejudging issues by means of capsule summaries or leading questions. They make no claim to provide continuity or depth. We consider it more constructive to suggest to the student—in the short introductory essay following the Table of Contents—the kinds of questions by which he can learn to come to grips with original sources for himself.

From its half-conscious inception to its final form, this four-volume anthology has been a collective venture on the part of three historians and one philosopher. Not only did all the editors participate in the detailed planning of each volume, but each of us has contributed selections and introductions to each of the four volumes. Our overriding concern has been to produce a collection of readings that would be interesting, unhackneyed, and enjoyable to use. We can only hope that we have succeeded.

Richard J. Burke, Jr.

Peter H. Amann
Melvin Cherno
Gerald M. Straka

Contents

III THE JUDAEO–CHRISTIAN TRADITION

IV THE EARLY GERMANS

On Reading Original Sources

TO THE STUDENT

A generation ago the historian Carl Becker shocked an after-dinner audience with a speech entitled, "Every Man His Own Historian." His audience was made up of members of the American Historical Association who had come to honor and hear their newly elected president. Yet Becker upset their mental equilibrium—and their digestion—by suggesting that history was not some secret art to be passed on to a cloistered initiate who would emerge years later from behind ivy walls with eyesight impaired and a Ph.D. to his name. Becker's point was that man's attempt to make sense of his own past was a natural and universal concern; that since no two men were alike, every man had to deal with the past—to be his own historian—in terms meaningful to himself. Yet Becker did not imply that all men were equally qualified for the task. Though the past is always seen through human eyes—by someone with interests, predilections, prejudices, and blind spots—there is nonetheless something like 20/20 vision in history as opposed to the myopia that results from lack of training. There are *some* tricks to the trade, and they can be learned.

One of the aims of any course using an anthology such as this is to provide you with some critical insight into the unavoidable job of being your own historian. All your life you will have to come to terms with the past, whether it be yesterday's personal encounter or the international roulette wheel stopping at your number. Even most family arguments boil down to historical controversy.

In dealing with the readings in this anthology, your first objective should be to master the technique of being your own *competent* historian. Here you are asked to make sense of a cultural tradition by analyzing documents illustrating different aspects of that tradition. The variety of documents that you will face is enormous. They may be roughly classified as follows:

1 History, biography, autobiography
2 Letters, journals, memoirs
3 Philosophical and scientific treatises
4 Speeches, sermons, manifestoes, public debates
5 Articles in periodicals
6 Essays, dialogues, poetry
7 Legal and constitutional documents
8 Diplomatic reports

You may best begin your analysis by following some rather basic considerations. Every one of these documents may be studied from various perspectives: each will have (1) an author, (2) a social and cultural context, (3) a purpose or function, (4) a subject matter, (5) a structure and method, and (6) relationships with and affiliations to other documents. You can make each of these "dimensions" of a document a focus for analysis, either by yourself or in class discussion. Each is a *direction* in which you can strike out; each suggests a *question* or a cluster of questions that you can raise about the document. If you learn to ask these questions habitually while reading, you are well on your way toward a critical understanding of history, even in its more difficult social and intellectual aspects.

Dimension 1: The Author. You may read a document as an expression of the author's point of view. A presidential message to Congress, for instance, is an expression of presidential policy on a given problem or problems. You may raise the question of the author's background, of his values and biases. In most cases this is a straightforward enough question. Sometimes this may be a crucial question, although at other times it is of minor importance or even altogether irrelevant.

Dimension 2: The Historical Context. You may read a document as reflecting the social and cultural milieu out of which it comes. When a Chinese leader makes a statement of national policy, for example, to what extent do his ideas and the way in which he puts them reflect the historical experience of China on the one hand, of the Chinese Communist movement on the other? This kind of question is related to the previous one, yet it is broader: it involves the ideas and values held during whole historical eras. You should learn to move back and forth between textbook and documents, evaluating the textbook interpretations of the Protestant Reformation or of the Industrial Revolution in terms of generalizations you have drawn from your original readings for each period.

Dimension 3: The Purpose. Not all documents aim simply to tell the truth, the whole truth, and nothing but the truth. Many of them, through the use of rhetorical devices, are designed to win a case, whether in an actual court, in formal debate, or in a wider forum of opinion. Many are pitched to a special audience to get some particular point across, for instance, a speech of Adolf Hitler's addressing a Nazi party rally Some are justifications of actions already taken, others exhortations for the future Clearly, all written documents are intelligible only in terms of the purpose or function they intended to serve and of the audience they attempted to reach.

Dimension 4: The Subject Matter. This may be the obvious question, yet it may not always be easy to answer. What is the reading about? You should practice summarizing documents in your own words and as briefly as possible, particularly when this is difficult to do. You may have to summarize ideas that have been advanced or to characterize institutions that have been described or exemplified. In historical or biographical narratives, subject matter is normally central. What were the ancient Germans like? What sort of man was Leonardo da Vinci? What was the structure of the ancient Roman Republic? What was life like at the court of Louis XIV of France

Dimension 5: Structure and Method. This is the *internal* dimension. How does a document hang together? What is the relation of the parts to the whole? *How* does the President present his case for certain legislation to Congress? In a straightforward historical narrative or a list of grievances, these internal relationships may be very simple; in a philosophical treatise or in a tragedy the internal structure may be very complex and artful. If a document presents an *argument,* then the question of its validity is perfectly in order, as is the question of the truth of its premises.

Dimension 6: Relationships to Other Documents. In this broad category fall all the questions about the influence of earlier writers on later ones and about similarities, contrasts, "climates of opinion," and traditions. How does the foreign policy statement of our Chinese Communist leader compare with earlier such announcements? With announced Russian Communist aims, recent and in Lenin's day? With the way non-Communist countries justify and announce their policy? Does our Chinese Communist seem to follow the guidelines for holding on to power suggested by Machiavelli in the sixteenth century? You may consider a given document as an effect of earlier developments and as a cause of subsequent ones. It may be combined with others of its own period to form a trend. It may be grouped in countless ways. As editors, we have already done some grouping by dividing the readings into four volumes and by choosing an arrangement within the volumes that is partly topical. Your instructor, by assigning some readings and not others, will have made yet another such grouping.

All this may seem very abstract and remote, until you really get down to cases. Take, as an example, the Declaration of Independence of July 4, 1776 (see Vol. III, pages 327–330). This document is at least vaguely familiar to most Americans, yet it reveals its full significance—as well as a nest of controversial issues—only when analyzed in terms of the six dimensions that have been suggested.

The Declaration of Independence was drafted chiefly by Thomas Jefferson, revised by a committee that included Benjamin Franklin and John Adams, and signed by all fifty-six delegates to the Second Continental Congress, the representatives of the "Thirteen" United States of America. Who, then, was its *author?* Does it really represent the views of all the inhabitants of those thirteen states? A majority of them? How were the delegates elected?

The social and cultural *context* of the document was the eighteenth-century Enlightenment, with its appeal to "self-evident truths" characteristic of that period's buoyant confidence in the power of human reason to apprehend objective fact. Could such an appeal carry any force today, after modern psychology has revealed the numberless ways in which we all deceive ourselves and after the history of modern wars and totalitarian regimes has demonstrated the folly of calling man the "rational animal"?

The *purpose* of the Declaration, as we are told explicitly, is to justify the revolution of the thirteen colonies against their mother country. But what is "justification"? Is it only a convenient cover-up for what they had undertaken? Was it an attempt to win support from other countries, perhaps from France?

As for its *subject matter,* most of it seems to be about the actions of "the present King of Great Britain." (This is puzzling in itself, for did not the Glorious Revolution of 1688–1689 establish the supremacy of Parliament over the King?) On closer examination, however, these actions all have one thing in common: they are allegedly violations of the "rights" of the colonists. With this as a clue, we see that the opening and closing sections of the document also deal with the concept of rights.

This leads to a consideration of the *structure* of the Declaration of Independence, which proves to be that of a "hypothetical syllogism": *if* any government fails to protect the rights of its citizens to life, liberty, and the pursuit of happiness, *then* such a government forfeits all claim to their allegiance; the English government *has* failed to protect our rights (the long list of grievances is intended to prove this); *therefore* we owe the English government no allegiance. This is Jefferson's argument reduced to its essentials. In form it is a logical argument: if *x* is true, then *y* is true; but *x* *is* true; therefore *y* is true. If its premises are also true—and this is quite another question—then its conclusion must be accepted. But what are these premises? How can we tell whether they are true?

Finally, the Declaration of Independence reveals the strong *influence* of John Locke's Second Treatise of Civil Government (see Vol. III, pages 44–64), and in turn the Declaration had an undoubted *effect* on the great French Revolution that broke out only thirteen years later. Did the Declaration also serve as the basis for the United States Constitution, or was that latter document founded on different philosophical premises? Did the Declaration establish political democracy? Did it have anything to say about capitalism? Have the principles set forth in the Declaration played any part in the current wave of colonial wars of independence in Africa and Asia?

Not all these dimensions are equally important in every document. Even so, you would do well to cultivate the habit of asking yourself all six questions about every document you encounter, before deciding which are the most significant in each particular case. In time this becomes second nature, yet to do this is to cultivate the critical faculty that is an essential part of an educated man.

Part One

Ancient Greece

◆ THE ILIAD

Homer

The first authentic voice in the history of Western civilization is that of the great poet who composed The Iliad *and* The Odyssey *out of the mass of legends that had accumulated about the Trojan War. That war itself probably occurred in the twelfth or thirteenth century* B.C.*, and may have been no more than a large-scale pirate raid. Yet to Homer, who lived about four centuries later, and to his readers throughout ancient times, the Trojan War was the first great contest between East and West as well as a proving ground for heroism. The Greeks looked upon these ancient warriors as the embodiment of every virtue, as paragons not only of bravery and physical strength but also of the wisdom needed to guide armies and lead whole peoples. Through Homer's epics a modern reader may gain insight not so much into early Greek society as it actually existed—for here inferences are hazardous—but into the prevailing ideals of behavior and association.*

These ideals are illustrated in the two selections from The Iliad *which follow. The first, which is Book I, opens in the ninth year of the great siege of Troy by the Achaeans (Greeks). We learn that an epidemic has broken out among the armies camped around the city, and a council of chiefs has been assembled to decide what to do about it. The quarrel that ensues, through which the drama of the rest of the poem unfolds, illuminates the fundamental principles of the society and that society's conception of the gods and their relationship to man.*

The second selection is a description of a fabulous shield made for Achilles by Hephaistos, the patron god of fire and the skills that make use of fire. On the shield is depicted the whole of human life: city and country, peace and war, nature and society.

BOOK I

Sing, O Goddess, of the wrath of Peleus' son Achilles, the deadly wrath that brought upon the Achaeans countless woes and sent many mighty souls of heroes down to the

Homer, *The Iliad*, trans. Alston Hurd Chase and William G. Perry, Jr. (Boston: Little, Brown and Company, 1950), pp. 3–20, 341–345.

house of Death and made their bodies prey for dogs and all the birds, as the will of Zeus was done, from the day when first the son of Atreus, king of men, and godlike Achilles parted in strife.

Which one of the gods, then, set them to angry quarreling? The son of Leto and Zeus. For in anger at the king he sent a grim plague throughout the army, and the men perished, because the son of Atreus scorned Chryses, the priest, who came to the swift ships of the Achaeans to free his daughter, bearing a boundless ransom and holding in his hands upon a golden staff the garlands of unerring Apollo. He entreated all the Achaeans, but especially the two sons of Atreus, the marshals of the people: "Sons of Atreus, and you other well-greaved Achaeans, may the gods, who have their homes upon Olympus, grant that you sack the city of Priam and go safely home. And may you release my dear child to me and accept these gifts of ransom, reverencing the son of Zeus, unerring Apollo."

Then all the rest of the Achaeans shouted their assent, to honor the priest and take the glorious ransom, but this did not please the heart of Agamemnon, Atreus' son; rather, he sent him rudely off and laid on him a harsh command: "Let me not find you, old man, beside the hollow ships, either lingering now or coming back hereafter, lest the staff and garland of the god avail you not. Her I will not set free. Sooner even shall old age come upon her in my home in Argos, far from her native land, as she paces before the loom and shares my bed. Now go, anger me not, that you may go the safer."

So he spoke, and the old man was afraid and obeyed his command and went in silence by the shore of the resounding sea. When he was far away, the aged man offered many a prayer to lord Apollo, whom fair-haired Leto bore: "Hear me, thou of the silver bow, who dost protect Chryse and hold Cilla and dost rule over Tenedos with might. Sminthian, if ever I roofed for thee a pleasant temple or if ever I burned for thee fat thighs of cattle and of goats, grant me this wish: may the Danaans pay for my tears beneath thy shafts."

So he spoke in prayer, and Phoebus Apollo heard him and came down from the peaks of Olympus angry at heart, his bow and covered quiver on his shoulders. The arrows rattled on the shoulders of the angry god as he sped, and he came like night. Then he sat down far from the ships and sent an arrow toward them; dreadful was the twang of his silver bow. First he shot the mules and the swift dogs, and then he sent a sharp arrow against the men and smote them. And the crowded pyres of the dead burned on, unceasing.

Nine days throughout the camp fell the missiles of the god, and on the tenth Achilles called the host to an assembly. For the white-armed goddess Hera had put the thought in his heart, since she pitied the Danaans as she saw them dying.

When they were gathered together, Achilles spoke to them: "Son of Atreus, now I think we shall be driven back and shall flee homeward, if indeed we escape from death, if war and plague alike are to destroy the Achaeans. Come, let us ask some prophet or priest or reader of dreams—for a dream, too, comes from Zeus—who might tell why Phoebus Apollo is so angered, whether he finds fault with some vow or offering, if possibly he may be willing to receive the fat of unblemished sheep or goats and ward off from us this plague."

So speaking, he sat down, and before them arose Calchas, Thestor's son, far best of readers of dreams, who knew things present, things to be, and things now past, and had guided the ships of the Achaeans to Ilium through his foresight which Phoebus Apollo gave him. With wise and kindly thought for them he spoke and said: "Achilles, dear to Zeus, you bid me explain the wrath of lord Apollo, the unerring. Therefore I shall speak; but for your part promise and swear to me loyally to protect me both by words and hands, for I expect to anger a man who rules mightily over all the Argives and whom the Achaeans obey. For a king is the mightier when he is angry with a lesser man. If he swallow his wrath on the day itself, still thereafter he nurses a grudge in his heart until he may satisfy it. Tell me if you will protect me."

Swift-footed Achilles answered him and said: "Be of good courage and declare the prophecy you know. For by Apollo, dear to Zeus, to whom you pray, Calchas, when you reveal to the Danaans the oracles of the gods, none of all the Danaans shall lay harsh hands upon you by the hollow ships as long as I live and look upon the earth, not even though you speak of Agamemnon, who now boasts to be by far the best of the Achaeans."

Then the blameless seer took courage and declared: "He finds no fault with us for vow or offering, but on his priest's account, whom Agamemnon scorned, neither did he free his daughter nor accept the ransom. Because of that the unerring one has sent suffering, and will yet send it until we give back the bright-eyed maiden to her father without price or ransom and take a sacred offering to Chryse. Then might we appease and win him."

So speaking, he sat down. Then before them arose the heroic son of Atreus, wide-ruling Agamemnon, furious; his dark heart was filled with rage and his eyes were like gleaming fire. First he addressed Calchas, with an evil glance: "Prophet of evil, never yet have you spoken a good omen to me. Always your heart loves evil prophecies and never have you spoken one good word, nor ever yet fulfilled one. Now, prophesying among the Danaans, you proclaim that for this cause the unerring one brings woe upon them, namely because I refused to take the splendid ransom for Chryses' maiden daughter, since it is my great desire to keep her in my home. I prefer her, indeed, to Clytemnestra, my wedded wife, since she is inferior to her neither in form nor stature nor in mind nor skill at work. Yet even so I am willing to give her back, if that be better, after all. I had rather the men be safe than that they die. But do you at once prepare for me a prize, that I alone among the Argives be not prizeless, since that is not fitting. For you all see what a prize of mine goes elsewhere."

Then swift-footed, godlike Achilles answered him: "Most noble son of Atreus, greediest of men, how shall the great-hearted Achaeans give you a prize? For we know of no great store of common goods; those things which we took from the sack of cities have been divided, nor is it fitting that the men should gather them again. But do you now surrender her to the god; then we Achaeans shall repay you three and four times over, if ever Zeus grant that we sack the well-walled city of Troy."

Mighty Agamemnon answered him and said: "Seek not thus in your heart to deceive me, brave though you be, godlike Achilles, since you shall not trick nor persuade me. Is it your wish, so that you may keep your prize, that I meanwhile sit tamely lacking mine, and do you bid me give her back? Yet, if the great-hearted

Achaeans will give a prize to suit my heart, one that will serve as well—but if they will not, then I myself will go and take your prize, or Ajax', or Odysseus', and bear it off. Angry will he be to whom I come. But we will think of this hereafter; now let us launch a black ship upon the shining sea, and let us quickly muster in its oarsmen and put in it an offering, and place on board the fair-cheeked Chryseis herself. Let one counsel-bearing warrior be its captain, Ajax or Idomeneus or godlike Odysseus or you, son of Peleus, most terrible of men, that you may offer sacrifice and appease for us the Warder."

Swift-footed Achilles looked at him scornfully and said: "Greedy one, clothed in shamelessness, how shall any of the Achaeans willingly obey your bidding, either to go a journey or stoutly to fight with men? For I did not come hither to do battle on account of the Trojan spearmen, since they are by no means guilty in my eyes. Never have they driven off my cattle or horses, never wasted the harvest in fertile Phthia, nurse of men, since in between lie many shadowy mountains and the resounding sea. No, it was you, utterly shameless, that we followed hither, to win revenge from the Trojans for Menelaus and for you, dog-face, that you might rejoice. But these things you neither care for nor consider. You even threaten to take away my prize yourself, the prize for which I labored much, and which the sons of the Achaeans gave me. Nor do I ever receive a prize equal to yours when the Achaeans sack some fair-lying city of the Trojans. The greater burden of furious war my hands sustain, yet whenever there comes division of the spoil, your prize is far the greater and I return to the ships with some small thing, but my own, when I am weary of war. Now I will go to Phthia, for it is far better to go home with the curved ships, nor do I intend unhonored to pile up wealth and riches here for you."

Then Agamemnon, king of men, replied to him: "Flee then, if your heart so bids you, nor will I beg you to remain for me. I have others who will honor me; above all, Zeus the counselor. You are the most hateful to me of Zeus-nurtured kings, for dear to you always are strife and wars and battles. If you are very strong, surely it is a god who made you so. Go home with your ships and your companions and rule over the Myrmidons; I do not care about you nor am I troubled by your anger. This warning I will give you: since Phoebus Apollo takes Chryseis from me, I will send her in my ship with my companions, but I will go myself and lead to my tent your prize, fair-cheeked Briseis, that you may know well how much I am your better, and that any other man may hate to speak as my equal and match himself against me face to face."

So he spoke, and anger arose in Peleus' son. His heart within his shaggy breast pondered two courses—whether, drawing his sharp sword from his thigh, he should disperse the others and slay the son of Atreus, or should quell his wrath and curb his spirit. While he was debating this in heart and mind and was drawing from the sheath his mighty sword, Athena came from heaven. The white-armed Hera sent her, she who loved and cherished in her heart both men alike. She stood behind the son of Peleus and grasped his yellow hair, appearing to him alone, and none of the others saw her. Achilles was amazed and turned about and at once knew Pallas Athena, for her eyes gleamed dreadfully. Addressing her, he spoke winged words: "Why hast thou come here, child of aegis-bearing Zeus? That thou mightest behold the insolence of Agamemnon, Atreus' son? This I will tell thee, and I think it will come to pass. By his overbearing pride he will soon destroy himself."

Then the bright-eyed goddess Athena addressed him: "I came from heaven to check your fury, if possibly you will obey. The white-armed goddess Hera sent me, she who loves and cherishes in her heart both men alike. Come, give up your wrath, draw not your sword in hand, but reproach him with words, even as it shall be hereafter, for thus I prophesy and thus shall it come to pass: some day you shall have thrice as many splendid gifts because of this piece of insolence; restrain yourself and obey us."

Swift-footed Achilles answered her and said: "I must respect your command, O goddess, though very angry at heart. For it is better thus. The gods give ear above all to him who obeys them."

So he spoke, and stayed his heavy hand upon the silver hilt and thrust the great sword back into its sheath, nor did he disobey the command of Athena. And she went toward Olympus to join the other gods in the house of aegis-bearing Zeus.

But the son of Peleus again with harsh words addressed the son of Atreus and still did not abate his wrath: "Sot, dog-eyed, deer-hearted, never has your spirit dared to arm for battle with the host nor to go forth to ambush with the best of the Achaeans. For this seems death to you. No doubt it is far better in the broad camp of the Achaeans to wrest away the prize of him who dares oppose you. A folk-devouring king you are, since you rule over men of no account; otherwise, son of Atreus, this would be your last insolence. But I shall speak out to you and swear a great oath upon it: By this scepter, which shall never put forth leaves and shoots once it has left its stump among the mountains nor shall it bloom again, for the bronze has stripped it of leaves and bark and now the sons of the Achaeans bear it in their hands, the judges, those who guard the laws that come from Zeus—and this shall be for you a mighty oath—truly a longing for Achilles shall some day come to all the sons of the Achaeans, and then, though you be frantic, you shall be able in no way to give aid when many fall in death before man-slaying Hector, and you shall rend your soul in rage within you that you paid no honor to the best of the Achaeans."

So spoke the son of Peleus and hurled the golden-studded scepter to the ground, and he himself sat down; and the son of Atreus faced him raging. Then among them arose Nestor, sweet of speech, the clear-voiced orator of the men of Pylos, from whose tongue the words flowed sweeter than honey. Already two generations of mortal men had passed before him, who were born and reared of old with him in sacred Pylos, and now he ruled among the third. With wise and kindly thought for them, he spoke and said: "Ah, a great sorrow has come upon the land of Achaea. Surely Priam and Priam's sons and the other Trojans would rejoice greatly in heart should they learn the full tale of this strife between you two, who are the leaders of the Danaans in council and in war. Come, listen to me, for you are both younger than I. Long ago I was the comrade of men far better than you and never did they scorn me. Never yet have I seen, nor shall I see, such warriors as Peirithous and Dryas, shepherd of the people, and Caeneus and Exadius and godlike Polyphemus and Theseus, Aegeus' son, like to the immortals. Mightiest of men reared on the earth were these, and with the mightiest they fought, the mountain-ranging centaurs, and fiercely they destroyed them. With these men was I companion when I came from Pylos, from a far distant land, for they summoned me themselves. I fought in single combat; with that foe no one of the mortals who are now upon the earth could fight. They listened to my counsels and heeded my word. So do you two heed it, for it is better to heed. Brave though you are, do not deprive him of his maiden, but let her be, as the Achaeans first gave her to him as a prize. Nor do you desire, son of Peleus, to struggle with a king on equal terms, for a sceptered king, to whom Zeus has granted glory, holds no common honor. Even if you be mighty and a goddess mother bore you, still is he mightier, since he rules over more. You, too, son of Atreus, cease your anger. I beg you, check your rage against Achilles, who for all Achaeans is a mighty bulwark against evil war."

Then mighty Agamemnon answered him and said: "Indeed, old man, you have spoken all these things with justice. But this man would surpass all others; he would rule over all and lord it over all and give orders to all, which I think someone will not obey. Even if the gods who live forever have made him a spearman, do they therefore suffer him to speak reproach?"

Then godlike Achilles interrupted him and answered: "I should be called cowardly and worthless if I yielded to everything you say. Lay these commands on others, give them not to me, for I no longer intend to obey you. I will tell you something else, and do you turn this over in your heart: I will not for the maiden's sake lift a hand in strife with you or any other, since you are taking from me what you gave. But of all the rest that is mine beside my swift, black ship, naught could you seize and take away against my will. Or come and try, so that these men too may know; at once will your dark blood flow about my spear."

So having striven against one another with hostile words, they arose and dismissed the assembly by the ships of the Achaeans. Peleus' son went to his tents and his fair-lined ships with the son of Menoetius and his comrades. But the son of Atreus had a swift ship launched upon the sea and chose twenty oarsmen for it and sent on board an offering for the god and brought the fair-cheeked Chryseis and placed her on the ship. As captain, many-wiled Odysseus went aboard.

These, then, embarked and sailed the watery ways, and the son of Atreus ordered the men to purify themselves. So they purified themselves and cast the defilement into the sea, and they made to Apollo unblemished offerings of bulls and goats by the shore of the barren sea, and the savor, eddying amid the smoke, arose to heaven.

Thus they toiled throughout the camp. But Agamemnon did not cease from the wrath with which he first threatened Achilles. He spoke to Talthybius and Eurybates, who were his heralds and ready servants: "Go to the tent of Achilles, Peleus' son, and take the fair-cheeked Briseis by the hand and bring her here. If he will not give her, then will I myself go with more men and take her, and that shall be the worse for him."

So he spoke, and sent them forth, and he laid on them a harsh command. Unwillingly they went along the shore of the barren sea and came to the tents and ships of the Myrmidons. They found Achilles seated near his tent and his black ship; nor was he glad to see them. The two stood fearful and awestruck before the king and neither spoke to him nor asked him anything. But he knew their errand in his heart and said: "Welcome, heralds, messengers of Zeus and men; draw near. For it is not you I blame, but rather Agamemnon, who sent you here for the maiden Briseis. Come, Zeus-born Patroclus, bring out the maid and give her to them to lead away. And do you two be witnesses before the blessed gods and mortal men and before that ruthless king, if ever hereafter there be need of me to ward off shameful ruin from the rest. For indeed he rages in his baneful heart and knows not how to look before and after, that his Achaeans may fight in safety by the ships."

So he spoke, and Patroclus obeyed his dear companion and brought the fair-cheeked Briseis from the tent and gave her to them to lead away. They went back past the ships of the Achaeans and the woman went with them, against her will. Then Achilles went apart from his companions and sat weeping upon the shore of the gray sea, looking out across the boundless deep. And stretching out his hands, he offered many a prayer to his dear mother: "Mother, since it was you who bore me, brief though my life may be, honor at least should high-thundering Zeus have granted me. But now he has not honored me in the least. For Atreus' son, wide-ruling Agamemnon, has insulted me. He has taken my prize and holds it, having wrested it away himself."

So he spoke, weeping, and his queenly mother heard him as she sat in the depths of the sea beside her aged father. Swiftly she rose from the gray sea like a mist and sat down beside him as he wept, and caressed him with her hand and spoke and said to him: "My child, why do you weep? What grief has come upon your heart? Speak, hide nothing in your mind, so that we both may know."

Swift-footed Achilles sighed heavily and said to her: "You know; why should I tell all this to you when you know it already? We went to Thebe, the holy city of Eëtion, and we sacked it and brought all the booty here. The sons of the Achaeans divided the rest fairly among themselves and put aside for Atreus' son fair-cheeked Chryseis. Then Chryses, priest of unerring Apollo, came to the swift ships of the bronze-clad Achaeans to free his daughter, bearing a boundless ransom and holding in his hands upon a golden staff the garlands of unerring Apollo. He entreated all the Achaeans, but especially the two sons of Atreus, the marshals of the people. Then all the rest of the Achaeans shouted their assent, to honor the priest and take the glorious ransom, but this did not please the heart of Agamemnon, Atreus' son; rather, he sent him rudely off and laid on him a harsh command. The old man went away in anger, and Apollo heard him when he prayed, for he was very dear to him, and he sent an evil bolt upon the Argives. Now the people died in swift succession, for the shafts of the god fell everywhere throughout the broad camp of the Achaeans. Then a prophet, well informed, delivered to us the oracle of unerring one. At once I was the first to urge that we appease the god. Then anger seized the son of Atreus, and straightway he arose and made a threat which has been fulfilled. For the bright-eyed Achaeans are sending the one maiden on a swift ship to Chryse and are bearing gifts to the god, but the heralds have just now departed from my tent taking the other maiden, the daughter of Briseus, whom the sons of the Achaeans gave to me. But do you, if you can, protect your son. Go to Olympus and petition Zeus, if ever you have gladdened his heart by word or deed. For often in my father's halls have I heard you boasting, as you said that alone among the immortals you warded off shameful ruin from the black-clouded son of Cronus when the other Olympians wished to bind him—Hera and Poseidon and Pallas Athena. But you, goddess, went to him and loosed him from his bonds, quickly summoning to high Olympus him of a hundred hands, whom the gods call Briareus but all men Aegaeon—indeed, he was greater in strength than his own father. He sat beside the son of Cronus, exulting in his glory. And the blessed gods took fright and tried no more to fetter Zeus. Reminding him of this, sit by him and clasp his knees, in the hope that he may consent to aid the Trojans and hem the Achaeans about the sterns of their ships along the sea as they are slain, that they may all enjoy their king, and that Atreus' son, wide-ruling Agamemnon, may know his folly in paying no honor to the best of the Achaeans."

Then Thetis, weeping, answered him: "Ah, my child, why did I rear you, accursed in your birth? Would that you might sit tearless and free from sorrow by the ships, since your lot is brief and not very long. Now you are both swift of doom and wretched beyond all. Therefore, to an evil fate did I bear you in our halls. To speak this word for you to Zeus, who delights in the thunder, I myself will go to snow-capped Olympus, in the hope that the may be persuaded. But do you sit beside the swift ships and nurse your wrath against the Achaeans and withhold entirely from war. For Zeus went yesterday to the Ocean to feast with the blameless Aethiopians, and all the gods went with him. But on the twelfth day he will come again to Olympus and then I will go on your behalf to the bronze-floored house of Zeus, and I will clasp his knees, and I think that I shall persuade him."

So speaking, she departed, and left him there angered at heart because of the fair-girdled woman whom they had taken from him by force, against his will.

Meanwhile, Odysseus was arriving at Chryse with the holy offering. When they had entered the deep harbor, they furled the sail and stowed it in the black ship, and they lowered the mast by the forestays and brought it quickly to its crutch, and rowed her to the anchorage with oars. Out they cast the mooring stones and tied the stern cables, and out they stepped themselves into the surf; out they brought the offering for Apollo, the unerring, and out stepped Chryses' daughter from the ship that fared the sea. Then the many-wiled Odysseus led her to an altar and gave her into the arms of her dear father and addressed him: "Chryses, Agamemnon, king of men, sent me to bring your child to you and to make to Phoebus a holy offering on behalf of the Danaans, that we may appease the lord who but now sent upon the Argives lamentable woes."

So speaking, he gave her into Chryses' arms, and he received his dear child with joy. Quickly they set the sacred offering for the god in due order about the well-buil altar. Then they washed their hands and took up the sacred barley, and before them Chryses lifted up his hands and prayed aloud: "Hear me, thou of the silver bow who dost protect Chryse and holy Cilla and dost rule over Tenedos with might. Truly thou didst hear me when I prayed to thee before, didst honor me, and didst fiercely smite the host of the Achaeans. So now as well grant me this wish. Dispel now from the Danaans the shameful pestilence."

So he spoke in prayer, and Phoebus Apollo heard him. Then, when they had prayed and had sprinkled the sacred barley, they first drew back the heads of th victims and slew and flayed them. The thighs they cut out and wrapped in fat, making two layers, and placed raw meat upon them. The old man burned them on split wood and poured upon them shining wine. And the young men at his side held five-pronged forks in their hands. Then, when the thighs were burned and they had tasted the entrails, they cut up the rest and placed it on spits and roasted it carefully and drew it all off. When they had ceased from their toil and had made the banquet ready, they ate, and no heart lacked due portion of the feast. But when they had put aside desire for food and drink, the youths filled brimming bowls with wine and served o all, having first filled the cups for the libations. So all the day long the sons of he Achaeans appeased the god with song and dance, singing a fair paean in praise of he Warder. And he rejoiced at heart to hear them.

But when the sun set and the twilight came, they lay down by the stern cables of he ship. When the early, rosy-fingered Dawn appeared, they set sail for the broad amp of the Achaeans. The Warder Apollo sent them a following breeze. They set p the mast and spread the white sail; the wind struck squarely upon the sail, and bout the stem the blue wave sang aloud as the ship sped on; across the swell she ran, naking good her course. When they came to the broad camp of the Achaeans, they lrew the black ship out upon the land, high upon the shingle, and placed long props eneath her, and they themselves scattered to their tents and ships.

But the Zeus-born son of Peleus, swift-footed Achilles, sat in anger beside the swift hips. Never did he go to man-ennobling council or to war, but he ate out his heart, biding there, and longed for the battle cry and war.

When the twelfth dawn after this arose, the gods, who live forever, came all ogether to Olympus, led by Zeus. Nor did Thetis forget the bidding of her son; she rose from a wave of the sea and early in the morning went up into high heaven and lympus. She found the far-thundering son of Cronus seated apart from the others n the highest peak of many-ridged Olympus. She sat down beside him and clasped is knees with her left hand, and, touching him beneath the chin with her right, she poke in supplication to lord Zeus, Cronus' son: "Father, Zeus, if ever by word or leed I have helped you among the immortals, grant me this wish: honor my son, who s brief-fated beyond all others. Yet now Agamemnon, king of men, has insulted him, or he has taken his prize and holds it, having wrested it away himself. But do you venge him, Olympian Zeus, the counselor. Give might to the Trojans until the chaeans reverence my son and pay him honor."

Thus she spoke, yet cloud-gathering Zeus did not address her but sat long in ilence. Still Thetis clasped his knees, still clung to him, and once again implored im: "Promise me this in truth and confirm it with your nod, or else deny me, since here is no fear in you, that I may know well how much I am the least in honor mong all the gods."

Then, greatly distressed, cloud-gathering Zeus addressed her: "This is a ruinous usiness, for you would bid me stir up strife with Hera, when she shall taunt me with eproachful words. Even as it is, she always nags at me among the immortal gods nd says that in battle I support the Trojans. But do you now go back, lest Hera notice. shall be my concern to carry out these things. Come now, I will nod to you, that ou may trust me. For this is the greatest pledge from me even among the immortals.

For I may not take back nor betray nor fail to carry out that pledge to which I nod my confirmation."

So speaking, the son of Cronus nodded with his black brows and the ambrosial locks flowed down from the lord's immortal head, and he made great Olympus tremble.

When they had plotted thus, they parted. She plunged to the deep sea from bright Olympus, and Zeus went to his home. All the gods arose from their seats before their father, nor did any dare abide his coming, but they all stood up to meet him. So he sat down there upon his throne; nor did Hera fail to realize, when she saw him, that silver-footed Thetis, daughter of the old man of the sea, had been taking counsel with him. At once she addressed Zeus, son of Cronus, with reproaches: "Which of the gods was taking counsel with you, deceitful one? Always it is your pleasure to sit apart from me and debate and pass judgment in secret. Never have you dared willingly to tell me what plan you are debating."

The father of gods and men replied to her: "Hera, do not expect to know all my words. For they will be hard for you, even though you be my wife. That which is suitable for you to hear, no one of gods or men shall learn before you. But that which I wish to consider apart from the gods, of this do you not always ask or question."

Then ox-eyed, queenly Hera answered him: "Most dreadful son of Cronus, what sort of word is this which you have uttered? I have never before asked of you or sought to know too much, but you consider, quite unmolested, what you will. Yet now I fear dreadfully in my heart lest silver-footed Thetis, daughter of the old man of the sea, may have beguiled you. For, early this morning, she sat beside you and clasped your knees. I think you gave her solemn promise by a nod to honor Achilles and destroy many beside the ships of the Achaeans."

Then cloud-gathering Zeus answered her and said, "Mad one, you are always suspicious, nor do I escape you; yet you shall be unable to do anything; you will be but the further from my heart, and that shall be the worse for you. If it be as you say, such is my pleasure. Sit down in silence and obey my order, lest all the gods who dwell upon Olympus avail you not if I come closer, when once I lay my invincible hands upon you."

So he spoke, and ox-eyed, queenly Hera was afraid. She sat down in silence, curbing her heart. The heavenly gods in the house of Zeus were troubled, and Hephaestus the famed artisan, began to address them, favoring his dear mother, white-armed Hera: "Truly this will be a ruinous business, no longer bearable, if these two strive thus because of mortals and bring wrangling among the gods. There will be no pleasure in our noble banquet, since the worse course prevails. But I advise my mother, who thinks the same herself, to humor my dear father, Zeus, that my father may not again be angry and trouble our feast. If the Olympian lord of lightning wishes to cast us from our seats, for he is mightiest by far—but soothe him yourself with soft words. Then straightway the Olympian will relent toward us."

So he spoke, and, springing up, he placed in his mother's hands the double-handled cup and said to her: "Take heart, Mother, and endure, though grieved, lest dear though you be, I see you struck before my eyes; then, however distressed, I shall be powerless to help you. For the Olympian is hard to counter. Already once before, when I tried to save you, he caught me by the foot and hurled me from his awful threshold

All day I fell, and with the setting sun dropped upon Lemnos, and little was the life till in me. But the Sintians straightway cared for me after my fall."

So he spoke, and the white-armed goddess Hera smiled, and smiling received the up in her hand from her son. Then going from left to right he poured sweet nectar or the other gods, drawing it from a bowl. And unquenchable laughter arose among he blessed gods as they watched Hephaestus bustling about the hall.

So all the day until the sun had set they feasted, and no heart lacked due portion of the feast, nor of the fair lyre which Apollo held, nor of the Muses, who sang in nswer with their lovely voices.

But when the bright light of the sun had set, each of them went home to sleep where lame Hephaestus, the renowned, had by his skillful cunning made for each a ouse. And Zeus, the Olympian lord of lightning, went to his bed, where of old he sed to rest when sweet sleep came upon him. There he went and slept, with Hera f the golden throne beside him.

OOK XVIII

. . First he made a great, stout shield, adorning it on every side, and put a threefold littering, shining rim about it, and fastened to it a silver strap. There were five ayers in the shield itself, and on it he set many devices with his cunning skill.

On it he fashioned earth and sea, the unwearying sun and the full moon, and all he wondrous signs that wreathe the heavens—the Pleiades and Hyades, mighty Orion, nd the Bear, that they also call the Wain, which turns in the same place watching rion, and has alone no share in Ocean's baths.

On it he fashioned two towns of mortal men, most fair. In one there was a wedding east, and they were escorting the brides from their chambers through the city by e light of shining torches, and the wedding hymn rose loudly. Dancing boys whirled ound and round, and in their midst the flutes and lyres made music. The women, ach in her doorway, watched with wonder. The people were gathered in the market lace, where a dispute had arisen, and two men were quarreling about the blood-price f some murdered man. One said that he had given all, explaining it to the people; e other denied receiving it; and each was eager to win his case before the judge. he people applauded both, as both sides had supporters. Heralds held back the eople, and the old men sat upon polished stones in a sacred circle and held the staves f loud-voiced heralds in their hands. Leaning on these, they rose and gave their rdict, each in turn. In the center lay two talents of gold, to give to him who spoke e straightest verdict.

About the other city sat two armies, gleaming in their armor. Their purpose lay tween two choices, to destroy the town or each to take the half of all the wealth the vely city held within it. But the citizens would not yet yield and were arming for ambush. Their dear wives and tender children stood upon the wall to guard it, d with them those men upon whom age had come. The warriors were starting out, d by Ares and Pallas Athena, both wrought in gold and clad in golden garments, d both fair and tall, and splendid in their arms, as gods should be. The soldiers were of lesser stature. When they came to the place where it suited them to set their ambush, by the river, at the watering place of all the flocks, there they sat down, wrapped in gleaming bronze. Two lookouts lay apart from the soldiers, waiting to see the sheep and crooked-horned cattle. These soon appeared, and with them came two herdsmen, playing on Panpipes, with no thought of treachery. When the men caught sight of them, they rushed upon them and quickly then cut off the herds of cattle and the fair flocks of shining sheep and slew the herdsmen by them. But when the besiegers, sitting before the assembly place, heard the great din about the cattle, they straightway leaped up behind high-stepping horses and drove toward it, arriving in a moment. Then they formed their lines and fought a battle by the river's bank and hurled their bronze-tipped spears at one another. Strife and Uproar moved among them, and baneful Fate as well, keeping one man alive though wounded, another free from wounds, while she dragged by the feet amid the din another who had perished and she wore upon her shoulders a robe all reddened with men's blood. Like living men they joined and fought, and dragged dead bodies from each other.

On it he placed a soft fallow earth, a rich plowland, wide and thrice plowed. Many plowmen plowed thereon this way and that, turning their teams about. And when they had turned and reached the field's edge once again, a man stepped up and put into their hands a cup of honey-sweet wine; and they turned again along the furrows eager to reach once more the edge of the deep fallow land. The earth was black behind them, and like earth freshly plowed, though wrought in gold. It was a very wondrous work.

On it he placed a royal field. Here reapers moved with sharp sickles in their hands Some handfuls fell to earth along the swath, and others the sheave binders tied with bands of straw. Three binders followed, and behind came children gleaning, who never ceased to give them armfuls. The king stood in their midst in silence by the swaths, holding his staff and glad at heart. Heralds were preparing dinner underneath a distant oak, and were dressing a great bull which they had sacrificed; and the women were strewing much white barley on the meat as a dinner for the reapers.

On it he placed a fair golden vineyard, heavy-laden with fruit. There were dar clusters on it, and it was all held on silver vine props. Around it he made a ditch o blue enamel and a fence of tin. There was only one pathway through it, along whic the vintagers would go when they harvested the vineyard. Light-hearted youths an maidens bore the honey-sweet fruit in woven baskets. In their midst a lad played o his lyre a tune to set one dreaming, and in a delicate voice sang a fair Linus song Stamping in unison, they followed with shouts and dancing, beating the measure.

On it he placed a herd of straight-horned cattle. These were wrought in gold an tin, and pressed lowing from the barnyard to their pasture on a singing river by a be of waving reeds. Four herdsmen in gold went with the cattle, followed by nin swift-footed dogs. Two grim lions had caught a bellowing bull among the foremo cattle, and he was bawling loudly as they dragged him off, and dogs and youths wen after him. The lions, having broken the hide of the great bull, were gulping dow the entrails and dark blood, and the herdsmen vainly set on the swift hounds wit their urgings. The dogs shrank from biting the lions, but stood close by and barke and then fell back.

On it the renowned lame god placed a great pasture of sheep in a fair glen—folds and roofed huts and pens.

On it the renowned lame god placed a dancing floor like that which once in broad Cnossus Daedalus made for Ariadne of the lovely tresses. There youths and dearly courted maidens danced, holding each other's wrists. The maids wore robes of fine linen and the lads well-woven shirts, just touched with olive oil. The maidens wore fair garlands and the lads bore golden daggers, hanging from silver belts. Sometimes they ran most easily on skillful feet, as when a potter sits and fits his hand about his wheel and tries it, if it run; sometimes they ran in lines toward one another. A great throng stood in delight about the charming dance, and among them a divine bard played on his lyre, and two tumblers, beginning their sport, spun through their midst.

On it he placed the great might of Ocean around the outer rim of the well-wrought shield.

◆§ THE PERSIAN WARS

Herodotus

With Herodotus of Halicarnassus (ca. 484–ca. 425 B.C.), *the Greeks became conscious of themselves as a people. Herodotus was born in Ionia on the west coast of Asia Minor (now Turkey); he spent many years travelling around the known world of that time. He called his book a "history," meaning an inquiry or an investigation, of the two unsuccessful attempts by the kings of Persia to invade and conquer Greece between 490 and 479* B.C. *But it contains much more than a simple account: Herodotus, like all true historians ever since, wanted to* understand *the wars—why they took place, and how the Greeks were able to hold off the vastly superior forces brought against them.*

The answer, he thought, lay in the difference in character between the Greek people and the "barbarians"—that is, everybody else in the world. (The word "barbarian" meant "those who go bar-bar, *which is the way all foreign languages sounded to the Greeks—harsh and unintelligible.) The Greeks, Herodotus said, knew the value of freedom and were ready to fight to the death for it; but the barbarians were by nature slavish and, like animals, needed a master. Probably every people has considered itself superior to its neighbors; the distinguishing feature of the Greeks of the fifth century* B.C. *is that they really were superior—and they proved it.*

A full two-thirds (about five hundred pages) of Herodotus' book consists of careful descriptions of the history and customs of all the peoples involved in the wars. These actually include everyone Herodotus had ever heard of, for he saw these wars as the culmination of all previous wars, the grand struggle between Asia and Europe. The descriptions are full, objective, and sometimes humorous. They display the Greek spirit o disinterested inquiry at its best, especially in view of the fact that Herodotu was at the same time constructing a latter-day epic of Greek heroism. We have included sections on two different types of barbarians: the overcivilized Medes and Persians, and the savage Scythians from the north

The climax comes with the war itself and the heroic stand at Thermopylae, where 300 Spartans fought to the last man to hold a narrow mountain pass against a huge invading army, in order to give the Greeks in the open plain behind them a few more days to organize their defense. The Persians eventually took the pass, as the selection indicates, by mean of treachery and overwhelming numbers; but they suffered crushing defeats at Plataea and Salamis, and finally were forced to withdraw in disgrace. The moral victory had been even greater than the military one. For the first time the Greeks had worked together as a united people, an the results had been spectacular. The magnificent art, literature and oratory of the ensuing fifty years in Greece are all tinged with the Greeks' justifiable pride and patriotism. And Herodotus, the Father of History, wa also the poet of their triumph.

BOOK I

This is a publication of the researches of Herodotus of Halicarnassus, in order th the actions of men may not be effaced by time, nor the great and wondrous dee displayed both by Greeks and barbarians deprived of renown:—and amongst the res for what cause they waged war upon each other.

The learned among the Persians assert that the Phoenicians were the original autho of the quarrel; for that they having migrated from that which is called the Red Se to the Mediterranean, and having settled in the country which they now inhabit, fort with applied themselves to distant voyages; and that having exported Egyptian an Assyrian merchandise, they touched at other places, and also at Argos. Now Arg at that period in every respect surpassed all those states which are now comprehende under the general appellation of Greece. *They say,* that on their arrival at Argos, t Phoenicians exposed their merchandise to sale, and that on the fifth or sixth day aft their arrival, and when they had almost disposed of their cargo, a great number women came down to the sea-shore, and among them the king's daughter, who name, as the Greeks also say, was Io daughter of Inachus. *They add,* that while the women were standing near the stern of the vessel, and were bargaining for su

Herodotus, *The Persian Wars*, trans. H. Cary (London: G. Ball & Sons, Ltd., Bohn's Classic Library, 1894), pp. 1–3, 11–15, 59–63, 257–261, 272–273, 410–413, 442–444, 479–488.

hings as most pleased them, the Phoenicians, having exhorted one another, made an .ttack upon them; and that most of the women escaped, but that Io, with some others, vas seized: and that they, having hurried them on board, set sail for Egypt.

Thus the Persians say that Io went to Egypt, not agreeing *herein* with the Phoeni- ians; and that this was the beginning of wrongs. After this, that certain Grecians, for they are unable to tell their name,) having touched at Tyre in Phoenicia, carried ›ff the king's daughter Europa. These must have been Cretans. Thus far they say hat they had only retaliated; but that after this the Greeks were guilty of the second ›rovocation; for that having sailed down in a vessel of war to Aea, a city of Colchis n the river Phasis, when they had accomplished the more immediate object of their xpedition, they carried off the king's daughter Medea; and that the king of Colchis, aving despatched a herald to Greece, demanded satisfaction for the rape, and the estitution of the princess; but the Greeks replied, that as they of Asia had not given ny satisfaction for the rape of Io, neither would they give any to them.

They say too, that in the second generation after this, Alexander the son of Priam, aving heard of these events, was desirous of obtaining a wife from Greece by means f violence, being fully persuaded that he should not have to give satisfaction, for that he Greeks had not done so. When therefore he had carried off Helen, *they say,* that he Greeks immediately sent messengers to demand her back again, and require satis- action for the rape; but that they, when they brought forward these demands, objected o them the rape of Medea; "that they who had not themselves given satisfaction, nor nade it when demanded, now wished others to give it to themselves."

Thus far then *they say* that there had only been rapes from each other; but that fter this the Greeks were greatly to blame, for that they levied war against Asia efore the Asiatics did upon Europe. Now, to carry off women by violence the Persians hink is the act of wicked men, but to trouble oneself about avenging them when so arried off is the act of foolish ones; and to pay no regard to them when carried off, f wise men: for that it is clear, that if they had not been willing, they could not have een carried off. Accordingly the Persians say, that they of Asia made no account of vomen that were carried off; but that the Greeks for the sake of a Lacedaemonian voman assembled a mighty fleet, and then having come to Asia overthrew the empire ›f Priam. That from this event they had always considered the Greeks as their enemies: or the Persians claim Asia and the barbarous nations that inhabit it, as their own, and onsider Europe and the people of Greece as totally distinct. . . .

When these nations were subdued, and Croesus had added them to the Lydians, ll the other wise men of that time, as each had opportunity, came from Greece to ardis, which had then attained to the highest degree of prosperity; and amongst them olon an Athenian, who having made laws for the Athenians at their request, absented imself for ten years, having sailed away under pretence of seeing the world, that e might not be compelled to abrogate any of the laws he had established: for the Athenians could not do it themselves, since they were bound by solemn oaths to observe or ten years whatever laws Solon should enact for them.

Solon therefore having gone abroad for these reasons, and for the purposes of bservation, arrived in Egypt at the court of Amasis, and afterwards at that of Croesus t Sardis. On his arrival he was hospitably entertained by Croesus, and on the third or fourth day, by order of the king, the attendants conducted him round the treasury and showed him all their grand and costly contents; and when he had seen and examined every thing sufficiently, Croesus asked him this question: "My Athenian guest, your great fame has reached even to us, as well of your wisdom as of your travels, how that as a philosopher you have travelled through various countries for the purpose of observation; I am therefore desirous of asking you, who is the most happy man you have seen?" He asked this question, because he thought himself the most happy of men. But Solon, speaking the truth freely, without any flattery, answered "Tellus the Athenian." Croesus, astonished at his answer, eagerly asked him, "On what account do you deem Tellus the happiest?" He replied, "Tellus, in the first place lived in a well-governed commonwealth; had sons who were virtuous and good; and he saw children born to them all, and all surviving: in the next place, when he had lived as happily as the condition of human affairs will permit, he ended his life in a most glorious manner. For coming to the assistance of the Athenians in a battle with their neighbours of Eleusis, he put the enemy to flight, and died nobly. The Athenians buried him at the public charge in the place where he fell, and honoured him greatly."

When Solon had roused the attention of Croesus by relating many and happy circumstances concerning Tellus, Croesus, expecting at least to obtain the second place asked, whom he had seen next to him. "Cleobis," said he, "and Biton, for they being natives of Argos, possessed a sufficient fortune, and had withal such strength of body that they were both alike victorious in the public games; and moreover the following story is related of them: when the Argives were celebrating a festival of Juno, it was necessary that their mother should be drawn to the temple in a chariot; but the oxen did not come from the field in time, the young men therefore, being pressed for time, put themselves beneath the yoke, and drew the car in which their mother sate and having conveyed it forty-five stades, they reached the temple. After they had done this in sight of the assembled people, a most happy termination was put to their lives and in them the Deity clearly showed, that it is better for a man to die than to live For the men of Argos, who stood round, commended the strength of the youths, and the women blessed her as the mother of such sons; but the mother herself, transported with joy both on account of the action and its renown, stood before the image and prayed, that the goddess would grant to Cleobis and Biton, her own sons, who had so highly honoured her, the greatest blessing man could receive. After this prayer when they had sacrificed and partaken of the feast, the youths fell asleep in the temple itself, and never awoke more, but met with such a termination of life. Upon this the Argives, in commemoration of their piety, caused their statues to be made and dedicated at Delphi."

Thus Solon adjudged the second place of felicity to these youths. But Croesus, being enraged, said, "My Athenian friend, is my happiness then so slighted by you as nothing worth, that you do not think me of so much value as private men?" He answered; "Croesus, do you inquire of me concerning human affairs—of me, who know that the divinity is always jealous, and delights in confusion. For in lapse of time men are constrained to see many things they would not willingly see, and to suffer many things *they would not willingly suffer*. Now I put the term of man's life at seventy years; these seventy years then give twenty-five thousand two hundred days without including the intercalary month; and if we add that month to every other year, in order that the seasons arriving at the proper time may agree, the intercalary months will be thirty-five more in the seventy years, and the days of these months will be one thousand and fifty. Yet in all this number of twenty-six thousand two hundred and fifty days, that compose these seventy years, one day produces nothing exactly the same as another. Thus, then, O Croesus, man is altogether the sport of fortune. You appear to me to be master of immense treasures, and king of many nations; but as relates to what you inquire of me, I cannot say, till I hear you have ended your life happily. For the richest of men is not more happy than he that has a sufficiency for a day, unless good fortune attend him to the grave, so that he ends his life in happiness. Many men, who abound in wealth, are unhappy; and many, who have only a moderate competency, are fortunate. He that abounds in wealth, and is yet unhappy, surpasses the other only in two things; but the other surpasses the wealthy and the miserable in many things. The former indeed is better able to gratify desire, and to bear the blow of adversity. But the latter surpasses him in this; he is not indeed equally able to bear misfortune or *satisfy* desire, but his good fortune wards off these things from him; and he enjoys the full use of his limbs, he is free from disease and misfortune, he is blessed with good children and a fine form, and if, in addition to all these things, he shall end his life well, he is the man you seek, and may justly be called happy; but before he die we ought to suspend our judgment, and not pronounce him happy, but fortunate. Now it is impossible for any one man to comprehend all these advantages: as no one country suffices to produce every thing for itself, but affords some and wants others, and that which affords the most is the best; so no human being is in all respects self-sufficient, but possesses one advantage, and is in need of another; he therefore who has constantly enjoyed the most of these, and then ends his life tranquilly, this man, in my judgment, O king, deserves the name of happy. We ought therefore to consider the end of every thing, in what way it will terminate; for the Deity having shown a glimpse of happiness to many, has afterwards utterly overthrown them."

When he spoke thus to Croesus, Croesus did not confer any favour on him, and holding him in no account, dismissed him; since he considered him a very ignorant man, because he overlooked present prosperity, and bade men look to the end of every thing. . . .

The Persians, according to my own knowledge, observe the following customs. It is not their practice to erect statues, or temples, or altars, but they charge those with folly who do so; because, as I conjecture, they do not think the gods have human forms, as the Greeks do. They are accustomed to ascend the highest parts of the mountains, and offer sacrifice to Jupiter, and they call the whole circle of the heavens by the name of Jupiter. They sacrifice to the sun and moon, to the earth, fire, water, and the winds. To these alone they have sacrificed from the earliest times: but they have since learnt from the Arabians and Assyrians to sacrifice to Venus Urania, whom the Assyrians call Venus Mylitta, the Arabians, Alitta, and the Persians, Mitra.

The following is the established mode of sacrifice to the above-mentioned deities: they do not erect altars nor kindle fires when about to sacrifice; they do not use libations, or flutes, or fillets, or cakes; but, when any one wishes to offer sacrifice to any one of these deities, he leads the victim to a clean spot, and invokes the god, usually having his tiara decked with mrytle. He that sacrifices is not permitted to pray for blessings for himself alone; but he is obliged to offer prayers for the prosperity of all the Persians, and the king, for he is himself included in the Persians. When he has cut the victim into small pieces, and boiled the flesh, he strews under it a bed of tender grass, generally trefoil, and then lays all the flesh upon it: when he has put every thing in order, one of the Magi standing by sings an ode concerning the original of the gods, which they say is the incantation; and without one of the Magi it is not lawful for them to sacrifice. After having waited a short time, he that has sacrificed carries away the flesh and disposes of it as he thinks fit.

It is their custom to honour their birth-day above all other days; and on this day they furnish their table in a more plentiful manner than at other times. The rich then produce an ox, a horse, a camel, and an ass, roasted whole in an oven; but the poor produce smaller cattle. They are moderate at their meals, but eat of many after dishes and those not served up together. On this account the Persians say, "that the Greeks rise hungry from table, because nothing worth mentioning is brought in after dinner and that if any thing were brought in, they would not leave off eating." The Persians are much addicted to wine; they are not allowed to vomit or make water in presence of another. These customs are observed to this day. They are used to debate the most important affairs when intoxicated; but whatever they have determined on in such deliberations, is on the following day, when they are sober, proposed to them by the master of the house where they have met to consult; and if they approve of it when sober also, then they adopt it; if not, they reject it. And whatever they have first resolved on when sober, they reconsider when intoxicated.

When they meet one another in the streets, one may discover by the following custom, whether those who meet are equals. For instead of accosting one another they kiss on the mouth; if one be a little inferior to the other, they kiss the cheek but if he be of a much lower rank, he prostrates himself before the other. They honour above all, those who live nearest to themselves; in the second degree, those that are second in nearness; and after that, as they go further off, they honour in proportion and least of all they honour those who live at the greatest distance; esteeming them selves to be by far the most excellent of men in every respect; and that others make approaches to excellence according to the foregoing gradations, but that they are the worst who live farthest from them. During the empire of the Medes, each nation ruled over its next neighbour, the Medes over all, and especially over those that were nearest to them; these again, over the bordering people, and the last in like manner over their next neighbours; and in the same gradations the Persians honour; for that nation went on extending its government and guardianship.

The Persians are of all nations most ready to adopt foreign customs; for they wear the Medic costume, thinking it handsomer than their own; and in war they use the Egyptian cuirass. And they practise all kinds of indulgences with which they become acquainted; amongst others, they have learnt from the Greeks a passion for boys they marry, each of them, many wives; and keep a still greater number of concubines

Next to bravery in battle, this is considered the greatest proof of manliness, to be able to exhibit many children; and to such as can exhibit the greatest number, the king sends presents every year; for numbers are considered strength. Beginning from the age of five years to twenty, they instruct their sons in three things only; to ride, to use the bow, and to speak truth. Before he is five years of age, a son is not admitted to the presence of his father, but lives entirely with the women: the reason of this custom is, that if he should die in childhood, he may occasion no grief to his father.

Now I much approve of the above custom, as also of the following, that not even the king is allowed to put any one to death for a single crime, nor any private Persian exercise extreme severity against any of his domestics for one fault, but if on examination he should find that his misdeeds are more numerous and greater than his services, he may in that case give vent to his anger. They say that no one ever yet killed his own father or mother, but whenever such things have happened they affirm, that if the matter were thoroughly searched into, they would be found to have been committed by supposititious children or those born in adultery, for they hold it utterly improbable that a true father should be murdered by his own son.

They are not allowed even to mention the things which it is not lawful for them to do. To tell a lie is considered by them the greatest disgrace; next to that, to be in debt; and this for many other reasons, but especially because they think that one who is in debt must of necessity tell lies. Whosoever of the citizens has the leprosy or scrofula, is not permitted to stay within a town, nor to have communication with other Persians; and they say that from having committed some offence against the sun a man is afflicted with these diseases. Every stranger that is seized with these distempers many of them even drive out of the country; and they do the same to white pigeons, making the same charge against them. They neither make water, nor spit, nor wash their hands in a river, nor defile the stream with urine, nor do they allow any one else to do so, but they pay extreme veneration to all rivers.

Another circumstance is also peculiar to them, which has escaped the notice of the Persians themselves, but not of us. Their names, which correspond with their personal forms and their rank, all terminate in the same letter which the Dorians call *San,* and the Ionians *Sigma* And if you inquire into this you will find, that all Persian names, without exception, end in the same letter.

These things I can with certainty affirm to be true, since I myself know them. But what follows, relating to the dead, is only secretly mentioned and not openly; viz. that the dead body of a Persian is never buried until it has been torn by some bird or dog; but I know for a certainty that the Magi do this, for they do it openly. The Persians then, having covered the body with wax, conceal it in the ground. The Magi differ very much from all other men, and particularly from the Egyptian priests, for the latter hold it matter of religion not to kill any thing that has life, except such things as they offer in sacrifice; whereas the Magi kill every thing with their own hands, except a dog or a man; and they think they do a meritorious thing, when they kill ants, serpents, and other reptiles and birds. And with regard to this custom, let it remain as it existed from the first. . . .

BOOK IV

[The] affairs [of the Scythians] are ordered as follows. When a Scythian overthrows his first enemy, he drinks his blood; and presents the king with the heads of the enemies he has killed in battle: for if he brings a head, he shares the booty that they take; but not, if he does not bring one. He skins it in the following manner. Having made a circular incision round the ears and taking hold of the skin, he shakes it from the skull; then having scraped off the flesh with the rib of an ox, he softens the skin with his hands; and having made it supple, he uses it as a napkin: each man hangs it on the bridle of the horse which he rides, and prides himself on it; for whoever has the greatest number of these skin napkins, is accounted the most valiant man. Many of them make cloaks of these skins, to throw over themselves, sewing them together like shepherd's coats; and many, having flayed the right hands of their enemies that are dead, together with the nails, make coverings for their quivers: the skin of a man, which is both thick and shining, surpasses almost all other skins in the brightness of its white. Many, having flayed men whole, and stretched the skin on wood, carry it about on horseback. Such usages are received amongst them.

The heads themselves, not indeed of all, but of their greatest enemies, they treat as follows: each, having sawn off all below the eye-brows, cleanses it, and if the man is poor, he covers only the outside with leather, and so uses it; but if he is rich, he covers it indeed with leather, and having gilded the inside, he so uses it for a drinking-cup. And they do this to their relatives, if they are at variance, and one prevails over another in the presence of the king. When strangers of consideration come to him, he produces these heads, and relates how, though they were his relatives, they made war against him, and he overcame them, considering this a proof of bravery.

Once in every year, the governor of a district, each in his own district, mingles a bowl of wine, from which those Scythians drink by when enemies have been captured: but they who have not achieved this, do not taste of this wine, but sit at a distance in dishonour; this is accounted the greatest disgrace: such of them as have killed very many men, having two cups at once, drink them together.

Soothsayers among the Scythians are numerous, who divine by the help of a number of willow rods, in the following manner. When they have brought with them large bundles of twigs, they lay them on the ground and untie them; and having placed each rod apart, they utter their predictions; and whilst they are pronouncing them, they gather up the rods again, and put them together again one by one. This is their national mode of divination. But the Enarees, or Androgyni, say that Venus gave them the power of divining. They divine by means of the bark of a linden-tree: when a man has split the linden-tree in three pieces, twisting it round his own fingers, and then untwisting it, he utters a response.

When the king of the Scythians is sick, he sends for three of the most famous of these prophets, who prophesy in the manner above mentioned; and they generally say as follows, that such or such a citizen has sworn falsely by the royal hearth, mentioning the name of the citizen of whom they speak: for it is a custom with the Scythians in general, to swear by the royal hearth, when they would use the most solemn oath. The person who, they say, has sworn falsely, is immediately seized, and brought forward; and when he is come, the prophets charge him with being clearly proved by their prophetic art to have sworn falsely by the royal hearth, and for this reason the king is ill. He denies it, affirming that he has not sworn falsely, and complains bitterly. On his denial, the king sends for twice as many more prophets; and if they also, examining into the prophetic art, condemn him with having sworn falsely, they straightway cut off his head, and the first prophets divide his property between them; but if the prophets who came last acquit him, other prophets are called in, and others after them. If, then, the greater number acquit the man, it is decreed that the first prophets shall be put to death.

They accordingly put them to death in the following manner: when they have filled a waggon with faggots, and have yoked oxen to it, having tied the feet of the prophets and bound their hands behind them, and having gagged them, they enclose them in the midst of the faggots; then having set fire to them, they terrify the oxen, and let them go. Many oxen therefore are burnt with the prophets, annd many escape very much scorched, when the pole has been burnt asunder. In this manner, and for other reasons, they burn the prophets, calling them false prophets. The king does not spare the children of those whom he puts to death, but kills all the males, and does not hurt the females.

The Scythians make solemn contracts in the following manner, with whomsoever they make them. Having poured wine into a large earthen vessel, they mingle with it blood taken from those who are entering into covenant, having struck with an awl or cut with a knife a small part of the body; then, having dipped a scimetar, some arrows, a hatchet, and a javelin in the vessel, when they have done this, they make many solemn prayers, and then both those who make the contract, and the most considerable of their attendants, drink up *the mixture.*

The sepulchres of the kings are in the country of the Gerrhi, as far as which the Borysthenes is navigable. There, when their king dies, they dig a large square hole in the ground; and having prepared this, they take up the corpse, having the body covered with wax, the belly opened and cleaned, filled with bruised cypress, incense, and parsley and anise-seed, and then sown up again, and carry it in a chariot to another nation: those who receive the corpse brought to them, do the same as the Royal Scythians; they cut off part of their ear, shave off their hair, wound themselves on the arms, lacerate their forehead and nose, and drive arrows through their left hand. Thence they carry the corpse of the king to another nation whom they govern; and those to whom they first came accompany them. When they have carried the corpse round all the provinces, they arrive among the Gerrhi, who are the most remote of the nations they rule over, and at the sepulchres. Then, when they have placed the corpse in the grave on a bed of leaves, having fixed spears on each side of the dead body, they lay pieces of wood over it, and cover it over with mats. In the remaining space of the grave they bury one of the king's concubines, having strangled her, and his cup-bearer, a cook, a groom, a page, a courier, and horses, and firstlings of every thing else, and golden goblets; they make no use of silver or brass. Having done this, they all heap up a large mound, striving and vying with each other to make it as large as possible.

When a year has elapsed, they then do as follows: having taken the most fitting of his remaining servants; they are all native Scythians; for they serve him whomsoever the king may order, and they have no servants bought with money: when therefore they have strangled fifty of these servants, and fifty of the finest horses, having taken out their bowels and cleansed them, they fill them with chaff, and sow them up again. Then having placed the half of a wheel, with its concave side uppermost, on two pieces of wood, and the other half on two other pieces of wood, and having fixed many of these in the same manner, then having thrust thick pieces of wood through the horses lengthwise, up to the neck, they mount them on the half-wheels; and of these the foremost part of the half-wheels supports the shoulders of the horses, and the hinder part supports the belly near the thighs, but the legs on both sides are suspended in the air: then having put bridles and bits on the horses, they stretch them in front, and fasten them to a stake; they then mount upon a horse each, one of the fifty young men that have been strangled, mounting them in the following manner: when they have driven a straight piece of wood along the spine as far as the neck, but a part of this wood projects from the bottom, they fix it into a hole bored in the other piece of wood that passes through the horse. Having placed such horsemen round the monument, they depart. . . .

The Tauri observe the following customs: they sacrifice to the virgin all who suffer shipwreck, and any Greeks they meet with driven on their coasts, in the following manner: having performed the preparatory ceremonies, they strike the head with a club; some say they throw the body down from a precipice, (for their temple is built on a precipice,) and impale the head; but others agree with respect to the head, but say that the body is not thrown from the precipice, but buried in the earth. The Tauri themselves say, that this deity to whom they sacrifice is Iphigenia, daughter of Agamemnon. Enemies whom they subdue they treat as follows: each having cut off a head, carries it home with him, then having fixed it on a long pole, he raises it far above the roof of his house, at all events above the chimney; they say that these are suspended as guards over the whole household. This people live by rapine and war.

The Agathyrsi are a most luxurious people, and wear a profusion of gold. They have promiscuous intercourse with women, to the end that they may be brethren one of another, and being all of one family, may not entertain hatred towards each other. In other respects they approach the usages of the Thracians.

The Neuri observe Scythian customs. One generation before the expedition of Darius, it happened to them to be driven out of their whole country by serpents; for their country produced many serpents, and a much greater number came down upon them from the deserts above; until, being hard pressed, they abandoned their territory, and settled among the Budini. These men seem to be magicians, for it is said of them by the Scythians and the Greeks settled in Scythia, that once every year each Neurian becomes a wolf for a few days, and then is restored again to the same state. Though they affirm this, however, they do not persuade me; they affirm it nevertheless, and support their assertion with an oath.

The Androphagi have the most savage customs of all men; they pay no regard to justice, nor make use of any established law. They are nomades, and wear a dress like the Scythian; *they speak* a peculiar language; and of these nations, are the only people that eat human flesh. . . .

BOOK VII

Xerxes, after the reduction of Egypt, when he was about to take in hand the expedition against Athens, convoked an assembly of the principal Persians, that he might both hear their opinions, and himself make known his intentions before them all. When they were assembled Xerxes addressed them as follows: "Men of Persia, I shall not be the first to introduce this custom among you, but shall adopt it, having received it from my forefathers. For, as I learn from older men, we have never remained inactive since we wrested the sovereign power from the Medes, and Cyrus overthrew Astyages: but the deity thus leads the way, and to us who follow his guidance many things result to our advantage. What deeds Cyrus, and Cambyses, and my father Darius have achieved, and what nations they have added to our empire, no one need mention to you who know them well. But I, since I have succeeded to the throne, have carefully considered this, in what way I may not fall short of my predecessors in this honour, nor acquire less additional power to the Persians. And on mature consideration, I find that we may at once acquire an increase of glory, and a country not inferior nor poorer, but even more productive than that we now possess; and at the same time that satisfaction and vengeance will accrue to us. Wherefore I have now called you together, that I may communicate to you what I purpose to do.

I intend to throw a bridge over the Hellespont, and to march an army through Europe against Greece, that I may punish the Athenians for the injuries they have done to the Persians and to my father. You have already seen Darius preparing to make war against those people; but he died, and had it not in his power to avenge himself. But I, in his cause and that of the other Persians, will not rest till I have taken and burnt Athens; for they first began by doing acts of injustice against my father and me. First of all having come to Sardis, with Aristagoras the Milesian, our servant, on their arrival they burnt down both the groves and the temples. And, secondly, how they treated us on our making a descent on their territory, when Datis and Artaphernes led our forces, you all know well enough.

For these reasons, therefore, I have resolved to make war upon them. And on reflection, I find the following advantages in this course: if we shall subdue them, and their neighbours, who inhabit the country of Pelops the Phrygian, we shall make the Persian territory co-extensive with the air of heaven; nor will the sun look down upon any land that borders on ours; but I, with your assistance, will make them all one territory, marching through the whole of Europe. For I am informed that such is the case; and that no city or nation of the world will remain, which will be able to come to a battle with us, when those whom I have mentioned have been brought into subjection. Thus, both those who are guilty, and those who are not guilty, must equally submit to the yoke of servitude.

But you, by doing what I require, will gratify me exceedingly; when I shall have informed you of the time, it will be the duty of each of you to come promptly. And whosoever shall appear with the best-appointed troops, to him I will give such presents as are accounted most honourable in our country. But that I may not appear to follow my own counsel only, I lay the matter before you, bidding any one of you who wishes, to declare his opinion." Having said this, he ceased.

After him Mardonius spoke: "Sir, not only are you the most excellent of all the Persians that have yet been, but even of all that ever shall be; you also, in other respects, have in speaking touched upon the most important topics and the most exact truth, and especially will not suffer the Ionians, who dwell in Europe, to mock us, worthless as they are. For it would indeed be a great indignity, if, having subdued the Sacae, Indians, Ethiopians, and Assyrians, and other nations, many and powerful, which never did the Persians any wrong, but, in order only to enlarge our dominions, we hold them in servitude; and yet shall not avenge ourselves on the Greeks, who were the first to commit injustice. Having what to fear? what confluence of numbers? what power of wealth?

We are acquainted with their manner of fighting; and we are acquainted with their power, that it is weak. We hold their children in subjection, those who dwell within our territories, and are called Ionians, Aeolians, and Dorians. I myself have made trial of these men already, marching against them at the command of your father; and when I advanced as far as Macedonia, and was within a short distance of reaching Athens itself, no one opposed me in battle.

And yet the Greeks are accustomed, as I am informed, to undertake wars without deliberation, from obstinacy and folly. For when they have declared war against one another, having found out the fairest and most level spot, they go down to it and fight; so that the conquerors depart with great loss, and of the conquered I say nothing at all, for they are utterly destroyed. Whereas, being of the same language, they ought, by the intervention of heralds and ambassadors, to adjust their differences, and in any way rather than by fighting. But if they must needs go to war with each other, they ought to find out where they are each least likely to be conquered, and there try *the issue of a battle.* The Greeks, accordingly, adopting a disadvantageous method, when I marched as far as Macedonia, never ventured so far as to come to a battle.

Will any one, then, O king, have recourse to war, and oppose you, when you lead the multitudes of Asia, and all her ships? In my opinion, indeed, the Grecians will never proceed to such a degree of audacity. But if I should happen to be deceived in my opinion, and they, elated by folly, should come to battle with us, they will learn, that of all men we are the most skilled in war. Let nothing then be untried; for nothing is accomplished of its own self, but all things are usually achieved by men through endeavours." Mardonius, having thus smoothed over the opinion of Xerxes, ceased to speak. . . .

Xerxes, when he had numbered his forces, and the army was drawn up, desired to pass through and inspect them in person. Accordingly he did so, and driving through on a chariot, by each separate nation, he made inquires, and his secretaries wrote down the answers; until he had gone from one extremity to the other, both of the horse and foot. When he had finished this, and the ships had been launched into the sea, Xerxes thereupon removing from his chariot to a Sidonian ship, sat under a gilded canopy, and then sailed by the prows of the ships, asking questions of each, as he had done with the land-forces, and having the answers written down. The captains of the ships having drawn their vessels about four plethra from the beach, lay to, all having turned their ships frontwise to land, and having armed the marines as if for a battle; but Xerxes, sailing between the prows and the beach, inspected them.

When he had sailed through them, and had landed from the ship, he sent for Demaratus, son of Ariston, who accompanied him in the expedition against Greece, and having called him, he addressed him thus: "Demaratus, it is now my pleasure to ask of you certain questions that I wish. You are a Greek, and, as I am informed by you, and other Greeks who have conversed with me, of a city neither the least nor the weakest. Now, therefore, tell me this, whether the Grecians will venture to lift their hands against me: for, as I think, if all the Grecians, and all the rest of the nations that dwell towards the west, were collected together, they would not be able to withstand my attack, unless they were united together. However, I am desirous to know what you say on this subject." Such was the question he asked; but Demaratus answering said, "O king, whether shall I speak truth to you, or what is pleasing?" He bade him speak truth, assuring him that he would not be at all less agreeable than he was before.

When Demaratus heard this, he spoke thus: "O king, since you positively require me to speak truth, I will say such things, as whoever should utter them, would not hereafter be convicted of falsehood. Poverty has ever been familiar to Greece, but virtue has been acquired, having been accomplished by wisdom and firm laws; by the aid of which, Greece has warded off poverty and tyranny. I commend, indeed, all those Greeks who dwell round those Doric lands; but I shall now proceed to speak, not of all, but of the Lacedaemonians only. In the first place, *I say* it is not possible that they should ever listen to your proposals, which bring slavery on Greece: secondly, that they will meet you in battle, even if all the rest of the Greeks should side with with you. With respect to their number, you need not ask how many they are, that they are able to do this; for whether a thousand men, or more, or even less, should have marched out, they will certainly give you battle."

Xerxes, having heard this, replied, "Demaratus, what have you said? that a thousand men will fight with such an army as this? Come, tell me, you say that you were yourself king of these men? Are you, then, willing on the spot to fight with ten men? And yet if all your citizens are such as you represent, you, who are their king, ought by your own institutions to be matched against twice that number; for if each of them is a match for ten men in my army, I expect that you should be a match for twenty, so the opinion you have given utterance to would prove correct. But if, being such as yourself, and of the same stature as you and other Greeks who have conversed with me, ye boast so much, beware that the opinion you have uttered be not an idle vaunt. For come, let us consider every probability: how could a thousand men, or even ten thousand, or even fifty thousand, being all equally free, and not subject to the command of a single person, resist such an army as this? for if they are five thousand, we are more than a thousand against one. Were they, indeed, according to our custom, subject to the command of a single person, they might, through fear of him, prove superior to their natural courage; and, compelled by the lash, might, though fewer, attack a greater number: but now, being left to their own free-will, they will do nothing of the kind. And I am of opinion, that even if they were equal in numbers, the Grecians would hardly contend with the Persians alone. For the valour that you speak of, exists amongst us; it is not, however, common, but rare. For there are Persians among my body-guards, who would readly encounter three Greeks at once; and you, having no experience of these men, talk very idly."

To this Demaratus replied, "O king, I knew from the first, that by adhering to the truth, I should not say what would be agreeable to you; but since you constrained me to speak the exact truth, I told you the real character of the Spartans. However, you yourself well know how tenderly I must love them, who, after they had deprived me of my paternal honours and dignity, have made me citiless and an exile; but your father, having received me, gave me maintenance and a home: it is not probable therefore that a prudent man should repel manifest benevolence, but should by all means cherish it. For my part, I do not pretend to be able to fight with ten men, nor with two; nor would I willingly fight with one. But if there was any necessity, or any great stake to rouse me, I would most willingly fight with one of those men, who pretend to be singly a match for three Grecians. In like manner the Lacedaemonians in single combat are inferior to none; but together are the bravest of all men. For though free, they are not absolutely free; for they have a master over them, the law, which they fear much more than your subjects do you. They do, accordingly, whatever it enjoins; and it ever enjoins the same thing, forbidding them to fly from battle before any number of men, but to remain in their ranks, and conquer or die. If I appear to you, in saying this, to talk idly, I will for the future observe silence on this subject, and now I have spoken through compulsion; however, may events, O king, turn out according to your wish." . . .

King Xerxes, then, encamped in the Trachinian territory of Malis, and the Greeks in the pass. This spot is called by most of the Greeks, Thermopylae, but by the inhabitants and neighbours, Pylae. Both parties, then, encamped in these places. The one was in possession of all the parts towards the north, as far as Trachis; and the others, of the parts which stretch towards the south and meridian, on this continent.

The following were the Greeks who awaited the Persian in this position. Of Spartans three hundred heavy-armed men; of Tegeans and Mantineans one thousand, half of each; from Orchomenus in Arcadia one hundred and twenty; and from the rest of Arcadia one thousand, there were so many Arcadians; from Corinth four hundred; from Phlius two hundred men, and from Mycenae eighty. These came from Peloponnesus. From Boeotia, of Thespians seven hundred, and of Thebans four hundred.

In addition to these, the Opuntian Locrians, being invited, came with all their forces, and a thousand Phocians. For the Greeks themselves had invited them, representing by their ambassadors that "they had arrived as forerunners of the others, and that the rest of the allies might be daily expected; that the sea was protected by them, being guarded by the Athenians, the Aeginetae, and others, who were appointed to the naval service; and that they had nothing to fear, for that it was not a god who invaded Greece, but a man; and that there never was, and never would be, any mortal who had not evil mixed with *his prosperity* from his very birth; and to the greatest of them the greatest *reverses happen*. That it must, therefore, needs be, that he who is marching against us, being a mortal, will be disappointed in his expectation." They, having heard this, marched with assistance to Trachis.

These nations had separate generals for their several cities; but the one most admired, and who commanded the whole army, was a Lacedaemonian, Leonidas, son of Anaxandrides, son of Leon, son of Eurycratides, son of Anaxander, son of Eurycrates, son of Polydorus, son of Alcamenes, son of Teleclus, son of Archelaus, son of Agesilaus, son of Doryssus, son of Leobotes, son of Echestratus, son of Agis, son of Eurysthenes, son of Aristodemus, son of Aristomachus, son of Cleodaeus, son of Hyllus, son of Hercules; who had unexpectedly succeeded to the throne of Sparta.

For as he had two elder brothers, Cleomenes and Dorieus, he was far from any thought of the kingdom. However, Cleomenes having died without male issue, and Dorieus being no longer alive, having ended his days in Sicily, the kingdom thus devolved upon Leonidas; both because he was older than Cleombrotus, (for he was the youngest son of Anaxandrides,) and also because he had married the daughter of Cleomenes. He then marched to Thermopylae, having chosen the three hundred men allowed by law, and such as had children. On his march he took with him the Thebans, whose numbers I have already reckoned, and whom Leontiades, son of Eurymachus commanded. For this reason Leonidas was anxious to take with him the Thebans alone of all the Greeks, because they were strongly accused of favouring the Medes: he, therefore, summoned them to the war, wishing to know whether they would send their forces with him, or would openly renounce the alliance of the Grecians. But they, though otherwise minded, sent assistance.

The Spartans sent these troops first with Leonidas, in order that the rest of the allies, seeing them, might take the field, and might not go over to the Medes, if they heard that they were delaying. But afterwards, for the Carnean festival was then an obstacle to them, they purposed, when they had kept the feast, to leave a garrison in Sparta, and to march immediately with their whole strength. The rest of the confederates likewise intended to act in the same manner; for the Olympic games occurred at the same period as these events. As they did not, therefore, suppose that the engagement at Thermopylae would so soon be decided, they despatched an advance-guard. Thus, then, they intended to do.

The Greeks at Thermopylae, when the Persians came near the pass, being alarmed, consulted about a retreat; accordingly, it seemed best to the other Peloponnesians to retire to Peloponnesus, and guard the Isthmus; but Leonidas, perceiving the Phocians and Locrians very indignant at this proposition, determined to stay there, and to despatch messengers to the cities, desiring them to come to their assistance, as being too few to repel the army of the Medes.

While they were deliberating on these matters, Xerxes sent a scout on horseback, to see how many they were, and what they were doing. For while he was still in Thessaly, he had heard that a small army had been assembled at that spot, and as to their leaders, that they were Lacedaemonians, and Leonidas, who was of the race of Hercules. When the horseman rode up to the camp, he reconnoitred, and saw not indeed the whole camp, for it was not possible that they should be seen who were posted within the wall, which, having rebuilt, they were now guarding: but he had a clear view of those on the outside, whose arms were piled in front of the wall. At this time the Lacedaemonians happened to be posted outside; and some of the men he saw performing gymnastic exercises, and others combing their hair. On beholding this he was astonished, and ascertained their number; and having informed himself of every thing accurately, he rode back at his leisure, for no one pursued him, and he met with general contempt. On his return he gave an account to Xerxes of all that he had seen.

When Xerxes heard this, he could not comprehend the truth, that the Grecians were preparing to be slain and to slay to the utmost of their power. But, as they appeared to behave in a ridiculous manner, he sent for Demaratus, son of Ariston, who was then in the camp; and when he was come into his presence, Xerxes questioned him as to each particular, wishing to understand what the Lacedaemonians were doing. Demaratus said, "You before heard me, when we were setting out against Greece, speak of these men; and when you heard, you treated me with ridicule, though I told you in what way I foresaw these matters would issue. For it is my chief aim, O king, to adhere to the truth in your presence; hear it, therefore, once more. These men have come to fight with us for the pass, and are now preparing themselves to do so. For such is their custom, when they are going to hazard their lives, then they dress their heads. But be assured, if you conquer these men, and those that remain in Sparta, there is no other nation in the world that will dare to raise their hands against you, O king. For you are now to engage with the noblest kingdom and city of all amongst the Greeks, and with the most valiant men." What was said seemed very incredible to Xerxes, and he asked again, "how, being so few in number, they could contend with his army." He answered, "O king, deal with me as with a liar, if these things do not turn out as I say."

By saying this he did not convince Xerxes. He therefore let four days pass, constantly expecting that they would betake themselves to flight. But on the fifth day, as they had not retreated, but appeared to him to stay through arrogance and rashness, he being enraged, sent the Medes and Cissians against them, with orders to take them alive, and bring them into his presence. When the Medes bore down impetuously upon the Greeks, many of them fell; others followed to the charge, and were not repulsed, though they suffered greatly. But they made it evident to every one, and not least of all to the king himself, that they were indeed many men, but few soldiers. The engagement lasted through the day.

When the Medes were roughly handled, they thereupon retired; and the Persians whom the king called "Immortal," and whom Hydarnes commanded, taking their place, advanced to the attack; thinking that they indeed should easily settle the business. But when they engaged with the Grecians, they succeeded no better than the Medic troops, but just the same, as they fought in a narrow space, and used shorter spears than the Greeks, and were unable to avail themselves of their numbers. The Lacedaemonians fought memorably both in other respects, showing that they knew how to fight with men who knew not, and whenever they turned their backs, they retreated in close order: but the barbarians seeing them retreat, followed with a shout and clamour; then they, being overtaken, wheeled round so as to front the barbarians, and having faced about, overthrew an inconceivable number of the Persians; and then some few of the Spartans themselves fell. So that when the Persians were unable to gain any thing in their attempt on the pass, by attacking in troops and in every possible manner, they retired.

It is said that during these onsets of the battle, the king, who witnessed them, thrice sprang from his throne, being alarmed for his army. Thus they strove at that time. On the following day the barbarians fought with no better success; for considering that the Greeks were few in number, and expecting that they were covered with wounds, and would not be able to raise their heads against them any more, they renewed the contest. But the Greeks were marshalled in companies and according to their several nations, and each fought in turn, except only the Phocians, they were stationed at the mountain to guard the pathway. When therefore the Persians found nothing different from what they had seen on the preceding day, they retired.

While the king was in doubt what course to take in the present state of affairs, Ephialtes, son of Eurydemus, a Malian, obtained an audience of him, expecting that he should receive a great reward from the king, and informed him of the path which leads over the mountain to Thermopylae; and by that means caused the destruction of those Greeks who were stationed there. But afterwards, fearing the Lacedaemonians, he fled to Thessaly; and when he had fled, a price was set on his head by the Pylagori, when the Amphictyons were assembled at Pylae. But some time after, he went down to Anticyra, and was killed by Athenades, a Trachinian. This Athenades killed him for another reason, which I shall mention in a subsequent part of my history; he was however rewarded none the less by the Lacedaemonians.

Another account is given, that Onetes, son of Phanagoras, a Carystian, and Corydallus of Anticyra, were the persons who gave this information to the king, and conducted the Persians round the mountain. But to me this is by no means credible: for in the first place we may draw that inference from this circumstance, that the Pylagori of the Grecians set a price on the head not of Onetes and Corydallus, but of Ephialtes the Trachinian, having surely ascertained the exact truth; and in the next place we know that Ephialtes fled on that account. Onetes indeed, though he was not a Malian, might be acquainted with this path, if he had been much conversant with the country; but it was Ephialtes who conducted them round the mountain by the path, and I charge him as the guilty person.

Xerxes, since he was pleased with what Ephialtes promised to perform, being exceedingly delighted, immediately despatched Hydarnes and the troops that Hydarnes commanded; and he started from the camp about the hour of lamp-lighting. The native Malians discovered this pathway; and having discovered it, conducted the Thessalians by it against the Phocians, at the time when the Phocians, having fortified the pass by a wall, were under shelter from an attack. From that time it appeared to have been of no service to the Malians.

This path is situated as follows: it begins from the river Asopus, which flows through the cleft; the same name is given both to the mountain and to the path, Anopaea; and this Anopaea extends along the ridge of the mountain, and ends near Alpenus, which is the first city of the Locrians towards the Malians, and by the rock called Melampygus, and by the seats of the Cercopes; and there the path is the narrowest.

Along this path, thus situate, the Persians, having crossed the Asopus, marched all night, having on their right the mountains of the Oetaeans, and on their left those of the Trachinians; morning appeared, and they were on the summit of the mountain. At this part of the mountain, as I have already mentioned, a thousand heavy-armed Phocians kept guard, to defend their own country, and to secure the pathway. For the lower pass was guarded by those before mentioned; and the Phocians had voluntarily promised Leonidas to guard the path across the mountain.

The Phocians discovered them after they had ascended, in the following manner; for the Persian ascended without being observed, as the whole mountain was covered with oaks; there was a perfect calm, and as was likely, a considerable rustling taking place from the leaves strewn under foot, the Phocians sprung up and put on their arms, and immediately the barbarians made their appearance. But when they saw men clad in armour they were astonished, for, expecting to find nothing to oppose them, they fell in with an army. Thereupon Hydarnes, fearing lest the Phocians might be Lacedaemonians, asked Ephialtes of what nation the troops were; and being accurately informed, he drew up the Persians for battle. The Phocians, when they were hit by many and thick-falling arrows, fled to the summit of the mountain, supposing that they had come expressly to attack them, and prepared to perish. Such was their determination. But the Persians, with Ephialtes and Hydarnes, took no notice of the Phocians, but marched down the mountain with all speed.

To those of the Greeks who were at Thermopylae, the augur Megistias, having inspected the sacrifices, first made known the death that would befall them in the morning; certain deserters afterwards came and brought intelligence of the circuit the Persians were taking; these brought the news while it was yet night, and, thirdly, the scouts running down from the heights, as soon as day dawned, *brought the same intelligence.* Upon this the Greeks held a consultation, and their opinions were divided. For some would not hear of abandoning their post, and others opposed that view. After this, when the assembly broke up, some of them departed, and being dispersed betook themselves to their several cities; but others of them prepared to remain there with Leonidas.

It is said that Leonidas himself sent them away, being anxious that they should not perish; but that he and the Spartans who were there could not honourably desert the post which they originally came to defend. For my own part, I am rather inclined to think, that Leonidas, when he perceived that the allies were averse and unwilling to share the danger with him, bade them withdraw; but that he considered it dishonourable for himself to depart: on the other hand, by remaining there, great renown would be left for him, and the prosperity of Sparta would not be obliterated. For it had been announced to the Spartans, by the Pythian, when they consulted the oracle concerning this war, as soon as it commenced, "that either Lacedaemon must be overthrown by the barbarians, or their king perish." This answer she gave in hexameter verses to this effect: "To you, O inhabitants of spacious Lacedaemon, either your vast, glorious city shall be destroyed by men sprung from Perseus, or, if not so, the confines of Lacedaemon mourn a king deceased of the race of Hercules. For neither shall the strength of bulls nor of lions withstand him, with force opposed to force; for he has the strength of Jove; and I say he shall not be restrained, before he has, certainly, obtained one of these for his share." I think, therefore, that Leonidas, considering these things, and being desirous to acquire glory for the Spartans alone, sent away the allies, rather than that those who went away differed in opinion, and went away in such an unbecoming manner.

The following in no small degree strengthens my conviction on this point. For not only *did he send away* the others, but it is certain, that Leonidas also sent away the augur who followed the army, Megistias the Acarnanian, who was said to have been originally descended from Melampus, the same who announced from an inspection of the victims what was about to befall them, in order that he might not perish with them. He, however, though dismissed, did not himself depart, but sent away his son, who served with him in the expedition, being his only child.

The allies accordingly, that were dismissed, departed, and obeyed Leonidas; but only the Thespians and the Thebans remained with the Lacedaemonians: the Thebans, indeed, remained unwillingly, and against their inclination, (for Leonidas detained them, treating them as hostages;) but the Thespians willingly, for they refused to go away and abandon Leonidas and those with him, but remained and died with them. Demophilus, son of Diadromas, commanded them.

Xerxes, after he had poured out libations at sun-rise, having waited a short time, began his attack about the time of full market; for he had been so instructed by Ephialtes; for the descent from the mountain is more direct, and the distance much shorter, than the circuit and ascent. The barbarians, therefore, with Xerxes, advanced; and the Greeks with Leonidas, marching out as if for certain death, now advanced much farther than before into the wide part of the defile. For the fortification of the wall had protected them, and they on the preceding days, having taken up their position in the narrow part, there fought. But now engaging outside the narrows, great numbers of the barbarians fell. For the officers of the companies from behind, having scourges, flogged every man, constantly urging them forward; in consequence, many of them falling into the sea, perished, and many more were trampled alive under foot by one another; and no regard was paid to any that perished. For the Greeks, knowing that death awaited them at the hands of those who were going round the mountain, being desperate, and regardless of their own lives, displayed the utmost possible valour against the barbarians.

Already were most of their javelins broken, and they had begun to despatch the Persians with their swords. In this part of the struggle fell Leonidas, fighting valiantly, and with him other eminent Spartans, whose names, seeing they were deserving men, I have ascertained; indeed I have ascertained the names of the whole three hundred. On the side of the Persians, also, many other eminent men fell on this occasion, and amongst them two sons of Darius, Abrocomes and Hyperanthes, born to Darius of Phrataguna, daughter of Artanes; but Artanes was brother to king Darius, and son of Hystaspes, son of Arsames. He, when he gave his daughter to Darius, gave him also all his property, as she was his only child.

Accordingly, two brothers of Xerxes fell at this spot, fighting for the body of Leonidas, and there was a violent struggle between the Persians and Lacedaemonians, until at last the Greeks rescued it by their valour, and four times repulsed the enemy. Thus the contest continued until those with Ephialtes came up. When the Greeks heard that they were approaching, from this time the battle was altered. For they retreated to the narrow part of the way, and passing beyond the wall, came and took up their position on the rising ground, all in a compact body, with the exception of the Thebans: the rising ground is at the entrance where the stone lion now stands to the memory of Leonidas. On this spot, while they defended themselves with swords, such as had them still remaining, and their hands and teeth, the barbarians overwhelmed them with missiles, some of them attacking them in front, and having thrown down the wall; and others surrounding and attacking them on every side.

☙ ANTIGONE
Sophocles

In ancient Greece, drama was more than entertainment, more even than art. It was religious ritual, performed with fitting solemnity at the great spring festival of Dionysus, the god of fertility. As such, it was far closer to the ritual dances of primitive tribes than to Broadway theater. In fifth-century Athens, at the hands of Aeschylus, Sophocles, and Euripides, tragedy was fashioned into a superb art form with a life of its own. To the spectators, however, it continued to be an event—and a highly significant one—in the annual life of the polis. Nowhere do Greek values receive a more searching treatment. In particular, one common theme is the conflicting claims of family, religion, and the polis; another is the potentiality of exceptional individuals to bring about harm as well as good. Greek tragedy was always "moralistic": it dealt with right and wrong to inculcate a moral lesson.

The Antigone *of Sophocles* (ca. *496–406* B.C.) *was first performed in 441* B.C., *at the height of Athenian influence. Critics, both then and in our own day, have disagreed about the meaning of the play.*

The scene is set in ancient Thebes before the Trojan War, but the problems raised are characteristic of the Age of Tyrants (seventh and sixth centuries B.C.). *As the play opens, Antigone and Ismene, the daughters of Oedipus, are mourning the deaths of their brothers Eteocles and Polynices, and discussing a recent edict by King Creon. Oedipus, whose life had borne witness to the futility of evading the decrees of the gods (see Sophocles'* Oedipus the King), *has finally died in the sacred grove at Colonus after twenty years of wandering in blindness. Soon afterward his sons, as if doomed by the family curse, quarreled over the kingdom. Polynices left Thebes, only to return at the head of seven armies to challenge his elder brother Eteocles for the throne. A siege ensued, and a climactic battle in which the two brothers killed each other. Creon, the brother of Jocasta (Oedipus' mother and wife), who had acted as regent while the boys were growing up, has now resumed the throne in his own right. He has issued an edict that the body of Polynices is to be left unburied, thus condemning his soul to wander endlessly instead of resting in Hades, as a dreadful deterrent to treason.*

characters

Ismene }
Antigone } daughters of Oedipus
Creon, King of Thebes
Haemon, son of Creon
Teiresias, a blind prophet
A Sentry
A Messenger
Eurydice, wife of Creon
Chorus of Theban elders
King's attendants
Queen's attendants
A boy leading Teiresias
Soldiers

Scene: Before the Palace at Thebes

Enter **Ismene** *from the central door of the Palace.* **Antigone** *follows, anxious and urgent; she closes the door carefully, and comes to join her sister.*

Antigone O sister! Ismene dear, dear sister Ismene!
You know how heavy the hand of God is upon us;
How we who are left must suffer for our father, Oedipus.
There is no pain, no sorrow, no suffering, no dishonour
We have not shared together, you and I.
And now there is something more. Have you heard this order,
This latest order that the King has proclaimed to the city?
Have you heard how our dearest are being treated like enemies?

Ismene I have heard nothing about any of those we love,
Neither good nor evil—not, I mean, since the death
Of our two brothers, both fallen in a day.
The Argive army, I hear, was withdrawn last night.
I know no more to make me sad or glad.

Antigone I thought you did not. That's why I brought you out here,
Where we shan't be heard, to tell you something alone.

Ismene What is it, Antigone? Black news, I can see already.

Antigone O Ismene, what do you think? Our two dear brothers . . .
Creon has given funeral honours to one,
And not to the other; nothing but shame and ignominy.
Eteocles has been buried, they tell me, in state,
With all honourable observances due to the dead.
But Polynices, just as unhappily fallen—the order
Says he is not to be buried, not to be mourned;
To be left unburied, unwept, a feast of flesh

Sophocles, *The Theban Plays,* trans. E. F. Watling (Baltimore: Penguin Books, Inc., 1947), pp. 126–162.

For keen-eyed carrion birds. The noble Creon!
It is against you and me he has made this order.
Yes, against me. And soon he will be here himself
To make it plain to those that have not heard it,
And to enforce it. This is no idle threat;
The punishment for disobedience is death by stoning.
So now you know. And now is the time to show
Whether or not you are worthy of your high blood.

Ismene My poor Antigone, if this is really true,
What more can *I* do, or undo, to help you?

Antigone *Will* you help me? Will you do something with me? Will you?

Ismene Help you do what, Antigone? What do you mean?

Antigone Would you help me lift the body . . . you and me?

Ismene You cannot mean . . . to bury him? Against the order?

Antigone Is he not my brother, and yours, whether you like it
Or not? *I* shall never desert him, never.

Ismene How could you dare, when Creon has expressly forbidden it?

Antigone He has no right to keep me from my own.

Ismene O sister, sister, do you forget how our father
Perished in shame and misery, his awful sin
Self-proved, blinded by his own self-mutilation?
And then his mother, his wife—for she was both—
Destroyed herself in a noose of her own making.
And now our brothers, both in a single day
Fallen in an awful exaction of death for death,
Blood for blood, each slain by the other's hand.
Now we two left; and what will be the end of us,
If we transgress the law and defy our king?
O think, Antigone; we are women; it is not for us
To fight against men; our rulers are stronger than we,
And we must obey in this, or in worse than this.
May the dead forgive me, I can do no other
But as I am commanded; to do more is madness.

Antigone No; then I will not ask you for your help.
Nor would I thank you for it, if you gave it.
Go your own way; I will bury my brother;
And if I die for it, what happiness!
Convicted of reverence—I shall be content
To lie beside a brother whom I love.
We have only a little time to please the living,
But all eternity to love the dead.
There I shall lie for ever. Live, if you will;
Live, and defy the holiest laws of heaven.

Ismene I do not defy them; but I cannot act
Against the State. I am not strong enough.

Antigone Let that be your excuse, then. I will go
And heap a mound of earth over my brother.

Ismene I fear for you, Antigone; I fear—

Antigone You need not fear for me. Fear for yourself.

Ismene At least be secret. Do not breathe a word.
I'll not betray your secret.

Antigone Publish it
To all the world! Else I shall hate you more.

Ismene Your heart burns! Mine is frozen at the thought.

Antigone I know my duty, where true duty lies.

Ismene If you can do it; but you're bound to fail.

Antigone When I have *tried* and failed, I shall have failed.

Ismene No sense in starting on a hopeless task.

Antigone Oh, I shall hate you if you talk like that!
And *he* will hate you, rightly. Leave me alone
With my own madness. There is no punishment
Can rob me of my honourable death.

Ismene Go then, if you are determined, to your folly.
But remember that those who love you . . . love you still.

__Ismene__ goes into the Palace.
__Antigone__ leaves the stage by a side exit.

Enter the __Chorus__ of Theban elders.

Chorus Hail the sun! the brightest of all that ever
Dawned on the City of Seven Gates, City of Thebes!
Hail the golden dawn over Dirce's river
Rising to speed the flight of the white invaders
Homeward in full retreat!

The army of Polynices was gathered against us,
In angry dispute his voice was lifted against us,
Like a ravening bird of prey he swooped around us
With white wings flashing, with flying plumes,
With armed hosts ranked in thousands.

At the threshold of seven gates in a circle of blood
His swords stood round us, his jaws were opened against us;
But before he could taste our blood, or consume us with fire,
He fled, fled with the roar of the dragon behind him
And thunder of war in his ears.

The Father of Heaven abhors the proud tongue's boasting;
He marked the oncoming torrent, the flashing stream
Of their golden harness, the clash of their battle gear;
He heard the invader cry Victory over our ramparts,
And smote him with fire to the ground.

Down to the ground from the crest of his hurricane onslaught
He swung, with the fiery brands of his hate brought low:
Each and all to their doom of destruction appointed
By the god that fighteth for us.

Seven invaders at seven gates seven defenders
Spoiled of their bronze for a tribute to Zeus; save two
Luckless brothers in one fight matched together
And in one death laid low.

Great is the victory, great be the joy
In the city of Thebes, the city of chariots.
Now is the time to fill the temples
With glad thanksgiving for warfare ended;
Shake the ground with the night-long dances,
Bacchus afoot and delight abounding.

But see, the King comes here,
Creon, the son of Menoeceus,
Whom the gods have appointed for us
In our recent change of fortune.
What matter is it, I wonder,
That has led him to call us together
By his special proclamation?

*The central door is opened, and **Creon** enters.*

Creon My councillors: now that the gods have brought our city
Safe through a storm of trouble to tranquillity,
I have called you especially out of all my people
To conference together, knowing that you
Were loyal subjects when King Laius reigned,
And when King Oedipus so wisely ruled us,
And again, upon his death, faithfully served
His sons, till they in turn fell—both slayers, both slain,
Both stained with brother-blood, dead in a day—
And I, their next of kin, inherited
The throne and kingdom which I now possess.
No other touchstone can test the heart of a man,
The temper of his mind and spirit, till he be tried
In the practice of authority and rule.
For my part, I have always held the view,
And hold it still, that a king whose lips are sealed
By fear, unwilling to seek advice, is damned.
And no less damned is he who puts a friend
Above his country; I have no good word for him.
As God above is my witness, who sees all,

When I see any danger threatening my people,
Whatever it may be, I shall declare it.
No man who is his country's enemy
Shall call himself my friend. Of this I am sure—
Our country is our life; only when she
Rides safely, have we any friends at all.
Such is my policy for our common weal.
In pursuance of this, I have made a proclamation
Concerning the sons of Oedipus, as follows:
Eteocles, who fell fighting in defence of the city,
Fighting gallantly, is to be honoured with burial
And with all the rites due to the noble dead.
The other—you know whom I mean—his brother Polynices,
Who came back from exile intending to burn and destroy
His fatherland and the gods of his fatherland,
To drink the blood of his kin, to make them slaves—
He is to have no grave, no burial,
No mourning from anyone; it is forbidden.
He is to be left unburied, left to be eaten
By dogs and vultures, a horror for all to see.
I am determined that never, if I can help it,
Shall evil triumph over good. Alive
Or dead, the faithful servant of his country
Shall be rewarded.

Chorus Creon, son of Menoeceus,
You have given your judgment for the friend and for the enemy.
As for those that are dead, so for us who remain,
Your will is law.

Creon See then that it be kept.

Chorus My lord, some younger would be fitter for that task.

Creon Watchers are already set over the corpse.

Chorus What other duty then remains for us?

Creon Not to connive at any disobedience.

Chorus If there were any so mad as to ask for death—

Creon Ay, that is the penalty. There is always someone
Ready to be lured to ruin by hope of gain.

*He turns to go. A **Sentry** enters from the side of the stage.*

***Creon** pauses at the Palace door.*

Sentry My lord: if I am out of breath, it is not from haste.
I have not been running. On the contrary, many a time
I stopped to think and loitered on the way,
Saying to myself 'Why hurry to your doom,
Poor fool?' and then I said 'Hurry, you fool.
If Creon hears this from another man,

Your head's as good as off.' So here I am,
As quick as my unwilling haste could bring me;
In no great hurry, in fact. So now I am here . . .
But I'll tell my story . . . though it may be nothing after all.
And whatever I have to suffer, it can't be more
Than what God wills, so I cling to that for my comfort.

Creon Good heavens, man, whatever is the matter?

Sentry To speak of myself first—I never did it, sir;
Nor saw who did; no one can punish me for that.

Creon You tell your story with a deal of artful precaution.
It's evidently something strange.

Sentry It is.
So strange, it's very difficult to tell.

Creon Well, out with it, and let's be done with you.

Sentry It's this, sir. The corpse . . . someone has just
Buried it and gone. Dry dust over the body
They scattered, in the manner of holy burial.

Creon What! Who dared to do it?

Sentry I don't know, sir.
There was no sign of a pick, no scratch of a shovel;
The ground was hard and dry—no trace of a wheel;
Whoever it was has left no clues behind him.
When the sentry on the first watch showed it us,
We were amazed. The corpse was covered from sight—
Not with a proper grave—just a layer of earth—
As it might be, the act of some pious passer-by.
There were no tracks of an animal either, a dog
Or anything that might have come and mauled the body.
Of course we all started pitching in to each other,
Accusing each other, and might have come to blows,
With no one to stop us; for anyone might have done it,
But it couldn't be proved against him, and all denied it.
We were all ready to take hot iron in hand
And go through fire and swear by God and heaven
We hadn't done it, nor knew of anyone
That could have thought of doing it, much less done it.
Well, we could make nothing of it. Then one of our men
Said something that made all our blood run cold—
Something we could neither refuse to do, nor do,
But at our own risk. What he said was 'This
Must be reported to the King; we can't conceal it.'
So it was agreed. We drew lots for it, and I,
Such is my luck, was chosen. So here I am,
As much against my will as yours, I'm sure;
A bringer of bad news expects no welcome.

Chorus My lord, I fear—I feared it from the first—
That this may prove to be an act of the gods.
Creon Enough of that! Or I shall lose my patience.
Don't talk like an old fool, old though you be.
Blasphemy, to say the gods could give a thought
To carrion flesh! Held him in high esteem,
I suppose, and buried him like a benefactor—
A man who came to burn their temples down,
Ransack their holy shrines, their land, their laws?
Is that the sort of man you think gods love?
Not they. No. There's a party of malcontents
In the city, rebels against my word and law,
Shakers of heads in secret, impatient of rule;
They are the people, I see it well enough,
Who have bribed their instruments to do this thing.
Money! Money's the curse of man, none greater.
That's what wrecks cities, banishes men from home,
Tempts and deludes the most well-meaning soul,
Pointing out the way to infamy and shame.
Well, they shall pay for their success.
(*To the* **Sentry**)
See to it!
See to it, you! Upon my oath, I swear,
As Zeus is my god above: either you find
The perpetrator of this burial
And bring him here into my sight, or death—
No, not your mere death shall pay the reckoning,
But, for a living lesson against such infamy,
You shall be racked and tortured till you tell
The whole truth of this outrage; so you may learn
To seek your gain where gain is yours to get,
Not try to grasp it everywhere. In wickedness
You'll find more loss than profit.
Sentry May I say more?
Creon No more; each word you say but stings me more.
Sentry Stings in your ears, sir, or in your deeper feelings?
Creon Don't bandy words, fellow, about my feelings.
Sentry Though I offend your ears, sir, it is not I
But he that's guilty that offends your soul.
Creon Oh, born to argue, were you?
Sentry Maybe so;
But still not guilty in this business.
Creon Doubly so, if you have sold your soul for money.
Sentry To think that thinking men should think so wrongly!
Creon Think what you will. But if you fail to find

The doer of this deed, you'll learn one thing:
Ill-gotten gain brings no one any good.

He goes into the Palace.

Sentry Well, heaven send they find him. But whether or no,
They'll not find me again, that's sure. Once free,
Who never thought to see another day,
I'll thank my lucky stars, and keep away.

Exit.

Chorus Wonders are many on earth, and the greatest of these
Is man, who rides the ocean and takes his way
Through the deeps, through wind-swept valleys of perilous seas
That surge and sway.

He is master of ageless Earth, to his own will bending
The immortal mother of gods by the sweat of his brow,
As year succeeds to year, with toil unending
Of mule and plough.

He is lord of all things living; birds of the air,
Beasts of the field, all creatures of sea and land
He taketh, cunning to capture and ensnare
With sleight of hand;

Hunting the savage beast from the upland rocks,
Taming the mountain monarch in his lair,
Teaching the wild horse and the roaming ox
His yoke to bear.

The use of language, the wind-swift motion of brain
He learnt; found out the laws of living together
In cities, building him shelter against the rain
And wintry weather.

There is nothing beyond his power. His subtlety
Meeteth all chance, all danger conquereth.
For every ill he hath found its remedy,
Save only death.

O wondrous subtlety of man, that draws
To good or evil ways! Great honour is given
And power to him who upholdeth his country's laws
And the justice of heaven.

But he that, too rashly daring, walks in sin
In solitary pride to his life's end.
At door of mine shall never enter in
To call me friend.

(*Severally, seeing some persons approach from a distance*)

O gods! A wonder to see!
Surely it cannot be—
It is no other—
Antigone!
Unhappy maid—
Unhappy Oedipus' daughter; it is she they bring.
Can she have rashly disobeyed
The order of our King?

Enter the **Sentry,** *bringing* **Antigone** *guarded by two more soldiers.*

Sentry We've got her. Here's the woman that did the deed.
We found her in the act of burying him. Where's the King?

Chorus He is just coming out of the palace now.

Enter **Creon.**

Creon What's this? What am I just in time to see?

Sentry My lord, an oath's a very dangerous thing.
Second thoughts may prove us liars. Not long since
I swore I wouldn't trust myself again
To face your threats; you gave me a drubbing the first time.
But there's no pleasure like an unexpected pleasure,
Not by a long way. And so I've come again,
Though against my solemn oath. And I've brought this lady,
Who's been caught in the act of setting that grave in order.
And no casting lots for it this time—the prize is mine
And no one else's. So take her; judge and convict her.
I'm free, I hope, and quit of the horrible business.

Creon How did you find her? Where have you brought her from?

Sentry She was burying the man with her own hands, and that's the truth.

Creon Are you in your senses? Do you know what your are saying?

Sentry I saw her myself, burying the body of the man
Whom you said not to bury. Don't I speak plain?

Creon How did she come to be seen and taken in the act?

Sentry It was this way.
After I got back to the place,
With all your threats and curses ringing in my ears,
We swept off all the earth that covered the body,
And left it a sodden naked corpse again;
Then sat up on the hill, on the windward side,
Keeping clear of the stench of him, as far as we could;
All of us keeping each other up to the mark,
With pretty sharp speaking, not to be caught napping this time.
So this went on some hours, till the flaming sun
Was high in the top of the sky, and the heat was blazing.
Suddenly a storm of dust, like a plague from heaven,
Swept over the ground, stripping the trees stark bare,
Filling the sky; you had to shut your eyes

To stand against it. When at last it stopped,
There was the girl, screaming like an angry bird,
When it finds its nest left empty and little ones gone.
Just like that she screamed, seeing the body
Naked, crying and cursing the ones that had done it.
Then she picks up the dry earth in her hands,
And pouring out of a fine bronze urn she's brought
She makes her offering three times to the dead.
Soon as we saw it, down we came and caught her.
She wasn't at all frightened. And so we charged her
With what she'd done before, and this. She admitted it,
I'm glad to say—though sorry too, in a way.
It's good to save your own skin, but a pity
To have to see another get into trouble,
Whom you've no grudge against. However, I can't say
I've ever valued anyone else's life
More than my own, and that's the honest truth.

Creon (*to* ***Antigone***) Well, what do you say—you, hiding your head there:
Do you admit, or do you deny the deed?

Antigone I do admit it. I do not deny it.

Creon (*to the* ***Sentry***) You—you may go. You are discharged from blame.

Exit ***Sentry.***

Now tell me, in as few words as you can,
Did you know the order forbidding such an act?

Antigone I knew it, naturally. It was plain enough.

Creon And yet you dared to contravene it?

Antigone Yes.
That order did not come from God. Justice,
That dwells with the gods below, knows no such law.
I did not think your edicts strong enough
To overrule the unwritten unalterable laws
Of God and heaven, you being only a man.
They are not of yesterday or to-day, but everlasting,
Though where they came from, none of us can tell.
Guilty of their transgression before God
I cannot be, for any man on earth.
I knew that I should have to die, of course,
With or without your order. If it be soon,
So much the better. Living in daily torment
As I do, who would not be glad to die?
This punishment will not be any pain.
Only if I had let my mother's son
Lie there unburied, then I could not have borne it.
This I can bear. Does that seem foolish to you?
Or is it you that are foolish to judge me so?

Chorus She shows her father's stubborn spirit: foolish
Not to give way when everything's against her.
Creon Ah, but you'll see. The over-obstinate spirit
Is soonest broken; as the strongest iron will snap
If over-tempered in the fire to brittleness.
A little halter is enough to break
The wildest horse. Proud thoughts do not sit well
Upon subordinates. This girl's proud spirit
Was first in evidence when she broke the law;
And now, to add insult to her injury,
She gloats over her deed. But, as I live,
She shall not flout my orders with impunity.
My sister's child—ay, were she even nearer,
Nearest and dearest, she should not escape
Full punishment—she, and her sister too,
Her partner, doubtless, in this burying.
Let her be fetched! She was in the house just now;
I saw her, hardly in her right mind either.
Often the thoughts of those who plan dark deeds
Betray themselves before the deed is done.
The criminal who being caught still tries
To make a fair excuse, is damned indeed.
Antigone Now you have caught, will you do more than kill me?
Creon No, nothing more; that is all I could wish.
Antigone Why then delay? There is nothing that you can say
That I should wish to hear, as nothing I say
Can weigh with you. I have given my brother burial.
What greater honour could I wish? All these
Would say that what I did was honourable,
But fear locks up their lips. To speak and act
Just as he likes is a king's prerogative.
Creon You are wrong. None of my subjects thinks as you do.
Antigone Yes, sir, they do; but dare not tell you so.
Creon And you are not only alone, but unashamed.
Antigone There is no shame in honouring my brother.
Creon Was not his enemy, who died with him, your brother?
Antigone Yes, both were brothers, both of the same parents.
Creon You honour one, and so insult the other.
Antigone He that is dead will not accuse me of that.
Creon He will, if you honour him no more than the traitor.
Antigone It was not a slave, but his brother, that died with him.
Creon Attacking his country, while the other defended it.
Antigone Even so, we have a duty to the dead.
Creon Not to give equal honour to good and bad.
Antigone Who knows? In the country of the dead that may be the law.

Creon An enemy can't be a friend, even when dead.
Antigone My way is to share my love, not share my hate.
Creon Go then, and share your love among the dead.
We'll have no woman's law here, while I live.

*Enter **Ismene** from the Palace.*

Chorus Here comes Ismene, weeping
In sisterly sorrow; a darkened brow,
Flushed face, and the fair cheek marred
With flooding rain.
Creon You crawling viper! Lurking in my house
To suck my blood! Two traitors unbeknown
Plotting against my throne. Do you admit
To a share in this burying, or deny all knowledge?
Ismene I did it—yes—if she will let me say so.
I am as much to blame as she is.
Antigone No.
That is not just. You would not lend a hand
And I refused your help in what I did.
Ismene But I am not ashamed to stand beside you
Now in your hour of trial, Antigone.
Antigone Whose was the deed, Death and the dead are witness.
I love no friend whose love is only words.
Ismene O sister, sister, let me share your death,
Share in the tribute of honour to him that is dead.
Antigone You shall not die with me. You shall not claim
That which you would not touch. One death is enough.
Ismene How can I bear to live, if you must die?
Antigone Ask Creon. Is not he the one you care for?
Ismene You do yourself no good to taunt me so.
Antigone Indeed no: even my jests are bitter pains.
Ismene But how, O tell me, how can I still help you?
Antigone Help yourself. I shall not stand in your way.
Ismene For pity, Antigone—can I not die with you?
Antigone You chose; life was your choice, when mine was death.
Ismene Although I warned you that it would be so.
Antigone Your way seemed right to some, to others mine.
Ismene But now both in the wrong, and both condemned.
Antigone No, no. You live. My heart was long since dead,
So it was right for me to help the dead.
Creon I do believe the creatures both are mad;
One lately crazed, the other from her birth.
Ismene Is it not likely, sir? The strongest mind
Cannot but break under misfortune's blows.
Creon Yours did, when you threw in your lot with hers.
Ismene How could I wish to live without my sister?

reon You have no sister. Count her dead already.
smene You could not take her—kill your own son's bride?
reon Oh, there are other fields for him to plough.
smene No truer troth was ever made than theirs.
reon No son of mine shall wed so vile a creature.
ntigone O Haemon, can your father spite you so?
reon You and your paramour, I hate you both.
horus Sir, would you take her from your own son's arms?
reon Not I, but death shall take her.
horus Be it so.
Her death, it seems, is certain.
reon Certain it is.
No more delay. Take them, and keep them within—
The proper place for women. None so brave
As not to look for some way of escape
When they see life stand face to face with death.

The women are taken away.

horus Happy are they who know not the taste of evil.
From a house that heaven hath shaken
The curse departs not
But falls upon all of the blood,
Like the restless surge of the sea when the dark storm drives
The black sand hurled from the deeps
And the Thracian gales boom down
On the echoing shore.

In life and in death is the house of Labdacus stricken.
Generation to generation,
With no atonement,
It is scourged by the wrath of a god.
And now for the dead dust's sake is the light of promise,
The tree's last root, crushed out
By pride of heart and the sin
Of presumptous tongue.

For what presumption of man can match thy power,
O Zeus, that art not subject to sleep or time
Or age, living for ever in bright Olympus?
To-morrow and for all time to come,
As in the past,
This law is immutable:
For mortals greatly to live is greatly to suffer.

Roving ambition helps many a man to good,
And many it falsely lures to light desires,

Till failure trips them unawares, and they fall
On the fire that consumes them. Well was it said,
Evil seems good
To him who is doomed to suffer;
And short is the time before that suffering comes.

But here comes Haemon,
Your youngest son.
Does he come to speak his sorrow
For the doom of his promised bride,
The loss of his marriage hopes?

Creon We shall know it soon, and need no prophet to tell us.

Enter ***Haemon.***

Son, you have heard, I think, our final judgment
On your late bethrothed. No angry words, I hope?
Still friends, in spite of everything, my son?

Haemon I am your son, sir; by your wise decisions
My life is ruled, and them I shall always obey.
I cannot value any marriage-tie
Above your own good guidance.

Creon Rightly said.
Your father's will should have your heart's first place.
Only for this do fathers pray for sons
Obedient, loyal, ready to strike down
Their fathers' foes, and love their fathers' friends.
To be the father of unprofitable sons
Is to be the father of sorrows, a laughing-stock
To all one's enemies. Do not be fooled, my son,
By lust and the wiles of a woman. You'll have bought
Cold comfort if your wife's a worthless one.
No wound strikes deeper than love that is turned to hate.
This girl's an enemy; away with her,
And let her go and find a mate in Hades.
Once having caught her in a flagrant act—
The one and only traitor in our State—
I cannot make myself a traitor too;
So she must die. Well may she pray to Zeus,
The God of Family Love. How, if I tolerate
A traitor at home, shall I rule those abroad?
He that is a righteous master of his house
Will be a righteous statesman. To transgress
Or twist the law to one's own pleasure, presume
To order where one should obey, is sinful,
And I will have none of it.
He whom the State appoints must be obeyed

To the smallest matter, be it right—or wrong.
And he that rules his household, without a doubt,
Will make the wisest king, or, for that matter,
The staunchest subject. He will be the man
You can depend on in the storm of war,
The faithfullest comrade in the day of battle.
There is no more deadly peril than disobedience;
States are devoured by it, homes laid in ruins,
Armies defeated, victory turned to rout.
While simple obedience saves the lives of hundreds
Of honest folk. Therefore, I hold to the law,
And will never betray it—least of all for a woman.
Better be beaten, if need be, by a man,
Than let a woman get the better of us.

Chorus To me, as far as an old man can tell,
It seems your Majesty has spoken well.

Haemon Father, man's wisdom is the gift of heaven,
The greatest gift of all. I neither am
Nor wish to be clever enough to prove you wrong,
Though all men might not think the same as you do.
Nevertheless, I have to be your watchdog,
To know what others say and what they do,
And what they find to praise and what to blame.
Your frown is a sufficient silencer
Of any word that is not for your ears.
But *I* hear whispers spoken in the dark;
On every side I hear voices of pity
For this poor girl, doomed to the cruellest death,
And most unjust, that ever woman suffered
For an honourable action—burying a brother
Who was killed in battle, rather than leave him naked
For dogs to maul and carrion birds to peck at.
Has she not rather earned a crown of gold?—
Such is the secret talk about the town.
Father, there is nothing I can prize above
Your happiness and well-being. What greater good
Can any son desire? Can any father
Desire more from his son? Therefore I say,
Let not your first thought be your only thought.
Think if there cannot be some other way.
Surely, to think your own the only wisdom,
And yours the only word, the only will,
Betrays a shallow spirit, an empty heart.
It is no weakness for the wisest man
To learn when he is wrong, know when to yield.

So, on the margin of a flooded river
Trees bending to the torrent live unbroken,
While those that strain against it are snapped off.
A sailor has to tack and slacken sheets
Before the gale, or find himself capsized.
So, father, pause, and put aside your anger.
I think, for what my young opinion's worth,
That, good as it is to have infallible wisdom,
Since this is rarely found, the next best thing
Is to be willing to listen to wise advice.

Chorus There is something to be said, my lord, for his point of view,
And for yours as well; there is much to be said on both sides.

Creon Indeed! Am I to take lessons at my time of life
From a fellow of his age?

Haemon No lesson you need be ashamed of.
It isn't a question of age, but of right and wrong.

Creon Would you call it right to admire an act of disobedience?

Haemon Not if the act were also dishonourable.

Creon And was not this woman's action dishonourable?

Haemon The people of Thebes think not.

Creon The people of Thebes!
Since when do I take my orders from the people of Thebes?

Haemon Isn't that rather a childish thing to say?

Creon No. I am king, and responsible only to myself.

Haemon A one-man state?
What sort of a state is that?

Creon Why, does not every state belong to its ruler?

Haemon You'd be an excellent king—on a desert island.

Creon Of course, if you're on the woman's side—

Haemon No, no—
Unless you're the woman. It's you I'm fighting for.

Creon What, villain, when every word you speak is against me?

Haemon Only because I know you are wrong, wrong.

Creon Wrong? To respect my own authority?

Haemon What sort of respect tramples on all that is holy?

Creon Despicable coward! No more will than a woman!

Haemon I have nothing to be ashamed of.

Creon Yet you plead her cause.

Haemon No, *yours,* and mine, and that of the gods of the dead.

Creon You'll never marry her this side of death.

Haemon Then, if she dies, she does not die alone.

Creon Is that a threat, you impudent—

Haemon Is it a threat
To try to argue against wrong-headedness?

Creon You'll learn what wrong-headedness is, my friend, to your cost.

Haemon O father, I could call you mad, were you not my father.
Creon Don't toady me, boy; keep that for your lady-love.
Haemon You mean to have the last word, then?
Creon I do.
And what is more, by all the gods in heaven,
I'll make you sorry for your impudence.
(*Calling to those within*)
Bring out that she-devil, and let her die
Now, with her bridegroom by to see it done!
Haemon That sight I'll never see. Nor from this hour
Shall you see me again. Let those that will
Be witness of your wickedness and folly.

Exit.

Chorus He is gone, my lord, in very passionate haste.
And who shall say what a young man's wrath may do?
Creon Let him go! Let him do! Let him rage as never man raged,
He shall not save those women from their doom.
Chorus You mean, then, sire, to put them both to death?
Creon No, not the one whose hand was innocent.
Chorus And to what death do you condemn the other?
Creon I'll have her taken to a desert place
Where no man ever walked, and there walled up
Inside a cave, alive, with food enough
To acquit ourselves of the blood-guiltiness
That else would lie upon our commonwealth.
There she may pray to Death, the god she loves,
And ask release from death; or learn at last
What hope there is for those who worship death.

Exit.

horus Where is the equal of Love?
Where is the battle he cannot win,
The power he cannot outmatch?
In the farthest corners of earth, in the midst of the sea,
He is there; he is here
In the bloom of a fair face
Lying in wait;
And the grip of his madness
Spares not god or man,

Marring the righteous man,
Driving his soul into mazes of sin
And strife, dividing a house.
For the light that burns in the eyes of a bride of desire
Is a fire that consumes.
At the side of the great gods

Aphrodite immortal
Works her will upon all.

The doors are opened and ***Antigone*** *enters, guarded.*

But here is a sight beyond all bearing,
At which my eyes cannot but weep;
Antigone forth faring
To her bridal-bower of endless sleep.

Antigone You see me, countrymen, on my last journey,
Taking my last leave of the light of day;
Going to my rest, where death shall take me
Alive across the silent river.
No wedding-day; no marriage-music;
Death will be all my bridal dower.

Chorus But glory and praise go with you, lady,
To your resting-place. You go with your beauty
Unmarred by the hand of consuming sickness,
Untouched by the sword, living and free,
As none other that ever died before you.

Antigone The daughter of Tantalus, a Phrygian maid,
Was doomed to a piteous death on the rock
Of Sipylus, which embraced and imprisoned her,
Merciless as the ivy; rain and snow
Beat down upon her, mingled with her tears,
As she wasted and died. Such was her story,
And such is the sleep that I shall go to.

Chorus She was a goddess of immortal birth,
And we are mortals; the greater the glory,
To share the fate of a god-born maiden,
A living death, but a name undying.

Antigone Mockery, mockery! By the gods of our fathers,
Must you make me a laughing-stock while I yet live?
O lordly sons of my city! O Thebes!
Your valleys of rivers, your chariots and horses!
No friend to weep at my banishment
To a rock-hewn chamber of endless durance,
In a strange cold tomb alone to linger
Lost between life and death for ever.

Chorus My child, you have gone your way
To the outermost limit of daring
And have stumbled against Law enthroned.
This is the expiation
You must make for the sin of your father.

Antigone My father—the thought that sears my soul—
The unending burden of the house of Labdacus.

Monstrous marriage of mother and son . . .
My father . . . my parents . . . O hideous shame!
Whom now I follow, unwed, curse-ridden,
Doomed to this death by the ill-starred marriage
That marred my brother's life.

Chorus An act of homage is good in itself, my daughter;
But authority cannot afford to connive at disobedience.
You are the victim of your own self-will.

Antigone And must go the way that lies before me.
No funeral hymn; no marriage-music;
No sun from this day forth, no light,
No friend to weep at my departing.

Enter ***Creon.***

Creon Weeping and wailing at the door of death!
There'd be no end of it, if it had force
To buy death off. Away with her at once,
And close her up in her rock-vaulted tomb.
Leave her and let her die, if die she must,
Or live within her dungeon. Though on earth
Her life is ended from this day, her blood
Will not be on our hands.

Antigone So to my grave,
My bridal-bower, my everlasting prison,
I go, to join those many of my kinsmen
Who dwell in the mansions of Persephone,
Last and unhappiest, before my time.
Yet I believe my father will be there
To welcome me, my mother greet me gladly,
And you, my brother, gladly see me come.
Each one of you my hands have laid to rest,
Pouring the due libations on your graves.
It was by this service to your dear body, Polynices,
I earned the punishment which now I suffer,
Though all good people know it was for your honour.
O but I would not have done the forbidden thing
For any husband or for any son.
For why? I could have had another husband
And by him other sons, if one were lost;
But, father and mother lost, where would I get
Another brother? For thus preferring you,
My brother, Creon condemns me and hales me away,
Never a bride, never a mother, unfriended,
Condemned alive to solitary death.
What law of heaven have I transgressed? What god
Can save me now? What help or hope have I,

In whom devotion is deemed sacrilege?
If this is God's will, I shall learn my lesson
In death; but if my enemies are wrong,
I wish them no worse punishment than mine.

Chorus Still the same tempest in the heart
Torments her soul with angry gusts.

Creon The more cause then have they that guard her
To hasten their work; or they too suffer.

Chorus Alas, that word had the sound of death.

Creon Indeed there is no more to hope for.

Antigone Gods of our fathers, my city, my home,
Rulers of Thebes! Time stays no longer.
Last daughter of your royal house
Go I, *his* prisoner, because I honoured
Those things to which honour truly belongs.

Antigone *is led away.*

Chorus Such was the fate, my child, of Danae
Locked in a brazen bower,
A prison secret as a tomb,
Where was no day.
Daughter of kings, her royal womb
Garnered the golden shower
Of life from Zeus. So strong is Destiny,
No wealth, no armoury, no tower,
No ship that rides the angry sea
Her mastering hand can stay.

And Dryas' son, the proud Edonian king,
Pined in a stony cell
At Dionysus' bidding pent
To cool his fire
Till, all his full-blown passion spent,
He came to know right well
What god his ribald tongue was challenging
When he would break the fiery spell
Of the wild Maenads' revelling
And vex the Muses' choir.

It was upon the side
Of Bosporus, where the Black Rocks stand
By Thracian Salmydessus over the twin tide,
That Thracian Ares laughed to see
How Phineus' angry wife most bloodily
Blinded his two sons' eyes that mutely cried
For vengeance; crazed with jealousy
The woman smote them with the weaving-needle in her hand.

Forlorn they wept away
Their sad step-childhood's misery
Predestined from their mother's ill-starred marriage-day.
She was of old Erechtheid blood,
Cave-dwelling daughter of the North-wind God;
On rocky steeps, as mountain ponies play,
The wild winds nursed her maidenhood.
On her, my child, the grey Fates laid hard hands, as upon thee.

Enter **Teiresias,** *the blind prophet, led by a boy.*

Teiresias Gentlemen of Thebes, we greet you, my companion and I,
Who share one pair of eyes on our journeys together—
For the blind man goes where his leader tells him to.

Creon You are welcome, father Teiresias. What's your news?

Teiresias Ay, news you shall have; and advice, if you can heed it.

Creon There was never a time when I failed to heed it, father.

Teiresias And thereby have so far steered a steady course.

Creon And gladly acknowledge the debt we owe to you.

Teresias Then mark me now; for you stand on a razor's edge.

Creon Indeed? Grave words from your lips, good priest.
Say on.

Teiresias I will; and show you all that my skill reveals.
At my seat of divination, where I sit
These many years to read the signs of heaven,
An unfamiliar sound came to my ears
Of birds in vicious combat, savage cries
In strange outlandish language, and the whirr
Of flapping wings; from which I well could picture
The gruesome warfare of their deadly talons.
Full of foreboding then I made the test
Of sacrifice upon the altar fire.
There was no answering flame; only rank juice
Oozed from the flesh and dripped among the ashes,
Smouldering and sputtering; the gall vanished in a puff,
And the fat ran down and left the haunches bare.
Thus (through the eyes of my young acolyte,
Who sees for me, that I may see for others)
I read the signs of failure in my quest.
And why? The blight upon us is *your* doing.
The blood that stains our altars and our shrines,
The blood that dogs and vultures have licked up,
It is none other than the blood of Oedipus
Spilled from the veins of his ill-fated son.
Our fires, our sacrifices, and our prayers
The gods abominate. How should the birds
Give any other than ill-omened voices,

Gorged with the dregs of blood that man has shed?
Mark this, my son: all men fall into sin.
But sinning, he is not for ever lost
Hapless and helpless, who can make amends
And has not set his face against repentance.
Only a fool is governed by self-will.
Pay to the dead his due. Wound not the fallen.
It is no glory to kill and kill again.
My words are for your good, as is my will,
And should be acceptable, being for your good.

Creon You take me for your target, reverend sir,
Like all the rest. I know your art of old,
And how you make me your commodity
To trade and traffic in for your advancement.
Trade as you will; but all the silver of Sardis
And all the gold of India will not buy
A tomb for yonder traitor. No. Let the eagles
Carry his carcase up to the throne of Zeus;
Even that would not be sacrilege enough
To frighten me from my determination
Not to allow this burial. No man's act
Has power enough to pollute the goodness of God.
But great and terrible is the fall, Teiresias,
Of mortal men who seek their own advantage
By uttering evil in the guise of good.

Teiresias Ah, is there any wisdom in the world?

Creon Why, what is the meaning of that wide-flung taunt?

Teiresias What prize outweighs the priceless worth of prudence?

Creon Ay, what indeed? What mischief matches the lack of it?

Teiresias And there you speak of your own symptom, sir.

Creon I am loth to pick a quarrel with you, priest.

Teiresias You do so, calling my divination false.

Creon I say all prophets seek their own advantage.

Teiresias All kings, say I, seek gain unrighteously.

Creon Do you forget to whom you say it?

Teiresias No.
Our king and benefactor, by my guidance.

Creon Clever you may be, but not therefore honest.

Teiresias Must I reveal my yet unspoken mind?

Creon Reveal all; but expect no gain from it.

Teiresias Does that still seem to you my motive, then?

Creon Nor is my will for sale, sir, in your market.

Teiresias Then hear this. Ere the chariot of the sun
Has rounded once or twice his wheeling way,
You shall have given a son of your own loins

To death, in payment for death—two debts to pay:
One for the life that you have sent to death,
The life you have abominably entombed;
One for the dead still lying above ground
Unburied, unhonoured, unblest by the gods below.
You cannot alter this. The gods themselves
Cannot undo it. It follows of necessity
From what you have done. Even now the avenging Furies,
The hunters of Hell that follow and destroy,
Are lying in wait for you, and will have their prey,
When the evil you have worked for others falls on you.
Do I speak this for my gain? The time shall come,
And soon, when your house will be filled with the lamentation
Of men and of women; and every neighbouring city
Will be goaded to fury against you, for upon them
Too the pollution falls when the dogs and vultures
Bring the defilement of blood to their hearths and altars.
I have done. You pricked me, and these shafts of wrath
Will find their mark in your heart. You cannot escape
The sting of their sharpness.
Lead me home, my boy.
Let us leave him to vent his anger on younger ears,
Or school his mind and tongue to a milder mood
Than that which now possesses him.
Lead on.

Exit.

Chorus He has gone, my lord. He has prophesied terrible things.
And for my part, I that was young and now am old
Have never known his prophecies proved false.

Creon It is true enough; and my heart is torn in two.
It is hard to give way, and hard to stand and abide
The coming of the curse. Both ways are hard.

Chorus If you would be advised, my good lord Creon—

Creon What must I do? Tell me, and I will do it.

Chorus Release the woman from her rocky prison.
Set up a tomb for him that lies unburied.

Creon Is it your wish that I consent to this?

Chorus It is, and quickly. The gods do not delay
The stroke of their swift vengeance on the sinner.

Creon It is hard, but I must do it. Well I know
There is no armour against necessity.

Chorus Go. Let your own hand do it, and no other.

Creon I will go this instant.
Slaves there! One and all.
Bring spades and mattocks out on the hill!

My mind is made; 'twas I imprisoned her,
And I will set her free. Now I believe
It is by the laws of heaven that man must live.

Exit.

Chorus O Thou whose name is many,
Son of the Thunderer, dear child of his Cadmean bride,
Whose hand is mighty
In Italia,
In the hospitable valley
Of Eleusis,
And in Thebes,
The mother-city of thy worshippers,
Where sweet Ismenus gently watereth
The soil whence sprang the harvest of the dragon's teeth;

Where torches on the crested mountains gleam,
And by Castalia's stream
The nymph-train in thy dance rejoices,
When from the ivy-tangled glens
Of Nysa and from vine-clad plains
Thou comest to Thebes where the immortal voices
Sing thy glad strains.

Thebes, where thou lovest most to be,
With her, thy mother, the fire-stricken one,
Sickens for need of thee.
Healer of all her ills;
Come swiftly o'er the high Parnassian hills,
Come o'er the sighing sea.

The stars, whose breath is fire, delight
To dance for thee; the echoing night
Shall with thy praises ring.
Zeus-born, appear! With Thyiads revelling
Come, bountiful
Iacchus, King!

Enter a ***Messenger,*** *from the side of the stage.*

Messenger Hear, men of Cadmus' city, hear and attend,
Men of the house of Amphion, people of Thebes!
What is the life of man? A thing not fixed
For good or evil, fashioned for praise or blame.
Chance raises a man to the heights, chance casts him down,
And none can foretell what will be from what is.
Creon was once an enviable man;
He saved his country from her enemies,
Assumed the sovereign power, and bore it well,

The honoured father of a royal house.
Now all is lost; for life without life's joys
Is living death; and such a life is his.
Riches and rank and show of majesty
And state, where no joy is, are empty, vain
And unsubstantial shadows, of no weight
To be compared with happiness of heart.

Chorus What is your news? Disaster in the royal house?

Messenger Death; and the guilt of it on living heads.

Chorus Who dead? And by what hand?

Messenger Haemon is dead,
Slain by his own—

Chorus His father?

Messenger His own hand.
His father's act it was that drove him to it.

Chorus Then all has happened as the prophet said.

Messenger What's next to do, your worships will decide.

The Palace door opens.

Chorus Here comes the Queen, Eurydice. Poor soul,
It may be she has heard about her son.

Enter **Eurydice,** *attended by women.*

Eurydice My friends, I heard something of what you were saying
As I came to the door. I was on my way to prayer
At the temple of Pallas, and had barely turned the latch
When I caught your talk of some near calamity.
I was sick with fear and reeled in the arms of my women.
But tell me what is the matter; what have you heard?
I am not unacquainted with grief, and I can bear it.

Messenger Madam, it was I that saw it, and will tell you all.
To try to make it any lighter now
Would be to prove myself a liar. Truth
Is always best.
It was thus. I attended your husband,
The King, to the edge of the field where lay the body
Of Polynices, in pitiable state, mauled by the dogs.
We prayed for him to the Goddess of the Roads, and to Pluto,
That they might have mercy upon him. We washed the remains
In holy water, and on a fire of fresh-cut branches
We burned all that was left of him, and raised
Over his ashes a mound of his native earth.
That done, we turned towards the deep rock-chamber
Of the maid that was married with death.
Before we reached it,
One that stood near the accursed place had heard
Loud cries of anguish, and came to tell King Creon.

As he approached, came strange uncertain sounds
Of lamentation, and he cried aloud:
'Unhappy wretch! Is my foreboding true?
Is this the most sorrowful journey that ever I went?
My son's voice greets me. Go, some of you, quickly
Through the passage where the stones are thrown apart,
Into the mouth of the cave, and see if it be
My son, my own son Haemon that I hear.
If not, I am the sport of gods.'
We went
And looked, as bidden by our anxious master.
There in the furthest corner of the cave
We saw her hanging by the neck. The rope
Was of the woven linen of her dress.
And, with his arms about her, there stood he
Lamenting his lost bride, his luckless love,
His father's cruelty.
When Creon saw them,
Into the cave he went, moaning piteously.
'O my unhappy boy,' he cried again,
'What have you done? What madness brings you here
To your destruction? Come away, my son,
My son, I do beseech you, come away!'
His son looked at him with one angry stare,
Spat in his face, and then without a word
Drew sword and struck out. But his father fled
Unscathed. Whereon the poor demented boy
Leaned on his sword and thrust it deeply home
In his own side, and while his life ebbed out
Embraced the maid in loose-enfolding arms,
His spurting blood staining her pale cheeks red.

Eurydice goes quickly back into the Palace.

Two bodies lie together, wedded in death,
Their bridal sleep a witness to the world
How great calamity can come to man
Through man's perversity.

Chorus But what is this?
The Queen has turned and gone without a word.

Messenger Yes. It is strange. The best that I can hope
Is that she would not sorrow for her son
Before us all, but vents her grief in private
Among her women. She is too wise, I think,
To take a false step rashly.

Chorus It may be.
Yet there is danger in unnatural silence

No less than in excess of lamentation.

Messenger I will go in and see, whether in truth
There is some fatal purpose in her grief.
Such silence, as you say, may well be dangerous.

He goes in.

Enter Attendants preceding the King.

Chorus The King comes here.
What the tongue scarce dares to tell
Must now be known
By the burden that proves too well
The guilt, no other man's
But his alone.

Enter **Creon** *with the body of* **Haemon.**

Creon The sin, the sin of the erring soul
Drives hard unto death.
Behold the slayer, the slain,
The father, the son.
O the curse of my stubborn will!
Son, newly cut off in the newness of youth,
Dead for my fault, not yours.

Chorus Alas, too late you have seen the truth.

Creon I learn in sorrow. Upon my head
God has delivered this heavy punishment,
Has struck me down in the ways of wickedness,
And trod my gladness under foot.
Such is the bitter affliction of mortal man.

Enter the **Messenger** *from the Palace.*

Messenger Sir, you have this and more than this to bear.
Within there's more to know, more to your pain.

Creon What more? What pain can overtop this pain?

Messenger She is dead—your wife, the mother of him that is dead—
The death-wound fresh in her heart. Alas, poor lady!

Creon Insatiable Death, wilt thou destroy me yet?
What say you, teller of evil?
I am already dead,
And is there more?
Blood upon blood?
More death? My wife?

The central doors open, revealing the body of **Eurydice.**

Chorus Look then, and see; nothing is hidden now.

Creon O second horror!
What fate awaits me now?
My child here in my arms . . . and there, the other . . .
The son . . . the mother . . .

Messenger There at the altar with the whetted knife

She stood, and as the darkness dimmed her eyes
Called on the dead, her elder son and this,
And with her dying breath cursed you, their slayer.

Creon O horrible . . .
Is there no sword for me,
To end this misery?

Messenger Indeed you bear the burden of two deaths.
It was her dying word.

Creon And her last act?

Messenger Hearing her son was dead, with her own hand
She drove the sharp sword home into her heart.

Creon There is no man can bear this guilt but I.
It is true, I killed him.
Lead me away, away. I live no longer.

Chorus 'Twere best, if anything is best in evil times.
What's soonest done, is best, when all is ill.

Creon Come, my last hour and fairest,
My only happiness . . . come soon.
Let me not see another day.
Away . . . away . . .

Chorus The future is not to be known; our present care
Is with the present; the rest is in other hands.

Creon I ask no more than I have asked.

Chorus Ask nothing.
What is to be, no mortal can escape.

Creon I am nothing. I have no life.
Lead me away . . .
That have killed unwittingly
My son, my wife.
I know not where I should turn,
Where look for help.
My hands have done amiss, my head is bowed
With fate too heavy for me.

Exit.

Chorus Of happiness the crown
And chiefest part
Is wisdom, and to hold
The gods in awe.
This is the law
That, seeing the stricken heart
Of pride brought down,
We learn when we are old.

Exeunt.

৩§ LIFE OF LYCURGUS

Plutarch

This selection could also be called "The Constitution of Sparta," for "Lycurgus" is only the name given by tradition to the legendary lawgiver who gave to Sparta its characteristic institutions, supposedly in the eighth century B.C. *Plutarch's "life" is thus little more than a summary of these institutions in their earliest known form. The institutions* do *have a unity and consistency of purpose that suggests a single mind; but whether Lycurgus existed or not is unimportant compared with the institutions themselves, which most certainly existed, and which the Greeks regarded as their finest achievement.*

The Greeks admired good laws *over any other human achievement, and by common consent the laws of Sparta (or "Lacedaemon," as the city, with its surroundings, was called) best combined justice, stability, and freedom. Although Athens may have produced more striking individuals, there was no question in Greek minds that Sparta was the better governed and more admirable city. Indeed, the Spartan emphasis on rigorous physical and moral discipline and on the readiness of individual citizens to sacrifice their own desires for the common good has influenced every utopia from Plato's to those of our own day.*

Plutarch of Chaeronea (A.D. ca. 46–ca. *120*) *was a learned Greek of the period of the Roman emperors Trajan and Hadrian, who encouraged a revival of Greek art and literature by their generous patronage.* Parallel Lives, *from which this selection is taken, is his major work. It is a series of volumes, each containing the life of one Greek and one Roman whose achievements were roughly analogous, and a brief comparison of the two. Lycurgus was paired with Numa Pompilius, the legendary king and lawgiver of early Rome. Plutarch was not scrupulous about his sources of information; his chief interest lay in moral character and in the educative force of the lives of great men taken as models for imitation. It is this, too, which made him one of the most widely read of all classical authors, especially among the aristocracy of the eighteenth and nineteenth centuries. His own aristocratic prejudices are not concealed in his* Lives.

. . . Among the many changes and alterations which Lycurgus made, the first and of greatest importance was the establishment of the senate, which, having a power equal to the kings' in matters of great consequence, and as Plato expresses it, allaying and qualifying the fiery genius of the royal office, gave steadiness and safety to the commonwealth. For the state, which before had no firm basis to stand upon, but leaned one while toward an absolute monarchy, when the kings had the upper hand, and another while toward a pure democracy, when the people had the better, found in this establishment of the senate a central weight, like ballast in a ship, which always kept things in a just equilibrium; the twenty-eight always adhering to the kings so far as to resist democracy, and, on the other hand, supporting the people against the establishment of absolute monarchy. . . .

Although Lycurgus had, in this manner, used all the qualifications possible in the constitution of his commonwealth, yet those who succeeded him found the oligarchical element still too strong and dominant, and to check its high temper and its violence, put, as Plato says, a bit in its mouth, which was the power of the ephori, established an hundred and thirty years after the death of Lycurgus. Elatus and his colleagues were the first who had this dignity conferred upon them, in the reign of king Theopompus, who, when his queen upbraided him one day that he would leave the regal power to his children less than he had received it from his ancestors, said, in answer, "No, greater; for it will last longer." For, indeed, their prerogative being thus reduced within reasonable bounds, the Spartan kings were at once freed from all further jealousies and consequent danger, and never experienced the calamities of their neighbors at Messene and Argos, who, by maintaining their prerogative too strictly, for want of yielding a little to the populace, lost it all.

Indeed, whosoever shall look at the sedition and misgovernment which befell these bordering nations to whom they were as near related in blood as situation, will find in them the best reason to admire the wisdom and foresight of Lycurgus. For these three states, in their first rise, were equal, or, if there were any odds, they lay on the side of the Messenians and Argives, who, in the first allotment, were thought to have been luckier than the Spartans; yet was their happiness but of small continuance, partly the tyrannical temper of their kings and partly the ungovernableness of the people quickly bringing upon them such disorders, and so complete an overthrow of all existing institutions, as clearly to show how truly divine a blessing the Spartans had had in that wise lawgiver who gave their government its happy balance and temper. But of this I shall say more in its due place.

After the creation of the thirty senators, his next task, and, indeed, the most hazardous he ever undertook, was the making a new division of their lands. For there was an extreme inequality among them, and their state was overloaded with a multitude of indigent and necessitous persons, while its whole wealth had centered upon a very few. To the end, therefore, that he might expel from the state arrogance and envy, luxury and crime, and those yet more inveterate diseases of want and superfluity, he obtained of them to renounce their properties, and to consent to a new division of the land, and that they should live all together on an equal footing; merit to be their

***Plutarch's Lives of Illustrious Men*, trans. J. Dryden, rev. ed. A. H. Clough (New York: Hurst and Co., 1859), pp. 90–113 *passim*.**

only road to eminence, and the disgrace of evil, and credit of worthy acts, the one measure of difference between man and man. . . .

Not contented with this, he resolved to make a division of their movables too, that there might be no odious distinction or inequality left among them; but finding that it would be very dangerous to go about it openly, he took another course, and defeated their avarice by the following stratagem: he commanded that all gold and silver coin should be called in, and that only a sort of money made of iron should be current, a great weight and quantity of which was but very little worth; so that to lay up twenty or thirty pounds there was required a pretty large closet, and, to remove it, nothing less than a yoke of oxen. With the diffusion of this money, at once a number of vices were banished from Lacedaemon; for who would rob another of such a coin? Who would unjustly detain or take by force, or accept as a bribe, a thing which it was not easy to hide, nor a credit to have, nor indeed of any use to cut in pieces? For when it was just red hot, they quenched it in vinegar, and by that mean spoiled it, and made it almost incapable of being worked.

In the next place, he declared an outlawry of all needless and superfluous arts; but here he might almost have spared his proclamation; for they of themselves would have gone after the gold and silver, the money which remained being not so proper payment for curious work; for, being of iron, it was scarcely portable, neither, if they should take the pains to export it, would it pass among the other Greeks, who ridiculed it. So there was now no more means of purchasing foreign goods and small wares; merchants sent no shiploads into Laconian ports; no rhetoric-master, no itinerant fortune-teller, no harlot-monger, or gold or silversmith, engraver, or jeweller, set foot in a country which had no money; so that luxury, deprived little by little of that which fed and fomented it, wasted to nothing, and died away of itself. For the rich had no advantage here over the poor, as their wealth and abundance had no road to come abroad by, but were shut up at home doing nothing. And in this way they became excellent artists in common, necessary things; bedsteads, chairs, and tables, and such like staple utensils in a family, were admirably well made there; their cup, particularly, was very much in fashion, and eagerly bought up by soldiers, as Critias reports; for its color was such as to prevent water, drunk upon necessity and disagreeable to look at, from being noticed; and the shape of it was such that the mud stuck to the sides, so that only the purer part came to the drinker's mouth. For this, also, they had to thank their lawgiver, who, by relieving the artisans of the trouble of making useless things, set them to show their skill in giving beauty to those of daily and indispensable use.

The third and most masterly stroke of this great lawgiver, by which he struck a yet more effectual blow against luxury and the desire of riches, was the ordinance he made, that they should all eat in common, of the same bread, and same meat, and of kinds that were specified, and should not spend their lives at home, laid on costly couches at splendid tables, delivering themselves up into the hands of their tradesmen and cooks, to fatten them in corners, like greedy brutes, and to ruin not their minds only but their very bodies, which, enfeebled by indulgence and excess, would stand in need of long sleep, warm bathing, freedom from work, and, in a word, of as much care and attendance as if they were continually sick. It was certainly an extraordinary thing to have brought about such a result as this, but a greater yet to have taken away from wealth, as Theophrastes observes, not merely the property of being coveted but its very nature of being wealth. For the rich, being obliged to go to the same table with the poor, could not make use of or enjoy their abundance, nor so much as please their vanity by looking at or displaying it. So that the common proverb, that Plutus, the god of riches, is blind, was nowhere in all the world literally verified but in Sparta. There, indeed, he was not only blind, but like a picture, without either life or motion. Nor were they allowed to take food at home first, and then attend the public tables, for every one had an eye upon those who did not eat and drink like the rest, and reproached them with being dainty and effeminate. This last ordinance in particular exasperated the wealthier men. They collected in a body against Lycurgus, and from ill words came to throwing stones, so that at length he was forced to run out of the market-place, and make to sanctuary to save his life; by good-hap he outran all, excepting one Alcander, a young man otherwise not ill accomplished, but hasty and violent, who came up so close to him, that, when he turned to see who was near him, he struck him upon the face with his stick, and put out one of his eyes. Lycurgus, so far from being daunted and discouraged by this accident, stopped short, and showed his disfigured face and eye beat out to his countrymen; they, dismayed and ashamed at the sight, delivered Alcander into his hands to be punished, and escorted him home, with expressions of great concern for his ill usage. Lycurgus, having thanked them for their care of his person, dismissed them all, excepting only Alcander; and, taking him with him into his house, neither did nor said anything severely to him, but, dismissing those whose place it was, bade Alcander to wait upon him at table. The young man, who was of an ingenuous temper, without murmuring, did as he was commanded; and being thus admitted to live with Lycurgus, he had an opportunity to observe in him, besides his gentleness and calmness of temper, an extraordinary sobriety and an indefatigable industry, and so, from an enemy, became one of his most zealous admirers, and told his friends and relations that Lycurgus was not that morose and ill-natured man they had formerly taken him for, but the one mild and gentle character of the world. And thus did Lycurgus, for chastisement of his fault, make of a wild and passionate young man one of the discreetest citizens of Sparta. . . .

They used to send their children to these tables as to schools of temperance; here they were instructed in state affairs by listening to experienced statesmen; here they learned to converse with pleasantry, to make jests without scurrility, and take them without ill-humor. In this point of good breeding, the Lacedaemonians excelled particularly, but if any man were uneasy under it, upon the least hint given, there was no more to be said to him. It was customary also for the eldest man in the company to say to each of them, as they came in, "Through this" (pointing to the door), "no words go out." When any one had a desire to be admitted into any of these little societies, he was to go through the following probation, each man in the company took a little ball of soft bread, which they were to throw into a deep basin, which a waiter carried round upon his head; those that liked the person to be chosen dropped their ball into the basin without altering its figure, and those who disliked him pressed it betwixt their fingers, and made it flat; and this signified as much as a negative voice. And if there were but one of these flattened pieces in the basin, the suitor was rejected, so desirous were they that all the members of the company should be agreeable to each other. . . .

Lycurgus would never reduce his laws into writing; nay, there is a Rhetra expressly to forbid it. For he thought that the most material points, and such as most directly tended to the public welfare, being imprinted on the hearts of their youth by a good discipline, would be sure to remain, and would find a stronger security, than any compulsion would be, in the principles of action formed in them by their best lawgiver, education. And as for things of lesser importance, as pecuniary contracts, and such like, the forms of which have to be changed as occasion requires, he thought it the best way to prescribe no positive rule or inviolable usage in such cases, willing that their manner and form should be altered according to the circumstances of time, and determinations of men of sound judgment. Every end and object of law and enactment it was his design education should effect.

One, then, of the Rhetras was, that their laws should not be written; another is particularly levelled against luxury and expensiveness, for by it it was ordained that the ceilings of their houses should only be wrought by the axe, and their gates and doors smoothed only by the saw. Epaminondas's famous dictum about his own table, that "Treason and a dinner like this do not keep company together," may be said to have been anticipated by Lycurgus. Luxury and a house of this kind could not well be companions. For a man must have a less than ordinary share of sense that would furnish such plain and common rooms with silver-footed couches and purple coverlets and gold and silver plate. Doubtless he had good reason to think that they would proportion their beds to their houses, and their coverlets to their beds, and the rest of their goods and furniture to these. It is reported that king Leotychides, the first of that name, was so little used to the sight of any other kind of work, that, being entertained at Corinth in a stately room, he was much surprised to see the timber and ceiling so finely carved and panelled, and asked his host whether the trees grew so in his country.

A third ordinance or Rhetra was, that they should not make war often, or long, with the same enemy, lest that they should train and instruct them in war, by habituating them to defend themselves. And this is what Agesilaus was much blamed for, a long time after; it being thought, that, by his continual incursions into Boeotia, he made the Thebans a match for the Lacedaemonians; and therefore Antalcidas, seeing him wounded one day, said to him, that he was very well paid for taking such pains to make the Thebans good soldiers, whether they would or no. These laws were called the Rhetras, to intimate that they were divine sanctions and revelations.

In order to the good education of their youth (which, as I said before, he thought the most important and noblest work of a lawgiver), he went so far back as to take into consideration their very conception and birth, by regulating their marriages. For Aristotle is wrong in saying, that, after he had tried all ways to reduce the women to more modesty and sobriety, he was at last forced to leave them as they were, because that in the absence of their husbands, who spent the best parts of their lives in the wars, their wives, whom they were obliged to leave absolute mistresses at home, took great liberties and assumed the superiority; and were treated with overmuch respect and called by the title of lady or queen. The truth is, he took in their case, also, all the care that was possible; he ordered the maidens to exercise themselves with wrestling, running, throwing the quoit, and casting the dart, to the end that the fruit they conceived might, in strong and healthy bodies, take firmer root and find better growth, and withal that they, with this greater vigor, might be the more able to undergo the pains of child-bearing. And to the end he might take away their over-great tenderness and fear of exposure to the air, and all acquired womanishness, he ordered that the young women should go naked in the processions, as well as the young men, and dance, too in that condition, at certain solemn feasts, singing certain songs, while the young men stood around, seeing and hearing them. On these occasions, they now and then made by jests, a befitting reflection upon those who had misbehaved themselves in the wars and again sang encomiums upon those who had done any gallant action, and by these means inspired the younger sort with an emulation of their glory. Those that were thus commended went away proud, elated, and gratified with their honor among the maidens; and those who were rallied were as sensibly touched with it as if they had been formally reprimanded; and so much the more, because the kings and the elders as well as the rest of the city, saw and heard all that passed. Nor was there any thing shameful in this nakedness of the young women; modesty attended them, and all wantonness was excluded. It taught them simplicity and a care for good health, and gave them some taste of higher feelings, admitted as they thus were to the field of noble action and glory. Hence it was natural for them to think and speak as Gorgo for example, the wife of Leonidas, is said to have done, when some foreign lady, as it would seem, told her that the women of Lacedaemon were the only women of the world who could rule men; "With good reason," she said, "for we are the only women who bring forth men."

These public processions of the maidens, and their appearing naked in their exercises and dancings, were incitements to marriage, operating upon the young with the rigor and certainty, as Plato says, of love, if not of mathematics. But besides all this, to promote it yet more effectually, those who continued bachelors were in a degree disfranchised by law; for they were excluded from the sight of those public processions in which the young men and maidens danced naked, and, in winter-time, the officers compelled them to march naked themselves round the market-place, singing as they went a certain song to their own disgrace, that they justly suffered this punishment for disobeying the laws. Moreover, they were denied that respect and observance which the younger men paid their elders; and no man, for example, found fault with what was said to Dercyllidas, though so eminent a commander; upon whose approach one day, a young man, instead of rising, retained his seat, remarking, "No child of yours will make room for me."

In their marriages, the husband carried off his bride by a sort of force; nor were their brides ever small and of tender years, but in their full bloom and ripeness. After this, she who superintended the wedding comes and clips the hair of the bride close round her head, dresses her up in man's clothes, and leaves her upon a mattress in the dark; afterward comes the bridegroom, in his everyday clothes, sober and composed, as having supped at the common table, and, entering privately into the room where the bride lies, untied her virgin zone, and takes her to himself; and, after staying some time together, he returns composedly to his own apartment, to sleep as usual with the other young men. And so he continues to do, spending his days, and, indeed, his nights with them, visiting his bride in fear and shame, and with circumspection, when he thought he should not be observed; she, also, on her part, using her wit to help and find favorable opportunities for their meeting, when company was out of the way. In this manner they lived a long time, insomuch that they sometimes had children by their wives before ever they saw their faces by daylight. Their interviews, being thus difficult and rare, served not only for continual exercise of their self-control, but brought them together with their bodies healthy and vigorous, and their affections fresh and lively, unsated and undulled by easy access and long continuance with each other; while their partings were always early enough to leave behind unextinguished in each of them some remainder fire of longing and mutual delight. After guarding marriage with this modesty and reserve, he was equally careful to banish empty and womanish jealousy. For this object, excluding all licentious disorders, he made it, nevertheless, honorable for men to give the use of their wives to those whom they should think fit, that so they might have children by them; ridiculing those in whose opinion such favors are so unfit for participation as to fight and shed blood and go to war about it. Lycurgus allowed a man who was advanced in years and had a young wife to recommend some virtuous and approved young man, that she might have a child by him, who might inherit the good qualities of the father, and be a son to himself. On the other side, an honest man who had love for a married woman upon account of her modesty and the well-favoredness of her children, might, without formality, beg her company of her husband, that he might raise, as it were, from this plot of good ground, worthy and well-allied children for himself. And indeed, Lycurgus was of a persuasion that children were not so much the property of their parents as of the whole commonwealth, and, therefore, would not have his citizens begot by the first comers, but by the best men that could be found: the laws of other nations seemed to him very absurd and inconsistent, where people would be so solicitous for their dogs and horses as to exert interest and pay money to procure fine breeding, and yet kept their wives shut up, to be made mothers only by themselves, who might be foolish, infirm, or diseased; as if it were not apparent that children of a bad breed would prove their bad qualities first upon those who kept and were rearing them, and well-born children, in like manner, their good qualities. These regulations, founded on natural and social grounds, were certainly so far from that scandalous liberty which was afterward charged upon their women, that they knew not what adultery meant. It is told, for instance, of Geradas, a very ancient Spartan, that, being asked by a stranger what punishment their law had appointed for adulterers, he answered, "There are no adulterers in our country." "But," replied the stranger, "suppose there were?" "Then," answered he, "the offender would have to give the plaintiff a bull with a neck so long as that he might drink from the top of Taygetus of the Eurotas river below it." The man, surprised at this, said, "Why, 'tis impossible to find such a bull." Geradas smilingly replied, "'Tis as possible as to find an adulterer in Sparta." So much I had to say of their marriages.

Nor was it in the power of the father to dispose of the child as he thought fit; he was obliged to carry it before certain triers at a place called Lesche; these were some of the elders of the tribe to which the child belonged; their business it was carefully to view the infant, and, if they found it stout and well made, they gave order for its rearing, and allotted to it one of the nine thousand shares of land above mentioned for its maintenance, but, if they found it puny and ill-shaped, ordered it to be taken to what was called the Apothetae, a sort of chasm under Taygetus; as thinking it neither for the good of the child itself, nor for the public interest, that it should b brought up, if it did not, from the very outset, appear made to be healthy and vigorous Upon the same account, the women did not bathe the new-born children with water as is the custom in all other countries, but with wine, to prove the temper and com plexion of their bodies; from a notion they had that epileptic and weakly childre faint and waste away upon their being thus bathed, while, on the contrary, those of strong and vigorous habit acquire firmness and get a temper by it, like steel. Ther was much care and art, too, used by the nurses; they had no swaddling bands; th children grew up free and unconstrained in limb and form, and not dainty and fanci ful about their food; not afraid in the dark, or of being left alone; and withou peevishness or ill humor or crying. Upon this account, Spartan nurses were ofte brought up, or hired by people of other countries; and it is recorded that she wh suckled Alcibiades was a Spartan; who, however, if fortunate in his nurse, was no so in his preceptor; his guardian, Pericles, as Plato tells us, chose a servant for tha office called Zopyrus, no better than any common slave.

Lycurgus was of another mind; he would not have masters bought out of the marke for his young Spartans, nor such as should sell their pains; nor was it lawful, indeed for the father himself to breed up the children after his own fancy; but as soon a they were seven years old they were to be enrolled in certain companies and classes where they all lived under the same order and discipline, doing their exercises an taking their play together. Of these, he who showed the most conduct and courag was made captain; they had their eyes always upon him, obeyed his orders, an underwent patiently whatsoever punishment he inflicted; so that the whole course o their education was one continued exercise of a ready and perfect obedience. The ol men, too, were spectators of their performances, and often raised quarrels and dis putes among them, to have a good opportunity of finding out their different charac ters, and of seeing which would be valiant, which a coward, when they should com to more dangerous encounters. Reading and writing they gave them, just enough t serve their turn; their chief care was to make them good subjects, and to teach them to endure pain and conquer in battle. To this end, as they grew in years, their disci pline was proportionably increased; their heads were close-clipped, they were accus tomed to go barefoot, and for the most part to play naked.

After they are twelve years old, they were no longer allowed to wear any under garment; they had one coat to serve them a year; their bodies were hard and dry, wit but little acquaintance of baths and unguents; these human indulgences they wer allowed only on some few particular days in the year. They lodged together in littl bands upon beds made of the rushes which grew by the banks of the river Eurotas which they were to break off with their hands without a knife; if it were winter, the mingled some thistle-down with their rushes, which it was thought had the propert of giving warmth. By the time they were come to this age, there was not any of th more hopeful boys who had not a lover to bear him company. The old men, too, ha an eye upon them coming often to the grounds to hear and see them contend eithe in wit or strength with one another, and this as seriously and with as much concer as if they were their fathers, their tutors, or their magistrates; so that there scarcel vas any time or place without some one present to put them in mind of their duty, nd punish them if they had neglected it.

Besides all this, there was always one of the best and honestest men in the city ppointed to undertake the charge and governance of them; he again arranged them nto their several bands, and set over each of them for their captain the most temerate and boldest of those they called Irens, who were usually twenty years old, two ears out of the boys; and the eldest of the boys, again, were Mell-Irens, as much as o say, who would shortly be men. This young man, therefore, was their captain when hey fought and their master at home, using them for the offices of his house; sending he oldest of them to fetch wood, and the weaker and less able, to gather salads and erbs, and these they must either go without or steal; which they did by creeping into he gardens, or conveying themselves cunningly and closely into the eating houses; if hey were taken in the fact, they were whipped without mercy, for thieving so ill and wkwardly. They stole, too, all other meat they could lay their hands on, looking out nd watching all opportunities, when people were asleep or more careless than usual. f they were caught, they were not only punished with whipping, but hunger, too, eing reduced to their ordinary allowance, which was but very slender, and so conrived on purpose, that they might set about to help themselves, and be forced to exerise their energy and address. This was the principal design of their hard fare; there vas another not inconsiderable, that they might grow taller; for the vital spirits, not eing overburdened and oppressed by to great a quantity of nourishment, which ecessarily discharges itself into thickness and breadth, do, by their natural lightness, ise; and the body, giving and yielding because it is pliant, grows in height. The same hing seems, also, to conduce to beauty of shape; a dry and lean habit is a better subect for nature's configuration, which the gross and over-fed are too heavy to submit o properly. Just as we find that women who take physic while they are with child, ear leaner and smaller but better-shaped and prettier children; the material they ome of having been more pliable and easily moulded. The reason, however, I leave thers to determine.

To return from whence we have digressed. So seriously did the Lacedaemonian hildren go about their stealing, that a youth, having stolen a young fox and hid it nder his coat, suffered it to tear out his very bowels with its teeth and claws, and lied upon the place, rather than let it be seen. What is practiced to this very day in Lacedaemon is enough to gain credit to this story, for I myself have seen several of the ouths endure whipping to death at the foot of the altar of Diana surnamed Orthia.

The Iren, or under-master, used to stay a little with them after supper, and one of hem he bade to sing a song, to another he put a question which required an advised nd deliberate answer; for example, Who was the best man in the city? What he hought of such an action of such a man? They used them thus early to pass a right udgment upon persons and things, and to inform themselves of the abilities or defects f their countrymen. If they had not an answer ready to the question, Who was a ood or who an ill-reputed citizen, they were looked upon as of a dull and careless lisposition, and to have little or no sense of virtue and honor; besides this, they were o give a good reason for what they said, and in as few words and as comprehensive

as might be; he that failed of this, or answered not to the purpose, had his thumb bi
by his master. Sometimes the Iren did this in the presence of the old men and magis
trates, that they might see whether he punished them justly and in due measure or not
and when he did amiss, they would not reprove him before the boys, but, when the
were gone, he was called to an account and underwent correction, if he had run fa
into either of the extremes of indulgence or severity.

Their lovers and favorers, too, had a share in the young boy's honor or disgrace; an
there goes a story that one of them was fined by the magistrate, because the lad whon
he loved cried out effeminately as he was fighting. And though this sort of love wa
so approved among them, that the most virtuous matrons would make professions of i
to young girls, yet rivalry did not exist, and if several men's fancies met in one person
it was rather the beginning of an intimate friendship, while they all jointly conspire
to render the object of their affection as accomplished as possible.

They taught them, also, to speak with a natural and graceful raillery, and to com
prehend much matter of thought in few words. For Lycurgus, who ordered, as w
saw, that a great piece of money should be but of an inconsiderable value, on th
contrary would allow no discourse to be current which did not contain in few word
a great deal of useful and curious sense; children in Sparta, by a habit of long silence
came to give just and sententious answers; for, indeed, as loose and incontinent liver
are seldom fathers of many children, so loose and incontinent talkers seldom originat
many sensible words. King Agis, when some Athenian laughed at their short swords
and said that the jugglers on the stage swallowed them with ease, answered him, "W
find them long enough to reach our enemies with;" and as their swords were shor
and sharp, so, it seems to me, were their sayings. They reach the point and arrest th
attention of the hearers better than any. Lycurgus himself seems to have been shor
and sententious, if we may trust the anecdotes of him; as appears by his answer t
one who by all means would set up democracy in Lacedaemon. "Begin, friend," sai
he, "and set it up in your family." Another asked him why he allowed of such mea
and trivial sacrifices to the gods. He replied, "That we may always have something t
offer to them." Being asked what sort of martial exercises or combats he approved of
he answered, "All sorts, except that in which you stretch out your hands." Simila
answers, addressed to his countrymen by letter, are ascribed to him; as, being consulte
how they might best oppose an invasion of their enemies, he returned this answer
"By continuing poor, and not coveting each man to be greater than his fellow." Bein
consulted again whether it were requisite to inclose the city with a wall, he sent then
word, "The city is well fortified which hath a wall of men instead of brick." Bu
whether these letters are counterfeit or not is not easy to determine. . . .

Nor was their instruction in music and verse less carefully attended to than thei
habits of grace and good breeding in conversation. And their very songs had a lif
and spirit in them that inflamed and possessed men's minds with an enthusiasm an
ardor for action; the style of them was plain and without affectation; the subjec
always serious and moral; most usually, it was in praise of such men as had died i
defense of their country, or in derision of those that had been cowards; the forme
they declared happy and glorified; the life of the latter they described as most miserabl
and abject. There were also vaunts of what they would do and boasts of what they ha

done, varying with the various ages, as, for example, they had three choirs in their olemn festivals, the first of the old men, the second of the young men, and the last of the children; the old men began thus:

> We once were young, and brave and strong;

he young men answered them, singing,

> And we're so now, come on and try;

he children came last and said,

> But we'll be strongest by and by.

Indeed, if we will take the pains to consider their compositions, some of which were still extant in our days, and the airs on the flute to which they marched when going to battle, we shall find that Terpander and Pindar had reason to say that musing and valor were allied. The first says of Lacedaemon—

> The spear and song in her do meet,
> And Justice walks about her street;

and Pindar—

> Councils of wise elders here,
> And the young men's conquering spear,
> And dance, and song, and joy appear;

both describing the Spartans as no less musical than warlike; in the words of one of their own poets—

> With the iron stern and sharp
> Comes the playing on the harp.

For, indeed, before they engaged in battle, the king first did sacrifice to the Muses, in all likelihood to put them in mind of the manner of their education, and of the udgment that would be passed upon their actions, and thereby to animate them to the performance of exploits that should deserve a record. At such times, too, the Lacedaemonians abated a little the severity of their manners in favor of their young men, suffering them to curl and adorn their hair, and to have costly arms, and fine clothes; and were well pleased to see them, like proud horses, neighing and pressing to the course. And therefore, as soon as they came to be well-grown, they took a great deal of care of their hair, to have it parted and trimmed, especially against a day of battle, pursuant to a saying recorded of their lawgiver, that a large head of hair added beauty to a good face, and terror to an ugly one.

When they were in the field, their exercises were generally more moderate, their fare not so hard, nor so strict a hand held over them by their officers, so that they were the only people in the world to whom war gave repose. When their army was drawn up in battle array and the enemy near, the king sacrificed a goat, commanded the soldiers to set their garlands upon their heads, and the pipes to play the tune of the hymn to Castor, and himself began the paean of advance. It was at once a magnificent and a terrible sight to see them march on to the tune of their flutes, without an disorder in their ranks, any discomposure in their minds or change in their counte nance, calmly and cheerfully moving with the music to the deadly fight. Men, in thi temper, were not likely to be possessed with fear or any transport of fury, but with th deliberate valor of hope and assurance, as if some divinity were attending and con ducting them. The king had always about his person some one who had been crowne in the Olympic games; and upon this account a Lacedaemonian is said to have refuse a considerable present, which was offered to him upon condition that he would no come into the lists; and when he had with much to-do thrown his antagonist, some o the spectators saying to him, "And now, Sir Lacedaemonian, what are you the bette for your victory?" he answered smiling, "I shall fight next the king." After they ha routed an enemy, they pursued him till they were well assured of the victory, and the they sounded a retreat, thinking it base and unworthy of a Grecian people to cut me in pieces, who had given up and abandoned all resistance. This manner of dealin with their enemies did not only show magnanimity, but was politic too; for, knowin that they killed only those who made resistance, and gave quarter to the rest, me generally thought it their best way to consult their safety by flight. . . .

To return to the Lacedaemonians. Their discipline continued still after they wer full-grown men. No one was allowed to live after his own fancy; but the city wa a sort of camp, in which every man had his share of provisions and business set out and looked upon himself not so much born to serve his own ends as the interest of hi country. Therefore if they were commanded nothing else, they went to see the boy perform their exercises, to teach them something useful or to learn it themselves o those who knew better. And indeed one of the greatest and highest blessings Lycurgu procured his people was the abundance of leisure which proceeded from his forbid ding to them the exercise of any mean and mechanical trade. Of the money-makin that depends on troublesome going about and seeing people and doing business the had no need at all in a state where wealth obtained no honor or respect. The Helot tilled their ground for them, and paid them yearly in kind the appointed quantity without any trouble of theirs. To this purpose there goes a story of a Lacedaemonia who, happening to be at Athens when the courts were sitting, was told of a citize that had been fined for living an idle life, and was being escorted home in much dis tress of mind, by his condoling friends; the Lacedaemonian was much surprised at i and desired his friend to show him the man who was condemned for living like a freeman. So much beneath them did they esteem the frivolous devotion of time an attention to the mechanical arts and to money-making.

It need not be said, that upon the prohibition of gold and silver, all lawsuits im mediately ceased, for there was now neither avarice nor poverty among them, bu equality, where every one's wants were supplied, and independence, because thos wants were so small. All their time, except when they were in the field, was taken u by the choral dances and the festivals, in hunting, and in attendance on the exercise grounds and the places of public conversation. Those who were under thirty years o age were not allowed to go into the market-place, but had the necessaries of thei family supplied by the care of their relations and lovers; nor was it for the credit o elderly men to be seen too often in the market-place; it was esteemed more suitabl 'or them to frequent the exercise-grounds and places of conversation, where they spent their leisure rationally in conversation, not on money-making and market-prices, out for the most part in passing judgment on some action worth considering; extolling the good, and censuring those who were otherwise, and that in a light and sportive manner, conveying, without too much gravity, lessons of advice and improvement. Nor was Lycurgus himself unduly austere; it was he who dedicated, says Sosibius, the little statue of Laughter. Mirth, introduced seasonably at their suppers and places of common entertainment, was to serve as a sort of sweetmeat to accompany their strict and hard life. To conclude, he bred up his citizens in such a way that they neither would or could live by themselves; they were to make themselves one with the public good, and, clustering like bees around their commander, be by their zeal and public spirit carried all but out of themselves, and devoted wholly to their country. What their sentiments were will better appear by a few of their sayings. Paedaretus, not being admitted into the list of the three hundred, returned home with a joyful face, well pleased to find that there were in Sparta three hundred better men than himself. And Polycratidas, being sent with some others ambassador to the lieutenants of the king of Persia, being asked by them whether they came in a private or in a public character, answered, "In a public, if we succeed; if not, in a private character." Argileonis, asking some who came from Amphipolis if her son Brasidas died courageously and as became a Spartan, on their beginning to praise him to a high degree, and saying there was not such another left in Sparta, answered, "Do not say so; Brasidas was a good and brave man, but there are in Sparta many better than he."

The senate, as I said before, consisted of those who were Lycurgus's chief aiders and assistants in his plans. The vacancies he ordered to be supplied out of the best and most deserving men past sixty years old, and we need not wonder if there was much striving for it; for what more glorious competition could there be among men, than one in which it was not contested who was swiftest among the swift or strongest of the strong, but who of many wise and good was wisest and best, and fittest to be intrusted for ever after, as the reward of his merits, with the supreme authority of the commonwealth, and with power over the lives, franchises, and highest interests of all his countrymen? The manner of their election was as follows: the people being called together, some selected persons were locked up in a room near the place of election, so contrived that they could neither see nor be seen, but could only hear the noise of the assembly without; for they decided this, as most other affairs of moment, by the shouts of the people. This done, the competitors were not brought in and presented all together, but one after another by lot, and passed in order through the assembly without speaking a word. Those who were locked up had writing-tables with them, in which they recorded and marked each shout by its loudness, without knowing in favor of which candidate each of them was made, but merely that they came first, second, third, and so forth. He who was found to have the most and loudest acclamations was declared senator duly elected. Upon this he had a garland set upon his head, and went in procession to all the temples to give thanks to the gods; a great number of young men followed him with applauses, and women, also, singing verses in his honor, and extolling the virtue and happiness of his life. As he went round the city in this manner, each of his relations and friends set a table before him, saying, "The city honors you with this banquet;" but he, instead of accepting, passed round to the common table where he formerly used to eat, and was served as before, excepting that now he had a second allowance, which he took and put by. By the time supper was ended, the women who were of kin to him had come about the door; and he, beckoning to her whom he most esteemed, presented to her the portion he had saved, saying, that it had been a mark of esteem to him, and was so now to her; upon which she was triumphantly waited upon home by the women.

Touching burials, Lycurgus made very wise regulations; for, first of all, to cut off all superstition, he allowed them to bury their dead within the city, and even round about their temples, to the end that their youth might be accustomed to such spectacles, and not be afraid to see a dead body, or imagine that to touch a corpse or to tread upon a grave would defile a man. In the next place, he commanded them to put nothing into the ground with them, except if they pleased, a few olive leaves, and the scarlet cloth that they were wrapped in. He would not suffer the names to be inscribed, except only of men who fell in the wars, or women who died in a sacred office. The time, too, appointed for mourning, was very short, eleven days; on the twelfth, they were to do sacrifice to Ceres, and leave it off; so that we may see, that as he cut off all superfluity, so in things necessary there was nothing so small and trivial which did not express some homage of virtue or scorn of vice. He filled Lacedaemon all through with proofs and examples of good conduct; with the constant sight of which from their youth up, the people would hardly fail to be gradually formed and advanced in virtue.

And this was the reason why he forbade them to trave abroad, and go about acquainting themselves with foreign rulers of morality, the habits of ill-educated people, and different views of government. Withal he banished from Lacedaemon all strangers who could not give a very good reason for their coming thither; not because he was afraid lest they should inform themselves of and imitate his manner of government (as Thucydides says), or learn any thing to their good; but rather lest they should introduce something contrary to good manners. With strange people, strange words must be admitted; these novelties produce novelties in thought; and on these follow views and feelings whose discordant character destroys the harmony of the state. He was as careful to save his city from the infection of foreign bad habits, as men usually are to prevent the introduction of a pestilence.

Hitherto I, for my part, see no sign of injustice or want of equity in the laws of Lycurgus, though some who admit them to be well contrived to make good soldiers pronounce them defective in point of justice. The Cryptia, perhaps (if it were one of Lycurgus's ordinances, as Aristotle says it was), gave both him and Plato, too, this opinion alike of the lawgiver and his government. By this ordinance, the magistrates despatched privately some of the ablest of the young men into the country, from time to time, armed only with their daggers, and taking a little necessary provision with them, in the daytime, they hid themselves in out-of-the-way places, and there lay close, but, in the night, issued out into the highways, and killed all the Helots they could light upon; sometimes they set upon them by day, as they were at work in the fields, and murdered them. As, also, Thucydides, in his history of the Peloponnesian war, tells us, that a good number of them, after being singled out for their bravery by the Spartans, garlanded, as enfranchised persons, and led about to all the temples in token of honors, shortly after disappeared all of a sudden, being about the number of two thousand; and no man either then or since could give an account how they came by their deaths. And Aristotle, in particular, adds, that the ephori, so soon as they were entered into their office, used to declare war against them, that they might be massacred without a breach of religion. It is confessed, on all hands, that the Spartans dealt with them very hardly; for it was a common thing to force them to drink to excess, and to lead them in that condition into their public halls, that the children might see what a sight a drunken man is; they made them to dance low dances, and sing ridiculous songs, forbidding them expressly to meddle with any of a better kind. And accordingly, when the Thebans made their invasion into Laconia, and took a great number of the Helots, they could by no means persuade them to sing the verses of Terpander, Aleman, or Spendon, "For," said they, "the masters do not like it." So that it was truly observed by one, that in Sparta he who was free was most so, and he that was a slave there, the greatest slave in the world. For my part, I am of opinion that these outrages and cruelties began to be exercised in Sparta at a later time, especially after the great earthquake, when the Helots made a general insurrection, and, joining with the Messenians, laid the country waste, and brought the greatest danger upon the city. For I cannot persuade myself to ascribe to Lycurgus so wicked and barbarous a course, judging of him from the gentleness of his disposition and justice upon all other occasions; to which the oracle also testified.

When he perceived that his more important institutions had taken root in the minds of his countrymen, that custom had rendered them familiar and easy, that his commonwealth was now grown up and able to go alone, then, as Plato somewhere tell us, the Maker of the world, when first he saw it existing and beginning its motion, felt joy, even so Lycurgus, viewing with joy and satisfaction the greatness and beauty of his political structure, now fairly at work and in motion, conceived the thought to make it immortal too and, as far as human forecast could reach, to deliver it down unchangeable to posterity. He called an extraordinary assembly of all the people, and told them that he now thought everything reasonably well established, both for the happiness and the virtue of the state; but that there was one thing still behind, of the greatest importance, which he thought not fit to impart unil he had consulted the oracle; in the meantime, his desire was that they would observe the laws without any the least alteration until his return, and then he would do as the god should direct him. They all consented readily, and bade him hasten his journey; but, before he departed, he administered an oath to the two kings, the senate, and the whole commons, to abide by and maintain the established form of polity until Lycurgus should be come back. This done, he set out for Delphi, and, having sacrificed to Apollo, asked him whether the laws he had established were good, and sufficient for a people's happiness and virtue. The oracle answered that the laws were excellent, and that the people, while it observed them, should live in the height of renown. Lycurgus took the oracle in writing, and sent it over to Sparta; and, having sacrificed the second time to Apollo, and taken leave of his friends and his son, he resolved that the Spartans should not be released from the oath they had taken, and that he would, of his own act, close his life where he was. He was now about that age in which life was still tolerable, and yet might be quitted with regret. Everything, moreover, about him was in a sufficiently prosperous condition. He, therefore, made an end of himself by a tota abstinence from food, thinking it a stateman's duty to make his very death, if possible an act of service to the state, and even in the end of his life to give some example o virtue and effect some useful purpose. He would, on the one hand, crown and con summate his own happiness by a death suitable to so honorable a life, and, on th other, would secure to his countrymen the enjoyment of the advantages he had spen his life in obtaining for them, since they had solemnly sworn the maintenance of hi institutions until his return. Nor was he deceived in his expectations for the city o Lacedaemon continued the chief city of all Greece for the space of five hundred years in strict observance of Lycurgus's laws, in all which time there was no manner o alteration made, during the reign of fourteen kings down to the time of Agis, the so of Archidamus. For the new creation of the ephori, though thought to be in favo of the people, was so far from diminishing, that it very much heightened, the aristo cratical character of the government.

In the time of Agis, gold and silver first flowed into Sparta, and with them al those mischiefs which attend the immoderate desire of riches. Lysander promoted thi disorder; for by bringing in rich spoils from the wars, although himself incorrupt, h yet by this means filled his country with avarice and luxury, and subverted the law and ordinances of Lycurgus; so long as which were in force, the aspect presented b Sparta was rather that of a rule of life followed by one wise and temperate man than of the political government of a nation. And as the poets feign of Hercules that, with his lion's skin and his club, he went over the world, punishing lawles and cruel tyrants, so it may be said of the Lacedaemonians, that, with a common sta and a coarse coat, they gained the willing and joyful obedience of Greece, throug whose whole extent they suppressed unjust usurpations and despotisms, arbitrated i war, and composed civil dissensions; and this often without so much as taking dow one buckler, but barely by sending some one single deputy to whose direction all a once submitted, like bees swarming and taking their places around their prince. Suc a fund of order and equity, enough and to spare for others, existing in their state

And therefore I cannot but wonder at those who say that the Spartans were goo subjects, but bad governors, and for proof of it allege a saying of king Theopompus who, when one said that Sparta held up so long because their kings could comman so well, replied, "Nay, rather because the people know so well how to obey." Fo people do not obey, unless rulers know how to command; obedience is a lesson taugh by commanders. A true leader himself creates the obedience of his own followers; a it is the last attainment in the art of riding to make a horse gentle and tractable, s is it of the science of government, to inspire men with a willingness to obey. The Lace daemonians inspired men not with a mere willingness, but with an absolute desire to be their subjects. For they did not send petitions to them for ships or money, or supply of armed men, but only for a Spartan commander; and, having obtained one used him with honor and reverence; so the Sicilians behaved to Gylippus, the Chal cidians to Brasidas, and all the Greeks in Asia to Lysander, Callicratidas, and Agesilaus they styled them the composers and chasteners of each people or prince they were sen to, and had their eyes always fixed upon the city of Sparta itself, as the perfect mode of good manners and wise government. The rest seemed as scholars, they the master of Greece; and to this Stratonicus pleasantly alluded, when in jest he pretended to make a law that the Athenians should conduct religious processions and the mysteries, the Eleans should preside at the Olympic games, and, if either did amiss, the Lacedaemonians be beaten. Antisthenes, too, one of the scholars * of Socrates, said, in earnest, of the Thebans, when they were elated by their victory at Leuctra, that they looked like schoolboys who had beaten their master.

However, it was not the design of Lycurgus that his city should govern a great many others; he thought rather that the happiness of a state, as a private man, consisted chiefly in the exercise of virtue, and in the concord of the inhabitants; his aim, therefore, in all his arrangements, was to make and keep them free-minded, self-dependent, and temperate. And therefore all those who have writen well on politics, as Plato, Diogenes, and Zeno, have taken Lycurgus for their model, leaving behind them, however, mere projects and words; whereas Lycurgus was the author, not in writing but in reality, of a government which none else could so much as copy; and while men in general have treated the individual philosophic character as unattainable, he, by the example of a complete philosophic state, raised himself high above all other lawgivers of Greece.

And so Aristotle says they did him less honor at Lacedaemon after his death than he deserved, although he has a temple there, and they offer sacrifices yearly to him as to a god.

* [I.e., followers. (*Ed.*)]

THE CONSTITUTION OF THE ATHENIANS

"The Old Oligarch"

No one knows who wrote The Constitution of the Athenians, *which is given here in its entirety. Modern scholars have given its anonymous author the nickname "the Old Oligarch" because of his sour view of Athenian democracy. Yet his grudgingly respectful analysis tells us more about the actual strengths and weaknesses of Athenian institutions than do the polished phrases of Pericles (see Thucydides, pages 90–94). The Old Oligarch was no doubt an Athenian citizen, probably a merchant, and he seems to speak from firsthand experience. He was a member of the aristocratic (or oligarchic) faction, and his judgments are inevitably colored by the conflict between democrats and oligarchs—"the many" and "the few"—that was a universal and all-important phenomenon in the Greek states.*

The term "constitution" in the title does not refer to a written document, but to the structure of the polis itself; that is, the arrangement of privileges and responsibilities within the state. In this sense every society has its constitution, and no two of these constitutions would be just alike, since each society is affected by its climate, geography, history, customs, etc. It is the influence of just such factors at Athens, particularly the importanc of its being a seaport, that is brought out in this text.

CHAPTER I

As for the constitution of the Athenians, their choice of this type of constitution I d not approve, for in choosing thus they chose that rascals should fare better than goo citizens. This then is why I do not approve. However this being their decision, I sha show how well they preserve their constitution, and how well otherwise they are actin where the rest of Greece thinks that they are going wrong.

First of all then I shall say that at Athens the poor and the commons seem just to have the advantage over the well-born and the wealthy; for it is the commons whic mans the fleet and has brought the state her power, and the steersmen and the boat swains and the shipmasters and the lookout-men and the ship-builders—these hav brought the state her power much rather than the infantry and the well-born and th good citizens. This being so it seems just that all should have a share in offices fille by lot or by election, and that any citizen who wishes should be allowed to speak.

Then in those offices which bring security to the whole commons if they are in th hands of good citizens, but if not ruin, the commons desires to have no share. The do not think that they ought to have a share through the lot in the supreme command or in the cavalry commands, for the commons realises that it reaps greater benef by not having these offices in its own hands, but by allowing men of standing t hold them. All those offices however whose end is pay and family benefits the com mons does seek to hold.

Secondly some folk are surprised that everywhere they give the advantage to rascal the poor and the democrats rather than to good citizens. This is just where the will be seen to be preserving the democracy. For if the poor and the common fol and the worse elements are treated well, the growth of these classes will exalt th democracy; whereas if the rich and the good citizens are treated well the democra strengthen their own opponents.

In every land the best element is opposed to democracy. Among the best element there is very little license and injustice, very great discrimination as to what is worth while among the commons there is very great ignorance, disorderliness and rascality for poverty tends to lead them to what is disgraceful, as does lack of education an the ignorance which befalls some men as a result of lack of means.

It may be said that they ought not to have allowed everyone in turn to make speeche or sit on the Council, but only those of the highest capability and quality. But i allowing even rascals to speak they are also very well advised. For if the goo citizens made speeches and joined in deliberations, good would result to those lik themselves and ill to the democrats. As it is anyone who wants, a rascally fellow mayb

"The Old Oligarch," *The Constitution of the Athenians*, trans. J. A. Petch (Oxford: Bas Blackwell & Mott, Ltd., n.d.), 15–29.

gets up and makes a speech, and devises what is to the advantage of himself and those like him.

Someone may ask how such a fellow would know what is to the advantage of himself or the commons. They know that this man's ignorance, rascality and goodwill are more beneficial than the good citizen's worth, wisdom and illwill.

From such procedure then a city would not attain the ideal, but the democracy would be best preserved thus. For it is the wish of the commons not that the state should be well ordered and the commons itself in complete subjection, but that the commons should have its freedom and be in control; disorderliness is of little consequence to it. From what you consider lack of order come the strength and the liberty of the commons itself.

If on the other hand you investigate good order, first of all you will see that the most capable make laws for them; then the good citizens will keep the rascals in check and will deliberate on matters of state, refusing to allow madmen to sit on the Council or make speeches or attend the general assemblies. Such advantages indeed would very soon throw the commons into complete subjection.

The license allowed to slaves and aliens at Athens is extreme and a blow is forbidden there, nor will a slave make way for you. I shall tell you why this is the custom of the country. If it were legal for a slave or an alien or a freedman to be beaten by a freeman, you would often have taken the Athenian for a slave and struck him; for the commons there does not dress better than the slaves and the aliens, and their general appearance is in no way superior.

If anyone is suprised also at their allowing slaves, that is some of them, to live luxuriously and magnificently there, here too they would be seen to act with wisdom. In a naval state slaves must serve for hire, *that we may receive the fee for their labour,* and we must let them go free. Where there are rich slaves it is no longer profitable that my slave should be afraid of you. In Sparta my slave is afraid of you. If your slave is afraid of me there will be a danger even of his giving his own money to avoid personal risks.

This then is why we placed even slaves on a footing of equality with free men; and we placed aliens on a footing of equality with citizens because the state has need of aliens owing to the number of skilled trades and because of the fleet. For this reason then we were right to place even the aliens on a footing of equality.

The commons has put down those who make a practice of athletics and music there. It considers this unseemly, realising that it is unable to practise these pursuits. On the other hand in the provision of dramatic choruses, the superintendence of athletics and the command of ships of the line, they know that it is the rich who provide choruses while the commons is supplied with men to provide the choruses, that it is the rich who superintend athletics and command ships of the line, while the commons is supplied with men to command and superintend. At any rate the commons demands pay for singing, running, dancing and voyaging, in order that its wealth may increase and the rich become less rich. In the law-courts they do not pay more heed to justice than to their own gain.

As for the allies, that the Athenians leave home and, as it is thought, bring false accusations against the good citizens and hate them—they know that the ruler cannot help but be hated by the ruled, and that if the rich and the good citizens in the various cities have control the rule of the commons at Athens will be very short-lived. This then is why they disfranchise the good citizens, rob them of their wealth, drive them into exile, or put them to death, while they exalt the rascals. The good citizens of Athens protect the good citizens in the allied cities, realizing that it is to their own advantage always to protect the best elements in the various cities.

It might be suggested that the ability of the allies to pay tribute is the strength of Athens. The democrats think it more advantageous that each individual Athenian should possess the wealth of the allies and the allies only enough to live on, and continue working without having the power to conspire.

The commons of Athens is also thought to be ill-advised in compelling the allies to travel to Athens to have their law-suits tried. They meet this criticism by reckoning up all the benefits to the Athenian commons that this involves: first of all the receipt of pay out of the court fees all the year round; then while remaining at home without sending out ships they manage the allied cities, and protect the party of the commons while they ruin their opponents in the courts. If each of the allies tried their law-suits at home, out of hatred for Athenians they would have destroyed those of their own people most friendly to the Athenian commons.

In addition the commons of Athens gains the following advantages from having the allied law-suits tried at Athens. First the five per cent. duty levied at the Peiraeus brings more in to the state; next anyone who has a lodging-house is more prosperous, and so is the man who has a couple of hacks or a slave for hire; then the heralds are more prosperous as a result of the visits of the allies. Above all this if the allies did not come to Athens for their law-suits they would honour only those Athenians who leave home—the generals, the naval commanders and envoys. As it is all the allies individually must fawn upon the Athenian commons, realizing that they must come to Athens and appear as defendant or prosecutor before the commons and the commons alone, for that forsooth is the law at Athens; and in the law-courts they must make supplications and grasp so-and-so by the hand as he enters. This then is why the allies are rather in the position of slaves of the Athenian commons.

Moreover owing to their over-seas possessions and appointments they have unconsciously learned to row, their attendants too. For on a voyage master and man must often take an oar and learn the nautical terms. They become good steersmen by experience of boats and by practise. Some get practise by steering a boat, others by steering a merchant-man, and some go on to command ships of the line. The mob however can go on board and at once set about rowing, for they have spent all their previous life in practise.

CHAPTER II

The situation with regard to their infantry, which is at Athens thought to be least favourably situated of all, is that they think themselves inferior to their enemies and less than them in numbers, but to the allies who bring in the tribute they are superior on land, and they consider the infantry sufficient if they have the upper hand of them

Moreover chance has brought about a state of affairs somewhat as follows. Subjects of a land power can form a union of small cities and fight together as one, whereas such subjects of a naval power as are islanders cannot unite their cities in one, for the sea lies between and their masters have command of it. Even if the islanders can come together secretly on one island, they will be starved out.

Of such mainland states as are subject to Athenian rule the large are in subjection because of fear, the small simply because of need; there is not a city which does not require both import and export trade, and it will not have that unless it is subject to the rulers of the sea.

Secondly a sea power can always do what a land power can do occasionally—that is ravage the territory of a more powerful state. It is possible for him to coast along wherever there are few or no enemy troops and if they approach sail off in his ship; such tactics cause less inconvenience to him than to the man who marches up a force on foot.

Again the sea power can sail away as far as you like from their own land, whereas the land power cannot undertake a march of many days away from their own country; for marching is slow, and a man on foot cannot carry provisions for a long period. He who marches on foot must march through friendly country or win a way with the sword, whereas the man aboard ship can disembark where he has the superior force, and where he has not can refrain from disembarking at this point, and sail along until he comes to friendly country or meets with forces inferior to his own.

Again the strongest land power is hard hit by the blighted crops which are of God, but not so the sea power. All countries do not suffer from blight simultaneously, so that to those who rule the sea come imports from the country with healthy crops.

If there is any need to mention less important facts too, command of the sea and contact with the different people of different countries were the first means of introducing luxurious ways of living. The delicacies of Sicily, Italy, Cyprus, Egypt, Lydia, Pontus, the Peloponnese, in fact of any country, all converge upon one point as a result of the command of the sea.

Then hearing every tongue they adopted a phrase from this tongue and a phrase from that. The Greeks as a whole enjoy a language, a way of life and a general appearance which is rather their own, the Athenians a hotch-potch of those of all the Greeks and foreigners.

Sacrifices, temples, feasts and sacred inclosures too—the commons realises that every poor man is not able individually to offer sacrifices, give feasts, found temples, and live in a city which is beautiful and great, so it has devised a way of attaining this. The state sacrifices many victims at the public charge, but it is the commons which partakes of the feasts and divides up the victims.

So with sports-grounds, baths and changing-rooms, some rich men have their own, but the commons gets many athletic grounds, changing-rooms and baths built for itself on its own account, and the rabble gets more enjoyment from these than do the few well-to-do.

They alone can possess the wealth of Greeks and foreigners. If a city is rich in ship-building timber where will it dispose of it unless it win the consent of the ruler of the sea? What if some city is rich in iron or bronze or cloth? Where will it dispose of it unless it win the consent of the ruler of the sea? These however are just the very things of which my ships are made—somebody's wood, somebody's iron, somebody's bronze, somebody's cloth and somebody's wax.

Moreover *they will not allow our rivals to take their goods elsewhere or* (*if they try*) *they will not use the sea.* I pass my time in idleness, and because of the sea I have all these products of the earth, whereas no other single city has two of these commodities; the same city does not possess both timber and cloth, but where cloth is plentiful the country is flat and treeless, nor do bronze and iron come from the same city, nor does one city possess two or three of the other commodities, but one has one, another has another.

Once more along every coastline there is either a projecting headland or an island off the shore, or some strait or other. Thus those who have command of the sea can lie off there and ravage those who dwell on the mainland.

They lack one advantage. If the Athenians lived on an island and held command of the sea, they would have had the power to inflict loss if they wished without suffering any themselves so long as they ruled the sea, either the ravaging of their land or the waiting for invasion. As it is the farmers and the rich Athenians cringe somewhat before the enemy, whereas the commons, knowing well enough that the enemy will not burn or ravage anything of theirs, lives without fear and without cringing to them.

In addition there is a second ground for fear from which they would have been free had they lived on an island, the fear that the city would ever be betrayed by a minority or the gates opened or the enemy gain a footing. For how would this come about if they lived on an island? There would be no fear of a rising against the commons if they lived on an island. At present a rising would be based upon the hope of being able to invite the enemy in by land, but if they lived on an island there would be no grounds for fear in this respect either.

As therefore they did not originally happen to settle on an island, what they do is to lay up their wealth in the islands, trusting in their sea power, while they put up with the ravaging of Attica, knowing that if they take pity on her they will lose other greater advantages.

Again oligarchical states must abide by their alliances and their oaths. If they do not keep to the agreement *penalties can be exacted* from the few who made it. But whenever the commons makes an agreement it can lay the blame on the individual speaker or proposer, and say to the other party that it was not present and does not approve what they know was agreed upon in full assembly; and should it be decided that this is not so, the commons has discovered a hundred excuses for not doing what they may not wish to do. If any ill result from a decision of the commons it lays the blame on a minority for opposing and working its ruin, whereas if any good results they take the credit to themselves.

They do not allow caricature and abuse of the commons, lest they should hear themselves evilly spoken of, but they do allow you to caricature any individual you wish to. They well know that generally the man who is caricatured is not of the commons or of the crowd, but someone rich or well-born or influential, and that few of the poor and democrats are caricatured, and they only because they are busy-bodies and try to over-reach the commons; so they are not angry when such men are caricatured either.

I say then that the commons at Athens realizes which citizens are good citizens and which rascals. With this knowledge they favour those who are friendly and useful to them, even if they are rascals, whereas they hate rather the good citizens. For they do not believe that their worth exists for the good but for the ill of the commons. Conversely certain men who in fact belong to the commons are not democratic by nature.

I pardon the commons itself its democracy, for it is pardonable that everyone should seek his own interest. But the man who is not of the commons yet chose to live in a democratic rather than in an oligarchical state sought opportunity for wrongdoing, and realized that it was more possible for his wickedness to go unnoticed in a democratic state than in an oligarchical.

CHAPTER III

The type of the constitution of the Athenians I do not approve, but as they saw fit to be a democracy in my opinion they preserve their democracy well by employing the means I have pointed out.

Further I notice that certain folk blame the Athenians because sometimes there the Council or the commons cannot deal with a man, though he waits about for a year.

This happens at Athens simply because they are unable owing to the multitude of their activities to deal with and dismiss everybody. How could they do so, seeing that first of all they have to celebrate more feasts than any other Greek state, and in the course of these feasts it is less possible to get state business through? Secondly they have to decide more private and public law-suits and official scrutinies than all the rest of the world together, and the Council has to deliberate on much relating to war, revenue, legislation, contemporary happenings at home and among the allies; it has also to receive the tribute and look after the dock-yards and the temples. Is it then to be wondered at that with so much on hand they are unable to deal with everyone?

It is said that if you approach the Council or the commons with a bribe your business will be dealt with. I would agree that much is got through at Athens by means of bribery, and that still more would be got through if still more people gave bribes. This however I am sure of, *that the state is not capable of getting through everybody's business when so much is needed,* even if you were to give them any amount of gold and silver.

Furthermore judgments must be given if anyone does not equip his ship, or if someone builds upon public land; there must be judgments upon appeals by patrons of choruses for the Dionysia, the Thargelia, the Panathenaia, the Promethia and the Hephaestia every year; four hundred naval commanders are appointed annually, and every year judgments must be given on appeals lodged by any of them. In addition to this there must be preliminary and final scrutinies of the magistrates, there is the examination of orphans and the appointment of the custodians of prisoners.

This is annual business. From time to time there must be decisions *about military service,* or if any unlooked for crime is committed, whether of unprecedented outrage or impiety. I pass over much, but the most important duties have been mentioned except the assessment of tribute. This generally takes place every four years. Well then must we not suppose that they ought to judge upon all these cases?

Let any man mention any case they ought not to judge upon there. If we must agree that they ought not to give all these judgments it must be done in the course of a year. Even now, when the courts sit throughout the year, they do not suffice to suppress crime because of the size of the population.

Well then, you will argue, they ought to give judgment but employ smaller juries. They must surely, unless they have few courts, have small juries in each. As a result it will be easy to trick the small jury and bribe them to give much less just decisions.

Moreover you must remember that the Athenians have to hold festivals also, in the course of which the courts cannot sit. They hold twice as many festivals as the rest of the world, but I consider them as equal to those of the city which holds the fewest.

This then being how matters stand, I maintain that the state of things at Athens cannot be otherwise than it is at present, unless it is possible in some small way to take away this and add that. It is not possible to make many alterations without robbing the democracy of power.

It is possible to devise many ways of improving the constitution, but to leave the democracy in existence and yet devise adequate ways of introducing better government is not easy, unless, as I said just now, it is by way of some small additions or subtractions.

The Athenians are also thought to be ill advised because they take sides with the worse elements in cities divided by faction. They do this with good reason. If they sided with the better elements they would not side with those who hold the same opinions as themselves, for in no city is the better element well inclined to the commons, but in each the worse element is well inclined to the commons; like favours like. This then is why the Athenians side with the elements akin to themselves.

As often as they attempted to side with the best it has brought them no profit: within a short time the Boeotian commons was in slavery, and again when they sided with the best at Miletus within a short time the latter broke away and massacred the commons. Then too when they sided with the Lacedaemonians against the Messenians within a short time the Lacedaemonians reduced the latter, and were at war with Athens.

It might be imagined that no one at all has been disfranchised at Athens unjustly. I maintain that there are those who have been unjustly disfranchised; however they are but few.

But it needs not a few to attack the democracy at Athens, the fact being that it is not those who have been disfranchised justly who care, but those who may have suffered unjustly. How then could anyone think that at Athens the majority have been disfranchised unjustly where it is the commons which holds office? Unjust administration, unjust speaking, unjust action are the causes of disfranchisement at Athens. Considering this it must not be imagined that there is anything to fear from the disfranchised at Athens.

THE PELOPONNESIAN WAR

Thucydides

In 431 B.C., *war broke out between an alliance of Greek cities headed by Athens and another such alliance headed by Sparta. It dragged on for twenty-seven years, ending in a costly victory for Sparta. Sparta herself was defeated by Thebes a few years later. The consequence of these wars was to shatter forever the loose but free union of independent city-states that had emerged fifty years earlier during the struggle against the Persian invaders.*

An Athenian admiral named Thucydides (ca. 460–400 B.C.), *who was relieved of command in the early years of the war for losing an important naval battle, employed his newly found leisure in writing a history of the war. He saw that the key to the understanding of the war was to be found not on the battlefields, but within the adversaries themselves: their customs, ideals, and social and political institutions. This much had been grasped already by Herodotus. But Thucydides saw also that the war produced a gradual change in these ideals and institutions, so that long before they were finally defeated, the Athenians had ceased to be the same people who had created the world's first democracy, built a thriving commercial empire, and produced some of the greatest poets, philosophers, and statesmen the world has ever seen. In his investigation Thucydides studied the social structure of the Greek cities—classes, factions, forms of government—with remarkable objectivity. (He refers to his own military activities, for example, without any attempt to make excuses for his failure, simply as those of "a certain Thucydides.")*

Our selections include the "Funeral Oration of Pericles," a speech put in the mouth of the Athenian leader. It commemorates the men who died fighting in the first year of the war, and attempts to formulate what they died for. Undoubtedly Pericles did give a speech of this kind at a public funeral; but how many of the expressions, and even the ideas, are those of Thucydides rather than Pericles, we shall probably never know. Regardless of who should get the credit for the speech, however, it stands as an eloquent defense of a political and social ideal.

The passages on the plague at Athens and on the revolution at Corcyra are masterpieces of reporting, combining accurate narrative with penetrating analysis. They reveal the influence on Thucydides of the methods of medical research developed by Hippocrates: not only the plague, but the revolution and the war itself are seen as diseases of the body politic, displaying symptoms which must be carefully noted and classified to facilitate diagnosis and cure.

"The Melian Dialogue," based on an event of 417 B.C., *is another imaginative but fundamentally historical passage. Here Thucydides underlines the bold cynicism of Athenian policy. The influence of the sophists is apparent (See the introduction to Plato's* Gorgias, *page 108).*

BOOK I

1 Thucydides, an Athenian, wrote the history of the war in which the Peloponnesians and the Athenians fought against one another. He began to write when they first took up arms, believing that it would be great and memorable above any previous war. For he argued that both states were then at the full height of their military power, and he saw the rest of the Hellenes either siding or intending to side with one or other of them. No movement ever stirred Hellas more deeply than this; it was shared by many of the Barbarians, and might be said even to affect the world at large. The character of the events which preceded, whether immediately or in more remote antiquity, owing to the lapse of time cannot be made out with certainty. But, judging from the evidence which I am able to trust after most careful enquiry, I should imagine that former ages were not great either in their wars or in anything else. . . .

18 At length the tyrants of Athens and of the rest of Hellas (which had been under their dominion long before Athens), at least the greater number of them, and with the exception of the Sicilian the last who ever ruled, were put down by the Lacedaemonians. For although Lacedaemon, after the conquest of the country by the Dorians who now inhabit it, remained long unsettled, and indeed longer than any country which we know, nevertheless she obtained good laws at an earlier period than any other, and has never been subject to tyrants; she has preserved the same form of government for rather more than four hundred years, reckoning to the end of the Peloponnesian War. It was the excellence of her constitution which gave her power, and thus enabled her to regulate the affairs of other states. Not long after the overthrow of the tyrants by the Lacedaemonians, the battle of Marathon was fought between the Athenians and the Persians; ten years later, the Barbarian returned with the vast armament which was to enslave Hellas. In the greatness of the impending danger, the Lacedaemonians, who were the most powerful state in Hellas, assumed the lead of the confederates. The Athenians, as the Persian host advanced, resolved to forsake their city, broke up their homes, and, taking to their ships, became sailors. The Barbarian was repelled by a common effort; but soon the Hellenes, as well those who had revolted from the King as those who formed the original confederacy, took different sides and became the allies, either of the Athenians or of the Lacedaemonians; for

Thucydides, *The Peloponnesian War*, trans. B. Jowett (2 vols.; Oxford: Clarendon Press, 1881), I, 1, 12–16, 117–128, 215–225, 397–407.

these were now the two leading powers, the one strong by land and the other by sea. The league between them was of short duration; they speedily quarrelled and, with their respective allies, went to war. Any of the other Hellenes who had differences of their own now resorted to one or other of them. So that from the Persian to the Peloponnesian War, the Lacedaemonians and the Athenians were perpetually fighting or making peace, either with one another or with their own revolted allies; thus they attained military efficiency, and learned experience in the school of danger.

19 The Lacedaemonians did not make tributaries of those who acknowledged their leadership, but took care that they should be governed by oligarchies in the exclusive interest of Sparta. The Athenians, on the other hand, after a time deprived the subject cities of their ships and made all of them pay a fixed tribute, except Chios and Lesbos. And the single power of Athens at the beginning of this war was greater than that of Athens and Sparta together at their greatest, while the confederacy remained intact.

20 Such are the results of my enquiry into the early state of Hellas. They will not readily be believed upon a bare recital of all the proofs of them. Men do not discriminate, and are too ready to receive ancient traditions about their own as well as about other countries. . . .

21 Yet any one who upon the grounds which I have given arrives at some such conclusion as my own about those ancient times, would not be far wrong. He must not be misled by the exaggerated fancies of the poets, or by the tales of chroniclers who seek to please the ear rather than to speak the truth. Their accounts cannot be tested by him; and most of the facts in the lapse of ages have passed into the region of romance. At such a distance of time he must make up his mind to be satisfied with conclusions resting upon the clearest evidence which can be had. And, though men will always judge any war in which they are actually fighting to be the greatest at the time, but, after it is over, revert to their admiration of some other which has preceded, still the Peloponnesian, if estimated by the actual facts, will certainly prove to have been the greatest ever known.

22 As to the speeches which were made either before or during the war, it was hard for me, and for others who reported them to me, to recollect the exact words. I have therefore put into the mouth of each speaker the sentiments proper to the occasion, expressed as I thought he would be likely to express them, while at the same time I endeavoured, as nearly as I could, to give the general purport of what was actually said. Of the events of the war I have not ventured to speak from any chance information, nor according to any notion of my own; I have described nothing but what I either saw myself, or learned from others of whom I made the most careful and particular enquiry. The task was a laborious one, because eye-witnesses of the same occurrences gave different accounts of them, as they remembered or were interested in the actions of one side or the other. And very likely the strictly historical character of my narrative may be disappointing to the ear. But if he who desires to have before his eyes a true picture of the events which have happened, and of the like events which may be expected to happen hereafter in the order of human things, shall pronounce what I have written to be useful, then I shall be satisfied. My history is an everlasting possession, not a prize composition which is heard and forgotten.

23 The greatest achievement of former times was the Persian War; yet even this was speedily decided in two battles by sea and two by land. But the Peloponnesian War was a protracted struggle, and attended by calamities such as Hellas had never known within a like period of time. Never were so many cities captured and depopulated—some by Barbarians, others by Hellenes themselves fighting against one another; and several of them after their capture were repeopled by strangers. Never were exile and slaughter more frequent, whether in the war or brought about by civil strife. And rumours, of which the like had often been current before, but rarely verified by fact, now appeared to be well grounded. There were earthquakes unparalleled in their extent and fury, and eclipses of the sun more numerous than are recorded to have happened in any former age; there were also in some places great droughts causing famines, and lastly the plague which did immense harm and destroyed numbers of the people. All these calamities fell upon Hellas simultaneously with the war, which began when the Athenians and Peloponnesians violated the thirty years' truce concluded by them after the recapture of Euboea. Why they broke it and what were the grounds of quarrel I will first set forth, that in time to come no man may be at a loss to know what was the origin of this great war. The real though unavowed cause I believe to have been the growth of the Athenian power, which terrified the Lacedaemonians and forced them into war; but the reasons publicly alleged on either side were as follows. . . .

BOOK II (431 B.C.): FUNERAL ORATION OF PERICLES

36 'I will speak first of our ancestors, for it is right and becoming that now, when we are lamenting the dead, a tribute should be paid to their memory. There has never been a time when they did not inhabit this land, which by their valour they have handed down from generation to generation, and we have received from them a free state. But if they were worthy of praise, still more were our fathers, who added to their inheritance, and after many a struggle transmitted to us their sons this great empire. And we ourselves asembled here to-day, who are still most of us in the vigour of life, have chiefly done the work of improvement, and have richly endowed our city with all things, so that she is sufficient for herself both in peace and war. Of the military exploits by which our various possessions were acquired, or of the energy with which we or our fathers drove back the tide of war, Hellenic or Barbarian, I will not speak; for the tale would be long and is familiar to you. But before I praise the dead, I should like to point out by what principles of action we rose to power, and under what institutions and through what manner of life our empire became great. For I conceive that such thoughts are not unsuited to the occasion, and that this numerous assembly of citizens and strangers may profitably listen to them.

37 'Our form of government does not enter into rivalry with the institutions of others. We do not copy our neighbours, but are an example to them. It is true that we are called a democracy, for the administration is in the hands of the many and not of the few. But while the law secures equal justice to all alike in their private disputes, the claim of excellence is also recognised; and when a citizen is in any way distinguished, he is preferred to the public service, not as a matter of privilege, but as the reward of merit. Neither is poverty a bar, but a man may benefit his country whatever be the obscurity of his condition. There is no exclusiveness in our public life, and in our private intercourse we are not suspicious of one another, nor angry with our neighbour if he does what he likes; we do not put on sour looks at him which, though harmless, are not pleasant. While we are thus unconstrained in our private intercourse, a spirit of reverence pervades our public acts; we are prevented from doing wrong by respect for authority and for the laws, having an especial regard to those which are ordained for the protection of the injured as well as to those unwritten laws which bring upon the transgressor of them the reprobation of the general sentiment.

38 'And we have not forgotten to provide for our weary spirits many relaxations from toil; we have regular games and sacrifices throughout the year; at home the style of our life is refined; and the delight which we daily feel in all these things helps to banish melancholy. Because of the greatness of our city the fruits of the whole earth flow in upon us; so that we enjoy the goods of other countries as freely as of our own.

39 'Then, again, our military training is in many respects superior to that of our adversaries. Our city is thrown open to the world, and we never expel a foreigner or prevent him from seeing or learning anything of which the secret if revealed to an enemy might profit him. We rely not upon management or trickery, but upon our own hearts and hands. And in the matter of education, whereas they from early youth are always undergoing laborious exercises which are to make them brave, we live at ease, and yet are equally ready to face the perils which they face. And here is the proof. The Lacedaemonians come into Attica not by themselves, but with their whole confederacy following; we go alone into a neighbour's country; and although our opponents are fighting for their homes and we on a foreign soil, we have seldom any difficulty in overcoming them. Our enemies have never yet felt our united strength; the care of a navy divides our attention, and on land we are obliged to send our own citizens everywhere. But they, if they meet and defeat a part of our army, are as proud as if they had routed us all, and when defeated they pretend to have been vanquished by us all.

40 'If then we prefer to meet danger with a light heart but without laborious training, and with a courage which is gained by habit and not enforced by law, are we not greatly the gainers? Since we do not anticipate the pain, although, when the hour comes, we can be as brave as those who never allow themselves to rest; and thus too our city is equally admirable in peace and in war. For we are lovers of the beautiful, yet simple in our tastes, and we cultivate the mind without loss of manliness. Wealth we employ, not for talk and ostentation, but when there is a real use for it. To avow poverty with us is no disgrace; the true disgrace is in doing nothing to avoid it. An Athenian citizen does not neglect the state because he takes care of his own household; and even those of us who are engaged in business have a very fair idea of politics. We alone regard a man who takes no interest in public affairs, not as a harmless, but as a useless character; and if few of us are originators, we are all sound judges of a policy. The great impediment to action is, in our opinion, not discussion, but the want of that knowledge which is gained by discussion preparatory to action. For we have a peculiar power of thinking before we act and of acting too, whereas other men are courageous from ignorance but hesitate upon reflection. And they are surely to be esteemed the bravest spirits who, having the clearest sense both of the pains and pleasures of life, do not on that account shrink from danger. In doing good, again, we are unlike others; we make our friends by conferring, not by receiving favours. Now he who confers a favour is the firmer friend, because he would fain by kindness keep alive the memory of an obligation; but the recipient is colder in his feelings, because he knows that in requiting another's generosity he will not be winning gratitude but only paying a debt. We alone do good to our neighbours not upon a calculation of interest, but in the confidence of freedom and in a frank and fearless spirit

41 'To sum up: I say that Athens is the school of Hellas, and that the individual Athenian in his own person seems to have the power of adapting himself to the most varied forms of action with the utmost versatility and grace. This is no passing and idle word, but truth and fact; and the assertion is verified by the position to which these qualities have raised the state. For in the hour of trial Athens alone among her contemporaries is superior to the report of her. No enemy who comes against her is indignant at the reverses which he sustains at the hands of such a city; no subject complains that his masters are unworthy of him. And we shall assuredly not be without witnesses; there are mighty monuments of our power which will make us the wonder of this and of succeeding ages; we shall not need the praises of Homer or of any other panegyrist whose poetry may please for the moment, although his representation of the facts will not bear the light of day. For we have compelled every land and every sea to open a path for our valour, and have everywhere planted eternal memorials of our friendship and of our enmity. Such is the city for whose sake these men nobly fought and died; they could not bear the thought that she might be taken from them; and every one of us who survive should gladly toil on her behalf.

42 'I have dwelt upon the greatness of Athens because I want to show you that we are contending for a higher prize than those who enjoy none of these privileges, and to establish by manifest proof the merit of these men whom I am now commemorating Their loftiest praise has been already spoken. For in magnifying the city I have magnified them, and men like them whose virtues made her glorious. And of how few Hellenes can it be said as of them, that their deeds when weighed in the balance have been found equal to their fame! Methinks that a death such as theirs has been given the true measure of a man's worth; it may be the first revelation of his virtues, but is at any rate their final seal. For even those who come short in other ways may justly plead the valour with which they have fought for their country; they have blotted out the evil with the good, and have benefited the state more by their public services than they have injured her by their private actions. None of these men were enervated by wealth or hesitated to resign the pleasures of life; none of them put off the evil day in the hope, natural to poverty, that a man, though poor, may one day become rich But, deeming that the punishment of their enemies was sweeter than any of these things, and that they could fall in no nobler cause, they determined at the hazard of their lives to be honourably avenged, and to leave the rest. They resigned to hope their unknown chance of happiness; but in the face of death they resolved to rely upon themselves alone. And when the moment came they were minded to resist and suffer rather than to fly and save their lives; they ran away from the word of dishonour, but on the battle-field their feet stood fast, and in an instant, at the height of their fortune, they passed away from the scene, not of their fear, but of their glory.

43 'Such was the end of these men; they were worthy of Athens, and the living need not desire to have a more heroic spirit, although they may pray for a less fatal issue. The value of such a spirit is not to be expressed in words. Any one can discourse to you for ever about the advantages of a brave defence which you know already. But instead of listening to him I would have you day by day fix your eyes upon the greatness of Athens, until you become filled with the love of her; and when you are impressed by the spectacle of her glory, reflect that this empire has been acquired by men who knew their duty and had the courage to do it, who in the hour of conflict had the fear of dishonour always present to them, and who, if ever they failed in an enterprize, would not allow their virtues to be lost to their country, but freely gave their lives to her as the fairest offering which they could present at her feast. The sacrifice which they collectively made was individually repaid to them; for they received again each one for himself a praise which grows not old, and the noblest of all sepulchres—I speak not of that in which their remains are laid, but of that in which their glory survives, and is proclaimed always and on every fitting occasion both in word and deed. For the whole earth is the sepulchre of famous men; not only are they commemorated by columns and inscriptions in their own country, but in foreign lands there dwells also an unwritten memorial of them, graven not on stone but in the hearts of men. Make them your examples, and, esteeming courage to be freedom and freedom to be happiness, do not weigh too nicely the perils of war. The unfortunate who has no hope of a change for the better has less reason to throw away his life than the prosperous who, if he survive, is always liable to a change for the worse, and to whom any accidental fall makes the most serious difference. To a man of spirit, cowardice and disaster coming together are far more bitter than death striking him unperceived at a time when he is full of courage and animated by the general hope.

44 'Wherefore I do not now commiserate the parents of the dead who stand here; I would rather comfort them. You know that your life has been passed amid manifold vicissitudes; and that they may be deemed fortunate who have gained most honour, whether an honourable death like theirs, or an honourable sorrow like yours, and whose days have been so ordered that the term of their happiness is likewise the term of their life. I know how hard it is to make you feel this, when the good fortune of others will too often remind you of the gladness which once lightened your hearts. And sorrow is felt at the want of those blessings, not which a man never knew, but which were a part of his life before they were taken from him. Some of you are of an age at which they may hope to have other children, and they ought to bear their sorrow better; not only will the children who may hereafter be born make them forget their own lost ones, but the city will be doubly a gainer. She will not be left desolate, and she will be safer. For a man's counsel cannot have equal weight or worth, when he alone has no children to risk in the general danger. To those of you who have passed their prime, I say: "Congratulate yourselves that you have been happy during the greater part of your days; remember that your life of sorrow will not last long, and be comforted by the glory of those who are gone. For the love of honour alone is ever young, and not riches, as some say, but honour is the delight of men when they are old and useless."

45 'To you who are the sons and brothers of the departed, I see that the struggle to emulate them will be an arduous one. For all men praise the dead, and, however pre-eminent your virtue may be, hardly will you be thought, I do not say to equal, but even to approach them. The living have their rivals and detractors, but when a man is out of the way, the honour and good-will which he receives is unalloyed. And, if I am to speak of womanly virtues to those of you who will henceforth be widows, let me sum them up in one short admonition: To a woman not to show more weakness than is natural to her sex is a great glory, and not to be talked about for good or for evil among men.

'I have paid the required tribute, in obedience to the law, making use of such fitting words as I had. The tribute of deeds has been paid in part; for the dead have been honourably interred, and it remains only that their children should be maintained at the public charge until they are grown up: this is the solid prize with which, as with a garland, Athens crowns her sons living and dead, after a struggle like theirs. For where the rewards of virtue are greatest, there the noblest citizens are enlisted in the service of the state. And now, when you have duly lamented, every one his own dead, you may depart.'

THE PLAGUE

47 Such was the order of the funeral celebrated in this winter, with the end of which ended the first year of the Peloponnesian War. As soon as summer returned, the Peloponnesian army, comprising as before two-thirds of the force of each confederate state, under the command of the Lacedaemonian king Archidamus, the son of Zeuxidamus, invaded Attica, where they established themselves and ravaged the country. They had not been there many days when the plague broke out at Athens for the first time. A similar disorder is said to have previously smitten many places, particularly Lemnos, but there is no record of such a pestilence occurring elsewhere, or of so great a destruction of human life. For a while physicians, in ignorance of the nature of the disease, sought to apply remedies; but it was in vain, and they themselves were among the first victims, because they oftenest came into contact with it. No human art was of any avail, and as to supplication in temples, enquiries of oracles, and the like, they were utterly useless, and at last men were overpowered by the calamity and gave them all up.

48 The disease is said to have begun south of Egypt in Aethiopia; thence it descended into Egypt and Libya, and after spreading over the greater part of the Persian empire, suddenly fell upon Athens. It first attacked the inhabitants of the Piraeus, and it was supposed that the Peloponnesians had poisoned the cisterns, no conduits having as yet been made there. It afterwards reached the upper city, and then the mortality became far greater. As to its probable origin or the causes which might or could have produced such a disturbance of nature, every man, whether a physician or not, will give his own opinion. But I shall describe its actual course, and the symptoms by which any one who knows them beforehand may recognise the disorder should it ever reappear. For I was myself attacked, and witnessed the sufferings of others.

49 The season was admitted to have been remarkably free from ordinary sickness; and if anybody was already ill of any other disease, it was absorbed in this. Many who were in perfect health, all in a moment, and without any apparent reason, were seized with violent heats in the head and with redness and inflammation of the eyes. Internally the throat and the tongue were quickly suffused with blood, and the breath became unnatural and fetid. There followed sneezing and hoarseness; in a short time the disorder, accompanied by a violent cough, reached the chest; then fastening lower down, it would move the stomach and bring on all the vomits of bile to which physicians have ever given names; and they were very distressing. An ineffectual retching producing violent convulsions attacked most of the sufferers; some as soon as the previous symptoms had abated, others not until long afterwards. The body externally was not so very hot to the touch, nor yet pale; it was of a livid colour inclining to red, and breaking out in pustules and ulcers. But the internal fever was intense; the sufferers could not bear to have on them even the finest linen garment; they insisted on being naked, and there was nothing which they longed for more eagerly than to throw themselves into cold water. And many of those who had no one to look after them actually plunged into the cisterns, for they were tormented by unceasing thirst, which was not in the least assuaged whether they drank little or much. They could not sleep; a restlessness which was intolerable never left them. While the disease was at its height the body, instead of wasting away, held out amid these sufferings in a marvellous manner, and either they died on the seventh or ninth day, not of weakness, for their strength was not exhausted, but of internal fever, which was the end of most; or, if they survived, then the disease descended into the bowels and there produced violent ulceration; severe diarrhoea at the same time set in, and at a later stage caused exhaustion, which finally with few exceptions carried them off. For the disorder which had originally settled in the head passed gradually through the whole body, and, if a person got over the worst, would often seize the extremities and leave its mark, attacking the privy parts and the fingers and the toes; and some escaped with the loss of these, some with the loss of their eyes. Some again had no sooner recovered than they were seized with a forgetfulness of all things and knew neither themselves nor their friends.

50 The malady took a form not to be described, and the fury with which it fastened upon each sufferer was too much for human nature to endure. There was one circumstance in particular which distinguished it from ordinary diseases. The birds and animals which feed on human flesh, although so many bodies were lying unburied, either never came near them, or died if they touched them. This was proved by a remarkable disappearance of the birds of prey, who were not to be seen either about the bodies or anywhere else; while in the case of the dogs the fact was even more obvious because they live with man.

51 Such was the general nature of the disease; I omit many strange peculiarities which characterised individual cases. None of the ordinary sicknesses attacked any one while it lasted, or, if they did, they ended in the plague. Some of the sufferers died from want of care, others equally who were receiving the greatest attention. No single remedy could be deemed a specific; for that which did good to one did harm to another. No constitution was of itself strong enough to resist or weak enough to escape the attacks; the disease carried off all alike and defied every mode of treatment. Most appalling was the despondency which seized upon any one who felt himself sickening; for he instantly abandoned his mind to despair and, instead of holding out, absolutely threw away his chance of life. Appalling too was the rapidity with which men caught the infection; dying like sheep if they attended on one another; and this was the principal cause of mortality. When they were afraid to visit one another, the sufferers died in their solitude, so that many houses were empty because there had been no one left to take care of the sick; or if they ventured they perished, especially those who aspired to heroism. For they went to see their friends without thought of themselves and were ashamed to leave them, even at a time when the very relations of the dying were at last growing weary and ceased to make lamentations, overwhelmed by the vastness of the calamity. But whatever instances there may have been of such devotion, more often the sick and the dying were tended by the pitying care of those who had recovered, because they knew the course of the disease and were themselves free from apprehension. For no one was ever attacked a second time, or not with a fatal result. All men congratulated them, and they themselves, in the excess of their joy at the moment, had an innocent fancy that they could not die of any other sickness.

52 The crowding of the people out of the country into the city aggravated the misery; and the newly-arrived suffered most. For, having no houses of their own, but inhabiting in the height of summer stifling huts, the mortality among them was dreadful, and they perished in wild disorder. The dead lay as they had died, one upon another, while others hardly alive wallowed in the streets and crawled about every fountain craving for water. The temples in which they lodged were full of the corpses of those who died in them; for the violence of the calamity was such that men, not knowing where to turn, grew reckless of all law, human and divine. The customs which had hitherto been observed at funerals were universally violated, and they buried their dead each one as best he could. Many, having no proper appliances, because the deaths in their household had been so frequent, made no scruple of using the burial-place of others. When one man had raised a funeral pile, others would come, and throwing on their dead first, set fire to it; or when some other corpse was already burning, before they could be stopped would throw their own dead upon it and depart.

53 There were other and worse forms of lawlessness which the plague introduced at Athens. Men who had hitherto concealed their indulgence in pleasure now grew bolder. For, seeing the sudden change,—how the rich died in a moment, and those who had nothing immediately inherited their property,—they reflected that life and riches were alike transitory, and they resolved to enjoy themselves while they could, and to think only of pleasure. Who would be willing to sacrifice himself to the law of honour when he knew not whether he would ever live to be held in honour? The pleasure of the moment and any sort of thing which conduced to it took the place both of honour and of expediency. No fear of God or law of man deterred a criminal.

Those who saw all perishing alike, thought that the worship or neglect of the Gods made no difference. For offences against human law no punishment was to be feared; no one would live long enough to be called to account. Already a far heavier sentence had been passed and was hanging over a man's head; before that fell, why should he not take a little pleasure? . . .

BOOK III (427 B.C.): THE CORCYRIAN SEDITION

70 Now Corcyra had been in an unsettled state ever since the return of the prisoners who were taken at sea in the Epidamnian war, and afterwards released by the Corinthians. They were nominally ransomed for a sum of eight hundred talents on the security of their proxeni, but in reality they had been induced to try and gain over Corcyra to the Corinthian interest. They went from one citizen to another, and solicited them to revolt from Athens. On the arrival of an Athenian and also of a Corinthian vessel conveying ambassadors, there was a discussion in the assembly, and the Corcyraeans voted that they would continue allies of Athens according to their agreement, but would renew their former friendship with the Peloponnesians. A certain Peithias, who voluntarily acted as the proxenus of the Athenians and was the popular leader, was summoned by the partisans of the Peloponnesians to take his trial, they affirming that he wanted to bring Corcyra under the yoke of Athens. He was acquitted, and then he in turn summoned their five richest men, declaring that they were in the habit of cutting poles for vines in the sacred precinct of Zeus and Alcinous; now for each pole the penalty was fixed at a stater. They were condemned; but the fine was so excessive that they went and sat as suppliants in the temple of Zeus and Alcinous, begging that they might pay the money by instalments. Peithias, who happened to be a member of the senate as well as the popular leader, persuaded the senators to put the law in execution. The culprits, knowing that the law was against them, and perceiving that Peithias as long as he remained in the senate would try to induce the people to make an alliance offensive and defensive with Athens, conspired together, and, rushing into the council chamber with daggers in their hands, slew him and others to the number of sixty, as well private persons as senators. A few who were of the same party with him took refuge in the Athenian trireme, which had not yet left.

71 The next step taken by the conspirators was to assemble the people and tell them that they had acted for the best, and in order to secure them against the tyranny of Athens. For the future they should receive neither Athenians nor Peloponnesians, unless they came peaceably with one ship; to bring more should be deemed the act of an enemy; and this proposal they compelled the people to ratify. They also sent envoys to Athens, who were to put the most favourable colour on the affair, and to dissuade the refugees who had fled thither from taking any inconvenient step which might lead to a counter-revolution.

72 When the envoys arrived, the Athenians arrested them as disturbers of the peace, and deposited them in Aegina, together with any of the refugees whom they had gained over. In the meantime, the Corcyraean oligarchs who were now in power, on the arrival of a Corinthian trireme and Lacedaemonian envoys, attacked and defeated the people, who at nightfall took refuge in the Acropolis and the higher parts of the city, and there concentrated their forces. They also held the Hyllaic harbour; the other party seized the Agora, where most of them lived, and the adjacent harbour which looked towards the continent.

73 On the following day they skirmished a little, and both parties sent messengers round the country inviting the slaves to join them, and promising them liberty; the greater number came to the aid of the people, while the other faction was reinforced by eight hundred auxiliaries from the mainland.

74 After resting a day they fought again, and the people, who had the advantage in numbers and in the strength of their positions, gained the victory. Their women joined vigorously in the fray, hurling tiles from the housetops, and showing amid the uproar a fortitude beyond their sex. The conflict was decided towards evening; the oligarchy, fearing lest the people should take the arsenal with a sudden rush and so make an end of them, set fire to the private houses which surrounded the Agora, as well as to the larger blocks of buildings, sparing neither their own property nor that of any one else in their determination to stop them. Much merchandise was burnt, and the whole city would have been destroyed if the wind had carried the flame in that direction. Both parties now left off fighting, and kept watch in their own positions during the night. When the popular cause triumphed, the Corinthian vessel stole away and most of the auxiliaries crossed over unobserved to the continent.

75 On the following day, Nicostratus the son of Diitrephes, an Athenian general, arrived from Naupactus with twelve ships and five hundred Messenian hoplites. He tried to effect a reconciliation between the two parties, and on his suggestion they agreed to bring to trial ten of the most guilty persons, who immediately fled. The rest were to live together, and to make a truce with one another, and with Athens an alliance offensive and defensive. Having accomplished his purpose he was about to sail away, when the leaders of the people induced him to leave five of his own vessels, that the enemy might be less inclined to stir, promising to man five ships of their own and send them with him. He agreed, and they selected the crews of the ships out of the opposite faction. But the men were afraid of being sent to Athens, and sat as suppliants in the temple of the Dioscuri. Nicostratus sought to raise them up and reassure them, but they would not trust him; whereupon the people armed themselves, arguing that their mistrust and unwillingness to sail was a proof of their evil designs. They took their enemies' arms out of their houses, and some of them whom they chanced to meet would have been slain if Nicostratus had not interfered. The rest, to the number of about four hundred, when they saw what was going on took refuge anew in the temple of Herè. But the people, fearing that they would resort to violence, persuaded them to rise and conveyed them at once to the island that lies in front of the temple of Herè, whither provisions were regularly sent to them.

76 At this stage of the revolution, on the fourth or fifth day after the suppliants had been conveyed to the island, the fifty-three Peloponnesian ships from Cyllene, which since the expedition to Ionia had been in harbour there, arrived on the scene, still under the command of Alcidas. Brasidas his adviser was on board. They anchored for the night at Sybota, a harbour on the mainland, and when the morning broke they sailed upon Corcyra.

77 The whole place was in an uproar; the people dreaded their enemies within the city no less than the Peloponnesian fleet. They hastened to equip sixty ships, and as fast as they were manned sent them out against the Peloponnesians, although the Athenians entreated to be allowed to sail out first, leaving them to follow as soon as they had got their fleet together. But when in this straggling fashion their ships approached the enemy, two of them at once deserted; in others the crews were fighting with one another, and everything was in disorder. The Peloponnesians, seeing the confusion, employed twenty ships only against the Corcyraeans, and opposed the remainder of their fleet to the twelve Athenian ships, of which two were the Salaminia and Paralus.

78 The Corcyraeans, coming up few at a time and in this disorderly fashion, had trouble enough among themselves. The Athenians, afraid of being surrounded by superior numbers, did not attack the main body nor the centre of those opposed to them, but fell upon the wings and sank a single ship; then, the enemy forming in a circle, they sailed round them and endeavoured to throw them into confusion. But those who were opposed to the Corcyraeans, seeing this movement and fearing a repetition of what happened at Naupactus, came to the rescue, and the united fleet charged the Athenians. Thereupon they rowed astern, hoping that by retreating very leisurely they might give the Corcyraeans time to escape, especially as the attack of the enemy was now directed against themselves. The naval engagement ended at sunset.

79 The Corcyraeans, who were afraid that the victorious enemy would sail to the city and have recourse to some decisive measure, such as taking on board the prisoners in the island, conveyed them back to the temple of Herè and guarded the city. But the Peloponnesians, although they had won the battle, did not venture to attack the city, but returned to their station on the mainland with thirteen Corcyraean ships which they had taken. On the next day they still hesitated, although there was great panic and confusion among the inhabitants. It is said that Brasidas advised Alcidas to make the attempt, but he had not an equal vote with him. So they only disembarked at the promontory of Leucimmè and ravaged the country.

80 Meanwhile the people of Corcyra, dreading that the fleet of the Peloponnesians would attack them, held a parley with the other faction, especially with the suppliants, in the hope of saving the city; they even persuaded some of them to go on board the fleet; for the Corcyraeans still contrived to man thirty ships. But the Peloponnesians, after devastating the land till about midday, retired. And at nightfall the approach of sixty Athenian vessels was signalled to them from Leucas. These had been sent by the Athenians under the command of Eurymedon the son of Thucles, when they heard of the revolution and of the intended expedition of Alcidas to Corcyra.

81 The Peloponnesians set out that very night on their way home, keeping close to the land, and transporting the ships over the Leucadian isthmus, that they might not be seen sailing round. When the Corcyraeans perceived that the Athenian fleet was approaching, while that of the enemy had disappeared, they took the Messenian troops, who had hitherto been outside the walls, into the city, and ordered the ships which they had manned to sail round into the Hyllaic harbour. These proceeded on their way. Meanwhile they killed any of their enemies whom they caught in the city. On the arrival of the ships they disembarked those whom they had induced to go on board, and despatched them; they also went to the temple of Herè, and persuading about fifty of the suppliants to stand their trial, condemned them all to death. The majority would not come out, and, when they saw what was going on, destroyed one another in the enclosure of the temple where they were, except a few who hung themselves on trees, or put an end to their own lives in any other way which they could. And, during the seven days which Eurymedon after his arrival remained with his sixty ships, the Corcyraeans continued slaughtering those of their fellow-citizens whom they deemed their enemies; they professed to punish them for their designs against the democracy, but in fact some were killed from motives of personal enmity, and some because money was owing to them, by the hands of their debtors. Every form of death was to be seen, and everything, and more than everything that commonly happens in revolutions, happened then. The father slew the son, and the suppliants were torn from the temples and slain near them; some of them were even walled up in the temple of Dionysus, and there perished. To such extremes of cruelty did revolution go; and this seemed to be the worst of revolutions, because it was the first.

82 For not long afterwards the whole Hellenic world was in commotion; in every city the chiefs of the democracy and of the oligarchy were struggling, the one to bring in the Athenians, the other the Lacedaemonians. Now in time of peace, men would have had no excuse for introducing either, and no desire to do so, but when they were at war and both sides could easily obtain allies to the hurt of their enemies and the advantage of themselves, the dissatisfied party were only too ready to invoke foreign aid. And revolution brought upon the cities of Hellas many terrible calamities, such as have been and always will be while human nature remains the same, but which are more or less aggravated and differ in character with every new combination of circumstances. In peace and prosperity both states and individuals are actuated by higher motives, because they do not fall under the dominion of imperious necessities; but war which takes away the comfortable provision of daily life is a hard master, and tends to assimilate men's characters to their conditions.

When troubles had once begun in the cities, those who followed carried the revolutionary spirit further and further, and determined to outdo the report of all who had preceded them by the ingenuity of their enterprises and the atrocity of their revenges. The meaning of words had no longer the same relation to things, but was changed by them as they thought proper. Reckless daring was held to be loyal courage; prudent delay was the excuse of a coward; moderation was the disguise of unmanly weakness; to know everything was to do nothing. Frantic energy was the true quality of a man. A conspirator who wanted to be safe was a recreant in disguise. The lover of violence was always trusted, and his opponent suspected. He who succeeded in a plot was deemed knowing, but a still greater master in craft was he who detected one. On the other hand, he who plotted from the first to have nothing to do with plots was a breaker up of parties and a poltroon who was afraid of the enemy. In a word, he who could outstrip another in a bad action was applauded, and so was he who encouraged to evil one who had no idea of it. The tie of party was stronger than the tie of blood, because a partisan was more ready to dare without asking why. (For party associations are not based upon any established law, nor do they seek the public good; they are formed in defiance of the laws and from self-interest.) The seal of good faith was not divine law, but fellowship in crime. If an enemy when he was in the ascendant offered fair words, the opposite party received them not in a generous spirit, but by a jealous watchfulness of his actions. Revenge was dearer than self-preservation. Any agreements sworn to by either party, when they could do nothing else, were binding as long as both were powerless. But he who on a favourable opportunity first took courage and struck at his enemy when he saw him off his guard, had greater pleasure in a perfidious than he would have had in an open act of revenge; he congratulated himself that he had taken the safer course, and also that he had overreached his enemy and gained the prize of superior ability. In general the dishonest more easily gain credit for cleverness than the simple for goodness; men take a pride in the one, but are ashamed of the other.

The cause of all these evils was the love of power, originating in avarice and ambition, and the party-spirit which is engendered by them when men are fairly embarked in a contest. For the leaders on either side used specious names, the one party professing to uphold the constitutional equality of the many, the other the wisdom of an aristocracy, while they made the public interests, to which in name they were devoted, in reality their prize. Striving in every way to overcome each other, they committed the most monstrous crimes; yet even these were surpassed by the magnitude of their revenges which they pursued to the very utmost, neither party observing any definite limits either of justice or public expediency, but both alike making the caprice of the moment their law. Either by the help of an unrighteous sentence, or grasping power with the strong hand, they were eager to satiate the impatience of party-spirit. Neither faction cared for religion; but any fair pretence which succeeded in effecting some odious purpose was greatly lauded. And the citizens who were of neither party fell a prey to both; either they were disliked because they held aloof, or men were jealous of their surviving.

83 Thus revolution gave birth to every form of wickedness in Hellas. The simplicity which is so large an element in a noble nature was laughed to scorn and disappeared. An attitude of perfidious antagonism everywhere prevailed; for there was no word binding enough, nor oath terrible enough to reconcile enemies. Each man was strong only in the conviction that nothing was secure; he must look to his own safety, and could not afford to trust others. Inferior intellects generally succeeded best. For, aware of their own deficiencies, and fearing the capacity of their opponents, for whom they were no match in powers of speech, and whose subtle wits were likely to anticipate them in contriving evil, they struck boldly and at once. But the cleverer sort, presuming in their arrogance that they would be aware in time, and disdaining to act when they could think, were taken off their guard and easily destroyed.

84 Now in Corcyra most of these deeds were perpetrated, and for the first time. There was every crime which men might be supposed to perpetrate in revenge who had been governed not wisely, but tyrannically, and now had the oppressor at their mercy. There were the dishonest designs of others who were longing to be relieved from their habitual poverty, and were naturally animated by a passionate desire for their neighbour's goods; and there were crimes of another class which men commit, not from covetousness, but from the enmity which equals foster towards one another until they are carried away by their blind rage into the extremes of pitiless cruelty.

At such a time the life of the city was all in disorder, and human nature, which is always ready to transgress the laws, having now trampled them under foot, delighted to show that her passions were ungovernable, that she was stronger than justice, and the enemy of everything above her. If malignity had not exercised a fatal power, how could any one have preferred revenge to piety, and gain to innocence? But, when men are retaliating upon others, they are reckless of the future, and do not hesitate to annul those common laws of humanity to which every individual trusts for his own hope of deliverance should he ever be overtaken by calamity; they forget that in their own hour of need they will look for them in vain. . . .

BOOK V (417 B.C.): THE MELIAN DIALOGUE

84 In the ensuing summer, Alcibiades sailed to Argos with twenty ships, and seized any of the Argives who were still suspected to be of the Lacedaemonian faction three hundred in number; and the Athenians deposited them in the subject islands near at hand. The Athenians next made an expedition against the island of Melos with thirty ships of their own, six Chian, and two Lesbian, twelve hundred hoplites and three hundred archers besides twenty mounted archers of their own, and about fifteen hundred hoplites furnished by their allies in the islands. The Melians are colonists of the Lacedaemonians who would not submit to Athens like the other islanders. At first they were neutral and took no part. But when the Athenians tried to coerce them by ravaging their lands, they were driven into open hostilities. The generals, Cleomedes the son of Lycomedes and Tisias the son of Tisimachus, encamped with the Athenian forces on the island. But before they did the country any harm they sent envoys to negotiate with the Melians. Instead of bringing these envoys before the people, the Melians desired them to explain their errand to the magistrates and to the chief men. They spoke as follows:—

85 'Since we are not allowed to speak to the people, lest, forsooth, they should be deceived by seductive and unanswerable arguments which they would hear set forth in a single uninterrupted oration (for we are perfectly aware that this is what you mean in bringing us before a select few), you who are sitting here may as well make assurance yet surer. Let us have no set speeches at all, but do you reply to each several statement of which you disapprove, and criticise it at once. Say first of all how you like this mode of proceeding.'

86 The Melian representatives answered:—'The quiet interchange of explanations is a reasonable thing, and we do not object to that. But your warlike movements, which are present not only to our fears but to our eyes, seem to belie your words. We see that, although you may reason with us, you mean to be our judges; and that at the end of the discussion, if the justice of our cause prevail and we therefore refuse to yield, we may expect war; if we are convinced by you, slavery.'

87 ***Ath.*** 'Nay, but if you are only going to argue from fancies about the future, or if you meet us with any other purpose than that of looking your circumstances in the face and saving your city, we have done; but if this is your intention we will proceed.'

88 ***Mel.*** 'It is an excusable and natural thing that men in our position should have much to say and should indulge in many fancies. But we admit that this conference has met to consider the question of our preservation; and therefore let the argument proceed in the manner which you propose.'

89 ***Ath.*** 'Well, then, we Athenians will use no fine words; we will not go out of our way to prove at length that we have a right to rule, because we overthrew the Persians; or that we attack you now because we are suffering any injury at your hands. We should not convince you if we did; nor must you expect to convince us by arguing that, although a colony of the Lacedaemonians, you have taken no part in their expeditions, or that you have never done us any wrong. But you and we should say what we really think, and aim only at what is possible, for we both alike know that into the discussion of human affairs the question of justice only enters where the pressure of necessity is equal, and that the powerful exact what they can, and the weak grant what they must.'

90 ***Mel.*** 'Well, then, since you set aside justice and invite us to speak of expediency, in our judgment it is certainly expedient that you should respect a principle which is for the common good; and that to every man when in peril a reasonable claim should be accounted a claim of right, and any plea which he is disposed to urge, even if failing of the point a little, should help his cause. Your interest in this principle is quite as great as ours, inasmuch as you, if you fall, will incur the heaviest vengeance, and will be the most terrible example to mankind.'

91 ***Ath.*** 'The fall of our empire, if it should fall, is not an event to which we look forward with dismay; for ruling states such as Lacedaemon are not cruel to their vanquished enemies. And we are fighting not so much against the Lacedaemonians, as against our own subjects who may some day rise up and overcome their former masters. But this is a danger which you may leave to us. And we will now endeavour to show that we have come in the interests of our empire, and that in what we are about to say we are only seeking the preservation of your city. For we want to make you ours with the least trouble to ourselves, and it is for the interests of us both that you should not be destroyed.'

92 ***Mel.*** 'It may be your interest to be our masters, but how can it be ours to be your slaves?'

93 ***Ath.*** 'To you the gain will be that by submission you will avert the worst; and we shall be all the richer for your preservation.'

94 ***Mel.*** 'But must we be your enemies? Will you not receive us as friends if we are neutral and remain at peace with you?'

95 ***Ath.*** 'No, your enmity is not half so mischievous to us as your friendship; for the one is in the eyes of our subjects an argument of our power, the other of our weakness.'

96 ***Mel.*** 'But are your subjects really unable to distinguish between states in which you have no concern, and those which are chiefly your own colonies, and in some cases have revolted and been subdued by you?'

97 ***Ath.*** 'Why, they do not doubt that both of them have a good deal to say for themselves on the score of justice, but they think that states like yours are left free because they are able to defend themselves, and that we do not attack them because we dare not. So that your subjection will give us an increase of security, as well as an extension of empire. For we are masters of the sea, and you who are islanders, and insignificant islanders too, must not be allowed to escape us.'

98 ***Mel.*** 'But do you not recognise another danger? For, once more, since you drive us from the plea of justice and press upon us your doctrine of expediency, we must show you what is for our interest, and, if it be for yours also, may hope to convince you:—Will you not be making enemies of all who are now neutrals? When they see how you are treating us they will expect you some day to turn against them; and if so, are you not strengthening the enemies whom you already have, and bringing upon you others who, if they could help, would never dream of being your enemies at all?'

99 ***Ath.*** 'We do not consider our really dangerous enemies to be any of the peoples inhabiting the mainland who, secure in their freedom, may defer indefinitely any measures of precaution which they take against us, but islanders who, like you, happen to be under no control, and all who may be already irritated by the necessity of submission to our empire—these are our real enemies, for they are the most reckless and most likely to bring themselves as well as us into a danger which they cannot but foresee.'

100 ***Mel.*** 'Surely then, if you and your subjects will brave all this risk, you to preserve your empire and they to be quit of it, how base and cowardly would it be in us, who retain our freedom, not to do and suffer anything rather than be your slaves.'

101 ***Ath.*** 'Not so, if you calmly reflect: for you are not fighting against equals to whom you cannot yield without disgrace, but you are taking counsel whether or no you shall resist an overwhelming force. The question is not one of honour but of prudence.'

102 ***Mel.*** 'But we know that the fortune of war is sometimes impartial, and not always on the side of numbers. If we yield now, all is over; but if we fight, there is yet a hope that we may stand upright.'

103 ***Ath.*** 'Hope is a good comforter in the hour of danger, and when men have something else to depend upon, although hurtful, she is not ruinous. But when her spendthrift nature has induced them to stake their all, they see her as she is in the moment of their fall, and not till then. While the knowledge of her might enable them to be ware of her, she never fails. You are weak and a single turn of the scale might be your ruin. Do not you be thus deluded; avoid the error of which so many are guilty, who, although they might still be saved if they would take the natural means, when visible grounds of confidence forsake them, have recourse to the invisible, to prophecies and oracles and the like, which ruin men by the hopes which they inspire in them.'

104 ***Mel.*** 'We know only too well how hard the struggle must be against your power, and against fortune, if she does not mean to be impartial. Nevertheless we do not despair of fortune; for we hope to stand as high as you in the favour of heaven, because we are righteous, and you against whom we contend are unrighteous; and we are satisfied that our deficiency in power will be compensated by the aid of our allies the Lacedaemonians; they cannot refuse to help us, if only because we are their kinsmen, and for the sake of their own honour. And therefore our confidence is not so utterly blind as you suppose.'

105 ***Ath.*** 'As for the Gods, we expect to have quite as much of their favour as ou: for we are not doing or claiming anything which goes beyond common opinion bout divine or men's desires about human things. For of the Gods we believe, and f men we know, that by a law of their nature wherever they can rule they will. This law was not made by us, and we are not the first who have acted upon it; ve did but inherit it and shall bequeath it to all time, and we know that you and all nankind, if you were as strong as we are, would do as we do. So much for the Gods; ve have told you why we expect to stand as high in their good opinion as you. And then as to the Lacedaemonians—when you imagine that out of very shame they vill assist you, we admire the simplicity of your idea, but we do not envy you the olly of it. The Lacedaemonians are exceedingly virtuous among themselves, and ccording to their national standard of morality. But, in respect of their dealings with thers, although many things might be said, a word is enough to describe them,—of ll men whom we know they are the most notorious for identifying what is pleasant vith what is honourable, and what is expedient with what is just. But how inconsistent s such a character with your present blind hope of deliverance!'

106 ***Mel.*** 'That is the very reason why we trust them; they will look to their nterest, and therefore will not be willing to betray the Melians, who are their own olonists, lest they should be distrusted by their friends in Hellas and play into the ands of their enemies.'

107 ***Ath.*** 'But do you not see that the path of expediency is safe, whereas ustice and honour involve danger in practice, and such dangers the Lacedaemonians eldom care to face?'

108 ***Mel.*** 'On the other hand, we think that whatever perils there may be, they vill be ready to face them for our sakes, and will consider danger less dangerous vhere we are concerned. For if they need our aid we are close at hand, and they can etter trust our loyal feeling because we are their kinsmen.'

109 ***Ath.*** 'Yes, but what encourages men who are invited to join in a conflict s clearly not the good-will of those who summon them to their side, but a decided uperiority in real power. To this no men look more keenly than the Lacedaemonians; o little confidence have they in their own resources, that they only attack their neighours when they have numerous allies, and therefore they are not likely to find their vay by themselves to an island, when we are masters of the sea.'

110 ***Mel.*** 'But they may send their allies: the Cretan sea is a large place; and the nasters of the sea will have more difficulty in overtaking vessels which want to escape han the pursued in escaping. If the attempt should fail they may invade Attica itself, nd find their way to allies of yours whom Brasidas did not reach: and then you vill have to fight, not for the conquest of a land in which you have no concern, but earer home, for the preservation of your confederacy and of your own territory.'

111 ***Ath.*** 'Help may come from Lacedaemon to you as it has come to others, and hould you ever have actual experience of it, then you will know that never once ave the Athenians retired from a siege through fear of a foe elsewhere. You told is that the safety of your city would be your first care, but we remark that, in this ong discussion, not a word has been uttered by you which would give a reasonable nan expectation of deliverance. Your strongest grounds are hopes deferred, and what ower you have is not to be compared with that which is already arrayed against you.

Unless after we have withdrawn you mean to come, as even now you may, to a wise conclusion, you are showing a great want of sense. For surely you cannot dream o flying to that false sense of honour which has been the ruin of so many when dange and dishonour were staring them in the face. Many men with their eyes still ope to the consequences have found the word "honour" too much for them, and hav suffered a mere name to lure them on, until it has drawn down upon them real and irre trievable calamities; through their own folly they have incurred a worse dishonou than fortune would have inflicted upon them. If you are wise you will not run thi risk; you ought to see that there can be no disgrace in yielding to a great city whic invites you to become her ally on reasonable terms, keeping your own land, an merely paying tribute; and that you will certainly gain no honour if, having to choos between two alternatives, safety and war, you obstinately prefer the worse. To main tain our rights against equals, to be politic with superiors, and to be moderate toward inferiors is the path of safety. Reflect once more when we have withdrawn, and sa to yourselves over and over again that you are deliberating about your one and onl country, which may be saved or may be destroyed by a single decision.'

112 The Athenians left the conference: the Melians, after consulting amon themselves, resolved to persevere in their refusal, and made answer as follows:—'Me of Athens, our resolution is unchanged; and we will not in a moment surrender tha liberty which our city, founded seven hundred years ago, still enjoys; we will trus to the good-fortune which, by the favour of the Gods, has hitherto preserved us, an for human help to the Lacedaemonians, and endeavour to save ourselves. We ar ready however to be your friends, and the enemies neither of you nor of the Lacedae monians, and we ask you to leave our country when you have made such a peace a may appear to be in the interest of both parties.'

113 Such was the answer of the Melians; the Athenians, as they quitted the con ference, spoke as follows:—'Well, we must say, judging from the decision at which yo have arrived, that you are the only men who deem the future to be more certai than the present, and regard things unseen as already realised in your fond anticipatior and that the more you cast yourselves upon the Lacedaemonians and fortune, and hope and trust them, the more complete will be your ruin.'

114 The Athenian envoys returned to the army; and the generals, when the found that the Melians would not yield, immediately commenced hostilities. They sur rounded the town of Melos with a wall, dividing the work among the several con tingents. They then left troops of their own and of their allies to keep guard bot by land and by sea, and retired with the greater part of their army; the remainde carried on the blockade.

115 About the same time the Argives made an inroad into Phliasia, and lo nearly eighty men, who were caught in an ambuscade by the Phliasians and the Argiv exiles. The Athenian garrison in Pylos took much spoil from the Lacedaemonian nevertheless the latter did not renounce the peace and go to war, but only notified by proclamation that if any one of their own people had a mind to make reprisals on th Athenians he might. The Corinthians next declared war upon the Athenians on som private grounds, but the rest of the Peloponnesians did not join them. The Meliar took that part of the Athenian wall which looked towards the agora by a nigl sault, killed a few men, and brought in as much corn and other necessaries as they ›uld; they then retreated and remained inactive. After this the Athenians set a better 'atch. So the summer ended.

116 In the following winter the Lacedaemonians had intended to make an ‹pedition into the Argive territory, but finding that the sacrifices which they offered the frontier were unfavourable they returned home. The Argives, suspecting that ›e threatened invasion was instigated by citizens of their own, apprehended some of ›em; others however escaped.

About the same time the Melians took another part of the Athenian wall; for the ›rtifications were insufficiently guarded. Whereupon the Athenians sent fresh troops, ›nder the command of Philocrates the son of Demeas. The place was now closely ›vested, and there was treachery among the citizens themselves. So the Melians were ›duced to surrender at discretion. The Athenians thereupon put to death all who were f military age, and made slaves of the women and children. They then colonised the land, sending thither five hundred settlers of their own.

GORGIAS

Plato

Almost every important philosophical idea in our tradition received its first clear formulation in the Dialogues *of Plato of Athens* (ca. 427–ca. 347 B.C.) *who invented and brought to perfection the method of "dialectic," a process of reasoning that aims at revealing the presuppositions and consequences of ideas in the hope of arriving at a formulation that can withstand all criticism. This method has been employed by almost all subsequent Western philosophers, even when they gave up trying to reproduce the dialogue form in which Plato set his dialectic, and even when they disagreed completely with his doctrines.*

While Plato was still a young man he came under the influence of Socrates (469–399 B.C.)*, that strange, magnetic genius. Socrates captivated an entire generation of Athenian intellectuals, but influenced them in a dozen different directions, making it extremely difficult for us to say just what he himself believed. To add to the difficulty, he never wrote a word; but Plato paid him the supreme compliment of making him the chief character in his own immortal* Dialogues, *as the embodiment of the "philosophic life": the passionate but selfless pursuit of truth. We do know that in 399* B.C. *Socrates was put to death by the Athenian people as a public nuisance. Plato reports that he made a magnificent speech ("The Apology of Socrates") in his own defense. It seems probable that* *the "Socrates" of Plato's* Dialogues *is at least partly a mouthpiece for Plato's own ideas.*

The selections that follow show Socrates in his customary role, subjecting the statements of others to careful dialectical examination. They also, however, show him developing some of the implications *of the philosophic life as he understands it. In the* Gorgias *these implications include a radical critique of Athenian democracy and of the theory he finds embedded in it—that the greatest good for man is pleasure. In* The Republic *he goes a step further and concludes that true justice could exist only in a society ruled by philosophers.*

The selection from the Gorgias *opens in the middle of the dialogue, as Socrates is summarizing the conclusions reached so far. He has been talking with Gorgias, a famous sophist and teacher of rhetoric, and with his prize pupil, Polus. (The "sophists" were traveling teachers of various kinds who amassed great prestige—and great wealth—during the fifth century* B.C. *by training people in the arts of worldly success.) First Gorgias and then Polus have been forced by Socrates' questioning to admit that rhetoric is not really a very useful skill after all, except when used by criminals to persuade judges to punish them! Callicles, a vigorous young politician, finds this paradox intolerable, and resolves to squelch Socrates and his "verbal quibbling" once and for all. As you read, bear in mind that Plato chose to write in dramatic form deliberately, and that the characters are therefore intended to be genuine personalities and not just disembodied intellects.*

Soc. Well, Polus, but if this is true, where is the great use of rhetoric? If we admit what has been just now said, every man ought in every way to guard himself against doing wrong, for he will thereby suffer great evil?

Pol. True.

Soc. And if he, or any one about whom he cares, does wrong, he ought of his own accord to go where he will be immediately punished; he will run to the judge, as he would to the physician, in order that the disease of injustice may not be rendered chronic and become the incurable cancer of the soul; must we not allow this consequence, Polus, if our former admissions are to stand:—is any other inference consistent with them?

Pol. To that, Socrates, there can be but one answer.

***The Dialogues of Plato,* trans. B. Jowett (2 vols.; New York: Random House, Inc., 1937), I, 540–554, 578–587.**

Soc. Then rhetoric is of no use to us, Polus, in helping a man to excuse his own ıjustice, or that of his parents or friends, or children or country; but may be of use) any one who holds that instead of excusing he ought to accuse—himself above all, nd in the next degree his family or any of his friends who may be doing wrong; e should bring to light the iniquity and not conceal it, that so the wrong-doer may ıffer and be made whole; and he should even force himself and others not to shrink, ut with closed eyes like brave men to let the physician operate with knife or searing on, not regarding the pain, in the hope of attaining the good and the honourable; t him who has done things worthy of stripes, allow himself to be scourged, if of onds, to be bound, if of a fine, to be fined, if of exile, to be exiled, if of death, to ie, himself being the first to accuse himself and his own relations, and using rhetoric) this end, that his and their unjust actions may be made manifest, and that they emselves may be delivered from injustice, which is the greatest evil. Then, Polus, hetoric would indeed be useful. Do you say 'Yes' or 'No' to that?

Pol. To me, Socrates, what you are saying appears very strange, though probably ı agreement with your premises.

Soc. Is not this the conclusion, if the premises are not disproven?

Pol. Yes; it certainly is.

Soc. And from the opposite point of view, if indeed it be our duty to harm another, vhether an enemy or not—I except the case of self-defence—then I have to be upon ıy guard—but if my enemy injures a third person, then in every sort of way, by word s well as deed, I should try to prevent his being punished, or appearing before the udge; and if he appears, I should contrive that he should escape, and not suffer pun-ishment: if he has stolen a sum of money, let him keep what he has stolen and spend on him and his, regardless of religion and justice; and if he have done things worthy f death, let him not die, but rather be immortal in his wickedness; or, if this is not ossible, let him at any rate be allowed to live as long as he can. For such purposes, olus, rhetoric may be useful, but is of small if of any use to him who is not intending o commit injustice; at least, there was no such use discovered by us in the previous iscussion.

Cal. Tell me, Chaerephon, is Socrates in earnest, or is he joking?

Chaer. I should say, Callicles, that he is in most profound earnest; but you may s well ask him.

Cal. By the gods, and I will. Tell me, Socrates, are you in earnest, or only in est? For if you are in earnest, and what you say is true, is not the whole of human ife turned upside down; and are we not doing, as would appear, in everything the pposite of what we ought to be doing?

Soc. O Callicles, if there were not some community of feelings among mankind, owever varying in different persons—I mean to say, if every man's feelings were eculiar to himself and were not shared by the rest of his species—I do not see how ve could ever communicate our impressions to one another. I make this remark ecause I perceive that you and I have a common feeling. For we are lovers both, nd both of us have two loves apiece:—I am the lover of Alcibiades, the son of leinias, and of philosophy; and you of the Athenian Demus, and of Demus the son f Pyrilampes. Now I observe that you, with all your cleverness, do not venture to contradict your favourite in any word or opinion of his; but as he changes you chang backwards and forwards. When the Athenian Demus denies anything that you a saying in the assembly, you go over to his opinion; and you do the same with Demu the fair young son of Pyrilampes. For you have not the power to resist the words an ideas of your loves; and if a person were to express surprise at the strangeness of wh you say from time to time when under their influence, you would probably reply him, if you were honest, that you cannot help saying what your loves say unless the are prevented; and that you can only be silent when they are. Now you must understan that my words are an echo too, and therefore you need not wonder at me; but if yo want to silence me, silence philosophy, who is my love, for she is always telling m what I am now tellng you, my friend; neither is she capricious like my other lov for the son of Cleinias says one thing to-day and another thing to-morrow, but philo ophy is always true. She is the teacher at whose words you are now wondering, an you have heard her yourself. Her you must refute, and either show, as I was sayin that to do injustice and to escape punishment is not the worst of all evils; or, if yo leave her word unrefuted, by the dog the god of Egypt, I declare, O Callicles, th Callicles will never be at one with himself, but that his whole life will be a discor And yet, my friend, I would rather that my lyre should be inharmonious, and th there should be no music in the chorus which I provided; aye or that the whole worl should be at odds with me, and oppose me rather than that I myself should be at od with myself, and contradict myself.

Cal. O Socrates, you are a regular declaimer, and seem to be running riot in t argument. And now you are declaiming in this way because Polus has fallen in the same error himself of which he accused Gorgias:—for he said that when Gorgi was asked by you, whether, if some one came to him who wanted to learn rhetori and did not know justice, he would teach him justice, Gorgias in his modesty replie that he would, because he thought that mankind in general would be displeased he answered 'No'; and then in consequence of this admission, Gorgias was compelle to contradict himself, that being just the sort of thing in which you delight. Whereupo Polus laughed at you deservedly, as I think; but now he has himself fallen into t same trap. I cannot say very much for his wit when he conceded to you that to do more dishonourable than to suffer injustice, for this was the admission which le to his being entangled by you; and because he was too modest to say what he though he had his mouth stopped. For the truth is, Socrates, that you, who pretend to b engaged in the pursuit of truth, are appealing now to the popular and vulgar notio of right, which are not natural, but only conventional. Convention and nature a generally at variance with one another: and hence, if a person is too modest to say wh he thinks, he is compelled to contradict himself; and you, in your ingenuity perceivin the advantage to be thereby gained, slyly ask of him who is arguing conventionally question which is to be determined by the rule of nature; and if he is talking of the ru of nature, you slip away to custom: as, for instance, you did in this very discussic about doing and suffering injustice. When Polus was speaking of the conventional dishonourable, you assailed him from the point of view of nature; for by the rule nature, to suffer injustice is the greater disgrace because the greater evil; but co ventionally, to do evil is the more disgraceful. For the suffering of injustice is not th art of a man, but of a slave, who indeed had better die than live; since when he wronged and trampled upon, he is unable to help himself, or any other about hom he cares. The reason, as I conceive, is that the makers of laws are the majority ho are weak; and they make laws and distribute praises and censures with a view themselves and to their own interests; and they terrify the stronger sort of men, nd those who are able to get the better of them, in order that they may not get the etter of them; and they say, that dishonesty is shameful and unjust; meaning, by the ord injustice, the desire of a man to have more than his neighbours; for knowing eir own inferiority, I suspect that they are too glad of equality. And therefore the ndeavour to have more than the many, is conventionally said to be shameful and unst, and is called injustice, whereas nature herself intimates that it is just for the better have more than the worse, the more powerful than the weaker; and in many ways e shows, among men as well as among animals, and indeed among whole cities nd races, that justice consists in the superior ruling over and having more than the ferior. For on what principle of justice did Xerxes invade Hellas, or his father the cythians? (not to speak of numberless other examples). Nay, but these are the men ho act according to nature; yes, by Heaven, and according to the law of nature: not, erhaps, according to that artificial law, which we invent and impose upon our fellows, f whom we take the best and strongest from their youth upwards, and tame them like oung lions,—charming them with the sound of the voice, and saying to them, that with quality they must be content, and that the equal is the honourable and the just. But if ere were a man who had sufficient force, he would shake off and break through and cape from all this; he would trample under foot all our formulas and spells and arms, and all our laws which are against nature: the slave would rise in rebellion nd be lord over us, and the light of natural justice would shine forth. And this I ke to be the sentiment of Pindar, when he says in his poem, that

> 'Law is the king of all, of mortals as well as of immortals;'

is, as he says,

> 'Makes might to be right, doing violence with highest hand; as I infer from the deeds of Heracles, for without buying them—'

-I do not remember the exact words, but the meaning is, that without buying them, nd without their being given to him, he carried off the oxen of Geryon, according to e law of natural right, and that the oxen and other possessions of the weaker and ferior properly belong to the stronger and superior. And this is true, as you may certain, if you will leave philosophy and go on to higher things: for philosophy, ocrates, if pursued in moderation and at the proper age, is an elegant accomplishment, ut too much philosophy is the ruin of human life. Even if a man has good parts, ill, if he carries philosophy into later life, he is necessarily ignorant of all those things hich a gentleman and a person of honour ought to know; he is inexperienced in the ws of the State, and in the language which ought to be used in the dealings of man ith man, whether private or public, and utterly ignorant of the pleasures and desires f mankind and of human character in general. And people of this sort, when they take themselves to politics or business, are as ridiculous as I imagine the politicians

to be, when they make their appearance in the arena of philosophy. For, as Euripide
says,

> 'Every man shines in that and pursues that, and devotes the greatest portion o
> the day to that in which he most excels,'

but anything in which he is inferior, he avoids and depreciates, and praises the opposit
from partiality to himself, and because he thinks that he will thus praise himself. Th
true principle is to unite them. Philosophy, as a part of education, is an excellent thing
and there is no disgrace to a man while he is young in pursuing such a study; but whe
he is more advanced in years, the thing becomes ridiculous, and I feel towards philos
ophers as I do towards those who lisp and imitate children. For I love to see a littl
child, who is not of an age to speak plainly, lisping at his play; there is an appearanc
of grace and freedom in his utterance, which is natural to his childish years. Bu
when I hear some small creature carefully articulating its words, I am offended; th
sound is disagreeable, and has to my ears the twang of slavery. So when I hear
man lisping, or see him playing like a child, his behaviour appears to me ridiculou
and unmanly and worthy of stripes. And I have the same feeling about students o
philosophy; when I see a youth thus engaged,—the study appears to me to be i
character, and becoming a man of liberal education, and him who neglects philosoph
I regard as an inferior man, who will never aspire to anything great or noble. But if
see him continuing the study in later life, and not leaving off, I should like to bea
him, Socrates; for, as I was saying, such a one, even though he have good natura
parts, becomes effeminate. He dies from the busy centre and the market-place, in which
as the poet says, men become distinguished; he creeps into a corner for the rest of hi
life, and talks in a whisper with three or four admiring youths, but never speaks ou
like a freeman in a satisfactory manner. Now I, Socrates, am very well inclined toward
you, and my feeling may be compared with that of Zethus towards Amphion, in th
play of Euripides, whom I was mentioning just now: for I am disposed to say t
you much what Zethus said to his brother, that you, Socrates, are careless about th
things of which you ought to be careful; and that you

> 'Who have a soul so noble, are remarkable for a puerile exterior;
> Neither in a court of justice could you state a case, or give any reason or proof
> Or offer valiant counsel on another's behalf.'

And you must not be offended, my dear Socrates, for I am speaking out of good-wil
towards you, if I ask whether you are not ashamed of being thus defenceless; whic
I affirm to be the condition not of you only but of all those who will carry the stud
of philosophy too far. For suppose that some one were to take you, or any one o
your sort, off to prison, declaring that you had done wrong when you had done n
wrong, you must allow that you would not know what to do:—there you would stan
giddy and gaping, and not having a word to say; and when you went up before th
Court, even if the accuser were a poor creature and not good for much, you would di
if he were disposed to claim the penalty of death. And yet, Socrates, what is the value o

> 'An art which converts a man of sense into a fool,'

ho is helpless, and has no power to save either himself or others, when he is in ne greatest danger and is going to be despoiled by his enemies of all his goods, and as to live, simply deprived of his rights of citizenship?—he being a man who, if I ay use the expression, may be boxed on the ears with impunity. Then, my good friend, ke my advice, and refute no more:

> 'Learn the philosophy of business, and acquire the reputation of wisdom.
> But leave to others these niceties,'

hether they are to be described as follies or absurdities:

> 'For they will only
> Give you poverty for the inmate of your dwelling.'

Cease, then, emulating these paltry splitters of words, and emulate only the man of ubstance and honour, who is well to do.

Soc. If my soul, Callicles, were made of gold, should I not rejoice to discover ne of those stones with which they test gold, and the very best possible one to which might bring my soul; and if the stone and I agreed in approving of her training, en I should know that I was in a satisfactory state, and that no other test was needed y me.

Cal. What is your meaning, Socrates?

Soc. I will tell you; I think that I have found in you the desired touchstone.

Cal. Why?

Soc. Because I am sure that if you agree with me in any of the opinions which y soul forms, I have at last found the truth indeed. For I consider that if a man to make a complete trial of the good or evil of the soul, he ought to have three ualities—knowledge, good-will, outspokenness, which are all possessed by you. any whom I meet are unable to make trial of me, because they are not wise as you e; others are wise, but they will not tell me the truth, because they have not the me interest in me which you have; and these two strangers, Gorgias and Polus, are ndoubtedly wise men and my very good friends, but they are not outspoken enough, d they are too modest. Why, their modesty is so great that they are driven to con- adict themselves, first one and then the other of them, in the face of a large company, n matters of the highest moment. But you have all the qualities in which these others e deficient, having received an excellent education; to this many Athenians can stify. And you are my friend. Shall I tell you why I think so? I know that you, allicles, and Tisander of Aphidnae, and Andron the son of Androtion, and Nausicydes f the deme of Cholarges, studied together: there were four of you, and I once heard u advising with one another as to the extent to which the pursuit of philosophy ould be carried, and, as I know, you came to the conclusion that the study should not e pushed too much into detail. You were cautioning one another not to be overwise; u were afraid that too much wisdom might unconsciously to yourselves be the ruin f you. And now when I hear you giving the same advice to me which you then ave to your most intimate friends, I have a sufficient evidence of your real good-will me. And of the frankness of your nature and freedom from modesty I am assured y yourself, and the assurance is confirmed by your last speech. Well then, the inference in the present case clearly is, that if you agree with me in an argument about any point that point will have been sufficiently tested by us, and will not require to be submitted to any further test. For you could not have agreed with me, either from lack of knowledge or from superfluity of modesty, nor yet from a desire to deceive me, for you are my friend, as you tell me yourself. And therefore when you and I are agreed the result will be the attainment of perfect truth. Now there is no nobler enquiry Callicles, than that which you censure me for making,—What ought the character of a man to be, and what his pursuits, and how far is he to go, both in maturer years and in youth? For be assured that if I err in my own conduct I do not err intentionally but from ignorance. Do not then desist from advising me, now that you have begun until I have learned clearly what this is which I am to practise, and how I may acquire it. And if you find me assenting to your words, and hereafter not doing that to which I assented, call me 'dolt,' and deem me unworthy of receiving further instruction. Once more, then, tell me what you and Pindar mean by natural justice: Do you not mean that the superior should take the property of the inferior by force; that the better should rule the worse, the noble have more than the mean? Am I not right in my recollection?

Cal. Yes; that is what I was saying, and so I still aver.

Soc. And do you mean by the better the same as the superior? for I could not make out what you were saying at the time—whether you meant by the superior the stronger, and that the weaker must obey the stronger, as you seemed to imply when you said that great cities attack small ones in accordance with natural right, because they are superior and stronger, as though the superior and stronger and better were the same; or whether the better may be also the inferior and weaker, and the superior the worse, or whether better is to be defined in the same way as superior: this is the point which I want to have cleared up. Are the superior and better and stronger the same or different?

Cal. I say unequivocally that they are the same.

Soc. Then the many are by nature superior to the one, against whom, as you were saying, they make the laws?

Cal. Certainly.

Soc. Then the laws of the many are the laws of the superior?

Cal. Very true.

Soc. Then they are the laws of the better; for the superior class are far better, as you were saying?

Cal. Yes.

Soc. And since they are superior, the laws which are made by them are by nature good?

Cal. Yes.

Soc. And are not the many of opinion, as you were lately saying, that justice is equality, and that to do is more disgraceful than to suffer injustice?—is that so or not? Answer, Callicles, and let no modesty be found to come in the way; do the many think, or do they not think thus?—I must beg of you to answer, in order that if you agree with me I may fortify myself by the assent of so competent an authority.

Cal. Yes; the opinion of the many is what you say.

Soc. Then not only custom but nature also affirms that to do is more disgraceful han to suffer injustice, and that justice is equality; so that you seem to have been vrong in your former assertion, when accusing me you said that nature and custom are pposed, and that I, knowing this, was dishonestly playing between them, appealing o custom when the argument is about nature, and to nature when the argument is bout custom?

Cal. This man will never cease talking nonsense. At your age, Socrates, are you ot ashamed to be catching at words and chuckling over some verbal slip? do you ot see—have I not told you already, that by superior I mean better: do you imagine ne to say, that if a rabble of slaves and nondescripts, who are of no use except perhaps or their physical strength, get together, their ipsissima verba are laws?

Soc. Ho! my philosopher, is that your line?

Cal. Certainly.

Soc. I was thinking, Callicles, that something of the kind must have been in your nind, and that is why I repeated the question,—What is the superior? I wanted to now clearly what you meant; for you surely do not think that two men are better han one, or that your slaves are better than you because they are stronger? Then please o begin again, and tell me who the better are, if they are not the stronger; and I will sk you, great Sir, to be a little milder in your instructions, or I shall have to run away rom you.

Cal. You are ironical.

Soc. No, by the hero Zethus, Callicles, by whose aid you were just now saying nany ironical things against me, I am not:—tell me, then, whom you mean by the etter?

Cal. I mean the more excellent.

Soc. Do you not see that you are yourself using words which have no meaning nd that you are explaining nothing?—will you tell me whether you mean by the etter and superior the wiser, or if not, whom?

Cal. Most assuredly, I do mean the wiser.

Soc. Then according to you, one wise man may often be superior to ten thousand ools, and he ought to rule them, and they ought to be his subjects, and he ought to ave more than they should. This is what I believe that you mean (and you must not uppose that I am word-catching), if you allow that the one is superior to the ten housand?

Cal. Yes; that is what I mean, and that is what I conceive to be natural justice—hat the better and wiser should rule and have more than the inferior.

Soc. Stop there, and let me ask you what you would say in this case: Let us uppose that we are all together as we are now; there are several of us, and we have large common store of meats and drinks, and there are all sorts of persons in our ompany having various degrees of strength and weakness, and one of us, being hysician, is wiser in the matter of food than all the rest, and he is probably stronger han some and not so strong as others of us—will he not, being wiser, be also better han we are, and our superior in this matter of food?

Cal. Certainly.

Soc. Either, then, he will have a larger share of the meats and drinks, because

he is better, or he will have the distribution of all of them by reason of his authorit
but he will not expend or make use of a larger share of them on his own person, o
if he does, he will be punished;—his share will exceed that of some, and be less tha
that of others, and if he be the weakest of all, he being the best of all will have th
smallest share of all, Callicles:—am I not right, my friend?

Cal. You talk about meats and drinks and physicians and other nonsense; I ar
not speaking of them.

Soc. Well, but do you admit that the wiser is the better? Answer 'Yes' or 'No

Cal. Yes.

Soc. And ought not the better to have a larger share?

Cal. Not of meats and drinks.

Soc. I understand: then, perhaps, of coats—the skilfullest weaver ought to hav
the largest coat, and the greatest number of them, and go about clothed in the bes
and finest of them?

Cal. Fudge about coats!

Soc. Then the skilfullest and best in making shoes ought to have the advantage i
shoes; the shoemaker, clearly, should walk about in the largest shoes, and have th
greatest number of them?

Cal. Fudge about shoes! What nonsense are you talking?

Soc. Or, if this is not your meaning, perhaps you would say that the wise an
good and true husbandman should actually have a larger share of seeds, and have a
much seed as possible for his own land?

Cal. How you go on, always talking in the same way, Socrates!

Soc. Yes, Callicles, and also about the same things.

Cal. Yes, by the Gods, you are literally always talking of cobblers and fulle
and cooks and doctors, as if this had to do with our argument.

Soc. But why will you not tell me in what a man must be superior and wiser i
order to claim a larger share; will you neither accept a suggestion, nor offer one?

Cal. I have already told you. In the first place, I mean by superiors not cobbler
or cooks, but wise politicians who understand the administration of a state, and wh
are not only wise, but also valiant and able to carry out their designs, and not the me
to faint from want of soul.

Soc. See now, most excellent Callicles, how different my charge against you i
from that which you bring against me, for you reproach me with always saying th
same; but I reproach you with never saying the same about the same things, for a
one time you were defining the better and the superior to be the stronger, then agai
as the wiser, and now you bring forward a new notion; the superior and the bette
are now declared by you to be the more courageous: I wish, my good friend, that yo
would tell me, once for all, whom you affirm to be the better and superior, and in wha
they are better?

Cal. I have already told you that I mean those who are wise and courageous i
the administration of a state—they ought to be the rulers of their states, and justic
consists in their having more than their subjects.

Soc. But whether rulers or subjects will they or will they not have more tha
themselves, my friend?

Cal. What do you mean?

Soc. I mean that every man is his own ruler; but perhaps you think that there is o necessity for him to rule himself; he is only required to rule others?

Cal. What do you mean by his 'ruling over himself'?

Soc. A simple thing enough; just what is commonly said, that a man should be mperate and master of himself, and ruler of his own pleasures and passions.

Cal. What innocence! you mean those fools,—the temperate?

Soc. Certainly:—any one may know that to be my meaning.

Cal. Quite so, Socrates; and they are really fools, for how can a man be happy ho is the servant of anything? On the contrary, I plainly assert, that he who would uly live ought to allow his desires to wax to the uttermost, and not to chastise them; ut when they have grown to their greatest he should have courage and intelligence minister to them and to satisfy all his longings. And this I affirm to be natural ustice and nobility. To this however the many cannot attain; and they blame the trong man because they are ashamed of their own weakness, which they desire to onceal, and hence they say that intemperance is base. As I have remarked already, hey enslave the nobler natures, and being unable to satisfy their pleasures, they praise emperance and justice out of their own cowardice. For if a man had been originally he son of a king, or had a nature capable of acquiring an empire or a tyranny or overeignty, what could be more truly base or evil than temperance—to a man like im, I say, who might freely be enjoying every good, and has no one to stand in his vay, and yet has admitted custom and reason and the opinion of other men to be ords over him?—must not he be in a miserable plight whom the reputation of justice nd temperance hinders from giving more to his friends than to his enemies, even hough he be a ruler in his city? Nay, Socrates, for you profess to be a votary of the ruth, and the truth is this:—that luxury and intemperance and licence, if they be rovided with means, are virtue and happiness—all the rest is a mere bauble, agreenents contrary to nature, foolish talk of men, nothing worth.

Soc. There is a noble freedom, Callicles, in your way of approaching the argument; or what you say is what the rest of the world think, but do not like to say. And I nust beg of you to persevere, that the true rule of human life may become manifest. 'ell me, then:—you say, do you not, that in the rightly-developed man the passions ught not to be controlled, but that we should let them grow to the utmost and omehow or other satisfy them, and that this is virtue?

Cal. Yes; I do.

Soc. Then those who want nothing are not truly said to be happy?

Cal. No indeed, for then stones and dead men would be the happiest of all.

Soc. But surely life according to your view is an awful thing; and indeed I think hat Euripides may have been right in saying,

> 'Who knows if life be not death and death life;'

nd that we are very likely dead; I have heard a philosopher say that at this moment ve are actually dead, and that the body is our tomb, and that the part of the soul which s the seat of the desires is liable to be tossed about by words and blown up and down; nd some ingenious person, probably a Sicilian or an Italian, playing with the word, invented a tale in which he called the soul—because of its believing and make-believe nature—a vessel, and the ignorant he called the uninitiated or leaky, and the place in the souls of the uninitiated in which the desires are seated, being the intemperate and incontinent part, he compared to a vessel full of holes, because it can never be satisfied. He is not of your way of thinking, Callicles, for he declares, that of all the souls in Hades, meaning the invisible world, hese uninitiated or leaky persons are the most miserable, and that they pour water into a vessel which is full of holes out of a colander which is similarly perforated. The colander, as my informer assures me, is the soul, and the soul which he compares to a colander is the soul of the ignorant which is likewise full of holes, and therefore incontinent, owing to a bad memory and want of faith. These notions are strange enough, but they show the principle which, if I can, I would fain prove to you; that you should change your mind, and instead of the intemperate and insatiate life, choose that which is orderly and sufficient and has a due provision for daily needs. Do I make any impression on you, and are you coming over to the opinion that the orderly are happier than the intemperate? Or do I fail to persuade you, and, however many tales I rehearse to you, do you continue of the same opinion still?

Cal. The latter, Socrates, is more like the truth.

Soc. Well, I will tell you another image, which comes out of the same school:—Let me request you to consider how far you would accept this as an account of the two lives of the temperate and intemperate in a figure:—There are two men, both of whom have a number of casks; the one man has his casks sound and full, one of wine another of honey, and a third of milk, besides others filled with other liquids, and the streams which fill them are few and scanty, and he can only obtain them with a great deal of toil and difficulty; but when his casks are once filled he has no need to feed them any more, and has no further trouble with them or care about them. The other, in like manner, can procure streams, though not without difficulty; but his vessels are leaky and unsound, and night and day he is compelled to be filling them and if he pauses for a moment, he is in an agony of pain. Such are their respective lives:—And now would you say that the life of the intemperate is happier than that of the temperate? Do I not convince you that the opposite is the truth?

Cal. You do not convince me, Socrates, for the one who has filled himself has no longer any pleasure left; and this, as I was just now saying, is the life of a stone he has neither joy nor sorrow after he is once filled; but the pleasure depends on the superabundance of the influx.

Soc. But the more you pour in, the greater the waste; and the holes must be large for the liquid to escape.

Cal. Certainly.

Soc. The life which you are now depicting is not that of a dead man, or of a stone, but of a cormorant; you mean that he is to be hungering and eating?

Cal. Yes.

Soc. And he is to be thirsting and drinking?

Cal. Yes, that is what I mean; he is to have all his desires about him, and to be able to live happily in the gratification of them.

Soc. Capital, excellent; go on as you have begun, and have no shame; I, too nust disencumber myself of shame: and first, will you tell me whether you include tching and scratching, provided you have enough of them and pass your life in cratching, in your notion of happiness?

Cal. What a strange being you are, Socrates! a regular mob-orator.

Soc. That was the reason, Callicles, why I scared Polus and Gorgias, until they were too modest to say what they thought; but you will not be too modest and will not be scared, for you are a brave man. And now, answer my question.

Cal. I answer, that even the scratcher would live pleasantly.

Soc. And if pleasantly, then also happily?

Cal. To be sure.

Soc. But what if the itching is not confined to the head? Shall I pursue the question? And here, Callicles, I would have you consider how you would reply if consequences are pressed upon you, especially if in the last resort you are asked, whether the life of a catamite is not terrible, foul, miserable? Or would you venture to say, that they too are happy, if they only get enough of what they want?

Cal. Are you not ashamed, Socrates, of introducing such topics into the argument?

Soc. Well, my fine friend, but am I the introducer of these topics, or he who says without any qualification that all who feel pleasure in whatever manner are happy, and who admits of no distinction between good and bad pleasures? And I would still ask, whether you say that pleasure and good are the same, or whether there is some pleasure which is not a good? . . .

Soc. Well, but if so, the truth is as I have said already, that in the Athenian State no one has ever shown himself to be a good statesman—you admitted that this was true of our present statesmen, but not true of former ones, and you preferred them to the others; yet they have turned out to be no better than our present ones; and therefore, if they were rhetoricians, they did not use the true art of rhetoric or of flattery, or they would not have fallen out of favour.

Cal. But surely, Socrates, no living man ever came near any one of them in his performances.

Soc. O, my dear friend, I say nothing against them regarded as the serving-men of the State; and I do think that they were certainly more serviceable than those who are living now, and better able to gratify the wishes of the State; but as to transforming those desires and not allowing them to have their way, and using the powers which they had, whether of persuasion or of force, in the improvement of their fellow-citizens, which is the prime object of the truly good citizen, I do not see that in these respects they were a whit superior to our present statesmen, although I do admit that they were more clever at providing ships and walls and docks, and all that. You and I have a ridiculous way, for during the whole time that we are arguing, we are always going round and round to the same point, and constantly misunderstanding one another. If I am not mistaken, you have admitted and acknowledged more than once, that there are two kinds of operations which have to do with the body, and two which have to do with the soul: one of the two is ministerial, and if our bodies are hungry provides food for them, and if they are thirsty gives them drink, or if they are cold supplies them with garments, blankets, shoes, and all that they crave. I use the same images as before intentionally, in order that you may understand me the better. The purveyor

of the articles may provide them either wholesale or retail, or he may be the maker o
any of them,—the baker, or the cook, or the weaver, or the shoemaker, or the currie
and in so doing, being such as he is, he is naturally supposed by himself and ever
one to minister to the body. For none of them know that there is another art—a
art of gymnastic and medicine which is the true minister of the body, and ought t
be the mistress of all the rest, and to use their results according to the knowledg
which she has and they have not, of the real good or bad effects of meats and drink
on the body. All other arts which have to do with the body are servile and menial an
illiberal; and gymnastic and medicine are, as they ought to be, their mistresses. Now
when I say that all this is equally true of the soul, you seem at first to know an
understand and assent to my words, and then a little while afterwards you com
repeating, Has not the State had good and noble citizens? and when I ask you wh
they are, you reply, seemingly quite in earnest, as if I had asked, Who are or hav
been good trainers?—and you had replied, Thearion, the baker, Mithoecus, who wrot
the Sicilian cookery-book, Sarambus, the vintner: these are ministers of the body, first
rate in their art; for the first makes admirable loaves, the second excellent dishes, an
the third capital wine;—to me these appear to be the exact parallel of the statesme
whom you mention. Now you would not be altogether pleased if I said to you, M
friend, you know nothing of gymnastics; those of whom you are speaking to me ar
only the ministers and purveyors of luxury, who have no good or noble notions o
their art, and may very likely be filling and fattening men's bodies and gaining thei
approval, although the result is that they lose their original flesh in the long run, an
become thinner than they were before; and yet they, in their simplicity, will nc
attribute their diseases and loss of flesh to their entertainers; but when in after year
the unhealthy surfeit brings the attendant penalty of disease, he who happens to b
near them at the time, and offers them advice, is accused and blamed by them, an
if they could they would do him some harm; while they proceed to eulogize the me
who have been the real authors of the mischief. And that, Callicles, is just wha
you are now doing. You praise the men who feasted the citizens and satisfied thei
desires, and people say that they have made the city great, not seeing that the swolle
and ulcerated condition of the State is to be attributed to these elder statesmen; fo
they have filled the city full of harbours and docks and walls and revenues and al
that, and have left no room for justice and temperance. And when the crisis of th
disorder comes, the people will blame the advisers of the hour, and applaud Themis
tocles and Cimon and Pericles, who are the real authors of their calamities; and if yo
are not careful they may assail you and my friend Alcibiades, when they are losin
not only their new acquisitions, but also their original possessions; not that you ar
the authors of these misfortunes of theirs, although you may perhaps be accessorie
to them. A great piece of work is always being made, as I see and am told, now as o
old, about our statesmen. When the State treats any of them as malefactors, I observ
that there is a great uproar and indignation at the supposed wrong which is done t
them; 'after all their many services to the State, that they should unjustly perish,'—s
the tale runs. But the cry is all a lie; for no statesman ever could be unjustly put t
death by the city of which he is the head. The case of the professed statesman is,
believe, very much like that of the professed sophist; for the sophists, although the

re wise men, are nevertheless guilty of a strange piece of folly; professing to e teachers of virtue, they will often accuse their disciples of wronging them, nd defrauding them of their pay, and showing no gratitude for their services. 'et what can be more absurd than that men who have become just and good, nd whose injustice has been taken away from them, and who have had justice nplanted in them by their teachers, should act unjustly by reason of the injustice which not in them? Can anything be more irrational, my friends, than this? You, Callicles, ompel me to be a mob-orator, because you will not answer.

Cal. And you are the man who cannot speak unless there is some one to answer?

Soc. I suppose that I can; just now, at any rate, the speeches which I am making re long enough because you refuse to answer me. But I adjure you by the god of riendship, my good sir, do tell me whether there does not appear to you to be a great nconsistency in saying that you have made a man good, and then blaming him for eing bad?

Cal. Yes, it appears so to me.

Soc. Do you never hear our professors of education speaking in this inconsistent nanner?

Cal. Yes, but why talk of men who are good for nothing?

Soc. I would rather say, why talk of men who profess to be rulers, and declare hat they are devoted to the improvement of the city, and nevertheless upon occasion eclaim against the utter vileness of the city:—do you think that there is any difference etween one and the other? My good friend, the sophist and the rhetorician, as I was aying to Polus, are the same, or nearly the same; but you ignorantly fancy that rhetoric a perfect thing, and sophistry a thing to be despised; whereas the truth is, that ophistry is as much superior to rhetoric as legislation is to the practice of law, or ymnastic to medicine. The orators and sophists, as I am inclined to think, are the nly class who cannot complain of the mischief ensuing to themselves from that which hey teach others, without in the same breath accusing themselves of having done no ood to those whom they profess to benefit. Is not this a fact?

Cal. Certainly it is.

Soc. If they were right in saying that they make men better, then they are the nly class who can afford to leave their remuneration to those who have been benefited y them. Whereas if a man has been benefited in any other way, if, for example, he as been taught to run by a trainer, he might possibly defraud him of his pay, if the rainer left the matter to him, and made no agreement with him that he should receive noney as soon as he had given him the utmost speed; for not because of any deficiency f speed do men act unjustly, but by reason of injustice.

Cal. Very true.

Soc. And he who removes injustice can be in no danger of being treated unjustly: e alone can safely leave the honorarium to his pupils, if he be really able to make hem good—am I not right?

Cal. Yes.

Soc. Then we have found the reason why there is no dishonour in a man receiving ay who is called in to advise about building or any other art?

Cal. Yes, we have found the reason.

Soc. But when the point is, how a man may become best himself, and best govern his family and state, then to say that you will give no advice gratis is held to be dishonourable?

Cal. True.

Soc. And why? Because only such benefits call forth a desire to requite them, and there is evidence that a benefit has been conferred when the benefactor receives a return; otherwise not. Is this true?

Cal. It is.

Soc. Then to which service of the State do you invite me? determine for me. Am I to be the physician of the State who will strive and struggle to make the Athenians as good as possible; or am I to be the servant and flatterer of the State? Speak out, my good friend, freely and fairly as you did at first and ought to do again, and tell me your entire mind.

Cal. I say then that you should be the servant of the State.

Soc. The flatterer? well, sir, that is a noble invitation.

Cal. The Mysian, Socrates, or what you please. For if you refuse, the consequence will be—

Soc. Do not repeat the old story—that he who likes will kill me and get my money; for then I shall have to repeat the old answer, that he will be a bad man and will kill the good, and that the money will be of no use to him, but that he will wrongly use that which he wrongly took, and if wrongly, basely, and if basely, hurtfully.

Cal. How confident you are, Socrates, that you will never come to harm! you seem to think that you are living in another country, and can never be brought into a court of justice, as you very likely may be brought by some miserable and mean person.

Soc. Then I must indeed be a fool, Callicles, if I do not know that in the Athenian State any man may suffer anything. And if I am brought to trial and incur the dangers of which you speak, he will be a villain who brings me to trial—of that I am very sure, for no good man would accuse the innocent. Nor shall I be surprised if I am put to death. Shall I tell you why I anticipate this?

Cal. By all means.

Soc. I think that I am the only or almost the only Athenian living who practises the true art of politics; I am the only politician of my time. Now, seeing that when I speak my words are not uttered with any view of gaining favour, and that I look to what is best and not to what is most pleasant, having no mind to use those arts and graces which you recommend, I shall have nothing to say in the justice court. And you might argue with me, as I was arguing with Polus:—I shall be tried just as a physician would be tried in a court of little boys at the indictment of the cook. What would he reply under such circumstances, if some one were to accuse him, saying, 'O my boys, many evil things has this man done to you: he is the death of you, especially of the younger ones among you, cutting and burning and starving and suffocating you, until you know not what to do; he gives you the bitterest potions, and compels you to hunger and thirst. How unlike the variety of meats and sweets on which I feasted you!' What do you suppose that the physician would be able to reply when he found himself in such a predicament? If he told the truth he could only say,

All these evil things, my boys, I did for your health,' and then would there not just be a clamour among a jury like that? How they would cry out!

Cal. I dare say.

Soc. Would he not be utterly at a loss for a reply?

Cal. He certainly would.

Soc. And I too shall be treated in the same way, as I well know, if I am brought before the court. For I shall not be able to rehearse to the people the pleasures which I have procured for them, and which, although I am not disposed to envy either the procurers or enjoyers of them, are deemed by them to be benefits and advantages. And if any one says that I corrupt young men, and perplex their minds, or that I speak evil of old men, and use bitter words towards them, whether in private or public, it is useless for me to reply, as I truly might:—'All this I do for the sake of justice, and with a view to your interest, my judges, and to nothing else.' And therefore there is no saying what may happen to me.

Cal. And do you think, Socrates, that a man who is thus defenceless is in a good position?

Soc. Yes, Callicles, if he have that defence, which as you have often acknowledged he should have—if he be his own defence, and have never said or done anything wrong, either in respect of gods or men; and this has been repeatedly acknowledged by us to be the best sort of defence. And if any one could convict me of inability to defend myself or others after this sort, I should blush for shame, whether I was convicted before many, or before a few, or by myself alone; and if I died from want of ability to do so, that would indeed grieve me. But if I died because I have no powers of flattery or rhetoric, I am very sure that you would not find me repining at death. For no man who is not an utter fool and coward is afraid of death itself, but he is afraid of doing wrong. For to go to the world below having one's soul full of injustice is the last and worst of all evils. And in proof of what I say, if you have no objection, I should like to tell you a story.

Cal. Very well, proceed; and then we shall have done.

Soc. Listen, then, as story-tellers say, to a very pretty tale, which I dare say that you may be disposed to regard as a fable only, but which, as I believe, is a true tale, for I mean to speak the truth. Homer tells us how Zeus and Poseidon and Pluto divided the empire which they inherited from their father. Now in the days of Cronos there existed a law respecting the destiny of man, which has always been, and still continues to be in Heaven,—that he who has lived all his life in justice and holiness shall go, when he is dead, to the Islands of the Blessed, and dwell there in perfect happiness out of the reach of evil; but that he who has lived unjustly and impiously shall go to the house of vengeance and punishment, which is called Tartarus. And in the time of Cronos, and even quite lately in the reign of Zeus, the judgment was given on the very day on which the men were to die; the judges were alive, and the men were alive; and the consequence was that the judgments were not well given. Then Pluto and the authorities from the Islands of the Blessed came to Zeus, and said that the souls found their way to the wrong places. Zeus said: 'I shall put a stop to this; the judgments are not well given, because the persons who are judged have their clothes on, for they are alive; and there are many who, having evil souls, are apparelle in fair bodies, or encased in wealth or rank, and, when the day of judgment arrives numerous witnesses come forward and testify on their behalf that they have live righteously. The judges are awed by them, and they themselves too have their clothe on when judging; their eyes and ears and their whole bodies are interposed as a vei before their own souls. All this is a hindrance to them; there are the clothes of th judges and the clothes of the judged.—What is to be done? I will tell you:—In th first place, I will deprive men of the foreknowledge of death, which they possess a present: this power which they have Prometheus has already received my orders t take from them: in the second place, they shall be entirely stripped before they ar judged, for they shall be judged when they are dead; and the judge too shall be naked that is to say, dead—he with his naked soul shall pierce into the other naked souls and they shall die suddenly and be deprived of all their kindred, and leave thei brave attire strewn upon the earth—conducted in this manner, the judgment will b just. I knew all about the matter before any of you, and therefore I have made m sons judges; two from Asia, Minos and Rhadamanthus, and one from Europe, Aeacus And these, when they are dead, shall give judgment in the meadow at the parting o the ways, whence the two roads lead, one to the Islands of the Blessed, and the othe to Tartarus. Rhadamanthus shall judge those who come from Asia, and Aeacus thos who come from Europe. And to Minos I shall give the primacy, and he shall hold court of appeal, in case either of the two others are in any doubt:—then the judgmen respecting the last journey of men will be as just as possible.'

From this tale, Callicles, which I have heard and believe, I draw the followin inferences:—Death, if I am right, is in the first place the separation from one anothe of two things, soul and body: nothing else. And after they are separated they retai their several natures, as in life; the body keeps the same habit, and the results o treatment or accident are distinctly visible in it: for example, he who by nature o training or both, was a tall man while he was alive, will remain as he was, afte he is dead; and the fat man will remain fat; and so on; and the dead man, who in lif had a fancy to have flowing hair, will have flowing hair. And if he was marked wit the whip and had the prints of the scourge, or of wounds in him when he was alive you might see the same in the dead body; and if his limbs were broken or misshape when he was alive, the same appearance would be visible in the dead. And in a word whatever was the habit of the body during life would be distinguishable after death either perfectly, or in a great measure and for a certain time. And I should imagin that this is equally true of the soul, Callicles; when a man is stripped of the body, al the natural or acquired affections of the soul are laid open to view.—And when the come to the judge, as those from Asia come to Rhadamanthus, he places them near hin and inspects them quite impartially, not knowing whose the soul is: perhaps he ma lay hands on the soul of the great king, or of some other king or potentate, who has no soundness in him, but his soul is marked with the whip, and is full of the print and scars of perjuries and crimes with which each action has stained him, and he is all crooked with falsehood and imposture, and has no straightness, because he has lived without truth. Him Rhadamanthus beholds, full of all deformity and disproportion which is caused by licence and luxury and insolence and incontinence, and despatches him ignominiously to his prison, and there he undergoes the punishment which he deserves.

Now the proper office of punishment is twofold: he who is rightly punished ought either to become better and profit by it, or he ought to be made an example to his fellows, that they may see what he suffers, and fear and become better. Those who are improved when they are punished by gods and men, are those whose sins are curable; and they are improved, as in this world so also in another, by pain and suffering; for there is no other way in which they can be delivered from their evil. But they who have been guilty of the worst crimes, and are incurable by reason of their crimes, are made examples; for, as they are incurable, the time has passed at which they can receive any benefit. They get no good themselves, but others get good when they behold them enduring for ever the most terrible and painful and fearful sufferings as the penalty of their sins—there they are, hanging up as examples, in the prison-house of the world below, a spectacle and a warning to all unrighteous men who come hither. And among them, as I confidently affirm, will be found Archelaus, if Polus truly reports of him, and any other tyrant who is like him. Of these fearful examples, most, as I believe, are taken from the class of tyrants and kings and potentates and public men, for they are the authors of the greatest and most impious crimes, because they have the power. And Homer witnesses to the truth of this; for they are always kings and potentates whom he has described as suffering everlasting punishment in the world below: such were Tantalus and Sisyphus and Tityus. But no one ever described Thersites, or any private person who was a villain, as suffering everlasting punishment, or as incurable. For to commit the worst crimes, as I am inclined to think, was not in his power, and he was happier than those who had the power. No, Callicles, the very bad men come from the class of those who have power. And yet in that very class there may arise good men, and worthy of all admiration they are, for where there is great power to do wrong, to live and to die justly is a hard thing, and greatly to be praised, and few there are who attain to this. Such good and true men, however, there have been, and will be again, at Athens and in other states, who have fulfilled their trust righteously; and there is one who is quite famous all over Hellas, Aristeides, the son of Lysimachus. But, in general, great men are also bad, my friend.

As I was saying, Rhadamanthus, when he gets a soul of the bad kind, knows nothing about him, neither who he is, nor who his parents are; he knows only that he had got hold of a villain; and seeing this, he stamps him as curable or incurable, and sends him away to Tartarus, whither he goes and receives his proper recompense. Or, again, he looks with admiration on the soul of some just one who has lived in holiness and truth; he may have been a private man or not; and I should say, Callicles, that he is most likely to have been a philosopher who has done his own work, and not troubled himself with the doings of other men in his lifetime; him Rhadamanthus sends to the Islands of the Blessed. Aeacus does the same; and they both have sceptres, and judge; but Minos alone has a golden sceptre and is seated looking on, as Odysseus in Homer declares that he saw him:

> 'Holding a sceptre of gold, and giving laws to the dead.'

Now I, Callicles, am persuaded of the truth of these things, and I consider how I shall present my soul whole and undefiled before the judge in that day. Renouncing the honours at which the world aims, I desire only to know the truth, and to live as well as I can, and, when I die, to die as well as I can. And, to the utmost of my power, I exhort all other men to do the same. And, in return for your exhortation of me, I exhort you also to take part in the great combat, which is the combat of life, and greater than every other earthly conflict. And I retort your reproach of me, and say, that you will not be able to help yourself when the day of trial and judgment, of which I was speaking, comes upon you; you will go before the judge, the son of Aegina, and, when he has got you in his grip and is carrying you off, you will gape and your head will swim round, just as mine would in the courts of this world, and very likely some one will shamefully box you on the ears, and put upon you any sort of insult.

Perhaps this may appear to you to be only an old wife's tale, which you will contemn. And there might be reason in your contemning such tales, if by searching we could find out anything better or truer: but now you see that you and Polus and Gorgias, who are the three wisest of the Greeks of our day, are not able to show that we ought to live any life which does not profit in another world as well as in this. And of all that has been said, nothing remains unshaken but the saying, that to do injustice is more to be avoided than to suffer injustice, and that the reality and not the appearance of virtue is to be followed above all things, as well in public as in private life; and that when any one has been wrong in anything, he is to be chastised, and that the next best thing to a man being just is that he should become just, and be chastised and punished; also that he should avoid all flattery of himself as well as of others, of the few or of the many: and rhetoric and any other art should be used by him, and all his actions should be done always, with a view to justice.

Follow me then, and I will lead you where you will be happy in life and after death, as the argument shows. And never mind if some one despises you as a fool, and insults you, if he has a mind; let him strike you, by Zeus, and do you be of good cheer, and do not mind the insulting blow, for you will never come to any harm in the practice of virtue, if you are a really good and true man. When we have practised virtue together, we will apply ourselves to politics, if that seems desirable, or we will advise about whatever else may seem good to us, for we shall be better able to judge then. In our present condition we ought not to give ourselves airs, for even on the most important subjects we are always changing our minds; so utterly stupid are we! Let us, then, take the argument as our guide, which has revealed to us that the best way of life is to practise justice and every virtue in life and death. This way let us go; and in this exhort all men to follow, not in the way to which you trust and in which you exhort me to follow you; for that way, Callicles, is nothing worth.

THE REPUBLIC

Plato

Plato (ca. *427*–ca. *347* B.C.; *see page 107*) *combined the imagination of the poet with powers of rigorous analysis. His most famous dialogue,* The Republic, *illustrates both these aspects of his genius. The passage that is given here, from the middle of Book VI to the middle of Book VII, is the heart of the work, in which Socrates delineates the wisdom sought by the true philosopher. Having started with the question, "What is justice?", he has decided that it must be a kind of proper balance, both in an individual and in a community. Such a community would have to be ruled by those who can tell the real from the counterfeit and the illusory in human life; that is, those who know what is really good for men and what only seems to be good. In a series of increasingly complex and powerful images—first the metaphor of the sun, then the "divided line," and finally the "parable of the cave"—he draws an unforgettable picture of the turning away ("conversion") of the soul from changing, deceptive things, and its gradual envisioning of a realm of timeless truth and essential reality.*

Plato's influence has been far-reaching: Christian theology in all its forms is essentially Platonic; the emphasis on mathematics as the key to the arts and sciences goes back to Plato; the utopian approach to social and political problems, which includes aspects of both liberalism and Communism, began with his Republic; *his school, the Academy, was the first in history to offer a "liberal" education; and so on and on.*

BOOK VI

And so with pain and toil we have reached the end of one subject, but more remains to be discussed;—how and by what studies and pursuits will the saviours of the constitution be created, and at what ages are they to apply themselves to their several studies?

Certainly.

I omitted the troublesome business of the possession of women, and the procreation of children, and the appointment of the rulers, because I knew that the perfect State would be eyed with jealousy and was difficult of attainment; but that piece of cleverness was not of much service to me, for I had to discuss them all the same. The women and children are now disposed of, but the other question of the rulers

***The Dialogues of Plato*, trans. B. Jowett (2 vols.; New York: Random House, Inc., 1937), I, 763–780.**

must be investigated from the very beginning. We were saying, as you will remember, that they were to be lovers of their country, tried by the test of pleasures and pains, and neither in hardships, nor in dangers, nor at any other critical moment were to lose their patriotism—he was to be rejected who failed, but he who always came forth pure, like gold tried in the refiner's fire, was to be made a ruler, and to receive honours and rewards in life and after death. This was the sort of thing which was being said, and then the argument turned aside and veiled her face; not liking to stir the question which has now arisen.

I perfectly remember, he said.

Yes, my friend, I said, and I then shrank from hazarding the bold word; but now let me dare to say—that the perfect guardian must be a philosopher.

Yes, he said, let that be affirmed.

And do not suppose that there will be many of them; for the gifts which were deemed by us to be essential rarely grow together; they are mostly found in shreds and patches.

What do you mean? he said.

You are aware, I replied, that quick intelligence, memory, sagacity, cleverness, and similar qualities, do not often grow together, and that persons who possess them and are at the same time high-spirited and magnanimous are not so constituted by nature as to live orderly and in a peaceful and settled manner; they are driven any way by their impulses, and all solid principle goes out of them.

Very true, he said.

On the other hand, those steadfast natures which can better be depended upon, which in a battle are impregnable to fear and immovable, are equally immovable when there is anything to be learned; they are always in a torpid state, and are apt to yawn and go to sleep over any intellectual toil.

Quite true.

And yet we were saying that both qualities were necessary in those to whom the higher education is to be imparted, and who are to share in any office or command.

Certainly, he said.

And will they be a class which is rarely found?

Yes, indeed.

Then the aspirant must not only be tested in those labours and dangers and pleasures which we mentioned before, but there is another kind of probation which we did not mention—he must be exercised also in many kinds of knowledge, to see whether the soul will be able to endure the highest of all, or will faint under them, as in any other studies and exercises.

Yes, he said, you are quite right in testing him. But what do you mean by the highest of all knowledge?

You may remember, I said, that we divided the soul into three parts; and distinguished the several natures of justice, temperance, courage, and wisdom?

Indeed, he said, if I had forgotten, I should not deserve to hear more.

And do you remember the word of caution which preceded the discussion of them?

To what do you refer?

We were saying, if I am not mistaken, that he who wanted to see them in their perfect beauty must take a longer and more circuitous way, at the end of which they would appear; but that we could add on a popular exposition of them on a level with the discussion which had preceded. And you replied that such an exposition would be enough for you, and so the enquiry was continued in what to me seemed to be a very inaccurate manner; whether you were satisfied or not, it is for you to say.

Yes, he said, I thought and the others thought that you gave us a fair measure of truth.

But, my friend, I said, a measure of such things which in any degree falls short of the whole truth is not fair measure; for nothing imperfect is the measure of anything, although persons are too apt to be contented and think that they need search no further.

Not an uncommon case when people are indolent.

Yes, I said; and there cannot be any worse fault in a guardian of the State and of the laws.

True.

The guardian then, I said, must be required to take the longer circuit, and toil at learning as well as at gymnastics, or he will never reach the highest knowledge of all which, as we were just now saying, is his proper calling.

What, he said, is there a knowledge still higher than this—higher than justice and and the other virtues?

Yes, I said, there is. And of the virtues too we must behold not the outline merely, as at present—nothing short of the most finished picture should satisfy us. When little things are elaborated with an infinity of pains, in order that they may appear in their full beauty and utmost clearness, how ridiculous that we should not think the highest truths worthy of attaining the highest accuracy!

A right noble thought; but do you suppose that we shall refrain from asking you what is this highest knowledge?

Nay, I said, ask if you will; but I am certain that you have heard the answer many times, and now you either do not understand me or, as I rather think, you are disposed to be troublesome; for you have often been told that the idea of good is the highest knowledge, and that all other things become useful and advantageous only by their use of this. You can hardly be ignorant that of this I was about to speak, concerning which, as you have often heard me say, we know so little; and, without which, any other knowledge or possession of any kind will profit us nothing. Do you think that the possession of all other things is of any value if we do not possess the good? or the knowledge of all other things if we have no knowledge of beauty and goodness?

Assuredly not.

You are further aware that most people affirm pleasure to be the good, but the finer sort of wits say it is knowledge?

Yes.

And you are aware too that the latter cannot explain what they mean by knowledge, but are obliged after all to say knowledge of the good?

How ridiculous!

Yes, I said, that they should begin by reproaching us with our ignorance of the good, and then presume our knowledge of it—for the good they define to be knowledge of the good, just as if we understood them when they use the term 'good'—this is of course ridiculous.

Most true, he said.

And those who make pleasure their good are in equal perplexity; for they are compelled to admit that there are bad pleasures as well as good.

Certainly.

And therefore to acknowledge that bad and good are the same?

True.

There can be no doubt about the numerous difficulties in which this question is involved.

There can be none.

Further, do we not see that many are willing to do or to have or to seem to be what is just and honourable without the reality; but no one is satisfied with the appearance of good—the reality is what they seek; in the case of the good, appearance is despised by every one.

Very true, he said.

Of this then, which every soul of man pursues and makes the end of all his actions, having a presentiment that there is such an end, and yet hesitating because neither knowing the nature nor having the same assurance of this as of other things, and therefore losing whatever good there is in other things,—of a principle such and so great as this ought the best men in our State, to whom everything is entrusted, to be in the darkness of ignorance?

Certainly not, he said.

I am sure, I said, that he who does not know how the beautiful and the just are likewise good will be but a sorry guardian of them; and I suspect that no one who is ignorant of the good will have a true knowledge of them.

That, he said, is a shrewd suspicion of yours.

And if we only have a guardian who has this knowledge our State will be perfectly ordered?

Of course, he replied; but I wish that you would tell me whether you conceive this supreme principle of the good to be knowledge or pleasure, or different from either?

Aye, I said, I knew all along that a fastidious gentleman like you would not be contented with the thoughts of other people about these matters.

True, Socrates; but I must say that one who like you has passed a lifetime in the study of philosophy should not be always repeating the opinions of others, and never telling his own.

Well, but has any one a right to say positively what he does not know?

Not, he said, with the assurance of positive certainty; he has no right to do that: but he may say what he thinks, as a matter of opinion.

And do you not know, I said, that all mere opinions are bad, and the best of them blind? You would not deny that those who have any true notion without intelligence are only like blind men who feel their way along the road?

Very true.

And do you wish to behold what is blind and crooked and base, when others will tell you of brightness and beauty?

Still, I must implore you, Socrates, said Glaucon, not to turn away just as you are reaching the goal; if you will only give such an explanation of the good as you have already given of justice and temperance and the other virtues, we shall be satisfied.

Yes, my friend, and I shall be at least equally satisfied, but I cannot help fearing that I shall fail, and that my indiscreet zeal will bring ridicule upon me. No, sweet sirs, let us not at present ask what is the actual nature of the good, for to reach what is now in my thoughts would be an effort too great for me. But of the child of the good who is likest him, I would fain speak, if I could be sure that you wished to hear —otherwise, not.

By all means, he said, tell us about the child, and you shall remain in our debt for the account of the parent.

I do indeed wish, I replied, that I could pay, and you receive, the account of the parent, and not, as now, of the offspring only; take, however, this latter by way of interest, and at the same time have a care that I do not render a false account, although I have no intention of deceiving you.

Yes, we will take all the care that we can: proceed.

Yes, I said, but I must first come to an understanding with you, and remind you of what I have mentioned in the course of this discussion, and at many other times.

What?

The old story, that there is a many beautiful and a many good, and so of other things which we describe and define; to all of them 'many' is applied.

True, he said.

And there is an absolute beauty and an absolute good, and of other things to which the term 'many' is applied there is an absolute; for they may be brought under a single idea, which is called the essence of each.

Very true.

The many, as we say, are seen but not known, and the ideas are known but not seen.

Exactly.

And what is the organ with which we see the visible things?

The sight, he said.

And with the hearing, I said, we hear, and with the other senses perceive the other objects of sense?

True.

But have you remarked that sight is by far the most costly and complex piece of workmanship which the artificer of the senses ever contrived?

No, I never have, he said.

Then reflect: has the ear or voice need of any third or additional nature in order that the one may be able to hear and the other to be heard?

Nothing of the sort.

No, indeed, I replied; and the same is true of most, if not all, the other senses— you would not say that any of them requires such an addition?

Certainly not.

But you see that without the addition of some other nature there is no seeing or being seen?

How do you mean?

Sight being, as I conceive, in the eyes, and he who has eyes wanting to see; colour being also present in them, still unless there be a third nature specially adapted to the purpose, the owner of the eyes will see nothing and the colours will be invisible.

Of what nature are you speaking?

Of that which you term light, I replied.

True, he said.

Noble, then, is the bond which links together sight and visibility, and great beyond other bonds by no small difference of nature; for light is their bond, and light is no ignoble thing?

Nay, he said, the reverse of ignoble.

And which, I said, of the gods in heaven would you say was the lord of this element? Whose is that light which makes the eye to see perfectly and the visible to appear?

You mean the sun, as you and all mankind say.

May not the relation of sight to this deity be described as follows?

How?

Neither sight nor the eye in which sight resides is the sun?

No.

Yet of all the organs of sense the eye is the most like the sun?

By far the most like.

And the power which the eye possesses is a sort of effluence which is dispensed from the sun?

Exactly.

Then the sun is not sight, but the author of sight who is recognised by sight.

True, he said.

And this is he whom I call the child of the good, whom the good begat in his own likeness, to be in the visible world, in relation to sight and the things of sight, what the good is in the intellectual world in relation to mind and the things of mind.

Will you be a little more explicit? he said.

Why, you know, I said, that the eyes, when a person directs them towards objects on which the light of day is no longer shining, but the moon and stars only, see dimly, and are nearly blind; they seem to have no clearness of vision in them?

Very true.

But when they are directed towards objects on which the sun shines, they see clearly and there is sight in them?

Certainly.

And the soul is like the eye: when resting upon that on which truth and being shine, the soul perceives and understands and is radiant with intelligence; but when turned towards the twilight of becoming and perishing, then she has opinion only, and goes blinking about, and is first of one opinion and then of another, and seems to have no intelligence?

Just so.

Now, that which imparts truth to the known and the power of knowing to the knower is what I would have you term the idea of good, and this you will deem to be the cause of science, and of truth in so far as the latter becomes the subject of knowledge; beautiful too, as are both truth and knowledge, you will be right in esteeming this other nature as more beautiful than either; and, as in the previous instance, light and sight may be truly said to be like the sun, and yet not to be the sun, so in this other sphere, science and truth may be deemed to be like the good, but not the good; the good has a place of honour yet higher.

What a wonder of beauty that must be, he said, which is the author of science and truth, and yet surpasses them in beauty; for you surely cannot mean to say that pleasure is the good?

God forbid, I replied; but may I ask you to consider the image in another point of view?

In what point of view?

You would say, would you not, that the sun is not only the author of visibilty in all visible things, but of generation and nourishment and growth, though he himself is not generation?

Certainly.

In like manner the good may be said to be not only the author of knowledge to all things known, but of their being and essence, and yet the good is not essence, but far exceeds essence in dignity and power.

Glaucon said, with a ludicrous earnestness: By the light of heaven, how amazing!

Yes, I said, and the exaggeration may be set down to you; for you made me utter my fancies.

And pray continue to utter them; at any rate let us hear if there is anything more to be said about the similitude of the sun.

Yes, I said, there is a great deal more.

Then omit nothing, however slight.

I will do my best, I said; but I should think that a great deal will have to be omitted.

You have to imagine, then, that there are two ruling powers, and that one of them is set over the intellectual world, the other over the visible. I do not say heaven, lest you should fancy that I am playing upon the name. May I suppose that you have this distinction of the visible and intelligible fixed in your mind?

I have.

Now take a line which has been cut into two unequal parts, and divide each of them again in the same proportion, and suppose the two main divisions to answer, one to the visible and the other to the intelligible, and then compare the subdivisions in respect of their clearness and want of clearness, and you will find that the first section in the sphere of the visible consists of images. And by images I mean, in the first place, shadows, and in the second place, reflections in water and in solid, smooth and polished bodies and the like: Do you understand?

Yes, I understand.

Imagine, now, the other section, of which this is only the resemblance, to include the animals which we see, and everything that grows or is made.

Very good.

Would you not admit that both the sections of this division have different degrees of truth, and that the copy is to the original as the sphere of opinion is to the sphere of knowledge?

Most undoubtedly.

Next proceed to consider the manner in which the sphere of the intellectual is to be divided.

In what manner?

Thus:—There are two subdivisions, in the lower of which the soul uses the figures given by the former division as images; the enquiry can only be hypothetical, and instead of going upwards to a principle descends to the other end; in the higher of the two, the soul passes out of hypotheses, and goes up to a principle which is above hypotheses, making no use of images as in the former case, but proceeding only in and through the ideas themselves.

I do not quite understand your meaning, he said.

Then I will try again; you will understand me better when I have made some preliminary remarks. You are aware that students of geometry, arithmetic, and the kindred sciences assume the odd and the even and the figures and three kinds of angles and the like in their several branches of science; these are their hypotheses, which they and every body are supposed to know, and therefore they do not deign to give any account of them either to themselves or others; but they begin with them, and go on until they arrive at last, and in a consistent manner, at their conclusion?

Yes, he said, I know.

And do you not know also that although they make use of the visible forms and reason about them, they are thinking not of these, but of the ideals which they resemble; not of the figures which they draw, but of the absolute square and the absolute diameter, and so on—the forms which they draw or make, and which have shadows and reflections in water of their own, are converted by them into images, but they are really seeking to behold the things themselves, which can only be seen with the eye of the mind?

That is true.

And of this kind I spoke as the intelligible, although in the search after it the soul is compelled to use hypotheses; not ascending to a first principle, because she is unable to rise above the region of hypothesis, but employing the objects of which the shadows below are resemblances in their turn as images, they having in relation to the shadows and reflections of them a greater distinctness, and therefore a higher value.

I understand, he said, that you are speaking of the province of geometry and the sister arts.

And when I speak of the other division of the intelligible, you will understand me to speak of that other sort of knowledge which reason herself attains by the power of dialectic, using the hypotheses not as first principles, but only as hypotheses—that is to say, as steps and points of departure into a world which is above hypotheses, in order that she may soar beyond them to the first principle of the whole; and clinging to this and then to that which depends on this, by successive steps she descends again without the aid of any sensible object, from ideas, through ideas, and in ideas she ends.

I understand you, he replied; not perfectly, for you seem to me to be describing a task which is really tremendous; but, at any rate, I understand you to say that knowledge and being, which the science of dialectic contemplates, are clearer than the notions of the arts, as they are termed, which proceed from hypotheses only: these are also contemplated by the understanding, and not by the senses: yet, because they start from hypotheses and do not ascend to a principle, those who contemplate them appear to you not to exercise the higher reason upon them, although when a first principle is added to them they are cognizable by the higher reason. And the habit which is concerned with geometry and the cognate sciences I suppose that you would term understanding and not reason, as being intermediate between opinion and reason.

You have quite conceived my meaning, I said; and now, corresponding to these four divisions, let there be four faculties in the soul—reason answering to the highest, understanding to the second, faith (or conviction) to the third, and perception of shadows to the last—and let there be a scale of them, and let us suppose that the several faculties have clearness in the same degree that their objects have truth.

I understand, he replied, and give my assent, and accept your arrangement.

BOOK VII

And now, I said, let me show in a figure how far our nature is enlightened or unenlightened:—Behold! human beings living in an underground den, which has a mouth open towards the light and reaching all along the den; here they have been from their childhood, and have their legs and necks chained so that they cannot move, and can only see before them, being prevented by the chains from turning round their heads. Above and behind them a fire is blazing at a distance, and between the fire and the prisoners there is a raised way; and you will see, if you look, a low wall built along the way, like the screen which marionette players have in front of them, over which they show the puppets.

I see.

And do you see, I said, men passing along the wall carrying all sorts of vessels, and statues and figures of animals made of wood and stone and various materials, which appear over the wall? Some of them are talking, others silent.

You have shown me a strange image, and they are strange prisoners.

Like ourselves, I replied; and they see only their own shadows, or the shadows of one another, which the fire throws on the opposite wall of the cave?

True, he said; how could they see anything but the shadows if they were never allowed to move their heads?

And of the objects which are being carried in like manner they would only see the shadows?

Yes, he said.

And if they were able to converse with one another, would they not suppose that they were naming what was actually before them?

Very true.

And suppose further that the prison had an echo which came from the other side, would they not be sure to fancy when one of the passers-by spoke that the voice which they heard came from the passing shadow?

No question, he replied.

To them, I said, the truth would be literally nothing but the shadows of the images.

That is certain.

And now look again, and see what will naturally follow if the prisoners are released and disabused of their error. At first, when any of them is liberated and compelled suddenly to stand up and turn his neck round and walk and look towards the light, he will suffer sharp pains; the glare will distress him, and he will be unable to see the realities of which in his former state he had seen the shadows; and then conceive some one saying to him, that what he saw before was an illusion, but that now, when he is approaching nearer to being and his eye is turned towards more real existence, he has a clearer vision,—what will be his reply? And you may further imagine that his instructor is pointing to the objects as they pass and requiring him to name them,—will he not be perplexed? Will he not fancy that the shadows which he formerly saw are truer than the objects which are now shown to him?

Far truer.

And if he is compelled to look straight at the light, will he not have a pain in his eyes which will make him turn away to take refuge in the objects of vision which he can see, and which he will conceive to be in reality clearer than the things which are now being shown to him?

True, he said.

And suppose once more, that he is reluctantly dragged up a steep and rugged ascent, and held fast until he is forced into the presence of the sun himself, is he not likely to be pained and irritated? When he approaches the light his eyes will be dazzled, and he will not be able to see anything at all of what are now called realities.

Not all in a moment, he said.

He will require to grow accustomed to the sight of the upper world. And first he will see the shadows best, next the reflections of men and other objects in the water, and then the objects themselves; then he will gaze upon the light of the moon and the stars and the spangled heaven; and he will see the sky and the stars by night better than the sun or the light of the sun by day?

Certainly.

Last of all he will be able to see the sun, and not mere reflections of him in the water, but he will see him in his own proper place, and not in another; and he will contemplate him as he is.

Certainly.

He will then proceed to argue that this is he who gives the season and the years, and is the guardian of all that is in the visible world, and in a certain way the cause of all things which he and his fellows have been accustomed to behold?

Clearly, he said, he would first see the sun and then reason about him.

And when he remembered his old habitation, and the wisdom of the den and his fellow-prisoners, do you not suppose that he would felicitate himself on the change, and pity them?

Certainly, he would.

And if they were in the habit of conferring honours among themselves on those who were quickest to observe the passing shadows and to remark which of them went before, and which followed after, and which were together; and who were therefore best able to draw conclusions as to the future, do you think that he would care for such honours and glories, or envy the possessors of them? Would he not say with Homer,

'Better to be the poor servant of a poor master,'

and to endure anything, rather than think as they do and live after their manner?

Yes, he said, I think that he would rather suffer anything than entertain these false notions and live in this miserable manner.

Imagine once more, I said, such an one coming suddenly out of the sun to be replaced in his old situation; would he not be certain to have his eyes full of darkness?

To be sure, he said.

And if there were a contest, and he had to compete in measuring the shadows with the prisoners who had never moved out of the den, while his sight was still weak, and before his eyes had become steady (and the time which would be needed to acquire this new habit of sight might be very considerable), would he not be ridiculous? Men would say of him that up he went and down he came without his eyes; and that it was better not even to think of ascending; and if any one tried to loose another and lead him up to the light, let them only catch the offender, and they would put him to death.

No question, he said.

This entire allegory, I said, you may now append, dear Glaucon, to the previous argument; the prison-house is the world of sight, the light of the fire is the sun, and you will not misapprehend me if you interpret the journey upwards to be the ascent of the soul into the intellectual world according to my poor belief, which, at your desire, I have expressed—whether rightly or wrongly God knows. But, whether true or false, my opinion is that in the world of knowledge the idea of good appears last of all, and is seen only with an effort; and, when seen, is also inferred to be the universal author of all things beautiful and right, parent of light and of the lord of light in this visible world, and the immediate source of reason and truth in the intellectual; and that this is the power upon which he who would act rationally either in public or private life must have his eye fixed.

I agree, he said, as far as I am able to understand you.

Moreover, I said, you must not wonder that those who attain to this beatific vision are unwilling to descend to human affairs; for their souls are ever hastening into the upper world where they desire to dwell; which desire of theirs is very natural, if our allegory may be trusted.

Yes, very natural.

And is there anything surprising in one who passes from divine contemplations to the evil state of man, misbehaving himself in a ridiculous manner; if, while his eyes are blinking and before he has become accustomed to the surrounding darkness, he is compelled to fight in courts of law, or in other places, about the images or the shadows of images of justice, and is endeavouring to meet the conceptions of those who have never yet seen absolute justice?

Anything but surprising, he replied.

Any one who has common sense will remember that the bewilderments of the eyes are of two kinds, and arise from two causes, either from coming out of the light or from going into the light, which is true of the mind's eye, quite as much as of th bodily eye; and he who remembers this when he sees any one whose vision is perplexe and weak, will not be too ready to laugh; he will first ask whether that soul of ma has come out of the brighter life, and is unable to see because unaccustomed to th dark, or having turned from darkness to the day is dazzled by excess of light. And h will count the one happy in his condition and state of being, and he will pity th other; or, if he have a mind to laugh at the soul which comes from below into th light, there will be more reason in this than in the laugh which greets him wh returns from above out of the light into the den.

That, he said, is a very just distinction.

But then, if I am right, certain professors of education must be wrong when the say that they can put a knowledge into the soul which was not there before, like sigh into blind eyes.

They undoubtedly say this, he replied.

Whereas, our argument shows that the power and capacity of learning exists i the soul already; and that just as the eye was unable to turn from darkness to ligh without the whole body, so too the instrument of knowledge can only by the movemen of the whole soul be turned from the world of becoming into that of being, and lear by degrees to endure the sight of being, and of the brightest and best of being, o in other words, of the good.

Very true.

And must there not be some art which will effect conversion in the easiest an quickest manner; not implanting the faculty of sight, for that exists already, but ha been turned in the wrong direction, and is looking away from the truth?

Yes, he said, such an art may be presumed.

And whereas the other so-called virtues of the soul seem to be akin to bodil qualities, for even when they are not originally innate they can be implanted later b habit and exercise, the virtue of wisdom more than anything else contains a divin element which always remains, and by this conversion is rendered useful and profitable or, on the other hand, hurtful and useless. Did you never observe the narrow intel ligence flashing from the keen eye of a clever rogue—how eager he is, how clearly hi paltry soul sees the way to his end; he is the reverse of blind, but his keen eye-sigh is forced into the service of evil, and he is mischievous in proportion to his cleverness

Very true, he said.

But what if there had been a circumcision of such natures in the days of thei youth; and they had been severed from those sensual pleasures, such as eating an drinking, which, like leaden weights, were attached to them at their birth, and whic drag them down and turn the vision of their souls upon the things that are below— if, I say, they had been released from these impediments and turned in the opposit direction, the very same faculty in them would have seen the truth as keenly as the see what their eyes are turned to now.

Very likely.

Yes, I said; and there is another thing which is likely, or rather a necessary inferenc from what has preceded, that neither the uneducated and uninformed of the truth nor yet those who never make an end of their education, will be able ministers o ꞩtate; not the former, because they have no single aim of duty which is the rule of .ll their actions, private as well as public; nor the latter, because they will not act at .ll except upon compulsion, fancying that they are already dwelling apart in the slands of the blest.

Very true, he replied.

Then, I said, the business of us who are the founders of the State will be to compel he best minds to attain that knowledge which we have already shown to be the ;reatest of all—they must continue to ascend until they arrive at the good; but when hey have ascended and seen enough we must not allow them to do as they do now.

What do you mean?

I mean that they remain in the upper world: but this must not be allowed; they nust be made to descend again among the prisoners in the den, and partake of their abours and honours, whether they are worth having or not.

But is not this unjust? he said; ought we to give them a worse life, when they night have a better?

You have again forgotten, my friend, I said, the intention of the legislator, who lid not aim at making any one class in the State happy above the rest; the happiness vas to be in the whole State, and he held the citizens together by persuasion and necessity, making them benefactors of the State, and therefore benefactors of one another; to this end he created them, not to please themselves, but to be his instruments n binding up the State.

True, he said, I had forgotten.

Observe, Glaucon, that there will be no injustice in compelling our philosophers to nave a care and providence of others; we shall explain to them that in other States, nen of their class are not obliged to share in the toils of politics: and this is reasonable, for they grow up at their own sweet will, and the government would rather not have hem. Being self-taught, they cannot be expected to show any gratitude for a culture which they have never received. But we have brought you into the world to be rulers of the hive, kings of yourselves and of the other citizens, and have educated you far better and more perfectly than they have been educated, and you are better able to share in the double duty. Wherefore each of you, when his turn comes, must go down to the general underground abode, and get the habit of seeing in the dark. When you have acquired the habit, you will see ten thousand times better than the inhabitants of the den, and you will know what the several images are, and what they represent, because you have seen the beautiful and just and good in their truth. And thus our State which is also yours will be a reality, and not a dream only, and will be administered in a spirit unlike that of other States, in which men fight with one another about shadows only and are distracted in the struggle for power, which in their eyes is a great good. Whereas the truth is that the State in which the rulers are most reluctant to govern is always the best and most quietly governed, and the State in which they are most eager, the worst.

Quite true, he replied.

And will our pupils, when they hear this, refuse to take their turn at the toils of State, when they are allowed to spend the greater part of their time with one another n the heavenly light?

Impossible, he answered; for they are just men, and the commands which we impose upon them are just; there can be no doubt that every one of them will take office as a stern necessity, and not after the fashion of our present rulers of State.

Yes, my friend, I said; and there lies the point. You must contrive for your future rulers another and a better life than that of a ruler, and then you may have a well-ordered State; for only in the State which offers this, will they rule who are truly rich, not in silver and gold, but in virtue and wisdom, which are the true blessings of life. Whereas if they go to the administration of public affairs, poor and hungering after their own private advantage, thinking that hence they are to snatch the chief good, order there can never be; for they will be fighting about office, and the civil and domestic broils which thus arise will be the ruin of the rulers themselves and of the whole State.

Most true, he replied.

And the only life which looks down upon the life of political ambition is that of true philosophy. Do you know of any other?

Indeed, I do not, he said.

And those who govern ought not to be lovers of the task? For, if they are, there will be rival lovers, and they will fight.

No question.

Who then are those whom we shall compel to be guardians? Surely they will be the men who are wisest about affairs of State, and by whom the State is best administered, and who at the same time have other honours and another and a better life than that of politics?

They are the men, and I will choose them, he replied.

❧ TIMAEUS

Plato

The Timaeus *is Plato's most unusual dialogue. In fact, it is hardly a dialogue at all. It begins as a continuation of* The Republic, *with Socrates summarizing what he had said there "yesterday," and reminding his guests that they had each promised to make a matching contribution to a "feast of reason." They decide that the next to speak should be Timaeus, an astronomer and statesman from Locris, in southern Italy. (His origin and interests indicate a connection with Pythagoras, the great philosopher and mathematician who had founded a kind of religious community in that area two centuries earlier, reflecting the influence of older religious ideas from the North and East.) Timaeus has "made the nature of the universe his special study," so he is eminently qualified to describe its origin and development in time, down to the creation of man. From there*

Critias, another guest, will take up the account, describing the heroic events of man's early history as narrated to him by his aged grandfather, who heard them from Solon, who in turn got the tale from the priests at Sais in Egypt, whose records go back before the beginning of Greece itself. (Once again the theme of ancient wisdom, in contrast to the dialectical inquiry of Socrates, is emphasized.)

Critias' story is given in a separate dialogue (called the Critias*), which has unfortunately come down to us incomplete. The entire account of Timaeus, however, of which the following excerpt constitutes about the first one-fourth, has survived intact, and was in fact the sole work by Plato to be preserved and read (in Latin translation) throughout the Dark Ages in Western Europe. As such, it is a document of incomparable historical importance. Until the recovery of the physical and metaphysical writings of Aristotle in the thirteenth century, the* Timaeus *served Roman and medieval students as an authoritative compendium of knowledge about the physical world, and was a basis for the researches of such men as Roger Bacon (see Vol. II, pages 257–258).*

This is ironic, because its significance to Plato himself was almost certainly quite different. Modern scholars have traced virtually every idea in the treatise to earlier religious writings, as far back as the ancient Babylonians and Egyptians. The opening invocation, the scope of the work, and the very conception of a genesis of all things, suggest comparison with the theogonies and cosmogonies of Hesiod, the Orphic writers, and the Babylonian "Hymn to Marduk," as well as with the first few chapters of the Book of Genesis (see pages 290–293). Even the emphases on astronomy, on mathematical proportions, on the conflict and blending of opposites, on the kinship of gods, men, and animals, and on the care of the soul as the highest duty of men (these last three ideas are developed in later sections of Timaeus' narrative) are characteristic of earlier religious thought, although at this time there were not yet any sharp distinctions between science, religion, and philosophy.

In this perspective, it is important to note Timaeus' insistence that his discourse is only a "likely story," since it is concerned with the world of change and becoming, in contrast to the realm of unchanging Forms about which alone true knowledge is possible. Perhaps Plato is here formulating the relationship between his own philosophy and Near Eastern religion. Medieval Christian thinkers likewise relegated such "physical" questions to second place, behind the revelations of Holy Scripture about eternal matters. In interpreting the Scriptures, however, they leaned heavily on works such as this one. In any case, it is fascinating to speculate on the significance of these ancient doctrines as seen by Plato, through whom they entered the Western tradition.

Critias Let me proceed to explain to you, Socrates, the order in which we have arranged our entertainment. Our intention is that Timaeus, who is the most of an astronomer among us, and has made the nature of the universe his special study, should speak first, beginning with the generation of the world and going down to the creation of man; next, I am to receive the men whom he has created, and of whom some will have profited by the excellent education which you have given them; and then, in accordance with the tale of Solon, and equally with his law, we will bring them into court and make them citizens, as if they were those very Athenians whom the sacred Egyptian record has recovered from oblivion, and thenceforward we will speak of them as Athenians and fellow citizens.

Socrates I see that I shall receive in my turn a perfect and splendid feast of reason. And now, Timaeus, you, I suppose, should speak next after duly calling up the gods.

Timaeus All men, Socrates, who have any degree or right feeling, at the beginning of every enterprise, whether small or great, always call upon God. And we, too, who are going to discourse of the nature of the universe, how created or how existing without creation, if we be not altogether out of our wits, must invoke the aid of gods and goddesses and pray that our words may be above all acceptable to them and in consequence to ourselves. Let this, then, be our invocation of the gods, to which I add an exhortation of myself to speak in such manner as will be most intelligible to you and will most accord with my own intent.

First then, in my judgment, we must make a distinction and ask, What is that which always is and has no becoming, and what is that which is always becoming and never is? That which is apprehended by intelligence and reason is always in the same state but that which is conceived by opinion with the help of sensation and without reason is always in a process of becoming and perishing and never really is. Now everything that becomes or is created must of necessity be created by some cause, for without a cause nothing can be created. The work of the creator, whenever he looks to the unchangeable and fashions the form and nature of his work after an unchangeable pattern, must necessarily be made fair and perfect but when he looks to the created only and uses a created pattern it is not fair or perfect. Was the heaven then or the world, whether called by this or by any other more appropriate name—assuming the name, I am asking a question which has to be asked at the beginning of an inquiry about anything—was the world, I say, always in existence and without beginning, or created, and had it a beginning? Created, I reply, being visible and tangible and having a body, and therefore sensible, and all sensible things are apprehended by opinion and sense, and are in a process of creation and created. Now that which is

***The Dialogues of Plato*, trans. B. Jowett (2 vols.; New York: Random House, Inc., 1937), II 12–28.**

reated must, as we affirm, of necessity be created by a cause. But the father and naker of all this universe is past finding out, and even if we found him, to tell of im to all men would be impossible. This question, however, we must ask about the vorld. Which of the patterns had the artificer in view when he made it—the pattern f the unchangeable or of that which is created? If the world be indeed fair and the rtificer good, it is manifest that he must have looked to that which is eternal, but f what cannot be said without blasphemy is true, then to the created pattern. Everyone vill see that he must have looked to the eternal, for the world is the fairest of creations nd he is the best of causes. And having been created in this way, the world has been ramed in the likeness of that which is apprehended by reason and mind and is nchangeable, and must therefore of necessity, if this is admitted, be a copy of omething. Now it is all-important that the beginning of everything should be ccording to nature. And in speaking of the copy and the original we may assume hat words are akin to the matter which they describe; when they relate to the lasting nd permanent and intelligible, they ought to be lasting and unalterable, and, as far s their nature allows, irrefutable and invincible—nothing less. But when they express nly the copy or likeness and not the eternal things themselves, they need only be ikely and analogous to the former words. As being is to becoming, so is truth to belief. f then, Socrates, amidst the many opinions about the gods and the generation of the niverse, we are not able to give notions which are altogether and in every respect xact and consistent with one another, do not be surprised. Enough if we adduce robabilities as likely as any others, for we must remember that I who am the speaker nd you who are the judges are only mortal men, and we ought to accept the tale vhich is probable and inquire no further.

Socrates Excellent, Timaeus, and we will do precisely as you bid us. The prelude s charming and is already accepted by us—may we beg of you to proceed to the strain?

Timaeus Let me tell you then why the creator made this world of generation. Ie was good, and the good can never have any jealousy of anything. And being free rom jealousy, he desired that all things should be as like himself as they could be. This is in the truest sense the origin of creation and of the world as we shall do well n believing on the testimony of wise men. God desired that all things should be ood and nothing bad, so far as this was attainable. Wherefore also finding the whole isible sphere not at rest, but moving in an irregular and disorderly fashion, out of isorder he brought order, considering that this was in every way better than the other. Now the deeds of the best could never be or have been other than the fairest, and the reator, reflecting on the things which are by nature visible, found that no unintelligent reature taken as a whole could ever be fairer than the intelligent taken as a whole, nd again that intelligence could not be present in anything which was devoid of soul. or which reason, when he was framing the universe, he put intelligence in soul, nd soul in body, that he might be the creator of a work which was by nature fairest nd best. On this wise, using the language of probability, we may say that the world ame into being—a living creature truly endowed with soul and intelligence by the rovidence of God.

This being supposed, let us proceed to the next stage. In the likeness of what animal id the creator make the world? It would be an unworthy thing to liken it to any ature which exists as a part only, for nothing can be beautiful which is like any imperfect thing. But let us suppose the world to be the very image of that whole of which all other animals both individually and in their tribes are portions. For the original of the universe contains in itself all intelligible beings, just as this world comprehends us and all other visible creatures. For the deity, intending to make this world like the fairest and most perfect of intelligible beings, framed one visible animal comprehending within itself all other animals of a kindred nature. Are we right in saying that there is one world, or that they are many and infinite? There must be one only if the created copy is to accord with the original. For that which includes all other intelligible creatures cannot have a second or companion; in that case there would be need of another living being which would include both, and of which they would be parts, and the likeness would be more truly said to resemble not them, but that other which included them. In order then that the world might be solitary, like the perfect animal, the creator made not two worlds or an infinite number of them, but there is and ever will be one only-begotten and created heaven.

Now that which is created is of necessity corporeal, and also visible and tangible. And nothing is visible where there is no fire, or tangible which has no solidity, and nothing is solid without earth. Wherefore also God in the beginning of creation made the body of the universe to consist of fire and earth. But two things cannot be rightly put together without a third; there must be some bond of union between them. And the fairest bond is that which makes the most complete fusion of itself and the things which it combines, and proportion is best adapted to effect such a union. For whenever in any three numbers, whether cube or square, there is a mean, which is to the last term what the first term is to it, and again, when the mean is to the first term as the last term is to the mean—then the mean becoming first and last and the first and last both becoming means, they will all of them of necessity come to be the same, and having become the same with one another will be all one. If the universal frame had been created a surface only and having no depth, a single mean would have sufficed to bind together itself and the other terms, but now, as the world must be solid, and solid bodies are always compacted not by one mean but by two, God placed water and air in the mean between fire and earth, and made them to have the same proportion so far as was possible—as fire is to air so is air to water, and as air is to water so is water to earth—and thus he bound and put together a visible and tangible heaven. And for these reasons, and out of such elements which are in number four, the body of the world was created, and it was harmonized by proportion, and therefore has the spirit of friendship, and having been reconciled to itself, it was indissoluble by the hand of any other than the framer.

Now the creation took up the whole of each of the four elements, for the creator compounded the world out of all the fire and all the water and all the air and all the earth, leaving no part of any of them nor any power of them outside. His intention was, in the first place, that the animal should be as far as possible a perfect whole and of perfect parts, secondly, that it should be one, leaving no remnants out of which another such world might be created, and also that it should be free from old age and unaffected by disease. Considering that if heat and cold and other powerful forces surround composite bodies and attack them from without, they decompose them before their time, and by bringing diseases and old age upon them make them waste away—

for this cause and on these grounds he made the world one whole, having every part entire, and being therefore perfect and not liable to old age and disease. And he gave to the world the figure which was suitable and also natural. Now to the animal which was to comprehend all animals, that figure would be suitable which comprehends within itself all other figures. Wherefore he made the world in the form of a globe, round as from a lathe, having its extremes in every direction equidistant from the center, the most perfect and the most like itself of all figures, for he considered that the like is infinitely fairer than the unlike. This he finished off, making the surface smooth all around for many reasons—in the first place, because the loving being had no need of eyes when there was nothing remaining outside him to be seen, nor of ears when there was nothing to be heard, and there was no surrounding atmosphere to be breathed, nor would there have been any use of organs by the help of which he might receive his food or get rid of what he had already digested, since there was nothing which went from him or came into him, for there was nothing besides him. Of design he was created thus—his own waste providing his own food, and all that he did or suffered taking place in and by himself. For the creator conceived that a being which was self sufficient would be far more excellent than one which lacked anything, and, as he had no need to take anything or defend himself against anyone, the creator did not think it necessary to bestow upon him hands, nor had he any need of feet, nor of the whole apparatus of walking. But the movement suited to his spherical form was assigned to him, being of all the seven that which is most appropriate to mind and intelligence and he was made to move in the same manner and on the same spot, within his own limits revolving in a circle. All the other six motions were taken away from him, and he was made not to partake of their deviations. And as this circular movement required no feet, the universe was created without legs and without feet.

Such was the whole plan of the eternal God about the god that was to be; he made it smooth and even, having a surface in every direction equidistant from the center, a body entire and perfect, and formed out of perfect bodies. And in the center he put the soul, which he diffused throughout the body, making it also to be the exterior environment of it, and he made the universe a circle moving in a circle, one and solitary, yet by reason of its excellence able to converse with itself, and needing no other friendship or acquaintance. Having these purposes in view he created the world a blessed god.

Now God did not make the soul after the body, although we are speaking of them in this order, for when he put them together he would never have allowed that the elder should be ruled by the younger, but this is a random manner of speaking which we have, because somehow we ourselves too are very much under the dominion of chance. Whereas he made the soul in origin and excellence prior to and older than the body, to be the ruler and mistress, of whom the body was to be the subject. And he made her out of the following elements and on this wise. From the being which is indivisible and unchangeable, and from that kind of being which is distributed among bodies, he compounded a third and intermediate kind of being. He did likewise with the same and the different, blending together the indivisible kind of each with that which is portioned out in bodies. Then, taking the three new elements, he mingled them all into one form, compressing by force the reluctant and unsociable nature o the different into the same. When he had mingled them with the intermediate kind o being and out of three made one, he again divided this whole into as many portion as was fitting, each portion being a compound of the same, the different, and being And he proceeded to divide after this manner. First of all, he took away one part o the whole [1], and then he separated a second part which was double the first [2] and then he took away a third part which was half as much again as the second an three times as much as the first [3], and then he took a fourth part which was twic as much as the second [4], and a fifth part which as three times the third [9], and sixth part which was eight times the first [8], and a seventh part which was twenty seven times the first [27]. After this he filled up the double intervals [that is, betwee 1, 2, 4, 8] and the triple [that is, between 1, 3, 9, 27], cutting off yet other portion from the mixture and placing them in the intervals, so that in each interval there wer two kinds of means, the one exceeding and exceeded by equal parts of its extreme [as for example, 1, $4/3$, 2, in which the mean $4/3$ is one third of 1 more than 1, an one third of 2 less than 2], the other being that kind of mean which exceeds and i exceeded by an equal number. Where there were intervals of $3/2$ and of $4/3$ and of $9/8$ made by the connecting terms in the former intervals, he filled up all the intervals o $4/3$ with the interval of $9/8$, leaving a fraction over, and the interval which this fractio expressed was in the ratio of 256 to 243. And thus the whole mixture out of which h cut these portions was all exhausted by him. This entire compound he divided length wise into two parts which he joined to one another at the center like the letter X, an bent them into a circular form, connecting them with themselves and each other a the point opposite to their original meeting point, and, comprehending them in uniform revolution upon the same axis, he made the one the outer and the othe the inner circle. Now the motion of the outer circle he called the motion of the same and the motion of the inner circle the motion of the other or diverse. The motion o the same he carried round by the side to the right, and the motion of the divers diagonally to the left. And he gave dominion to the motion of the same and like for that he left single and undivided, but the inner motion he divided in six place and made seven unequal circles having their intervals in ratios of two and three, thre of each, and bade the orbits proceed in a direction opposite to one another. And thre [sun, Mercury, Venus] he made to move with equal swiftness, and the remaining fou [moon, Saturn, Mars, Jupiter] to move with unequal swiftness to the three and to on another, but in due proportion.

Now when the creator had framed the soul according to his will, he formed withi her the corporeal universe, and brought the two together and united them center t center. The soul, interfused everywhere from the center to the circumference of heaven of which also she is the external envelopment, herself turning in herself, began divine beginning of never-ceasing and rational life enduring throughout all time. Th body of heaven is visible, but the soul is invisible and partakes of reason and harmony and, being made by the best of intellectual and everlasting natures, is the best of thing created. And because she is composed of the same and of the different and of bein these three, and is divided and united in due proportion, and in her revolution returns upon herself, the soul, when touching anything which has being, whethe lispersed in parts or undivided, is stirred through all her powers to declare the ;ameness or difference of that thing and some other, and to what individuals are elated, and by what affected, and in what way and how and when, both in the world of generation and in the world of immutable being. And when reason, which works vith equal truth, whether she be in the circle of the diverse or of the same—in voiceess silence holding her onward course in the sphere of the self-moved—when reason, say, is hovering around the sensible world and when the circle of the diverse also noving truly imparts the intimations of sense to the whole soul, then arise opinions ınd beliefs sure and certain. But when reason is concerned with the rational, and the ircle of the same moving smoothly declares it, then intelligence and knowledge are necessarily achieved. And if anyone affirms that in which these two are found to be other than the soul, he will say the very opposite of the truth.

When the father and creator saw the creature which he had made moving and iving, the created image of the eternal gods, he rejoiced, and in his joy determined o make the copy still more like the original, and as this was an eternal living being, ne sought to make the universe eternal, so far as might be. Now the nature of the deal being was everlasting, but to bestow this attribute in its fullness upon a creature vas impossible. Wherefore he resolved to have a moving image of eternity, and when ne set in order the heaven, he made this image eternal but moving according to ıumber, while eternity itself rests in unity, and this image we call time. For there vere no days and nights and months and years before the heaven was created, but vhen he constructed the heaven he created them also. They are all parts of time, and he past and future are created species of time, which we unconsciously but wrongly ransfer to eternal being, for we say that it 'was,' or 'is,' or 'will be,' but the truth is hat 'is' alone is properly attributed to it, and that 'was' and 'will be' are only to be poken of becoming in time, for they are motions, but that which is immovably the ame forever cannot become older or younger by time, nor can it be said that it came nto being in the past, or has come into being now, or will come into being in the uture, nor is it subject at all to any of those states which affect moving and sensible hings and of which generation is the cause. These are the forms of time, which mitates eternity and revolves according to a law of number. Moreover, when we ay that what has become *is* become and what becomes *is* becoming, and that what vill become *is* about to become and that the nonexistent *is* nonexistent—all these are naccurate modes of expression. But perhaps this whole subject will be more suitably liscussed on some other occasion.

Time, then, and the heaven came into being at the same instant in order that, naving been created together, if ever there was to be a dissolution of them, they might oe dissolved together. It was framed after the pattern of the eternal nature—that it night resemble this as far as was possible, for the pattern exists from eternity, and the reated heaven has been and is and will be in all time. Such was the mind and thought of God in the creation of time. The sun and moon and five other stars, which are alled the planets, were created by him in order to distinguish and preserve the numbers of time, and when he had made their several bodies, he placed them in the orbits in vhich the circle of the other was revolving—in seven orbits seven stars. First, there vas the moon in the orbit nearest the earth, and the next the sun, in the second orbit above the earth; then came the morning star and the star said to be sacred to Hermes, moving in orbits which have an equal swiftness with the sun, but in an opposite direction, and this is the reason why the sun and Hermes and Lucifer regularly overtake and are overtaken by each other. To enumerate the places which he assigned to the other stars and to give all the reasons why he assigned them, although a secondary matter, would give more trouble than the primary. These things at some future time, when we are at leisure, may have the consideration which they deserve, but not at present.

Now, when each of the stars which were necessary to the creation of time had come to its proper orbit, and they had become living creatures having bodies fastened by vital chains, and learned their appointed task—moving in the motion of the diverse, which is diagonal and passes through and is governed by the motion of the same—they revolved, some in a larger and some in a lesser orbit, those which had the lesser orbit revolving faster, and those which had the larger more slowly. Now by reason of the motion of the same, those which revolved fastest appeared to be overtaken by those which moved slower although they really overtook them, for the motion of the same made them all turn in a spiral, and, because some went one way and some another, that which receded most slowly from the sphere of the same, which was the swiftest, appeared to follow it most nearly. That there might be some visible measure of their relative swiftness and slowness as they proceeded in their eight courses, God lighted a fire, which we now call the sun, in the second from the earth of these orbits, that it might give light to the whole of heaven, and that the animals, as many as nature intended, might participate in number, learning arithmetic from the revolution of the same and the like. Thus, then, and for this reason the night and the day were created, being the period of the one most intelligent revolution. And the month is accomplished when the moon has completed her orbit and overtaken the sun, and the year when the sun has completed his own orbit. Mankind, with hardly an exception, have not remarked the periods of the other stars, and they have no name for them, and do not measure them against one another by the help of number, and hence they can scarcely be said to know that their wanderings, being of vast number and admirable for their variety, make up time. And yet there is no difficulty in seeing that the perfect number of time fulfills the perfect year when all the eight revolutions, having their relative degrees of swiftness, are accomplished together and attain their completion at the same time, measured by the rotation of the same and equally moving. After this manner, and for these reasons, came into being such of the stars as in their heavenly progress received reversals of motion, to the end that the created heaven might be as like as possible to the perfect and intelligible animal, by imitation of its eternal nature.

Thus far and until the birth of time the created universe was made in the likeness of the original, but inasmuch as all animals were not yet comprehended therein, it was still unlike. Therefore, the creator proceeded to fashion it after the nature of the pattern in this remaining point. Now as in the ideal animal the mind perceives ideas or species of a certain nature and number, he thought that this created animal ought to have species of a like nature and number. There are four such. One of them is the heavenly race of the gods; another, the race of birds whose way is in the air; the third, the watery species; and the fourth, the pedestrian and land creatures. Of the heavenly and divine, he created the greater part out of fire, that they might be the brightest of all things and fairest to behold, and he fashioned them after the likeness of the universe in the figure of a circle, and made them follow the intelligent motion of the supreme, distributing them over the whole circumference of heaven, which was to be a true cosmos or glorious world spangled with them all over. And he gave to each of them two movements—the first, a movement on the same spot after the same manner, whereby they ever continue to think consistently the same thoughts about the same things, in the same respect; the second, a forward movement, in which they are controlled by the revolution of the same and the like—but by the other five motions they were unaffected, in order that each of them might attain the highest perfection. And for this reason the fixed stars were created, to be divine and eternal animals, ever abiding and revolving after the same manner and on the same spot, and the other stars which reverse their motion and are subject to deviations of this kind were created in the manner already described. The earth, which is our nurse, clinging around the pole which is extended through the universe, he framed to be the guardian and artificer of night and day, first and eldest of gods that are in the interior of heaven. Vain would be the attempt to tell all the figures of them circling as in dance, and their juxtapositions, and the return of them in their revolutions upon themselves, and their approximations, and to say which of these deities in their conjunctions meet, and which of them are in opposition, and in what order they get behind and before one another, and when they are severally eclipsed to our sight and again reappear, sending terrors and intimations of the future to those who cannot calculate their movements—to attempt to tell of all this without a visible representation of the heavenly system would be labor in vain. Enough on this head, and now let what we have said about the nature of the created and visible gods have an end.

To know or tell the origin of the other divinities is beyond us, and we must accept the traditions of the men of old time who affirm themselves to be the offspring of the gods—that is what they say—and they must surely have known their own ancestors. How can we doubt the word of the children of the gods? Although they give no probable or certain proofs, still, as they declare that they are speaking of what took place in their own family, we must conform to custom and believe them. In this manner, then, according to them, the genealogy of these gods is to be received and set forth.

Oceanus and Tethys were the children of Earth and Heaven, and from these sprang Phorcys and Cronus and Rhea, and all that generation, and from Cronus and Rhea sprang Zeus and Hera, and all those who are said to be their brethren, and others who were the children of these.*

Now, when all of them, both those who visibly appear in their revolutions as well as those other gods who are of a more retiring nature, had come into being, the creator of the universe addressed them in these words. Gods, children of gods, who are my works and of whom I am the artificer and father, my creations are indissoluble, if so I will. All that is bound may be undone, but only an evil being would wish to undo that which is harmonious and happy. Wherefore, since ye are but creatures, ye

* [These lines are taken from the *Theogony* by Hesiod, a Greek poet who, together with Homer, was accepted by most Greeks as authoritative on religious matters. Plato is obviously making fun of such beliefs. (*Ed.*)]

are not altogether immortal and indissoluble, but ye shall certainly not be dissolved, nor be liable to the fate of death, having in my will a greater and mightier bond than those with which ye were bound at the time of your birth. And now listen to my instructions. Three tribes of mortal beings remain to be created—without them the universe will be incomplete, for it will not contain every kind of animal which it ought to contain, if it is to be perfect. On the other hand, if they were created by me and received life at my hands, they would be on an equality with the gods. In order then that they may be mortal, and that this universe may be truly universal, do ye, according to your natures, betake yourselves to the formation of animals, imitating the power which was shown by me in creating you. The part of them worthy of the name immortal, which is called divine and is the guiding principle of those who are willing to follow justice and you—of that divine part I will myself sow the seed, and having made a beginning, I will hand the work over to you. And do ye then interweave the mortal with the immortal and make and beget living creatures, and give them food and make them to grow, and receive them again in death.

Thus he spoke, and once more into the cup in which he had previously mingled the soul of the universe he poured the remains of the elements, and mingled them in much the same manner; they were not, however, pure as before, but diluted to the second and third degree. And having made it he divided the whole mixture into souls equal in number to the stars and assigned each soul to a star, and having there placed them as in a chariot he showed them the nature of the universe and declared to them the laws of destiny, according to which their first birth would be one and the same for all—no one should suffer a disadvantage at his hands. They were to be sown in the instruments of time severally adapted to them, and to come forth the most religious of animals, and as human nature was of two kinds, the superior race was of such and such a character, and would hereafter be called man. Now, when they should be implanted in bodies by necessity and be always gaining or losing some part of their bodily substance, then, in the first place, it would be necessary that they should all have in them one and the same faculty of sensation, arising out of irresistible impressions; in the second place, they must have love, in which pleasure and pain mingle—also fear and anger, and the feelings which are akin or opposite to them. If they conquered these they would live righteously, and if they were conquered by them, unrighteously. He who lived well during his appointed time was to return and dwell in his native star, and there he would have a blessed and congenial existence. But if he failed in attaining this, at the second birth he would pass into a woman, and if, when in that state of being, he did not desist from evil, he would continually be changed into some brute who resembled him in the evil nature which he had acquired, and would not cease from his toils and transformations until he helped the revolution of the same and the like within him to draw in its train the turbulent mob of later accretions made up of fire and air and water and earth, and by this victory of reason over the irrational returned to the form of his first and better state. Having given all these laws to his creatures, that he might be guiltless of future evil in any of them, the creator sowed some of them in the earth, and some in the moon, and some in the other instruments of time. And when he had sown them he committed to the younger gods the fashioning of their mortal bodies, and desired them to furnish what was still lacking to the human soul, and having made all the suitable additions, to rule over them, and to pilot the mortal animal in the best and wisest manner which they could and avert from him all but self-inflicted evils.

When the creator had made all these ordinances he remained in his own accustomed nature, and his children heard and were obedient to their father's word, and receiving from him the immortal principle of a mortal creature, in imitation of their own creator they borrowed portions of fire and earth and water and air from the world, which were hereafter to be restored—these they took and welded them together, not with the indissoluble chains by which they were themselves bound, but with little pegs too small to be visible, making up out of all the four elements each separate body, and fastening the courses of the immortal soul in a body which was in a state of perpetual influx and efflux. Now these courses, detained as in a vast river, neither overcame nor were overcome, but were hurrying and hurried to and fro, so that the whole animal was moved and progressed, irregularly however and irrationally and anyhow, in all the six directions of motion, wandering backward and forward, and right and left, and up and down, and in all the six directions. For great as was the advancing and retiring flood which provided nourishment, the affections produced by external contact caused still greater tumult—when the body of anyone met and came into collision with some external fire or with the solid earth or the gliding waters, or was caught in the tempest borne on the air—and the motions produced by any of these impulses were carried through the body to the soul. All such motions have consequently received the general name of 'sensations,' which they still retain. And they did in fact at that time create a very great and mighty movement; uniting with the ever-flowing stream in stirring up and violently shaking the courses of the soul, they completely stopped the revolution of the same by their opposing current and hindered it from predominating and advancing, and they so disturbed the nature of the other or diverse that the three double intervals [that is, between 1, 2, 4, 8] and the three triple intervals [that is, between 1, 3, 9, 27], together with the mean terms and connecting links which are expressed by the ratios of 3:2 and 4:3 and of 9:8—these, although they cannot be wholly undone except by him who united them, were twisted by them in all sorts of ways, and the circles were broken and disordered in every possible manner, so that when they moved they were tumbling to pieces and moved irrationally, at one time in a reverse direction, and then again obliquely, and then upside down, as you might imagine a person who is upside down and has his head leaning upon the ground and his feet up against something in the air, and when he is in such a position, both he and the spectator fancy that the right of either is his left, and the left right. If, when powerfully experiencing these and similar effects, the revolutions of the soul come in contact with some external thing, either of the class of the same or of the other, they speak of the same or of the other in a manner the very opposite of the truth, and they become false and foolish, and there is no course or revolution in them which has a guiding or directing power. And if again any sensations enter in violently from without and drag after them the whole vessel of the soul, then the courses of the soul, though they seem to conquer, are really conquered.

And by reason of all these affections, the soul, when incased in a mortal body, now, as in the beginning, is at first without intelligence, but when the flood of growth and nutriment abates and the courses of the soul, calming down, go their own way and become steadier as time goes on, then the several circles return to their natural form and their revolutions are corrected, and they call the same and the other by their right names and make the possessor of them to become a rational being. And if these combine in him with any true nurture or education, he attains the fullness and health of the perfect man, and escapes the worst disease of all, but if he neglects education he walks lame to the end of his life and returns imperfect and good for nothing to the world below. This, however, is a later stage; at present we must treat more exactly the subject before us, which involves a preliminary inquiry into the generation of the body and its members, and how the soul was created—for what reason and by what providence of the gods—and holding fast to probability we must pursue our way.

First, then, the gods, imitating the spherical shape of the universe, enclosed the two divine courses in a spherical body, that, namely, which we now term the head, being the most divine part of us and the lord of all that is in us; to this the gods, when they put together the body, gave all the other members to be servants, considering that it must partake of every sort of motion. In order then that it might not tumble about among the high and deep places of the earth, but might be able to get over the one and out of the other, they provided the body to be its vehicle and means of locomotion, which consequently had length and was furnished with four limbs extended and flexible. These God contrived to be instruments of locomotion with which it might take hold and find support, and so be able to pass through all places, carrying on high the dwelling place of the most sacred and divine part of us. Such was the origin of legs and hands, which for this reason were attached to every man, and the gods, deeming the front part of man to be more honorable and more fit to command than the hinder part, made us to move mostly in a forward direction. Wherefore man must needs have his front part unlike and distinguished from the rest of his body. And so in the vessel of the head, they first of all put a face in which they inserted organs to minister in all things to the providence of the soul, and they appointed this part, which has authority, to be the natural front. And of the organs they first contrived the eyes to give light, and the principle according to which they were inserted was as follows. So much of fire as would not burn, but gave a gentle light, they formed into a substance akin to the light of everyday life, and the pure fire which is within us and related thereto they made to flow through the eyes in a stream smooth and dense, compressing the whole eye and especially the center part, so that it kept out everything of a coarser nature and allowed to pass only this pure element. When the light of day surrounds the stream of vision, then like falls upon like, and they coalesce, and one body is formed by natural affinity in the line of vision, wherever the light that falls from within meets with an external object. And the whole stream of vision, being similarly affected in virtue of similarity, diffuses the motions of what it touches or what touches it over the whole body, until they reach the soul, causing that perception which we call sight. But when night comes on and the external and kindred fire departs, then the stream of vision is cut off, for going forth to an unlike element it is changed and extinguished, being no longer of one nature with the surrounding atmosphere which is now deprived of fire, and so the eye no longer sees, and we feel disposed to sleep. For when the eyelids, which the gods invented for the preservation of sight, are closed, they keep in the internal fire, and the power of the fire diffuses and equalizes the inward motions; when they are equalized, there is rest, and when the rest is profound, sleep comes over us scarce disturbed by dreams, but where any greater motions still remain, according to their nature and locality, they engender within us corresponding visions in dreams, which are remembered by us when we awaken to the external world. And now there is no longer any difficulty in understanding the creation of images in mirrors and all smooth and bright surfaces. For from the communion of the internal and external fires, and again from the union of them and their numerous transformations when they meet in the mirror, all these appearances of necessity arise when the fire from the face coalesces with the fire from the eye on the bright and smooth surface. And right appears left and left right, because the visual rays come into contact with the rays emitted by the object in a manner contrary to the usual mode of meeting. But the right appears right, and the left left, when the position of one of the two concurring lights is reversed, and this happens when the mirror is concave and its smooth surface repels the right stream of vision to the left side, and the left to the right. Or if the mirror be turned vertically, then the concavity makes the countenance appear to be all upside down, and the lower rays are driven upward and the upper downward.

All these are to be reckoned among the second and co-operative causes which God, carrying into execution the idea of the best as far as possible, uses as his ministers. They are thought by most men not to be the second, but the prime causes of all things, because they freeze and heat, and contract and dilate, and the like. But they are not so, for they are incapable of reason or intellect; the only being which can properly have mind is the invisible soul, whereas fire and water, and earth and air, are all of them visible bodies. The lover of intellect and knowledge ought to explore causes of intelligent nature first of all, and, secondly, of those things which, being moved by others, are compelled to move others. And this is what we too must do. Both kinds of causes should be acknowledged by us, but a distinction should be made between those which are endowed with mind and are the workers of things fair and good, and those which are deprived of intelligence and always produce chance effects without order or design. Of the second or co-operative causes of sight, which help to give to the eyes the power which they now possess, enough has been said. I will therefore now proceed to speak of the higher use and purpose for which God has given them to us. The sight in my opinion is the source of the greatest benefit to us, for had we never seen the stars and the sun and the heaven, none of the words which we have spoken about the universe would ever have been uttered. But now the sight of day and night, and the months and the revolutions of the years have created number and have given us a conception of time, and the power of inquiring about the nature of the universe. And from this source we have derived philosophy, than which no greater good ever was or will be given by the gods to mortal man. This is the greatest boon of sight, and of the lesser benefits why should I speak? Even the ordinary man if he were deprived of them would bewail his loss, but in vain. Thus much let me say however. God invented and gave us sight to the end that we might behold the courses of intelligence in the heaven, and apply them to the courses of our own intelligence which are akin to them, the unperturbed to the perturbed, and that we, learning them and partaking

of the natural truth of reason, might imitate the absolutely unerring courses of Go
and regulate our own vagaries. The same may be affirmed of speech and hearing. The
have been given by the gods to the same end and for a like reason. For this is th
principal end of speech, whereto it most contributes. Moreover, so much of musi
as is adapted to the sound of the voice and to the sense of hearing is granted t
us for the sake of harmony. And harmony, which has motions akin to the revolution
of our souls, is not regarded by the intelligent votary of the Muses as given by the
with a view to irrational pleasure, which is deemed to be the purpose of it in our day
but as meant to correct any discord which may have arisen in the courses of the soul
and to be our ally in bringing her into harmony and agreement with herself, an
rhythm too was given by them for the same reason, on account of the irregular an
graceless ways which prevail among mankind generally, and to help us against them

PARTS OF ANIMALS

Aristotle

The contribution of Aristotle (384–322 B.C.*) to our tradition is second only to that of Plato, his teacher. Dante called him "the master of those wh know," and in the Middle Ages he was known to Arabs and Christians alike as simply "The Philosopher." In modern terminology, however, it might more fittingly be "The Scientist," since his great achievement was to create systematic bodies of knowledge where only isolated facts and scattered insights had existed before. If Herodotus is called the Fathe of History, Aristotle should be called the Father of Physics, Biology, Psychology, Political Science, Logic, Rhetoric, Aesthetics, Ethics, and Metaphysics. Unlike Plato's Academy, which seems to have been no mor than a community of friends, Aristotle's Lyceum was an institute of scientific research.*

Parts of Animals *might also have been called "Comparative Anatomy"; it is a treatise on the structure of animals, stressing the way in which their various organs must function harmoniously in order to sustain life. We can see this idea of harmony of functions in Plato, and even earlier; but for Aristotle it becomes a principle guiding the painstaking collection of data about all kinds of animals. The introduction to the treatise, which appears here, sets forth the principles and methodology that must govern this branch of science, according to its particular subjec matter. Thus Aristotle is at pains to establish that* living *things cannot be studied as if they were lifeless—in modern terms, as simple collections of atoms and molecules—because the "life principle" (the "soul," in ancien*

Greek) is exactly what makes them the sorts of things they are: animals. The theory presented here, of various kinds of cause and necessity, dominated all the sciences until the seventeenth century, and it is still a live issue in discussions of scientific method today.

BOOK I

Chapter 1

There are, as it seems, two ways in which a person may be competent in respect of any study or investigation, whether it be a noble one or a humble: he may have either what can rightly be called a scientific knowledge of the subject; or he may have what is roughly described as an educated person's competence, and therefore be able to judge correctly which parts of an exposition are satisfactory and which are not. That, in fact, is the sort of person we take the "man of general education" to be; his "education" consists in the ability to do this. In this case, however, we expect to find in the one individual the ability to judge of almost all subjects, whereas in the other case the ability is confined to some special science; for of course it is possible to possess this ability for a limited field only. Hence it is clear that in the investigation of Nature, or Natural science, as in every other, there must first of all be certain defined rules by which the acceptability of the method of exposition may be tested, apart from whether the statements made represent the truth or do not. I mean, for instance, should we take each single species severally by turn (such as Man, or Lion, or Ox, or whatever it may be), and define what we have to say about it, in and by itself; or should we first establish as our basis the attributes that are common to all of them because of some common character which they possess?—there being many attributes which are identical though they occur in many groups which differ among themselves, *e.g.* sleep, respiration, growth, decay, death, together with those other remaining affections and conditions which are of a similar kind. I raise this, for at present discussion of these matters is an obscure business, lacking any definite scheme. However, thus much is plain, that even if we discuss them species by species, we shall be giving the same descriptions many times over for many different animals, since every one of the attributes I mentioned occurs in horses and dogs and human beings alike. Thus, if our description proceeds by taking the attributes for every species, we shall be obliged to describe the same ones many times over, namely, those which although they occur in different species of animals are themselves identical and present no difference whatever. Very likely, too, there are other attributes, which, though they come under the same general head, exhibit specific differences;—for example, the locomotion of animals: of which there are plainly more species than one—*e.g.* flight, swimming, walking, creeping.

Aristotle, *Parts of Animals*, trans. A. L. Peck (Cambridge, Mass.: Harvard University Press, Loeb Classical Library, 1961), pp. 53–79, 97–103.

Therefore we must make up our minds about the method of our investigation and decide whether we will consider first what the whole group has in common, and afterwards the specific peculiarities; or begin straightway with the particular species. Hitherto this has not been definitely settled. And there is a further point which has not yet been decided: should the student of Nature follow the same sort of procedure as the mathematician follows in his astronomical expositions—that is to say, should he consider first of all the phenomena which occur in animals, and the parts of each of them, and having done that go on to state the reasons and the causes; or should he follow some other procedure? Furthermore, we see that there are more causes than one concerned in the formation of natural things: there is the Cause *for the sake of which* the thing is formed, and the Cause to which *the beginning of the motion* is due. Therefore another point for us to decide is which of these two Causes stands first and which comes second. Clearly the first is that which we call the "Final" Cause—that for the sake of which the thing is formed—since that is the *logos* of the thing—its rational ground, and the *logos* is always the principle for products of Nature as well as for those of Art. The physician or the builder sets before himself something quite definite—the one, health, apprehensible by the mind, the other, a house, apprehensible by the senses; and once he has got this, each of them can tell you the causes and the rational grounds for everything he does, and why it must be done as he does it. Yet the Final Cause (purpose) and the Good * is more fully present in the works of Nature than in the works of Art. And moreover the factor of Necessity is not present in all the works of Nature in a similar sense. Almost all philosophers endeavour to carry back their explanations to Necessity; but they omit to distinguish the various meanings of Necessity. There is "absolute" Necessity, which belongs to the eternal things; and there is "conditional" Necessity, which has to do with everything that is formed by the processes of Nature, as well as with the products of Art, such as houses and so forth. If a house, or any other End, is to be realized, it is necessary that such and such material shall be available; one thing must first be formed, and set in motion, and then another thing; and so on continually in the same manner up to the End, which is the Final Cause, for the sake of which every one of those things is formed and for which it exists. The things which are formed in Nature are in like case. . . .

We must also decide whether we are to discuss the processes by which each animal comes to be formed—which is what the earlier philosophers studied—or rather the animal as it actually is. Obviously there is a considerable difference between the two methods. I said earlier that we ought first to take the phenomena that are observed in each group, and then go on to state their causes. This applies just as much to the subject of the process of formation: here too we ought surely to begin with things as they are actually observed to be when completed. Even in building the fact is that the particular stages of the process come about because the Form of the house is such and such, rather than that the house is such and such because the process of its formation follows a particular course: the process is for the sake of the actual thing, the thing is not for the sake of the process. So Empedocles was wrong when he said that many of the characteristics which animals have are due to some accident in the

* [The word here translated "good" also meant "beautiful" and "fitting" in Greek. There is no precise equivalent in English for this most important concept. (*Ed.*)]

process of their formation, as when he accounts for the vertebrae of the backbone by saying "the fetus gets twisted and so the backbone is broken into pieces": he was unaware (*a*) that the seed which gives rise to the animal must to begin with have the appropriate specific character; and (*b*) that the producing agent was pre-existent: it was chronologically earlier as well as logically earlier: in other words, men are begotten by men, and therefore the process of the child's formation is what it is because its parent was a man. . . . So the best way of putting the matter would be to say that *because* the essence of man is what it is, *therefore* a man has such and such parts, since there cannot be a man without them. If we may not say this, then the nearest to it must do, viz. that there cannot be a man at all otherwise than with them, or, that is well that a man should have them. And upon this these considerations follow: *Because* man is such and such, *therefore* the process of his formation must of necessity be such and such and take place in such a manner; which is why first this part is formed, then that. And thus similarly with all the things that are constructed by Nature.

Now those who were the first to study Nature in the early days spent their time in trying to discover what the material principle or the material Cause was, and what it was like; they tried to find out how the Universe is formed out of it; what set the process going (Strife, it might be, or Friendship, Mind, or Spontaneity); assuming throughout that the underlying material had, by necessity, some definite nature: *e.g.* that the nature of Fire was hot, and light; of Earth, cold, and heavy. At any rate, that is how they actually explain the formation of the world-order. In a like manner they describe the formation of animals and plants, saying (*e.g.*) that the stomach and every kind of receptacle for food and for residue is formed by the water flowing in the body, and the nostril openings are forcibly made by the passage of the breath. Air and water, of course, according to them, are the material of which the body is made: they all say that Nature is composed of substances of this sort. Yet if man and the animals and their parts are products of Nature, then account must be taken of flesh, bone, blood, in fact of all the "uniform parts," and indeed of the "non-uniform parts" too, viz. face, hand, foot; and it must be explained how it comes to pass that each of these is characterized as it is, and by what force this is effected. It is not enough to state simply the substances out of which they are made, as "Out of fire," or "Out of earth." If we were describing a bed or any other like article, we should endeavour to describe the form of it rather than the matter (bronze, or wood)—or, at any rate, the matter, if described, would be described as belonging to the concrete whole. For example, "a bed" is a certain form in certain matter, or, alternatively, certain matter that has a certain form; so we should have to include its shape and the manner of its form in our description of it—because the "formal" nature is of more fundamental importance than the "material" nature.

If, then, each animal and each of its parts is what it is in virtue of its shape and its colour, what Democritus says will be correct, since that was apparently his view, if one understands him aright when he says that it is evident to everyone what "man" is like as touching his shape, for it is by his shape and his colour that a man may be told. Now a corpse has the same shape and fashion as a living body; and yet it is not a man. Again, a hand constituted in any and every manner, *e.g.*, a bronze or wooden one, is not a hand except in name; and the same applies to a physician depicted on canvas, or a flute carved in stone. None of these can perform the functions appropriate to the things that bear those names. Likewise, the eye or the hand (or any other part) of a corpse is not really an eye or a hand. Democritus's statement, therefore, needs to be qualified, or a carpenter might as well claim that a hand made of wood really was a hand. The physiologers,* however, when they describe the formation and the causes of the shape of animal bodies, talk in this selfsame vein. Suppose we ask the carver "By what agency was this hand fashioned?" Perhaps his answer will be "By my axe" or "By my auger," just as if we ask the physiologer "By what agency was this body fashioned?" he will say "By air" and "By earth." But of the two the craftsman will give a better answer, because he will not feel it is sufficient to say merely that a cavity was created here, or a level surface there, by a blow from his tool. He will state the reason on account of which, and the purpose for the sake of which, he made the strokes he did; and that will be, in order that the wood might finally be formed into this or that shape.

It must now be evident that the statements of the physiologers are unsatisfactory. We have to state how the animal is characterized, *i.e.,* what is the essence and character of the animal itself, as well as describing each of its parts; just as with the bed we have to state its Form.

Now it may be that the Form of any living creature is Soul,† or some part of Soul, or something that involves Soul. At any rate, when its Soul is gone, it is no longer a living creature, and none of its parts remains the same, except only in shape, just like the animals in the story that were turned into stone. If, then, this is really so, it is the business of the student of Natural science to inform himself concerning Soul, and to treat of it in his exposition; not, perhaps, in its entirety, but of that special part of it which causes the living creature to be such as it is. He must say what Soul, or that special part of Soul, is; and when he has said what its essence is, he must treat of the attributes which are attached to an essence of that character. This is especially necessary, because the term "nature" is used—rightly—in two senses: (*a*) meaning "matter," and (*b*) meaning "essence" (the latter including both the "moving" Cause and the "End"). It is, of course, in this latter sense that the entire Soul or some part of it is the "nature" of a living creature. Hence on this score especially it should be the duty of the student of Natural science to deal with Soul in preference to matter, inasmuch as it is the Soul that enables the matter to "be the nature" of an animal (that is, *potentially,* in the same way as a piece of wood "is" a bed or a stool) rather than the matter which enables the Soul to do so. . . .

Further, no abstraction can be studied by Natural science, because whatever Nature makes she makes to serve some purpose; for it is evident that, even as art is present in the objects produced by art, so in things themselves there is some principle or cause of a like sort, which came to us from the universe around us, just as our material constituents (the hot, the cold, etc.) did. Wherefore there is better reason for holding that the Heaven was brought into being by some such cause—if we may assume that

* [I.e., the early writers on "Nature" mentioned above. (*Ed.*)]
† [By "soul" the Greeks meant "life principle." (*Ed.*)]

it came into being at all—and that through that cause it continues to be, than for holding the same about the mortal things it contains—the animals; at any rate, there is much clearer evidence of definite ordering in the heavenly bodies than there is in us; for what is mortal bears the marks of change and chance. Nevertheless, there are those * who affirm that, while every living creature has been brought into being by Nature and remains in being thereby, the heaven in all its glory was constructed by mere chance and came to be spontaneously, although there is no evidence of chance or disorder in it. And whenever there is evidently an End towards which a motion goes forward unless something stands in its way, then we always assert that the motion has the End for its purpose. From this it is evident that something of the kind really exists—that, in fact, which we call "Nature," because in fact we do not find any chance creature being formed from a particular seed, but *A* comes from *a,* and *B* from *b;* nor does any chance seed come from any chance individual. Therefore the individual from which the seed comes is the source and the cause of that which comes out of the seed. The reason is, that these things are so arranged by Nature; at any rate, the offspring *grows* out of the seed. Nevertheless, logically prior to the seed stands that of which it is the seed, because the End is an actual thing, and the seed is but a formative process. But further, prior to both of them stands the creature out of which the seed comes. (Note that a seed is the seed "of" something in two senses—two quite distinct senses: it is the seed "of" that out of which it came—*e.g.* a horse—as well as "of" that which will arise out of itself—*e.g.* a mule). Again, the seed is something *by potentiality,* and we know what is the relation of potentiality to actuality.†. . .

It is, therefore, evident that of Causation there are two modes; and that in our treatise both of them must be described, or at least an attempt must be made to describe them; and that those who fail herein tell us practically nothing of any value about "Nature," for a thing's "nature" is much more its principle than is matter. (Indeed, in some places even Empedocles, being led and guided by Truth herself, stumbles upon this, and is forced to assert that it is the *logos* which is a thing's essence or nature. For instance, when he is explaining what Bone is, he says not that it is any one of the Elements,‡ or any two, or three, or even all of them, but that it is "the *logos* of the mixture" of the Elements. And it is clear that he would explain in the same way what Flesh and each of such parts is. Now the reason why earlier thinkers did not arrive at this method of procedure was that in their time there was no notion of "essence" and no way of defining "being." The first to touch upon it was Democritus; and he did so, not because he thought it necessary for the study of Nature, but because he was carried away by the subject in hand and could not avoid it. In Socrates' time an advance was made so far as the method was concerned; but at that time philosophers gave up the study of Nature and turned to the practical subject of "virtue" and to political science.) . . .

* [E.g., Democritus. (*Ed.*)]

† [*Viz.,* actuality is more fundamental than potentiality. Aristotle explains this in his *Metaphysics.* (*Ed.*)]

‡ [The "elements" were fire, air, earth, and water. Many educated Greeks of Aristotle's time accepted these as the four basic materials of which everything in the universe was composed. (*Ed.*)]

Chapter 5

Of the works of Nature there are, we hold, two kinds: those which are brought into being and perish, and those which are free from these processes throughout all ages. The latter are of the highest worth and are divine, but our opportunities for the study of them are somewhat scanty, since there is but little evidence available to our senses to enable us to consider them and all the things that we long to know about. We have better means of information, however, concerning the things that perish, that is to say, plants and animals, because we live among them; and anyone who will but take enough trouble can learn much concerning every one of their kinds. Yet each of the two groups has its attractiveness. For although our grasp of the eternal things is but slight, nevertheless the joy which it brings is, by reason of their excellence and worth, greater than that of knowing all things that are here below; just as the joy of a fleeting and partial glimpse of those whom we love is greater than that of an accurate view of other things, no matter how numerous or how great they are. But inasmuch as it is possible for us to obtain more and better information about things here on the earth, our knowledge of them has the advantage over the other; and moreover, because they are nearer to us and more akin to our Nature, they are able to make up some of their leeway as against the philosophy which contemplates the things that are divine. Of "things divine" we have already treated and have set down our views concerning them; * so it now remains to speak of animals and their Nature. So far as in us lies, we will not leave out any one of them, be it never so mean; for though there are animals which have no attractiveness for the senses, yet for the eye of science, for the student who is naturally of a philosophic spirit and can discern the causes of things, Nature which fashioned them provides joys which cannot be measured. If we study mere likenesses of these things and take pleasure in so doing, because then we are contemplating the painter's or the carver's Art which fashioned them, and yet fail to delight much more in studying the works of Nature themselves, though we have the ability to discern the actual causes—that would be a strange absurdity indeed. Wherefore we must not betake ourselves to the consideration of the meaner animals with a bad grace, as though we were children; since in all natural things there is something of the marvellous. There is a story which tells how some visitors once wished to meet Heracleitus, and when they entered and saw him in the kitchen, warming himself at the stove, they hesitated; but Heracleitus said, "Come in; don't be afraid; there are gods even here." In like manner, we ought not to hesitate nor to be abashed, but boldly to enter upon our researches concerning animals of every sort and kind, knowing that in not one of them is Nature or Beauty lacking.

I add "Beauty," † because in the works of Nature purpose and not accident is predominant; and the purpose or end for the sake of which those works have been constructed or formed has its place among what is beautiful. If, however, there is anyone who holds that the study of the animals is an unworthy pursuit, he ought to go further and hold the same opinion about the study of himself, for it is not possible without

* [In other treatises, especially his *On the Heavens*. (*Ed.*)]

† [This is the word *kalos* again, translated "Good" on page 156. Here the context makes "Beauty" the closest English equivalent to what Aristotle wants to say. (*Ed.*)]

considerable disgust to look upon the blood, flesh, bones, blood-vessels, and suchlike parts of which the human body is constructed. In the same way, when the discussion turns upon any one of the parts or structures, we must not suppose that the lecturer is speaking of the material of them in itself and for its own sake; he is speaking of the whole conformation. Just as in discussing a house, it is the whole figure and form of the house which concerns us, not merely the bricks and mortar and timber; so in Natural science, it is the composite thing, the thing as a whole, which primarily concerns us, not the materials of it, which are not found apart from the thing itself whose materials they are.

First of all, our business must be to describe the attributes found in each group; I mean those "essential" attributes which belong to all the animals, and after that to endeavour to describe the causes of them. It will be remembered that I have said already that there are many attributes which are common to many animals, either identically the same (*e.g.* organs like feet, feathers, and scales, and affections similarly), or else common by analogy only (*i.e.* some animals have lungs, others have no lungs but something else to correspond instead of them; again, some animals have blood, while others have its counterpart, which in them has the same function as blood in the former). And I have pointed out above that to treat separately of all the particular species would mean continual repetition of the same things, if we are going to deal with all their attributes, as the same attributes are common to many animals. Such, then, are my views on this matter.

Now, as each of the parts of the body, like every other instrument, is for the sake of some purpose, viz. some action, it is evident that the body as a whole must exist for the sake of some complex action. Just as the saw is there for the sake of sawing and not sawing for the sake of the saw, because sawing is the using of the instrument, so in some way the body exists for the sake of the soul, and the parts of the body for the sake of those functions to which they are naturally adapted. . . .

☙ POLITICS

Aristotle

Aristotle's Politics *seems to be a composite work, including notes for a series of lectures—or several series—to be delivered in his Lyceum, and a draft of an unfinished book. It is uneven in style and even inconsistent, suggesting that the various sections date from different periods of Aristotle's life and must have been put together haphazardly. The purely traditional arrangement has been abandoned in the selection that follows, which substitutes a more logical sequence: Book VII, Books I and III, and Book IV. (Books II, V, VI, and VII are omitted.)*

Book VII is a sketch of an ideal state ("polis"). It has its own introductory section (Chapters 1–3), which is a summary of ethics—the theory of the good life for individuals. This approach to politics by way of ethics is characteristic of Plato, as is the attempt to delineate the ideal state, and scholars have concluded that Aristotle probably wrote Book VII (and Book VIII) first, while he was still a student in Plato's Academy. His discussion of the various classes in the ideal state, and of its appropriate size, activities, and organization, reveals many characteristically Greek assumptions about communities.

Books I and III, in which he carefully distinguishes the polis from other forms of community, and develops a classification of "constitutions" ("forms of polis" in Greek), mark the advent of a genuinely Aristotelian science of politics as the theory of the polis.

Finally, in Book IV, he says that politics must consider not only the best *state, and not only the various* possible *types of states (still an abstract, theoretical question), but also the* actual *varieties, their advantages and disadvantages in various circumstances, and how to maintain desirable forms and change undesirable ones. This project is carried out, at least in outline, in Books IV, V, and VI. Politics has now become a practical, empirical science—almost a technique, but based on theoretical principles.*

In this context, it should not be surprising to learn that Aristotle's Lyceum carried on extensive research into the histories and constitutions of 154 Greek cities, and compiled a monograph on each one—an invaluable reference library for prospective rulers or revolutionaries. There is even some evidence that it may have been used for just that purpose by some of Aristotle's students. Unfortunately, these monographs have all been lost, with the lucky exception of the one we wanted most (rediscovered only in 1890): Athens.

BOOK VII

1 He who would duly enquire about the best form of a state ought first to determine which is the most eligible life; while this remains uncertain the best form of the state must also be uncertain; for, in the natural order of things, those may be expected to lead the best life who are governed in the best manner of which their circumstances

***The Politics of Aristotle*, trans. B. Jowett (2 vols.; Oxford: Clarendon Press, 1885), I, 206–213, 218–223, 229–237, 1–5, 77–80, 107–110.**

admit. We ought therefore to ascertain, first of all, which is the most generally eligible life, and then whether the same life is or is not best for the state and for individuals.

Assuming that enough has been already said in exoteric discourses concerning the best life, we will now only repeat the statements contained in them. Certainly no one will dispute the propriety of that partition of goods which separates them into three classes, viz. external goods, goods of the body, and goods of the soul, or deny that the happy man must have all three. For no one would maintain that he is happy who has not in him a particle of courage or temperance or justice or prudence, who is afraid of every insect which flutters past him, and will commit any crime, however great, in order to gratify his lust of meat or drink, who will sacrifice his dearest friend for the sake of half-a-farthing, and is as feeble and false in mind as a child or a madman. These propositions are universally acknowledged as soon as they are uttered, but men differ about the degree or relative superiority of this or that good. Some think that a very moderate amount of virtue is enough, but set no limit to their desires of wealth, property, power, reputation, and the like. To whom we reply by an appeal to facts, which easily prove that mankind do not acquire or preserve virtue by the help of external goods, but external goods by the help of virtue, and that happiness, whether consisting in pleasure or virtue, or both, is more often found with those who are most highly cultivated in their mind and in their character, and have only a moderate share of external goods, than among those who possess external goods to a useless extent but are deficient in higher qualities; and this is not only matter of experience, but, if reflected upon, will easily appear to be in accordance with reason. For, whereas external goods have a limit, like any other instrument, and all things useful are of such a nature that where there is too much of them they must either do harm, or at any rate be of no use, to their possessors, every good of the soul, the greater it is, is also of greater use, if the epithet useful as well as noble is appropriate to such subjects. No proof is required to show that the best state of one thing in relation to another is proportioned to the degree of excellence by which the natures corresponding to those states are separated from each other: so that, if the soul is more noble than our possessions or our bodies, both absolutely and in relation to us, it must be admitted that the best state of either has a similar ratio to the other. Again, it is for the sake of the soul that goods external and goods of the body are eligible at all, and all wise men ought to choose them for the sake of the soul, and not the soul for the sake of them.

Let us acknowledge then that each one has just so much of happiness as he has of virtue and wisdom, and of virtuous and wise action. God is a witness to us of this truth, for he is happy and blessed, not by reason of any external good, but in himself and by reason of his own nature. And herein of necessity lies the difference between good fortune and happiness; for external goods come of themselves, and chance is the author of them, but no one is just or temperate by or through chance. In like manner, and by a similar train of argument, the happy state may be shown to be that which is [morally] best and which acts rightly; and rightly it cannot act without doing right actions, and neither individual nor state can do right actions without virtue and wisdom. Thus the courage, justice, and wisdom of a state have the same form and nature as the qualities which give the individual who possesses them the name of just, wise, or temperate.

Thus much may suffice by way of preface: for I could not avoid touching upon these questions, neither could I go through all the arguments affecting them; these must be reserved for another discussion.

Let us assume then that the best life, both for individuals and states, is the life of virtue, having external goods enough for the performance of good actions. If there are any who controvert our assertion, we will in this treatise pass them over, and consider their objections hereafter.

2 There remains to be discussed the question, Whether the happiness of the individual is the same as that of the state, or different? Here again there can be no doubt—no one denies that they are the same. For those who hold that the well-being of the individual consists in his wealth, also think that riches make the happiness of the whole state, and those who value most highly the life of a tyrant deem that city the happiest which rules over the greatest number; while they who approve an individual for his virtue say that the more virtuous a city is, the happier it is. Two points here present themselves for consideration: first (1), which is the more eligible life, that of a citizen who is a member of a state, or that of an alien who has no political ties; and again (2), which is the best form of constitution or the best condition of a state, either on the supposition that political privileges are given to all, or that they are given to a majority only? Since the good of the state and not of the individual is the proper subject of political thought and speculation, and we are engaged in a political discussion, while the first of these two points has a secondary interest for us, the latter will be the main subject of our enquiry.

Now it is evident that the form of government is best in which every man, whoever he is, can act for the best and live happily. But even those who agree in thinking that the life of virtue is the most eligible raise a question, whether the life of business and politics is or is not more eligible than one which is wholly independent of external goods, I mean than a contemplative life, which by some is maintained to be the only one worthy of a philosopher. For these two lives—the life of the philosopher and the life of the statesman—appear to have been preferred by those who have been most keen in the pursuit of virtue, both in our own and in other ages. Which is the better is a question of no small moment; for the wise man, like the wise state, will necessarily regulate his life according to the best end. There are some who think that while a despotic rule over others is the greatest injustice, to exercise a constitutional rule over them, even though not unjust, is a great impediment to a man's individual well-being. Others take an opposite view; they maintain that the true life of man is the practical and political, and that every virtue admits of being practised, quite as much by statesmen and rulers as by private individuals. Others, again, are of opinion that arbitrary and tyrannical rule alone consists with happiness; indeed, in some states the entire aim of the laws is to give men despotic power over their neighbours. And, therefore, although in most cities the laws may be said generally to be in a chaotic state, still, if they aim at anything, they aim at the maintenance of power: thus in Lacedaemon and Crete the system of education and the greater part of the laws are framed with a view to war. And in all nations which are able to gratify their ambition military power is held in esteem, for example among the Scythians and Persians and Thracians and Celts. In some nations there are even laws tending to stimulate the warlike virtues, as at

Carthage, where we are told that men obtain the honour of wearing as many rings as they have served campaigns. There was once a law in Macedonia that he who had not killed an enemy should wear a halter, and among the Scythians no one who had not slain his man was allowed to drink out of the cup which was handed round at a certain feast. Among the Iberians, a warlike nation, the number of enemies whom a man has slain is indicated by the number of obelisks which are fixed in the earth round his tomb; and there are numerous practices among other nations of a like kind, some of them established by law and others by custom. Yet to a reflecting mind it must appear very strange that the statesman should be always considering how he can dominate and tyrannize over others, whether they will or not. How can that which is not even lawful be the business of the statesman or the legislator? Unlawful it certainly is to rule without regard to justice, for there may be might where there is no right. The other arts and sciences offer no parallel; a physician is not expected to persuade or coerce his patients, nor a pilot the passengers in his ship. Yet many appear to think that a despotic government is a true political form, and what men affirm to be unjust and inexpedient in their own case they are not ashamed of practising towards others; they demand justice for themselves, but where other men are concerned they care nothing about it. Such behaviour is irrational; unless the one party is born to command, and the other born to serve, in which case men have a right to command, not indeed all their fellows, but only those who are intended to be subjects; just as we ought not to hunt mankind, whether for food or sacrifice, but only the animals which are intended for food or sacrifice, that is to say, such wild animals as are eatable. And surely there may be a city happy in isolation, which we will assume to be well-governed (for it is quite possible that a city thus isolated might be well-administered and have good laws); but such a city would not be constituted with any view to war or the conquest of enemies,—all that sort of thing must be excluded. Hence we see very plainly that warlike pursuits, although generally to be deemed honourable, are not the supreme end of all things, but only means. And the good lawgiver should enquire how states and races of men and communities may participate in a good life, and in the happiness which is attainable by them. His enactments will not be always the same; and where there are neighbours he will have to deal with them according to their characters, and to see what duties are to be performed towards each. The end at which the best form of government should aim may be properly made a matter of future consideration.

3 Let us now address those who, while they agree that the life of virtue is the most eligible, differ about the manner of practising it. For some renounce political power, and think that the life of the freeman is different from the life of the statesman and the best of all; but others think the life of the statesman best. The argument of the latter is that he who does nothing cannot do well, and that virtuous activity is identical with happiness. To both we say: 'you are partly right and partly wrong.' The first class are right in affirming that the life of the freeman is better than the life of the despot; for there is nothing grand or noble in having the use of a slave, in so far as he is a slave; or in issuing commands about necessary things. But it is an error to suppose that every sort of rule is despotic like that of a master over slaves, for there is as great a difference between the rule over freemen and the rule over slaves as there is between slavery by nature and freedom by nature, about which I have said enough at the commencement of this treatise. And it is equally a mistake to place inactivity above action, for happiness is activity, and the actions of the just and wise are the realization of much that is noble.

But perhaps some one, accepting these premises, may still maintain that supreme power is the best of all things, because the possessors of it are able to perform the greatest number of noble actions. If so, the man who is able to rule, instead of giving up anything to his neighbour, ought rather to take away his power; and the father should make no account of his son, nor the son of his father, nor friend of friend; they should not bestow a thought on one another in comparison with this higher object, for the best is the most eligible and 'doing well' is the best. There might be some truth in such a view if we assume that robbers and plunderers attain the chief good. But this can never be; and hence we infer the view to be false. For the actions of a ruler cannot really be honourable, unless he is as much superior to other men as a husband is to a wife, or a father to his children, or a master to his slaves. And therefore he who violates the law can never recover by any success, however great, what he has already lost in departing from virtue. For equals share alike in the honourable and the just, as is just and equal. But that the unequal should be given to equals, and the unlike to those who are like, is contrary to nature, and nothing which is contrary to nature is good. If, therefore, there is any one superior in virtue and in the power of performing the best actions, him we ought to follow and obey, but he must have the capacity for action as well as virtue.

If we are right in our view, and happiness is assumed to be virtuous activity, the active life will be the best, both for the city collectively, and for individuals. Not that a life of action must necessarily have relation to others, as some persons think, nor are those ideas only to be regarded as practical which are pursued for the sake of practical results, but much more the thoughts and contemplations which are independent and complete in themselves; since virtuous activity, and therefore action, is an end, and even in the case of external actions the directing mind is most truly said to act. Neither, again, is it necessary that states which are cut off from others and choose to live alone should be inactive; for there may be activity also in the parts; there are many ways in which the members of a state act upon one another. The same thing is equally true of every individual. If this were otherwise, God and the universe, who have no external actions over and above their own energies, would be far enough from perfection. Hence it is evident that the same life is best for each individual, and for states, and for mankind collectively. . . .

7 Having spoken of the number of the citizens, we will proceed to speak of what should be their character. This is a subject which can be easily understood by any one who casts his eye on the more celebrated states of Hellas, and generally on the distribution of races in the habitable world. Those who live in a cold climate and in [northern] Europe are full of spirit, but wanting in intelligence and skill; and therefore they keep their freedom, but have no political organization, and are incapable of ruling over others. Whereas the natives of Asia are intelligent and inventive, but they are wanting in spirit, and therefore they are always in a state of subjection and slavery. But the Hellenic race, which is situated between them, is likewise intermediate in character, being high-spirited and also intelligent. Hence it continues free, and is the best-governed of any nation, and, if it could be formed into one state, would be able to rule the world. There are also similar differences in the different tribes of Hellas; for some of them are of a one-sided nature, and are intelligent or courageous only, while in others there is a happy combination of both qualities. And clearly those whom the legislator will most easily lead to virtue may be expected to be both intelligent and courageous. Some [like Plato] say that the guardians should be friendly towards those whom they know, fierce towards those whom they do not know. Now, passion is the quality of the soul which begets friendship and inspires affection; notably the spirit within us is more stirred against our friends and acquaintances than against those who are unknown to us, when we think that we are despised by them; for which reason Archilochus, complaining of his friends, very naturally addresses his soul in these words,

'For wert thou not plagued on account of friends?'

The power of command and the love of freedom are in all men based upon this quality, for passion is commanding and invincible. Nor is it right to say that the guardians should be fierce towards those whom they do not know, for we ought not to be out of temper with any one; and a lofty spirit is not fierce by nature, but only when excited against evil-doers. And this, as I was saying before, is a feeling which men show most strongly towards their friends if they think they have received a wrong at their hands: as indeed is reasonable; for, besides the actual injury, they seem to be deprived of a benefit by those who owe them one. Hence the saying,

'Cruel is the strife of brethren;'

and again,

'They who love in excess also hate in excess.'

Thus we have nearly determined the number and character of the citizens of our state, and also the size and nature of their territory. I say 'nearly,' for we ought not to require the same minuteness in theory as in fact.

8 As in other natural compounds the conditions of a composite whole are not necessarily organic parts of it, so in a state or in any other combination forming a unity not everything is a part, which is a necessary condition. The members of an association have necessarily some one thing the same and common to all, in which they share equally or unequally; for example, food or land or any other thing. But where there are two things of which one is a means and the other an end, they have nothing in common except that the one receives what the other produces. Such, for example, is the relation in which workmen and tools stand to their work; the house and the builder have nothing in common, but the art of the builder is for the sake of the house. And so states require property, but property, even though living beings are included in it, is no part of a state; for a state is not a community of living beings only, but a community of equals, aiming at the best life possible. Now, whereas happiness is the highest good, being a realization and perfect practice of virtue, which some attain, while others have little or none of it, the various qualities of men are clearly the reason why there are various kinds of states and many forms of government; for different men seek after happiness in different ways and by different means, and so make for themselves different modes of life and forms of government. We must see also how many things are indispensable to the existence of a state, for what we call the parts of a state will be found among them. Let us then enumerate the functions of a state, and we shall easily elicit what we want:

First, there must be food; secondly, arts, for life requires many instruments; thirdly, there must be arms, for the members of a community have need of them in order to maintain authority both against disobedient subjects and against external assailants; fourthly, there must be a certain amount of revenue, both for internal needs, and for the purposes of war; fifthly, or rather first, there must be a care of religion, which is commonly called worship; sixthly, and most necessary of all, there must be a power of deciding what is for the public interest, and what is just in men's dealings with one another.

These are the things which every state may be said to need. For a state is not a mere aggregate of persons, but a union of them sufficing for the purposes of life; and if any of these things be wanting, it is simply impossible that the community can be self-sufficing. A state then should be framed with a view to the fulfilment of these functions. There must be husbandmen to procure food, and artisans, and a warlike and a wealthy class, and priests, and judges to decide what is just and expedient.

9 Having determined these points, we have in the next place to consider whether all ought to share in every sort of occupation. Shall every man be at once husbandman, artisan, councillor, judge, or shall we suppose the several occupations just mentioned assigned to different persons? or, thirdly, shall some employments be assigned to individuals and others common to all? The question, however, does not occur in every state; as we were saying, all may be shared by all, or not all by all, but only some by some; and hence arise the differences of states, for in democracies all share in all, in oligarchies the opposite practice prevails. Now, since we are here speaking of the best form of government, and that under which the state will be most happy (and happiness, as has been already said, cannot exist without virtue), it clearly follows that in the state which is best governed the citizens who are absolutely and not merely relatively just men must not lead the life of mechanics or tradesmen, for such a life is ignoble and inimical to virtue. Neither must they be husbandmen, since leisure is necessary both for the development of virtue and the performance of political duties.

Again, there is in a state a class of warriors, and another of councillors, who advise about the expedient and determine matters of law, and these seem in an especial manner parts of a state. Now, should these two classes be distinguished, or are both functions to be assigned to the same persons? Here again there is no difficulty in seeing that both functions will in one way belong to the same, in another, to different persons. To different persons in so far as their employments are suited to different ages of life, for the one requires wisdom, and the other strength. But on the other hand, since it is an impossible thing that those who are able to use or to resist force should be willing to remain always in subjection, from this point of view the persons are the same; for those who carry arms can always determine the fate of the constitution.

t remains therefore that both functions of government should be entrusted to the ame persons, not, however, at the same time, but in the order prescribed by nature, vho has given to young men strength and to older men wisdom. Such a distribution f duties will be expedient and also just, and is founded upon a principle of proporion. Besides, the ruling class should be the owners of property, for they are citizens, nd the citizens of a state should be in good circumstances; whereas mechanics or any ther class whose art excludes the art of virtue have no share in the state. This follows rom our first principle, for happiness cannot exist without virtue, and a city is not o be termed happy in regard to a portion of the citizens, but in regard to them all. And clearly property should be in their hands, since the husbandmen will of necessity e slaves or barbarians or Perioeci.

Of the classes enumerated there remain only the priests, and the manner in which heir office is to be regulated is obvious. No husbandman or mechanic should be ppointed to it; for the Gods should receive honour from the citizens only. Now since he body of the citizens is divided into two classes, the warriors and the councillors; nd it is beseeming that the worship of the Gods should be duly performed, and also rest provided in their service for those who from age have given up active life—to he old men of these two classes should be assigned the duties of the priesthood.

We have shown what are the necessary conditions, and what the parts of a state: usbandmen, craftsmen, and labourers of all kinds are necessary to the existence of tates, but the parts of the state are the warriors and councillors. And these are listinguished severally from one another, the distinction being in some cases pernanent, in others not. . . .

13 Returning to the constitution itself, let us seek to determine out of what nd what sort of elements the state which is to be happy and well-governed should e composed. There are two things in which all well-being consists, one of them s the choice of a right end and aim of action, and the other the discovery of the actions vhich are means towards it; for the means and the end may agree or disagree. Sometimes the right end is set before men, but in practice they fail to attain it; in other ases they are successful in all the means, but they propose to themselves a bad end, nd sometimes they fail in both. Take, for example, the art of medicine; physicians lo not always understand the nature of health, and also the means which they use nay not effect the desired end. In all arts and sciences both the end and the means hould be equally within our control.

The happiness and well-being which all men manifestly desire, some have the power f attaining, but to others, from some accident or defect of nature, the attainment of hem is not granted; for a good life requires a supply of external goods, in a less degree vhen men are in a good state, in a greater degree when they are in a lower state. Others again, who possess the condition of happiness, go utterly wrong from the first n the pursuit of it. But since our object is to discover the best form of government, hat, namely, under which a city will be best governed, and since the city is best overned which has the greatest opportunity of obtaining happiness, it is evident that ve must clearly ascertain the nature of happiness.

We have said in the Ethics, if the arguments there adduced are of any value, that appiness is the realization and perfect exercise of virtue, and this not conditional, but absolute. And I used the term 'conditional' to express that which is indispensable, and 'absolute' to express that which is good in itself. Take the case of just actions; just punishments and chastisements do indeed spring from a good principle, but they are good only because we cannot do without them—it would be better that neither individuals nor states should need anything of the sort—but actions which aim at honour and advantage are absolutely the best. The conditional action is only the choice of a lesser evil; whereas these are the foundation and creation of good. A good man may make the best even of poverty and disease, and the other ills of life; but he can only attain happiness under the opposite conditions. As we have already said in the Ethics, the good man is he to whom, because he is virtuous, the absolute good is his good. It is also plain that this use of other goods must be virtuous and in the absolute sense good. This makes men fancy that external goods are the cause of happiness, yet we might as well say that a brilliant performance on the lyre was to be attributed to the instrument and not to the skill of the performer.

It follows then from what has been said that some things the legislator must find ready to his hand in a state, others he must provide. And therefore we can only say: May our state be constituted in such a manner as to be blessed with the goods of which fortune disposes (for we acknowledge her power): whereas virtue and goodness in the state are not a matter of chance but the result of knowledge and purpose. A city can be virtuous only when the citizens who have a share in the government are virtuous, and in our state all the citizens share in the government; let us then enquire how a man becomes virtuous. For even if we could suppose all the citizens to be virtuous, and not each of them, yet the latter would be better, for in the virtue of each the virtue of all is involved.

There are three things which make men good and virtuous: these are nature, habit, reason. In the first place, every one must be born a man and not some other animal; in the second place, he must have a certain character, both of body and soul. But some qualities there is no use in having at birth, for they are altered by habit, and there are some gifts of nature which may be turned by habit to good or bad. Most animals lead a life of nature, although in lesser particulars some are influenced by habit as well. Man has reason, in addition, and man only. Wherefore nature, habit, reason must be in harmony with one another; [for they do not always agree]; men do many things against habit and nature, if reason persuades them that they ought. We have already determined what natures are likely to be most easily moulded by the hands of the legislator. All else is the work of education; we learn some things by habit and some by instruction.

14 Since every political society is composed of rulers and subjects, let us consider whether the relations of one to the other should interchange or be permanent. For the education of the citizens will necessarily vary with the answer given to this question. Now, if some men excelled others in the same degree in which gods and heroes are supposed to excel mankind in general, having in the first place a great advantage even in their bodies, and secondly in their minds, so that the superiority of the governors over their subjects was patent and undisputed, it would clearly be better that once for all the one class should rule and the others serve. But since this is unattainable, and kings have no marked superiority over their subjects, such as Scylax affirms

.o be found among the Indians, it is obviously necessary on many grounds that all .he citizens alike should take their turn of governing and being governed. Equality :onsists in the same treatment of similar persons, and no government can stand which s not founded upon justice. For [if the government be unjust] every one in the :ountry unites with the governed in the desire to have a revolution, and it is an mpossibility that the members of the government can be so numerous as to be stronger han all their enemies put together. Yet that governors should excel their subjects is ındeniable. How all this is to be effected, and in what way they will respectively share n the government, the legislator has to consider. The subject has been already menioned. Nature herself has given the principle of choice when she made a difference)etween old and young (though they are really the same in kind), of whom she itted the one to govern and the others to be governed. No one takes offence at being ;overned when he is young, nor does he think himself better than his governors, :specially if he will enjoy the same privilege when he reaches the required age.

We conclude that from one point of view governors and governed are identical, and rom another different. And therefore their education must be the same and also lifferent. For he who would learn to command well must, as men say, first of all learn o obey. As I observed in the first part of this treatise, there is one rule which is for he sake of the rulers and another rule which is for the sake of the ruled; the former s a despotic, the latter a free government. Some commands differ not in the thing ommanded, but in the intention with which they are imposed. Wherefore, many ıpparently menial offices are an honour to the free youth by whom they are performed; or actions do not differ as honourable or dishonourable in themselves so much as in he end and intention of them. But since we say that the virtue of the citizen and uler is the same as that of the good man, and that the same person must first be a ubject and then a ruler, the legislator has to see that they become good men, and by vhat means this may be accomplished, and what is the end of the perfect life.

Now the soul of man is divided into two parts, one of which has reason in itself, ınd the other, not having reason in itself, is able to obey reason. And we call a man ;ood because he has the virtues of these two parts. In which of them the end is more ikely to be found is no matter of doubt to those who adopt our division; for in the vorld both of nature and of art the inferior always exists for the sake of the better or uperior, and the better or superior is that which has reason. The reason too, in our ordinary way of speaking, is divided into two parts, for there is a practical and a speclative reason, and there must be a corresponding division of actions; the actions of he naturally better principle are to be preferred by those who have it in their power o attain to both or to all, for that is always to every one the most eligible, which is the ıighest attainable by him. The whole of life is further divided into two parts, business .nd leisure, war and peace, and all actions into those which are necessary and useful, .nd those which are honourable. And the preference given to one or the other class of actions must necessarily be like the preference given to one or other part of the soul .nd its actions over the other; there must be war for the sake of peace, business for the ake of leisure, things useful and necessary for the sake of things honourable. All hese points the statesman should keep in view when he frames his laws; he should onsider the parts of the soul and their functions, and above all the better and the end; he should also remember the diversities of human lives and actions. For me must engage in business and go to war, but leisure and peace are better; they mus do what is necessary and useful, but what is honourable is better. In such principle children and persons of every age which requires education should be trained. Wherea even the Hellenes of the present day, who are reputed to be best governed, and th legislators who gave them their constitutions, do not appear to have framed thei governments with a regard to the best end, or to have given them laws and educatio with a view to all the virtues, but in a vulgar spirit have fallen back on those whic promised to be more useful and profitable. Many modern writers have taken a simila view: they commend the Lacedaemonian constitution, and praise the legislator fo making conquest and war his sole aim, a doctrine which may be refuted by argumen and has long ago been refuted by facts. For most men desire empire in the hope o accumulating the goods of fortune; and on this ground Thibron and all those who hav written about the Lacedaemonian constitution have praised their legislator, because th Lacedaemonians, by a training in hardships, gained great power. But surely they ar not a happy people now that their empire has passed away, nor was their legislato right. How ridiculous is the result, if, while they are continuing in the observance of hi laws and no one interferes with them, they have lost the better part of life. Thes writers further err about the sort of government which the legislator should approve for the government of freemen is noble, and implies more virtue than despotic govern ment. Neither is a city to be deemed happy or a legislator to be praised because h trains his citizens to conquer and obtain dominion over their neighbours, for ther is great evil in this. On a similar principle any citizen who could, would obviousl try to obtain the power in his own state,—the crime which the Lacedaemonians accus king Pausanias of attempting, although he had so great honour already. No suc principle and no law having this object is either statesmanlike or useful or right. Fo the same things are best both for individuals and for states, and these are the thing which the legislator ought to implant in the minds of his citizens. Neither shoul men study war with a view to the enslavement of those who do not deserve to b enslaved; but first of all they should provide against their own enslavement, and i the second place obtain empire for the good of the governed, and not for the sake o exercising a general despotism, and in the third place they should seek to be master only over those who deserve to be slaves. Facts, as well as arguments, prove that th legislator should direct all his military and other measures to the provision of leisur and the establishment of peace. For most of these military states are safe only whil they are at war, but fall when they have acquired their empire; like unused iron the rust in time of peace. And for this the legislator is to blame, he never having taugh them how to lead the life of peace.

15 Since the end of individuals and of states is the same, the end of the best ma and of the best state must also be the same; it is therefore evident that there ought t exist in both of them the virtues of leisure; for peace, as has been often repeated is the end of war, and leisure of toil. But leisure and cultivation may be promoted not only by those virtues which are practiced in leisure, but also by some of thos which are useful to business. For many necessaries of life have to be supplied befor we can have leisure. Therefore a city must be temperate and brave, and able t ndure: for truly, as the proverb says, 'There is no leisure for slaves,' and those who annot face danger like men are the slaves of any invader. Courage and endurance are equired for business and philosophy for leisure, temperance and justice for both, ore especially in times of peace and leisure, for war compels men to be just and emperate, whereas the enjoyment of good fortune and the leisure which comes with eace tends to make them insolent. Those then, who seem to be the best-off and to e in the possession of every good, have special need of justice and temperance,—for xample, those (if such there be, as the poets say) who dwell in the Islands of the lest; they above all will need philosophy and temperance and justice, and all the ore leisure they have, living in the midst of abundance. There is no difficulty in eeing why the state that would be happy and good ought to have these virtues. If it e disgraceful in men not to be able to use the goods of life, it is peculiarly disgraceful ot to be able to use them in time of peace,—to show excellent qualities in action and var, and when they have peace and leisure to be no better than slaves. Wherefore we hould not practise virtue after the manner of the Lacedaemonians. For they, while greeing with other men in their conception of the highest goods, differ from the rest f mankind in thinking that they are to be obtained by the practice of a single virtue. nd since these goods and the enjoyment of them are clearly greater than the enjoyment derived from the virtues of which they are the end, we must now consider how nd by what means they are to be attained.

We have already determined that nature and habit and reason are required, and what hould be the character of the citizens has also been defined by us. But we have still to onsider whether the training of early life is to be that of reason or habit, for these wo must accord, and when in accord they will then form the best of harmonies. eason may make mistakes and fail in attaining the highest ideal of life, and there ay be a like evil influence of habit. Thus much is clear in the first place, that, as in ll other things, birth implies some antecedent principle, and that the end of anything as a beginning in some former end. Now, in men reason and mind are the end owards which nature strives, so that the birth and moral discipline of the citizens ought o be ordered with a view to them. In the second place, as the soul and body are wo, we see also that there are two parts of the soul, the rational and the irraonal, and two corresponding states—reason and appetite. And as the body is rior in order of generation to the soul, so the irrational is prior to the rational. he proof is that anger and will and desire are implanted in children from their very irth, but reason and understanding are developed as they grow older. Wherefore, he care of the body ought to precede that of the soul, and the training of the appetitive art should follow: none the less our care of it must be for the sake of the reason, nd our care of the body for the sake of the soul.

OOK I

Every state is a community of some kind, and every community is established with view to some good; for mankind always act in order to obtain that which they think ood. But, if all communities aim at some good, the state or political community, which is the highest of all, and which embraces all the rest, aims, and in a greater degree than any other, at the highest good.

Now there is an erroneous opinion that a statesman, king, householder, and master are the same, and that they differ, not in kind, but only in the number of their subjects. For example, the ruler over a few is called a master; over more, the manager of a household; over a still larger number, a statesman or king, as if there were no difference between a great household and a small state. The distinction which is made between the king and the statesman is as follows: When the government is personal the ruler is a king; when, according to the principles of the political science, the citizens rule and are ruled in turn, then he is called a statesman.

But all this is a mistake; for governments differ in kind, as will be evident to any one who considers the matter according to the method which has hitherto guided us. As in other departments of science, so in politics, the compound should always be resolved into the simple elements or least parts of the whole. We must therefore look at the elements of which the state is composed, in order that we may see in what they differ from one another, and whether any scientific distinction can be drawn between the different kinds of rule.

2 He who thus considers things in their first growth and origin, whether a state or anything else, will obtain the clearest view of them. In the first place (1) there must be a union of those who cannot exist without each other; for example, of male and female, that the race may continue; and this is a union which is formed, not of deliberate purpose, but because, in common with other animals and with plants, mankind have a natural desire to leave behind them an image of themselves. And (2) there must be a union of natural ruler and subject, that both may be preserved. For he who can foresee with his mind is by nature intended to be lord and master, and he who can work with his body is a subject, and by nature a slave; hence master and slave have the same interest. Nature, however, has distinguished between the female and the slave. For she is not niggardly, like the smith who fashions the Delphian knife for many uses; she makes each thing for a single use, and every instrument is best made when intended for one and not for many uses. But among barbarians no distinction is made between women and slaves, because there is no natural ruler among them: they are a community of slaves, male and female. Wherefore the poets say,—

> 'It is meet that Hellenes should rule over barbarians;'

as if they thought that the barbarian and the slave were by nature one.

Out of these two relationships between man and woman, master and slave, the family first arises, and Hesiod is right when he says,—

> 'First house and wife and an ox for the plough,'

for the ox is the poor man's slave. The family is the association established by nature for the supply of men's every day wants, and the members of it are called by Charondas 'companions of the cupboard' and by Epimenides the Cretan, 'companions of the manger.' But when several families are united, and the association aims at something more than the supply of daily needs, then comes into existence the village. And the most natural form of the village appears to be that of a colony from the family composed of the children and grandchildren, who are said to be 'suckled with the same milk.' And this is the reason why Hellenic states were originally governed by kings; because the Hellenes were under royal rule before they came together, as the barbarians still are. Every family is ruled by the eldest, and therefore in the colonies of the family the kingly form of government prevailed because they were of the same blood. As Homer says [of the Cyclopes]:—

> 'Each one gives law to his children and to his wives.'

For they lived dispersedly, as was the manner in ancient times. Wherefore men say that the Gods have a king, because they themselves either are or were in ancient times under the rule of a king. For they imagine, not only the forms of the Gods, but their ways of life to be like their own.

When several villages are united in a single community, perfect and large enough to be nearly or quite self-sufficing, the state comes into existence, originating in the bare needs of life, and continuing in existence for the sake of a good life. And therefore, if the earlier forms of society are natural, so is the state, for it is the end of them, and the [completed] nature is the end. For what each thing is when fully developed, we call its nature, whether we are speaking of a man, a horse, or a family. Besides, the final cause and end of a thing is the best, and to be self-sufficing is the end and the best.

Hence it is evident that the state is a creation of nature, and that man is by nature a political animal. And he who by nature and not by mere accident is without a state, is either above humanity, or below it; he is the

> 'Tribeless, lawless, hearthless one,'

whom Homer denounces—the outcast who is a lover of war; he may be compared to a bird which flies alone.

Now the reason why man is more of a political animal than bees or any other gregarious animals is evident. Nature, as we often say, makes nothing in vain, and man is the only animal whom she has endowed with the gift of speech. And whereas mere sound is but an indication of pleasure or pain, and is therefore found in other animals (for their nature attains to the perception of pleasure and pain and the intimation of them to one another, and no further), the power of speech is intended to set forth the expedient and inexpedient, and likewise the just and the unjust. And it is a characteristic of man that he alone has any sense of good and evil, of just and unjust, and the association of living beings who have this sense makes a family and a state.

Thus the state is by nature clearly prior to the family and to the individual, since the whole is of necessity prior to the part; for example, if the whole body be destroyed, there will be no foot or hand, except in an equivocal sense, as we might speak of a stone hand; for when destroyed the hand will be no better. But things are defined by their working and power; and we ought not to say that they are the same when they are no longer the same, but only that they have the same name. The proof that the state is a creation of nature and prior to the individual is that the individual, when isolated, is not self-sufficing; and therefore he is like a part in relation to the whole.

But he who is unable to live in society, or who has no need because he is sufficient fo
himself, must be either a beast or a god: he is no part of a state. A social instinct i
implanted in all men by nature, and yet he who first founded the state was the greates
of benefactors. For man, when perfected, is the best of animals, but, when separate
from law and justice, he is the worst of all; since armed injustice is the more dangerou
and he is equipped at birth with the arms of intelligence and with moral qualitie
which he may use for the worst ends. Wherefore, if he have not virtue, he is th
most unholy and the most savage of animals, and the most full of lust and glutton
But justice is the bond of men in states, and the administration of justice, which i
the determination of what is just, is the principle of order in political society. . .

BOOK III

6 Having determined these questions, we have next to consider whether there i
only one form of government ["constitution"] or many, and if many, what they ar
and how many, and what are the differences between them.

A constitution is the arrangement of magistracies in a state, especially of the highes
of all. The government is everywhere sovereign in the state, and the constitution is i
fact the government. For example, in democracies the people are supreme, but i
oligarchies, the few; and, therefore, we say that these two forms of government ar
different: and so in other cases.

First, let us consider what is the purpose of a state, and how many forms of govern
ment there are by which human society is regulated. We have already said, in th
former part of this treatise, when drawing a distinction between household-manage
ment and the rule of a master, that man is by nature a political animal. And therefore
men, even when they do not require one another's help, desire to live together all th
same, and are in fact brought together by their common interests in proportion as the
severally attain to any measure of well-being. This is certainly the chief end, both o
individuals and of states. And also for the sake of mere life (in which there is possibl
some noble element) mankind meet together and maintain the political communit
so long as the evils of existence do not greatly overbalance the good. And we all se
that men cling to life even in the midst of misfortune, seeming to find in it a natura
sweetness and happiness.

There is no difficulty in distinguishing the various kinds of authority; they hav
been often defined already in popular works. The rule of a master, although the slav
by nature and the master by nature have in reality the same interests, is nevertheles
exercised primarily with a view to the interest of the master, but accidentally consider
the slave, since, if the slave perish, the rule of the master perishes with him. On th
other hand, the government of a wife and children and of a household, which w
have called household-management, is exercised in the first instance for the good of th
governed or for the common good of both parties, but essentially for the good of th
governed, as we see to be the case in medicine, gymnastic, and the arts in genera
which are only accidentally concerned with the good of the artists themselves. (Fo
there is no reason why the trainer may not sometimes practice gymnastics, and th
pilot is always one of the crew.) The trainer or the pilot considers the good of thos

ommitted to his care. But, when he is one of the persons taken care of, he accidentally articipates in the advantage, for the pilot is also a sailor, and the trainer becomes one f those in training. And so in politics: when the state is framed upon the principle f equality and likeness, the citizens think that they ought to hold office by turns. n the order of nature every one would take his turn of service; and then again, omebody else would look after his interest, just as he, while in office, had looked fter theirs. But now-a-days, for the sake of the advantage which is to be gained rom the public revenues and from office, men want to be always in office. One might nagine that the rulers, being sickly, were only kept in health while they continued in ffice; in that case we may be sure that they would be hunting after places. The con- lusion is evident: that governments, which have a regard to the common interest, are onstituted in accordance with strict principles of justice, and are therefore true forms; ut those which regard only the interest of the rulers are all defective and perverted orms, for they are despotic, whereas a state is a community of freemen.

7 Having determined these points, we have next to consider how many forms of overnment there are, and what they are; and in the first place what are the true orms, for when they are determined the perversions of them will at once be apparent. he words constitution and government have the same meaning, and the government, hich is the supreme authority in states, must be in the hands of one, or of a few, r of many. The true forms of government, therefore, are those in which the one, or e few, or the many, govern with a view to the common interest; but governments hich rule with a view to the private interest, whether of the one, or of the few, r of the many, are perversions. For citizens, if they are truly citizens, ought to par- cipate in the advantages of a state. Of forms of government in which one rules, we all that which regards the common interests, kingship or royalty; that in which more an one, but not many, rule, aristocracy [the rule of the best]; and it is so called, ither because the rulers are the best men, or because they have at heart the best terests of the state and of the citizens. But when the citizens at large administer the ate for the common interest, the government is called by the generic name,—a con- itution. And there is a reason for this use of language. One man or a few may excel virtue; but of virtue there are many kinds: and as the number increases it becomes ore difficult for them to attain perfection in every kind, though they may in military irtue, for this is found in the masses. Hence, in a constitutional government the ghting-men have the supreme power, and those who possess arms are the citizens.

Of the above-mentioned forms, the perversions are as follows:—of royalty, tyranny; f aristocracy, oligarchy; of constitutional government, democracy. For tyranny is a ind of monarchy which has in view the interest of the monarch only; oligarchy has view the interest of the wealthy; democracy, of the needy: none of them the common ood of all. . . .

OOK IV

In all arts and sciences which embrace the whole of any subject, and are not stricted to a part only, it is the province of a single art or science to consider all that ppertains to a single subject. For example, the art of gymnastic considers not only

the suitableness of different modes of training to different bodies (2), but what so
is absolutely the best (1); (for the absolutely best must suit that which is by natur
best and best furnished with the means of life), and also what common form c
training is adapted to the great majority of men (4). And if a man does not desir
the best habit of body or the greatest skill in gymnastics, which might be attained b
him, still the trainer or the teacher of gymnastics should be able to impart any lowe
degree of either (3). The same principle equally holds in medicine and ship-building
and the making of clothes, and in the arts generally.

Hence it is obvious that government too is the subject of a single science, whic
has to consider what kind of government would be best and most in accordance wit
our aspirations, if there were no external impediment, and also what kind of goverr
ment is adapted to particular states. For the best is often unattainable, and therefor
the true legislator and statesman ought to be acquainted, not only with (1) th
which is best in the abstract, but also with (2) that which is best relative to circum
stances. We should be able further to say how a state may be constituted under an
given conditions (3); both how it is originally formed and, when formed, how
may be longest preserved; the supposed state being so far from the very best that
is unprovided even with the conditions necessary for the very best; neither is it th
best under the circumstances, but of an inferior type.

He ought, moreover, to know (4) the form of government which is best suite
to states in general; for political writers, although they have excellent ideas, are ofte
unpractical. We should consider, not only what form of government is best, but als
what is possible and what is easily attainable by all. There are some who would hav
none but the most perfect; for this many natural advantages are required. Other
again, speak of a more attainable form, and, although they reject the constitutic
under which they are living, they extol some one in particular, for example th
Lacedaemonian. Any change of government which has to be introduced should be or
which men will be both willing and able to adopt, since there is quite as much troub
in the reformation of an old constitution as in the establishment of a new one, ju
as to unlearn is as hard as to learn. And therefore, in addition to the qualifications c
the statesman already mentioned, he should be able to find remedies for the defects
existing constitutions. This he cannot do unless he knows how many forms of a gover
ment there are. It is often supposed that there is only one kind of democracy an
one of oligarchy. But this is a mistake; and, in order to avoid such mistakes, we mu
ascertain what differences there are in the constitutions of states, and in how mar
ways they are combined. The same political insight will enable a man to know whic
laws are the best, and which are suited to different constitutions; for the laws are, an
ought to be, relative to the constitution, and not the constitution to the laws.
constitution is the organization of offices in a state, and determines what is to be th
governing body, and what is the end of each community. But laws are not to b
confounded with the principles of the constitution: they are the rules according
which the magistrates should administer the state, and proceed against offenders. S
that we must know the number and varieties of the several forms of government,
only with a view to making laws. For the same laws cannot be equally suited to a
oligarchies and to all democracies, and there is certainly more than one form bo
of democracy and of oligarchy.

2 In our original discussion about governments we divided them into three true rms: kingly rule, aristrocracy, and constitutional government, and three correspond-g perversions—tyranny, oligarchy, and democracy. Of kingly rule and of aristocracy e have already spoken, for the enquiry into the perfect state is the same thing with e discussion of the two forms thus named, since both imply a principle of virtue rovided with external means. We have already determined in what aristocracy and ngly rule differ from one another, and when the latter should be established. In what llows we have to describe the so-called constitutional government, which bears the mmon name of all constitutions, and the other forms, tyranny, oligarchy, and mocracy.

It is obvious which of the three perversions is the worst, and which is the next in dness. That which is the perversion of the first and most divine is necessarily the orst. And just as a royal rule, if not a mere name, must exist by virtue of some great rsonal superiority in the king, so tyranny, which is the worst of governments, is cessarily the farthest removed from a well-constituted form; oligarchy is a little tter, but a long way from aristocracy, and democracy is the most tolerable of the ree.

A writer who preceded me [Plato] has already made these distinctions, but his int of view is not the same as mine. For he lays down the principle that of all good nstitutions (under which he would include a virtuous oligarchy and the like) mocracy is the worst, but the best of bad ones. Whereas we maintain that they are l defective, and that one oligarchy is not to be accounted better than another, but ly less bad.

Not to pursue this question further at present, let us begin by determining (1) w many varieties of states there are (since of democracy and oligarchy there are veral); (2) what constitution is the most generally acceptable, and what is eligible the next degree after the perfect or any other aristocratical and well-constituted rm of government—if any other there be—which is at the same time adapted to ates in general; (3) of the other forms of government to whom is each suited. For mocracy may meet the needs of some better than oligarchy, and conversely. In the xt place (4) we have to consider in what manner a man ought to proceed who sires to establish some one among these various forms, whether of democracy or of igarchy; and lastly, (5) having briefly discussed these subjects to the best of our wer, we will endeavour to ascertain whence arise the ruin and preservation of states, th generally and in individual cases, and to what causes they are to be attributed. . . .

11 We have now to enquire what is the best constitution for most states, and the st life for most men, neither assuming a standard of virtue which is above ordinary rsons, nor an education which is exceptionally favoured by nature and circumstances, r yet an ideal state which is an aspiration only, but having regard to the life in hich the majority are able to share, and to the form of government which states in neral can attain. As to those aristocracies, as they are called, of which we were just w speaking, they either lie beyond the possibilities of the greater number of states, they approximate to the so-called constitutional government, and therefore need separate discussion. And in fact the conclusion at which we arrive respecting all ese forms rests upon the same grounds. For if it has been truly said in the Ethics at the happy life is the life according to unimpeded virtue, and that virtue is a mean,

then the life which is in a mean, and in a mean attainable by every one, must be th best. And the same principles of virtue and vice are characteristic of cities and c constitutions; for the constitution is in a figure the life of the city.

Now in all states there are three elements; one class is very rich, another very poo and a third in a mean. It is admitted that moderation and the mean are best, an therefore it will clearly be best to possess the gifts of fortune in moderation; for i that condition of life men are most ready to listen to reason. But he who great excels in beauty, strength, birth or wealth, or on the other hand who is very poor, c very weak, or very much disgraced, finds it difficult to follow reason. Of these tw the one sort grow into violent and great criminals, the others into rogues and pett rascals. And two sorts of offences correspond to them, the one committed from violenc the other from roguery. The petty rogues are disinclined to hold office, whether militar or civil, and their aversion to these two duties is as great an injury to the state as the tendency to crime. Again, those who have too much of the goods of fortune, strengt wealth, friends, and the like, are neither willing nor able to submit to authority. Th evil begins at home: for when they are boys, by reason of the luxury in which the are brought up, they never learn, even at school, the habit of obedience. On the othe hand, the very poor, who are in the opposite extreme, are too degraded. So that th one class cannot obey, and can only rule despotically; the other knows not how t command and must be ruled like slaves. Thus arises a city, not of freemen, but c masters and slaves, the one despising, the other envying; and nothing can be more fat to friendship and good fellowship in states than this: for good fellowship tends t friendship; when men are at enmity with one another, they would rather not eve share the same path. But a city ought to be composed, as far as possible, of equals an similars; and these are generally the middle classes. Wherefore the city which is con posed of middle-class citizens is necessarily best governed; they are, as we say, th natural elements of a state. And this is the class of citizens which is most secure in state, for they do not, like the poor, covet their neighbours' goods; nor do othe covet theirs, as the poor covet the goods of the rich; and as they neither plot again others, nor are themselves plotted against, they pass through life safely. Wisely the did Phocylides pray,—

'Many things are best in the mean; I desire to be of a middle condition in my city

Thus it is manifest that the best political community is formed by citizens of th middle class, and that those states are likely to be well-administered, in which th middle class is large, and larger if possible than both the other classes, or at any ra than either singly; for the addition of the middle class turns the scale, and preven either of the extremes from being dominant. Great then is the good fortune of state in which the citizens have a moderate and sufficient property; for where som possess much, and the others nothing, there may arise an extreme democracy, or pure oligarchy; or a tyranny may grow out of either extreme,—either out of th most rampant democracy, or out of an oligarchy; but it is not so likely to arise ou of a middle and nearly equal condition. I will explain the reason of this hereafte when I speak of the revolutions of states. The mean condition of states is clearly bes for no other is free from faction; and where the middle class is large, there are lea kely to be factions and dissensions. For a similar reason large states are less liable to action than small ones, because in them the middle class is large; whereas in small tates it is easy to divide all the citizens into two classes who are either rich or poor, nd to leave nothing in the middle. And democracies are safer and more permanent han oligarchies, because they have a middle class which is more numerous and has greater share in the government; for when there is no middle class, and the poor reatly exceed in number, troubles arise, and the state soon comes to an end. A proof f the superiority of the middle class is that the best legislators have been of a middle ondition; for example, Solon, as his own verses testify; and Lycurgus, for he was not king; and Charondas, and almost all legislators.

These considerations will help us to understand why most governments are either emocratical or oligarchical. The reason is that the middle class is seldom numerous n them, and whichever party, whether the rich or the common people, transgresses the neans and predominates, draws the government to itself, and thus arises either oligarchy r democracy. There is another reason—the poor and the rich quarrel with one another, nd whichever side gets the better, instead of establishing a just or popular government, regards political supremacy as the prize of victory, and the one party sets up a emocracy and the other an oligarchy. Both the parties which had the supremacy in Iellas looked only to the interest of their own form of government, and established n states, the one, democracies, and the other, oligarchies; they thought of their own dvantage, of the public not at all. For these reasons the middle form of government as rarely, if ever, existed, and among a very few only. One man alone of all who ver ruled in Hellas was induced to give this middle constitution to states. But it has ow become a habit among the citizens of states, not even to care about equality; all nen are seeking for dominion, or, if conquered, are willing to submit.

SCEPTICISM: OUTLINES OF PYRRHONISM

Sextus Empiricus

Very little is known of Sextus Empiricus (A.D. ca. *200*) *besides the fact that he is the author of the fullest summary of ancient scepticism. His three surviving works*—Outlines of Pyrrhonism, Against the Dogmatists, *and* Against the Professors—*all say essentially the same thing: No certain knowledge has been attained by man, yet neither can it be shown definitely that certain knowledge is impossible. We must therefore suspend judgment about all things and keep on looking.*

Pyrrho of Elis (ca. *360–275* B.C.), *after whom the* Outlines of Pyrrhonism *is named, was regarded as the founder of this "school" (although by its very nature it could hardly be a school in the same sense as the others), but the sceptical turn of mind is evident in Socrates, if not earlier. The selection we have chosen deals with religious beliefs, and is of intere not only for its scepticism, but also for the evidence it provides of the remarkable variety of religious ideas and customs existing under the Roman* imperium. *Note that the Jews are mentioned, but not the Christians; apparently in* A.D. *200 the Christians were not yet numero or distinctive enough to merit attention from philosophers.*

. . . Around all matters of religion and theology also, there rages violent controvers For while the majority declare that gods exist, some deny their existence, like Diagor of Melos, and Theodorus, and Critias the Athenian. And of those who maintain t existence of gods, some believe in the ancestral gods, others in such as are construct in the Dogmatic systems—as Aristotle asserted that God is incorporeal and "the lin of heaven," the Stoics that he is a breath which permeates even through things fo Epicurus that he is anthropomorphic, Xenophanes that he is an impassive spher Some, too, hold that he cares for human affairs, others that he does not so care; f Epicurus declares that "what is blessed and incorruptible neither feels trouble itse nor causes it to others." Hence ordinary people differ also, some saying that the is one god, others that there are many gods and of various shapes; in fact, they ev come to share the notions of the Egyptians who believe in gods that are dog-faced, hawk-shaped, or cows or crocodiles or anything else.

Hence, too, sacrificial usages, and the ritual of worship in general, exhibit gre diversity. For things which are in some cults accounted holy are in others accounte unholy. But this would not have been so if the holy and the unholy existed by natur Thus, for example, no one would sacrifice a pig to Sarapis, but they sacrifice it Heracles and Asclepius. To sacrifice a sheep to Isis is forbidden, but it is offered up honour of the so-called Mother of the gods and of the other deities. To Cronos a huma victim is sacrificed (at Carthage), although this is regarded by most as an impious ac In Alexandria they offer a cat to Horus and a beetle to Thetis—a thing which no o here would do. To Poseidon they sacrifice a horse; but to Apollo (especially t Didymaean Apollo) that animal is an abomination. It is an act of piety to offer goa to Artemis, but not to Asclepius. And I might add a host of similar instances, but forbear since my aim is to be brief. Yet surely, if a sacrifice had been holy by natu or unholy, it would have been deemed so by all men alike.

Examples similar to these may also be found in the religious observances with rega to human diet. For a Jew or an Egyptian priest would sooner die than eat swine flesh; by a Libyan it is regarded as a most impious thing to taste the meat of a shee by some of the Syrians to eat a dove, and by others to eat sacrificial victims. And certain cults it is lawful, but in others impious, to eat fish. And amongst the Egyptiar some of those who are reputed to be sages believe it is sinful to eat an animal's hea

Sextus Empiricus, *Outlines of Pyrrhonism,* trans. R. G. Bury (Cambridge, Mass.: Harva University Press, Loeb Classical Library, 1933), Vol. I, 471–485.

thers the shoulder, others the foot, others some other part. And no one would bring n onion as an offering to Zeus Casius of Pelusium, just as no priest of the Libyan phrodite would taste garlic. And in some cults they abstain from mint, in others from atmint, in others from parsley. And some declare that they would sooner eat their athers' heads than beans. Yet, amongst others, these things are indifferent. Eating og's flesh, too, is thought by us to be sinful, but some of the Thracians are reported be dog-eaters. Possibly this practice was customary also amongst the Greeks; and on nis account Diocles, too, starting from the practices of the Asclepiadae, prescribes nat hounds' flesh should be given to certain patients. And some, as I have said, ven eat human flesh indifferently, a thing which with us is accounted sinful. Yet, if ne rules of ritual and of unlawful foods had existed by nature, they would have een observed by all men alike.

A similar account may be given of reverence towards the departed. Some wrap the ead up completely and then cover them with earth, thinking that it is impious to xpose them to the sun; but the Egyptians take out their entrails and embalm them nd keep them above ground with themselves. The fish-eating tribes of the Ethiopians ast them into the lakes, there to be devoured by the fish; the Hyrcanians expose them s a prey to dogs, and some of the Indians to vultures. And they say that some of the roglodytes take the corpse to a hill, and then after tying its head to its feet cast stones pon it amidst laughter, and when they have made a heap of stones over it they leave there. And some of the barbarians slay and eat those who are over sixty years old, ut bury in the earth those who die young. Some burn the dead; and of these some ecover and preserve their bones, while others show no care but leave them scattered bout. And they say that the Persians impale their dead and embalm them with nitre, fter which they wrap them round in bandages. How much grief others endure for e dead we see ourselves.

Some, too, believe death itself to be dreadful and horrible, others do not. Thus uripides says:

> Who knows if life be but the state of death,
> And death be counted life in realms below?

nd Epicurus declares: "Death is nothing to us; for what is dissolved is senseless, nd what is senseless is nothing to us." They also declare that, inasmuch as we are ompounded of soul and body, and death is a dissolution of soul and body, when we xist death does not exist (for we are not being dissolved), and when death xists we do not exist, for through the cessation of the compound of soul and ody we too cease to exist. And Heracleitus states that both life and death exist oth in our state of life and in our state of death; for when we live our souls are dead nd buried within us, and when we die our souls revive and live. And some even uppose that dying is better for us than living. Thus Euripides says:

> Rather should we assemble to bewail
> The babe new-born, such ills has he to face;
> Whereas the dead, who has surcease from woe,
> With joy and gladness we should bear from home.

These lines, too, spring from the same sentiment:

> Not to have been begotten at all were the best thing for mortals,
> Nor to have lookèd upon fiery rays of the sun:
> Or, if begotten, to hasten amain to the portals of Hades,
> And to lie unmoved robèd in masses of earth.

We know, too, the facts about Cleobis and Biton which Herodotus relates in his story of the Argive priestess. It is reported, also, that some of the Thracians sit round the new-born babe and chant dirges. So, then, death should not be considered a thing naturally dreadful, just as life should not be considered a thing naturally good. Thus none of the things mentioned above is naturally of this character or of that, but all are matters of convention and relative.

The same method of treatment may be applied also to each of the other customs which we have not now described owing to the summary character of our exposition. And even if, in regard to some of them, we are unable to declare their discrepancy offhand, we ought to observe that disagreement concerning them may possibly exist amongst certain nations that are unknown to us. For just as, if we had been ignorant, say, of the custom amongst the Egyptians of marrying sisters, we should have asserted wrongly that it was universally agreed that men ought not to marry sisters,—even so, in regard to those practices wherein we notice no discrepancy, it is not proper for us to affirm that there is no disagreement about them, since, as I said, disagreement about them may possibly exist amongst some of the nations which are unknown to us.

Accordingly, the Sceptic, seeing so great a diversity of usages, suspends judgement as to the natural existence of anything good or bad or (in general) fit or unfit to be done, therein abstaining from the rashness of dogmatism; and he follows undogmatically the ordinary rules of life, and because of this he remains impassive in respect of matters of opinion, while in conditions that are necessitated his emotions are moderate; for though, as a human being, he suffers emotion through his senses, yet because he does not also opine that what he suffers is evil by nature, the emotion he suffers is moderate. For the added opinion that a thing is of such a kind is worse than the actual suffering itself, just as sometimes the patients themselves bear a surgical operation, while the bystanders swoon away because of their opinion that it is a horrible experience. But in fact, he who assumes that there exists by nature something good or bad or, generally fit or unfit to be done, is disquieted in various ways. For when he experiences what he regards as natural evils he deems himself to be pursued by Furies, and when he becomes possessed of what seems to him good things he falls into no ordinary state of disquiet both through arrogance and through fear of losing them, and through trying to guard against finding himself again amongst what he regards as natural evils; for those who assert that goods are incapable of being lost we shall put to silence by means of the doubts raised by their dissension. Hence we conclude that if what is productive of evil is evil and to be shunned, and the persuasion that these things are good, those evil, by nature produces disquiet, then the assumption and persuasion that anything is in its real nature, either bad or good is evil and to be shunned.

For the present, then, this account of things good, evil, and indifferent is sufficient

☙ EPICUREANISM: THE NATURE OF THE UNIVERSE

Lucretius

Titus Lucretius Carus (ca. *98–53* B.C.) *was a Roman aristocrat who withdrew from the violent political struggles of the first century* B.C. *to write a long philosophical poem,* De Rerum Natura *(literally, "On the Nature of Things"). This poem, as Lucretius himself tells us, was the work of an enthusiastic disciple rather than an original thinker: it proclaims the peace of soul to be had by following the doctrines of the Greek philosopher Epicurus.*

Epicurus (341–270 B.C.) *founded a school at Athens, called "The Garden," in 306* B.C. *He accepted even women and slaves as students, and taught that the proper life for mankind was not warfare, politics, or business, but the quiet enjoyment of simple pleasures of mind and body in the company of a few good friends. Diogenes Laertius tells us that Epicurus wrote over 300 books, including treatises on logic and science; but his interest in these things was only as a means to an end: tranquillity of mind. If it could be shown, he thought, that everything in the world is composed of tiny particles of matter (called "atoms"; this idea he got from Democritus, a great philosopher who lived almost two centuries earlier), that all processes take place according to definite natural laws of cause and effect, and that it is therefore irrational to fear death or the gods, then men would be freed from the bondage of their own emotions and could lead peaceful, happy lives.*

Lucretius' poem is addressed to one Gaius Memmius, a prominent politician. This is only a literary device, however; in reality he hopes to convert as many readers as possible to Epicureanism. In this he was singularly unsuccessful. Until the seventeenth century, when men like Gassendi and Spinoza began to entertain similar ideas under the impact of scientific discoveries, Lucretius was regarded as an agent of the devil, and even as a madman. Today he is recognized as one of the greatest of Latin poets, and even his philosophy has been finding adherents.

BOOK II

What joy it is, when out at sea the stormwinds are lashing the waters, to gaze from the shore at the heavy stress some other man is enduring! Not that anyone's afflictions are

Lucretius, *The Nature of the Universe*, trans. R. E. Latham (Baltimore: Penguin Books, Inc., 1951), pp. 60–63, 173–178, 183–186, 194–209, 215–216.

in themselves a source of delight; but to realize from what troubles you yourself ar free is joy indeed. What joy, again, to watch opposing hosts marshalled on the field o battle when you have yourself no part in their peril! But this is the greatest joy o all: to stand aloof in a quiet citadel, stoutly fortified by the teaching of the wise, an to gaze down from that elevation on others wandering aimlessly in a vain searc for the way of life, pitting their wits one against another, disputing for precedence struggling night and day with unstinted effort to scale the pinnacles of wealth an power. O joyless hearts of men! O minds without vision! How dark and dangerou the life in which this tiny span is lived away! Do you not see that nature is clamourin for two things only, a body free from pain, a mind released from worry and fear fo the enjoyment of pleasurable sensations?

So we find that the requirements of our bodily nature are few indeed, no more tha is necessary to banish pain. To heap pleasure upon pleasure may heighten men's enjoyment at times. But what matter if there are no golden images of youths about th house, holding flaming torches in their right hands to illumine banquets prolonge into the night? What matter if the hall does not sparkle with silver and gleam wit gold, and no carved and gilded rafters ring to the music of the lute? Nature does n miss these luxuries when men recline in company on the soft grass by a running strea under the branches of a tall tree and refresh their bodies pleasurably at small expens Better still if the weather smiles upon them and the season of the year stipples th green herbage with flowers. Burning fevers flee no swifter from your body if yo toss under figured counterpanes and coverlets of crimson than if you must lie in rud homespun.

If our bodies are not profited by treasures or titles or the majesty of kingship, w must go on to admit that neither are our minds. Or tell me, Memmius, when you se your legions thronging the Campus Martius in the ardour of mimic warfare, supporte by ample auxiliaries, magnificently armed and fired by a common purpose, does tha sight scare the terrors of superstition from your mind? Does the fear of death retir from your breast and leave it carefree at the moment when you sight your warship ranging far and wide? Or do we not find such resources absurdly ineffective? The fear and anxieties that dog the human breast do not shrink from the clash of arms or th fierce rain of missiles. They stalk unabashed among princes and potentates. They ar not awe-struck by the gleam of gold or the bright sheen of purple robes.

Can you doubt then that this power rests with reason alone? All life is a struggl in the dark. As children in blank darkness tremble and start at everything, so we i broad daylight are oppressed at times by fears as baseless as those horrors whic children imagine coming upon them in the dark. This dread and darkness of the min cannot be dispelled by the sunbeams, the shining shafts of day, but only by an understanding of the outward form and inner workings of nature.

And now to business. I will explain *the motion by which the generative bodies o matter give birth to various things,* and, after they are born, dissolve them once more the force that compels them to do this; and the power of movement through the boundless void with which they are endowed. It is for you to devote yourself attentively t my words.

Be sure that matter does not stick together in a solid mass. For we see that every hing grows less and seems to melt away with the lapse of time and withdraw its old .ge from our eyes. And yet we see no diminution in the sum of things. This is because he bodies that are shed by one thing lessen it by their departure but enlarge another y their coming; here they bring decay, there full bloom, but they do not linger there. o the sum of things is perpetually renewed. Mortals live by mutual interchange. One ace increases by another's decrease. The generations of living things pass in swift uccession and like runners hand on the torch of life.

If you think that the atoms can stop and by their stopping generate new motions in hings, you are wandering far from the path of truth. Since the atoms are moving reely through the void, they must all be kept in motion either by their own weight or n occasion by the impact of another atom. For it must often happen that two of hem in their course knock together and immediately bounce apart in opposite direc- ions, a natural consequence of their hardness and solidity and the absence of anything ehind to stop them.

As a further indication that all particles of matter are on the move, remember that he universe is bottomless: there is no place where the atoms could come to rest. As I ave already shown by various arguments and proved conclusively, space is without nd or limit and spreads out immeasurably in all directions alike.

It clearly follows that no rest is given to the atoms in their course through the depths f space. Driven along in an incessant but variable movement, some of them bounce ar apart after a collision while others recoil only a short distance from the impact. rom those that do not recoil far, being driven into a closer union and held there by he entanglement of their own interlocking shapes, are composed firmly rooted rock, he stubborn strength of steel and the like. Those others that move freely through larger racts of space, springing far apart and carried far by the rebound—these provide for s thin air and blazing sunlight. Besides these, there are many other atoms at large in mpty space which have been thrown out of compound bodies and have nowhere even een granted admittance so as to bring their motions into harmony.

This process, as I might point out, is illustrated by an image of it that is continually aking place before our very eyes. Observe what happens when sunbeams are admitted nto a building and shed light on its shadowy places. You will see a multitude of tiny articles mingling in a multitude of ways in the empty space within the light of the eam, as though contending in everlasting conflict, rushing into battle rank upon rank vith never a moment's pause in a rapid sequence of unions and disunions. From this ou may picture what it is for the atoms to be perpetually tossed about in the illimitable oid. To some extent a small thing may afford an illustration and an imperfect image f great things. . . .

BOOK V

The next stage in the argument is this. I must first demonstrate that the world also vas born and is composed of a mortal body. Then I must deal with the concourse of natter that laid the foundation of land, sea and sky, stars and sun and the globe of he moon. I must show what living things have existed on earth, and which have never been born; how the human race began to employ various utterances among themselves for denoting various things; and how there crept into their minds that fear of the gods which, all the world over, sanctifies temples and lakes, groves and altars and images of the gods. After that, I will explain by what forces nature steers the courses of the sun and the journeyings of the moon, so that we shall not suppose that they run their yearly races between heaven and earth of their own free will with the amiable intention of promoting the growth of crops and animals, or that they are rolled round in furtherance of some divine plan. For it may happen that men who have learnt the truth about the carefree existence of the gods fall to wondering by what power the universe is kept going, especially those movements that are seen overhead in the borderland of ether. Then the poor creatures are plunged back into their old superstitions and saddle themselves with cruel masters whom they believe to be all-powerful. All this because they do not know what can be and what cannot: how a limit is fixed to the power of everything and an immovable frontier post.

And now, Memmius, I will not hold you off any longer with promises. First of all then, cast your eyes on sea, lands and sky. These three bodies so different in nature, three distinct forms, three fabrics such as you behold—all these a single day will blot out. The whole substance and structure of the world, upheld through many years, will crash. I am well aware how novel and strange in its impact on the mind is this impending demolition of heaven and earth, and how hard it is for my words to carry conviction. This is always so when you bring to men's ears something outside their experience—something you cannot set before their eyes or lay hold of by hand, which is the shortest highway for belief to enter the human breast and the compartments of the mind. But, for all that, I will proclaim it. It may be that force will be given to my arguments by the event itself; that your own eyes will see those violent earthquakes in a brief space dash the whole world to fragments. From such a fate may guiding fortune steer us clear! May reason rather than the event itself convince you that the whole world can collapse with one ear-splitting crack!

Before I attempt to utter oracles on this theme, with more sanctity and far surer reason than those the Delphic prophetess pronounces, drugged by the laurel fumes from Apollo's tripod, I will first set your mind at rest with words of wisdom. Do not imagine under the spell of superstition, that lands and sun and sky, sea, stars and moon, must endure for ever because they are endowed with a divine body. Do not for that reason think it right that punishment appropriate to a monstrous crime should be imposed, as on the rebellious Titans, on all those who by their reasoning breach the ramparts of the world and seek to darken heaven's brightest luminary, the sun, belittling with mortal speech immortal beings. In fact these objects are so far from divinity, so unworthy of a place among the gods, that they may rather serve to impress upon us the type of the lifeless and the insensible. Obviously, it is only with certain bodies that mind and intelligence can co-exist. A tree cannot exist in the ether, or clouds in the salt sea, as fishes cannot live in the fields or blood flow in wood or sap in stones. There is a determined and allotted place for the growth and presence of everything. So mind cannot arise alone without body or apart from sinews and blood. If it could do this, then surely it could much more readily function in head or shoulders or the tips of the heels or be born in any other part, so long as it was held in the same container, that is to say, in the same man. Since, however, even in the human body we see a determined and allotted place set aside for the growth and presence of spirit and mind, we have even stronger grounds for denying that they can survive apart from all body or animal form in the crumbling clods of earth or the fire of the sun or in water or the high borderland of ether. These objects, therefore, are not endowed with divine consciousness, since they cannot even possess living spirits.

Furthermore, you must not suppose tht the holy dwelling-places of the gods are anywhere within the limits of the world. For the flimsy nature of the gods, far removed from our senses, is scarcely visible even to the perception of the mind. Since it eludes the touch and pressure of our hands, it can have no contact with anything that is tangible to us. For what cannot be touched cannot touch. Therefore their dwelling-places also must be unlike ours, of the same flimsy texture as their bodies, as I will prove to you at length later on.

Next, the theory that they deliberately created the world in all its natural splendour for the sake of man, so that we ought to praise this eminently praiseworthy piece of divine workmanship and believe it eternal and immortal and think it a sin to unsettle by violence the everlasting abode established for mankind by the ancient purpose of the gods and to worry it with words and turn it topsy-turvy—this theory, Memmius, with all its attendant fictions is sheer nonsense. For what benefit could immortal and blessed beings reap from our gratitude, that they should undertake any task on our behalf? Or what could tempt those who had been at peace so long to change their old life for a new? The revolutionary is one who is dissatisfied with the old order. But one who has known no trouble in the past, but spent his days joyfully—what could prick such a being with the itch for novelty? Or again, what harm would it have done us to have remained uncreated? Are we to suppose that our life was sunk in gloom and grief till the light of creation blazed forth? True that, once a man is born, he must will to remain alive so long as beguiling pleasure holds him. But one who has never tasted the love of life, or been enrolled among the living, what odds is it to him if he is never created?

Here is a further point. On what pattern did the gods model their creation? From what source did an image of human beings first strike upon them, so that they might know and see with their minds what they wished to make? How was the power of the atoms made known to them, and the potential effect of their various combinations, unless nature itself provided a model of the creation? So many atoms, clashing together in so many ways as they are swept along through infinite time by their own weight, have come together in every possible way and realized everything that could be formed by their combinations. No wonder, then, if they have actually fallen into those groupings and movements by which the present world through all its changes is kept in being.

Even if I knew nothing of the atoms, I would venture to assert on the evidence of the celestial phenomena themselves, supported by many other arguments, that the universe was certainly not created for us by divine power: it is so full of imperfections. In the first place, of all that is covered by the wide sweep of the sky, part has been greedily seized by mountains and the woodland haunts of wild beasts. Part is usurped by crags and desolate bogs and the sea that holds far asunder the shores of the lands. Almost two-thirds are withheld from mankind by torrid heat and perennial deposits of frost. The little that is left of cultivable soil, if the force of nature had its way would be choked with briars, did not the force of man oppose it. It is man's way, for the sake of life, to groan over the stout mattock and cleave the earth with down-pressed plough. Unless we turn the fruitful clods with the coulter and break up the soil to stimulate the growth of the crops, they cannot emerge of their own accord into the open air. Even so, when by dint of hard work all the fields at last burst forth into leaf and flower, then either the fiery sun withers them with intemperate heat, or sudden showers and icy frosts destroy them and gales of wind batter them with hurricane force. Again, why does nature feed and breed the fearsome brood of wild beasts, a menace to the human race by land and sea? Why do the changing seasons bring pestilence in their train? Why does untimely death roam abroad? The human infant, like a shipwrecked sailor cast ashore by the cruel waves, lies naked on the ground, speechless, lacking all aids to life, when nature has first tossed him with pangs of travail from his mother's womb upon the shores of the sunlit world. He fills the air with his piteous wailing, and quite rightly, considering what evils life holds in store for him. But beasts of every kind, both tame and wild, have no need of rattles or a nurse to lull them with inarticulate babble. They do not want to change their clothes at every change in the weather. They need no armaments or fortifications to guard their possessions, since all the needs of all are lavishly supplied by mother earth herself and nature, the great artificer. . . .

I will now set out in order *the stages by which the initial concentration of matter laid the foundations of earth and sky,* of the ocean depths and the orbits of sun and moon. Certainly the atoms did not post themselves purposefully in due order by an act of intelligence, nor did they stipulate what movements each should perform. But multitudinous atoms, swept along in multitudinous courses through infinite time by mutual clashes and their own weight, have come together in every possible way and realized everything that could be formed by their combinations. So it comes about that a voyage of immense duration, in which they have experienced every variety of movement and conjunction, has at length brought together those whose sudden encounter normally forms the starting-point of substantial fabrics—earth and sea and sky and the races of living creatures.

At that time the sun's bright disc was not to be seen here, soaring aloft and lavishing its light, nor the stars that crowd the far-flung firmament, nor sea nor sky nor earth nor air nor anything in the likeness of the things we know—nothing but a hurricane raging in a newly congregated mass of atoms of every sort. From their disharmony sprang conflict, which maintained a turmoil in their interspaces, courses, unions, thrusts, impacts, collisions and motions, because owing to their diversity of shape and pattern they could not all remain in the combinations in which they found themselves or mutually reconcile their motions. From this medley they started to sort themselves out, like combining with like, and to rough out the main features of a world composed of distinct parts: they began, in fact, to separate the heights of heaven from the earth, to single out the sea as a receptacle for water detached from the mass and to set apart the fires of pure and isolated ether.

In the first place all the particles of earth, because they were heavy and intertangled, collected in the middle and took up the undermost stations. The more closely they cohered and clung together, the more they squeezed out the atoms that went to the making of sea and stars, sun and moon and the outer walls of this great world. For all these are composed of smooth round seeds, much smaller than the particles of earth. The first element to break out of the earth through the pores in its spongy crust and to shoot up aloft was ether, the generator of fire. Owing to its lightness, it carried off with it a quantity of fire. We may compare a sight we often see when the sun's golden rays glow with the first flush of dawn among the dew-spangled herbage: the lakes and perennial watercourses exhale a vapour, while at times we see the earth itself steaming. It is these vapours, when they all coalesce and combine their substance in the upper air, that weave a cloudy curtain under the sky. Just so in those days the ethereal fire, buoyant and diffusive, coalesced at the circumference and trickled this way and that till it became generally diffused and enveloped the other elements in an ardent embrace.

On this ensued the birth of the sun and moon, whose globes revolve at middle height in the atmosphere. The earth did not claim them for itself, nor did the transcendent ether, because they were neither heavy enough to sink and settle nor light enough to soar in the uppermost zone. Yet in their midway station they are so placed as to revolve actual bodies and to form parts of the world as a whole. Just so in our own bodies, while some members remain fixed at their posts, others are free to move.

When these elements had withdrawn, the earth suddenly caved in, throughout the zone now covered by the blue extent of sea, and flooded the cavity with surging brine. Day by day the encircling ethereal fires and the sun's rays by continual bombardment of the outer crust from every quarter compressed the earth into an ever narrower compass, so that it shrank into itself in its middle reaches and cohered more compactly. So even ampler floods of salty fluid were exuded from its body to swell the billowy plain of ocean. Ever fresh contingents of those particles of heat and air of which I have spoken slipped out to reinforce the sparkling vault of heaven far up above the earth. As the plains settled down, the mountain steeps grew more prominent; for the crags could not sink in, and it was not possible for every part to subside to the same extent.

So the earth by its weight and the coalescing of its substance came to rest. All the sediment of the world, because it was heavy, drifted downwards together and settled at the bottom like dregs. Then sea and air and fiery ether itself were each in turn left unalloyed in their elemental purity, one being lighter than another. Ether, as the clearest and the lightest, floats upon the gusty air and does not mingle its clear substance with the air's tempestuous tumult. It leaves the lower regions to be spun round by eddying whirlwinds, tossed to and fro by veering squalls. It bears its own fires on a steady course as it glides along. The possibility of such a regular and constant flow as this of ether is demonstrated by the Bosporus, a sea which flows with a uniform tide, maintaining perpetually the single tenor of its current. . . .

I have explained the processes by which the various phenomena may be brought about in the blue expanses of the firmament. I have made intelligible the forces that may actuate the movements of the sun and the moon's wanderings. I have shown how both may suffer eclipse through the obscuration of their light and plunge the unexpecting earth in gloom, as though they blinked and then with reopened eye surveyed the world, aglow with limpid radiance. I return now to the childhood of the world, to consider what fruits the tender fields of earth in youthful parturition first ventured to fling up into the light of day and entrust to the fickle breezes.

First of all, the earth girdled its hills with a green glow of herbage, and over every plain the meadows gleamed with verdure and with bloom. Then trees of every sort were given free rein to join in an eager race for growth into the gusty air. As feathers, fur and bristles are generated at the outset from the bodies of winged and four-footed creatures, so then *the new-born earth first flung up herbs and shrubs. Next in order it engendered the various breeds of mortal creatures,* manifold in mode of origin as in form. The animals cannot have fallen from the sky, and those that live on land cannot have emerged from the briny gulfs. We are left with the conclusion that the name of mother has rightly been bestowed on the earth, since out of the earth everything is born.

Even now multitudes of animals are formed out of the earth with the aid of showers and the sun's genial warmth. So it is not surprising if more and bigger ones took shape and developed in those days, when earth and ether were young. First, the various breeds of winged birds were hatched out of eggs in the spring season, just as now the cicadas in summer crawl out spontaneously from their tubular integuments in quest of sustenance and life. Then it was that the earth brought forth the first mammals. There was a great superfluity of heat and moisture in the soil. So, wherever a suitable spot occurred, there grew up wombs, clinging to the earth by roots. These, when the time was ripe, were burst open by the maturation of the embryos, rejecting moisture now and struggling for air. Then nature directed towards that spot the pores of the earth, making it open its veins and exude a juice resembling milk, just as nowadays every female when she has given birth is filled with sweet milk because all the flow of nourishment within her is directed into the breasts. The young were fed by the earth, clothed by the warmth and bedded by the herbage, which was then covered with abundance of soft down. The childhood of the world provoked no hard frosts or excessive heats or winds of boisterous violence. For all things keep pace in their growth and the attainment of their full strength. Here then, is further proof that the name of mother has rightly been bestowed on the earth, since it brought forth the human race and gave birth at the appointed season to every beast that runs wild among the high hills and at the same time to the birds of the air in all their rich variety.

Then, because there must be an end to such parturition, the earth ceased to bear, like a woman worn out with age. For the nature of the world as a whole is altered by age. Everything must pass through successive phases. Nothing remains for ever what it was. Everything is on the move. Everything is transformed by nature and forced into new paths. One thing, withered by time, decays and dwindles. Another emerges from ignominy, and waxes strong. So the nature of the world as a whole is altered by age. The earth passes through successive phases, so that it can no longer bear what it could, and it can now what it could not before.

In those days the earth attempted also to produce a host of monsters, grotesque in build and aspect—hermaphrodites, halfway between the sexes yet cut off from either, creatures bereft of feet or dispossessed of hands, dumb, mouthless brutes, or eyeless and blind, or disabled by the adhesion of their limbs to the trunk, so that they could neither do anything nor go anywhere nor keep out of harm's way nor take what they needed. These and other such *monstrous and misshapen births were created. But all in vain.* Nature debarred them from increase. They could not gain the coveted flower of maturity nor procure food nor be coupled by the arts of Venus. For it is evident that many contributory factors are essential to the reproduction of a species. First, it must have a food-supply. Then it must have some channel by which the procreative seeds can travel outward through the body when the limbs are relaxed. Then, in order that male and female may couple, they must have some means of interchanging their mutual delight.

In those days, again, *many species must have died out altogether* and failed to reproduce their kind. Every species that you now see drawing the breath of life has been protected and preserved from the beginning of the world either by cunning or by prowess or by speed. In addition, there are many that survive under human protection because their usefulness has commended them to our care. The surly breed of lions, for instance, in their native ferocity have been preserved by prowess, the fox by cunning and the stag by flight. The dog, whose loyal heart is alert even in sleep, all beasts of burden of whatever breed, fleecy sheep and horned cattle, over all these, my Memmius, man has established his protectorate. They have gladly escaped from predatory beasts and sought peace and the lavish meals, procured by no effort of theirs with which we recompense their service. But those that were gifted with none of these natural assets, unable either to live on their own resources or to make any contribution to human welfare, in return for which we might let their race feed in safety under our guardianship—all these, trapped in the toils of their own destiny, were fair game and an easy prey for others, till nature brought their race to extinction.

But *there never were,* nor ever can be, Centaurs—*creatures with a double nature,* combining organs of different origin in a single body so that there may be a balance of power between attributes drawn from two distinct sources. This can be inferred by the dullest wit from these facts. First, a horse reaches its vigorous prime in about three years, a boy far from it: for often even at that age he will fumble in sleep for his mother's suckling breasts. Then, when the horse's limbs are flagging and his mettle is fading with the onset of age and the ebbing of life, then is the very time when the boy is crowned with the flower of youth and his cheeks are clothed with a downy bloom. You need not suppose, therefore, that there can ever be a Centaur, compounded of man and draught-horse, or a Scylla, half sea-monster, with a girdle of mad dogs, or any other such monstrous hybrid between species whose bodies are obviously incompatible. They do not match in their maturing, in gaining strength or in losing it with advancing years. They respond diversely to the flame of Venus. Their habits are discordant. Their senses are not gratified by the same stimuli. You may even see bearded goats battening on hemlock, which to man is deadly poison. Since flame sears and burns the tawny frames of lions no less than any other form of flesh and blood that exists on earth, how could there be a Chimaera with three bodies rolled into one, in front a lion, at the rear a serpent, in the middle the she-goat that her name implies, belching from her jaws a dire flame born of her body? If anyone pretends that such monsters could have been begotten when earth was young and the sky new, pinning his faith merely on that empty word 'young', he is welcome to trot out a string of fairy tales of the same stamp. Let him declare that rivers of gold in those days flowed in profusion over the earth; that the trees bore gems for blossoms, or that a man was born with such a stretch of limbs that he could bestride the high seas and spin the whole firmament around him with his hands. The fact that there were abundant seeds of things in the earth at the time when it first gave birth to living creatures is no indication that beasts could have been created of intermingled shapes with limbs compounded from different species. The growths that even now spring profusely from the soil—the varieties of herbs and cereals and lusty trees—cannot be produced in this composite fashion: each species develops according to its own kind, and they all guard their specific characters in obedience to the laws of nature.

The *human beings* that peopled these fields were far tougher than the men of to-day, as became the offspring of tough earth. They were built on a framework of bigger and solider bones, fastened through their flesh to stout sinews. They were relatively insensitive to heat and cold, to unaccustomed diet and bodily ailments in general. Through many decades of the sun's cyclic course they lived out their lives in the fashion of wild beasts roaming at large. No one spent his strength in guiding the curved plough. No one knew how to cleave the earth with iron, or to plant young saplings in the soil or lop the old branches from tall trees with pruning hooks. Their hearts were well content to accept as a free gift what the sun and showers had given and the earth had produced unsolicited. Often they stayed their hunger among the acorn-laden oaks. Arbutus berries, whose scarlet tint now betrays their winter ripening, were then produced by the earth in plenty and of a large size. In addition the lusty childhood of the earth yielded a great variety of tough foods, ample for afflicted mortals. Rivers and springs called to them to slake their thirst, as nowadays a clamorous cataract of water, tumbling out of the high hills, summons from far away the thirsty creatures of the wild. They restored to those woodland sanctuaries of the nymphs, familiar to them in their wandering, from which they knew that trickling streams of water issued to bathe the dripping rocks in a bountiful shower, sprinkled over green moss, and gushed out here and there over the open plain.

They did not know as yet how to enlist the aid of fire, or to make use of skins, or to clothe their bodies with trophies of the chase. They lived in thickets and hillside caves and forests and stowed their rugged limbs among bushes when driven to seek shelter from the lash of wind and rain.

They could have no thought of the common good, no notion of the mutual restraint of morals and laws. The individual, taught only to live and fend for himself, carried off on his own account such prey as fortune brought him. Venus coupled the bodies of lovers in the greenwood. Mutual desire brought them together, or the male's mastering might and overriding lust, or a payment of acorns or arbutus berries or choice pears. Thanks to their surpassing strength of hand and foot, they hunted the woodland beasts by hurling stones and wielding ponderous clubs. They were more than a match for many of them; from a few they took refuge in hiding-places.

When night overtook them, they flung their jungle-bred limbs naked on the earth like bristly boars, and wrapped themselves round with a coverlet of leaves and branches. It is not true that they wandered panic-stricken over the countryside through the darkness of night, searching with loud lamentations for the daylight and the sun. In fact they waited, sunk in quiet sleep, till the sun with his rose-red torch should bring back radiance to the sky. Accustomed as they were from infancy to seeing the alternate birth of darkness and light, they could never have been struck with amazement or misgiving whether the withdrawal of the sunlight might not plunge the earth in everlasting night. They were more worried by the peril to which unlucky sleepers were often exposed from predatory beasts. Turned out of house and home by the intrusion of a slavering boar or a burly lion, they would abandon their rocky roofs at dead of night and yield up their leaf-strewn beds in terror to the savage visitor.

The proportion of mortal men that relinquished the dear light of life before it was all spent was not appreciably higher then than now. Then it more often happened that an individual victim would furnish living food to a beast of prey: engulfed in its jaws, he would fill thicket and mountainside and forest with his shrieks, at the sight of his living flesh entombed in a living sepulchre. Those who saved their mangled bodies by flight would press trembling palms over ghastly sores, calling upon death in heart-rending voices, till life was wrenched from them by racking spasms. In their ignorance of the treatment that wounds demand, they could not help themselves. But it never happened then that many thousands of men following the standards were led to death on a single day. Never did the ocean levels, lashed into tumult, hurl ships and men together upon the reefs. Here, time after time, the sea would rise and vainly vent its fruitless ineffectual fury, then lightly lay aside its idle threats. The crafty blandishment of the unruffled deep could not tempt any man to his undoing with its rippling laughter. Then, when the mariner's presumptuous art lay still unguessed, it was lack of food that brought failing limbs at last to death. Now it is superfluity that proves too much for them. The men of old, in their ignorance, often served poison to themselves. Now, with greater skill, they administer it to others.

As time went by, men began to build huts and to use skins and fire. Male and female learnt to live together in a stable union and to watch over their joint progeny. Then it was that humanity first began to mellow. Thanks to fire, their chilly bodies could no longer so easily endure the cold under the canopy of heaven. Venus subdued brute strength. Children by their wheedling easily broke down their parents' stubborn temper. Then neighbours began to form *mutual alliances,* wishing neither to do nor to suffer violence among themselves. They appealed on behalf of their children and womenfolk, pointing out with gestures and inarticulate cries that it is right for everyone to pity the weak. It was not possible to achieve perfect unity of purpose. Yet a substantial majority kept faith honestly. Otherwise the entire human race would have been wiped out there and then instead of being propagated, generation after generation, down to the present day.

As for the various sounds of *spoken language,* it was nature that drove men to utter these, and practical convenience that gave a form to the names of objects. We see a similar process at work when babies are led by their speechless plight to employ gestures, such as pointing with a finger at objects in view. For every creature has a sense of the purposes for which he can use his own powers. A bull-calf, before ever his horns have grown and sprouted from his forehead, butts and thrusts with them aggressively when his temper is roused. Panther and lion cubs tussle with paws and jaws when their claws and teeth are scarcely yet in existence. We see every species of winged bird trust in its wings and seek faint-hearted aid from flight. To suppose that someone on some particular occasion allotted names to objects, and that by this means men learnt their first words, is stark madness. Why should we suppose that one man had this power of indicating everything by vocal utterances and emitting the various sounds of speech when others could not do it? Besides, if others had not used such utterances among themselves, from what source was the mental image of its use implanted in him? Whence did this one man derive the power in the first instance of seeing with his mind what he wanted to do? One man could not subdue a greater number and induce them by force to learn his names for things. It is far from easy to convince deaf listeners by any demonstration what needs to be done. They would not endure it or submit for long on any terms to have incomprehensible noises senselessly dinned into their ears.

And what, after all, is so surprising in the notion that the human race, possessed of a vigorous voice and tongue, should indicate objects by various vocal utterances expressive of various feelings? Even dumb cattle and wild beasts utter distinct and various sounds when they are gripped by fear or pain or when joy wells up within them. Indeed we have direct evidence of such distinctions. Molossian hounds, for instance, when first their gaping flabby jowls are drawn back in a grim snarl that bares their hard teeth, give vent to a gruff growl. Very different is the sound when the growl has grown to a loud-mouthed reverberating bay. Different again is the soft crooning with which they fondle their pups when they fall to licking them lovingly with their tongues or toss them with their paws, snapping with open jaws in a playful pretence of gobbling them up with teeth that never close. And different from all these are their howls when left alone in the house, or the whimpering with which they shrink and cringe to avoid the whip. In the same way, when a stallion in the prime of his youth is let loose among the mares, smarting from the prick of winged Cupid's darts, and snorts defiance to his rivals through distended nostrils, his neigh is surely not the same that shakes his limbs on other occasions. So also with the various species of winged birds. The hawks and ospreys and gulls that seek a livelihood among the salt sea-waves all have distinctive cries that show when they are squabbling over their booty or struggling to master a quarry. Some birds even vary their note according to the weather. So the hoarse-throated cawing of long-lived ravens and gregarious rooks varies from time to time according as they are clamouring for showers of rain, as it is said, or summoning wind and storm. If the animals, dumb though they be, are impelled by different feelings to utter different cries, how much the more reason to suppose that men in those days had the power of distinguishing between one thing and another by distinctive utterances! . . .

As time went by, men learnt to change their old way of life by means of fire and other new inventions, instructed by those of outstanding ability and mental energy. *Kings began to found cities* and establish citadels for their own safeguard and refuge. They parcelled out cattle and lands, giving to each according to his looks, his strength and his ability; for good looks were highly prized and strength counted for much. Later came the invention of property and the discovery of gold, which speedily robbed the strong and the handsome of their pre-eminence. The man of greater riches finds no lack of stalwart frames and comely faces to follow in his train. And yet, if a man would guide his life by true philosophy, he will find ample riches in a modest livelihood enjoyed with a tranquil mind. Of that little he need never be beggared. Men craved for fame and power so that their fortune might rest on a firm foundation and they might live out a peaceful life in the enjoyment of plenty. An idle dream. In struggling to gain the pinnacle of power they beset their own road with perils. And then from the very peak, as though by a thunderbolt, they are cast down by envy into a foul abyss of ignominy. For envy, like the thunderbolt, most often strikes the highest and all that stands out above the common level. Far better to lead a quiet life in subjection than to long for sovereign authority and lordship over kingdoms. So leave them to the blood and sweat of their wearisome unprofitable struggle along the narrow pathway of ambition. Since they savour life through another's mouth and choose their target rather by hearsay than by the evidence of their own senses, it avails them now, and will avail them, no more than it has ever done.

So the kings were killed. Down in the dust lay the ancient majesty of thrones, the haughty sceptres. The illustrious emblem of the sovereign head, dabbled in gore and trampled under the feet of the rabble, mourned its high estate. What once was feared too much is now as passionately downtrodden. So the conduct of affairs sank back into the turbid depths of mob-rule, with each man struggling to win dominance and supremacy for himself. Then some men showed how to form a constitution, based on fixed rights and recognized laws. Mankind, worn out by a life of violence and enfeebled by feuds, was the more ready to submit of its own free will to the bondage of laws and institutions. This distaste for a life of violence came naturally to a society in which every individual was ready to gratify his anger by a harsher vengeance than is now tolerated by equitable laws. Ever since then the enjoyment of life's prizes has been tempered by the fear of punishment. A man is enmeshed by his own violence and wrong-doing, which commonly recoil upon their author. It is not easy for one who breaks by his acts the mutual compact of social peace to lead a peaceful and untroubled life. Even if he hides his guilt from gods and men, he must feel a secret misgiving that it will not rest hidden for ever. He cannot forget those oft-told tales of men betraying themselves by words spoken in dreams or delirium that drag out long-buried crimes into the daylight.

Let us now consider why *reverence for the gods* is widespread among the nations. What has crowded their cities with altars and inaugurated those solemn rites that are in vogue to-day in powerful states and busy resorts? What has implanted in mortal hearts that chill of dread which even now rears new temples of the gods the wide world over and packs them on holy days with pious multitudes? The explanation is not far to seek. Already in those early days men had visions when their minds were awake, and more clearly in sleep, of divine figures, dignified in mien and impressive in stature. To these figures they attributed sentience, because they were seen to move their limbs and give voice to lordly utterances appropriate to their stately features and stalwart frames. They further credited them with eternal life, because the substance of their shapes was perpetually renewed and their appearance unchanging and in general because they thought that beings of such strength could not lightly be subdued by any force. They pictured their lot as far superior to that of mortals, because none of them was tormented by the fear of death, and also because in dreams they saw them perform all sorts of miracles without the slightest effort.

Again, men noticed the orderly succession of celestial phenomena and the round of the seasons and were at a loss to account for them. So they took refuge in handing over everything to the gods and making everything dependent on their whim. They chose the sky to be the home and headquarters of the gods because it is through the sky that the moon is seen to tread its cyclic course with day and night and night's ominous constellations and the night-flying torches and soaring flames of the firmament, clouds and sun and rain, snow and wind, lightning and hail, the sudden thunder-crash and the long-drawn intimidating rumble.

Poor humanity, to saddle the gods with such responsibilities and throw in a vindictive temper! What griefs they hatched then for themselves, what festering sores for us, what tears for our posterity! This is not piety, this oft-repeated show of bowing a veiled head before a graven image; this bustling to every altar; this kow-towing and prostration on the ground with palms outspread before the shrines of the gods; this deluging of altars with the blood of beasts; this heaping of vow on vow. True piety lies rather in the power to contemplate the universe with a quiet mind.

When we gaze up at the supernal regions of this mighty world, at the ether poised above, studded with flashing stars, and there comes into our minds the thought of the sun and moon and their migrations, then in hearts already racked by other woes a new anxiety begins to waken and rear up its head. We fall to wondering whether we may not be subject to some unfathomable divine power, which speeds the shining stars along their various tracks. It comes as a shock to our faltering minds to realize how little they know about the world. Had it a birth and a beginning? Is there some limit in time, beyond which its bastions will be unable to endure the strain of jarring motion? Or are they divinely gifted with everlasting surety, so that in their journey through the termless tract of time they can mock the stubborn strength of illimitable age?

Again, who does not feel his mind quailing and his limbs unnerved with shuddering dread of the gods when the parched earth reels at the dire stroke of the thunderbolt and tumult rolls across the breadth of heaven? Do not multitudes quake and nations tremble? Do not proud monarchs flinch, stricken in every limb by terror of the gods and the thought that the time has come when some foul deed or arrogant word must pay its heavy price?

Or picture a storm at sea, the wind scouring the water with hurricane force and some high admiral of the fleet swept before the blast with all his lavish complement of troops and battle elephants. How he importunes the peace of the gods with vows! How fervently he prays in his terror that the winds, too, may be at peace and favouring breezes blow! But, for all his prayers, the tornado does not relax its grip, and all too often he is dashed upon the reefs of death. So irresistibly is human power ground to dust by some unseen force, which seems to mock at the majestic rods and ruthless axes of authority and trample on them for its sport.

Lastly, when the whole earth quakes beneath their feet, when shaken cities fall in ruins or hang hesitantly tottering, what wonder if mortal men despise themselves and find a place in nature for superhuman forces and miraculous divine powers with supreme control over the universe? . . .

It was the sun and moon, the watchmen of the world, encircling with their light that vast rotating vault, who taught men that the seasons of the year revolve and that there is a constant pattern in things and a constant sequence.

By this time men were living their lives fenced by fortifications and tilling an earth already parcelled out and allotted. The sea was aflutter with flying sails. Societies were bound together by compacts and alliances. Poets were beginning to record history in song. But letters were still a recent invention. Therefore our age cannot look back to see what happened before this stage, except in so far as its traces can be uncovered by reason.

So we find that not only such arts as sea-faring and agriculture, city walls and laws, weapons, roads and clothing, but also without exception the amenities and refinements of life, songs, pictures, and statues, artfully carved and polished, *all were taught gradually by usage* and the active mind's experience as men groped their way forward step by step. So each particular development is brought gradually to the fore by the advance of time, and reason lifts it into the light of day. Men saw one notion after another take shape within their minds until by their arts they scaled the topmost peak.

METAMORPHOSES

Apuleius

Lucius Apuleius (born A.D. ca. *125) came from Madaura, not far from Carthage in Africa. He received an excellent education in Carthage, Athens, and Rome, and devoted his life to writing and lecturing on a wide variety of subjects; he was a kind of Roman sophist. His primary interest was religion, however, and especially the ancient and mystical religions of the Near East.*

In his Metamorphoses *(also called* The Golden Ass*) this religious interest receives an ingenious treatment that combines allegory, autobiography, and satire. The central character, also named Lucius, is a wealthy young playboy who has a way with women. He becomes involved with a beautiful lady who, however, is also a sorceress, and he is accidentally transformed into an ass. The antidote is not readily available, and meanwhile Lucius is kidnapped by someone who mistakes him for an ordinary ass. He escapes, but has to wander from place to place in this embarrassing shape for some time. His adventures form a satirical portrait of the Roman world in the second century. Our selection begins as*

Lucius is about to be forced to play the male lead in a public fertility rite, opposite a voluptuous young maiden representing Venus.

The allegorical character of the work seems obvious enough: Lucius' bestial lust and laziness make an ass out of him, but he finally comes to see himself for the moral brute he is, and is metamorphosed (or converted) into a humble and pious man. Apuleius' choice of Isis rather than Christ to represent the height of moral purity seems to have blinded many Christian critics to the fact that this is a story about how one man found his God; it has repeatedly been dismissed as a collection of ribald tales. It is probably the only masterpiece of religious literature to be condemned as pornographic. St. Augustine, however, who was born two centuries later in the same region as Apuleius, seems to have recognized it for what it is: the pagan counterpart to his own Confessions.

BOOK TEN

. . . And now behold, the day destined for the show came; and amid shouts of applause, a long train escorting me, I was led to the amphitheatre. During the first part of the performance, which was devoted to the joyous choral dances of the players, I was placed outside the gate, and was glad to crop some very fresh grass which grew just at the entrance; while I every now and then delighted my curious eyes with a most agreeable view of the spectacle through the open gate.

Beautiful boys and maidens, in the bloom of youth, splendidly dressed, moved with great elegance of gesture through the graceful evolutions of the Greek Pyrrhic dance. Now they revolved in a circle; now they deployed into an oblique line, with hands joined; at times they formed a wedge-like figure enclosing an open square; then they parted into two troops, and went through a variety of intricate movements, till they ceased at the sound of the trumpet. Then the screen was lowered, the hangings were drawn aside, and a dramatic scene was exhibited.

There was a wooden structure formed in imitation of that celebrated mountain, Ida, of which the poet Homer has sung. It was a fabric of considerable height, covered over with turf and with growing trees up to the very top, whence, by the contrivance of the artist, a fountain was made to flow and pour down a stream of water. A few goats cropped the grass, and a young man, handsomely arrayed in flowing Barbaric vestments, and having his head covered with a golden tiara, in resemblance of Paris, the Phrygian shepherd, appeared to be employed in pastoral pursuits. A beautiful boy then came forward, his only garment being the mantle generally worn by striplings, which covered his left shoulder. His beautiful yellow hair flowed loosely, and from the midst of it issued a pair of little golden wings; these and the caduceus he carried showed him to be Mercury. He danced forward, holding in his hand a golden apple, which he

The Works of Apuleius **(London: G. Bell & Sons, Ltd., 1881), pp. 215–233.**

presented to the performer who personated Paris, made known to him by signs what Jove commanded, and gracefully retired. A girl then made her appearance, of noble features, representing the goddess Juno: for her head was surrounded with a white diadem, and she bore a sceptre in her hand. Another then entered, who was easy to be recognized as Minerva, having on her head a shining helmet, encircled with a wreath of olive. She raised her shield aloft, and brandished her spear, like that goddess when engaged in battle. After these came another female, of surpassing beauty; the loveliness of her divine complexion declared her to be Venus, and Venus such as she was while yet a virgin. Her perfect form was naked, all but some charms imperfectly concealed by a gauze scarf, which the wind played with amorously, sometimes uncovering the beauties beneath it, sometimes pressing it against the limbs, and displaying their delicious contour. The goddess appeared in two different colours; her body was dazzlingly white, because she had descended from the heavens, while her silken garment was azure, because she had emerged from the sea.

The virgins who represented the goddesses were accompanied by their respective attendants: Juno by two young players, representing Castor and Pollux, whose heads were covered with helmets of semi-oval form, graced with a cluster of stars. She advanced with a calm and unaffected air to the warbling of the flute, and promised the shepherd, with modest gestures, that she would bestow on him the empire of all Asia, if he adjudged to her the prize of beauty.

She who personated Minerva was attended by two armed youths, Terror and Fear, who danced before her with drawn swords. Behind her a piper played a martial air, mingling shrill and deep-braying tones, and excited the agility of the dancers as with the blast of the trumpet. With restless head and threatening glances, Pallas bounded forward, and with animated gesture signified to Paris that if he pronounced her victorious in the contest of beauty, she would render him illustrious for his valour, and his achievements in war.

Greeted with vast applause from the spectators, Venus advanced with a sweet smile, and stood still in a graceful attitude in the middle of the stage, surrounded by a throng of merry little boys, such plump, round-limbed, fair-skinned little fellows, you would have sworn they were real Cupids, who had just flown from heaven or from the sea; for they had little wings, and arrows, and all other accoutrements conformable; and they carried gleaming torches before their mistress, as if to light her way to a nuptial banquet. She had also in her train a lovely choir of virgins, the charming Graces and the Hours, who strewed the path of their goddess with loose flowers and bouquets, and propitiated the queen of pleasure with the pleasant offerings of the spring.

Presently the flutes began to breathe soft Lydian airs, that thrilled the audience with delight; but greater still was their delight, when Venus began to move in concert with the music, and with slow lingering steps, and gentle sinuous flexure of the spine and head, and graceful movements of the arms, to respond to the soft modulations of the flutes; while now her eyes swam with voluptuous languor, now flashed with the ardour of passion, and sometimes she seemed, as it were, to dance with her eyes alone. As soon as she had approached close to the judge, she was understood to promise, by the movements of her arms, that if she was preferred to the other goddesses, she would bestow on Paris a wife surpassing all women in beauty, in a word, one like herself.

Gladly, then, did the young Phrygian deliver to her the golden apple he held in his hand, as a token of her victory.

What wonder is it, then, you vilest of people, forensic cattle rather, vultures clad in gowns, if all judges now sell their decisions for a price? Even in the early ages of the world, favour was able to corrupt judgment in a question agitated between Gods and men, and a young man, a rustic and a shepherd, elected judge by the counsels of mighty Jupiter, bartered the first judicial decision for the lucre of lust, ensuring thereby the destruction of all his race. Ay, by Hercules, and another such judgment was given in later times, by the illustrious leaders of the Greeks, when Palamedes, renowned for wisdom and learning, was condemned on false accusations as a traitor; as also when the mendicant Ulysses was preferred to the mighty Ajax, who excelled in military prowess. And what sort of judgment was that given by those renowned lawgivers, the Athenians, those clever people, and masters of all the sciences? Was not that divinely wise old man, whom the Delphic god pronounced superior in wisdom to all men, circumvented by the treachery and envy of a most famous faction, as a declared corrupter of youth, though he restrained their excesses as with a bridle? Was he not cut off by the deadly juice of a pestilential herb, leaving to his fellow-citizens the stain of indelible ignominy? For even at this day the most excellent philosophers make choice of his most holy sect before all others, and swear by his name, in their highest aspirations for consummate happiness.

Lest, however, any one blame this outburst of indignation, and say to himself, Look ye now, are we to suffer an ass to philosophize to us? I shall again return to the point in the narrative from which I digressed. After that judgment of Paris was finished, Juno and Minerva retired from the stage in sorrow and anger; and showed by their gestures the indignation they felt at being rejected; but Venus, full of joy and merriment, testified her gladness by dancing with all her choir. Then wine, mixed with saffron, burst forth on high from the summit of the mountain, through a pipe that lay concealed, and flowing in scattered streams, besprinkled as it fell, with an odoriferous shower, the goats that fed around, and changed their native whiteness for a more beautiful yellow tint. And now, the whole theatre exhaling a sweet odour, a chasm of the earth absorbed the wooden mountain.

One of the soldiers now ran down the street, to fulfil the demands of the people, and bring from the public prison the woman before-mentioned, who, as I have stated, was condemned to the wild beasts, on account of her manifold crimes, and destined to be my illustrious bride. What was intended also to be our genial bed was already prepared. It was brilliantly adorned with the Indian tortoise-shell, swelling with feathery heaps, and decorated with a silken coverlet. As for me, besides the shame of being thus publicly exhibited, and besides the contact of that wicked and polluted woman, I was also in the highest degree tormented with the fear of death; for it struck me that if, while we were performing our prescribed part in the exhibition, any wild beast should be let in on purpose to destroy the woman, it would not be so remarkably well trained or sagacious, or so temperate and abstemious, as to tear the woman to pieces who was at my side, and spare me, as being uncondemned, and guilty of no crime.

Being therefore alarmed, not on grounds of delicacy alone, but on account of my life, while my master was intent on preparing for the representation, and all his servants were partly engaged in getting ready for the spectacle of hunting, and partly in gazing at the grandeur of the show: and as no one thought that so tame an ass required to be so very attentively watched, and I was free to follow my own devices, accordingly little by little I stole away softly and quietly. When I reached the nearest gate, I hurried along at a most rapid pace. And after I had travelled a hot gallop of six miles, I arrived at Cenchreae; a city which has the reputation of being the most noble colony of the Corinthians, and is washed by the Aegean and Saronic sea. Here, also, there is a port, which is a most safe harbour for ships, and frequented by a vast concourse of people.

Avoiding, therefore, the crowds, and choosing a sequestered spot on the sea-shore, close to the spray of the waves, I stretched my weary body on the soft bosom of the sand. The chariot of the sun had sped onward to the end of its course; and I resigned myself to repose, and was soon wrapped in sweet sleep.

BOOK ELEVEN

Awaking in sudden alarm about the first watch of the night, I beheld the full orb of the moon shining with remarkable brightness, and just then emerging from the waves of the sea. Availing myself, therefore, of the silence and solitude of night, as I was also well aware that the great primal goddess possessed a transcendent majesty, and that human affairs are entirely governed by her providence; and that not only cattle and wild beasts, but likewise things inanimate, are invigorated by the divine influence of her light; that the bodies likewise which are on the earth, in the heavens, and in the sea, at one time increase with her increments, and at another lessen duly with her wanings; being well assured of this, I determined to implore the august image of the goddess then present, Fate, as I supposed, being now satiated with my many and great calamities, and holding out to me at last some prospect of relief.

Shaking off all drowsiness, therefore, I rose with alacrity, and directly, with the intention of purifying myself, began bathing in the sea. Having dipped my head seven times in the waves, because, according to the divine Pythagoras, that number is especially adapted to religious purposes, I joyously and with alacrity thus supplicated with a tearful countenance the transcendently powerful Goddess:—

"Queen of heaven, whether thou art the genial Ceres, the prime parent of fruits, who, joyous at the discovery of thy daughter, didst banish the savage nutriment of the ancient acorn, and pointing out a better food, dost now till the Eleusinian soil; or whether thou art celestial Venus, who, in the first origin of things, didst associate the different sexes, through the creation of mutual love, and having propagated an eternal offspring in the human race, art now worshipped in the sea-girt shrine of Paphos; or whether thou art the sister of Phoebus, who, by relieving the pangs of women in travail by soothing remedies, hast brought into the world multitudes so innumerable, and art now venerated, in the far-famed shrines of Ephesus; or whether thou art Proserpine, terrific with midnight howlings, with triple features checking the attack of the ghosts, closing the recesses of the earth, and who wandering over many a grove, art propitiated by various modes of worship; with that feminine brightness of thine, illuminating the walls of every city, and with thy vaporous beams nurturing the joyous seeds of plants, and for the revolutions of the sun ministering thy fitful gleams: by whatever name, by whatever ceremonies, and under whatever form it is lawful to invoke thee; do thou graciously succour me in this my extreme distress, support my fallen fortune, and grant me rest and peace, after the endurance of so many sad calamities. Let there be an end of my sufferings, let there be an end of my perils. Remove from me the dire form of a quadruped, restore me to the sight of my kindred, restore me to Lucius, my former self. But if any offended deity pursues me with inexorable cruelty, may it at least be allowed me to die, if it is not allowed me to live."

Having after this manner poured forth my prayers and added bitter lamentations, sleep again overpowered my stricken feelings on the same bed. Scarcely had I closed my eyes, when behold! a divine form emerged from the middle of the sea, and disclosed features that even the gods themselves might venerate. After this, by degrees, the vision, resplendent throughout the whole body, seemed gradually to take its stand before me, rising above the surface of the sea. I will even make an attempt to describe to you its wondrous appearance, if, indeed, the poverty of human language will afford me the power of appropriately setting it forth; or, if the Divinity herself will supply me with a sufficient stock of eloquent diction.

In the first place, then, her hair, long and hanging in tapered ringlets, fell luxuriantly on her divine neck; a crown of varied form encircled the summit of her head, with a diversity of flowers, and in the middle of it, just over her forehead, there was a flat circlet, which resembled a mirror, or rather emitted a white refulgent light, thus indicating that she was the moon. Vipers rising from furrows of the earth, supported this on the right hand and on the left, while ears of corn projected on either side. Her garment was of many colours, woven of fine flax; in one part it was resplendent with a clear white colour, in another it was yellow like the blooming crocus, and in another flaming with a rosy redness. And then, what riveted my gaze far more than all, was her mantle of the deepest black, that shone with a glossy lustre. It was wrapped around her, and passing from below her right side over the left shoulder, was fastened in a knot that resembled the boss of a shield, while a part of the robe fell down in many folds, and gracefully floated with its little knots of fringe that edged its extremities. Glittering stars were dispersed along the embroidered extremities of the robe, and over its whole surface; and in the middle of them a moon of two weeks old breathed forth its flaming fires. Besides this, a garland, wholly consisting of flowers and fruits of every kind, adhered naturally to the border of this beautiful mantle, in whatever direction it was wafted by the breeze.

The objects which she carried in her hands were of a different description. In her right hand she bore a brazen sistrum, through the narrow rim of which, winding just like a girdle for the body, passed a few little rods, producing a sharp shrill sound, while her arm imparted motion to the triple chords. An oblong vessel, made of gold, in the shape of a boat, hung down from her left hand, on the handle of which, in that part in which it met the eye, was an asp raising its head erect, and with its throat puffed out on either side. Shoes, too, woven from the palm, the emblem of victory, covered her ambrosial feet.

Such was the appearance of the mighty goddess, as, breathing forth the fragrant perfumes of Arabia the happy, she deigned with her divine voice thus to address me: "Behold me, Lucius; moved by thy prayers, I appear to thee; I, who am Nature, the parent of all things, the mistress of all the elements, the primordial offspring of time, the supreme among Divinities, the queen of departed spirits, the first of the celestials, and the uniform manifestation of the Gods and Goddesses; who govern by my nod the luminous heights of heaven, the salubrious breezes of the ocean, and the anguished silent realms of the shades below: whose one sole divinity the whole orb of the earth venerates under a manifold form, with different rites, and under a variety of appellations. Hence the Phrygians, that primaeval race, call me Pessinuntica, the Mother of the Gods; the Aborigines of Attica, Cecropian Minerva; the Cyprians, in their sea-girt isle, Paphian Venus; the arrow-bearing Cretans, Diana Dictynna; the three-tongued Sicilians, Stygian Proserpine; and the Eleusinians, the ancient Goddess Ceres. Some call me Juno, others Bellona, others Hecate, and others Rhamnusia. But those who are illumined by the earliest rays of that divinity, the Sun, when he rises, the Aethiopians, the Arii, and the Egyptians, so skilled in ancient learning, worshipping me with ceremonies quite appropriate, call me by my true name, Queen Isis. Behold then, commiserating your calamities, I am come to thy assistance; favouring and propitious I am come. Away, then, with tears; leave your lamentations; cast off all sorrow. Soon, through my providence, shall the day of deliverance shine upon you. Listen, therefore, attentively to these my instructions.

"Eternal religion has consecrated to me the day which will be born from this night; to-morrow my priests offer to me the first fruits of the opened navigation, and dedicate to me a new ship, for that the wintry tempests are now appeased, and the stormy waves of the ocean lulled, and the sea itself has become navigable. That sacred ceremonial you must await, with a mind neither full of anxiety, nor intent upon subjects that are profane. For the priests, at my command, will carry in the procession a crown of roses, attached to the sistrum in his right hand. Without delay, then, pushing the crowd aside, join my procession, and put your trust in my gracious disposition; then, having approached close, as though to kiss the hand of the priest, gently pluck the roses, and at once divest yourself of the hide of that abominable beast, which I have long looked upon with detestation.

"Nor hold in dread any thing pertaining to my concerns as difficult. For even at this very same instant of time in which I appear to you here present, I am giving orders also to my priest how to bring about the things that are to take place hereafter. By my command, the dense crowds of people shall give way before you. Neither, amid the joyous rites and festive scenes, will any one view with abhorrence the unsightliness of the figure which you bear, or malignantly accuse you, by putting a sinister interpretation on the sudden change of your form. Only remember, and always keep it fast in the very depths of your heart, that the remaining period of your life must be dedicated to me, even to the moment of your latest breath. Nor is it unjust that you should devote your whole life to that goddess, by whose assistance you will have been restored to human form. But under my protection you will live happy, you will live glorious: and when, having passed through the allotted period of your life, you shall descend to the realms beneath, there, also, in the subterranean hemisphere, you, dwelling in the

Elysian fields, shall frequently adore me whom you now behold thus propitious to you, and shall there see me shining amidst the darkness of Acheron, and reigning in the Stygian realms. And further, if you shall be found to deserve the protection of my divinity by sedulous obedience, religious devotion, and inviolable chastity, you shall be sensible that it is possible for me, and me alone, to extend your life beyond the limits that have been appointed to it by your destiny."

The venerable oracle having thus concluded, the invincible divinity dissolved into herself. Instantly shaking off sleep, I arose, in a state of fear and joy, and bathed in perspiration. Astonished in the highest degree at so evident a manifestation of the powerful goddess, having sprinkled myself with the spray of the sea, and intent on her high commands, I tried to recall to mind the successive particulars of her injunctions. Soon after this, the golden sun arose, and put to flight the clouds of dark night: and now, behold, a crowd of people filled all the streets with a religious procession, conducted in a style of triumph. All things likewise, independently of my own delight, seemed to me to be affected with the greatest hilarity, insomuch that I thought even the cattle of all kinds, every house, and the day itself, wore an aspect of gladness and serenity; for a sunny and placid day had suddenly succeeded to the frost of the previous one; so that, allured by the warmth of the spring, the tuneful little birds sang sweetly, and with their merry warbling soothed Her who was the mother of the stars, the parent of the seasons, and the mistress of the whole universe. And then the trees, too, both those prolific and those which only yielded a shade, unbound from their wintry sleep by the warm southern breezes, and embellished with young foliage, sent forth a sweet rustling sound from their branches. The waves of the sea, no longer heaving turbidly to the roaring blast of the tempest, gently washed the shore; the dark clouds were dispersed, and the heavens shone with the serene splendour of of their native light.

And now, behold, the prelude to the grand procession came gradually into action. The persons who composed it were all finely caparisoned in various ways, each according to his own taste and inclination. This man, being girded with a belt, represented a soldier; another was equipped as a hunter, with a short scarf, a hunting-knife, and javelin. Another, wearing gilded sandals, a silken garment, and precious female ornaments, and with false hair on his head, personated a woman by his appearance and his gait. Another, with his boots, his shield, his helmet, and his sword, appeared as though he had come straight from the school of the gladiators. There was one who played the part of a magistrate, with the fasces and the purple robe; another that of a philosopher, with his cloak, his staff, his wooden-clogged shoes, and his goatish beard; two persons, with dissimilar reeds, represented, the one a fowler with bird-lime, and the other a fisherman with his hook. I also saw a tame she-bear, wearing the dress of a woman, and carried in a chair; an ape, too, with a plaited straw hat on its head, and clothed with a Phrygian garment of saffron colour, carrying in its hand a golden cup, and representing the shepherd Ganymede; likewise an ass, on which wings were glued, and which walked near a feeble old man; so that you would certainly have said that the one was Bellerophon, and the other Pegasus; but still you would have enjoyed your laugh at both.

Amid this merry masquerade of the swarming people, the procession proper of the guardian Goddess now advanced. Females, splendidly arrayed in white garments, expressing their joy by various gestures, and adorned with vernal chaplets, scattered flowers on the ground from their bosoms, along the path of the sacred procession. Others, again, with mirrors upon their backs, showed all who followed to the Goddess, with their faces towards her as if they were coming to meet her. Others, carrying ivory combs, imitated the combing and bedecking of her regal hair, with the motion of their arms, and the twisting of their fingers. There were others, too, who sprinkled the streets with drops of genial balsam, and other kinds of perfume. In addition to all this, there was a great multitude of men and women, who propitiated the Goddess, offspring of the celestial stars, by bearing lamps, torches, wax-tapers, and other kinds of artificial light. Next came musicians, playing sweetly on pipes and flutes. A graceful choir of chosen youths, in snow-white garments, followed them, repeating a beautiful song, which an excellent poet had composed under favour of the Muses, the words of which explained the first origin of the votive procession. Pipers also, consecrated to the great Serapis, played an air appropriate to the worship of the god, on pipes with transverse mouth-pieces, and tubes held obliquely towards their right ears. There were, also, a number of persons, whose office it was to give notice that room should be left for the sacred procession to pass. Then came a multitude of those who had been initiated into the sacred rites of the goddess, consisting of men and women of all classes and ages, resplendent with the pure whiteness of their linen garments. The women had their anointed hair enveloped in a transparent covering; but the men had shaven and shining pates; earthly stars were these of extreme sanctity, who kept up a shrill and incessant tinkling upon brazen, silver, and even gold sistra. But the chief ministers of the sacred rites, clothed in garments of white linen, drawn close over the breast, and hanging down to their feet, carried the insignia of the mighty Gods, exposed full to view. The first held aloft a brilliant lamp, not by any means resembling those lamps of ours which illumine banquets at night; but it was of gold, of a boat-like form, and emitted a flame of considerable magnitude, from an aperture in the middle. The second was arrayed in a similar manner, but carried in both his hands models of altars, to which the auxiliary providence of the supreme goddess gave the appropriate name of "auxilia." The third bore a palm tree, the leaves of which were beautifully wrought in gold, as also the caduceus of Mercury. The fourth displayed the symbol of Equity, a left hand, fashioned with the palm expanded; which seems to be more adapted to administering Equity than the right, from its natural inertness, and its being endowed with no craft and no subtlety. The same person also carried a golden vessel, which was rounded in the shape of the female breast, and from which he poured forth milk on the ground. The fifth bore a golden corn-fan, made with thickset branches of gold; while another carried an amphora.

In the next place, appeared the gods that deigned to walk with the feet of men. Here, dreadful to view, was the messenger of the gods above, and of those of the realms beneath, standing erect, with a face partly black, and partly of a golden hue, bearing in his left hand a caduceus, and shaking in his right a green branch of palm; close upon whose footsteps followed a cow, in an erect position; this cow being the prolific resemblance of the all-parent goddess, and seated on the shoulders of one of the blessed devotees of this divinity, who acted gesticulatingly as he walked. Another carried a chest, containing the secret utensils of this stupendous mystery. Another bore in his beatified bosom a venerable effigy of his supreme Divinity, bearing no resemblance to any bird or beast, wild or tame, or even to man; but worthy of all veneration for the exquisite art with which it was wrought, as also for its very originality, and an ineffable symbol of a sublime religion, the mysteries of which were ever to be kept in deep silence. It was of burnished gold, after the following manner: there was a small urn, hollowed out in a most artistic manner, with a bottom quite round, and which outside was covered with the wonderful hieroglyphics of the Egyptians. The spout of this urn was very long, not much elevated; a handle was attached to the other side, and projected from the urn with a wide sweep. On this lay an asp, uplifting its scaly, wrinkled, and swollen throat, and embraced it with its winding folds.

At last the moment was at hand, when I was to experience the blessing promised me by the most potent goddess; and the priest, attired just as she had described, approached with the means of my deliverance. In his right hand he carried the sistrum of the goddess, and a crown of roses; and by Hercules, a crown it was for me; since by the providence of the mighty goddess, after having endured so many hardships, and escaped so many dangers, I should now achieve a victory over my cruel enemy, Fortune.

Still, however, though agitated by a sudden burst of joy, I did not rush forward at once, lest the tranquil order of the sacred procession should be disturbed by the impetuosity of a quadruped; but passed through the crowd with a quiet and altogether human step, and a sidelong movement of my body, and as the people gave way, through the interference, no doubt, of the goddess, I gradually crept nearer and nearer. But the priest, as I could plainly perceive, recollecting the nocturnal oracle, and struck with wonder at the coincidence with the duty which he had been commanded to perform, instantly stood still, and extending his right hand of his own accord, presented the chaplet to my very mouth. Trembling, and with a great beating of my heart, I seized the bright rosy chaplet, and greedily, most greedily devoured it.

Nor did the celestial promise deceive me; for immediately my unsightly and brutal figure left me. First of all, my rough hair fell off, and next my thick skin became thin; my big belly shrank in; my hoofs spread out into feet and toes; my hands were no longer feet, but ready for the duties of their elevated position. My long neck was shortened; my face and my head became round; my enormous ears were restored to their former small dimensions; my stony teeth returned to the diminutive size of those of men; and the tail, which before especially annoyed me, was no where to be seen. The people were astonished, and the religious adored the power of the supreme Divinity, so manifested in the facility of my restoration which resembled the visions of a dream. Extending their hands towards the heavens, they attested, with a loud and unanimous voice, the favour of the goddess thus signally displayed.

As for me, I stood riveted to the spot in excessive astonishment, my mind being unable to contain a delight so sudden and so great, quite at a loss what first and in especial to say, how to make a commencement with a new voice, how most auspiciously to prepare my address, my tongue being now born again, and in what words sufficiently to express my thanks to a Goddess so great. The priest, however, who through the divine admonition knew all my misfortunes from the beginning, though he himself also was in a state of utter astonishment at this remarkable miracle, at once signified ais wish by nodding his head, and ordered that a linen garment should be given me, or the purpose of covering my nakedness. For, the very instant that the ass had laid .side his abominable covering, I carefully shaded myself with a natural screen, as nuch as it was possible for a naked person to do, by closely compressing my thighs, .nd applying my hands. Upon this one of the throng of devotees promptly throwing ne his upper tunic, covered me therewith; which being done, the priest with a benign ountenance, and, by Hercules, astonished at my perfectly human appearance, thus .ddressed me:—

"At last, Lucius, you have arrived at the haven of peace and the altar of mercy, after he many and various hardships you have undergone, and all the buffetings of stormy ortune. Neither the nobility of your descent, nor your dignified position, nor even the earning in which you excel, have benefited you in the slightest degree; but falling nto the slavery of pleasure, in the wantonness of buxom youth, you have reaped the nauspicious reward of your ill-fated curiosity. Nevertheless, blind Fortune, while iarassing you with the worst of dangers, has conducted you, in her short-sighted nalice, to this state of religious beatitude. Let her go now, and rage with all her fury, ınd let her seek some other object for her cruelty, for direful calamity has no power ver those whose lives the majesty of our Goddess has claimed for her own service. What dvantage has unscrupulous Fortune derived from the robbers, from the wild beasts, rom the servitude, from the long toils on rugged roads, and from the fear of death o which you were daily exposed? You are now received under the guardianship of ortune, but of a Fortune who can see, and who even illuminates the other Deities vith the splendour of her light. Assume henceforth a more joyous countenance, such .s befits that white garment which you wear. Follow the train of the Goddess your leliverer with triumphant steps. Let the irreligious see, let them see and acknowledge heir error. Behold now, Lucius, rejoicing in the providence of great Isis, and freed rom his former miseries, triumphs over his destiny. Nevertheless, that you may be nore secure and better protected, enroll your name in this holy militia, which you will iereafter rejoice to belong to; dedicate yourself to the service of our religion, and voluntarily bend your neck to the yoke of this ministry; for when you have once begun o serve the Goddess, you will then in a still higher degree enjoy the fruit of your iberty."

The worthy priest having uttered these words, while his breath heaved with inspira- ion, concluded his address, and I mingling with the throng of devotees, accompanied he procession; an object of curiosity to the whole city. All pointed at me with their ingers and heads, and said, "This day has the august power of all-mighty God restored hat person to the human form. Happy, by Hercules! and thrice blessed he, to have nerited, by the innocence and probity of his past life, such special patronage of ieaven; in that, being after a manner born again, he is immediately affianced to the ervice of the sacred ministry."

Part Two

Ancient Rome

THE GENERAL HISTORY OF THE WARS OF THE ROMANS

Polybius

The most reliable and best-informed account of Rome's rise to world power was written by a non-Roman. Polybius (ca. 208–ca. 125 B.C.) *was a Greek aristocrat born in Megalopolis who, like his father, became an official in the Achaean League, the leading federation of Greek city-states. In this capacity Polybius advocated a middle-of-the-road policy of friendly neutrality toward the Romans, as against open resistance or the unconditional collaboration championed by the democratic faction. This benevolent neutrality was, however, not appreciated by the Romans, who followed up their victory over the Macedonians in 168* B.C. *by deporting a thousand leading Greeks, including Polybius, to Italy. Nominally a prisoner at Rome, Polybius was fortunate in being accepted into the leading aristocratic circles, where he gained insight into some of the events that he was to include in his history. Even after his repatriation in 151* B.C., *he remained in touch with Roman leaders, while endearing himself to his countrymen by using his influence in their behalf.*

Polybius' history deals with the period from 264 to 146 B.C., *the latter date being that of the final destruction of Carthage and, quite independently, of the autonomy of the Greek city-states. Of the forty books originally published by Polybius, only five have survived intact, although fragments and excerpts from many of the others have also come down to us. Our selections are from the first chapter of Book I and from an extensive fragment of Book VI.*

In evaluating Polybius' view of the Roman constitution, you must remember his purpose in writing his History: *to acquaint his Greek countrymen with the country that had conquered them; and, by acquainting them, to reconcile them to Roman supremacy. His problem, therefore, was to explain Roman* success, *rather than to give arguments for or against Roman institutions. That Polybius' presentation was overly cheerful may be demonstrated by the era of violent civil strife which began just about the time of his death. Polybius himself had been a leader of the aristocratic party in Greece and had moved in the highest aristocratic circles while in Rome. It is not very surprising, therefore, that he saw Roman institutions through the eyes of a powerful and satisfied senatorial nobility.*

Polybius' cyclical theory of history makes no claim to originality. Cyclical theories had been sketched by Aristotle and Plato, and were antiquity's dominant way of looking at history.

If those who have been employed before me, in relating the transactions of former times, had been altogether silent concerning the singular use and excellence of history, it might perhaps be necessary to begin this work with advising all mankind to apply themselves with earnestness to that kind of study; since the knowledge of past events affords the best instructions for the regulation and good conduct of human life. But as the greater part, or rather all of them, have taken every occasion to declare, repeating it, as we may say, from one end of their writings to the other, that history supplies the only proper discipline to train and exercise the minds of those who are inclined to enter into public affairs, and that the evil accidents which are there recorded to have befallen other men contain the wisest and most effectual lessons for enabling us to support our own misfortunes with dignity and courage, there is little need to repeat again what others have so often urged with eloquence and force. But, indeed, the subject itself which I am engaged to treat may well exempt me from this task; since it is of a kind so new and singular, that it cannot fail to excite the attention of every reader. For what man is there so sordid and insensible, that he would not wish to be informed in what manner, and through what kind of government, almost the whole habitable world, in less than the course of fifty-three years, was reduced to the Roman yoke? an event of which there is no example in any former time. Or who, on the other hand, is so passionately fond of any other kind of speculation, or of any branch of science, as to think it more worthy of his care and pains than this inquiry?

That the subject of this work deserves more than a common share of attention and regard, on account both of its novelty and greatness, will most evidently appear, if we take a view of all the ancient states that are chiefly celebrated in history, and compare them with the Roman.

The Persians were, for some time, possessed of a very wide dominion; but whenever they laboured to extend it beyond the bounds of Asia, the attempt was always unsuccessful, and, indeed, almost proved fatal to them. The Lacedaemonians, after many struggles, obtained the sovereignty of Greece, but within twelve years were again divested of it. The Macedonian kingdom was at first extended from the provinces that border on the Asiatic coast, as far as to the Danube; the whole including but a small and inconsiderable part of Europe. After some time, indeed, they found means to break the Persian monarchy, and joined Asia to their empire. But though the general opinion of mankind may, perhaps, have taught us always to regard this people as a very flourishing and potent state, it cannot be denied a great part of the world was totally exempted from their sway. Africa, Sicily, and Sardinia, were never

***The General History of the Wars of the Romans by Polybius*, trans. Hampton (London, 1812), pp. 17–19, 363–376, 392–393, 397–402.**

visited by their arms; and these fierce and warlike nations, who possessed the western parts of Europe, were utterly unknown and undiscovered by them. But the Romans, disdaining to confine their conquests within the limits of a few countries only, have forced almost the whole habitable world to pay submission to their laws, and have raised their empire to that vast height of power which is so much the wonder of the present age, and which no future times can ever hope to exceed. And this is the event which I design to explain, in the following narration: and from thence it will be evident what great advantages may be derived from an attentive and close perusal of political history. . . .

Now, before this period, the great transactions of the world were single, distinct, and unconnected, both in place and time, while each proceeded from motives peculiar to itself, and was directed to its own proper end. But from this time history assumes an entire and perfect body: the affairs of Italy and Africa were now conjoined with those of Asia and Greece, and all moved together towards one fixed and single point. And this it was that first determined me to choose this era for the beginning of my work; for it was not till after they had broken the strength of Carthage, in the war just mentioned, that the Romans, imagining that by this success they had accomplished the chief and most important part of their intended enterprise, and opened to themselves the way to universal empire, now first resolved to enlarge their conquests, and spread their armies over Greece and Asia.

If mankind were already sufficiently acquainted with the condition and past fortunes of these republics, which contended thus together for the sovereignty of the world, there would, perhaps, be no occasion to have recourse to the former parts of their story, in order to explain the strength and number of their forces, or the probable hopes of success, by which they severally were excited to so great and difficult an undertaking. But because the Greeks are, for the most part, strangers to the ancient state, power, and exploits, both of the Carthaginians and Romans, I thought it necessary to prefix this book, and that which follows, to the body of my history to remove all doubts that might occur, and to exhibit clearly to the reader's view the councils, strength, resources, upon which the Romans supported those great designs, which rendered them the masters of the world, both by land and sea. For, from the recital which I design to make in these preliminary books, it will be seen, beyond all doubt, that this vast project was neither formed nor carried into execution, but upon reasons the most fair and solid, and which gave strong assurances of success. . . .

I am aware that some will wonder why I have deferred until the present occasion my account of the Roman constitution, thus being obliged to interrupt the due course of my narrative. Now, that I have always regarded this account as one of the essential parts of my whole design, I have, I am sure, made evident in numerous passages and chiefly in the prefatory remarks dealing with the fundamental principles of this history, where I said that the best and most valuable result I aim at is that readers of my work may gain a knowledge how it was and by virtue of what peculiar political institutions that in less than fifty-three years nearly the whole world was overcome and fell under the single dominion of Rome, a thing the like of which had never happened before. Having made up my mind to deal with the matter, I found no occasion more suitable than the present for turning my attention to the constitution and testing the truth of what I am about to say on the subject. For just as those who pronounce in private on the characters of bad or good men, do not, when they really resolve to put their opinion to the test, choose for investigation those periods of their life which they passed in composure and repose, but seasons when they were afflicted by adversity or blessed with success, deeming the sole test of a perfect man to be the power of bearing high-mindedly and bravely the most complete reverses of fortune, so it should be in our judgement of states. Therefore, as I could not see any greater or more violent change in the fortunes of the Romans than this which has happened in our own times, I reserved my account of the constitution for the present occasion. . . .

What chiefly attracts and chiefly benefits students of history is just this—the study of causes and the consequent power of choosing what is best in each case. Now the chief cause of success or the reverse in all matters is the form of a state's constitution; for springing from this, as from a fountain-head, all designs and plans of action not only originate, but reach their consummation. . . .

With regard, indeed, to those states of Greece which have been often raised to a high degree of strength and power, and again as frequently have suffered an entire reverse of fortune, it would be no hard task either to treat of the events that have happened among them in past times, or to speak with some assurance concerning those that must hereafter happen. For it is easy to recount transactions that are known, and obvious likewise, from an attentive view of former accidents, to derive a foresight of the future. But, with regard to the republic of the Romans, as the present condition of the government, on account of that variety of parts of which it is composed, cannot be explained without great labour; so, on the other hand, the want of being sufficiently acquainted both with the general institutions, and particular conduct, that have prevailed among this people in former times, renders it not less difficult to pronounce concerning their future fortune. It will be necessary, therefore, to employ the closest pains, in order to obtain a distinct and comprehensive knowledge of the advantages that are peculiar to the constitution of this state.

Among those, then, who have treated of these matters in the way of science, the greatest part distinguished civil government into three several kinds, royalty, aristocracy, and democracy. But, it may very reasonably be demanded of these writers, whether they speak of these as the only kinds, or simply as the best. In either case, indeed, they must be charged with error. For first, that kind of government is undoubtedly to be esteemed the best, which is composed of all the three now mentioned. The proof of this is evident, from experience and from fact, as well as reason. Such, for example, was the system first invented by Lycurgus, and established by him in Sparta. Nor is it true, on the other hand, that these are the only kinds. For many are the examples of monarchical and tyrannical governments, which are greatly different from royalty; though they appear indeed to bear some kind of resemblance to it: which gives occasion to all monarchs, to cover themselves, as well as they are able, under this disguise, and falsely to assume the regal name. There are likewise many oligarchical states, which seem to approach nearly in their form to aristocracies; though these are in truth very widely distant from them. The same observation may be made, with respect also to democracies. The following illustration will serve more clearly to explain my meaning.

It is not every government, which is conducted by a single sovereign, that is immediately to be termed a royalty; but that alone, which was at first bestowed by the consent of those who governed; and which is administered according to right reason, rather than by force and terror. In the same manner, neither is every state to be called an aristocracy, which places the supreme direction of affairs in the hands of a few; but that only, in which those who are most distinguished by their prudence and integrity are appointed by free choice to govern. Nor, lastly, is that to be esteemed a democracy, in which the whole multitude usurp the liberty of pursuing their own counsels and designs without control. But when we see a people, who, from the ancient manners of the country, are accustomed to pay due worship to the gods, to revere their parents, to show respect to the aged, and to obey the laws; when, in the assemblies of citizens like these, the resolutions of the greater part are made the rule of government; then we behold the form of a just democracy.

There are therefore six different kinds of government: three, which are in the mouths of all men, and which have now been mentioned; and three more, that are allied to those by nature; monarchy, oligarchy, and the government of the multitude. Of all these, the first in order is monarchy; which is established by the bare work of nature, without any preparation or design. From monarchy arises royalty; when art has been applied to correct the vices of the former. And when royalty has degenerated into its congenial evil, which is tyranny; the destruction of the latter gives birth to aristocracy. This again being changed, according to the natural order of things, into oligarchy; the subjects, roused to vengeance by oppression, resist the injustice of their governors, and establish a democracy. And, in the last place, when the people themselves become haughty and untractable, and reject all law; to democracy succeeds, in the course of time, the government of the multitude.

That this deduction is agreeable to truth, will be clear to every one, who considers with attention the commencement and first rise, as well as the changes, which nature has appropriated to each particular kind of government. And indeed there is no other way, but by observing what was the natural birth of every state, to judge with certainty concerning the progress of it towards perfection, and from thence to decline and ruin; and to discern, at what time, in what manner, and into what different form it will at last be changed. Above all others, the Roman government may best be illustrated by such a method of inquiry: because this state, both in its first establishment, and subsequent increase, displays a close conformity with the settled laws, and regular course of nature.

I am not ignorant indeed, that Plato, and some other philosophers, have already treated with the greatest accuracy, of the several forms of government, and their alternate revolutions. But as there are but few, that are able to comprehend the length of their discourses, and the variety of matter which they contain; I shall endeavour rather to give a summary account of those more obvious principles, which are adapted both to common apprehension, and to the purpose of civil history. And in case that any obscurity or defect should be found in the general view, the particular detail, which I shall afterwards subjoin, will afford ample compensation, by removing every difficulty.

What then are the commencements, and what the original rise, of political societies?

When a deluge, a pestilential disease, a famine, or any other similar cause, has brought destruction upon the human race, as tradition assures us it has happened in former times, and as it is probable it will again hereafter happen; and when all arts and institutions are extinguished also in the same calamity, from the few that are left alive another progeny of men springs up, who, being conscious of their natural weakness, and attracted, like all other animals, to a union with their own kind, associate themselves together in a body. At this time, therefore, it is manifest, that he who is superior both in strength and courage must govern and conduct the rest. For that this is indeed the genuine work of nature is most clearly seen in the examples of the several kinds of animals, which are led by natural instinct only, unimproved by reason. Such are cocks, bulls, and boars, as well as other kinds; among all which, those that are confessedly the first in strength are placed at the head of all the herd. Such, therefore, is the original state of men, when they assemble together in a manner not unlike to that of the other animals, and are led by those that are the bravest and the most powerful. And this state may properly be called a monarchy, in which the authority of those that govern is measured by their strength. But afterwards, when in these societies a common education and mutual intercourse have produced new sentiments and habits, then first commences royalty; then first arise in the human mind the notions of honourable and base, of just and unjust. These sentiments, and this change of government, are formed in the following manner:

From the union of the two sexes, to which all are naturally inclined, children are born. When any of these, therefore, being arrived at perfect age, instead of yielding suitable returns of gratitude and assistance to those by whom they have been bred, on the contrary attempt to injure them, either by words or actions, it is manifest that those who behold the wrong, after having also seen the sufferings and the anxious care that were sustained by the parents in the nourishment and education of these children must be greatly offended and displeased at such proceeding. For man, who, among all the various kinds of animals is alone endowed with the faculty of reason, cannot, like the rest, pass over such actions with indifference; but will make reflection on what he sees; and, comparing likewise the future with the present, will not fail to express his indignation at this injurious treatment, to which, as he foresees, he also may at some time be exposed. Thus again, when any one, who has been succoured by another in the time of danger, instead of showing the like kindness to his benefactor, endeavours, at any time, to destroy or hurt him, it is certain, that all men must be shocked by such ingratitude, through sympathy with the resentment of their neighbour, and from an apprehension also, that the case may be their own. And from hence arises, in the mind of every man, a certain sense of the nature and force of duty, in which consists both the beginning and the end of justice. In the same manner, likewise, the man, who, in the defence of others, is seen to throw himself the foremost into every danger, and even to sustain the fury of the fiercest animals, never fails to obtain the loudest acclamations of applause and veneration from all the multitude; while he, who shows a different conduct, is pursued with censure and reproach. And thus it is that the people begin to discern the nature of things honourable or base, and in what consists the difference between them; and to perceive that the former, on account of the advantage that attends them, are fit to be admired and imitated, and the latter to be detested and avoided. When he, therefore, who possesses the greatest power, and is placed at the head of all the rest, is found always to comply with the general sentiments, in supporting fortitude and merit, and in distributing to every one impartial justice; the people no longer dreading his superior force, but paying a willing obedience to his wisdom, submit themselves to his authority, and, with one consent, maintain him in his government against all invaders, even to extreme old age. And thus the monarch, by insensible degrees, becomes a king; when reason takes the rule, in the place of strength and violence. Such are the first perceptions among mankind of justice and injustice, of base and honourable; and such the origin and rise of genuine royalty. For the people not only confirm these leaders in the possession of the power to which they have been raised, but preserve it to their children likewise; being persuaded, that those who have received their birth and education from virtuous parents cannot but resemble them in manners. And if, at any time, they are displeased at the conduct of these descendants, they then choose other magistrates and kings. But having been taught to discern by past experience the difference between external faculties and the endowments of the mind, they now appoint to the supreme command, not those that excel in bodily strength and vigour, but those who are distinguished by their wisdom and superior reason.

In ancient times, then, those who had once been judged worthy to be invested with the regal dignity, continued, during the remainder of their lives, in the undisturbed possession and exercise of government; fortifying all the advantageous posts; inclosing their towns with walls, and obtaining such an increase of territory as was necessary for their security, or the plentiful subsistence of their subjects. And as they assumed no great distinction either in their dress or table, but lived a life that was comformable in every point to that of the other citizens, they raised against themselves no envy, nor afforded any matter of offence. But their descendants, having received the sovereignty in the course of hereditary succession, and finding that all things already were obtained that were convenient for defence, and that the abundance of all necessaries exceeded the demands of nature, were soon hurried, by the wantonness of ease and plenty, into an open gratification of every passion. They then began to be persuaded that it was necessary that kings should be distinguished from their subjects by more splendid habits, and be served with more costly and luxurious tables; and pursued also with full career the indulgence of their amours, however lawless, without admitting any control. The first of these disorders soon excited envy and offence, and the latter wrath and unrelenting hatred. And from hence the royalty being now converted into tyranny, the dissolution of it was begun by machinations formed against the persons of the sovereigns. These conspiracies were at first contrived, not by men of obscure or low condition, but by those of noblest birth, and who were the most distinguished by their courage and exalted spirit: for such are at all times most impatient of the insolence of princes. But the people being not less offended also and enraged, having once obtained such leaders, readily joined their forces in the same attempt. And thus the form of royalty and monarchy being utterly destroyed, an aristocracy grew up, and was established in its place.

For the people, moved with present gratitude towards those who had delivered them from tyranny, resolved to invest them with the government, and submitted themselves to their guidance and dominion. And these, being on their part also not less satisfied with the honour that was bestowed upon them, regarded the good of the community as the only rule of their administration, and employed their whole care and pains to promote the happiness of individuals, as well as to advance the common interests of all. But when again the children of these governors were raised in the course of succession likewise to the same authority, unpractised, as they had always been, in hardship or misfortune, and inexperienced also in that equality and liberty upon which the government was founded; having been nurtured from their birth in the pre-eminence and honours of their parents, they began, some of them, to accumulate inordinate wealth by fraud and violence, while others, allowing a full indulgence to their passions, abandoned themselves without restraint to riot and intemperance, adulteries and rapes.

And thus the aristocracy being now changed into an oligarchy, the passions of the multitude were once more inflamed; and the same destruction followed that had before fallen upon the kings, when they had degenerated into tyrants. For no sooner was there found a single citizen, who, being encouraged by the general discontent and hatred that such a conduct had occasioned, was bold enough, either by words or actions, to attempt any thing against the governors, than the people, with one consent, were ready to concur in the design. And when they had killed or driven into banishment their oppressors, not daring to establish royalty on account of the misconduct of the former kings, and being deterred also by the mischiefs which they still more lately had experienced, from yielding the sovereignty to any certain number, they were then forced to have recourse to the only single expedient which was left untried, and to place in themselves alone their confidence of safety. And, having assumed into their own hands the conduct and the trust of government, they thus framed a democracy upon the ruins of the oligarchy.

During some time afterwards, and while any of those remained alive who had beheld the miseries that flowed from the former unequal government, the people were all well pleased to maintain this popular state; and thought that nothing was more valuable than equality and liberty. But, after the course of one or two successions, as new men sprang up, even these enjoyments, now become familiar to them, began, through long use and habit, to be lessened in their esteem, and to give place to the desire of pre-eminence and power. Above all the rest, those who had acquired the greatest wealth, being eager likewise to possess the sovereign rule, and not able to obtain it by their own strength and virtue, endeavoured to draw the people to their side; scattering among them, with profusion, all their riches, and employing every method of corruption; till, by degrees, they had taught them to fix their whole attention upon the gifts by which they were sustained, and rendered their avidity subservient to the views of their own wild ambition. And thus the frame of the democracy was dissolved; and gave place to the rule of violence and force. For when once the people are accustomed to be fed without any cost or labour, and to derive all the means of their subsistence from the wealth of other citizens; if, at this time, some bold and enterprising leader should arise, whose poverty has shut him out from all the honours of the state, then commences the government of the multitude; who run together in tumultuous assemblies, and are hurried into every kind of violence; assassinations, banishments, and divisions of lands: till, being reduced at last to a state of savage anarchy, they once more find a master and a monarch, and submit themselves to arbitrary sway.

Such is the circle in which political societies are revolved, and such the natural order in which the several kinds of government are varied, bound to obey their commands. They introduce ambassadors into the senate. They propose also to the senate the subjects of debate; and direct all the forms that are observed in making the decrees. Nor is it less a part of their office likewise, to attend to those affairs that are transacted by the people; to call together general assemblies; to report to them the resolutions of the senate; and to ratify whatever is determined by the greater number. In all the preparations that are made for war, as well as in the whole administration in the field, they possess an almost absolute authority. For to them it belongs, to impose upon the allies whatever services they judge expedient; to appoint the military tribunes; to enrol the legions, and make the necessary levies; and to inflict punishments in the field, upon all that are subject to their command. Add to this, that they have the power likewise to expend whatever sums they may think convenient from the public treasure; being attended for that purpose by a quaestor, who is always ready to receive and execute their orders. When any one therefore directs his view to this part of the constitution, it is very reasonable for him to conclude, that the government is no other than a simple royalty. Let me only observe, that if in some of these particular points, or in those that will be hereafter mentioned, any change should be either now remarked, or should happen at some future time, such an alteration will not destroy the general principles of this discourse.

To the senate belongs, in the first place, the sole care and management of the public money. For all the returns that are brought into the treasury, as well as all the payments that are issued from it, are directed by their orders. Nor is it allowed to the quaestors to apply any part of the revenue to particular occasions as they arise, without a decree of the senate; those sums alone excepted, which are expended in the service of the consuls. And even those more general, as well as greatest disbursements, which are employed, at the return of every five years, in building and repairing the public edifices, are assigned to the censors for that purpose, by the express permission of the senate. To the senate also is referred the cognizance of all the crimes committed in any part of Italy, that demand a public examination and inquiry: such as treasons, conspiracies, poisonings, and assassinations. Add to this, that when any controversies arise, either between private men, or any of the cities of Italy, it is the part of the senate to adjust all disputes; to censure those that are deserving of blame; and to yield assistance to those who stand in need of protection and defence. When any embassies are sent out of Italy; either to reconcile contending states; to offer exhortations and advice; or even, as it sometimes happens, to impose commands; to propose conditions of a treaty; or to make a denunciation of war; the care and conduct of all these transactions is intrusted wholly to the senate. When any ambassadors also arrive at Rome, it is the senate likewise that determines, in what manner they shall be received and treated, and what answer shall be given to their demands. In all these things, that have now been mentioned, the people has no share. To those therefore, who come to reside in Rome during the absence of the consuls, the government appears to be purely aristocratical. Many of the Greeks especially, and of the foreign princes, are easily led into this persuasion: when they perceive that almost all the affairs, which they are forced to negotiate with the Romans, are determined by the senate.

And now it may well be asked, what part is left to the people in this government: since the senate, on the one hand, is vested with the sovereign power, in the several instances that have been here enumerated, and more especially in all things that concern the management and disposal of the public treasure; and since the consuls, on the other hand, are intrusted with the absolute direction of the preparations that are made for war, and exercise an uncontrolled authority in the field. There is, however, a part still allotted to the people; and indeed the most important part. For first, the people are the sole dispensers of rewards and punishments; which are the only bands by which states and kingdoms, and, in a word, all human societies are held together. For when the difference between these is overlooked, or when they are distributed without due distinction, nothing but disorder can ensue. Nor is it possible, indeed, that government should be maintained, if the wicked stand in equal estimation with the good. The people then, when any offences demand such punishment, frequently condemn the citizens to the payment of a fine: those especially who have been invested with the dignities of the state. To the people alone belongs the right to sentence any one to die. Upon this occasion they have a custom which deserves to be mentioned with applause. The person accused is allowed to withdraw himself in open view, and embrace a voluntary banishment, if only a single tribe remains, that has not yet given judgment; and is suffered to retire in safety to Proeneste, Tibur, Naples, or any other of the confederate cities. The public magistracies are allotted also by the people to those who are esteemed worthy of them: and these are the noblest rewards that any government can bestow on virtue. To the people belongs the power of approving or rejecting laws: and, which is still of greater importance, peace and war are likewise fixed by their deliberations. When any alliance is concluded, any war ended, or treaty made; to them the conditions are referred, and by them either annulled or ratified. And thus again, from a view of all these circumstances, it might with reason be imagined, that the people had engrossed the largest portion of the government, and that the state was plainly a democracy.

Such are the parts of the administration, which are distinctly assigned to each of the three forms of government that are united in the commonwealth of Rome. It now remains to be considered, in what manner each several form is enabled to counteract the others, or to co-operate, with them.

When the consuls, invested with the power that has been mentioned, lead the armies into the field, though they seem indeed to hold such absolute authority as is sufficient for all purposes, yet are they in truth so dependent both on the senate and on the people, that without their assistance they are by no means able to accomplish any design. It is well known that armies demand a continual supply of necessaries. But neither corn, nor habits, nor even the military stipends, can at any time be transmitted to the legions, unless by an express order of the senate. Any opposition, therefore, or delay, on the part of this assembly, is sufficient always to defeat the enterprises of the generals. It is the senate likewise, that either compels the consuls to leave their designs imperfect, or enables them to complete the projects which they have formed, by sending a successor into each of their several provinces, upon the expiration of the annual term, or by continuing them in the same command. The senate also has the power to aggrandize and amplify the victories that are gained, or, on the contrary, to depreciate and debase them. For that which is called among the Romans a triumph, in which a sensible representation of the actions of the generals is exposed in solemn procession to the view of all the citizens, can neither be exhibited with due pomp and splendour, nor indeed be in any manner celebrated, unless the consent of the senate be first obtained, together with the sums that are requisite for the expense. Nor is it less necessary, on the other hand, that the consuls, however far they may happen to be removed from Rome, should be careful to preserve the good affections of the people. For the people, as we have already mentioned, annuls or ratifies all treaties. But that which is of greatest moment is, that the consuls, at the time of laying down their office, are bound also to submit their past administration to the judgment of the people. And thus these magistrates can at no time think themselves secure, if they neglect to gain the approbation both of the senate and of the people.

In the same manner the senate also, though invested with so great authority, is bound to yield a certain attention to the people, and to act in concert with them, in all affairs that are of great and general importance. With regard to those offences which are especially committed against the state, and which demand a capital punishment, no inquiry can be perfected, nor any judgment carried into execution, unless the people confirm what the senate has before decreed. Nor are the things which more immediately regard the senate itself less subject to the same control. For if a law should at any time be proposed, to lessen the received authority of the senators; to detract from their honours and pre-eminence; or even to deprive them of part of their possessions; it belongs wholly to the people to establish or reject it. And even still more; the interposition of a single tribune is sufficient, not only to suspend the deliberations of the senate, but to prevent them also from holding any meeting or assembly. Now the peculiar office of the tribunes is, to declare those sentiments that are most pleasing to the people; and principally to promote their interests and designs. And thus the senate, on account of all these reasons, is forced to cultivate the favour, and gratify the inclinations of the people.

The people again, on their part, are held in a dependence on the senate, and are obliged to pay a certain deference, both to the particular members, and to the general body. In every part of Italy there are works of various kinds, which are let to farm by the censors; such as the building or repairing of the public edifices, which are almost innumerable; the care of rivers, harbours, gardens, mines, and lands; every thing, in a word, that falls beneath the dominion of the Romans. In all these things the people are the undertakers; insomuch that there are scarcely any to be found, that are not in some degree involved, either in the contracts, or in the management of the works. For some take farms of the censors at a certain price: others become partners with the first. Some again engage themselves as sureties to the farmers; and others, in support also of these sureties, pledge their own fortunes to the state. Now the supreme direction of all these affairs is placed wholly in the senate. The senate has the power to allot a longer time; to lighten the conditions of the agreement, in case that any accident has intervened; or even to release the contractors from their bargain, if the terms should be found impracticable. There are also many other circumstances, in which those that are engaged in any of these public works may be either greatly injured or greatly benefited by the senate; since to this body, as we have already observed, all things that belong to these transactions are constantly referred. But there is still another advantage of much greater moment. For from this order likewise judges are selected, in almost every accusation of considerable weight, whether it be of a public or a private nature. The people, therefore, being by these means held under due subjection and restraint, and doubtful of obtaining that protection, which they foresee that they may at sometime want, are always cautious of exciting any opposition to the measures of the senate. Nor are they, on the other hand, less ready to pay obedience to the orders of the consuls; through the dread of that supreme authority, to which the citizens in general, as well as each particular man, are obnoxious in the field.

Thus, while each of these separate parts is enabled either to assist or obstruct the rest, the government, by the apt contexture of them all in the general frame, is so well secured against every accident, that it seems scarcely possible to invent a more perfect system. For when the dread of any common danger that threatens from abroad, constrains all the orders of the state to unite together, and co-operate with joint assistance; such is the strength of the republic, that as, on the one hand, no measures that are necessary are neglected, while all men fix their thoughts upon the present exigency; so neither is it possible, on the other hand, that their designs should at any time be frustrated through the want of due celerity, because all in general, as well as every citizen in particular, employ their utmost efforts to carry what has been determined into execution. Thus the government, by the very form and peculiar nature of its constitution, is equally enabled to resist all attacks, and to accomplish every purpose. And when again all apprehensions of foreign enemies are past, and the Romans being now settled in tranquillity, and enjoying at their leisure all the fruits of victory, begin to yield to the seduction of ease and plenty, and, as it happens usually in such conjunctures, become haughty and ungovernable; then chiefly we may observe in what manner the same constitution likewise finds in itself a remedy against the impending danger. For whenever either of the separate parts of the republic attempts to exceed its proper limits, excites contentions and dispute, and struggles to obtain a greater share of power than that which is assigned to it by the laws, it is manifest, that since no one single part, as we have shown in this discourse, is in itself supreme or absolute, but that on the contrary the powers which are assigned to each are still subject to reciprocal control, the part which thus aspires must soon be reduced again within its own just bounds, and not be suffered to insult or depress the rest. And thus the several orders of which the state is framed, are forced always to maintain their due position; being partly counterworked in their designs; and partly also restrained from making any attempt, by the dread of falling under that authority to which they are exposed.

Some peculiar excellencies in the Roman government and manners, illustrated by a comparison of them with those of other states.

The states, which almost all writers have transmitted to us with applause, are those of Lacedaemon, Mantinea, Crete, and Carthage. To these some have also added the government of Thebes, and Athens. With regard to the first, it may be allowed, perhaps, that they merit some distinction. But the republics of Thebes and Athens very little deserve, in my opinion, to be made the subject of any particular discourse; because they neither rose by natural steps to greatness, nor remained for any long continuance in a prosperous state, nor sunk again by a gradual decline. But having owed all their exaltation merely to some favourable seasons, and borrowed a kind of transient splendour from the times, in that very moment which saw them flourish, and which seemed to promise a lasting confirmation of their power, they were thrown back again by fortune into a contrary state. . . . The same observation may be applied as justly to the commonwealth of Athens, which flourished indeed at many other particular seasons; but having been raised by the able conduct of Themistocles to the greatest height of glory, within a short time afterwards was sunk again in weakness and disgrace. The cause of this sudden change was no other than the irregular constitution of the government. For the Athenian state may very aptly be compared to a ship in which there is no person that commands. In such a vessel, when the mariners, either through the dread of enemies, or the impending dangers of a storm, are compelled to act together in concert, and attend to the orders of the pilot, all things that are necessary are performed by them with diligence and skill. But no sooner are these apprehensions past than they begin to reject all control, and engage in mutual contest, such as the diversity of their sentiments inspires. And while some among them are earnest for continuing their course, and others not less urgent with the pilot to cast anchor; while the first unfurl the sails, and the latter interpose with violence, and command them to be furled; this spirit of contention and seditious obstinacy not only affords a shameful spectacle to those that observe it at a distance, but renders the safety likewise of those who are embarked in the vessel so precarious, that very frequently when they have escaped the dangers of the greatest seas and most dreadful tempests, they are at last wrecked even in the harbour, and when they had just gained the land. In the same manner the Athenian state, after having been conducted, by the virtue of the governors and the people, through all the difficulties of the most threatening seasons, has often unaccountably been overset in times of perfect safety and tranquillity. There is no need, therefore, to say more concerning this republic, or that of Thebes; in both of which the multitude disposes all things as the impulse of their own peculiar passions prompts them: the people in the one, being naturally precipitate and eager above the rest of men; and in the other trained up to habits of force and violence. . . .

The government of Carthage seems also to have been originally well contrived with regard to those general forms that have been mentioned. For there were kings in this government, together with a senate, which was vested with aristocratical authority. The people likewise enjoy the exercise of certain powers that were appropriated to them. In a word, the entire frame of the republic very much resembled those of Rome and Sparta. But at the time of the war of Annibal the Carthaginian constitution was worse in its condition than the Roman. For as nature has assigned to every body, every government, and every action, three successive periods: the first, of growth; the second, of perfection; and that which follows, of decay; and as the period of perfection is the time in which they severally display their greatest strength; from hence arose the difference that was then found between the two republics. For the government of Carthage, having reached the highest point of vigour and perfection much sooner than that of Rome, had now declined from it in the same proportion: whereas the Romans, at this very time, had just raised their constitution to the most flourishing and perfect state. The effect of this difference was, that among the Carthaginians the people possessed the greatest sway in all deliberations, but the senate among the Romans. And as, in the one republic, all measures were determined by the multitude; and, in the other, by the most eminent citizens; of so great force was this advantage in the conduct of affairs, that the Romans, though brought by repeated losses into the greatest danger, became, through the wisdom of their counsels, superior to the Carthaginians in the war. . . .

Add to this, that they have among them certain institutions by which the young men are greatly animated to perform acts of bravery. It will be sufficient to mention one of these, as a proof the attention that is shown by the Roman government, to infuse such a spirit into the citizens as shall lead them to encounter every kind of danger for the sake of obtaining reputation in their country. When any illustrious person dies, he is carried in procession with the rest of the funeral pomp, to the rostra in the forum; sometimes placed conspicuous in an upright posture; and sometimes, though less frequently, reclined. And while the people are all standing round, his son, if he has one of sufficient age, and who is then at Rome, or, if otherwise, some person of his kindred, ascends the rostra, and extols the virtues of the deceased, and the great deeds that were performed by him in his life. By this discourse, which recals his past actions to remembrance, and places them in open view before all the multitude, not those alone who were sharers in his victories, but even the rest who bore no part in his exploits are moved to such sympathy of sorrow, that the accident seems rather to be a public misfortune, than a private loss. He is then buried with the usual rites; and afterwards an image, which, both in features and complexion, expresses an exact resemblance of his face, is set up in the most conspicuous part of the house, inclosed in a shrine of wood. Upon solemn festivals, these images are uncovered, and adorned with the greatest care. And when any other person of the same family dies, they are carried also in the funeral procession, with a body added to the bust, that the representation may be just, even with regard to size. They are dressed likewise in the habits, that belonged to the ranks which they severally filled when they were alive. If they were consuls or praetors, in a gown bordered with purple: if censors, in a purple robe: and if they had triumphed, or obtained any similar honour, in a vest embroidered with gold. Thus apparelled, they are drawn along in chariots preceded by the rods and axes, and other ensigns of their former dignity. And when they arrive at the forum, they are all seated upon chairs of ivory; and there exhibit the noblest object that can be offered to a youthful mind, warmed with the love of virtue and of glory. For who can behold without emotion the forms of so many illustrious men, thus living, as it were, and breathing together in his presence? Or what spectacle can be conceived more great and striking? The person also that is appointed to harangue, when he has exhausted all the praises of the deceased, turns his discourse to the rest, whose images are before him; and, beginning with the most ancient of them, recounts the fortunes and the exploits of every one in turn. By this method, which renews continually the remembrance of men celebrated for their virtue, the fame of every great and noble action becomes immortal; and the glory of those, by whose services their country has been benefited, is rendered familiar to the people, and delivered down to future times. But the chief advantage is, that by the hope of obtaining this honourable fame, which is reserved for virtue, the young men are animated to sustain all danger, in the cause of the common safety. For from hence it has happened that many among the Romans have voluntarily engaged in single combat, in order to decide the fortune of an entire war. Many also have devoted themselves to inevitable death; some of them in battle, to save the lives of other citizens; and some in time of peace, to rescue the whole state from destruction. Others again, who have been invested with the highest dignities, have, in defiance of all law and custom, condemned their own sons to die, showing greater regard to the advantage of their country, than to the bonds of nature, and the closest ties of kindred. . . .

In all things that regard the acquisition of wealth, the manners also, and the customs of the Romans, are greatly preferable to those of the Carthaginians. Among the latter, nothing is reputed infamous, that is joined with gain. But among the former nothing is held more base than to be corrupted by gifts, or to covet an increase of wealth by means that are unjust. For as much as they esteem the possession of honest riches to be fair and honourable, so much on the other hand, all those that are amassed by unlawful arts are viewed by them with horror and reproach. The truth of this fact is clearly seen in the following instance. Among the Carthaginians, money is openly employed to obtain the dignities of the state; but all such proceeding is a capital crime in Rome. As the rewards, therefore, that are proposed to virtue in the two republics are so different, it cannot but happen, that the attention of the citizens to form their minds to virtuous actions must be also different.

But among all the useful institutions that demonstrate the superior excellence of the Roman government, the most considerable, perhaps, is the opinion which the people are taught to hold concerning the gods; and that which other men regard as an object of disgrace appears, in my judgment, to be the very thing by which this republic chiefly is sustained. I mean, superstition: which is impressed with all its terrors: and influences both the private actions of the citizens, and the public administration also of the state, in a degree that can scarcely be exceeded. This may appear astonishing to many. To me it is evident that this contrivance was at first adopted for the sake of the multitude. For if it were possible that a state could be composed of wise men only, there would be no need, perhaps, of any such invention. But as the people universally are fickle and inconstant, filled with irregular desires, precipitate in their passions, and prone to violence; there is no way left to restrain them, but by the dread of things unseen, and by the pageantry of terrifying fiction. The ancients therefore acted not absurdly, nor without good reason, when they inculcated the notions concerning the gods, and the belief of infernal punishments; but much more those of the present age are to be charged with rashness and absurdity, in endeavouring to extirpate these opinions. For, not to mention other effects that flow from such an institution; if, among the Greeks, for example, a single talent only be intrusted to those who have the management of any of the public money; though they give ten written sureties, with as many seals, and twice as many witnesses, they are unable to discharge the trust reposed in them with integrity. But the Romans, on the other hand, who, in the course of their magistracies, and in embassies, disburse the greatest sums, are prevailed on, by the single obligation of an oath, to perform their duty with inviolable honesty. And as, in other states, a man is rarely to be found whose hands are pure from public robbery; so, among the Romans, it is no less rare to discover one that is tainted with this crime.

But all things are subject to decay and change. This is a truth so evident, and so demonstrated by the perpetual and the necessary course of nature, that it needs no other proof. Now there are two ways by which every kind of government is destroyed; either by some accident that happens from without, or some evil that arises within itself. What the first will be is not always easy to foresee; but the latter is certain and determinate. We have already shown what are the original and in what manner also they are reciprocally converted each into the other. Whoever, therefore, is able to connect the beginning with the end in this inquiry will be able to declare, with some assurance, what will be the future fortune of the Roman government; at least, in my judgment, nothing is more easy. For when a state, having passed with safety through many and great dangers, arrives at the highest degree of power, and possesses an entire and undisputed sovereignty, it is manifest that the long continuance of prosperity must give birth to costly and luxurious manners, and that the minds of men will be heated with ambitious contests, and become too eager and aspiring in the pursuit of dignities. And as these evils are continually increased, the desire of power and rule and the imagined ignominy of remaining in a subject state, will first begin to work the ruin of the republic; arrogance and luxury will afterwards advance it; and, in the end, the change will be completed by the people; when the avarice of some is found to injure and oppress them, and the ambition of others swells their vanity, and poisons them with flattering hopes. For then, being inflamed with hopes, and following only the dictates of their passions, they no longer will submit to any control, or be contented with an equal share of the administration, in conjunction with their rulers; but will draw to themselves the entire sovereignty and supreme direction of all affairs. When this is done, the government will assume, indeed, the fairest of all names, that of a free and popular state; but will, in truth, be the greatest of all evils,—the government of the multitude.

As we have thus sufficiently explained the constitution and the growth of the Roman government; have marked the causes of that greatness in which it now subsists; and shown, by comparison, in what view it may be judged inferior, and in what superior, to other states; we shall here close this discourse.

LIFE OF MARCUS CATO

Plutarch

Marcus Porcius Cato (234–149 B.C.*) was both a historical character and a kind of folk hero around whom legends grow. By the time of Plutarch, a Greek philosopher writing some 250 years after Cato's death, fact and fancy had become inextricably intertwined. Plutarch, though he had access to reliable sources that have since disappeared, was not a critical historian but a moralist. The heroes of his biographies were meant to edify the reader by illustrating some dominant moral quality in action, though Plutarch did not hide their human foibles altogether. (For more about Plutarch, see page 63.)*

In "Marcus Cato," Plutarch depicted the embodiment of civic virtue. Plutarch drew attention to the peculiarly Roman characteristics of his hero, not all of which appealed to the Greek moralist. In any case, during antiquity Cato was widely accepted as a symbol of Roman republican virtue. With the revival of interest in classical history during the early modern period, the ideal of the stern and sober citizen regained its hold on the Western imagination. From the days of Machiavelli in the early sixteenth century to those of Robespierre at the end of the eighteenth, it was generally assumed that the success of republican institutions depended upon the prevalence of civic virtue of Cato's type.

Marcus Cato, we are told, was born at Tusculum, though (till he betook himself to civil and military affairs) he lived and was bred up in the country of the Sabines, where his father's estate lay. His ancestors seeming almost entirely unknown, he himself praises his father Marcus, as a worthy man and a brave soldier, and Cato, his great grandfather too, as one who had often obtained military prizes, and who, having lost five horses under him, received, on the account of his valor, the worth of them out of the public exchequer. Now it being the custom among the Romans to call those who, having no repute by birth, made themselves eminent by their own exertions, new men or upstarts, they called even Cato himself so, and so he confessed himself to be as to any public distinction or employment, but yet asserted that in the exploits and virtues of his ancestors he was very ancient. His third name originally was not Cato, but Priscus, though afterwards he had the surname of Cato, by reason of his abilities; for the Romans call a skilful or experienced man, *Catus.* He was of a ruddy com-

Plutarch's Lives, trans. called Dryden's, rev. A. H. Clough (Boston: Little, Brown and Company, 1875), Vol. II, 316–324, 326–329, 334–347, 351–352.

plexion, and grey-eyed. . . . He gained, in early life, a good habit of body by working with his own hands, and living temperately, and serving in war; and seemed to have an equal proportion both of health and strength. And he exerted and practised his eloquence through all the neighborhood and little villages; thinking it as requisite as a second body, and an all but necessary organ to one who looks forward to something above a mere humble and inactive life. He would never refuse to be counsel for those who needed him, and was, indeed, early reckoned a good lawyer, and, ere long, a capable orator.

Hence his solidity and depth of character showed itself gradually, more and more to those with whom he was concerned, and claimed, as it were, employment in great affairs, and places of public command. Nor did he merely abstain from taking fees for his counsel and pleading, but did not even seem to put any high price on the honor which proceeded from such kind of combats, seeming much more desirous to signalize himself in the camp and in real fights; and while yet but a youth, had his breast covered with scars he had received from the enemy; being (as he himself says) but seventeen years old, when he made his first campaign; in the time when Hannibal, in the height of his success, was burning and pillaging all Italy. In engagements he would strike boldly, without flinching, stand firm to his ground, fix a bold countenance upon his enemies, and with a harsh threatening voice accost them, justly thinking himself and telling others, that such a rugged kind of behavior sometimes terrifies the enemy more than the sword itself. In his marches, he bore his own arms on foot, whilst one servant only followed, to carry the provisions for his table, with whom he is said never to have been angry or hasty, whilst he made ready his dinner or supper, but would, for the most part, when he was free from military duty, assist and help him himself to dress it. When he was with the army, he used to drink only water; unless, perhaps, when extremely thirsty, he might mingle it with a little vinegar; or if he found his strength fail him, take a little wine.

The little country house of Manius Curius, who had been thrice carried in triumph, happened to be near his farm; so that often going thither, and contemplating the small compass of the place, and plainness of the dwelling, he formed an idea of the mind of the person, who, being one of the greatest of the Romans, and having subdued the most warlike nations, nay, had driven Pyrrhus out of Italy, now, after three triumphs, was contented to dig in so small a piece of ground, and live in such a cottage. Here it was that the ambassadors of the Samnites, finding him boiling turnips in the chimney corner, offered him a present of gold; but he sent them away with this saying; that he, who was content with such a supper, had no need of gold; and that he thought it more honorable to conquer those who possessed the gold, than to possess the gold itself. Cato, after reflecting upon these things, used to return, and reviewing his own farm, his servants, and housekeeping, increase his labor, and retrench all superfluous expenses. . . .

There was a man of the highest rank, and very influential among the Romans, called Valerius Flaccus, who was singularly skilful in discerning excellence yet in the bud, and, also, much disposed to nourish and advance it. He, it seems, had lands bordering upon Cato's; nor could he but admire, when he understood from his servants the manner of his living, how he labored with his own hands, went on foot betimes in the morning to the courts to assist those who wanted his counsel; how, returning home again, when it was winter, he would throw a loose frock over his shoulders, and in the summer time would work without any thing on among his domestics, sit down with them, eat of the same bread, and drink of the same wine. When they spoke, also, of other good qualities, his fair dealing and moderation, mentioning also some of his wise sayings, he ordered, that he should be invited to supper; and thus becoming personally assured of his fine temper and his superior character which, like a plant, seemed only to require culture and a better situation, he urged and persuaded him to apply himself to state affairs at Rome. Thither, therefore, he went, and by his pleading soon gained many friends and admirers; but, Valerius chiefly assisting his promotion, he first of all got appointed tribune in the army, and afterwards was made quaestor, or treasurer. And now becoming eminent and noted, he passed, with Valerius himself, through the greatest commands, being first his colleague as consul, and then censor. . . .

Cato grew more and more powerful by his eloquence, so that he was commonly called the Roman Demosthenes; but his manner of life was yet more famous and talked of. For oratorical skill was, as an accomplishment, commonly studied and sought after by all young men; but he was very rare who would cultivate the old habits of bodily labor, or prefer a light supper, and a breakfast which never saw the fire; or be in love with poor clothes and a homely lodging, or could set his ambition rather on doing without luxuries than on possessing them. For now the state, unable to keep its purity by reason of its greatness, and having so many affairs, and people from all parts under its government, was fain to admit many mixed customs, and new examples of living. With reason, therefore, everybody admired Cato, when they saw others sink under labors, and grow effeminate by pleasures; and yet beheld him unconquered by either, and that not only when he was young and desirous of honor, but also when old and greyheaded, after a consulship and triumph; like some famous victor in the games, persevering in his exercise and maintaining his character to the very last. He himself says, that he never wore a suit of clothes which cost more than a hundred drachmas; and that, when he was general and consul, he drank the same wine which his workmen did; and that the meat or fish which was bought in the market for his dinner, did not cost above thirty *asses.* All which was for the sake of the commonwealth, that so his body might be the hardier for the war. Having a piece of embroidered Babylonian tapestry left him, he sold it; because none of his farm-houses were so much as plastered. Nor did he ever buy a slave for above fifteen hundred drachmas; as he did not seek for effeminate and handsome ones, but able, sturdy workmen, horse-keepers and cow-herds: and these he thought ought to be sold again, when they grew old, and no useless servants fed in a house. In short, he reckoned nothing a good bargain, which was superfluous; but whatever it was, though sold for a farthing, he would think it a great price, if you had no need of it; and was for the purchase of lands for sowing and feeding, rather than grounds for sweeping and watering.

Some imputed these things to petty avarice, but others approved of him, as if he had only the more strictly denied himself for the rectifying and amending of others. Yet certainly, in my judgment, it marks an over-rigid temper, for a man to take the work out of his servants as out of brute beasts, turning them off and selling them in their old age, and thinking there ought to be no further commerce between man and man, than whilst there arises some profit by it. We see that kindness or humanity has a larger field than bare justice to exercise itself in; law and justice we cannot, in the nature of things, employ on others than men; but we may extend our goodness and charity even to irrational creatures; and such acts flow from a gentle nature, as water from an abundant spring. It is doubtless the part of a kind-natured man to keep even worn-out horses and dogs, and not only take care of them when they are foals and whelps, but also when they are grown old. . . .

Yet Cato for all this glories that he left that very horse in Spain, which he used in the wars when he was consul, only because he would not put the public to the charge of his freight. Whether these acts are to be ascribed to the greatness or pettiness of his spirit, let every one argue as they please.

For his general temperance, however, and self-control, he really deserves the highest admiration. For when he commanded the army, he never took for himself, and those that belonged to him, above three bushels of wheat for a month, and somewhat less than a bushel and a half a day of barley for his baggage-cattle. And when he entered upon the government of Sardinia, where his predecessors had been used to require tents, bedding, and clothes upon the public account, and to charge the state heavily with the cost of provisions and entertainments for a great train of servants and friends, the difference he showed in his economy was something incredible. There was nothing of any sort for which he put the public to expense; he would walk without a carriage to visit the cities, with one only of the common town officers, who carried his dress, and a cup to offer libation with. Yet, though he seemed thus easy and sparing to all who were under his power, he, on the other hand, showed most inflexible severity and strictness, in what related to public justice, and was rigorous, and precise in what concerned the ordinances of the commonwealth; so that the Roman government, never seemed more terrible, nor yet more mild, than under his administration.

His very manner of speaking seemed to have such a kind of idea with it; for it was courteous, and yet forcible; pleasant, yet overwhelming; facetious, yet austere; sententious, and yet vehement: like Socrates, in the description of Plato, who seemed outwardly to those about him to be but a simple, talkative, blunt fellow; whilst at the bottom he was full of such gravity and matter, as would even move tears, and touch the very hearts of his auditors. . . .

His interest being entreated by Scipio, on account of Polybius, for the Achaean exiles, and there happening to be a great discussion in the senate about it, some being for, and some against their return; Cato, standing up, thus delivered himself: "Here do we sit all day long, as if we had nothing to do, but beat our brains whether these old Greeks should be carried to their graves by the bearers here, or by those in Achaea." The senate voting their return, it seems that a few days after Polybius's friends further wished that it should be moved in the senate, that the said banished persons should receive again the honors which they first had in Achaea; and, to this purpose, they sounded Cato for his opinion; but he, smiling, answered, that Polybius, Ulysses like, having escaped out of the Cyclops' den, wanted, it would seem, to go back again because he had left his cap and belt behind him. He used to assert, also, that wise men profited more by fools, than fools by wise men: for that wise men avoided the faults of fools, but that fools would not imitate the good examples of wise men. He would profess, too, that he was more taken with young men that blushed, than with those who looked pale; and that he never desired to have a soldier that moved his hands too much in marching, and his feet too much in fighting; or snored louder than he shouted. Ridiculing a fat overgrown man: "What use," said he, "can the state turn a man's body to, when all between the throat and groin is taken up by the belly?" When one who was much given to pleasures desired his acquaintance, begging his pardon, he said, he could not live with a man whose palate was of a quicker sense than his heart. He would likewise say, that the soul of a lover lived in the body of another: and that in his whole life he most repented of three things; one was, that he had trusted a secret to a woman; another, that he went by water when he might have gone by land; the third, that he had remained one whole day without doing any business of moment. Applying himself to an old man who was committing some vice: "Friend," said he, "old age has of itself blemishes enough; do not you add to it the deformity of vice." Speaking to a tribune, who was reputed a poisoner, and was very violent for the bringing in of a bill, in order to make a certain law: "Young man," cried he, "I know not which would be better, to drink what you mix, or confirm what you would put up for a law." Being reviled by a fellow who lived a profligate and wicked life: "A contest," replied he, "is unequal between you and me; for you can hear ill words easily, and can as easily give them; but it is unpleasant to me to give such, and unusual to hear them." Such was his manner of expressing himself in his memorable sayings.

Being chosen consul, with his friend and familiar Valerius Flaccus, the government of that part of Spain which the Romans call the Hither Spain, fell to his lot. Here, as he was engaged in reducing some of the tribes by force, and bringing over others by good words, a large army of barbarians fell upon him, so that there was danger of being disgracefully forced out again. He therefore called upon his neighbors, the Celtiberians, for help; and on their demanding two hundred talents for their assistance, everybody else thought it intolerable, that ever the Romans should promise barbarians a reward for their aid; but Cato said, there was no discredit or harm in it; for if they overcame, they would pay them out of the enemy's purse, and not out of their own; but if they were overcome, there would be nobody left either to demand the reward or to pay it. However, he won that battle completely, and after that, all his other affairs succeeded splendidly. . . .

In civil policy, he was of opinion, that one chief duty consisted in accusing and indicting criminals. He himself prosecuted many, and he would also assist others who prosecuted them, nay would even procure such, as he did the Petilii against Scipio; but not being able to destroy him, by reason of the nobleness of his family, and the real greatness of his mind, which enabled him to trample all calumnies underfoot, Cato at last would meddle no more with him; yet joining with the accusers against Scipio's brother Lucius, he succeeded in obtaining a sentence against him, which condemned him to the payment of a large sum of money to the state; and being insolvent, and in danger of being thrown into jail, he was, by the interposition of the tribunes of the people, with much ado dismissed. It is also said of Cato, that when he met a certain youth, who had effected the disgrace of one of his father's enemies, walking in the market-place, he shook him by the hand, telling him, that this was what we ought to sacrifice to our dead parents—not lambs and goats, but the tears and condemnations of their adversaries. But neither did he himself escape with impunity in his management of affairs; for if he gave his enemies but the least hold, he was still in danger, and exposed to be brought to justice. He is reported to have escaped at least fifty indictments; and one above the rest, which was the last, when he was eighty-six years old, about which time he uttered the well-known saying, that it was hard for him who had lived with one generation of men, to plead now before another. Neither did he make this the last of his lawsuits; for, four years after, when he was fourscore and ten, he accused Servilius Galba: so that his life and actions extended, we may say, as Nestor's did, over three ordinary ages of man. For, having had many contests, as we have related, with Scipio the Great, about affairs of state, he continued them down even to Scipio the younger, who was the adopted grandson of the former, and the son of that Paulus, who overthrew Perseus and the Macedonians.

Ten years after his consulship, Cato stood for the office of censor, which was indeed the summit of all honor, and in a manner the highest step in civil affairs; for besides all other power, it had also that of an inquisition into every one's life and manners. For the Romans thought that no marriage, or rearing of children, nay, no feast or drinking-bout ought to be permitted according to every one's appetite or fancy, without being examined and inquired into; being indeed of opinion, that a man's character was much sooner perceived in things of this sort, than in what is done publicly and in open day. They chose, therefore, two persons, one out of the patricians, the other out of the commons, who were to watch, correct, and punish, if any one ran too much into voluptuousness, or transgressed the usual manner of life of his country; and these they called Censors. They had power to take away a horse,[1] or expel out of the senate any one who lived intemperately and out of order. It was also their business to take an estimate of what every one was worth, and to put down in registers everybody's birth and quality; besides many other prerogatives. And therefore the chief nobility opposed his pretensions to it. Jealousy prompted the patricians, who thought that it would be a stain to everybody's nobility, if men of no original honor should rise to the highest dignity and power; while others, conscious of their own evil practices, and of the violation of the laws and customs of their country, were afraid of the austerity of the man; which, in an office of such great power was likely to prove most uncompromising and severe. And so consulting among themselves, they brought forward seven candidates in opposition to him, who sedulously set themselves to court the people's favor by fair promises, as though what they wished for was indulgent and easy government. Cato, on the contrary, promising no such mildness, but plainly threatening evil livers, from the very hustings openly declared himself; and exclaiming, that the city needed a great and thorough purgation, called upon the people, if they were wise, not to choose the gentlest, but the roughest of physicians; such a one, he said, he was, and Valerius Flaccus, one of the patricians, another; together with him, he doubted not but he should do something worth the while, and that, by cutting to

[1] *To inflict on any member of the order of horsemen or* equites, *the forfeiture of the horse that was allowed him: in other words, to degrade from the equestrian dignity.*

pieces and burning like a hydra,[2] all luxury and voluptuousness. He added, too, that he saw all the rest endeavoring after the office with ill intent, because they were afraid of those who would exercise it justly, as they ought. And so truly great and so worthy of great men to be its leaders was, it would seem, the Roman people, that they did not fear the severity and grim countenance of Cato, but rejecting those smooth promisers who were ready to do all things to ingratiate themselves, they took him, together with Flaccus; obeying his recommendations not as though he were a candidate, but as if he had had the actual power of commanding and governing already. . . .

Manilius, also, who, according to the public expectation, would have been next consul, he threw out of the senate, because, in the presence of his daughter, and in open day, he had kissed his wife. He said, that as for himself, his wife never came into his arms except when there was great thunder; so that it was a jest with him, that it was a pleasure for him, when Jupiter thundered.

His treatment of Lucius, likewise, the brother of Scipio, and one who had been honored with a triumph, occasioned some odium against Cato; for he took his horse from him, and was thought to do it with a design of putting an affront on Scipio Africanus, now dead. But he gave most general annoyance, by retrenching people's luxury; for though (most of the youth being thereby already corrupted) it seemed almost impossible to take it away with an open hand and directly, yet going, as it were, obliquely around, he caused all dress, carriages, women's ornaments, household furniture, whose price exceeded one thousand five hundred drachmas, to be rated at ten times as much as they were worth; intending by thus making the assessments greater, to increase the taxes paid upon them. He also ordained that upon every thousand *asses* of property of this kind, three should be paid, so that people, burdened with these extra charges, and seeing others of as good estates, but more frugal and sparing, paying less into the public exchequer, might be tired out of their prodigality. And thus, on the one side, not only those were disgusted at Cato, who bore the taxes for the sake of their luxury, but those, too, who on the other side laid by their luxury for fear of the taxes. For people in general reckon, that an order not to display their riches, is equivalent to the taking away their riches; because riches are seen much more in superfluous, than in necessary, things. . . .

Cato, notwithstanding, being little solicitous as to those who exclaimed against him, increased his austerity. He caused the pipes, through which some persons brought the public water into their own houses and gardens, to be cut, and threw down all buildings which jutted out into the common streets. He beat down also the price in contracts for public works to the lowest, and raised it in contracts for farming the taxes to the highest sum; by which proceedings he drew a great deal of hatred on himself. Those who were of Titus Flamininus's party cancelled in the senate all the bargains and contracts made by him for the repairing and carrying on of the sacred and public buildings, as unadvantageous to the commonwealth. They incited also the boldest of the tribunes of the people to accuse him, and to fine him two talents. They likewise much opposed him in building the court or basilica, which he caused to be erected

[2] *Wherever Hercules cut off one head from the Lernaean hydra, two new ones sprung up in its place; until he applied fire and cauterized the wounds.*

at the common charge, just by the senate-house, in the market-place, and called by his own name, the Porcian. However, the people, it seems, liked his censorship wondrously well; for, setting up a statue for him in the temple of the goddess of Health, they put an inscription under it, not recording his commands in war or his triumph, but to the effect, that this was Cato the Censor, who, by his good discipline and wise and temperate ordinances, reclaimed the Roman commonwealth when it was declining and sinking down into vice. Before this honor was done to himself, he used to laugh at those who loved such kind of things, saying, that they did not see that they were taking pride in the workmanship of brass-founders and painters; whereas the citizens bore about his best likeness in their breasts. And when any seemed to wonder, that he should have never a statue, while many ordinary persons had one; "I would," said he, "much rather be asked, why I have not one, than why I have one." In short, he would not have any honest citizen endure to be praised, except it might prove advantageous to the commonwealth. Yet still he had passed the highest commendation on himself; for he tells us that those who did any thing wrong, and were found fault with, used to say, it was not worth while to blame them; for they were not Catos. He also adds, that they who awkwardly mimicked some of his actions, were called left-handed Catos; and that the senate in perilous times would cast their eyes on him, as upon a pilot in a ship, and that often when he was not present they put off affairs of greatest consequence. These things are indeed also testified of him by others; for he had a great authority in the city, alike for his life, his eloquence, and his age.

He was also a good father, an excellent husband to his wife, and an extraordinary economist; and as he did not manage his affairs of this kind carelessly, and as things of little moment, I think I ought to record a little further whatever was commendable in him in these points. He married a wife more noble than rich; being of opinion that the rich and the high-born are equally haughty and proud; but that those of noble blood, would be more ashamed of base things, and consequently more obedient to their husbands in all that was fit and right. A man who beat his wife or child laid violent hands, he said, on what was most sacred; and a good husband he reckoned worthy of more praise than a great senator; and he admired the ancient Socrates for nothing so much, as for having lived a temperate and contented life with a wife who was a scold, and children who were half-witted.

As soon as he had a son born, though he had never such urgent business upon his hands, unless it were some public matter, he would be by when his wife washed it and dressed it in its swaddling clothes. For she herself suckled it, nay, she often too gave her breast to her servants' children, to produce, by sucking the same milk, a kind of natural love in them to her son. When he began to come to years of discretion, Cato himself would teach him to read, although he had a servant, a very good grammarian, called Chilo, who taught many others; but he thought not fit, as he himself said, to have his son reprimanded by a slave, or pulled, it may be, by the ears when found tardy in his lesson: nor would he have him owe to a servant the obligation of so great a thing as his learning; he himself, therefore, (as we were saying,) taught him his grammar, law, and his gymnastic exercises. Nor did he only show him, too, how to throw a dart, to fight in armor, and to ride, but to box also and to endure both heat and cold, and to swim over the most rapid and rough rivers. He says, likewise, that he wrote histories, in large characters, with his own hand, that so his son, without stirring out of the house, might learn to know about his country-men and forefathers: nor did he less abstain from speaking any thing obscene before his son, than if it had been in the presence of the sacred virgins, called vestals. Nor would he ever go into the bath with him; which seems indeed to have been the common custom of the Romans. Sons-in-law used to avoid bathing with fathers-in-law, disliking to see one another naked: but having, in time, learned of the Greeks to strip before men, they have since taught the Greeks to do it even with the women themselves.

Thus, like an excellent work, Cato formed and fashioned his son to virtue; nor had he any occasion to find fault with his readiness and docility; but as he proved to be of too weak a constitution for hardships, he did not insist on requiring of him any very austere way of living. However, though delicate in health, he proved a stout man in the field, and behaved himself valiantly when Paulus Aemilius fought against Perseus; where when his sword was struck from him by a blow, or rather slipped out of his hand by reason of its moistness, he so keenly resented it, that he turned to some of his friends about him, and taking them along with him again, fell upon the enemy; and having by a long fight and much force cleared the place, at length found it among great heaps of arms, and the dead bodies of friends as well as enemies piled one upon another. Upon which Paulus, his general, much commended the youth; and there is a letter of Cato's to his son, which highly praises his honorable eagerness for the recovery of his sword. Afterwards he married Tertia, Aemilius Paulus's daughter, and sister to Scipio; nor was he admitted into this family less for his own worth than his father's. So that Cato's care in his son's education came to a very fitting result.

He purchased a great many slaves out of the captives taken in war, but chiefly bought up the young ones, who were capable to be, as it were, broken and taught like whelps and colts. None of these ever entered another man's house, except sent either by Cato himself or his wife. If any one of them were asked what Cato did, they answered merely, that they did not know. When a servant was at home, he was obliged either to do some work or sleep; for indeed Cato loved those most who used to lie down often to sleep, accounting them more docile than those who were wakeful, and more fit for any thing when they were refreshed with a little slumber. Being also of opinion, that the great cause of the laziness and misbehavior of slaves was their running after their pleasures, he fixed a certain price for them to pay for permission amongst themselves, but would suffer no connections out of the house. At first, when he was but a poor soldier, he would not be difficult in any thing which related to his eating, but looked upon it as a pitful thing to quarrel with a servant for the belly's sake; but afterwards, when he grew richer, and made any feasts for his friends and colleagues in office, as soon as supper was over he used to go with a leathern thong and scourge those who had waited or dressed the meat carelessly. He always contrived, too, that his servants should have some difference one among another, always suspecting and fearing a good understanding between them. Those who had committed any thing worthy of death, he punished, if they were found guilty by the verdict of their fellow-servants. But being after all much given to the desire of gain, he looked upon agriculture rather as a pleasure than profit; resolving, therefore, to lay out his money in safe and solid things, he purchased ponds, hot baths, grounds full of fuller's earth, remunerative lands, pastures, and woods; from all which he drew large returns, nor could Jupiter himself, he used to say, do him much damage. He was also given to the form of usury, which is considered most odious, in traffic by sea; and that thus:— he desired that those whom he put out his money to, should have many partners and when the number of them and their ships came to be fifty, he himself took one share through Quintio his freedman, who therefore was to sail with the adventurers and take part in all their proceedings; so that thus there was no danger of losing his whole stock, but only a little part, and that with a prospect of great profit. He likewise lent money to those of his slaves who wished to borrow, with which they bought also other young ones, whom, when they had taught and bred up at his charges, they would sell again at the year's end; but some of them Cato would keep for himself, giving just as much for them as another had offered. To incline his son to be of this kind of temper, he used to tell him, that it was not like a man, but rather like a widow woman to lessen an estate. But the strongest indication of Cato's avaricious humor was when he took the boldness to affirm, that he was a most wonderful, nay, a godlike man who left more behind him than he had received.

He was now grown old, when Carneades the Academic, and Diogenes the Stoic came as deputies from Athens to Rome, praying for release from a penalty of five hundred talents laid on the Athenians, in a suit, to which they did not appear, in which the Oropians were plaintiffs, and Sicyonians judges. All the most studious youth immediately waited on these philosophers, and frequently, with admiration heard them speak. But the gracefulness of Carneades's oratory, whose ability was really greatest, and his reputation equal to it, gathered large and favorable audiences and erelong filled, like a wind, all the city with the sound of it. So that it soon began to be told, that a Greek, famous even to admiration, winning and carrying all before him, had impressed so strange a love upon the young men, that quitting all their pleasures and pastimes, they ran mad, as it were, after philosophy; which indeed much pleased the Romans in general; nor could they but with much pleasure see the youth receive so welcomely the Greek literature, and frequent the company of learned men But Cato, on the other side, seeing this passion for words flowing into the city, from the beginning, took it ill, fearing lest the youth should be diverted that way, and so should prefer the glory of speaking well before that of arms, and doing well. And when the fame of the philosophers increased in the city, and Caius Acilius, a person of distinction, at his own request, became their interpreter to the senate at their first audience, Cato resolved, under some specious pretence, to have all philosophers cleared out of the city; and, coming into the senate, blamed the magisrates for letting these deputies stay so long a time without being despatched, though they were persons that could easily persuade the people to what they pleased; that therefore in all haste something should be determined about their petition, that so they might go home again to their own schools, and declaim to the Greek children, and leave the Roman youth to be obedient, as hitherto, to their own laws and governors.

Yet he did this not out of any anger, as some think, to Carneades; but because he wholly despised philosophy, and out of a kind of pride, scoffed at the Greek studies and literature; as, for example, he would say, that Socrates was a prating seditious fellow, who did his best to tyrannize over his country, to undermine the ancient customs, and to entice and withdraw the citizens to opinions contrary to the laws. Ridiculing the school of Isocrates, he would add, that his scholars grew old men before they had done learning with him, as if they were to use their art and plead causes in the court of Minos in the next world. And to frighten his son from any thing that was Greek, in a more vehement tone than became one of his age, he pronounced, as it were, with the voice of an oracle, that the Romans would certainly be destroyed when they began once to be infected with Greek literature; though time indeed has shown the vanity of this his prophecy; as, in truth, the city of Rome has risen to its highest fortune, while entertaining Grecian learning. Nor had he an aversion only against the Greek philosophers, but the physicians also; for having, it seems, heard how Hippocrates, when the king of Persia sent for him, with offers of a fee of several talents, said, that he would never assist barbarians who were enemies to the Greeks; he affirmed, that this was now become a common oath taken by all physicians, and enjoined his son to have a care and avoid them; for that he himself had written a little book of prescriptions for curing those who were sick in his family; he never enjoined fasting to any one, but ordered them either vegetables, or the meat of a duck, pigeon, or leveret; such kind of diet being of light digestion, and fit for sick folks, only it made those who ate it, dream a little too much; and by the use of this kind of physic, he said, he not only made himself and those about him well, but kept them so.

ON THE LAWS

Cicero

Marcus Tullius Cicero (106–43 B.C.) *was one of the outstanding Roman political leaders of his day. As a moderate compromiser in an age of violence he ultimately failed—he was murdered for political reasons. As a letter writer whose voluminous correspondence has been preserved, he provides a uniquely vivid portrait of politics during the declining decades of the Roman Republic. Cicero was recognized as the greatest of Latin orators, and his speeches remained the supreme model for aspiring politicians well into the nineteenth century. Finally, as the most productive and influential Roman philosopher, he became the chief interpreter of Greek thought to the Latin world.*

The Laws *came from Cicero the philosopher, although Cicero drew as much on his training as a Roman lawyer as on contemporary Greek philosophers whose work has since been lost. In form the treatise is modeled after Plato's dialogues; indeed, Cicero freely acknowledges his debt. The chief speaker, the figure of Marcus, is Cicero himself; the other participants are*

*Atticus, his long-time friend and a self-proclaimed Epicurean (**see page 185**), and Quintus, Cicero's own brother.*

The first and major part of the selection is drawn from Book I and deals with the concept of natural law, which Cicero derived from Stoic philosophy. This vision of an orderly, moral universe in which man is a partner has been among the most durable and influential of philosophic ideas. Although Roman law had originated in a primitive society far removed from such rational notions, by Cicero's day legislation increasingly came under the influence of natural law in its emphasis on reason and universality; and this process continued under the Principate, after the fall of the Republic. In the last section, taken from Book III, we see how Cicero envisages the application of these principles to the Rome of his time.

Atticus Let us go, then, and enter on our investigations, as we walk along the bank of the river under the shadow of its foliage. And now begin, I beg of you, to explain to us your opinion respecting the nature of Civil Law.

Marcus My opinion? Why, that we have had many great men in Rome, who have made it their profession to expound it to the people, and explain its doctrines and practice. But though they professed to be acquainted with its great principles, they were in reality familiar rather with its minuter technicalities. For what can be grander or nobler than the jurisprudence of a state? or what can be so insignificant as the office of those men who are consulted as advocates, necessary as it is for the people? Not that I think that those who adopt this profession have been altogether ignorant of the principles of universal legislation, but they have united their practice of this civil law, as they call it, to just so much as gives them a hold on the interests of the people. But the great principles of jurisprudence are unknown, and less necessary in practice. What, then, is it that you invite me to? or what are you exhorting me to? to write treatises on the rights of common sewers and partition walls? or to compose formulas of stipulations and judgments? These have been already most diligently prepared by many persons, and are lower than the topics which, I suppose, you expect me to discuss.

Atticus But, if you ask what I expect, I should reply, that after having given us a treatise on the Commonwealth, it appears a natural consequence that you should also write one on the Laws. For this is what I see was done by your illustrious favourite Plato, the philosopher whom you admire and prefer to all others, and love with an especial affection.

Marcus Do you wish, then, that, as he conversed at Crete with Clinias, and Megillus of Lacedaemon, on that summer's day, as he describes it, in the cypress groves and sylvan avenues of Cnossus, often objecting to, and at times approving of, the estab

The Treatises of M. T. Cicero, **trans. C. D. Yonge (London: G. Bell & Sons, Ltd., 1872), pp. 404–412, 417–421, 431–432, 461–466.**

ished laws and customs of commonwealths, and discussed what were the best laws; so we also, walking beneath these lofty poplars, along the green and umbrageous banks, and sometimes sitting down, should investigate the same subjects somewhat more copiously than is required by the practice of the courts of law?

Atticus I should like to hear such a discussion.

Marcus But what says Quintus?

Quintus There is no subject which I would rather hear argued.

Marcus And you are quite right. For, take my word for it, in no kind of discussion can it be more advantageously displayed how much has been bestowed upon man by nature, and how great a capacity for the noblest enterprises is implanted in the mind of man, for the sake of cultivating and perfecting which we were born and sent into the world, and what beautiful association, what natural fellowship, binds men together by reciprocal charities: and when we have explained these grand and universal principles of morals, then the true fountain of laws and rights can be discovered.

Atticus In your opinion, then, it is not in the edict of the magistrate, as the majority of our modern lawyers pretend, nor in the Twelve Tables, as the ancients maintained, but in the sublimest doctrines of philosophy, that we must seek for the true source and obligation of jurisprudence.

Marcus For in this discussion of ours, my Atticus, we are not inquiring how we may take proper caution in law, or what we are to answer in each consultation,—that may indeed be an important affair, as in truth it is; and at one time it was supported by many great men, and is at present expounded by one most eminent lawyer with admirable ability and skill.

But the whole subject of universal law and jurisprudence must be comprehended in this discussion, in order that this which we call civil law, may be confined in some one small and narrow space of nature. For we shall have to explain the true nature of moral justice, which must be traced back from the nature of man. And laws will have to be considered by which all political states should be governed. And last of all, shall we have to speak of those laws and customs of nations, which are framed for the use and convenience of particular countries, (in which even our own people will not be omitted,) which are known by the title of civil laws.

Quintus You take a noble view of the subject, my brother, and go to the fountain-head, in order to throw light on the subject of our consideration; and those who treat civil law in any other manner, are not so much pointing out the paths of justice as those of litigation.

Marcus That is not quite the case, my Quintus. It is not so much the science of law that produces litigation, as the ignorance of it. But more of this by-and-by. At present let us examine the first principles of Right.

Now, many learned men have maintained that it springs from law. I hardly know if their opinion be not correct, at least according to their own definition; for "law," say they, "is the highest reason implanted in nature, which prescribes those things which ought to be done, and forbids the contrary." And when this same reason is confirmed and established in men's minds, it is then law.

They therefore conceive that prudence is a law, whose operation is to urge us to good actions, and restrain us from evil ones. And they think, too, that the Greek name for law (νόμος), which is derived from νέμω, to distribute, implies the very nature of the thing, that is, to give every man his due. The Latin name, *lex,* conveys the idea of selection, *a legendo*. According to the Greeks, therefore, the name of law implies an equitable distribution: according to the Romans, an equitable selection. And, indeed, both characteristics belong peculiarly to law.

And if this be a correct statement, which it seems to me for the most part to be, then the origin of right is to be sought in the law. For this is the true energy of nature,— this is the very soul and reason of a wise man, and the test of virtue and vice. But since all this discussion of ours relates to a subject, the terms of which are of frequent occurrence in the popular language of the citizens, we shall be sometimes obliged to use the same terms as the vulgar, and to call that law, which in its written enactments sanctions what it thinks fit by special commands or prohibitions.

Let us begin, then, to establish the principles of justice on that supreme law, which has existed from all ages before any legislative enactments were drawn up in writing, or any political governments constituted.

Quintus That will be more convenient, and more sensible with reference to the subject of the discussion which we have determined on.

Marcus Shall we, then, seek for the origin of justice at its fountain-head? when we have discovered which, we shall be in no doubt to what these questions which we are examining ought to be referred.

Quintus Such is the course I would advise.

Atticus I also subscribe to your brother's opinion.

Marcus Since, then, we wish to maintain and preserve the constitution of that republic which Scipio, in those six books which I have written under that title, has proved to be the best, and since all our laws are to be accommodated to the kind of political government there described, we must also treat of the general principles of morals and manners, and not limit ourselves on all occasions to written laws; but I purpose to trace back the origin of right from nature itself, who will be our best guide in conducting the whole discussion.

Atticus You will do right, and when she is our guide it is absolutely impossible for us to err.

Marcus Do you then grant, my Atticus, (for I know my brother's opinion already,) that the entire universe is regulated by the power of the immortal Gods, that by their nature, reason, energy, mind, divinity, or some other word of clearer signification, if there be such, all things are governed and directed? for if you will not grant me this, that is what I must begin by establishing.

Atticus I grant you all you can desire. But owing to this singing of birds and babbling of waters, I fear my fellow-learners can scarcely hear me.

Marcus You are quite right to be on your guard; for even the best men occasionally fall into a passion, and they will be very indignant if they hear you denying the first article of that notable book, entitled "The Chief Doctrines of Epicurus," in which he says "that God takes care of nothing, neither of himself nor of any other being!"

Atticus Pray proceed, for I am waiting to know what advantage you mean to take of the concession I have made you.

Marcus I will not detain you long. This is the bearing which they have on our subject. This animal—prescient, sagacious, complex, acute, full of memory, reason, and counsel, which we call man—has been generated by the supreme God in a most transcendent condition. For he is the only creature among all the races and descriptions of animated beings who is endued with superior reason and thought, in which the rest are deficient. And what is there, I do not say in man alone, but in all heaven and earth, more divine than reason, which, when it becomes right and perfect, is justly termed wisdom?

There exists, therefore, since nothing is better than reason, and since this is the common property of God and man, a certain aboriginal rational intercourse between divine and human natures. But where reason is common, there right reason must also be common to the same parties; and since this right reason is what we call law, God and men must be considered as associated by law. Again, there must also be a communion of right where there is a communion of law. And those who have law and right thus in common, must be considered members of the same commonwealth.

And if they are obedient to the same rule and the same authority, they are even much more so to this one celestial regency, this divine mind and omnipotent deity. So that the entire universe may be looked upon as forming one vast commonwealth of gods and men. And, as in earthly states certain ranks are distinguished with reference to the relationships of families, according to a certain principle which will be discussed in its proper place, that principle, in the nature of things, is far more magnificent and splendid by which men are connected with the Gods, as belonging to their kindred and nation.

For when we are reasoning on universal nature, we are accustomed to argue (and indeed the truth is just as it is stated in that argument) that in the long course of ages, and the uninterrupted succession of celestial revolutions, there arrived a certain ripe time for the sowing of the human race; and when it was sown and scattered over the earth, it was animated by the divine gift of souls. And as men retained from their terrestrial origin those other particulars by which they cohere together, which are frail and perishable, their immortal spirits were ingenerated by the Deity. From which circumstance it may be truly said, that we possess a certain consanguinity, and kindred, and fellowship with the heavenly powers. And among all the varieties of animals, there is not one except man which retains any idea of the Divinity. And among men themselves, there is no nation so savage and ferocious as not to admit the necessity of believing in a God, however ignorant they may be what sort of God they ought to believe in. From whence we conclude that every man must recognise a Deity, who has any recollection and knowledge of his own origin.

Now, the law of virtue is the same in God and man, and in no other disposition besides them. This virtue is nothing else than a nature perfect in itself, and wrought up to the most consummate excellence. There exists, therefore, a similitude between God and man. And as this is the case, what connection can there be which concerns us more nearly, and is more certain?

Therefore, nature has supplied such an abundance of supplies suited to the convenience and use of men, that the things which are thus produced appear to be designedly bestowed on us, and not fortuitous productions. Nor does this observation apply only to the fruits and vegetables which gush from the bosom of the earth, but likewise to cattle and the beasts of the field, some of which, it is clear, were intended for the use of mankind, others for propagation, and others for the food of man. Innumerable arts have likewise been discovered by the teaching of nature, whom reason has imitated, and thus skilfully discovered all things necessary to the happiness of life.

With respect to man, this same bountiful nature hath not merely allotted him a subtle and active spirit, but also physical senses, like so many servants and messengers. And she has laid bare before him the obscure but necessary explanation of many things, which are, as it were, the foundation of practical knowledge; and in all respects she has given him a convenient figure of body, suited to the bent of the human character. For while she has kept down the countenances of other animals, and fixed their eyes on their food, she has bestowed on man alone an erect stature, and prompted him to the contemplation of heaven, the ancient home of his kindred immortals. So exquisitely, too, has she fashioned the features of the human face, as to make them indicate the most recondite thoughts and sentiments. For our eloquent eyes speak forth every impulse and passion of our souls; and that which we call *expression,* which cannot exist in any other animal but man, betrays all our feelings, the power of which was well known to the Greeks, though they have no name for it.

I will not enlarge on the wonderful faculties and qualities of the rest of the body, the modulation of the voice, and the power of oratory, which is the greatest instrument of influence upon human society. For these matters do not all belong to the present occasion or the present subject, and I think that Scipio has already sufficiently explained them in those books of mine which you have read.

Since, then, the Deity has been pleased to create and adorn man to be the chief and president of all terrestrial creatures, so it is evident, without further argument, that human nature has also made very great advances by its own intrinsic energy; that nature, which without any other instruction than her own, has developed the first rude principles of the understanding, and strengthened and perfected reason to all the appliances of science and art.

Atticus Oh ye immortal Gods! to what a distance back are you tracing the principles of justice! However, you are discoursing in such a style that I will not show any impatience to hear what I expect you to say on the Civil Law. But I will listen patiently, even if you spend the whole day in this kind of discourse; for assuredly these, which perhaps you are embracing in your argument for the sake of others, are grander topics than even the subject itself for which they prepare the way.

Marcus You may well describe these topics as grand, which we are now briefly discussing. But of all the questions which are ever the subject of discussion among learned men, there is none which it is more important thoroughly to understand than this, that man is born for justice, and that law and equity have not been established by opinion, but by nature. This truth will become still more apparent if we investigate the nature of human association and society.

For there is no one thing so like or so equal to another, as in every instance man is to man. And if the corruption of customs, and the variation of opinions, did not induce an imbecility of minds, and turn them aside from the course of nature, no one would more nearly resemble himself than all men would resemble all men. Therefore, whatever definition we give of man, will be applicable to the whole human race. And this is a good argument that there is no dissimilarity of kind among men; because if this were the case, one definition could not include all men.

In fact, reason, which alone gives us so many advantages over beasts, by means of which we conjecture, argue, refute, discourse, and accomplish and conclude our designs, is assuredly common to all men; for the faculty of acquiring knowledge is similar in all human minds, though the knowledge itself may be endlessly diversified. By the same senses we all perceive the same objects, and those things which move the senses at all, do move in the same way the senses of all men. And those first rude elements of intelligence which, as I before observed, are the earliest developments of thought, are similarly impressed upon all men; and that faculty of speech which is the interpreter of the mind, agrees in the ideas which it conveys, though it may differ in the words by which it expresses them. And therefore there exists not a man in any nation, who, if he adopts nature for his guide, may not arrive at virtue.

Nor is this resemblance which all men bear to each other remarkable in those things only which are in accordance with right reason, but also in errors. For all men alike are captivated by pleasure, which, although it is a temptation to what is disgraceful, nevertheless bears some resemblance to natural good; for, as by its delicacy and sweetness it is delightful, it is through a mistake of the intellect adopted as something salutary.

And by an error scarcely less universal, we shun death as if it were a dissolution of nature, and cling to life because it keeps us in that existence in which we were born. Thus, likewise, we consider pain as one of the greatest evils, not only on account of its present asperity, but also because it seems the precursor of mortality. Again, on account of the apparent resemblance between renown with honour, those men appear to us happy who are honoured, and miserable who happen to be inglorious. In like manner our minds are all similarly susceptible of inquietudes, joys, desires, and fears; nor if different men have different opinions, does it follow that those who deify dogs and cats, do not labour under superstition equally with other nations, though they may differ from them in the forms of its manifestation.

Again, what nation is there which has not a regard for kindness, benignity, gratitude, and mindfulness of benefits? What nation is there in which arrogance, malice, cruelty, and unthankfulness, are not reprobated and detested? And while this uniformity of opinions proves that the whole race of mankind is united together, the last point is that a system of living properly makes men better. If what I have said meets your approbation, I will proceed; or if any doubts occur to you, we had better clear them up first.

Atticus There is nothing which strikes us, if I may reply for both of us. . . .

Marcus But if justice consists in submission to written law and national customs, and if, as the same school affirms, everything must be measured by utility alone, he who thinks that such conduct will be advantageous to him will neglect the laws, and break them if it is in his power. And the consequence is, that real justice has really no existence if it have not one by nature, and if that which is established as such on account of utility is overturned by some other utility.

But if nature does not ratify law, then all the virtues may lose their sway. For what becomes of generosity, patriotism, or friendship? Where will the desire of benefitting our neighbours, or the gratitude that acknowledges kindness, be able to exist at all? For all these virtues proceed from our natural inclination to love mankind. And this is the true basis of justice, and without this not only the mutual charities of men, but the religious services of the Gods, would be at an end; for these are preserved, as I imagine, rather by the natural sympathy which subsists between divine and human beings, than by mere fear and timidity.

But if the will of the people, the decrees of the senate, the adjudications of magistrates, were sufficient to establish rights, then it might become right to rob, right to commit adultery, right to substitute forged wills, if such conduct were sanctioned by the votes or decrees of the multitude. But if the opinions and suffrages of foolish men had sufficient weight to outbalance the nature of things, then why should they not determine among them, that what is essentially bad and pernicious should henceforth pass for good and beneficial? Or why, since law can make right out of injustice, should it not also be able to change evil into good?

But we have no other rule by which we may be capable of distinguishing between a good or a bad law than that of nature. Nor is it only right and wrong which are discriminated by nature, but generally all that is honourable is by this means distinguished from all that is shameful; for common sense has impressed in our minds the first principles of things, and has given us a general acquaintance with them, by which we connect with virtue every honourable quality, and with vice all that is disgraceful.

But to think that these differences exist only in opinion, and not in nature, is the part of an idiot. For even the virtue of a tree or a horse, in which expression there is an abuse of terms, does not exist in our opinion only, but in nature; and if that is the case, then what is honourable and disgraceful, must also be discriminated by nature.

For if opinion could determine respecting the character of universal virtue, it might also decide respecting particular or partial virtues. But who will dare to determine that a man is prudent and cautious, not from his general conduct, but from some external appearances? For virtue evidently consists in perfect reason, and this certainly resides in nature. Therefore so does all honour and honesty in the same way.

For as what is true and false, creditable and discreditable, is judged of rather by their essential qualities than their external relations; so the consistent and perpetual course of life, which is virtue, and the inconsistency of life, which is vice, are judged of according to their own nature,—and that inconstancy must necessarily be vicious.

We form an estimate of the opinions of youths, but not by their opinions. Those virtues and vices which reside in their moral natures must not be measured by opinions. And so of all moral qualities, we must discriminate between honourable and dishonourable by reference to the essential nature of the things themselves.

The good we commend, must needs contain in itself something commendable; for as I before stated, goodness is not a mode of opinion, but of nature. For if it were otherwise, opinion alone might constitute virtue and happiness, which is the most absurd of suppositions. And since we judge of good and evil by their nature, and since good and evil are the first principles of nature, certainly we should judge in the same manner of all honourable and all shameful things, referring them all to the law of nature.

But we are often too much disturbed by the dissensions of men and the variation of opinions. And because the same thing does not happen with reference to our senses, we look upon them as certain by nature. Those objects, indeed, which sometimes presents to us one appearance, sometimes another, and which do not always appear to the same people in the same way, we term fictions of the senses; but it is far otherwise. For neither parent, nor nurse, nor master, nor poet, nor drama, deceive our senses; nor do popular prejudices seduce them from the truth. But all kinds of snares are laid for the mind, either by those errors which I have just enumerated, which, taking possession of the young and uneducated, imbue them deeply, and bend them any way they please; or by that pleasure which is the imitator of goodness, being thoroughly and closely implicated with all our senses—the prolific mother of all evils. For she so corrupts us by her blandishments, that we no longer perceive some things which are essentially excellent, because they have none of this deliciousness and pruriency.

It follows that I may now sum up the whole of this argument by asserting, as is plain to every one from these positions which have been already laid down, that all right and all that is honourable is to be sought for its own sake. In truth, all virtuous men love justice and equity for what they are in themselves; nor is it like a good man to make a mistake, and love that which does not deserve their affection. Right, therefore, is desirable and deserving to be cultivated for its own sake; and if this be true of right, it must be true also of justice. What then shall we say of liberality? Is it exercised gratuitously, or does it covet some reward and recompense? If a man does good without expecting any recompense for his kindness, then it is gratuitous: if he does expect compensation, it is a mere matter of traffic. Nor is there any doubt that he who truly deserves the reputation of a generous and kind-hearted man, is thinking of his duty, not of his interest. In the same way the virtue of justice demands neither emolument nor salary, and therefore we desire it for its own sake. And the case of all the moral virtues is the same, and so is the opinion formed of them.

Besides this, if we weigh virtue by the mere utility and profit that attend it, and not by its own merit, the one virtue which results from such an estimate will be in fact a species of vice. For the more a man refers all his actions especially to his own advantage, the further he recedes from probity; so that they who measure virtue by profit, acknowledge no other virtue than this, which is a kind of vice. For who can be called benevolent, if no one ever acts kindly for the sake of another? And where are we to find a grateful person, if those who are disposed to be so can find no benefactor to whom they can show gratitude? What will become of sacred friendship, if we are not to love our friend for his own sake with all our heart and soul, as people say? if we are even to desert and discard him, as soon as we despair of deriving any further assistance or advantage from him. What can be imagined more inhuman than this conduct? But if friendship ought rather to be cultivated on its own account, so also for the same reason are society, equality, and justice, desirable for their own sakes. If this be not so, then there can be no such thing as justice at all; for the most unjust thing of all is to seek a reward for one's just conduct.

What then shall we say of temperance, sobriety, continence, modesty, bashfulness, and chastity? Is it the fear of infamy, or the dread of judgments and penalties, which prevent men from being intemperate and dissolute? Do men then live in innocence and moderation, only to be well spoken of, and to acquire a certain fair reputation? Modest men blush even to speak of indelicacy. And I am greatly ashamed of those philosophers, who assert that there are no vices to be avoided but those which the laws have branded with infamy. For what shall I say? Can we call those persons truly chaste, who abstain from adultery merely for the fear of public exposure, and that disgrace which is only one of its many evil consequences? For what can be either praised or blamed with reason, if you depart from that great law and rule of nature, which makes the difference between right and wrong? Shall corporal defects, if they are remarkable, shock our sensibilities, and shall those of the soul make no impression on us?—of the soul, I say, whose turpitude is so evidently proved by its vices. For what is there more hideous than avarice, more brutal than lust, more contemptible than cowardice, more base than stupidity and folly? Well, then, are we to call those persons unhappy, who are conspicuous for one or more of these, on account of some injuries, or disgraces, or sufferings to which they are exposed, or on account of the moral baseness of their sins? And we may apply the same test in the opposite way to those who are distinguished for their virtue.

Lastly, if virtue be sought for on account of some other things, it necessarily follows that there is something better than virtue. Is it money, then? is it fame, or beauty, or health? all of which appear of little value to us when we possess them; nor can it be by any possibility certainly known how long they will last. Or is it (what it is shameful even to utter) that basest of all, pleasure? Surely not; for it is in the contempt and disdain of pleasure that virtue is most conspicuous.

Do not you see what a long series of facts and arguments I have brought forward, and how perfect is the connection between one and another? I should have proceeded further still, if I had not kept myself in check. . . .

Marcus This, then, as it appears to me, has been the decision of the wisest philosophers,—that law was neither a thing contrived by the genius of man, nor established by any decree of the people, but a certain eternal principle, which governs the entire universe, wisely commanding what is right and prohibiting what is wrong. Therefore they called that aboriginal and supreme law the mind of God, enjoining or forbidding each separate thing in accordance with reason. On which account it is, that this law, which the Gods have bestowed on the human race, is so justly applauded. For it is the reason and mind of a wise Being equally able to urge us to good and to deter us from evil.

Quintus You have, on more than one occasion, already touched on this topic. But before you come to treat of the laws of nations, I wish you would endeavour to explain the force and power of this divine and celestial law, lest the torrent of custom should overwhelm our understanding, and betray us into the vulgar method of expression.

Marcus From our childhood we have learned, my Quintus, to call such phrases as this, "that a man appeals to justice, and goes to law," and many similar expressions, law; but, nevertheless, we should understand that these, and other similar commandments and prohibitions, have sufficient power to lead us on to virtuous actions and to call us away from vicious ones. Which power is not only far more ancient than any existence of states and peoples, but is coeval with God himself, who beholds and governs both heaven and earth. For it is impossible that the divine mind can exist in a state devoid of reason; and divine reason must necessarily be possessed of a power to determine what is virtuous and what is vicious. Nor, because it was nowhere written, that one man should maintain the pass of a bridge against the enemy's whole army, and that he should order the bridge behind him to be cut down, are we therefore to imagine that the valiant Cocles did not perform this great exploit agreeably to the laws of nature and the dictates of true bravery. Again, though in the reign of Tarquin there was no written law concerning adultery, it does not therefore follow that Sextus Tarquinius did not offend against the eternal law when he committed a rape on Lucretia, daughter of Tricipitinus. For, even then he had the light of reason deduced from the nature of things, that incites to good actions and dissuades from evil ones; and which does not begin for the first time to be a law when it is drawn up in writing, but from the first moment that it exists. And this existence of moral obligation is co-eternal with that of the divine mind. Therefore, the true and supreme law, whose commands and prohibitions are equally authoritative, is the right reason of the Sovereign Jupiter.

Quintus I grant you, my brother, that whatever is just is also at all times the true law; nor can this true law either be originated or abrogated by the written forms in which decrees are drawn up.

Marcus Therefore, as that Divine Mind, or reason, is the supreme law, so it exists in the mind of the sage, so far as it can be perfected in man. But with respect to civil laws, which are drawn up in various forms, and framed to meet the occasional requirements of the people, the name of law belongs to them not so much by right as by the favour of the people. For men prove by some such arguments as the following, that every law which deserves the name of a law, ought to be morally good and laudable. It is clear, say they, that laws were originally made for the security of the people, for the preservation of states, for the peace and happiness of society; and that they who first framed enactments of that kind, persuaded the people that they would write and publish such laws only as should conduce to the general morality and happiness, if they would receive and obey them. And then such regulations, being thus settled and sanctioned, they justly entitled *Laws.* From which we may reasonably conclude, that those who made unjustifiable and pernicious enactments for the people, acted in a manner contrary to their own promises and professions, and established anything rather than *laws,* properly so called, since it is evident that the very signification of the word *law,* comprehends the whole essence and energy of justice and equity. . . .

Marcus I shall, therefore, imitate that divine man, who has inspired me with such admiration that I eulogise him perhaps oftener than is necessary.

Atticus You mean Plato.

Marcus The very man, my Atticus.

Atticus Indeed you do not exaggerate your compliments, nor bestow them too frequently, for even my Epicurean friends, who do not like any one to be praised but their own master, still allow me to love Plato as much as I like.

Marcus They do well to grant you this indulgence, for what can be so suitable to the elegance of your taste as the writings of Plato?—who in his life and manners appears to me to have succeeded in that most difficult combination of gravity and politeness.

Atticus I am glad I interrupted you, since you have availed yourself of an opportunity of giving this splendid testimonial of your judgment respecting him; but pursue the subject as you began.

Marcus Let us begin, then, with praising the law itself, with those commendations which are both deserved and appropriate to the subject.

Atticus That is but fair, since you did the same in the case of our ecclesiastical jurisprudence.

Marcus You see, then, that this is the duty of magistrates, to superintend and prescribe all things which are just and useful, and in accordance with the law. For as the law is set over the magistrate, even so are the magistrates set over the people. And therefore, it may be truly said, "that the magistrate is a speaking law, and the law a silent magistrate."

Moreover, nothing is so conformable to justice and to the condition of nature (and when I use that expression, I wish it to be understood that I mean the law, and nothing else,) as sovereign power; without which, neither house, nor commonwealth, nor nation, nor mankind itself, nor the entire nature of things, nor the universe itself could exist. For this universe is obedient to God, and land and sea are submissive to the universe; and human life depends on the just administration of the laws of order.

But to come to considerations nearer home, and more familiar to us, all ancient nations have been at one time or other under the dominion of kings. Which kind of authority was at first conferred on the wisest and justest men. (And this rule mainly prevailed in our own commonwealth, as long as the regal power lasted.) Afterwards the authority of kings was handed down in succession to their descendants, and this practice remains to this day in those which are governed by kings. And even those to whom the regal domination was distasteful, did not desire to be obedient to no one, but only not to be always under the authority of the same person.

For ourselves, then, as we are proposing laws for a free people, and as we have already set forth in six books all our own opinions about the best kind of commonwealth, we shall on the present occasion endeavour to accommodate our laws to that constitutional government of which we have expressed our approval.

It is clear, then, that magistrates are absolutely necessary; since, without their prudence and diligence, a state cannot exist; and since it is by their regulations that the whole commonwealth is kept within the bounds of moderation. But it is not enough to prescribe them a rule of domination, unless we likewise prescribe the citizens a rule of obedience. For he who commands well, must at some time or other have obeyed; and he who obeys with modesty appears worthy of some day or other being allowed to command. It is desirable, therefore, that he who obeys should expect that some day he will come to command, and that he who commands should bear in mind that ere long he may be called to the duty of submission.

We would not, however, limit ourselves to requiring from the citizens submission and obedience towards their magistrates; we would also enjoin them by all means to honour and love their rulers, as Charondas prescribes in his code. Our Plato likewise declares that they are of the race of the Titans, who, as they rebelled against the heavenly deities, do in like manner oppose their magistrates. These points being granted, we will, if you please, advance to the examination of the laws themselves.

Atticus I certainly do please, and the arrangement seems advisable.

Marcus "Let all authorities be just, and let them be honestly obeyed by the people with modesty and without opposition. Let the magistrate restrain the disobedient and mischievous citizens, by fine, imprisonment, and corporal chastisement; unless some equal or greater power, or the people forbid it; for there should be an appeal thereto. If the magistrate shall have decided, and inflicted a penalty, let there be a public appeal to the people respecting the penalty and fine imposed.

"With respect to the army, and the general that commands it by martial law, there should be no appeal from his authority. And whatever he who conducts the war commands, shall be absolute law, and ratified as such.

"As to the minor magistrates, let there be such a distribution of their legal duties, that each may more effectively superintend his own department of justice. In the army let those who are appointed command, and let them have tribunes. In the city, let men be appointed as superintendents of the public treasury. Let some devote their attention to the prison disciplines, and capital punishments. Let others supervise the public coinage of gold, and silver, and copper. Let others judge of suits and arbitrations; and let others carry the orders of the senate into execution.

"Let there likewise be aediles, curators of the city, the provisions, and the public games, and let these offices be the first steps to higher promotions of honour.

"Let the censors take a census of the people, according to age, offspring, family, and property. Let them have the inspection of the temples, the streets, the aqueducts, the rates, and the customs. Let them distribute the citizens, according to their tribes: after that let them divide them with reference to their fortunes, ages, and ranks. Let them keep a register of the families of those of the equestrian and plebeian orders. Let them impose a tax on celibates. Let them guard the morals of the people. Let them permit no scandal in the senate. Let the number of such censors be two. Let their magistracy continue five years. Let the other magistrates be annual, but their offices themselves should be perpetual.

"Let the judge of the law who shall decide private actions, or send them for decision to the praetor—let him be the proper guardian of civil jurisprudence. Let him have as many colleagues, of equal power, as the senate think necessary, and the people allows him.

"Let two magistrates be invested with sovereign authority; from their presiding, judging, and counselling, let them be called praetors, judges, or consuls. Let them have supreme authority over the army, and let them be subject to none; for the safety of the people is the supreme law; and no one should succeed to this magistracy till it has been held ten years—regulating the duration by an annual law.

"When a considerable war is undertaken, or discord is likely to ensue among the citizens, let a single supreme magistrate be appointed, who shall unite in his own person the authority of both consuls, if the senate so decrees, for six months only. And when such a magistrate has been proclaimed under favourable auspices, let him be the master of the people. Let him have for a colleague, with equal powers with himself, a knight whomsoever he may choose to appoint, as a judge of the law. And when such a dictator or master of the people is created the other magistracies shall be suppressed.

"Let the auspices be observed by the senate, and let them authorize persons of their own body to elect the consuls in the comitia, according to the established ceremonials.

"Let the commanders, generals, and lieutenants, leave the city whenever the senate decrees or the people orders that they shall do so. Let them properly prosecute all just wars. Let them spare our allies, and restrain themselves and their subordinates. Let them increase the glory of our country. Let them return home with honour. Let no one be made an ambassador with a view to his own interest.

"Let the ten officers whom the people elect to protect them against oppression be their tribunes; and let all their prohibitions and adjudications be established, and their persons considered inviolable, so that tribunes may never be wanting to the people.

"Let all magistrates possess their auspices and jurisdictions, and let the senate be composed of these legitimate authorities. Let its ordinances be absolute, and let its enactments be written and ratified, unless an equal or greater authority disannul them. Let the order of the senators be free from reproach and scandal, and let them be an example of virtue to all.

"In the creation of magistrates, the judgment of the accused, and the reception or rejection of laws, when suffrages are employed, let the suffrages be at once notorious to the nobles, and free to the people.

"If any question occur out of the established jurisdiction of the magistrates, let another magistrate be appointed by the people, whose jurisdiction shall expressly extend thereto. Let the consul, the praetor, the censor, the master of the people and of the knights, and he to whom the senate has committed the election of consuls, have full liberty to treat both with the senate and the people, and endeavour to reconcile the interests of all parties. Let the tribunes of the people likewise have free access to the senate, and advocate the interests of the people in all their deliberations. Let a just moderation predominate in the opinions and declarations of those who would thus act as mediators between the senate and the people. Let a senator who does not attend the senate, either show cause of his non-attendance, or submit to an appropriate fine. Let a senator speak in his turn, with all moderation, and let him be thoroughly acquainted with the interests of the people.

"By all means avoid violence among the people. Let the greatest authority have the greatest weight in decisions. If any one shall disturb the public harmony, and foment party quarrels, let him be punished as a criminal. To act the intercessor in cases of offence should be considered the part of a good citizen. Let those who act observe the auspices; obey the public augur; and carry into effect all proclamations, taking care that they are exhibited in the treasury, and generally known. Let the public consultations be concentrated in one point at a time, let them instruct the people in the nature of the question, and let all the magistrates and the people be permitted to advise on the subject.

"Let them permit no monopolies, or privileges. With respect to the capital punishment of any citizen, let it not take place, unless by the adjudication of the high courts of justice, and the ministry of those whom the censors have placed over the popular orders. Let no bribes be given or received, either in soliciting, discharging, or resigning an official situation.

"If any one shall infringe any of these laws, let him be liable to a penalty. Let these regulations be committed to the charge of the censors. Let public officers, on their retiring from their posts, give these censors an account of their conduct, but let them not by this means escape from legal prosecution if they have been guilty of corruption."

I have here recited the whole law; now, consider the question, and give your votes.

Quintus With what conciseness, my brother, have you brought before our eyes the duties and offices of all magistrates! But your system of laws is almost that of our own commonwealth, although a little that is new has also been added by you.

Marcus Your observation is very just, my Quintus, for this is the very system of a commonwealth which Scipio eulogises in my treatise, and which he mainly approves —and which cannot be kept in operation but by a successive order of magistrates, such as we have described. For you may take it for granted that it is the establishment of magistrates that gives its form to a commonwealth, and it is exactly by this distribution and subordination that we must determine the nature of the constitution. Which establishment being very wisely and discreetly settled by our ancestors, there is nothing, or at all events very little alteration that I think necessary in the laws. . . .

Roman Law— Ideal and Reality

Cicero's Third Philippic *is best viewed against the background of prolonged social and political crisis of the Roman Republic, a crisis sketched by the Greek historian Appian of Alexandria* (A.D. ca. *95–165*) *in introducing his account of the Roman civil wars.*

What this crisis meant to a contemporary—in this case a member of the senatorial ruling class shouldered aside by military strong men—may be seen in the speech that Cicero (for biographical details, see pages 239–240) delivered to the Roman Senate on December 20, 44 B.C., *a speech known to us as the* Third Philippic against Marcus Antonius. *Nine months earlier, in March of 44* B.C., *a band of conservative republican conspirators headed by Marcus Junius Brutus had assassinated the dictator Julius Caesar. Caesar, seemingly on the point of making himself king, had rekindled the traditional Roman hostility to monarchy. Almost immediately after the elimination of Caesar, the republican conspirators were challenged by Marcus Antonius (Shakespeare's "Mark Antony"), who had been Caesar's co-consul and now set himself up as his heir. Not long afterwards Octavianus, Caesar's nephew and adoptive son, took his uncle's magically popular name, Gaius Caesar, and joined the race for the succession. A three-cornered civil war was on.*

Though sympathetic to the republicanism of Brutus and the other assassins, Cicero had not been involved in the conspiracy. On the other hand, by the time of this speech, he had definitely and irrevocably broken with Marcus Antonius. Cicero at this time hoped to promote an alliance of young Caesar Octavianus and Decimus Brutus, a kinsman of Marcus, against Marcus Antonius. Unfortunately for Cicero, another combination emerged instead: Caesar Octavianus and Marcus Antonius joined forces temporarily to eliminate both of the Brutuses and the other republican conspirators. In the proscriptions that followed, Cicero himself was murdered on Marcus Antonius' orders about one year after delivering the Third Philippic.

HISTORY OF ROME

Appian

The plebeians and Senate of Rome [in the olden time] were often at strife with each other concerning the enactment of laws, the cancelling of debts, the division of lands, or the election of magistrates. Internal discord did not bring them to blows, however; these were dissensions merely and contests within the law, which they composed by making mutual concessions, and with much respect for each other. Once when the plebeians were going to a war they fell into such a controversy, but they did not use the weapons in their hands, but withdrew to the hill, which from this time on was called the Sacred Mount. Even then no violence was done, but they created a magistrate for their protection and called him the tribune of the plebs, to serve especially as a check upon the consuls, who were chosen by the Senate, so that the political power should not be exclusively in their hands. Whence arose still greater bitterness, and the magistrates were arrayed in stronger animosity to each other after this event, and the Senate and plebeians took sides with them, each believing that it would prevail over the other by augmenting the power of its own magistrates. In the midst of contests of this kind Marcius Coriolanus, having been banished contrary to justice, took refuge with the Volsci and levied war against his country.

This is the only case of armed strife that can be found in the ancient seditions, and this was caused by an exile. The sword was never carried into the assembly, and there was no civil butchery until Tiberius Gracchus, while serving as tribune and bringing forward new laws, was the first to fall a victim to internal commotion; and

***The Roman History of Appian of Alexandria*, trans. H. White (London: The Macmillan Company, 1899), Vol. II, 1–5.**

many others besides, who were assembled with him at the Capitol, were slain around the temple. Sedition did not end with this abominable deed. Repeatedly the parties came into open conflict, often carrying daggers; and occasionally in the temples, or the assemblies, or the forum, some one serving as tribune, or praetor, or consul, or a candidate for those offices, or some person otherwise distinguished, would be slain. Unseemly violence prevailed almost constantly, together with shameful contempt for law and justice. As the evil gained in magnitude open insurrections against the government and large warlike expeditions against the country were undertaken by exiles, or criminals, or persons contending against each other for some office or military command. There were chiefs of factions in different places aspiring to supreme power, some of them refusing to disband the troops intrusted to them by the people, others levying forces against each other on their own account, without public authority. Whichever of them first got possession of the city, the others made war nominally against their adversaries, but actually against their country. They asailed it like a foreign enemy. Ruthless and indiscriminate massacres of citizens were perpetrated. Men were proscribed, others banished, property was confiscated, and some were even subjected to excruciating tortures.

No unseemly deed was wanting until, about fifty years after the death of Gracchus, Cornelius Sulla, one of these chiefs of factions, doctoring one evil with another, made himself the absolute master of the state for an indefinite period. Such officials were formerly called dictators—an office created in the most perilous emergencies for six months only, and long since fallen into disuse. Sulla, although nominally elected, became dictator for life by force and compulsion. Nevertheless he became satiated with power and was the first man, so far as I know, holding supreme power, who had the courage to lay it down voluntarily and to declare that he would render an account of his stewardship to any who were dissatisfied with it. And so, for a considerable period, he walked to the forum as a private citizen in the sight of all and returned home unmolested, so great was the awe of his government still remaining in the minds of the onlookers, or their amazement at his laying it down. Perhaps they were ashamed to call for an accounting, or entertained other good feeling toward him, or a belief that his despotism had been beneficial to the state. Thus there was a cessation of factions for a short time while Sulla lived, and a compensation for the evils which Sulla had wrought.

After his death the troubles broke out afresh and continued until Gaius Caesar, who had held the command in Gaul by election for some years, was ordered by the Senate to lay down his command. He charged that it was not the wish of the Senate, but of Pompey, his enemy, who had command of an army in Italy, and was scheming to depose him. So he sent a proposal that both should retain their armies, so that neither need fear the other's enmity, or that Pompey should dismiss his forces also and live as a private citizen under the laws in like manner with himself. Both requests being refused, he marched from Gaul against Pompey in the Roman territory, entered it, put him to flight, pursued him into Thessaly, won a brilliant victory over him in a great battle, and followed him to Egypt. After Pompey had been slain by the Egyptians Caesar set to work on the affairs of Egypt and remained there until he had settled the dynasty of that country. Then he returned to Rome. Having overpowered by war his principal rival, who had been surnamed the Great on account of his brilliant military exploits, he now ruled without disguise, nobody daring any longer to dispute him about anything, and was chosen, next after Sulla, dictator for life. Again all civil dissensions ceased until Brutus and Cassius, envious of his great power and desiring to restore the government of their fathers, slew in the Senate this most popular man, who was also the one most experienced in the art of government. The people mourned for him greatly. They scoured the city in pursuit of his murderers. They buried him in the middle of the forum and built a temple on the place of his funeral pile, and offered sacrifice to him as a god.

And now civil discord broke out again worse than ever and increased enormously. Massacres, banishments, and proscriptions of both senators and the so-called knights took place straightway, including great numbers of both classes, the chief of factions surrendering their enemies to each other, and for this purpose not sparing even their friends and brothers; so much does animosity toward rivals overpower the love of kindred. So in the course of events the Roman empire was partitioned, as though it had been their private property, by these three men: Antony, Lepidus, and the one who was first called Octavius, but afterward Caesar from his relationship to the other Caesar and adoption in his will. Shortly after this division they fell to quarrelling among themselves, as was natural, and Octavius, who was the superior in understanding and skill, first deprived Lepidus of Africa, which had fallen to his lot, and afterward, as the result of the battle of Actium, took from Antony all the provinces lying between Syria and the Adriatic gulf. Thereupon, while all the world was filled with astonishment at these wonderful displays of power, he sailed to Egypt and took that country, which was the oldest and at that time the strongest possession of the successors of Alexander, and the only one wanting to complete the Roman empire as it now stands. In consequence of these exploits he was at once elevated to the rank of a deity while still living, and was the first to be thus distinguished by the Romans, and was called by them Augustus. He assumed to himself an authority like Caesar's over the country and the subject nations, and even greater than Caesar's, not needing any form of election, or authorization, or even the pretence of it. His government being strengthened by time and mastery, and himself successful in all things and revered by all, he left a lineage and succession that held the supreme power in like manner after him.

Thus, out of multifarious civil commotions, the Roman state passed into solidarity and monarchy. To show how these things came about I have written and compiled this narrative, which is well worth the study of those who wish to know the measureless ambition of men, their dreadful lust of power, their unwearying perseverance, and the countless forms of evil. . . .

THIRD PHILIPPIC

Cicero

We have been assembled at length, O conscript fathers,* altogether later than the necessities of the republic required; but still we are assembled; a measure which I, indeed, have been every day demanding; inasmuch as I saw that a nefarious war against our altars and our hearths, against our lives and our fortunes, was, I will not say being prepared, but being actually waged by a profligate and desperate man. People are waiting for the first of January. But Antonius is not waiting for that day, who is now attempting with an army to invade the province of Decimus Brutus, a most illustrious and excellent man. And when he has procured reinforcements and the equipments there, he threatens that he will come to this city. What is the use then of waiting, or of even a delay for the very shortest time? For although the first of January is at hand, still a short time is a long one for people who are not prepared. For a day, or I should rather say an hour, often brings great disasters, if no precautions are taken. And it is not usual to wait for a fixed day for holding a council, as it is for celebrating a festival. But if the first of January had fallen on the day when Antonius first fled from the city, or if people had not waited for it, we should by this time have no war at all. For we should easily have crushed the audacity of that frantic man by the authority of the senate and the unanimity of the Roman people. And now, indeed, I feel confident that the consuls elect will do so, as soon as they enter on their magistracy. For they are men of the highest courage, of the most consummate wisdom, and they will act in perfect harmony with each other. But my exhortations to rapid and instant action are prompted by a desire not merely for victory, but for speedy victory.

For how long are we to trust to the prudence of an individual to repel so important, so cruel, and so nefarious a war? Why is not the public authority thrown into the scale as quickly as possible?

Caius Caesar, a young man, or, I should rather say, almost a boy, endued with an incredible and godlike degree of wisdom and valour, at the time when the frenzy of Antonius was at its height, and when his cruel and mischievous return from Brundusium was an object of apprehension to all, while we neither desired him to do so, nor thought of such a measure, nor ventured even to wish it, (because it did not seem practicable,) collected a most trustworthy army from the invincible body of veteran soldiers, and has spent his own patrimony in doing so. Although I have not used the expression which I ought,—for he has not spent it,—he has invested it in the safety of the republic.

And although it is not possible to requite him with all the thanks to which he is entitled, still we ought to feel all the gratitude towards him which our minds are capable of conceiving. For who is so ignorant of public affairs, so entirely indifferent

***The Orations of Marcus Tullius Cicero*, trans. C. D. Yonge (London: G. Bell & Sons, Ltd., 1872), Vol. IV, 70–75, 77–85.**

* [The formal title by which Roman Senators were addressed. (*Ed.*)]

to all thoughts of the republic, as not to see that, if Marcus Antonius could have come with those forces which he made sure that he should have, from Brundusium to Rome, as he threatened, there would have been no description of cruelty which he would not have practised? A man who in the house of his entertainer at Brundusium ordered so many most gallant men and virtuous citizens to be murdered, and whose wife's face was notoriously besprinkled with the blood of men dying at his and her feet. Who is there of us, or what good man is there at all, whom a man stained with this barbarity would ever have spared; especially as he was coming hither much more angry with all virtuous men than he had been with those whom he had massacred there? And from this calamity Caesar has delivered the republic by his own individual prudence, (and, indeed, there were no other means by which it could have been done). And if he had not been born in this republic we should, owing to the wickedness of Antonius, now have no republic at all.

For this is what I believe, this is my deliberate opinion, that if that one young man had not checked the violence and inhuman projects of that frantic man, the republic would have been utterly destroyed. And to him we must, O conscript fathers, (for this is the first time, met in such a condition, that, owing to his good service, we are at liberty to say freely what we think and feel,) we must, I say, this day give authority, so that he may be able to defend the republic, not because that defence has been voluntarily undertaken by him but also because it has been entrusted to him by us.

Nor (since now after a long interval we are allowed to speak concerning the republic) is it possible for us to be silent about the Martial legion. For what single man has ever been braver, what single man has ever been more devoted to the republic than the whole of the Martial legion? which, as soon as it had decided that Marcus Antonius was an enemy of the Roman people, refused to be a companion of his insanity; deserted him though consul; which, in truth, it would not have done if it had considered him as consul, who, as it saw, was aiming at nothing and preparing nothing but the slaughter of the citizens, and the destruction of the state. And that legion has encamped at Alba. What city could it have selected either more suitable for enabling it to act, or more faithful, or full of more gallant men, or of citizens more devoted to the republic?

The fourth legion, imitating the virtue of this legion, under the leadership of Lucius Egnatuleius, the quaestor, a most virtuous and intrepid citizen, has also acknowledged the authority and joined the army of Caius Caesar.

We, therefore, O conscript fathers, must take care that those things which this most illustrious young man, this most excellent of all men has of his own accord done, and still is doing, be sanctioned by our authority; and the admirable unanimity of the veterans, those most brave men, and of the Martial and of the fourth legion, in their zeal for the reestablishment of the republic, be encouraged by our praise and commendation. And let us pledge ourselves this day that their advantage, and honours, and rewards shall be cared for by us as soon as the consuls elect have entered on their magistracy.

And the things which I have said about Caesar and about his army, are, indeed, already well known to you. For by the admirable valour of Caesar, and by the firmness of the veteran soldiers, and by the admirable discernment of those legions which have followed our authority, and the liberty of the Roman people, and the valour of Caesar, Antonius has been repelled from his attempts upon our lives. But these things, as I have said, happened before; but this recent edict of Decimus Brutus, which has just been issued, can certainly not be passed over in silence. For he promises to preserve the province of Gaul in obedience to the senate and people of Rome. O citizen, born for the republic; mindful of the name he bears; imitator of his ancestors! Nor, indeed, was the acquisition of liberty so much an object of desire to our ancestors when Tarquinius was expelled, as, now that Antonius is driven away, the preservation of it is to us. Those men had learnt to obey kings ever since the foundation of the city, but we from the time when the kings were driven out have forgotten how to be slaves. And that Tarquinius, whom our ancestors expelled, was not either considered or called cruel or impious, but only The Proud. That vice which we have often borne in private individuals, our ancestors could not endure even in a king.

Lucius Brutus could not endure a proud king. Shall Decimus Brutus submit to the kingly power of a man who is wicked and impious? What atrocity did Tarquinius ever commit equal to the innumerable acts of the sort which Antonius has done and is still doing? Again, the kings were used to consult the senate; nor, as is the case when Antonius holds a senate, were armed barbarians ever introduced into the council of the king. The kings paid due regard to the auspices, which this man, though consul and augur, has neglected, not only by passing laws in opposition to the auspices, but also by making his colleague (whom he himself had appointed irregularly, and had falsified the auspices in order to do so) join in passing them. Again, what king was ever so preposterously impudent as to have all the profits, and kindnesses, and privileges of his kingdom on sale? But what immunity is there, what rights of citizenship, what rewards that this man has not sold to individuals, and to cities, and to entire provinces? We have never heard of anything base or sordid being imputed to Tarquinius. But at the house of this man gold was constantly being weighed out in the spinning room, and money was being paid, and in one single house every soul who had any interest in the business was selling the whole empire of the Roman people. We have never heard of any executions of Roman citizens by the orders of Tarquinius; but this man both at Suessa murdered the man whom he had thrown into prison, and at Brundusium massacred about three hundred most gallant men and most virtuous citizens. Lastly, Tarquinius was conducting a war in defence of the Roman people at the very time when he was expelled. Antonius was leading an army against the Roman people at the time when, being abandoned by the legions, he cowered at the name of Caesar and at his army, and neglecting the regular sacrifices, he offered up before daylight vows which he could never mean to perform; and at this very moment he is endeavouring to invade a province of the Roman people. The Roman people, therefore, has already received and is still looking for greater services at the hand of Decimus Brutus than our ancestors received from Lucius Brutus, the founder of this race and name which we ought to be so anxious to preserve.

But, while all slavery is miserable, to be slave to a man who is profligate, unchaste, effeminate, never, not even while in fear, sober, is surely intolerable. He, then, who keeps this man out of Gaul, especially by his own private authority, judges, and judges most truly, that he is not consul at all. We must take care, therefore, O conscript fathers, to sanction the private decision of Decimus Brutus by public authority. Nor, indeed, ought you to have thought Marcus Antonius consul at any time since the Lupercalia.* For on the day when he, in the sight of the Roman people, harangued the mob, naked, perfumed, and drunk, and laboured moreover to put a crown on the head of his colleague, on that day he abdicated not only the consulship, but also his own freedom. At all events he himself must at once have become a slave, if Caesar had been willing to accept from him that ensign of royalty. Can I then think him a consul, can I think him a Roman citizen, can I think him a freeman, can I even think him a man, who on that shameful and wicked day showed what he was willing to endure while Caesar lived, and what he was anxious to obtain himself after he was dead?

Nor it is possible to pass over in silence the virtue and the firmness and the dignity of the province of Gaul. For that is the flower of Italy; that is the bulwark of the empire of the Roman people; that is the chief ornament of our dignity. But so perfect is the unanimity of the municipal towns and colonies of the province of Gaul, that all men in that district appear to have united together to defend the authority of this order, and the majesty of the Roman people. Wherefore, O tribunes of the people, although you have not actually brought any other business before us beyond the question of protection, in order that the consuls may be able to hold the senate with safety on the first of January, still you appear to me to have acted with great wisdom and great prudence in giving an opportunity of debating the general circumstances of the republic. For when you decided that the senate could not be held with safety without some protection or other, you at the same time asserted by that decision that the wickedness and audacity of Antonius was still continuing its practices within our walls.

Wherefore, I will embrace every consideration in my opinion which I am now going to deliver, a course to which you, I feel sure, have no objection; in order that authority may be conferred by us on admirable generals, and that hope of reward may be held out by us to gallant soldiers, and that a formal decision may be come to, not by words only, but also by actions, that Antonius is not only not a consul, but is even an enemy. For if he be consul, then the legions which have deserted the consul deserve beating to death. Caesar is wicked, Brutus is impious, since they of their own heads have levied an army against the consul. But if new honours are to be sought out for the soldiers on account of their divine and immortal merits, and if it is quite impossible to show gratitude enough to the generals, who is there who must not think that man a public enemy, whose conduct is such that those who are in arms against him are considered the saviours of the republic? . . .

But what is it that he has done himself? When he had published all these edicts, he issued another, that the senate was to meet in a full house on the twenty-fourth of November. On that day he himself was not present. But what were the terms of his edict? These, I believe, are the exact words of the end of it: "If any one fails to attend, all men will be at liberty to think him the adviser of my destruction and of

* [A Roman fertility festival that took place in February. (*Ed.*)]

most ruinous counsels." What are ruinous counsels? those which relate to the recovery of the liberty of the Roman people? Of those counsels I confess that I have been and still am an adviser and prompter to Caesar. Although he did not stand in need of any one's advice; but still I spurred on the willing horse, as it is said. For what good man would not have advised putting you to death, when on your death depended the safety and life of every good man, and the liberty and dignity of the Roman people?

But when he had summoned us all by so severe an edict, why did he not attend himself? Do you suppose that he was detained by any melancholy or important occasion? He was detained drinking and feasting. If, indeed, it deserves to be called a feast, and not rather gluttony. He neglected to attend on the day mentioned in his edict; and he adjourned the meeting to the twenty-eighth. He then summoned us to attend in the Capitol; and at that temple he did arrive himself, coming up through some mine left by the Gauls. Men came, having been summoned, some of them indeed men of high distinction, but forgetful of what was due to their dignity. For the day was such, the report of the object of the meeting such, such too the man who had convened the senate, that it was discreditable for a senate to feel no fear for the result. And yet to those men who had assembled he did not dare to say a single word about Caesar, though he had made up his mind to submit a motion respecting him to the senate. There was a man of consular rank who had brought a resolution ready drawn up. Is it not now admitting that he is himself an enemy, when he does not dare to make a motion respecting a man who is leading an army against him while he is consul? For it is perfectly plain that one of the two must be an enemy; nor is it possible to come to a different decision respecting adverse generals. If then Caius Caesar be an enemy, why does the consul submit no motion to the senate? If he does not deserve to be branded by the senate, then what can the consul say, who, by his silence respecting him, has confessed that he himself is an enemy? In his edicts he styles him Spartacus,* while in the senate he does not venture to call him even a bad citizen. . . .

I ask now, why all on a sudden he became so gentle in the senate, after having been so fierce in his edicts? For what was the object of threatening Lucius Cassius, a most fearless tribune of the people, and a most virtuous and loyal citizen, with death if he came to the senate? of expelling Decimus Carfulenus, a man thoroughly attached to the republic, from the senate by violence and threats of death? of interdicting Titus Canutius, by whom he had been repeatedly and deservedly harassed by most legitimate attacks not only from the temple itself but from all approach to it? What was the resolution of the senate which he was afraid that they would stop by the interposition of their veto? That, I suppose, respecting the supplication in honour of Marcus Lepidus, a most illustrious man! Certainly there was a great danger of our hindering an ordinary compliment to a man on whom we were every day thinking of conferring some extraordinary honour. However, that he might not appear to have had no reason at all for ordering the senate to meet, he was on the point of bringing forward some motion about the republic, when the news about the fourth legion came. . . .

How miserable was his flight! how shameful! how infamous! Splendid, too, were

* [The leader of a great slave insurrection about twenty years before the date of this speech. (*Ed.*)]

the decrees of the senate passed on the evening of that very day; very religiously solemn was the allotment of the provinces; and heavenly indeed was the opportunity, when every one got exactly what he thought most desirable. You are acting admirably, therefore, O tribunes of the people, in bringing forward a motion about the protection of the senate and consuls, and most deservedly are we all bound to feel and to prove to you the greatest gratitude for your conduct. . . .

O Caius Caesar, (I am speaking of the young man,) what safety have you brought to the republic! How unforeseen has it been! how sudden! for if he did these things when flying, what would he have done when he was pursuing? In truth, he had said in a harangue that he would be the guardian of the city; and that he would keep his army at the gates of the city till the first of May. What a fine guardian (as the proverb goes) is the wolf of the sheep! Would Antonius have been a guardian of the city, or its plunderer and destroyer? And he said too that he would come into the city and go out as he pleased. What more need I say? Did he not say, in the hearing of all the people, while sitting in front of the temple of Castor, that no one should remain alive but the conqueror?

On this day, O conscript fathers, for the first time after a long interval do we plant our foot and take possession of liberty. Liberty, of which, as long as I could be, I was not only the defender, but even the saviour. But when I could not be so, I rested; and I bore the misfortunes and misery of that period without abjectness, and not without some dignity. But as for this most foul monster, who could endure him, or how could any one endure him? What is there in Antonius except lust, and cruelty, and wantonness, and audacity? Of these materials he is wholly made up. There is in him nothing ingenuous, nothing moderate, nothing modest, nothing virtuous. Wherefore, since the matter has come to such a crisis that the question is whether he is to make atonement to the republic for his crimes, or we are to become slaves, let us at last, I beseech you, by the immortal gods, O conscript fathers, adopt our fathers' courage, and our fathers' virtue, so as either to recover the liberty belonging to the Roman name and race, or else to prefer death to slavery. We have borne and endured many things which ought not to be endured in a free city: some of us out of a hope of recovering our freedom, some from too great a fondness for life. But if we have submitted to these things, which necessity and a sort of force which may seem almost to have been put on us by destiny, have compelled us to endure; though, in point of fact, we have not endured them; are we also to bear with the most shameful and inhuman tyranny of this profligate robber?

What will he do in his passion, if ever he has the power, who, when he is not able to show his anger against any one, has been the enemy of all good men? What will he not dare to do when victorious, who, without having gained any victory, has committed such crimes as these since the death of Caesar? has emptied his well-filled house? has pillaged his gardens? has transferred to his own mansion all their ornaments? has sought to make his death a pretext for slaughter and conflagration? who, while he has carried two or three resolutions of the senate which have been advantageous to the republic, has made everything else subservient to his own acquisition of gain and plunder? who has put up exemptions and annuities to sale? who has released cities from obligations? who has removed whole provinces from subjection to the Roman empire? who has restored exiles? who has passed forged laws in the name of Caesar, and has continued to have forged decrees engraved on brass and fixed up in the Capitol, and has set up in his own house a domestic market for all things of that sort? who has imposed laws on the Roman people? and who, with armed troops and guards, has excluded both the people and the magistrates from the forum? who has filled the senate with armed men? and has introduced armed men into the temple of Concord when he was holding a senate there? who ran down to Brundusium to meet the legions, and then murdered all the centurions in them who were well affected to the republic? who endeavoured to come to Rome with his army to accomplish our massacre and the utter destruction of the city? . . .

He is leading his mutilated army into Gaul; with one legion, and that too wavering in its fidelity to him, he is waiting for his brother Lucius, as he cannot find any one more nearly like himself than him. . . .

Will you open your gates to these most infamous brothers? will you ever admit them into the city? will you not rather, now that the opportunity is offered to you, now that you have generals ready, and the minds of the soldiers eager for the service, and all the Roman people unanimous, and all Italy excited with the desire to recover its liberty,—will you not, I say, avail yourself of the kindness of the immortal gods? You will never have an opportunity if you neglect this one. He will be hemmed in in the rear, in the front, and in flank, if he once enters Gaul. Nor must he be attacked by arms alone, but by our decrees also. Mighty is the authority, mighty is the name of the senate when all its members are inspired by one and the same resolution. Do you not see how the forum is crowded? how the Roman people is on tiptoe with the hope of recovering its liberty? which now, beholding us, after a long interval, meeting here in numbers, hopes too that we are also met in freedom. . . .

Now then that this opportunity is afforded to you, O conscript fathers, I entreat you in the name of the immortal gods, seize upon it; and recollect at last that you are the chief men of the most honourable council on the whole face of the earth. Give a token to the Roman people that your wisdom shall not fail the republic, since that too professes that its valour shall never desert it either. There is no need for my warning you: there is no one so foolish as not to perceive that if we go to sleep over this opportunity we shall have to endure a tyranny which will be not only cruel and haughty, but also ignominious and flagitious. You know the insolence of Antonius; you know his friends; you know his whole household. To be slaves to lustful, wanton, debauched, profligate, drunken gamblers, is the extremity of misery combined with the extremity of infamy. And if now (but may the immortal gods avert the omen!) that worst of fates shall befal the republic, then, as brave gladiators take care to perish with honour, let us too, who are the chief men of all countries and nations, take care to fall with dignity rather than to live as slaves with ignominy.

There is nothing more detestable than disgrace; nothing more shameful than slavery. We have been born to glory and to liberty; let us either preserve them or die with dignity. Too long have we concealed what we have felt: now at length it is revealed: every one has plainly shown what are his feelings to both sides, and what are his inclinations. There are impious citizens, measured by the love I bear my country, too many; but in proportion to the multitude of well-affected ones, very few; and the immortal gods have given the republic an incredible opportunity and chance for destroying them. For, in addition to the defences which we already have, there will soon be added consuls of consummate prudence, and virtue, and concord, who have already deliberated and pondered for many months on the freedom of the Roman people. With these men for our advisers and leaders, with the gods assisting us, with ourselves using all vigilance and taking great precautions for the future, and with the Roman people acting with unanimity, we shall indeed be free in a short time, and the recollection of our present slavery will make liberty sweeter. . . .

THE ANNALS

Tacitus

Little is known about the background and life of Tacitus (A.D. ca. 55–ca. 116). *It is assumed that he came from a family of established wealth and standing. We do know that he enjoyed a very successful political career that culminated in his consulship* A.D. ca. 97, *a career that was apparently not interrupted even by the reign of terror directed by the Emperor Domitian* (A.D. 81–96) *against the senatorial class.*

This experience, or perhaps simply his membership in a class that had once ruled but now only reigned, colors Tacitus' Histories *and his* Annals, *both of which depict the new regime—the Principate—that had supplanted the traditional Roman Republic at the conclusion of a century of civil strife. His description of the Principate is less the work of a dispassionate historian than that of a brilliant prosecuting attorney summing up for posterity.*

The opening passage of the Annals, *dealing with the rulership of Octavian (better known as Augustus), is not concerned merely with presenting the chief events of Augustus' reign, but with evaluating this new form of government in the person of its founder. The selection presupposes some acquaintance with Roman politics in the last decades of the Republic (**see Appian, pages 254–256**), and with the powers of certain traditional Roman offices, such as the tribunate.*

In the beginning, Rome was ruled by Kings. Lucius Brutus established liberty and the Consulship. The Dictatorship was resorted to in emergencies. The authority of the Decemvirs lasted for only two years; that of the Military Tribunes with Consular Powers for no long period. The tyrannies of Cinna and of Sulla were short-lived; the ascendency of Pompeius and Crassus passed quickly on to Caesar, the swords of Lepidus and Antonius made way before Augustus: who under the title of 'Princeps' took the whole world, worn out by civil conflict, under Imperial rule.

The story of ancient Rome, in her triumphs and reverses, has been related by illustrious writers; nor were men of genius wanting to tell of Augustus and his times, until the rising spirit of sycophancy bid them beware. The histories of Tiberius and Gaius, of Claudius and Nero, were either falsified through fear, if written during their lifetime; or composed under feelings of fresh hatred after their fall. I purpose, therefore, to write shortly of Augustus and his end, and then narrate the reigns of Tiberius and his successors; unmoved, as I have no reason to be moved, by either hatred or partiality.

When the last army of the Republic had fallen with Brutus and Cassius on the field; when Sextus Pompeius had been crushed in Sicily; and when the deposition of Lepidus, followed by the death of Antonius, had left Augustus sole leader of the Julian party, he laid aside the title of Triumvir, assumed the Consulship, and professed himself content with the Tribunitian Power for the protection of the plebs. But when he had won the soldiery by bounties, the populace by cheap corn, and all classes alike by the sweets of peace, he rose higher and higher by degrees, and drew into his own hands all the functions of the Senate, the magistrates and the laws. And there was no one to oppose; for the most ardent patriots had fallen on the field, or in the proscriptions; and the rest of the nobles, advanced in wealth and place in proportion to their servility, and drawing profit out of the new order of affairs, preferred the security of the present to the hazards of the past.

Nor did the provinces resent the change; for the rule of the Senate and the People had become odious to them from the contests between great leaders, and the greed of magistrates, against whom the laws, upset by force, by favour, and, in fine, by bribery, were powerless to protect them.

Meanwhile Augustus, as buttresses to his rule, advanced Claudius Marcellus, his sister's son, to the priesthood and Curule Aedileship, while yet a lad; and bestowed the honour of two Consulships on Marcus Agrippa—a man of ignoble birth, but a stout soldier, and partner in his victories. When Marcellus died, he took Agrippa as his son-in-law; and distinguished his two step-sons, Tiberius Nero and Claudius Drusus, with Imperatorial titles, though as yet there was no lack of heirs in his own family.

For he had adopted the two sons of Agrippa, Gaius and Lucius, into the family of the Caesars; and before they assumed the manly gown, had caused them to be styled 'Chiefs of the Youth,' and to be designated Consuls—honours which he had affected to decline, but had most ardently coveted for them. But first Agrippa died; then the two Caesars were cut off—whether by an untimely fate, or through the

The Annals of Tacitus, trans. G. G. Ramsey (London: John Murray (Publishers), Ltd., 1904), pp. 1–25.

machinations of their step-mother Livia—the younger of them on his way to join the Spanish army, the elder when returning wounded from Armenia. Tiberius was now the sole surviving step-son of Augustus; for his brother Drusus had perished long before. On him therefore all hopes were centred. He was adopted as a son, made colleague in the 'Imperium,' admitted to share the Tribunitian Power, and exhibited to all the armies: his mother no longer intriguing for him in secret, but affording him open encouragement.

For Livia had acquired such an ascendency over Augustus in his old age, that he cast out on the island of Planasia his only surviving grandson, Agrippa Postumus: an uncultured youth, no doubt, with nothing but brute bodily strength to recommend him, but one who had never been found guilty of any open misdemeanour. And yet so anxious was Augustus to strengthen his position that he appointed Germanicus, the son of Drusus, to the command of the eight legions on the Rhine, and ordered his adoption by Tiberius, although Tiberius had a young son of his own.

All wars had now ceased except that against the Germans; and even that was being continued rather to wipe out the disgrace of the loss of Quintilius Varus and his legions, than from a desire to extend the empire, or for any profitable end. Tran-quillity reigned at home; the magistrates were called by their old names; the younge generation had been born since Actium, the elder, for the most part, during the cours of the Civil Wars: how many were there left who had beheld the Republic?

Thus a revolution had been accomplished. The old order had passed away; every thing had suffered change. The days of equality were gone: men looked to the Princ for his commands, having no anxiety for the present, so long as Augustus was of th age, and had the strength, to keep himself, his house and the public peace secure. Bu when he advanced in years, when his health and strength failed, and his approachin end gave birth to new hopes, some few discoursed idly on the blessings of liberty many dreaded war; some longed for it.

But the greater number pulled to pieces the characters of their future masters wit comments such as these:—

Agrippa, they said, was a savage, exasperated by contumelious treatment; he ha neither the years nor the experience to bear the weight of empire. Tiberius Nero wa of ripe age, and a tried warrior: but he had all the old pride of the Claudii in hi blood; and, however carefully suppressed, many indications of a cruel temper ha escaped him. He had been brought up from infancy in a reigning house; Consulship and Triumphs had been heaped upon him in his youth: even during the years of exil which he had spent in Rhodes, under violence of retreat, he had done nothing bu brood over his resentments, or practise hypocrisy and solitary debauch. And then ther was his mother, with all the ungovernable passions of her sex: they would have t serve a woman, and two striplings into the bargain, who would begin by oppressin the commonwealth, and end by rending it asunder.

Amid speculations such as these, the health of Augustus began to fail. Some sus pected foul play on the part of his wife. For a rumour had got abroad that Augustu some months before, with the privity of a few special friends, and with Fabius Max mus as sole companion, had journeyed to Planasia to see Agrippa. It was said th many tears had been shed, many signs of affection exchanged, between the two; an hopes were raised that the young man might be restored to his grandfather's hom

The secret of this visit, it was reported, had been betrayed by Maximus to his wife Marcia, and by her to Livia. This had come to the ears of Augustus; and when Maxi-mus died not long after (whether by his own hand or not was a matter of doubt), Marcia had been overheard lamenting at his funeral, and blaming herself for her usband's death.

Be that as it may, Tiberius had scarcely reached Illyricum when he was recalled in aste by a message from his mother. Whether on arriving at Nola he found Augustus till alive, or already dead, was never known. For Livia had placed a strict guard upon he palace and its approaches; favourable bulletins were issued from time to time; ntil, when every necessary precaution had been taken, it was announced in one and he same breath that Augustus was dead, and that Tiberius was in possession of the overnment.

The opening crime of the new reign was the murder of Agrippa Postumus. He was aken by surprise, and was unarmed; yet the centurion, though a determined man, had ome difficulty in despatching him. Tiberius made no communication on the subject to he Senate. His father, he pretended, had left orders with the officer in charge to put Agrippa to death so soon as he himself should breathe his last. Now Augustus, no doubt, had said many harsh things about the young man's character, and had caused he Senate to decree his banishment; but he never hardened himself so far as to put ny of his own family to death, nor is it credible that he should have slain his grand-on to secure a step-son's safety. It is more probable that this hurried murder of a outh detested equally by Tiberius and by Livia, was the work of both; the former noved by fear, the latter by her hatred as a step-mother.

When the centurion reported, according to military custom, that he had executed he order, Tiberius replied that he had never given any such order; and that the man vould have to answer to the Senate for his conduct. When this became known to Sal-ustius Crispus, who was in the secret—it was he who had sent the written instruc-ons to the Tribune—he was afraid that the charge would be shifted on to his own houlders, in which case, whether he should tell the truth or not, he would be in equal eril. He therefore warned Livia that the secrets of the palace, the private advice of iends, and the services of the soldiery, were things not to be published abroad:—iberius must not weaken the powers of Principate by referring everything to the enate. The condition of Imperial rule was this: that every one should be accountable o one man, and to one only.

Meanwhile all at Rome—Consuls, Senators, and Knights—were plunging into servi-ude. Men bearing the most illustrious names were the foremost with false professions; omposing their features so as not to show too much pleasure at the death of the one rince, or too little at the accession of the other; blending tears with their smiles, and attery with their lamentations. The Consuls, Sextus Pompeius and Sextus Appuleius, ere the first to take the oath of allegiance, which they in turn administered to Seius trabo and Gaius Turranius—the former Commandant of the Praetorian Cohorts, the tter, Superintendent of the corn-market. Then came the Senate, the soldiers, and the eople. For Tiberius left all initiative with the Consuls, as though the old Republic ere still standing, and as if he himself had not made up his mind to assume the Em-ire: even the edict by which he summoned the Senate he only put forth in virtue of e Tribunitian authority conferred on him in the lifetime of Augustus.

The edict itself was short, and moderate in tone:—He desired to take their advic
as to the honours to be paid to his father; he himself would not leave the body, no
undertake any other public duty. And yet, no sooner was Augustus dead, than he ha
given the password to the Praetorians as their commander; he had surrounded himsel
with guards and sentinels and all the paraphernalia of a court; he was escorted b
soldiers to the Forum and to the Senate-house, and he had issued a proclamation to th
army as though he were already Emperor: nowhere did he show hesitation save in hi
language to the Senate.

His chief reason for this attitude was his fear of Germanicus. That prince had man
legions under his command, and a vast force of allies; he was the darling of th
people; and it might be that he would prefer possession to expectation. Tiberius ha
regard also to public opinion. He wanted men to believe that he had been chosen an
called to power by his countrymen, rather than that he had crept into it through th
intrigues of a wife, or as the adopted son of a dotard. It transpired afterwards that th
air of hesitation was assumed deliberately, for the purpose of fathoming the feeling
of the leading men; for Tiberius would distort a word or a look into an offence, an
treasure it up in his memory.

At the first meeting of the Senate, Tiberius permitted no business to be transacte
except that relating to the obsequies of Augustus. The testament was carried in by th
Vestal Virgins. Tiberius and Livia were appointed heirs. Livia was to be adopted int
the Julian house, and to receive the title of 'Augusta.' His grandsons and great
grandsons came next in the succession; in the third rank were many names of distinc
tion, mostly those of personal enemies, inserted in a spirit of vain-glory, with an ey
to the approbation of posterity. The amount bequeathed was not above the scale of
private fortune; but a sum of forty-three and a half million sesterces was left to th
people and to the plebs. Each soldier of the Praetorian Cohorts was to receive on
thousand sesterces; the soldiers of the Urban Cohorts five hundred; the legionarie
and the members of the Cohorts raised from Roman citizens, three hundred sesterc
apiece.

The question of funeral honours was then considered. The most outstanding pr
posals were that of Gallus Asinius, that the procession should pass through the Tr
umphal Gate; and that of Lucius Arruntius, that the titles of the laws passed by th
deceased, and the names of the nations which he had conquered, should be born
before the body. To these Messalla Valerius added that the oath of allegiance t
Tiberius should be renewed every year; and when challenged by Tiberius to sa
whether that motion had been made at his instigation, he replied that no man ha
prompted him: nor would he follow any counsel but his own in public matters, eve
though he might give offence thereby. Such was the only form of flattery still left u
tried!

It was carried by acclamation that the body should be borne to the pyre by senator
an honour which Tiberius waived, in a tone of arrogant condescension. And to th
people he issued a proclamation, praying them not to think of burning the body in th
Forum, rather than at its appointed resting-place in the Campus Martius, nor to r
peat the disturbances caused by excess of affection at the obsequies of the Immort
Julius.

On the funeral day, the troops were drawn up on guard, amid the derision of those vho had themselves beheld or had heard their elders describe the day when Rome, ınripe as yet for slavery, had struck that ill-fated blow for freedom—the day when ome regarded the assassination of Caesar as a foul crime, others as a most glorious chievement: whereas now an aged emperor, after a long lease of power, and after roviding his heirs with resources against the Commonwealth, had need of a guard of oldiers to keep order over his grave!

There followed much talk about Augustus. People idly marvelled that he had died pon the same day as that on which he had first entered on power; in the same house, a the very room, at Nola, in which his father Octavius had breathed his last. They welt upon the number of his consulships, equal to those of Valerius Corvus and Gaius Marius put together; they recounted how the Tribunitian Power had been con- inued to him for thirty-seven years; how the title of 'Imperator' had been conferred pon him one-and-twenty times: how other distinctions had been heaped on him, or ıvented in his honour.

Reflecting men discussed his career in various tones of praise or blame. Some ıaintained:—

That he had been forced into civil war by regard for his father's memory, and by he exigencies of public affairs, which left no room for law: and civil war was a thing vhich none could bring about or carry on clean-handed. He had made many conces- ions to Antonius, many also to Lepidus, in order to secure vengeance on his father's ıurderers; but when the latter became old and lethargic, and the former lost himself ı debauch, no resource was left for the distracted country but the rule of one man. 'et even so, Augustus had not set up his government as King or Dictator, but under ıe name of 'Princeps.' Under his rule, the frontiers had been pushed forward to the)cean or to distant rivers; the provinces, the armies, and the fleets of the Empire had een brought into communication with one another. Justice had been dispensed at ome; consideration had been shewn to the allies; the city itself had been sumptu- usly adorned: and, if some few acts of violence had been committed, it had been in rder to secure the general tranquillity.

On the other side it was said:—

The pleas of filial duty and political necessity were but pretexts. It was lust of ower which had prompted Augustus to attract the veterans by bribes, to collect an rmy while he was still a stripling and without office, to tamper with the troops of the onsul, and to affect sympathy with the Pompeian party. After that, by virtue of a ecree of the Senate, he had usurped the Praetorship, with its military and judicial owers; and when Hirtius and Pansa were slain in battle—whether or no those enerals were indeed so slain: or had died, the latter, of a poisoned wound, the former, the hands of his own soldiers treacherously set on by Octavianus—he had assumed ommand of both armies; he had forced the Senate to make him Consul against its will, ıd having received an army to oppose Antonius, had turned it against his own coun- y: the proscriptions, the confiscations, were measures which not even their perpetra- rs could approve. The deaths of Brutus and Cassius, indeed, might be deemed a ibute of vengeance to his father; though even so it were right for private hatred to ve way before the public good. But he had tricked Sextus Pompeius by a pretence

of peace, and Lepidus under the guise of friendship; later on, he had entrappe
Antonius by the treaties of Tarentum and Brundisium and by giving him his ow
sister in marriage—a treacherous alliance which Antonius had paid for with hi
blood. Peace, no doubt, had followed, but it was a peace stained with blood: ther
had been the disasters of Lollius and of Varus abroad; at home, the executions of
Varro, an Egnatius, and a Iulus.

Nor was his private life spared:—

He had torn Livia, when pregnant, from her husband, going through the farce o
consulting the augurs whether she could rightfully marry without waiting for th
child to be born; he had permitted the extravagance of a Quintus Tedius and a Vediu
Pollio. And lastly, there was Livia: a very scourge to the Commonwealth as a mothe
no less a scourge to the house of the Caesars as a step-mother. What honours were lef
for the Gods, when Augustus ordained temples and images to be set up to himself a
to a Deity, with Flamens and Priests to worship him? Even in adopting Tiberius as hi
successor, he had not been moved by affection, or by care for the public good; bu
having sounded the depths of that proud and cruel nature, he had sought to win glor
for himself by contrast with an execrable successor.

For not many years before, when Augustus was asking the Senate to confer ane
the Tribunitian Power on Tiberius, though he spoke of him in terms of complimen
he had let fall some observations about his bearing, his manners and style of living
which under guise of an apology bore all the character of a reproach.

The obsequies were carried out in due form; and a temple, with religious worshi
was voted in his honour.

The Senate then turned to Tiberius with entreaties. He replied in various strain
He spoke of the vastness of the Empire; of his want of confidence in himself: no min
but that of the Divine Augustus could cope with so huge a task. Having been himse
invited to share that monarch's cares, he had learned by experience how grievous, ho
precarious, the burden of universal rule. A State which had so many distinguishe
men on whom to lean, should not place all power in one man's hands; the business o
government would be easier were it divided among several partners.

Grand words these; but there was little sincerity in them. For whether by nature o
by habit, Tiberius was at all times ambiguous and obscure in his utterances, eve
when he had nothing to conceal; and on the present occasion, when he was doing hi
utmost to hide his meaning, his language was more involved and unintelligible tha
ever.

Meantime the Senators, whose only terror was that they should appear to unde
stand what he meant, broke out into tears, prayers, and protestations; they held o
their hands in supplication to the Gods, to the statues of Augustus, and to the kne
of Tiberius himself. Upon that he ordered a document to be brought in and read, co
taining a statement of the public resources; an enumeration of the troops under arm
whether Roman or allied, and of the naval forces; of the Provinces and Protect
States, of the direct and indirect taxes, of the public burdens and state largesses. A
this Augustus had written out with his own hand; appending to it a recommendati
—whether prompted by timidity or jealousy—that the empire should be kept withi
its present limits.

LETTERS

Pliny the Younger

Pliny the Younger (A.D. ca. *61–113*) *enjoyed a career typical of the successful politician-administrator under the Principate. Born into the provincial Italian nobility, Pliny first made a name for himself in pleading lawsuits, then moved up the hierarchy of Roman political offices culminating in the consulship, which he attained by* A.D. *100 and which qualified him for a provincial governorship.*

About A.D. *111 Pliny was appointed governor of Bithynia, a province in what today would be Turkish Asia Minor along the southern coast of the Black Sea. He went there as the personal representative of the Emperor Trajan* (*reigned* A.D. *97–117*), *who had become perturbed by the maladministration of Bithynia under previous governors who had answered only to the Senate. For this reason, the relationship illustrated by this exchange of letters between provincial administrator and Roman emperor may have been closer than was customary. The letters show the problems and methods of Roman administration at the height of the Pax Romana* (*the "Roman Peace"*) *under an emperor who is rated among the very ablest. Some of the other letters from Pliny that have survived were clearly written with an eye to publication, but unlike these the official correspondence of Pliny and Trajan seems genuine and unstudied. It was presumably published after Pliny's death.*

etter VI. To the Emperor Trajan

[H]aving been attacked last year by a severe and dangerous illness, I employed a physi-an, whose care and diligence, Sir, I cannot sufficiently reward, but by your gracious ssistance. I intreat you therefore to make him a denizen of Rome; for as he is the eedman of a foreigner, he is, consequently, himself also a foreigner. His name is [H]arpocras; his patroness (who has been dead a considerable time) was Thermuthis e daughter of Theon. I farther intreat you to bestow the full privileges of a Roman tizen upon Helia and Antonia Harmeris the freedwomen of Antonia Maximilla, a dy of great merit. It is at her desire I make this request.

etter VII. To the Emperor Trajan

return you thinks, Sir, for your ready compliance with my desire, in granting the mplete privileges of a Roman, to the freedwomen of a lady to whom I am allied, d making Harpocras my physician a denizen of Rome. But when, agreeable to your

he Letters of Pliny the Consul, trans. William Melmoth (4th ed.; London: R. and J. Dodsley, '57), Vol. II, 585–588, 594–598, 610–611, 613–614, 616–629, 671–677.

directions, I gave in an account of his age and estate, I was informed by those who ar
better skilled in these affairs than I pretend to be, that as he is an Egyptian, I ought firs
to have obtained for him the freedom of Alexandria, before he was made free o
Rome. I confess, indeed, as I was ignorant of any difference in this case betwee
those of Egypt and other countries, I contented myself with only acquainting you, tha
he had been manumized by a foreign lady, long since deceased. However, it is an igno
rance I cannot regret, since it affords me an opportunity of receiving from you a doubl
obligation in favor of the same person. That I may legally therefore enjoy the benef
of your goodness, I beg you would be pleased to grant him the freedom of the city o
Alexandria, as well as that of Rome. And that your gracious intentions may not mee
with any farther obstacles, I have taken care, as you directed, to send an account t
your freedman of his age and fortunes.

Letter VIII. The Emperor Trajan to Pliny

It is my resolution, in pursuance of the maxim observed by the princes my predece
sors, to be extremely cautious in granting the freedom of the city of Alexandria: how
ever, since you have obtained of me the freedom of Rome for your physician Harpo
cras, I cannot refuse you this other request. You must let me know to what district h
belongs, that I may give you a letter to my good friend Pompeius Planta, governo
of Egypt.

Letter IX. To the Emperor Trajan

I cannot express, Sir, the pleasure your letter gave me, by which I am informed th
you have made my physician Harpocras a denizen of Alexandria; notwithstandin
your resolution to follow the maxim of your predecessors in this point, by being ex
tremely cautious in granting that privilege. Agreeably to your directions, I acquai
you that Harpocras belongs to the district of Memphis. I intreat you then, most gra
cious Emperor, to send me, as you promised, a letter to your good friend Pompeiu
Planta, governor of Egypt.

As I purpose (in order to have the earliest enjoyment of your presence, so ardentl
wished for here) to come to meet you; I beg, Sir, you would permit me to extend m
journey as far as possible.

Letter XIV. To the Emperor Trajan

Having safely passed the promonotory of Malea, I am arrived at Ephesus with all m
my train, notwithstanding I was detained for some time by contrary winds: an inform
tion, Sir, in which, I trust, you will think yourself concerned. I design to pursue th
remainder of my journey to the province, partly in light vessels, and partly in pos
chaises: for as the excessive heats will prevent my travelling altogether by land, so th
Etesian winds, which are now set-in, will not permit me to proceed entirely by sea.

Letter XV. Trajan to Pliny

Your information, my dear Pliny, was extremely agreeable to me; as it is much m
concern to know in what manner you arrive at your province. I well approve of yo
intention to travel either by sea or land, as you shall find most convenient.

etter XVI. *To the Emperor Trajan*

s I had a very favorable voyage to Ephesus, so in travelling post from thence I was xtremely incommoded by the heats, which threw me into a fever, and kept me some ime at Pergamum. From thence, Sir, I took ship again; but being detained by con- rary winds, I did not arrive at Bithynia so soon as I hoped. However I have no reason o complain of this delay, since (which indeed was the most auspicious circumstance hat could attend me) I reached the province in time to celebrate your birth-day. I am t present engaged in examining into the finances of the Prusenses, their disbursements nd credits; and the farther I proceed in this affair, the more I am convinced of the ecessity of my enquiry. Several large sums of money are owing to the city from private ersons, which they neglect to pay upon various pretences; as on the other hand, I ind the public funds are, in some instances, very unwarrantly applied. This, Sir, I vrite to you immediately on my arrival. I entered this province on the 17th of Sep- ember, and found it in those sentiments of obedience and loyalty, which you justly nerit from all mankind. You will consider, Sir, whether it would not be proper to send ither a surveyor; for I am inclined to think, much might be deducted from what is harged by those who have the conduct of the public works, if a faithful admeasure- nent were to be taken: at least I am of that opinion from what I have already seen of he accounts of this city, which I am now examining, with the assistance of Maximus.

etter XVII. *Trajan to Pliny*

should have rejoiced to have hear'd that you arrived at Bithynia without inconven- ence to yourself or any of your train; and that your journey from Ephesus had been as asy, as your voyage to that place was favorable. For the rest, your letter informs me, ny dear Pliny, what day you reached Bithynia. The people of that province will be onvinced, I persuade myself, that I am attentive to their interest; as your conduct to- wards them will make it manifest, that I could have chosen no person more proper to upply my place. Your first inquiry ought, no doubt, to turn upon the state of the public finances; for that they have been abused, is but too evident. I have scarce sur- veyors enough to inspect those works which I am carrying on at Rome, and in the neighbourhood: but persons of integrity and skill in this art may be found, most cer- tainly, in every province; so that you cannot be at a loss in that point, if you will make due enquiry.

Letter XXX. *To the Emperor Trajan*

I beg your determination, Sir, in a point wherein I am greatly doubtful: it is, whether I should place the public slaves as sentinels round the prisons of the several cities in this province (as has been hitherto the practice) or employ a party of soldiers for that purpose? On the one hand, I am afraid the public slaves will not attend this duty with the fidelity they ought; and on the other, that it will engage too large a body of the soldiery: in the mean while I have joined a few of the latter with the former. I suspect however, there may be some danger that this method will occasion a general neglect of duty, as it will afford them a mutual pretence of throwing the blame upon each other.

Letter XXXI. Trajan to Pliny

There is no occasion, my dear Pliny, to draw off any soldiers in order to guard th prisons. Let us rather persevere in the ancient customs observed by this province, o employing the public slaves for that purpose: and the fidelity with which they shal execute their duty will depend much upon your care and strict discipline. It is greatl to be feared, as you observe, if the soldiers should be mixed with the public slaves they will mutually trust to each other, and by that means grow so much the more negli gent. But the principal objection I have, is, that as few soldiers as possible should b called off from their colors.

Letter XXXIV. To the Emperor Trajan

The Prusenses, Sir, have an ancient and ruinous bath, which they desire your leave t repair. Upon examining into the condition of it, I find it ought to be rebuilt. I thin therefore you may indulge them in this request, as there will be a sufficient fund fo that purpose, partly from those debts which are due from private persons to the public which I am now calling in; and partly from what they raise among themselves toward furnishing the bath with oil, which they are willing to apply to the carrying on of thi building: a work which the dignity of the city, and the splendor of your times seem to demand.

Letter XXXV. Trajan to Pliny

If the erecting a public bath will not be too great a charge upon the Prusenses, w may comply with their request: provided, however, that no new tax be levied for thi purpose, nor any of those taken off which are applied for necessary services.

Letter XXXVIII. To the Emperor Trajan

Sempronius Caelianus (whose merit I must always mention with esteem) having dis covered two slaves among the recruits, has sent them to me. But I deferred passing sen tence till I had conferred with you, the glorious founder, and firm support of militar discipline, concerning the punishment proper to be inflicted upon them. My principa doubt is, that tho' they have taken the military oath, they are not yet entered into an particular legion. I beg therefore, Sir, you would let me know what method I shal pursue, especially as it is an affair in which example is concerned.

Letter XXXIX. Trajan to Pliny

Sempronius Caelianus has acted agreeably to my orders, in sending such persons t be tried before you as appear to deserve capital punishment. It is material however, i the case in question, to enquire, whether these slaves inlisted themselves voluntarily, o were chosen by the officers, or presented as proxies for others. If they were chosen, th officer is guilty; if they are proxies, the blame rests with those who deputed them but if, conscious of the legal inabilities of their station, they presented themselves vol untarily, the punishment must fall upon their own heads. That they are not yet entere into any legion, makes no great difference in their case; for they ought to have give true account of themselves immediately, upon their being approved as fit for the ervice.

etter XL. *To the Emperor Trajan*

As I have your permission, Sir, to address myself to you in all my doubts, you will ot esteem it below your dignity to descend to those affairs, which concern the adminstration of my post. I find there are in several cities, particularly those of Nicomedia nd Nicea, certain persons who take upon themselves to act as public slaves, and reeive an annual stipend accordingly; notwithstanding they have been condemned either o the mines, the public games, or other punishments of the like nature. Having reeived information of this abuse, I have been long debating with myself, how I should ct. On the one hand, to send them back again to their respective punishments, (many f them being now grown old, and behaving, as I am assured, with sobriety and modsty) would, I thought, be proceeding against them too severely; on the other, to etain convicted criminals in the public service, seemed not altogether so decent. I onsidered at the same time, to support these people in idleness, would be an useless xpence to the public; and to leave them to starve, would be dangerous. I was obliged herefore to suspend the determination of this matter, 'till I could consult with you. You will be desirous, perhaps, to be informed, how it happened that these persons scaped the punishments to which they were condemned. This enquiry I have also nade myself, but cannot return you my satisfactory answer. The decrees against them vere indeed produced; but no record appears of their having ever been reversed. It vas asserted, however, that these people were pardoned upon their petition to the proconsuls, or their lieutenants; which seems likely enough to be the truth, as it is mprobable any person should have dared to set them at liberty without authority.

Letter XLI. *Trajan to Pliny*

You will remember you were sent into Bithynia, for the particular purpose of corecting those many abuses with which it appeared to be over-run. Now none stands nore in need of reformation, than that criminals, who have been sentenced to punishnent, should, not only be set at liberty (as your letter informs me) without authority; out even appointed to employments, which ought alone to be exercised by persons vhose characters are irreproachable. Those therefore among them who have been convicted within these ten years, and whose sentence has not been reversed by proper uthority, must be sent back again to their respective punishments: but where more han ten years have elapsed since their conviction, and they are grown old and infirm, et them be disposed of in such employments, as are but few degrees removed from he punishments to which they were sentenced; that is, either to attend upon the public baths, cleanse the common shores, or repair the streets and highways, the usual offices o which such persons are assigned.

Letter XLII. *To the Emperor Trajan*

While I was making a progress in a different part of the province, a prodigious fire broke out at Nicomedia, which not only consumed several private houses, but also

two public buildings; the town-house and the temple of Isis, tho' they stood on con
trary sides of the street. The occasion of its spreading thus far, was partly owing t
the violence of the wind, and partly to the indolence of the people, who I am wel
assured, stood fixed and idle spectators of this terrible calamity. The truth is, the cit
was not provided either with engines, buckets, or any one single instrument proper t
extinguish fires; which I have now however given directions to have prepared. Yo
will consider, Sir, whether it may not be advisable to institute a company of fire-men
consisting only of one hundred and fifty members. I will take care none but those o
that business shall be admitted into it; and that the privileges granted them shall nc
be extended to any other purpose. As this incorporated body will consist of so smal
a number, it will be easy enough to keep them under proper regulation.

Letter XLIII. Trajan to Pliny

You are of opinion it would be proper to constitute a company of fire-men in Nico
media, agreeably to what has been practised in several other cities. But it is to be re
member'd, that this sort of societies have greatly disturb'd the peace of that provinc
in general, and of those cities in particular. Whatever name we give them, and fo
whatever purposes they may be founded, they will not fail to form themselves int
assemblies, however short their meetings may be. It will therefore be safer, to provid
such machines as are of service in extinguishing fires, enjoining the owners of house
to assist upon such occasions; and if it shall be necessary, to call in the help of th
populace.

Letter XLIV. To the Emperor Trajan

We have acquitted, Sir, and renewed our vows, for your prosperity, in which that o
the public is necessarily included; imploring the Gods to grant us ever thus to pay
and thus to repeat them.

Letter XLV. Trajan to Pliny

I received the satisfaction, my dear Pliny, of being informed by your letter, that you
together with the people under your government, have both paid and renewed you
vows to the immortal Gods, for my health and happiness.

Letter XLVI. To the Emperor Trajan

The city of Nicomedia, Sir, have expended three millions three hundred and twent
nine sesterces building an aquaeduct; but, not being able to finish it, the works ar
entirely falling to ruin. They made a second attempt in another place, where they lai
out two millions. But this likewise is discontinued; so that after having been at a
immense charge to no purpose, they must still be at a farther expence, in order to b
accommodated with water. I have examined a fine spring from whence the water ma
be conveyed over arches (as was done in their first design) in such a manner that th
higher, as well as level and low parts of the city may be supplied. There are but ver
few of the old arches remaining; the square stones, however, employed in the forme
building, may be used in turning the new ones. I am of opinion part should be raise

ith brick, as that will be the easier and cheaper method. But that this work may not e carried on with the same ill success as the former, it will be necessary to send here n architect and an engineer. And I will venture to say, from the beauty and usefulness f the design, it will be a work well worthy the splendor of your times.

etter XLVII. Trajan to Pliny

are must be taken to supply the city of Nicomedia with water; and you will do so, am well persuaded, with all the diligence you ought. But it is most certainly no less ncumbent upon you to examine, by whose misconduct it has happened, that such large ums have been thrown away upon this work, left by appliying the money to private urposes, this aquaeduct should likewise be left unfinished. You will let me know the esult of your enquiry.

etter XLVIII. To the Emperor Trajan

he citizens of Nicea, Sir, are building a theatre, which, tho' it is not yet finished, has lready exhausted, as I am informed (for I have not examined the account myself) bove ten millions of sesterces; and, what is worse, I fear to no purpose. For either rom the foundation being laid in a marshy ground, or that the stones themselves were ecayed, the walls are crack'd from top to bottom. It deserves your consideration herefore, whether it be best to carry on this work, or entirely discontinue it; or ather, perhaps, whether it would not be most prudent absolutely to destroy it: for the oundations upon which this building is immediately supported, appear to me more xpensive than solid. Several private persons have undertaken to build the compartnents of this theatre at their own expence, some engaging to erect the portico, others he galleries beyond the pit: but this design cannot be executed, as the principal fabric s now at a stand. This city is also rebuilding, upon a more enlarged plan, the Gymnaium, which was burnt down before my arrival in the province. They have already een at some (and, I doubt, a fruitless) expence. The structure is not only irregular nd ill-disposed, but the present architect (who it must be owned is a rival to the erson who was first employed) asserts, that the walls, tho' they are twenty-two feet hick, are not strong enough to support the superstructure, as they are not incrusted *vithout,* nor the intermediate space properly cemented *within.* The inhabitants of laudiopolis are sinking (for I cannot call it erecting) a large public bath, upon a low pot of ground which lies at the foot of a mountain. The fund appropriated for the arrying on this work, arises from the money which those honorary members you were leased to add to their senate, paid (or at least are ready to pay whenever I call upon hem) for their admission. As I am afraid therefore the public money in one place, and what is infinitely more valuable than any pecuniary consideration) your benefaction n the other, should be ill applied, I am obliged to desire you would send hither an rchitect to inspect, not only the theatre, but the bath; in order to consider whether, fter all the expence which has already been laid out, it will be better to finish them pon the present plan, or reform the one, and remove the other: for otherwise we may ossibly throw away our future cost, by endeavoring not to lose what we have lready expended.

Letter XLIX. Trajan to Pliny

You who are upon the spot, will best be able to consider and determine what i proper to be done concerning the theatre, which the inhabitants of Nicea are building as for myself, it will be sufficient if you let me know your resolution. With respect t the particular parts of this theatre which are to be raised at a private charge; you wil see those engagements fulfilled, when the body of the building, to which they are t be annexed, shall be finished.—These paltry Greeks are, I know, immoderately fon of Gymnastic diversions, and therefore, perhaps, the citizens of Nicea have enlarge their fabric for this purpose, beyond its due proportion; however, they must be con tented with such a one as will be sufficient to answer their occasions.

I entirely leave it to you to persuade the Claudiopolitani as you shall think prope with relation to their bath, which they have placed, it seems, in a very improper situa tion. As there is no province that is not furnished with men of skill and ingenuity, yo cannot possibly want architects; unless you think it the shortest way to get them fron Rome, when it is generally from Greece that they come hither.

Letter XCVII. To the Emperor Trajan

It is a rule, Sir, which I inviolably observe, to refer myself to you in all my doubts for who is more capable of removing my scruples, or informing my ignorance? Hav ing never been present at any trials concerning those who profess Christianity, I an unacquainted not only with the nature of their crimes, or the measure of their punish ment, but how far it is proper to enter into an examination concerning them. Whethe therefore any difference is usually made with respect to the ages of the guilty, or n distinction is to be observed between the young and the adult; whether repentanc intitles them to a pardon; or if a man has been once a Christian, it avails nothing t desist from his error; whether the very profession of Christianity, unattended with an criminal act, or only the crimes themselves inherent in the profession are punishable in all these points I am greatly doubtful. In the mean while the method I have ob served towards those who have been brought before me as Christians, is this: I inter rogated them whether they were Christians; if they confessed I repeated the questio twice again, adding threats at the same time; when, if they still persevered, I ordere them to be immediately punished: for I was persuaded, whatever the nature of thei opinions might be, a contumacious and inflexible obstinacy certainly deserved correc tion. There were others also brought before me possessed with the same infatuation but being citizens of Rome, I directed them to be carried thither. But this crime spread ing (as is usually the case) while it was actually under prosecution, several instance of the same nature occurred. An information was presented to me without any nam subscribed, containing a charge against several persons, who upon examination denie they were Christians, or had ever been so. They repeated after me an invocation to th gods, and offered religious rites with wine and frankincense before your statue (which for the purpose I had ordered to be brought together with those of the gods) and even reviled the name of Christ: whereas there is no forcing, it is said, those wh are really Christians, into a compliance with any of these articles: I thought prope therefore to discharge them. Some among those who were accused by a witness in peron, at first confessed themselves Christians, but immediately after denied it; while he rest own'd indeed that they had been of that number formerly, but had now some above three, others more, and a few above twenty years ago) forsaken that rror. They all worshipped your statue and the images of the gods, throwing out mprecations at the same time against the name of Christ. They affirmed, the whole of heir guilt, or their error, was, that they met on a certain stated day before it was ight, and addressed themselves in a form of prayer to Christ, as to some God, binding hemselves by a solemn oath, not for the purposes of any wicked design, but never to ommit any fraud, theft, or adultery, never to falsify their word, nor deny a trust when hey should be called upon to deliver it up; after which, it was their custom to sepa-ate, and then reassemble, to eat in common a harmless meal. From this custom, how-ver, they desisted after the publication of my edict, by which, according to your rders, I forbade the meeting of any assemblies. After receiving this account, I judged t so much the more necessary to endeavor to extort the real truth, by putting two emale slaves to the torture, who were said to administer in their religious functions: ut I could discover nothing more than an absurd and excessive superstition. I thought roper therefore to adjourn all farther proceedings in this affair, in order to consult with you. For it appears to be a matter highly deserving your consideration; more specially as great numbers must be involved in the danger of these prosecutions, this nquiry having already extended, and being still likely to extend, to persons of all anks and ages, and even of both sexes. For this contagious superstition is not con-ined to the cities only, but has spread its infection among the country villages. Never-heless, it still seems possible to remedy this evil and restrain its progress. The emples, at least, which were once almost deserted, begin now to be frequented; and he sacred solemnities, after a long intermission, are again revived; while there is a eneral demand for the victims, which for some time past have met with but few urchasers. From hence it is easy to imagine, what numbers might be reclaimed from his error, if a pardon were granted to those who shall repent.

etter XCVIII. Trajan to Pliny

The method you have pursued, my dear Pliny, in the proceedings against those Christians which were brought before you, is extremely proper; as it is not possible o lay down any fixed plan by which to act in all cases of this nature. But I would ot have you officiously enter into any enquiries concerning them. If indeed they should e brought before you, and the crime is proved, they must be punished; with the estriction however that where the party denies himself to be a Christian, and shall nake it evident that he is not, by invoking our Gods, let him (notwithstanding any ormer suspicion) be pardoned upon his repentance. Information without the accuser's ame subscribed, ought not to be received in prosecutions of any sort, as it is introduc-ng a very dangerous precedent, and by no means agreeable to the equity of my govern-nent.

Roman Slavery—
Theory and Practice

Slaves were very much part of the Greek, the Roman, and indeed the whole Mediterranean economy and society. At the end of the reign of Augustus they made up about one-third of the population of Italy. Varro's treatise on the use of slaves in agriculture dates from around 34 B.C.*, and Seneca's letter on slavery was written some eighty years later; nothing indicates that slavery as an institution underwent any dramatic changes in this interval. There is no evidence that Seneca's humane prescriptions were characteristic of the later period, although it is true that during the Principate the spectacular slave uprisings (like that of Spartacus) that had threatened the established order during Varro's day did not recur.*

The two works are very different in scope and intent. Marcus Terentius Varro (116–27 B.C.*), who had gained recognition as senator, military commander, and the most prolific and erudite of all Roman authors, wrote his treatise on agriculture as a practical handbook based on a lifetime of personal experience as a gentleman farmer. Varro therefore treats slavery as one of many practical problems of sound agricultural management. Lucius Annaeus Seneca (*ca. 5 B.C.–A.D. 65*), on the other hand, as an intellectual strongly influenced by Stoic philosophy, deliberately approached the treatment of slaves as a moral problem.*

ON AGRICULTURE

Varro

CONCERNING THE EQUIPMENT OF A FARM

I have spoken of the four points of husbandry which relate to the land to be cultivated and also of those other four points which have to do with the outside relations of that land: now I will speak of those things which pertain to the cultivation of the land. Some divide this subject into two parts, men and those assistants to men without which agriculture cannot be carried on. Others divide it into three parts, the instruments of agriculture which are articulate, inarticulate and mute: the articulate being the servants,

***Roman Farm Management—The Treatises of Cato and Varro,* anon. trans. (New York: The Macmillan Company, 1913), pp. 107–115.**

the inarticulate the draught animals, and the mute being the wagons and other such implements.

Of Agricultural Labourers

All men carry on agriculture by means of slaves or freemen or both. The freemen who cultivate the land do so either on their own account, as do many poor people with the aid of their own children, or for wages, as when the heaviest farm operations, like the vintage and the harvest, are accomplished with the aid of hired freemen: in which class may be included those bond servants whom our ancestors called *obaerati,* a class which may still be found in Asia, in Egypt and in Illyricum. With respect to the use of freemen in agriculture, my own opinion is that it is more profitable to use hired hands than one's own slaves in cultivating unhealthy lands, and, even where the country is salubrious, they are to be preferred for the heaviest kind of farm work, such as harvesting and storing grapes and corn. Cassius has this to say on the subject: "Select for farm hands those who are fitted for heavy labour, who are not less than twenty-two years of age and have some aptitude for agriculture, which can be ascertained by trying them on several tasks and by enquiring as to what they did for their former master." Slaves should be neither timid nor overconfident. The foreman should have some little education, a good disposition and economical habits, and it is better that they should be some what older than the hands, for then they will be listened to with more respect than if they were boys. It is most important to choose as foremen those who are experienced in agricultural work, for they should not merely give orders but lend a hand at the work, so that the labourers may learn by imitation and may also appreciate that it is greater knowledge and skill which entitles the foreman to command. The foreman should never be authorized to enforce his discipline with the whip if he can accomplish his result with words.

Avoid having many slaves of the same nation, for this gives rise to domestic rows.

The foremen will work more cheerfully if rewards are offered them, and particularly pains must be taken to see that they have some property of their own, and that they marry wives among their fellow servants, who may bear them children, some thing which will make them more steady and attach them to the place. On account of such relationships families of Epirote slaves are esteemed the best and command the highest prices.

Marks of consideration by the master will go far in giving happiness to your hands: as, for instance, by asking the opinion of those of them who have done good work, as to how the work ought to be done, which has the effect of making them think less that they are looked down upon, and encourages them to believe that they are held in some estimation by the master.

Those slaves who are most attentive to their work should be treated more liberally either in respect of food or clothes, or in holidays, or by giving them permission to graze some cattle of their own on the place, or some thing of that kind. Such liberality tempers the effect of a harsh order or a heavy punishment, and restores the slaves' good will and kindly feeling towards their master.

On the subject of the number of slaves one will require for operating a farm, Cato lays down the two measures of the extent of the farm and the kind of farming to be carried on. Writing about the cultivation of olives and vines he gives these formulas, viz.:

For carrying on an olive farm of two hundred and forty jugera, thirteen slaves are necessary, to-wit: an overseer, a housekeeper, five labourers, three teamsters, an ass driver, a swineherd and a shepherd: for carrying on a vineyard of one hundred jugera, fifteen slaves are necessary, to-wit: an overseer, a housekeeper, ten labourers, a teamster, an ass driver and a swineherd.

On the other hand Saserna says that one man is enough for every eight jugera,[1] as a man should cultivate that much land in forty-five days: for while one man can cultivate a jugerum in four days, yet he allows thirteen days extra for the entire eight jugera to provide against the chance of bad weather, the illness or idleness of the labourer and the indulgence of the master."

At this Licinius Stolo put in.

"Neither of these writers has given us an adequate rule," he said. "For if Cato intended, as he doubtless did, that we should add to or subtract from what he prescribes in proportion as our farm is of greater or less extent than that he describes, he should have excluded the overseer and the housekeeper from his enumeration. If you cultivate less than two hundred and forty jugera of olives you cannot get along with less than one overseer, while if you cultivate twice or more as much land you will not require two or three overseers. It is the number of labourers and teamsters only which must be added to or diminished in proportion to the size of the farm, and this applies only if the land is all of the same character, for if part of it is of a kind which cannot be ploughed, as for example very rocky, or on a steep hillside, there is that much less necessity for teams and teamsters. I pass over the fact that Cato's example of a farm of two hundred and forty jugera is neither a fair nor a comparable unit. The true unit for comparison of farms is a centuria, which contains two hundred jugera, but if one deducts forty jugera, or one-sixth, from Cato's two hundred and forty jugera, I do not see how in applying this rule one can deduct also one-sixth of his thirteen slaves; or, even if we leave out the overseer and the housekeeper, how one can deduct one-sixth of eleven slaves. Again, Cato says that one should have fifteen slaves for one hundred jugera of vineyard, but suppose one had a centuria half in vines and half in olives, then, according to Cato's rule, one would require two overseers and two housekeepers, which is absurd. Wherefore it is necessary to find another measure than Cato's for determining the number of slaves, and I myself think better of Saserna's rule, which is that for each jugerum it suffices to provide four days work of one hand. Yet, if this was a good rule on Saserna's farm in Gaul, it might not apply on a mountain farm in Liguria. In fine you will best determine what number of slaves and what other equipment you will require if you diligently consider three things, that is to say, what kind of farms are there in your neighbourhood, how large are they, and how many hands are engaged in cultivating them, and you should add to or subtract from that number in proportion as you take up more or less work. For nature gave us two schools of agriculture, which are experience and imitation. The most ancient farmers established many principles by experiment and their descendants for the most part have simply imitated them. We should do both these things: imitate

[1] *Saserna's rule would be the equivalent of one hand to every five acres cultivated.*

›thers and on our own account make experiments, following always some principle, ıot chance: thus we might work our trees deeper or not so deep as others do to see what the effect would be. It was with such intelligent curiosity that some farmers first :ultivated their vines a second and a third time, and deferred grafting the figs from ·pring to summer."

)f Draught Animals

.n respect of those instruments of agriculture which are called inarticulate, Saserna ays that two yokes of oxen will be enough for two hundred jugera of arable land, vhile Cato prescribes three yokes for two hundred and forty jugera in olives.

ON THE TREATMENT OF SLAVES

Seneca

:PISTLE XLVII

)n the Treatment of Servants

t by no means displeases me, *Lucilius,* to hear from those you converse with; that you ive in some sort of familiarity with your servants: this becomes your prudence, your rudition. *Are they slaves?* No; they are men; they are comrades; they are humble riends: *Are they slaves?* Nay, rather fellow-servants; if you reflect on the equal ›ower of Fortune over both you and them. I therefore laugh at those, who think it candalous, for a gentleman, to permit, at times his servant to sit down with him at upper: why should he not? but that proud custom hath ordained, that the master hould sup in state; surrounded at least by a dozen servants; with greediness he loads is distended paunch, now disused to do its proper office (of digestion.) So that it osts him more pains to evacuate than to gormandize; while the poor servants are ot allowed to open their lips, so much as to speak: the scourge restrains every nurmur; nor are mere accidents excused, such as a cough, a sneezing, an hiccup; ilence interrupted by a word is sure to be punished severely: so that they must stand, erhaps the whole night, without taking a bit of any thing, or speaking a word. Whence it often happens, that such as are not allowed to speak before their masters, vill speak disrespectfully of them behind their backs: whereas they who have been llowed not only to speak before their masters, but sometimes with them; whose nouths were not always sewed up, have been ready to incur the most imminent anger, even to the sacrificing their lives, for their master's safety; they have talked t an entertainment; the rack cannot extort a word from them. Besides, from the orementioned arrogance, arises the proverbial saying. *Totidem esse hostes, quot servos: ls many slaves, so many enemies;* not that they are naturally enemies, but we make ıem such.

'he Epistles of Lucius Annaeus Seneca, trans. T. Morell (London, 1786), Vol. I, 158–162. light revisions of the translation by the editor.

I pass by the more cruel and inhuman actions, wherein we treat slaves, not as men, but as beasts of burthen; and need only mention, that while we are indulging our appetites, one is employed to wipe up our spawlings; another, down upon his knees, gathers up the scraps and broken bottles; another carves up some choice birds, and, dissecting them with a dexterous hand, lays the breasts and rumps in delicate order; wretched is the man, who lives to no other purpose, than to cut up with dexterity a fat fowl; unless he is more wretched who teaches this art out of mere voluptuousness, than he who learns it to get his bread; [Another, who serving the wine is forced to dress like a woman and struggle with his advancing age; unable to get away from his boyhood, he is always dragged back to it; and though he already has the look of a soldier, he is kept beardless by having his hair shaved or plucked out by the roots and he must stay awake throughout the night, dividing his time between his master's drunkenness and his lust; in the bedroom he must be a man, at the feast a boy.] Another who is allowed the freedom of playing the buffoon, and censuring the guests goes on in his wretched state of life, expecting every day, that his ability to flatter to drink, and prattle, will induce some one to invite him again to-morrow; add to these the caterers, who have an exquisite knowledge of their master's taste; what relish best provokes his appetite; what will most please his eye; what dainty will suit his stomach; what he loaths from satiety; and what such a day he will eat greedily; and yet their master disdains to sup with them, thinking it a diminution of his grandeur to admit a servant to the same table. The Gods are most just, who to repay their wonted arrogance, have sometimes given *them* masters, even from those whom they so much despised. Before the door of *Calistus,* have I seen his former Lord waiting and even the man, who once fixed a label on his breast, and set him to sale among his rejected slaves, excluded, while others were admitted: the servant, who was put in the first rank of abject slaves, whom to make vendible the cryer was obliged to exert his voice, hath now returned the compliment; in his turn rejected his master, and thought him not worthy to enter his house. His master sold *Calistus,* but how many things since hath *Calistus* sold his master?

Were you to consider, that he, whom you call your slave, is sprung from the same origin, enjoys the same climate, breathes the same air, and is subject to the same condition of life and death, you might as well think it possible for you to see *him* a gentleman, as he to see *you* a slave. In the fall of *Varus,* how many born of the most splendid parentage, and not unjustly expecting, for their exploits in war, a senatorial degree, hath fortune cast down? She hath made of one a shepherd, of another a cottager. And can you now despise the man, whose fortune is such, into which, while you despise it, you may chance to fall?

I will not enter into so large a field of discourse, as to dispute on the use of servants whom we are apt to treat with contumely, pride and cruelty: but this is the sum of what I would prescribe; *live so with an inferior, as you would have a superior live with you.* As often as you think on the power you have over a servant, reflect on the power your master has over you. But you say you *have no master;* be it so; the world goes well at present; it may not do so always; you may, one day, be a servant yourself Do you know at what time *Hecuba* became a slave? as also *Croesus;* and the mother of

Darius; and *Plato,* and *Diogenes?* * Live therefore courteously with your servant; vouchsafe him conference; admit him to counsel, and even to your table. I know the whole band of fops will cry out upon me, alledging, that nothing can be more mean, nothing more scandalous: and yet I have caught some of these kissing the hand of another's servant.

See you not by what means our ancestors withdrew all manner of envy from masters, and contumely from servants? They called a master, *pater familias, the father of a family;* and servants, *Familiares,* (as the word is still used in our *Mimes*) their *familiars.* They instituted certain festivals, when the servants not only sat at table with their masters, but were allowed to bear honourable rule in the House, and enact laws; in short they looked upon a family as a little commonwealth. What then, shall I admit all servants to my table? Yes, as well as all your children: you are mistaken if you think I would reject even those of the meaner sort; suppose, the groom, or the cow-keeper; I esteem them not according to their vocation, but their manners: the manners are a man's own; his vocation, such as it is, is the gift of Fortune; let some sit down with you, because they are worthy, and others that they may become so; what remains in them of low and servile conversation, may be thrown off by conversing with their betters.

There is no reason, my *Lucilius,* that you should seek a friend only in the *Forum,* or at Court; if you search diligently, you may possibly find a truer friend at home: good materials are often lost for want of a workman; for once make the experiment: as he is a fool, who, when buying a horse, inspects or examines nothing more than the bridle and saddle, he is as great a fool who esteems a man from his dress, or his condition in life, which is also a sort of dress. *Is he a slave?* His mind may yet be free: *is he a slave?* Why should this prejudice you against him? Shew me the man who is not a slave. One is a slave to lust; another to covetousness; another to ambition; and all to fear. I can shew you a man of consular dignity, a slave to an old woman; a very rich man a slave to his handmaid; and many a young gentleman, who are the very bond-slaves of players. No slavery is more infamous than that which is voluntary: there is no reason, therefore, that some over-nice persons should deter you from shewing yourself affable and good-humour'd to your servants; instead of carrying yourself proudly as their superior: let them rather honour you than fear you.

Some one now will say that I am inviting every slave to assume the cap (*of Liberty*), and degrading every master from his proper station, because I have said, rather let them respect, than fear you; what, says he, must they only reverence him, as his clients, and such as attend his rising? He that will say this, forgets, that what satisfies God, may well satisfy a master: God is reverenced and loved: love cannot accord with fear. I think therefore you act justly in not requiring your servants to fear you; and in chastizing them with words only; it is for brutes to be corrected by the scourge: not every thing that offends, hurts us: daintiness compells us to outrage; so that the least thing that thwarts our inclination can put us in a passion; we take upon us to

* [Hecuba was one of the Trojan women who was given to Ulysses after the fall of the city. Both Plato and the philosopher Diogenes are said to have been sold into slavery, though both of them were soon redeemed. (*Ed.*)]

act like Kings; who not considering their own strength, and the weakness of others, are causelessly enraged as if they received an injury; when the greatness of their state hath rendered them quite secure against any such danger: this they know, but by an unjust complaint, they pretend to have received an injury, in order to commit one themselves. I am unwilling to detain you any longer; for I think you have no need of exhortation. Good morals, among other advantages, have this quality; they enjoy self-complacency, and are always steady; but a wicked disposition is ever light and changeable; no matter whether the change be for the better, a change is enough.

Part Three

The Judaeo-Christian Tradition

GENESIS

The historical books of the Old Testament represent an epic-like attempt on the part of the ancient Hebrews to place themselves in the universe. Their conception of themselves was that they were a nation chosen by God to fulfill a special role in the operation of His scheme of things. The main portion of the books from Genesis through Kings describes the origins and wanderings of the nation and its eventual establishment of a kingdom, in a special location selected by God. But it is as much a record of failure as of success in living up to the divinely chosen role, and the books end with the destruction of the kingdom, first by civil war and then by captivity.

The whole account is preceded by an even more fundamental presentation of the origin of all things—the creation of the world in an orderly fashion, with man as a culmination of creation, and the origin of various human institutions. Our selection includes the major portion of these opening passages, including the stories of the fall of Adam and Eve, the murder of Abel, and the Flood.

For many people Genesis remains a controversial account: some dispute the evidence that it is a composite work; the nature of Adam's and Cain's sins are open questions; etc. Although leaving these issues for discussion, we have opted for one side on the issue of the translation of the opening sentence. Many modern scholars have rejected the traditional "In the beginning God created . . . ," as does the important American translation of the Bible, published in the early 1930s by the University of Chicago Press, from which our selection is taken.

Like the rest of the Pentateuch (the first five books of the Bible), Genesis is a compilation of many sources, some as early as the period before 1200 B.C.*, which were finally edited by 400* B.C.*, when the Pentateuch as we now know it was canonized (officially accepted by Jewish leaders as a divine work). Our particular excerpts from Genesis were apparently put into their present form around 500* B.C.*, with the bulk of the narrative stemming from the period 1000–900* B. C.

When God began to create the heavens and the earth, the earth was a desolate waste, with darkness covering the abyss and a tempestuous wind raging over the surface of the waters. Then God said,

The Complete Bible: An American Translation **(Chicago: The University of Chicago Press, 1948); The Old Testament, ed. and trans. J. M. P. Smith, pp. 1–8.**

"Let there be light!"

And there was light; and God saw that the light was good. God then separated the light from the darkness. God called the light day, and the darkness night. Evening came, and morning, the first day.

Then God said,

"Let there be a firmament in the middle of the waters to divide the waters in two!"

And so it was. God made the firmament, dividing the waters that were below the firmament from those that were above it; and God called the firmament sky. Evening came, and morning, the second day.

Then God said,

"Let the waters below the sky be gathered into one place so that the dry land may appear!"

And so it was. God called the dry land earth, and the gathered waters seas. God saw that it was good.

Then God said,

"Let the earth produce vegetation, seed-bearing plants and the various kinds of fruit-trees that bear fruit containing their seed!"

And so it was. The earth brought forth vegetation, the various kinds of seed-bearing plants and the various kinds of trees that bear fruit containing their seed. God saw that it was good. Evening came, and morning, the third day.

Then God said,

"Let there be luminaries in the firmament of the sky to separate day from night; let them serve as signs and as indicators of times, days, and years; and let them serve as luminaries in the firmament of the sky to shed light on the earth!"

And so it was. God made the two great luminaries, the greater luminary to rule the day and the smaller one to rule the night—and the stars also. God set them in the firmament of the sky to shed light on the earth, to rule by day and by night, and to separate the light from the darkness. God saw that it was good. Evening came, and morning, the fourth day.

Then God said,

"Let the waters teem with shoals of living creatures, and let birds fly over the earth across the firmament of the sky!"

And so it was. God created the great sea-monsters and all the various kinds of living, gliding creatures with which the waters teem, and all the various kinds of winged birds. God saw that it was good, and God blessed them, saying,

"Be fruitful, multiply, and fill the waters in the seas; and let the birds multiply on the earth!"

Evening came, and morning, the fifth day.

Then God said,

"Let the earth bring forth the various kinds of living creatures, the various kinds of domestic animals, reptiles, and wild beasts!"

And so it was. God made the various kinds of wild beasts, the various kinds of domestic animals, and all the various kinds of land reptiles; and God saw that it was good.

Then God said,

"Let us make man in our image, after our likeness, and let him have dominion over the fish of the sea, the birds of the air, the domestic animals, the wild beasts, and all the land reptiles!"

So God created man in his own image; in the image of God he created him; he created both male and female. Then God blessed them, and God said to them,

"Be fruitful, multiply, fill the earth, and subdue it; have dominion over the fish of the sea, the birds of the air, the domestic animals, and all the living things that crawl on the earth!"

Further, God said,

"See, I give you all the seed-bearing plants that are found all over the earth, and all the trees which have seed-bearing fruit; it shall be yours to eat. To all the wild beasts of the earth, to all the birds of the air, and to all the land reptiles, in which there is a living spirit, I give all the green plants for food."

And so it was. God saw that all that he had made was very good. Evening came, and morning, the sixth day.

Thus the heavens and the earth were finished, and all their host. On the seventh day God brought his work to an end on which he had been engaged, desisting on the seventh day from all the work in which he had been engaged. So God blessed the seventh day, and consecrated it, because on it he had desisted from all his work, in doing which God had brought about creation.

The following are the origins of the heavens and the earth in their creation.

At the time when the LORD God made the earth and the heavens, there were as yet no field shrubs on the earth, and no field plants had as yet sprung up; for the LORD God had sent no rain on the earth, and there was no man to till the soil—although a mist used to rise from the earth and water all the surface of the ground. Then the LORD God molded man out of the dust of the ground, and breathed into his nostrils the breath of life, so that man became a living being. Then the LORD God planted a garden in Eden, to the east, and put there the man whom he had molded. Out of the ground the LORD God made all sorts of trees grow that were pleasant to the sight and good for food, as well as the tree of life in the middle of the garden, and the tree of the knowledge of good and evil.

There was a river flowing out of Eden to water the garden, and leaving there it divided into four branches; the name of the first being Pishon (the one which encircles all the land of Havilah, where there is gold—the gold of that land is fine—and bdellium and onyx stone); the name of the second river, Gihon (the one which encircles all the land of Cush); the name of the third river, the Tigris (the one which flows east of Ashur); and the name of the fourth river, the Euphrates.

The LORD God took the man and put him in the garden of Eden to till it and look after it; and the LORD God laid this command upon the man:

"From any tree in the garden you are free to eat; but from the tree of the knowledge of good and evil you must not eat; for the day that you eat of it you shall certainly die."

Then the LORD God said,

"It is not good for the man to be alone; I must make a helper for him who is like him."

So the LORD God molded out of the ground all the wild beasts and all the birds of the air, and brought them to the man to see what he would call them; whatever the man called each living creature, that was its name. So the man gave names to all the domestic animals, the birds of the air, and all the wild beasts; but for man himself no helper was found who was like him. Then the LORD God had a trance fall upon the man; and when he had gone to sleep, he took one of his ribs, closing up its place with flesh. The rib which he took from the man the LORD God built up into a woman, and brought her to the man, whereupon the man said,

"This at last is bone of my bone,
And flesh of my flesh;
She shall be called woman,
For from man was she taken."

(That is why a man leaves his father and mother, and clings to his wife, so that they form one flesh.)

Both of them were naked, the man and his wife, but they felt no shame.

Now the serpent was the most clever of all the wild beasts that the LORD God had made.

"And so God has said that you are not to eat from any tree in the garden?" he said to the woman.

"From the fruit of the trees in the garden we may eat," the woman said to the serpent; "it is only concerning the fruit of the tree which is in the middle of the garden that God has said, 'You may not eat any of it, nor touch it, lest you die.' "

But the serpent said to the woman,

"You would not die at all; for God knows that the very day you eat of it, your eyes will be opened, and you will be like gods who know good from evil."

So when the woman realized that the tree was good for food and attractive to the eye, and further, that the tree was desirable for its gift of wisdom, she took some of its fruit, and ate it; she also gave some to her husband with her, and he ate. Then the eyes of both of them were opened, and they realized that they were naked; so they sewed fig-leaves together, and made themselves girdles. But when they heard the sound of the LORD God taking a walk in the garden for the breezes of the day, the man and his wife hid themselves from the LORD God among the trees in the garden. The LORD God called to the man.

"Where are you?" he said to him.

"I heard the sound of you in the garden," he replied, "and I was afraid, because I was naked; so I hid myself."

"Who told you that you were naked?" he said. "Have you eaten from the tree from which I commanded you not to eat?"

The man said,

"The woman whom you set at my side, it was she who gave me fruit from the tree; so I ate it."

Then the LORD God said to the woman,
"What ever have you done?"
The woman said,
"It was the serpent that misled me, and so I ate it."
So the LORD God said to the serpent,
"Because you have done this,
The most cursed of all animals shall you be,
And of all wild beasts.
On your belly you shall crawl, and eat dust,
As long as you live.
I will put enmity between you and the woman,
And between your posterity and hers;
They shall attack you in the head,
And you shall attack them in the heel."
To the woman he said,
"I will make your pain at child-birth very great;
In pain shall you bear children;
And yet you shall be devoted to your husband,
While he shall rule over you."
And to the man he said,
"Because you followed your wife's suggestions, and ate from the tree from which I commanded you not to eat,
Cursed shall be the ground through you,
In suffering shall you gain your living from it as long as you live;
Thorns and thistles shall it produce for you,
So that you will have to eat wild plants.
By the sweat of your brow shall you earn your living,
Until you return to the ground,
Since it was from it that you were taken;
For dust you are,
And to dust you must return."

The man called his wife's name Eve [mother], because she was the mother of all living beings.

The LORD God made skin tunics for the man and his wife, and clothed them.

Then the LORD God said,

"See, the man has become like one of us, in knowing good from evil; and now, suppose he were to reach out his hand and take the fruit of the tree of life also, and eating it, live forever!"

So the LORD God expelled him from the garden of Eden, to till the ground from which he had been taken; he drove the man out, and stationed the cherubs east of the garden of Eden, with the flaming, whirling sword to guard the way to the tree of life.

The man had intercourse with his wife Eve; so she conceived and bore Cain. Then she said,

"I have won back my husband; the LORD is with me!'

Later she bore his brother, Abel. Abel was a shepherd, while Cain was a farmer.

In the course of time Cain brought some produce of the soil as an offering to the LORD, while Abel on his part brought some firstlings from his flock, that is, some fat pieces from them. The LORD took notice of Abel and his offering; but of Cain and his offering he took no notice. So Cain became very angry and downcast. Then the LORD said to Cain,

"Why are you angry, and why are you downcast? If you have been doing right, should you not be happy? But if you have not, sin will be lurking at the door. And yet he is devoted to you, while you rule over him."

Then Cain said to his brother Abel,

"Let us go off into the country."

When they were out in the country, Cain attacked his brother Abel, and murdered him.

Then the LORD said to Cain,

"Where is your brother Abel?"

"I do not know," he said. "Am I my brother's keeper?"

Whereupon he said,

"What have you done? Hark, your brother's blood is crying to me from the ground! And now, cursed shall you be in banishment from the soil which has opened its mouth to receive your brother's blood from your hand. Though you were to till the soil, never again would it yield you its full produce; a vagrant and a vagabond shall you be on the earth."

Cain said to the LORD,

"My punishment is too great to bear. Seeing that thou hast today driven me off the soil, I must remain hidden from thee; I must be a vagrant and a vagabond in the earth, and then anyone who comes across me will kill me."

So the LORD said to him,

"In that case, sevenfold vengeance shall be taken on anyone who kills Cain."

Then the LORD prescribed a mark for Cain, to prevent anyone who came across him from hurting him. So Cain left the presence of the LORD, and settled in the land of Nod, east of Eden.

Cain had intercourse with his wife; so she conceived and bore Enoch. Then he became the builder of a city, and named the city after his son, Enoch. To Enoch was born Irad; and Irad was the father of Mehujael. Mehujael was the father of Methushael, and Methushael of Lamech. Lamech married two wives, the name of one being Adah, and the name of the other Zillah. Adah bore Jabal, who was the ancestor of those who live in tents as shepherds; his brother's name was Jubal, who was the ancestor of all who play the lyre and pipe. Zillah in turn bore Tubal-cain, the forger of bronze and iron utensils; and the sister of Tubal-cain was Naamah. . . .

Presently when men began to grow numerous over the earth, and had daughters born to them, the gods noticed that the daughters of men were attractive; so they married those whom they liked best. Then the LORD said,

"My spirit must not remain in man forever, inasmuch as he is flesh. Accordingly, his lifetime shall be one hundred and twenty years."

In those days, as well as afterwards, there were giants in the earth, who were born to the gods whenever they had intercourse with the daughters of men; these were the heroes who were men of note in days of old.

When the LORD saw that the wickedness of man on the earth was great, and that the whole bent of his thinking was never anything but evil, the LORD regretted that he had ever made man on the earth, and he was grieved to the heart. So the LORD said,

"I will blot the men that I have created off the face of the ground, both men and animals, reptiles, and birds of the air; for I regret that I ever made them."

Noah, however, had found favor with the LORD.

Noah alone among his contemporaries was a pious and exceedingly good man; Noah walked with God. Noah had three sons born to him, Shem, Ham, and Japheth. Now in God's sight, the earth was corrupt; the earth was full of wrong-doing; God saw that the earth was corrupt; for every mortal on the earth had corrupted his life. So God said to Noah,

"I have resolved on the extermination of all mortals; for the earth is full of wrong-doing through them; I am going to exterminate them from the earth. Make yourself an ark of oleander wood; make the ark with cabins, and smear it with bitumen inside and out. This is how you are to make it: the length of the ark is to be three hundred cubits, its breadth fifty cubits, and its height thirty cubits; you are to make a roof for the ark, finishing it off on top to the width of a cubit; and the doorway of the ark you are to put in its side; you are to make it with lower, second, and third decks. I on my part am about to bring a flood upon the earth, to destroy every mortal from under the heavens, who has the breath of life in him; everything that is on the earth shall perish. But with you I will make a covenant; you shall enter the ark, accompanied by your sons, your wife, and your sons' wives. Also, of all living creatures, of all animals, you must have two of every kind enter the ark, to keep them alive with you; they are to be a male and a female. Of the various kinds of birds, the various kinds of animals, and all the various kinds of reptiles, two of every kind are to join you, that you may keep them alive. Take also some of every kind of edible food, and store it by you, to be food for yourself and them."

Noah did so; he did just as God had commanded him.

The LORD said to Noah,

"Enter the ark, with all your household; for you alone of the present age have I found righteous. Of all clean animals, you are to take seven pairs, a male with its mate; but of the animals that are not clean a pair, a male with its mate; likewise, of the of the birds of the air seven pairs, a male and a female—to keep their kind alive all over the earth. For in seven days' time I am going to make it rain for forty days and nights on the earth, to blot off the face of the earth every living thing that I have made."

Noah did just as God had commanded him.

Noah was six hundred years old when the flood came on the earth.

Noah, with his sons, his wife, and his sons' wives, went into the ark to escape the waters of the flood. Of the clean animals and of those that were not clean, of the birds, and of all the reptiles, a pair of each, a male and a female, joined Noah in the ark, as

God had commanded Noah. Then, at the end of the seven days the waters of the flood came on the earth.

In the six hundredth year of Noah's life, on the seventeenth day of the second month, on that very day the fountains of the great abyss were all broken open, and the windows of the heavens were opened. (The rain fell on the earth for forty days and nights.) That same day Noah, with Shem, Ham, and Japheth, Noah's sons, and Noah's wife, and the three wives of his sons accompanying them, went into the ark, together with all the various kinds of wild beasts, all the various kinds of domestic animals, all the various kinds of land reptiles, and all the various kinds of birds, everything with feathers and wings; of all creatures in which there was the breath of life, a pair of each joined Noah in the ark. Those that entered were a male and a female of every kind of animal, as God had commanded him. Then the LORD shut him in.

The flood continued for forty days upon the earth. The waters mounted, and lifted the ark so that it rose above the earth. The waters rose and increased greatly on the earth, so that the ark floated on the surface of the waters. The waters rose higher and higher on the earth, until the highest mountains everywhere under the heavens were all covered. Fifteen cubits above them the waters rose, so that the mountains were covered. Every creature that moved on the earth perished, including birds, domestic animals, wild beasts, all the land reptiles, and all mankind. Of all that was on the land, everything in whose nostrils was the breath of life died; every living thing was blotted off the face of the earth, both men and animals and reptiles and birds; they were blotted off the earth, so that Noah alone was left, and those that were with him in the ark. The waters rose on the earth for one hundred and fifty days.

Then God remembered Noah, and all the wild and domestic animals that were with him in the ark; so God made a wind blow over the earth, and the waters subsided. Likewise, the fountains of the abyss and the windows of the heavens were closed. The rain from the heavens ceased, and the waters abated steadily from the earth. At the end of one hundred and fifty days the waters subsided, so that on the seventeenth day of the seventh month the ark grounded on the mountains of Ararat. The waters subsided steadily until the tenth month; and on the first day of the tenth month the tops of the mountains became visible.

At the end of forty days Noah opened the window that he had made in the ark, and released a raven, which went flying back and forth until the waters had dried off the earth. Then he released a dove, to see whether the waters had subsided from the surface of the land; but the dove could find no resting-place for the sole of her foot, so she came back to him into the ark; for there was water all over the earth. He put out his hand, and catching her, drew her into the ark with him. After waiting another seven days, he again released the dove from the ark; in the evening the dove came back to him, and there, in her beak, was a freshly picked olive leaf! So Noah knew that the waters had subsided off the earth. After waiting another seven days, he released the dove, but she never came back to him. By the first day of the first month of the six hundred and first year of Noah's life the waters had dried off the earth. So Noah removed the covering of the ark to look out, and found that the surface of the ground was quite dry. By the twenty-seventh day of the second month the earth was dry.

Then God said to Noah,

"Come out of the ark, your wife, your sons, and your sons' wives accompanying you; bring out with you every animal of every sort that is with you, birds, quadrupeds, and all land reptiles, that they may breed freely on the earth, and be fruitful and multiply on the earth."

So Noah came out, his sons, his wife, and his sons' wives accompanying him. Every animal, every reptile, and every bird, everything that moves on the earth came out of the ark by their species.

Then Noah built an altar to the LORD, and taking some clean animals and birds of every kind, he offered them as burnt-offerings on the altar. When the LORD smelled the soothing odor, the LORD said to himself,

"I will never again curse the soil because of man, though the bent of man's mind may be evil from his very youth; nor will I ever again destroy all life, as I have just done. As long as the earth endures, seedtime and harvest, cold and heat, summer and winter, day and night, shall never cease."

God blessed Noah and his sons, and said to them,

"Be fruitful, multiply, and fill the earth. The fear and dread of you shall be on every beast of the earth and on every bird of the air; as in the case of all the reptiles on the ground and all the fish of the sea, they have been delivered into your power. Everything that moves, that is alive, is to be food for you; as I once gave you the green plants, I now give you everything. Only, you must never eat flesh with the life (that is, the blood) in it. For your own life-blood, however, I will require an account; I will hold every animal accountable for it, and I will hold men accountable for one another's lives; whoever sheds the blood of man, by man shall his blood be shed; for God made man in his own image. As for you then, be fruitful, and multiply; be prolific in the earth and multiply in it."

God then said to Noah and to his sons with him,

"As for me, I do hereby establish my covenant with you and your descendants, and with every living creature that is with you, the birds, the domestic animals, and all the wild beasts with you, as many of them as came out of the ark; I establish my covenant with you, that never again shall all flesh be destroyed by the waters of a flood, and never again shall there be a flood to ravage the earth."

Further, God said,

"This shall be the symbol of the covenant which I am making between myself and you and every living creature that is with you, to endless generations: I will put my rainbow in the clouds, and it shall be a symbol of the covenant between myself and the world. Whenever I bring clouds over the earth, the rainbow will appear in the clouds, and then I will remember my covenant, which obtains between myself and you and every living creature of every sort, and the waters shall never again become a flood to destroy all flesh. When the rainbow appears in the clouds, I will see it, and remember the everlasting covenant between God and every living creature of every sort that is on the earth."

God said to Noah,

"This shall be the symbol of the covenant which I am making between myself and all flesh that is on the earth."

The sons of Noah who came out of the ark were Shem, Ham, and Japheth; and Ham was the father of Canaan. These three were the sons of Noah, and from them sprang the whole world. Now Noah was the first farmer to plant a vineyard. Having drunk some of the wine, he became intoxicated, and lay uncovered in his tent. When Ham, the father of Canaan, saw his father lying naked, he told his two brothers outside; whereupon Shem and Japheth took a robe, which they put on their shoulders, and walking backward, they covered up their father's nakedness, their faces being turned away so that they could not see their father's nakedness. When Noah awoke from his wine, and learned what his youngest son had done to him, he said,

"Cursed be Canaan!
The meanest of slaves shall he be to his brothers."

Also he said,

"Blessed of the LORD my God may Shem be;
And let Canaan be his slave!
May God expand Japheth, and dwell in the tents of Shem;
But let Canaan be his slave!"

Noah lived three hundred and fifty years after the flood; thus Noah lived altogether nine hundred and fifty years, and then he died.

DEUTERONOMY

Interspersed with the historical narrative of the Old Testament are summations of law codes, developed over a long period of time but presented in these books as a single revelation by God to Moses, the great Hebrew lawgiver. A collection of ritualistic, economic, military, judicial, and ethical pronouncements, the Pentateuchal laws are a major source of Western conceptions of law as a religious responsibility.

The Book of Deuteronomy is what the title implies: a second account (after the one in the three preceding books) of the giving of the Law by God to His chosen people. Since it is in effect a summation of legal obligations and since it is placed in an oratorical and literary setting, Deuteronomy may serve to illustrate the Hebrew conception of Law, or Torah—a conception different from earlier, less spiritual Babylonian ideas of law, and also from the Roman conception illustrated later in this volume. The Mishnah and Paul's letters represent further developments of this Hebrew tradition.

Our selections are of two kinds: first, from the framework of the book, part of Moses' oration to the people just before they entered the Promised Land, in which he presents the Ten Commandments and points out the historical significance of God's selection of the Hebrews; second, a collection of laws on an amazingly wide variety of topics. Many of the provisions, which might otherwise appear arbitrary, are the result of a direct reaction against the observance of pagan practices; the ban on boiling a kid in its mother's milk, for example, is undoubtedly an outgrowth of an earlier ritual, the meaning of which is now lost. Many are borrowings from other peoples; many, such as the sanctity of human and animal life or sympathy for the downtrodden, are the result of the direct application of exalted ethical principles.

Moses summoned all Israel, and said to them,

"Hear, O Israel, the statutes and ordinances which I am delivering in your hearing :oday, that you may learn them, and be careful to observe them. The LORD our God nade a covenant with us at Horeb; it was not with our forefathers that the LORD nade this covenant, but with ourselves, with those of us who are all here alive today. The LORD talked with you face to face out of the fire at the mountain, myself standing between the LORD and you at the time, to communicate to you the words of the LORD; for you stood in fear of the fire, and did not ascend the mountain. He said,

" 'I, the LORD, am your God, who brought you out of the land of Egypt, out of a state of slavery. You must have no other gods beside me.

" 'You must not carve an image for yourself in the shape of anything that is in the heavens above, or that is on the earth below, or that is in the waters under the earth; you must not pay homage to them, nor serve them; for I, the LORD your God, am a jealous God, punishing children for the sins of their fathers, to the third or fourth generation of those who hate me, but showing grace to the thousandth generation of those who love me and keep my commands.

" 'You must not invoke the name of the LORD your God to evil intent; for the LORD will not excuse anyone who invokes his name to evil intent.

" 'Be careful to keep the sabbath day holy, as the LORD your God commanded you. Six days you are to labor and do all your work, but on the seventh day, a sabbath to the LORD your God, you must not do any work at all, neither you, nor your son, nor your daughter, nor your male or female slave, nor your ox, nor your ass, nor any of your cattle, nor the alien in your employ residing in your community, that your male and female slaves may rest as well as you. You must remember that you were once a slave yourself in the land of Egypt, and that the LORD your God brought you out

The Complete Bible: An American Translation (Chicago: The University of Chicago Press, 1948); The Old Testament, ed. and trans. J. M. P. Smith, pp. 163–166, 169–174, 176–181.

from there by a strong hand and an outstretched arm; that is why the LORD your God has commanded you to observe the sabbath day.

" 'Honor your father and mother, as the LORD your God has commanded you, that you may live long and prosper in the land that the LORD your God is giving you.

" 'You must not commit murder.

" 'You must not commit adultery.

" 'You must not steal.

" 'You must not bring a false charge against your fellow.

" 'You must not lust after your neighbor's wife, nor covet your neighbor's home, his fields, his male or female slave, his ox, his ass, or anything at all that is your neighbor's.'

"These words, and nothing more, the LORD spoke to all your assemblage at the mountain with a loud voice out of the midst of the fire, cloud, and gloom; and he wrote them on two stone tablets, which he gave to me. When you heard the voice out of the darkness, the mountain being aflame with fire, you came up to me, that is, all the heads of your tribes and your elders, and said, 'Seeing that the LORD our God has let us see his glory and his greatness, and that it is his voice which we have heard out of the fire, we know now that God can speak with man, and he still live. Why then should we die? For this great fire is going to consume us! If we continue to hear the voice of the LORD our God any longer, we shall die! For what mortal at all is there that has ever heard the voice of the living God speak out of fire, as we have, and has still lived? Do you go near, and hear all that the LORD our God has to say, and then tell us whatever the LORD our God tells you; when we hear it, we will observe it.'

"When the LORD heard your protestations when you spoke to me, the LORD said to me, 'I have heard the protestations which this people have made to you. They have spoken quite properly. O that their present attitude might lead them always to stand in awe of me and keep all my commands, that it might go well with them and with their children for all time! Go and say to them, "Go home to your tents"; but do you stand here beside me, that I may tell you the whole charge, the statutes and ordinances, that you are to teach them to observe in the land which I am about to give them to occupy.'

"Be careful, then, to do as the LORD your God has commanded you, swerving neither to the right nor to the left. You must walk wholly in the way that the LORD your God has appointed you, that you may live, and prosper, and live long in the land that you are to occupy.

"Now this is the charge, the statutes and ordinances, which the LORD your God commanded that you be taught to observe in the land into which you are crossing for conquest, a land abounding in milk and honey, that you, with your son and your grandson, may stand in awe of the LORD your God all your life by observing all his statutes and commands which I am giving you, and that you may live long. Therefore heed them, O Israel, and be careful to observe them, that you may prosper, and multiply greatly, as the LORD, the God of your fathers, promised you.

"Listen, O Israel; the LORD is our God, the LORD alone; so you must love the LORD your God with all your mind and all your heart and all your strength. These instructions that I am giving you today are to be fixed in your mind; you must impress them on your children, and talk about them when you are sitting at home, and when you go off on a journey, when you lie down and when you get up; you must bind them on your hand as a sign, and they must be worn on your forehead as a mark; you must inscribe them on the door-posts of your house and on your gates.

"When the LORD your God brings you into the land which he promised on oath to your fathers, Abraham, Isaac, and Jacob, to give you great and splendid cities which you did not build, houses full of all kinds of goods with which you did not fill them, cisterns already hewn out, which you did not hew out, and vineyards and olive groves which you did not plant, but from which you may eat your fill, then take care not to forget the LORD who brought you out of the land of Egypt, out of a state of slavery. You must stand in awe of the LORD your God; him you must serve; and by his name you must swear. You must not run after alien gods, any of the gods of the nations that surround you, lest the anger of the LORD your God blaze against you, and he wipe you off the face of the earth; for the LORD your God who is in your midst is a jealous God.

"You must not put the LORD your God to the test, as you did at Massah. You must be sure to keep the commands of the LORD your God, as well as his decrees and statutes which he commanded you. You must do what is right and good in the sight of the LORD, that you may prosper, and go in and occupy the fine land concerning which the LORD swore to your fathers that he would drive all your enemies out of your way, as the LORD promised.

"When your son asks you in time to come, 'What is the significance of the decrees, statutes, and ordinances which the LORD our God has commanded you? you must say to your son, 'When we were Pharaoh's slaves in Egypt, the LORD brought us out of Egypt by a strong hand. The LORD displayed before our eyes great and ominous signs and portents against Egypt, against Pharaoh and all his court, but he brought us out from there that he might bring us into a position to give us the land which he promised on oath to our fathers. So the LORD commanded us to observe all these statutes, by standing in awe of the LORD our God for our good always, that he might keep us alive, as at this day. Hence it will stand to our credit with the LORD our God to be careful to observe all this charge, as he commanded us.'

"When the LORD your God brings you into the land which you are invading for conquest, and clears out of your way great nations like the Hittites, Girgashites, Amorites, Canaanites, Perizzites, Hivvites, and Jebusites, seven nations greater and stronger than yourselves; when the LORD your God puts them at your mercy, and you defeat them, you must be sure to exterminate them, without making a covenant with them, or giving them any quarter; you must not intermarry with them, neither giving your daughters in marriage to their sons, nor receiving their daughters for your sons; for they would turn your sons from following me to serving alien gods, and then the anger of the LORD would blaze against you, and he would quickly destroy you. But this is how you are to treat them: you must tear down their altars, smash their sacred pillars, cut down their sacred poles, and burn up their carved images. For you are a people consecrated to the LORD your God, the LORD your God having chosen you out of all the peoples that are on the face of the earth to be a people of his very own. It was not because you were the greatest of all peoples that the LORD set his heart on you and chose you—for you were the smallest of all peoples—but it was because the LORD loved you, and would keep the oath that he swore to your fathers, that the LORD brought you out by a strong hand, and rescued you from a state of slavery, from the power of Pharaoh, king of Egypt. Be assured, then, that the LORD your God is God, a trustworthy God, who to a thousand generations keeps loving faith with those that love him and keep his commands, but one who immediately requites anyone who hates him, by destroying him, never delaying with anyone who hates him, but requiting him immediately. So be careful to observe the charge, the statutes and ordinances, that I am enjoining on you today.

"It will be because you heed these ordinances, and are careful to observe them, that the LORD your God will keep loving faith with you, as he swore to your fathers; he will love you, bless you, and multiply you; he will bless the offspring of your body and the produce of your soil, your grain and wine and oil, the issue of your cattle, and the progeny of your flock, in the land which he swore to your fathers to give you. Blessed shall you be above all peoples, not a male or female being barren among you or your cattle. The LORD will also free you from all sickness, and none of the malignant diseases of Egypt, with which you are acquainted, will he inflict on you; but he will inflict them on all who hate you. You must annihilate all the peoples whom the LORD your God surrenders to you, without giving them any quarter, so that you may not serve their gods; for that would be dangerous for you.

"Though you say to yourselves, 'These nations are greater than I; how can I conquer them?' you must not be afraid of them; remembering rather what the LORD your God did to Pharaoh and all Egypt; the great tests which you saw with your own eyes, the signs and portents, the strong hand and outstretched arm, by means of which the LORD your God brought you out. So shall the LORD your God do to all the peoples of whom you stand in fear. In fact, the LORD your God will send leprosy among them, until any that are left or hidden perish from your way. You must not stand in terror of them; for the LORD your God is in your midst, a great and awful God. The LORD your God, however, will only clear these nations out of your way little by little; you are not to be allowed to put an end to them all at once, lest the wild beasts grow too numerous for you. But the LORD your God will put them at your mercy, and will throw them into great confusion, until they are destroyed. He will deliver their kings into your power, so that you shall obliterate their very name from under the heavens, not one being able to hold his own against you, until you have destroyed them. The carved images of their gods you must burn up; you must not covet the silver or the gold on them, nor appropriate it for yourselves, lest you be ensnared by it; for it is abominable to the LORD your God, and you must not bring anything abominable into your house, and so become a doomed thing like it; you must rather loathe it and abhor it; for it is a doomed thing.

"All the charge that I am enjoining on you today, you must be careful to observe that you may live and multiply, and go in and occupy the land which the LORD promised on oath to your fathers. You must remember all the experiences through which the LORD your God has led you for the past forty years in the desert, that he might bring afflictions on you to test you, to find out whether it was your intention to keep his commands or not. So he brought afflictions on you, and let you hunger, and then fed you with manna, with which you were not acquainted, nor were your fathers, that he might make you understand that it is not on bread alone that man lives, but on everything produced by decree of the LORD. Your clothing did not become too worn for you to wear, nor did your feet swell during the past forty years. Be assured, then, in your mind that the LORD your God has been disciplining you as a man disciplines his son. You must keep the commands of the LORD your God by walking in his ways and by standing in awe of him; for the LORD your God is bringing you into a fine land, a land with streams of water, with springs and pools, welling up in the valleys and on the hills; a land of wheat and barley, of vines, fig-trees, and pomegranates; a land of oil-producing olives and honey; a land where you may eat food without stint, lacking nothing in it; a land whose stones contain iron, and out of whose hills you can dig copper. When you have eaten your fill, you must thank the LORD your God for the fine land that he has given you. Take care not to forget the LORD your God by not keeping his commands, ordinances, and statutes, which I am commanding you today; and when you have eaten your fill, and have built fine houses to live in, and your herds and flocks multiply, and your silver and gold increase, and all that you have increases, not to become haughty, and forget the LORD your God who brought you out of the land of Egypt, out of a state of slavery, who led you through the great and terrible desert with its venomous serpents and scorpions and thirsty waterless ground, who brought water for you out of the flinty rock, who fed you in the desert with manna, with which your fathers were not acquainted, that he might bring afflictions on you and test you, in order to make you prosper in the end; and then say to yourselves, 'My own power and the strength of my own hand have gained this wealth for me.' You must remember that it is the LORD your God who is giving you power to gain wealth, that he may carry out his covenant which he swore to your fathers, as is the case today.

"If you ever forget the LORD your God, and run after alien gods, and serve them and pay homage to them, I warn you today that you shall most certainly perish. Like the nations that the LORD is to wipe out of your way, so shall you perish, since you would not listen to the injunctions of the LORD your God.". . .

"The following are the statutes and ordinances which you must be careful to observe in the land which the LORD, the God of your fathers, shall give you to hold as long as you live on earth.

"You must be sure to destroy all the sanctuaries where the nations whom you are to dispossess served their gods, on high mountains, on hills, and under every leafy tree; you must tear down their altars, smash their sacred pillars, burn up their sacred poles, and cut down the carved images of their gods, obliterating the very name of them from that sanctuary. You must not act like this toward the LORD your God, but to the sanctuary which the LORD your God chooses out of all your tribes as the seat of his presence, to his habitation you must resort; there you must go, and there bring your burnt-offerings, your sacrifices, your dues, your personal contributions, your votive offerings, your voluntary offerings, and the firstlings of your herd and flock; and there you must eat before the LORD your God, and with your households rejoice over all your undertakings, in which the LORD your God has blessed you. . . .

"If a prophet or an interpreter of dreams appears among you, offering you a sign or portent, and the sign or portent comes true, in connection with which he said to you, 'Let us follow alien gods—of whom you have had no experience—and let us serve them,' you must not heed the words of that prophet or that interpreter of dreams; for the LORD your God is testing you to find out whether you really love the LORD your God with all your mind and heart. It is the LORD your God that you must follow; of him you must stand in awe; his commands you must keep; his injunctions you must heed; him you must serve; and to him you must hold fast. But that prophet or that interpreter of dreams must be put to death, because he spoke falsely against the LORD your God, who brought you out of the land of Egypt, and rescued you from a state of slavery, in order to allure you from the path in which the LORD your God commanded you to walk. Thus shall you eradicate the wicked person from your midst.

"If your brother, the son of your mother, or your son, or your daughter, or the wife of your bosom, or your friend who is as precious as your own life, entices you in secret, saying, 'Let us go and serve alien gods!'—of whom you have had no experience, nor have your fathers, namely, any of the gods of the peoples who surround you, either near you or far away from you, from one end of the earth to the other—you must not yield to him, nor heed him; you must not show him any mercy, nor spare him, nor shield him; but you must be sure to kill him; your own hand to be the first against him to put him to death, and then the hands of all the people. You must stone him to death, because he tried to allure you away from the LORD your God, who brought you out of the land of Egypt, out of a state of slavery; and when all Israel hears of it, they will be afraid, and never again do such a wicked thing as this in your midst. . . .

"You must not eat anything abominable. The following are animals that you may eat: the ox, the sheep, the goat, the deer, the gazelle, the roebuck, the wild-goat, the ibex, the antelope, and the mountain-sheep. Also, you may eat any animal with a cloven hoof, that has the hoof divided completely in two, and that chews the cud. However, of those that chew the cud or have the hoof completely cloven, you must not eat the following: the camel, the hare, and the rock-badger, because, although chewing the cud, they do not have the hoof cloven—they are unclean for you; also the pig, because although having the hoof cloven, it does not chew the cud—it is unclean for you. Of their flesh you must not eat, and their carcasses you must not touch.

"Of all things that live in the water you may eat the following: whatever has fins and scales you may eat; but whatever has not fins and scales you must not eat; it is unclean for you.

"You may eat any clean bird; but the following are the ones of which you must not eat: the griffon, the vulture, the eagle, the buzzard, the kite in its several species, the raven in all its species, the ostrich, the night-hawk, the sea-mew, the hawk in its several species, the screech-owl, the eagle-owl, the horned owl, the jackdaw, the carrion vulture, the cormorant, the stork, the heron in its several species, the bittern, and the bat. Also, all winged insects are unclean for you; they must not be eaten. Any winged thing that is clean you may eat.

"You must not eat anything that has died a natural death; for you are a people consecrated to the LORD your God; you may give it to any alien residing in your community to eat, or sell it to a foreigner.

"You must not boil a kid in its mother's milk. . . .

"Every seventh year you must observe a remission; and the operation of the remission is to be as follows: every creditor who has a claim against his fellow-countryman is to remit it; he is not to press it against his fellow-countryman or kinsman; for a remission has been proclaimed by the LORD. Against an alien you may press it; but anything of yours that is in the possession of your kinsman you must remit. However, there shall be no poor among you; for the LORD will be sure to bless you in the land which the LORD your God is giving you as a heritage to occupy, if you but heed the injunctions of the LORD your God by being careful to observe all this charge which I am enjoining on you today. When the LORD your God blesses you, as he has promised you, you shall have many nations obligated to you, but you shall never be obligated to them; you shall rule over many nations, but they shall never rule over you.

"If there is a needy person among you, any of your fellow-countrymen in any of your communities in the land which the LORD your God is giving you, must not steel your heart, nor shut your hand against your needy countryman; but you must open wide your hand to him, and freely lend him sufficient for the needs that he has. Take care lest a base thought enter your head like this: 'The seventh year, the year of remission, is near!' and you behave meanly to your needy countryman by not giving him anything, and he cries to the LORD against you, and you incur guilt. You must give to him freely; and you are not to begrudge it when you give him something, because the LORD your God for this very thing will bless you in all your work and all your undertakings. For the poor will never cease to be in your land; that is why I am commanding you to open wide your hand to your poor and needy fellow-countryman in your land.

"If a countryman of yours, a Hebrew man or woman, is sold to you, he is to work six years for you, but in the seventh year you must set him free from your service. And when you set him free from your service, you must not send him away empty-handed; you must provision him liberally out of your flock, threshing-floor, and wine-press, supplying him as the LORD your God has blessed you. You must remember that you were once a slave yourself in the land of Egypt, and that the LORD your God rescued you; that is why I am giving you this command today. If, however, he says to you, 'I will not leave your service'—because he is fond of you and your household, and has fared well with you—then you must take an awl, and drive it through his ear into the door; he shall then be your slave permanently. You shall do the same with your female slave. You must not begrudge it when you set him free from your service; for he has worked six years for you at half the cost of a hired laborer. Then shall the LORD your God bless you in all that you undertake. . . .

"In all the communities which the LORD your God is giving you, you are to appoint judges and officials for your various tribes, to judge the people aright. You must not pervert justice; you must not show partiality, nor take a bribe; for a bribe blinds the eyes of the learned, and subverts even a just case. Justice, and justice only, you must strive for, in order that you may live, and take possession of the land which the LORD your God is giving you. . . .

"When you reach the land that the LORD your God is giving you, and occupy it and settle down in it, and then declare, 'I must have a king over me like all the nations surrounding me,' you must be sure to make him king over you whom the LORD your God chooses. You must make one of your own countrymen king over you; you may not put a foreigner over you, who is not a countryman of yours. However, he must not provide himself with many horses, nor have the people enter into relations with Egypt again, to provide himself with many horses, since the LORD means that you are never again to go back that way. Neither must he provide himself with many wives, so that his heart may not be estranged; nor must he provide himself with great quantities of silver and gold. As soon as he has taken his seat on his royal throne, he must write for himself in a book a copy of this code as approved by the Levitical priests; he must keep it with him, and peruse it all the days of his life, that he may learn to stand in awe of the LORD his God, by being careful to observe all the provisions of this code and these statutes, that he may not consider himself more exempt than his fellow-countrymen, and that he may not swerve from the charge to the right or to the left, in order that he with his descendants may continue long on the throne in Israel. . . .

"A single witness shall not convict a man in the case of any crime or offense of any kind whatsoever that he has committed; it is only on the evidence of two or three witnesses that a charge can be sustained.

"If a plaintiff with a grudge appears against a man to accuse him falsely, the two parties who have the dispute must appear before the LORD, that is, before the priests, and the judges that are in office at that time; the judges shall make a thorough investigation, and if it turns out that the plaintiff is false, having falsely accused his fellow, you must do to him as he meant to do to his fellow. Thus shall you eradicate the wicked person from your midst; and when those that are left hear of it, they will be afraid, and never again do such a wicked thing as this in your midst. So you must show no mercy—life for life, eye for eye, tooth for tooth, hand for hand, foot for foot.

"When you go out to battle against your enemies, and see horses, and chariots, forces greater than your own, you must not be afraid of them; for the LORD your God who brought you up from the land of Egypt is on your side. . . . Then the officers shall say to the people, 'Whoever has built a new house, but has not dedicated it, may leave and return home, lest he die in the battle, and another dedicate it. Whoever has planted a vineyard, but has not had the use of it, may leave and return home, lest he die in the battle, and another get the use of it. Whoever has betrothed a wife, but has not married her, may leave and return home, lest he die in the battle and another marry her.' The officers shall say further to the people, 'Whoever is afraid and faint-hearted must leave and return home, so that his fellows may not become faint-hearted like him.' As soon as the officers have finished addressing the people, the army commanders shall place themselves at the head of the people.

"When you invest a city, you must offer it terms of peace. If it agrees to make peace with you, and surrenders to you, then all the people to be found in it shall become forced laborers for you, and serve you. But if it will not make peace with you, but wages war with you, you are to besiege it, and when the LORD your God delivers it up to you, you must put every male in it to the sword; but the women and children and live stock and everything that is in the city, that is, all its spoil, you may take as your booty, and yourselves use the spoil of your enemies which the LORD your God gives you. So shall you treat all the cities that are very far away from you, that do not belong to the cities of the nations here. However, in the cities of the peoples here, which the LORD your God is giving you as a heritage, you must not spare a living soul; but you must be sure to exterminate them, Hittites, Amorites, Canaanites, Perizzites, Hivvites, and Jebusites, as the LORD your God commanded you, so that they may not teach you to imitate all the abominable practices that they have carried on for their gods, and so sin against the LORD your God. . . .

"You must not see your fellow-countryman's ox or sheep go astray without showing concern for it; you must be sure to take it home to your fellow-countryman. If, however, your fellow-countryman is not a tribesman of yours and you do not know him, you must take it home with you, and keep it until your fellow-countryman claims it; then you must give it back to him. You must do the same with his ass, with his garment, and with anything lost by a fellow-countryman of yours, which he has lost and you have found; you are not to be without concern for it.

"You must not see your fellow-countryman's ass or ox foundered on the road without showing concern for it; you must be sure to help him to raise it up.

"A woman must never wear any article belonging to a man, nor must a man put on a woman's garment; for whosoever does such things is abominable to the LORD your God.

"If you should happen to come upon a bird's nest in any tree, or on the ground, with young ones or eggs, and the mother sitting on the young or the eggs, you must not take the mother with the young. You must rather let the mother go, and only take the young, that you may prosper, and live long.

"When you build a new house, you must make a parapet for your roof, that you may not bring the guilt of blood upon your house, in case anyone should fall from it. . . .

"If a man is caught lying with a married woman, both of them shall die, the man who lay with the woman and the woman herself; thus shall you eradicate the wicked person from Israel.

"If there happens to be a girl who is a virgin betrothed to a husband, and a man runs across her in the city and lies with her, you must take them both out to the gate of that city, and stone them to death; the girl, because she did not call for help although in the city, and the man, because he seduced another's wife. Thus shall you eradicate the wicked person from your midst. If, however, it is in the open country that the man runs across the betrothed girl, and the man seizes her, and lies with her, then simply the man who lay with her shall die; you must do nothing to the girl, since no sin deserving of death attaches to the girl; for this case is like that of a man attacking his neighbor and murdering him; because it was in the open country that he ran across her; the betrothed girl may have called for help, but there was no one to save her.

"If a man runs across a girl, a virgin who is not betrothed, and seizes her, and lies with her, and they are caught, the man who lay with her must pay the girl's father fifty shekels of silver, and she shall be his wife as long as he lives, without his being able to divorce her, because he violated her.

"A man must not marry his father's wife, nor have intercourse with her who belongs to his father. . . .

"You must not turn a slave over to his master when he has escaped from his master to you; he shall live right in your midst with you, in any place that he chooses in one of your communities as being advantageous to him; you must not mistreat him.

"None of the Israelite women shall become a temple-prostitute, nor shall any of the Israelite men become a temple-prostitute. You must never bring the gains of a harlot or the earnings of a male prostitute as a votive offering to the temple of the LORD your God; for both are abominable to the LORD your God.

"You must not exact interest on loans to a fellow-countryman of yours, interest in money, food, or anything else that might be exacted as interest. . . .

"Fathers are not to be put to death with their children, nor are children to be put to death with their fathers. Everyone is to be put to death for his own sin.

"You must not pervert the justice due the resident alien, or the orphan, nor take a widow's garment in pledge. You must remember that you were once a slave yourself in Egypt, and the LORD your God rescued you from there; that is why I am commanding you to do this.

"When you reap your harvest in your field, and forget a sheaf in the field, you must not go back to get it; it is to go to the resident alien, the orphan, and the widow, that the LORD your God may bless you in all your enterprises. When you beat your olive-trees, you must not go over them a second time; that is to go to the resident alien, the orphan, and the widow. When you pick the grapes of your vineyard, you must not go over it a second time; that is to go to the resident alien, the orphan, and the widow. You must remember that you were once a slave yourself in the land of Egypt; that is why I am commanding you to do this. . . .

"You must not have weights of different sizes in your bag, a large one and a small one; you must not have different sized ephahs in your house, a large one and a small one; you must have a full, just weight; you must have a full, just ephah, that you may live long in the land which the LORD your God is giving you; for everyone given to these practices, everyone given to dishonesty, is abominable to the LORD your God. . . .

MICAH

The Hebrew Prophets were a remarkable group of moral and religious innovators. Viewed by themselves and society as spokesmen for God, they should not be thought of as mere fortune-tellers. Their function was to make clear in a time of great national crisis the course of action most in accord with the divine scheme of things, and to reveal which human agents were on the side of God, which were not, and which were being used by God as the instruments of his constant intervention in human history.

Very frequently the Prophets forsook questions of political history and turned their attention to more personal acts of economic and social injustice. They were fearless and relentless in their vituperation, and perhaps this is the side of their activity we usually think of as their major contribution. Our present selection, the Book of Micah in its entirety, is preponderantly in this category.

In times of very severe national collapse, as during the period when many Jews had been exiled to Babylonia (sixth century B.C.*), the Prophets played yet a third role as the proclaimers of a message of deliverance, hope, and comfort. Although this tradition reached its great culmination in the later Prophets (notably the author of the second part of the Book of Isaiah), it is also present to some extent in Micah.*

The form of the prophetic books is often troublesome to anyone who wants to read them as unified literary works. In fact, they are compilations of flashes of oratory delivered at various places on various occasions, sometimes with and sometimes without adequate divisions and headings in the text. You should not be too concerned about frequent shifts or specific contexts; be open to the powerful rhetoric and imagery while seeking the ethical presuppositions underlying the prophet's message.

In Micah's time (he prophesied from 740 to 692 B.C.*), the Jewish kingdom had been rent by a civil war and there existed two rival kingdoms, with their capitals in Samaria and Jerusalem. Micah's position is that moral decay will inevitably lead to the collapse of both kingdoms at the hands of foreign enemies, and that subsequently a remnant of the faithful will be ruled by a divinely ordained leader.*

The messages of the Prophets are entirely in verse. The principle of the verse is simple and flexible: parallelism of concept, in which pairs of phrases or clauses, either repetitive or contrasting in thought, are conjoined. Lacking rhyme and meter, Hebrew poetry can easily arise from prose and flow back to prose again; this quality makes for exceptionally brilliant oratory, especially when the customary elaborate imagery creates a very vivid and concrete mode of discourse.

In addition to the so-called literary prophets (Amos, Isaiah, Jeremiah, etc.), the Bible mentions "seers" (who were in fact fortune-tellers) and at least two other kinds of prophets—the itinerant preachers and miracle-workers (Jonah, Elijah) and the advisers resident in the royal palace (Nathan the Prophet). Taken all together, these do not form a unified school, but indicate the various kinds of divine inspiration developed in Hebrew society during the period from 800 to 500 B.C.

The word of the Lord which came to Micah, the Morashtite, in the days of Jotham, Ahaz, and Hezekiah, kings of Judah, which he prophesied against Samaria and Jerusalem.

Hear, O peoples, all of you!
Give heed, O earth, and everything in it!
And let the LORD GOD be a witness against you,
The Lord from his holy temple.

For, lo, the LORD is coming forth from his place;
And he will descend and tread upon the heights of the earth;
And the mountains shall melt under him,
And the valleys be cloven asunder,
Like wax before the fire,
Like waters poured down a precipice.

For the transgression of Jacob is all this,
And for the sin of the house of Judah.
What is Jacob's transgression?
Is it not Samaria?
And what is Judah's sin?
Is it not Jerusalem?

So I will turn Samaria into a ruin of the field,
Into a planted vineyard.
And I will pour down her stones into the valley,
And lay bare her foundations.

All her carved images shall be smashed to pieces;
And all her images shall be burned with fire;
And all her idols I will lay waste.
For from the harlot's hire they were gathered,
And unto the harlot's hire they shall return.

For this let me lament and wail;
Let me go barefoot and stripped.
Let me make lamentation like the jackals,
And mourning like the ostriches.

For her stroke is incurable;
For it has come even to Judah;

The Complete Bible: An American Translation **(Chicago: The University of Chicago Press, 1948); The Old Testament, ed. and trans. J. M. P. Smith, pp. 852–857.**

It reaches the gate of my people,
Even to Jerusalem.

Tell it not in Gath!
Weep bitterly in Bethel;
Roll yourselves in dust.
They sound the trumpet abroad for you,
O inhabitant of Shaphir.
From her city she comes not forth,
The inhabitant of Zaanan.
Beth-ezel is taken from its foundations,
From the site where it stood.
How can she hope for good,
The inhabitant of Maroth?
For disaster will come down from the LORD,
To the gate of Jerusalem.
Harness the steed to the chariot,
O inhabitant of Lachish;
(The beginning of sin was she
To the daughter of Zion.)
For in you are found
The transgressions of Israel.
Therefore you shall give parting gifts
To Moresheth Gath.
Beth Achzib has become a snare
To the kings of Israel.
I will again bring the conqueror to you,
O inhabitant of Mareshah.
Unto Adullam shall come
The glory of Israel.
Make yourself bald, tear out your hair,
For the children you delight in;
Enlarge your baldness like the eagle's,
For they will go into exile from you.

Woe to them who devise wrong,
And work out wickedness upon their beds.
In the morning light they do it,
Because it is in their power.
They covet fields and seize them,
And houses, and carry them off.
So they crush a yeoman and his house,
A man and his possessions.

Therefore, thus says the LORD,
"Behold, I am planning disaster against this family,

Which you will be unable to remove from your necks,
Nor will you be able to walk erect;
For it will be a disastrous time."

In that day a taunt-song shall be sung over you,
And a lamentation shall be wailed, as follows:
"The possession of my people is parcelled out,
With none to restore it;
To our captors our soil is allotted;
We are utterly ruined."
Therefore, you shall have no one stretching the line,
Or casting the lot, in the assembly of the LORD.
"Do not keep on harping," they harp;
"One should not be harping upon such things;
Shame will not overtake us,"
Says the house of Jacob.
"Is the LORD's spirit impatient,
Or are such things his deeds?
Do not his words mean good
To his people Israel?"

But you are my people's foe;
You rise against those who are at peace.
You strip off from those who pass through in confidence
Spoils of war.
The women of my people you expel
From their comfortable homes.
From their children you take away
My glory forever.

Arise, and go!
For this is not your resting place!
For the sake of a mere trifle,
You take a heavy mortgage.
If a man, walking in a false spirit, should lie,
"I will prophesy to you of wine and strong drink,"
He would be this people's prophet!

I will completely assemble Jacob, all of him;
I will fully gather the remnant of Israel.
Moreover, I will make them like a flock of Bozrah,
Like a herd in the midst of the pasture;
And they shall go forth from Edom.
The breaker shall go up before them;
They shall break through the gate and go forth thereby;
Their king shall pass on before them,
With the LORD at their head.

And I said,
"Hear now, you heads of Jacob,
And rulers of the house of Israel,
Is it not your place to know justice,
You who hate the good, and love wickedness,
Snatching their skin from upon them,
And their flesh from upon their bones?"

They eat the flesh of my people,
And strip them of their flesh,
And lay bare their bones and break them,
Like meat in the pot and flesh within the cauldron."

Then shall they cry unto the LORD,
And he will not answer them,
But will hide his face from them, at that time,
Inasmuch as they have done wicked deeds.

Thus has the LORD said,
Regarding the prophets who lead my people astray,
Who preach prosperity when their mouth is filled;
But if one does not put something in their mouths,
They declare war against him!

"Therefore, it shall be night for you, without vision,
And darkness for you, without divination.
For the sun shall set upon the prophets,
And the day shall become dark over them.

"The seers shall be abashed,
And the diviners shall blush;
And they shall all cover the upper lip,
Because there is no answer from God."

But I am full of power,
The spirit of the LORD, justice, and strength,
To declare to Jacob his crimes,
And to Israel his sins.

Hear this, now, you heads of the house of Jacob,
And rulers of the house of Israel,
Who abhor justice,
And distort everything that is right;
Who build Zion with blood,
And Jerusalem with guilt.

Her chiefs pronounce judgment for a bribe,
And her priests declare oracles for hire,
And her prophets divine for cash.

Yet they lean upon the LORD, saying,
"Is not the LORD in the midst of us?
No misfortune can befall us."

Therefore, because of you,
Zion shall be plowed like a field,
And Jerusalem shall become a ruin,
And the temple hill a high place in a forest.

It shall come to pass in the coming days,
That the mountain of the house of the LORD will be
Established as the highest mountain,
And elevated above the hills.
Peoples will flow unto it,
And many nations will come, saying,

"Come, let us go up to the mount of the LORD,
And to the house of the God of Jacob;
That he may teach us of his ways,
So that we may walk in his paths."
For from Zion shall the law go forth,
And the word of the LORD from Jerusalem.

And he shall judge between many peoples,
And arbitrate for great nations, at a distance.
And they will beat their swords into plowshares,
And their spears into pruning-hooks.
Nation shall not lift up sword against nation,
Nor shall they learn war any more.

And they shall sit each one under his vine,
And under his fig tree, with none to alarm them.
For the mouth of the LORD of hosts has spoken.
For all the peoples walk,
Each in the name of his god;
But we will walk in the name of the LORD,
Our God, forever and ever.

"In that day," it is the oracle of the LORD,
"I will gather the lame,
And assemble the outcast,
And her whom I have afflicted.
And I will make the lame a remnant;
And the sick, a strong nation.
And the LORD shall rule over them in Mount Zion,
From now on and forever.
And you, O tower of the flock,

Height of the daughter of Zion,
To you shall come the former dominion,
And there shall come the kingdom of the daughter of Jerusalem.

Wherefore, now, do you cry so loud?
Is there no king among you?
Or, has your counsellor perished,
That agony has laid hold of you like a woman in travail?
Writhe and bring forth,
O daughter of Zion, like a woman in travail;
For soon you must go forth from the city,
And dwell in the field,
And go to Babylon.
There you shall be rescued;
There the LORD will ransom you,
From the power of your foes.

Soon there shall be gathered against you
Many nations, saying, 'Let her be desecrated,
And let our eyes fasten upon Zion.'
But they know not the purposes of the LORD,
Nor do they understand his plan,
That he has gathered them like grain to the threshing-floor.

Arise and thresh, O daughter of Zion;
For I will make your horn iron,
And your hoofs will I make bronze.
You shall crush many peoples,
And devote their spoil to the LORD,
And their wealth to the Lord of all the earth.

Now you will cut yourselves deeply;
They will lay siege against us;
With the rod they will strike upon the cheek,
The ruler of Israel.

And you, O Bethlehem Ephrathah,
Too little to be among the clans of Judah,
From you, one shall come forth for me,
Who shall be ruler over Israel,
Whose origins are from of old,
From ancient days.
Therefore he will give them up
Until the time when she who is with child shall have borne;
And the rest of his brothers shall return to the Israelites.
But he shall stand fast and feed his flock in the strength of the LORD,
In the majesty of the name of the LORD, his God.

And they shall endure;
For now shall he be great unto the ends of the earth.

And this shall be our protection from Assyria:
When he comes into our land,
And treads upon our soil,
Then we will raise up against him seven shepherds
And eight princes of men;
And they shall shepherd the land of Assyria with the sword,
And the land of Nimrod with the drawn sword;
And they shall rescue us from Assyria
When he comes into our land,
And treads upon our border.

The remnant of Jacob shall be,
In the midst of many peoples,
Like the dew from the LORD,
Like the showers upon the grass,
Which waits not for man,
Nor tarries for the children of men.

And the remnant of Jacob shall be among the nations,
In the midst of many peoples,
Like the lion among the beasts of the forest,
Like the young lion among the flocks of sheep,
Who, if he passes through,
Tramples and tears, with none to deliver.

Your hand shall be high above your foes,
And all your enemies shall be cut off.
"It shall come to pass in that day,"
It is the oracle of the LORD,
"That I will cut off your horses from the midst of you,
And destroy your chariots.
And I will cut off the cities of your land,
And lay waste all your fortresses.
I will cut off the sorceries from your hand,
And you shall have no soothsayers.
And I will cut off your images
And your pillars from the midst of you;
And you shall bow down no more
To the work of your hands.
And I will uproot your Asherahs from the midst of you,
And destroy your cities.
And I will execute vengeance in anger and wrath,
Upon the nations which have not hearkened."

Hear, now, what the LORD says,
"Arise, present your case before the mountains,
And let the hills hear your voice!
Hear, O mountains, the argument of the LORD,
And give ear, O foundations of the earth.
For the LORD has an argument with his people,
And a controversy with Israel.

"My people, what have I done to you?
And how have I wearied you? Answer me!
For I brought you up from the land of Egypt;
And delivered you from the prison house;
And I sent before you Moses,
Aaron, and Miriam.

"My people, remember, now, what Balak, king of Moab, planned;
And what Balaam, son of Beor, answered him,
From Shittim to Gilgal;
That you may understand the righteous deeds of the LORD."

Wherewith shall I come before the LORD,
And bow myself before God most high?
Shall I come before him with burnt-offerings,
With calves a year old?
Will the LORD be pleased with thousands of rams,
With myriads of streams of oil?
Shall I give my first-born for my transgression,
The fruit of my body for the sin of my soul?
You have been told, O man, what is good:
Yet what does the LORD require of you,
But to do justice, and to love kindness,
And to walk humbly with your God?

Hark! the LORD calls to the city:
(And "success" is fearing thy name!)
"Hear, O tribe, and assembly of the city:
Whose rich men are full of violence;
And her inhabitants speak falsehood;
And their tongue is deceit in their mouths.

"Can I forget the wicked treasures in the house of the wicked,
And the short measure that is accursed?
Can I treat as pure him with the wicked scales,
And with the bag of false weights?

"So I will begin to smite you,
To lay you in ruins because of your sins.

You shall eat, but not be satisfied.
You shall conceive, but not bear;
And what you may bear, I will give to the sword.
You shall sow, but not reap.
You shall trample the olives, but not anoint yourselves with oil;
And tread out the grapes, but drink no wine.

"For you have kept the decrees of Omri,
And all the doings of the house of Ahab,
And you have walked by their counsels,
So that I may give you over to ruin,
And your inhabitants to scorn.
The mockery of the peoples you shall bear."

Woe is me! For I am become
Like those that gather summer fruit,
In the gleanings of the vintage,
When there is not a cluster to eat,
Nor an early fig that my appetite craves.

The godly has perished from the land,
And there is none righteous among men.
They all lie in wait for blood;
Each one hunts his brother with a net.

They solemnly swear that bad is good;
The prince and the judge demand a bribe;
And the great man expresses his desire;
And they pervert justice.

The best of them are like a brier;
The most upright of them are like a hedge.
The day of their watchmen, their punishment, is come;
Soon shall be their havoc.

Put no confidence in a friend;
Trust not an intimate.
From her who lies in your bosom
Guard the doors of your mouth.

For the son insults his father;
The daughter rises up against her mother;
The daughter-in-law against her mother-in-law.
A man's foes are the members of his own household.

I, indeed, shall wait confidently for the LORD;
I shall hope for the God of my deliverance;
My God will hear me.

Rejoice not, O my foe, over me!
Though I have fallen, I shall arise.
Though I sit in darkness,
The LORD will be my light.

The anger of the LORD I must bear—
For I have sinned against him—
Until he shall take up my case,
And do me justice.

He will bring me forth to the light;
I shall see his vindication.
My foe shall see,
And shame shall cover her.

She that said unto me,
"Where is the LORD, your God?"
My eyes will gaze upon her;
Soon shall she be trampled upon,
Like the mud of the streets.

There shall be a day for rebuilding your walls;
In that day the frontier shall be far distant.
A day there shall be when unto you they will come
From Assyria even unto Egypt,
From Egypt even to the river,
From sea to sea,
And from mountain to mountain.
But the earth shall become a waste,
Because of its inhabitants,
On account of the fruit of their deeds.

Shepherd thy people with thy staff,
The flock of thy inheritance,
That dwells alone, a jungle
In the midst of a garden.
May they feed in Bashan and in Gilead,
As in the days of old.
As in the days when thou didst come forth from the land of Egypt,
Show us wonderful things.
May the nations see, and be ashamed
Of all their power.
May they lay their hand upon their mouths,
And may their ears be deaf.
May they lick the dust like the serpent,
Like crawling things of the earth.

May they come trembling from their dens unto the LORD, our God;
May they quake and fear because of thee.

Who is a god like thee, forgiving guilt,
And passing by transgression to the remnant of his inheritance?
He will not hold his anger forever,
For he delights in kindness.
He will again show us mercy,
He will tread down our iniquities.
Thou wilt cast into the depths of the sea,
All their sins.
Thou wilt show faithfulness to Jacob,
Grace toward Abraham,
As thou hast sworn to our fathers,
From days of old.

THE JEWISH WAR

Flavius Josephus

*From the very beginning the Jewish community had been divided by important doctrinal cleavages, often closely connected with political conflict. As early as the rebellion of Korah (Numbers 16) and the civil war described in the Books of Kings, controversy was a major problem. In the centuries immediately preceding the birth of Jesus, the disputants seem to have been grouped in something like a threefold division. The Jewish historian Flavius Josephus, writing at the time of the Jewish rebellion against Roman rule (*A.D. ca. 70*), describes the cleavage as he saw it. He placed most emphasis on the most unusual group—the Essens (or Essenes)—who are in fact of the greatest interest to us because of their apparent connection with the movement led by John the Baptist and Jesus of Nazareth. Of the other two groups, the relatively little-known Sadducees ceased to play an important role soon after this account, and the Pharisees, rather mercilessly treated by the authors of the New Testament, formed the nucleus of the regular rabbinical tradition in Judaism (see the Mishnah, pages 325–332).*

We have no answer to some questions about the Essenes: for example, the identity of their "legislator," referred to by Josephus and, apparently in the Dead Sea Scrolls, as the Teacher of Righteousness; or the extent to which they borrowed from non-Jewish sources. The Dead Sea Scrolls

—now available in inexpensive English editions—are the next source to turn to if you are interested in pursuing this subject.

BOOK TWO CHAPTER VIII

The three sects of the Jews There are three philosophical sects among the Jews. The followers of the first of which are the Pharisees, of the second the Sadducees, and the third sect, which pretends to a severe discipline, are called Essens. These last are Jews by birth, and seem to have a greater affection for one another than the other sects have. These Essens reject pleasures as an evil, but esteem continence and the conquest over our passions to be virtue. They neglect wedlock, but choose out other persons' children while they are pliable and fit for learning, and esteem them to be of their kindred, and form them according to their own manners. They do not absolutely deny the fitness of marriage, and the succession of mankind thereby continued; but they guard against the lascivious behaviour of women, and are persuaded that none of them preserve their fidelity to one man.

These men are despisers of riches, and their communism raises our admiration. Nor is there any one to be found among them who hath more than another; for it is a law among them, that those who come to them must let what they have be common to the whole order, insomuch that among them all there is no appearance of poverty, or excess of riches, but everyone's possessions are intermingled with every other's possessions, and so there is, as it were, one patrimony among all the brethren. They think that oil is a defilement, and if anyone of them be anointed, without his own intention, he wipes his body; for they think to be unwashed is a good thing, as they do also to be clothed in white garments. They also have stewards appointed by vote to take care of their common affairs, who every one of them have no separate business for any, but what is for the uses of them all.

They have no one certain city, but many of them dwell in every city; and if any of their sect come from other places, what they have lies open for them, just as if it were their own, and they go into such as they never knew before, as if they had been ever so long acquainted with them. For which reason they carry nothing at all with them when they travel into remote parts, though still they take their weapons with them, for fear of thieves. Accordingly, there is, in every city where they live, one appointed particularly to take care of strangers, and to provide garments and other necessaries for them. But the habit and management of their bodies is such as children use who are trained under terror. Nor do they allow of the change of garments or of shoes, till they first be entirely torn to pieces, or worn out by time. Nor do they either buy or sell anything to one another, but everyone of them gives what he hath to him that wanteth it, and receives from him again in lieu of it what may be convenient for himself; and although there be no requital made, they are fully allowed to take what they want of whomsoever they please.

Flavius Josephus, *De Bello Judaico*, trans. W. Whiston and D. S. Marjoliouth (London, 1906), pp. 76–80.

And as for their piety towards God, it is very extraordinary: for, before sun-rising, they speak not a word about profane matters, but put up certain prayers which they have received from their forefathers, as if they made a supplication for its rising. After this everyone of them is sent away by their curators to exercise some of those arts wherein they are skilled, in which they labour with great diligence till the fifth hour. After which they assemble themselves together again into one place, and when they have girt themselves with linen coverings, they then bathe their bodies in cold water. And after this purification is over, they meet together in an apartment of their own, into which it is not permitted to any of another sect to enter; while they go, after a pure manner, into the dining-room, as though it were into a holy temple, and quietly set themselves down; upon which the baker lays them loaves in order; the cook also brings a single plate of one sort of food, and sets it before every one of them; but a priest says grace before meat, and it is unlawful for anyone to taste of the food before grace be said. The same priest, when he hath dined, says grace again after meat, and when they begin, and when they end, they praise God, as him that bestows their food upon them; after which they lay aside their [white] garments as though they were sacred, and betake themselves to their labours again till the evening, then they return home to supper, after the same manner, and if there be any strangers there, they sit down with them. Nor is there ever any clamour or disturbance to pollute their house, but they give everyone leave to speak in their turn; which silence thus kept in their house, appears to foreigners like some tremendous mystery; the cause of which is that perpetual sobriety they exercise, and the same settled measure of meat and drink that is allotted them, and that such as is abundantly sufficient for them.

And truly, as for other things, they do nothing but according to the injunctions of their curators; only these two things are done among them at everyone's own free-will, which are to assist those that want it, and to shew mercy; for they are permitted of their own accord to afford succour to such as deserve it, when they stand in need of it, and to bestow food on those that are in distress; but they cannot give anything to their kindred without the curators. They dispense their anger after a just manner, and restrain their passion. They are eminent for fidelity, and are the ministers of peace, whatsoever they say also is firmer than an oath; but swearing is avoided by them, and they esteem it worse than perjury; for they say, that he who cannot be believed, without [swearing by] God, is already condemned. They also take great pains in studying the writings of the ancients, and choose out of them what is most for the advantage of their soul and body, and therefore for the cure of distempers they seek out such roots as may be effective and inquire into the properties of stones.

But now, if anyone hath a mind to come over to their sect, he is not immediately admitted, but he is prescribed the same method of living which they use, for a year, while he continues excluded, and they give him a small hatchet, and the forementioned girdle, and the white garment. And when he hath given evidence, during that time, that he can observe their continence, he approaches nearer to their way of living, and is made a partaker of the waters of purification; yet he is not even now admitted to live with them; for after this demonstration of his fortitude, his temper is tried two more years, and if he appear to be worthy, they then admit him into their society.

And before he is allowed to touch their common food, he is obliged to take tremendous oaths, that in the first place he will exercise piety towards God, and then, that he will observe justice towards men, and that he will do no harm to anyone, either of his own accord, or by the command of others; that he will always hate the wicked, and be an assistant to the righteous, that he will ever show fidelity to all men, and especially to those in authority; because no one obtains the government, without God's assistance; and that if he be in authority, he will in no time whatever abuse his authority, nor endeavour to outshine his subjects, either in his garments or any other finery; that he will be perpetually a lover of truth, and reprove those that tell lies; that he will keep his hands clear from theft, and his soul from unlawful gains; and that he will neither conceal anything from those of his own sect, nor discover any of their doctrines to others; no, not though any one should compel him so to do at the hazard of his life. Moreover he swears to communicate their doctrines to no one any otherwise than as he received them himself; that he will abstain from robbery, and will equally preserve the books belonging to their sect, and the names of the angels [or messengers]. These are the oaths by which they secure their proselytes to themselves.

But for those that are caught in any heinous sins, they cast them out of their society, and he who is thus separated from them, does often die after a miserable manner; for as he is bound by the oath he had taken, and by the customs he hath been engaged in, he is not at liberty to partake of that food that he meets with elsewhere, but is forced to eat grass, and to let his body famish with hunger, till he perish; for which reason they receive many of them again, when they are at their last gasp, out of compassion to them, as thinking the miseries they have endured till they came to the very brink of death, to be a sufficient punishment for the sins they had been guilty of.

But in the judgments they exercise they are most accurate and just, nor do they pass sentence by the votes of a court that is fewer than a hundred. And as to what is once determined by that number, it is unalterable. What they most of all honour, after God himself, is the name of their legislator, whom if any one blaspheme, he is punished capitally. They also think it a good thing to obey their elders and the major part. Accordingly, if ten of them be sitting together, no one of them will speak while the other nine are against it. . . . Moreover, they are stricter than any other of the Jews in resting from their labours on the seventh day; for they not only get their food ready the day before, that they may not be obliged to kindle a fire on that day, but they will not remove any vessel out of its place, nor go to stool thereon. . . .

Now after the time of their preparatory trial is over, they are parted into four classes; and so far are the juniors inferior to the seniors, that if the seniors should be touched by the juniors, they must wash themselves, as if they had intermixed themselves with the company of a foreigner. They are long-lived also, insomuch that most of them live above a hundred years, by means of the simplicity of their diet, nay, as I think, by means of the regular course of life they observe also. They contemn the miseries of life, and are above pain, by the generosity of their mind. And as for death, if it will come with glory, they esteem it better than immortality; and indeed our war with the Romans gave abundant evidence what great souls they had in their trials wherein, although they were tortured and distorted, burnt and torn to pieces, and went through all kinds of instruments of torment, that they might be forced either to blaspheme their legislator, or to eat what was forbidden them, yet could they not be made to do either of them, no nor once to flatter their tormentors, or to shed a tear; but they smiled in their very pains, and laughed those to scorn who inflicted the torments upon them, and resigned up their souls with great alacrity, as expecting to receive them again.

For the opinion is strongly held among them, that bodies are corruptible, and that the matter they are made of is not permanent; but that the souls are immortal, and continue forever, and that they come out of the most subtile air, and are united to their bodies as to prisons, into which they are drawn by a certain natural enticement; but that when they are set free from the bonds of the flesh, they then, as released from a long bondage, rejoice and mount upward. And their opinion is like that of the Greeks, that good souls have their habitations beyond the ocean, in a region that is neither oppressed with storms of rain or snow, or with intense heat, but that this place is such as is refreshed by the gentle breathing of a west wind, that is perpetually blowing from the ocean; while they allot to bad souls a dark and tempestuous den, full of never-ceasing punishments. . . . These are the divine doctrines of the Essens about the soul, whereby they lay an unavoidable bait for such as have once had a taste of their philosophy.

There are also those among them who undertake to foretell things to come, by reading holy books, and using several sorts of purifications, and being perpetually conversant with the discourses of the prophets; and it is but seldom that they miss in their predictions.

Moreover, there is another order of Essens, who agree with the rest as to their way of living, and customs, and laws, but differ from them in the point of marriage, as thinking that by not marrying they cut off the principal part of human life, which is the prospect of succession; nay rather, that if all men should be of the same opinion, the whole race of mankind would fail. However, they try their spouses for three years, and if they find that they have their natural purgations thrice, as trials that they are likely to be fruitful, they then actually marry them. But they do not use to accompany with their wives when they are with child, as a demonstration that they do not marry out of regard to pleasure, but for the sake of posterity. Now the women go into the baths with some of their garments on, as the men do with somewhat girded about them. And these are the customs of this order of Essens.

But then as to the two other orders at first mentioned, the Pharisees are those who are esteemed most skilful in the exact explication of their laws, and are regarded the first sect. These ascribe all to fate, and to God, and yet allow, that to act as is right, or the contrary, is principally in the power of men: although fate does co-operate in every action. They say, that all souls are incorruptible, but that the souls of good men only are removed into other bodies, but that the souls of bad men are subject to eternal punishment. But the Sadducees are those that compose the second order, and take away fate entirely, and suppose that God is not concerned in our doing or not doing what is evil; and they say, that to act what is good or what is evil, is at men's own choice, and each man attaches himself to the one or the other as he will. They also take away the belief of the immortal duration of the soul, and the punishments and rewards in Hades. Moreover, the Pharisees are friendly to one another, and are for the exercise of concord, and regard for the public; but the behaviour of the Sadducees one towards another is in some degree wild, and their conversation with those that are of their own party is as barbarous as if they were strangers to them. And this is what I had to say concerning the philosophic sects among the Jews.

THE MISHNAH

In contrast to the Sadducees, who adhered stringently and exclusively to the Written Law (i.e., the legal parts of the Old Testament), the Pharisees, with their concept of the Oral Law, left open the possibility of constant religious development. *That is to say, their view was that in addition to the Scriptures, God had passed on from Moses to current rabbinical leaders an inspired gift of interpretation and expansion of the written word. The deliberations of the rabbinical academies, necessary to spell out in countless ways the rather generally expressed Scriptural commands in order to make them applicable to a full-scale national life, thus received a divine sanction which gave them great status in the minds of the people. (One of our selections indicates that observation of the Oral Law is an even more strict requirement than that of the Written Law.)*

The Mishnah is a compilation of interpretations and commentaries, delivered over a period of several centuries and put into writing, only because of the increasingly staggering burden on the memory, some time in the second century after Christ. Many Jews were afraid that writing it down might petrify the Oral Law and make further religious inquiry difficult. This fear may very well have been justifiable; certainly the principles involved in this point are at the center of much later controversy over reformism within Judaism as well as Christianity.

Our selections are mostly from two parts of the Mishnah: the section "Sanhedrin," on judicial procedure; and the section "Aboth," from which the subsection "The Acquisition of the Torah" is included almost in its entirety. We have tried to illustrate the legalism, the flexibility, and the devotion to Torah (Law) of these early Fathers. Notice the tendency to drift into general speculation not directly connected with legal disputation. Among the authorities quoted in the Mishnah are Rabbi Gamaliel II, one of the teachers of Paul, and Rabbi Hillel, a remarkable spiritual leader many of whose ethical precepts, such as his stress on the golden rule, foreshadow those of Jesus.

KETUBOTH

There were two judges of civil law in Jerusalem, Admon and Hanan b. [ben=son of] Abishalom. Hanan gave two decisions and Admon seven. If a man went beyond the sea and his wife claimed maintenance, Hanan says: Let her swear [to her claim] at the end [of the time] and let her not swear at the beginning. But the Sons of the High Priests disputed with him and said, 'Let her swear at the beginning and let her not swear at the end'. R. [Rabbi] Dosa b. Harkinas decided according to their opinion. R. Johanan b. Zakkai said: Hanan said well: let her swear only at the end.

If a man went beyond the sea and another rose up and maintained his wife, Hanan said: His money is lost to him. But the Sons of the High Priests disputed with him and said, 'Let him swear on oath how much he has expended and let him recover it'. R. Dosa b. Harkinas decided according to their opinion. R. Johanan b. Zakkai said: Hanan said well: the man laid his money on the horn of the gazelle.

Admon gave seven decisions. If a man died and left sons and daughters, and the property was great, the sons inherit and the daughters receive maintenance; but if the property was small the daughters receive maintenance and the sons go a-begging. Admon says: [The son may say] 'Must I suffer loss because I am a male!' Rabban Gamaliel said: I approve the words of Admon. . . .

GITTIN

If a man was half bondman and half freedman he should labour one day for his master and one day for himself. So the School of Hillel. The School of Shammai said to them: Ye have ordered it well for his master, but for him ye have not ordered it well: [thus] he cannot marry a bondwoman since he is half freedman, and he cannot marry a freedwoman since he is half bondman. May he never marry? And was not the world only created for fruition and increase, as it is written, *He created it not a waste; he formed it to be inhabited?* But as a precaution for the general good they should compel his master and he sets him free; and the bondman writes him a bond of indebtedness for half his value. The School of Hillel changed their opinion and taught according to the opinion of the School of Shammai. . . .

SANHEDRIN

Non-capital and capital cases are alike in examination and inquiry, for it is written, *Ye shall have one manner of law.* In what do non-capital cases differ from capital

The Mishnah, ed. and trans. H. Danby (London: Oxford University Press, 1933), pp. 262, 311, 386–388, 392–395, 399–400, 459–461.

cases? Non-capital cases [are decided] by three and capital cases by three and twenty [judges]. Non-capital cases may begin either with reasons for acquittal or for conviction, but capital cases must begin with reasons for acquittal and may not begin with reasons for conviction. In non-capital cases they may reach a verdict either of acquittal or of conviction by the decision of a majority of one; but in capital cases they may reach a verdict of acquittal by the decision of a majority of one, but a verdict of conviction only by the decision of a majority of two. In non-capital cases they may reverse a verdict either [from conviction] to acquittal or [from acquittal] to conviction; but in capital cases they may reverse a verdict [from conviction] to acquittal but not [from acquittal] to conviction. In non-capital cases all may argue either in favour of conviction or of acquittal; but in capital cases all may argue in favour of acquittal but not in favour of conviction. In non-capital cases he that had argued in favour of conviction may afterward argue in favour of acquittal, or he that had argued in favour of acquittal may afterward argue in favour of conviction; in capital cases he that had argued in favour of conviction may afterward argue in favour of acquittal, but he that had argued in favour of acquittal cannot afterward change and argue in favour of conviction. In non-capital cases they hold the trial during the daytime and the verdict may be reached during the night; in capital cases they hold the trial during the daytime and the verdict also must be reached during the daytime. In non-capital cases the verdict, whether of acquittal or of conviction, may be reached the same day; in capital cases a verdict of acquittal may be reached on the same day, but a verdict of conviction not until the following day. Therefore trials may not be held on the eve of a Sabbath or on the eve of a Festival-day. . . .

How did they admonish the witnesses in capital cases? They brought them in and admonished them, [saying,] 'Perchance ye will say what is but supposition or hearsay or at secondhand, or [ye may say in yourselves], We heard it from a man that was trustworthy. Or perchance ye do not know that we shall prove you by examination and inquiry? Know ye, moreover, that capital cases are not as non-capital cases: in non-capital cases a man may pay money and so make atonement, but in capital cases the witness is answerable for the blood of him [that is wrongfully condemned] and the blood of his posterity [that should have been born to him] to the end of the world. For so have we found it with Cain that slew his brother, for it is written, *The bloods of thy brother cry.* It says not 'The blood of thy brother', but *The bloods of thy brother*—his blood and the blood of his posterity. (Another saying is: *Bloods of thy brother*—because his blood was cast over the trees and stones.) Therefore but a single man was created in the world, to teach that if any man has caused a single soul to perish from Israel Scripture imputes it to him as though he had caused a whole world to perish; and if any man saves alive a single soul from Israel Scripture imputes it to him as though he had saved alive a whole world. Again [but a single man was created] for the sake of peace among mankind, that none should say to his fellow, 'My father was greater than thy father'; also that the heretics should not say, 'There are many ruling powers in heaven'. Again [but a single man was created] to proclaim the greatness of the Holy One, blessed is he; for man stamps many coins with the one seal and they are all like one another; but the King of kings, the Holy One, blessed is he, has stamped every man with the seal of the first man, yet not one of them is like his fellow. Therefore every one must say, For my sake was the world created. And if perchance ye would say, Why should we be at these pains?—was it not once written, *He being a witness, whether he hath seen or known, [if he do not utter it, then shall he bear his iniquity]*? And if perchance ye would say, Why should we be guilty of the blood of this man?—was it not once written, *When the wicked perish there is rejoicing?* . . .

'The blasphemer' is not culpable unless he pronounces the Name itself. R. Joshua b. Karha says: On every day [of the trial] they examined the witnesses with a substituted name, [such as] 'May Jose smite Jose'. When sentence was to be given they did not declare him guilty of death [on the grounds of evidence given] with the substituted name, but they sent out all the people and asked the chief among the witnesses and said to him, 'Say expressly what thou heardest', and he says it; and the judges stand up on their feet and rend their garments, and they may not mend them again. And the second witness says, 'I also heard the like', and the third says, 'I also heard the like'.

'The idolator' [is culpable] no matter whether he worships or sacrifices or burns incense or pours out a libation or bows himself down to it or accepts it as his god or says to it, Thou art my god. But he that puts his arms around it or kisses it or sweeps it or besprinkles it or washes it or anoints it or clothes it or shoes it transgresses [only] a negative command. He that makes a vow in its name or takes an oath in its name transgresses a negative command. But if a man excretes to Baal Peor [he is to be stoned, because] this is how it is worshipped. He that throws a stone at a *Merkolis* [is to be stoned, because] this is how it is worshipped. . . .

'He that profanes the Sabbath' [is liable, after warning, to death by stoning] if he committed an act which renders him liable to Extirpation if he acted wantonly, or to a Sin-offering if he acted in error. 'He that curses his father or his mother' is not culpable unless he curses them with the Name. If he cursed them with a substituted name R. Meir declares him culpable but the Sages declare him not culpable.

'He that has connection with a girl that is betrothed' is not culpable unless she is still in her girlhood, and a virgin, and betrothed, and still in her father's house. If two had connection with her the first is [liable to death] by stoning, but the second [only] by strangling.

'He that beguiles [others to idolatry]'—such is a common man that beguiles another common man. If he said to another, 'There is a god in such a place that eats this, drinks that, does good in this way and does harm in that way'—they may not place witnesses in hiding against any that become liable to the death-penalties enjoined in the Law save in this case alone. If he spoke [after this fashion] to two, and they are such that can bear witness against him, they bring him to the court and stone him. If he spoke so to one only he may reply, 'I have companions that are so minded'; and if the other was crafty and would not speak before them, witnesses may be placed in hiding behind a wall. Then he says to the other, 'Say [again] what thou didst say to me in private', and the other speaks to him [as before] and he replies, 'How shall we leave our God that is in Heaven and go and worship wood and stone?' If he retracted it shall be well with him, but if he said, 'It is our duty and it is seemly so to do', they that are behind the wall bring him to the court and stone him. If a man said, 'I will worship [another god]' or 'I will go and worship it' or 'Let us go and worship it', or

I will sacrifice to it' or 'I will go and sacrifice to it' or 'Let us go and sacrifice to it', or I will burn incense to it' or 'I will go and burn incense to it' or 'Let us go and burn ncense to it', or 'I will make a libation to it' or 'I will go and make a libation to it' or Let us go and make a libation to it', or 'I will bow myself down before it' or 'I will go and bow myself down before it' or 'Let us go and bow ourselves down before it', such a one is culpable]. 'He that leads [a whole town] astray' is he that says, 'Let us go and worship idols'.

'The sorcerer'—he that performs some act is culpable, and not he that [only] de-eives the eyes. R. Akiba in the name of R. Joshua says: If two were gathering cucum-ers [by sorcery] one gatherer may not be culpable and the other gatherer may be ulpable: he that [indeed] performed the act is culpable, but he that [only] deceived he eyes is not culpable.

'A stubborn and rebellious son'—when can he be condemned as a stubborn and ebellious son? From the time that he can produce two hairs until he grows a beard the lower one and not the upper one [is meant]; howbeit the Sages spoke in modest anguage), for it is written, *If a man have a son;*—a son and not a daughter, a son and not a man; a minor is exempt since he has not yet come within the scope of the com-nandments.

When is he culpable? After he has eaten a *tritimor* of flesh and drunk a half-*log* f Italian wine. R. Jose says: A *mina* of flesh and a *log* of wine. If he consumed it at gathering that was a religious duty, or at the intercalation of the month, or if he onsumed it as Second Tithe in Jerusalem, or if he ate carrion or flesh that was *terefah* r forbidden beasts or creeping things, if by consuming it he had fulfilled a command r had committed a transgression, if he ate any foodstuff but did not eat flesh, or drank ny liquid but did not drink wine, he cannot be condemned as a stubborn and rebel-ious son; but only if he eats flesh and drinks wine, for it is written, *A glutton and a runkard.* And though there is no proof for this, there is an indication, for it is written, *e not among winebibbers; among gluttonous eaters of flesh.*

If he stole it from his father and ate it in his father's domain, or from others and te it in the others' domain, or from others and ate it in his father's domain, he cannot e condemned as a stubborn and rebellious son; but only if he steals from his father nd eats it in the others' domain. R. Jose the son of R. Judah says: Only if he steals rom his father and from his mother.

If his father was willing [to accuse him] but his mother was not willing, or if his ather was not willing but his mother was willing, he cannot be condemned as a stub-orn and rebellious son; but only if they both were willing. R. Judah says: If his nother was not fit for his father he cannot be condemned as a stubborn and rebellious on. If either of them was maimed in the hand, or lame or dumb or blind or deaf, he nnot be condemned as a stubborn and rebellious son, for it is written, *Then shall is father and his mother lay hold on him*—so they were not maimed in the hand; *nd bring him out*—so they were not lame; *and they shall say*—so they were not umb; *this our son*—so they were not blind; *he will not obey our voice*—so they were ot deaf. They must warn him, and scourge him before three [judges]. If he again ehaved evilly he must be tried before three and twenty [judges]; and he may only stoned if the first three are there, for it is written, *This our son,* to wit, this is he that was beaten before you. If he ran away before sentence was passed on him and afterward grew the lower beard, he is exempt; but if he ran away after sentence was passed on him and afterward grew the lower beard, he is still liable.

A stubborn and rebellious son is condemned because of [what he may become in] the end: the Law has said, Let him die innocent and let him not die guilty; for the death of the ungodly is a benefit to them and a benefit to the world, but the death of the righteous is a misfortune to them and a misfortune to the world. The wine and sleep of the ungodly are a benefit to them and a benefit to the world, but the wine and sleep of the righteous are a misfortune to them and a misfortune to the world. The dispersion of the ungodly is a benefit to them and a benefit to the world, but the dispersion of the righteous is a misfortune to them and a misfortune to the world. The gathering together of the ungodly is a misfortune to them and a misfortune to the world, but the gathering together of the righteous is a benefit to them and a benefit to the world. Peacefulness for the ungodly is a misfortune to them and a misfortune to the world, but peacefulness for the righteous is a benefit to them and a benefit to the world.

The thief that is found breaking through is condemned because of [what he may do in] the end. If in his breaking through he broke a jar and there would be bloodguiltiness [if the householder killed him], he is liable [to make restitution]; if there would be no bloodguiltiness he is exempt.

These may be delivered [from transgression] at the cost of their lives: he that pursues after his fellow to kill him, or after a male, or after a girl that is betrothed; but he that pursue after a beast, or that profanes the Sabbath, or that commits idolatry—they may not be delivered [from transgression] at the cost of their lives. . . .

'The elder that rebels against the decision of the court'—as it is written, *If there arise a matter too hard for thee in judgement, between blood and blood, between plea and plea* . . . Three courts were there [in Jerusalem]: one used to sit at the gate of the Temple Mount, one used to sit at the gate of the Temple Court, and one used to sit in the Chamber of Hewn Stone. They used to come first to the court that was at the gate of the Temple Mount, and the one would say, 'In this way have I expounded and in that way have my fellows expounded; in this way have I taught and in that way have my fellows taught.' If they [of that court] had heard a tradition, they told it to them; otherwise they betook themselves to them of the court that was at the gate of the Temple Court, and the one would say, 'In this way have I expounded and in that way have my fellows expounded; in this way have I taught and in that way have my fellows taught'. If they [of that court] had heard a tradition, they told it to them; otherwise they both came in to the Great Court that was in the Chamber of Hewn Stone, whence the Law goes forth to all Israel, as it is written, *From that place which the Lord shall choose.* If [any one of the elders that went up to Jerusalem to inquire] returned to his own city and again taught as he was wont to teach, he is not yet culpable; but if he gave a decision concerning what should be done, he is culpable, for it is written, *And the man that doeth presumptuously* . . . ; he is not culpable unless he gives a decision concerning what should be done. If a disciple gave a decision concerning what should be done he is not culpable, thus the greater stringency that applies to him on the one hand is seen to serve as leniency on the other.

Greater stringency applies to [the observance of] the words of the Scribes than to [the observance of] the words of the [written] Law. If a man said, 'There is no obligation to wear phylacteries' so that he transgresses the words of the Law, he is not culpable; [but if he said], 'There should be in them five partitions', so that he adds to the words of the Scribes, he is culpable. . . .

Rabbi Meir said: He that occupies himself in the study of the Law for its own sake merits many things, and, still more, he is deserving of the whole world. He is called friend, beloved [of God], lover of God, lover of mankind; and it clothes him with humility and reverence and fits him to become righteous, saintly, upright, and faithful; and it keeps him far from sin and brings him near to virtue, and from him men enjoy counsel and sound knowledge, understanding and might, for it is written, *Counsel is mine and sound knowledge, I am understanding, I have might.* And it gives him kingship and dominion and discernment in judgement; to him are revealed the secrets of the Law, and he is made like to a never-failing spring and like to a river that flows ever more mightily; and he becomes modest, longsuffering, and forgiving of insult; and it magnifies him and exalts him above all things. . . .

Greater is [learning in] the Law than priesthood or kingship; for kingship is acquired by thirty excellences and the priesthood by twenty-four; but [learning in] the Law by forty-eight. And these are they: by study, by the hearing of the ear, by the ordering of the lips, by the understanding of the heart, by the discernment of the heart, by awe, by reverence, by humility, by cheerfulness; by attendance on the Sages, by consorting with fellow-students, by close argument with disciples; by assiduity, by [knowledge of] Scripture and Mishnah; by moderation in business, worldly occupation, pleasure, sleep, conversation, and jesting; by longsuffering, by a good heart, by faith in the Sages, by submission to sorrows; [by being] one that recognizes his place and that rejoices in his lot and that makes a fence around his words and that claims no merit for himself; [by being one that is] beloved, that loves God, that loves mankind, that loves well-doing, that loves rectitude, that loves reproof, that shuns honour and boasts not of his learning, and delights not in making decisions; that helps his fellow to bear his yoke, and that judges him favourably, and that establishes him in the truth and establishes him in peace; and that occupies himself assiduously in his study; [by being one] that asks and makes answer, that hearkens and adds thereto; that learns in order to teach and that learns in order to practice; that makes his teacher wiser, that retells exactly what he has heard and reports a thing in the name of him that said it. So, thou hast learnt that he that tells a thing in the name of him that said it brings deliverance unto the world, for it is written, *And Esther told the king thereof in Mordecai's name.*

Great is the Law, for it gives life to them that practice it both in this world and in the world to come, as it is written, *For they are life unto those that find them, and health to all their flesh;* and it says, *It shall be health to thy navel and marrow to thy bones;* and it says, *She is a tree of life to them that lay hold upon her, and happy is everyone that retaineth her;* and it says, *For they shall be a chaplet of grace unto thine head, and chains about thy neck;* and it says, *She shall give to thine head a chaplet of grace, a crown of glory shall she deliver to thee;* and it says, *For by me thy days shall be multiplied and the years of thy life shall be increased;* and it says, *Length of days is in her right hand; in her left hand are riches and honour;* and it says, *For length of days, and years of life, and peace, shall they add to thee. . . .*

R. Jose b. Kisma said: I was once walking by the way and a man met me and greeted me and I returned his greeting. He said to me, 'Rabbi, from what place are thou?' I answered, 'I come from a great city of Sages and scribes'. He said to me, 'If thou wilt dwell with us in our place I will give thee a thousand golden *denars* and precious stones and pearls'. I answered, 'If thou gavest me all the silver and gold and precious stones and pearls in the world I would not dwell save in a place of the Law'. And thus it is written in the Book of Psalms by David, king of Israel, *The Law of thy mouth is better unto me than thousands of gold and silver.* Moreover at the time of a man's departure, neither silver nor gold nor precious stones nor pearls go with him, but only [his knowledge of] the Law and good works; for it is written, *When thou walkest, it shall lead thee; when thou sleepest, it shall watch over thee; and when thou awakest it shall talk with thee. When thou walkest it shall lead thee*—in this world; *when thou sleepest, it shall watch over thee*—in the grave; *and when thou awakest, it shall talk with thee*—in the world to come. And it says, *The silver is mine, and the gold is mine, saith the Lord of hosts.*

THE GOSPEL ACCORDING TO LUKE

The career of Jesus of Nazareth has been presented to us in four early accounts, known as the Gospels ("good news"). Written from slightly differing points of view and addressed to different audiences, these works introduce us to a remarkable spiritual leader as well as to the cultural environment in which he appeared and worked. The Gospel of Mark is distinguished by its clarity and conciseness, as well as by its relatively early date; Matthew, by its rhetoric and its classic presentations of the important events of Jesus' life. These two accounts were apparently designed for a predominantly Hebraic audience; Matthew especially is filled with references to the fulfilment of Old Testament prophecies. Luke's account, apparently primarily directed at a Greek audience, contains all the influential ideas of Jesus and is an example of great narrative and organizational skill; Luke has been called one of the great historians of the ancient world. Luke vividly presents Jesus' role in the religious ferment of his day; the Sadducees and Pharisees are shown clearly as the enemies of the movement represented by John the Baptist and Jesus, a movement obviously growing out of the same soil as that of the Essenes described by Josephus (see pages 321–324). As is tru of Paul's teachings (see the Epistle to the Romans, pages 357–364), th teachings of Jesus are properly understood only in terms of the sectarian tensions within Judaism.

It must, of course, be remembered that, like Plato's Socratic dialogues, this account is entirely the work of a friendly witness. With all due allowance for that fact, there is no reason not to accept it in the main as an accurate portrayal of Jesus and his doctrines. Remember that Judea was a province in the great Roman Empire, then at about its acme. Herod, the king of Judea, was a Jew; Pilate, a Roman agent. We do not know who the Theophilus was to whom Luke addressed the book.

Many writers have undertaken to compose accounts of the movement which has developed among us, just as the original eye-witnesses who became teachers of the message have handed it down to us. For that reason, Theophilus, and because I have investigated it all carefully from the beginning, I have determined to write a connected account of it for Your Excellency, so that you may be reliably informed about the things you have been taught.

In the days when Herod was king of Judea, there was a priest named Zechariah who belonged to the division of Abijah. His wife was also a descendant of Aaron, and her name was Elizabeth. They were both upright in the sight of God, blamelessly observing all the Lord's commands and requirements. They had no children, for Elizabeth was barren; and they were both advanced in life.

Once when he was acting as priest before God, when his division was on duty, it fell to his lot, according to the priests' practice, to go into the sanctuary of the Lord and burn the incense, while all the throng of people was outside, praying at the hour of the incense offering. And an angel of the Lord appeared to him, standing at the right of the altar of incense. When Zechariah saw him he was startled and overcome with fear. And the angel said to him,

"Do not be afraid, Zechariah, for your prayer has been heard. Your wife Elizabeth will bear you a son, and you are to name him John. This will bring gladness and delight to you, and many will rejoice over his birth. For he will be great in the sight of the Lord. He will drink no wine or strong drink, but he will be filled with the holy Spirit from his very birth, and he will turn many of Israel's descendants to the Lord their God. He will go before him with the spirit and the power of Elijah, to reconcile fathers to their children, and to bring the disobedient back to the wisdom of upright men, to make a people perfectly ready for the Lord.". . .

Soon afterward his wife Elizabeth began to expect a child, and she kept herself in seclusion for five months.

The Complete Bible: An American Translation (Chicago: The University of Chicago Press, 1948); The New Testament, trans. E. J. Goodspeed, pp. 92–101, 103–109, 113–115, 118–119, 121–130, 133, 139–149.

"This is what the Lord has done for me," she said, "now that he has deigned to remove the disgrace I have endured."

In the sixth month the angel Gabriel was sent by God to a town in Galilee called Nazareth, to a maiden there who was engaged to be married to a man named Joseph, a descendant of David. The maiden's name was Mary. And the angel went into the town and said to her,

"Good morning, favored woman! The Lord be with you!"

But she was startled at what he said, and wondered what this greeting meant. And the angel said to her,

"Do not be afraid, Mary, for you have gained God's approval. You are to become a mother and you will give birth to a son, and you are to name him Jesus. He will be great and will be called the Son of the Most High. The Lord God will give him the throne of his forefather David, and he will reign over Jacob's house forever; his reign will have no end."

Mary said to the angel,

"How can this be, when I have no husband?"

The angel answered,

"The holy Spirit will come over you, and the power of the Most High will overshadow you. For that reason your child will be called holy, and the Son of God. And your relative, Elizabeth, although she is old, is going to give birth to a son, and this is the sixth month with her who was said to be barren. For nothing is ever impossible for God.

And Mary said,

"I am the Lord's slave. Let it be as you say."

Then the angel left her.

In those days Mary set out and hurried to the hill-country, to a town in Judah, and she went to Zechariah's house and greeted Elizabeth. When Elizabeth heard Mary's greeting, the babe stirred within her. And Elizabeth was filled with the holy Spirit and she gave a great cry, and said,

"You are the most favored of women,
And blessed is your child!
Who am I,
To have the mother of my Lord come to me?

"For the moment your greeting reached my ears,
The child stirred with joy within me!
Blessed is she who has believed,
For what the Lord has promised her will be fulfilled!"

And Mary said,

"My heart extols the Lord,
My spirit exults in God my Savior.
For he has noticed his slave in her humble station,
For from this time all the ages will think me favored!

"For the Almighty has done wonders for me,
How holy his name is!

He shows his mercy age after age
To those who fear him.

"He has done mighty deeds with his arm,
He has routed the proud-minded,
He has dethroned monarchs and exalted the poor,
He has satisfied the hungry with good things, and sent the rich away empty-handed.

"He has helped his servant Israel,
Remembering his mercy,
As he promised our forefathers
To have mercy on Abraham and his descendants forever!"

So Mary stayed with her about three months, and then returned home.

Now the time came for Elizabeth's child to be born, and she gave birth to a son. Ier neighbors and relatives heard of the great mercy the Lord had shown her, and ıey came and congratulated her. On the eighth day they came to circumcise the ıild, and they were going to name him Zechariah, after his father. But his mother ıid,

"No! He is to be named John."

They said to her,

"There is no one among your relatives who bears that name."

But they made signs to the child's father and asked him what he wished to have the ıild named. He asked for a writing tablet, and wrote,

"His name is John."

And they were all amazed. Then his voice and the use of his tongue were immediely restored, and he blessed God aloud. And all their neighbors were overcome with ːar, and all over the hill-country of Judea all these stories were told, and everyone ho heard them kept them in mind, and said,

"What is this child going to be?" For the Lord's hand was with him.

And his father Zechariah was filled with the holy Spirit and he uttered a divine essage, saying,

"Blessings on the Lord, the God of Israel,
Because he has turned his attention to his people, and brought about their deliverance,
And he has produced a mighty Savior for us
In the house of his servant David. . . .

"And you, my child, will be called a prophet of the Most High,
For you will go before the Lord to make his way ready,
Bringing his people the knowledge of salvation
Through the forgiveness of their sins.

"Because the heart of our God is merciful,
And so the day will dawn upon us from on high,
To shine on men who sit in darkness and the shadow of death,
And guide our feet into the way of peace."

And the child grew up and became strong in the Spirit, and he lived in the deser until the day when he proclaimed himself to Israel.

In those days an edict was issued by the Emperor Augustus that a census of th whole world should be taken. It was the first census, taken when Quirinius was gov ernor of Syria. So everyone went to his own town to register. And Joseph went u from Galilee from the town of Nazareth to Judea to the city of David called Bethle hem, because he belonged to the house and family of David, to register with Mary who was engaged to him and who was soon to become a mother. While they wer there, the time came for her child to be born, and she gave birth to her first-bor son; and she wrapped him up, and laid him in a manger, for there was no room fo them at the inn.

There were some shepherds in that neighborhood keeping watch through the nigh over their flock in the open fields. And an angel of the Lord stood by them, and th glory of the Lord shone around them, and they were terribly frightened. The ange said to them,

"Do not be frightened, for I bring you good news of a great joy that is to be fe by all the people, for today, in the town of David, a Savior for you has been bor who is your Messiah and Lord. And this will prove it to you: You will find a bab wrapped up and lying in a manger."

Suddenly there appeared with the angel a throng of the heavenly army, praisin God, saying,

"Glory to God in heaven and on earth!
Peace to the men he favors!"

When the angels left them and returned to heaven, the shepherds said to one an other,

"Come! Let us go over to Bethlehem, and see this thing that has happened, that th Lord has told us of!"

And they hurried there, and found Mary and Joseph, with the baby lying in th manger. When they saw this, they told what had been said to them about this chil And all who heard it were amazed at what the shepherds told them, but Mary trea ured up all they had said, and pondered over it. And the shepherds went back glor fying God and praising him for all that they had heard and seen in fulfilment what they had been told.

When he was eight days old and it was time to circumcise him, he was name Jesus, as the angel had named him, before his birth was first expected.

When their purification period under the Law of Moses was over, they took hi up to Jerusalem to present him to the Lord, in fulfilment of the requirement of th Law of the Lord, "Every first-born male shall be considered consecrated to the Lord and to offer the sacrifice prescribed in the Law of the Lord, "A pair of turtle-doves two young pigeons."

Now there was a man in Jerusalem named Symeon, an upright, devout man, wh was living in expectation of the comforting of Israel, and under the influence of th holy Spirit. It had been revealed to him by the holy Spirit that he should not die wit out seeing the Lord's Messiah. And under the Spirit's influence he went into t

Temple, and when Jesus' parents brought him there to do for him what the Law equired, Symeon also took him in his arms and blessed God, and said,

"Now, Master, you will let your slave go free
In peace, as you promised,
For my eyes have seen your salvation
Which you have set before all the nations,
A light of revelation for the heathen,
And a glory to your people Israel!"

The child's father and mother were astonished at what Symeon said. And he gave hem his blessing, and said to Mary, the child's mother,

"This child is destined to cause the fall and rise of many in Israel, and to be a ›ortent that will be much debated—you yourself will be pierced to the heart—and so he thoughts of many minds will be revealed.". . .

When they had done everything that the Law of the Lord required, they returned o Galilee, to their own town of Nazareth.

And the child grew up and became strong and thoughtful, with God's blessing esting on him. . . .

In the fifteenth year of the reign of the Emperor Tiberius, when Pontius Pilate was governor of Judea, and Herod governor of Galilee, while his brother Philip was gov-ernor of the territory of Iturea and Trachonitis, and Lysanias was governor of Abilene, n the high priesthood of Annas and Caiaphas, a message from God came to Zech-ariah's son John in the desert. And he went all through the Jordan Valley preaching epentance and baptism in order to obtain the forgiveness of sins, as the book of the ermons of the prophet Isaiah says,

"Hark! Someone is shouting in the desert,
Get the Lord's way ready!
Make his paths straight.
Every hollow must be filled up,
And every mountain and hill leveled.
What is crooked is to be made straight,
And the rough roads are to be made smooth,
And all mankind is to see how God can save!"

So he would say to the crowds that came out there to be baptized by him,

"You brood of snakes! Who warned you to fly from the wrath that is coming? Then produce fruit that will be consistent with your professed repentance! And do not begin to say to yourselves, 'We have Abraham for our forefather,' for I tell you, God can produce descendants for Abraham right out of these stones! But the axe is already ying at the roots of the trees. Any tree that fails to produce good fruit is going to be cut down and thrown into the fire."

The crowds would ask him,

"Then what ought we to do?"

And he answered,

"The man who has two shirts must share with the man who has none, and the man who has food must do the same."

Even tax-collectors came to be baptized, and they said to him,

"Master, what ought we to do?"

He said to them,

"Do not collect any more than you are authorized to."

And soldiers would ask him,

"And what ought we to do?"

He said to them,

"Do not extort money or make false charges against people, but be satisfied with your pay."

As all this aroused people's expectations, and they were all wondering in thei hearts whether John was the Christ, John said to them all,

"I am only baptizing you in water, but someone is coming who is stronger than am, whose shoes I am not fit to untie. He will baptize you in the holy Spirit and in fire. He has his winnowing fork in his hand, to clean up his threshing-floor, and store his wheat in his barn, but he will burn up the chaff with inextinguishable fire."

So with many varied exhortations he would preach the good news to the people but Herod the governor, whom he condemned because of Herodias, his brother' wife, and all the wicked things Herod had done, crowned them all by putting John in prison.

Now when all the people were baptized and when Jesus also after his baptism was praying, heaven opened and the holy Spirit came down upon him in the material shape of a dove, and there came a voice from heaven,

"You are my Son, my Beloved! You are my Chosen!"

Jesus himself was about thirty years old when he began his work. . . .

Jesus returned from the Jordan full of the holy Spirit, and he was led about in the desert for forty days by the Spirit, and was tempted by the devil. In all those days he ate nothing, and when they were over he was famished. And the devil said to him,

"If you are God's son, tell this stone to turn into bread!"

Jesus answered,

"The Scripture says, 'Not on bread alone is man to live!' "

And he took him up and showed him in an instant all the kingdoms of the world And the devil said to him,

"I will give you all this power and their splendor, for it has been turned over to me, and I can give it to anyone I please. If you will do homage before me, it shall all be yours."

Jesus answered,

"The Scripture says, 'You must do homage before the Lord your God, and worship him alone.' "

And he took him to Jerusalem, and made him stand on the summit of the Temple and said to him,

"If you are God's son, throw yourself down from here, for the Scripture says, 'H will give his angels orders about you, to protect you,' and, 'They will lift you up with their hands, so that you may never strike your foot against a stone.' "

Jesus answered,

"We have been told, 'You shall not try the Lord your God.' "

When the devil had tried every kind of temptation he left him till another time.

Under the power of the Spirit Jesus returned to Galilee, and news of him went all over that region. And he taught in their synagogues, and was honored by them all. . . .

Once as the crowd was pressing about him to hear God's message, he happened to be standing by the Lake of Gennesaret, and he saw two boats on the shore of the lake, for the fishermen had gotten out of them and were washing their nets. And he got into one of the boats, which belonged to Simon, and asked him to push out a little from the shore. Then he sat down and taught the crowds of people from the boat. When he stopped speaking, he said to Simon,

"Push out into deep water, and then put down your nets for a haul."

Simon answered,

"Master, we worked all night and caught nothing, but as you tell me to do it, I will put down the nets."

So they did so, and inclosed such a shoal of fish that their nets began to break. And they signaled to their comrades in the other boat to come and help them. And they came, and they filled both boats so full that they began to sink. When Simon Peter saw it, he fell down at Jesus' feet and said,

"Leave me, Master, for I am a sinful man."

For he and all the men with him were perfectly amazed at the haul of fish they had made, and so were Zebedee's sons, James and John, who were Simon's partners. Jesus said to Simon,

"Do not be afraid. From now on you are to catch men!"

And they brought the boats to land and left everything and followed him. . . .

Yet the news about him spread more and more, and great crowds gathered to hear him and to be cured of their diseases. But Jesus himself would retire into the desert and pray.

One day as he was teaching, there were some Pharisees and experts in the Law sitting near by, who had come from every village in Galilee and Judea and from Jerusalem. The power of the Lord was there, so that he might cure people. Some men came up carrying on a bed a man who was paralyzed, and they tried to get him in and lay him before Jesus. And as they could find no way to get him in, on account of the crowd, they went upon the roof and let him down with his mat through the tiles, among the people in front of Jesus. When he saw their faith, he said,

"Friend, your sins are forgiven!"

And the scribes and the Pharisees began to debate and say,

"Who is this man who talks blasphemy? Who can forgive sins but God alone?"

But Jesus saw what they were discussing, and said to them,

"What are you pondering over in your minds? Which is easier, to say, 'Your sins are forgiven,' or to say, 'Get up and walk'? But to let you know that the Son of Man has authority to forgive sins on earth"—turning to the man who was paralyzed he said to him—"I tell you, get up, pick up your mat, and go home!"

And he got up at once before them all, and picked up what he had been lying on, and went home, praising God. They were all seized with astonishment, and praised God, and filled with awe they said,

"We have seen something wonderful today!"

After this he went out, and he saw a tax-collector named Levi sitting at the toll-house, and he said to him,

"Follow me!"

And he left everything and got up and followed him. Then Levi gave a great entertainment for him in his house, and there was a great throng of tax-collectors and others who were at table with them. And the Pharisees and their scribes grumbled about it to his disciples, and said,

"Why do you eat and drink with tax-collectors and irreligious people?"

Jesus answered them,

"It is not well people but the sick who have to have the doctor. I have not come to invite the pious but the irreligious to repentance!"

They said to him,

"John's disciples observe frequent fasts and offer prayers, and so do the disciples of the Pharisees, but your disciples eat and drink."

Jesus said to them,

"Can you make wedding guests fast while the bridegroom is with them? But other days will come, and when the bridegroom is taken away from them, in those days they will fast."

He used this figure also in speaking to them:

"No one tears a piece from a new coat and sews it on an old one, or if he does, he will both tear the new one and the piece from the new one will not match the old one. And nobody puts new wine into old wine-skins, or if he does, the new wine will burst the skins and run out, and the skins will be spoiled. New wine has to be put into fresh skins. No one after drinking old wine wants new, for he says, 'The old is better!' "

One Sabbath he happened to be passing through the wheat fields, and his disciples were picking the heads of wheat, and eating them, rubbing them in their hands. And some of the Pharisees said,

"Why do you do what it is against the Law to do on the Sabbath?"

Jesus answered,

"Have you not read even what David did, when he and his companions were hungry? How he went into the house of God and took the Presentation Loaves, which it was against the Law for anyone but the priests to eat, and ate them with his companions?" And he said to them, "The Son of Man is master of the Sabbath."

On another Sabbath he happened to go to the synagogue and teach. There was a man there whose right hand was withered. And the scribes and the Pharisees were on the watch to see whether he would cure people on the Sabbath, in order to find a charge to bring against him. But he knew what they were thinking, and he said to the man with the withered hand,

"Get up and stand in front."

And he got up and stood there. Jesus said to them,

"I want to ask you, Is it allowable on the Sabbath to do people good or to do them harm? to save life or to destroy it?"

And he looked around at them all and said to the man,

"Hold out your hand!"

And he did so, and his hand was restored.

But they were perfectly furious, and discussed with one another what they could do to Jesus.

It was in those days that he went up on the mountain to pray, and passed the whole night in prayer to God. When day came, he called his disciples to him, and chose twelve of them whom he named apostles: Simon, whom he named Peter, his brother Andrew, James, John, Philip, Bartholomew, Matthew, Thomas, James, the son of Alpheus, Simon, who was called the Zealot, Judas, the son of James, and Judas Iscariot, who turned out a traitor. And he came down with them and took his stand on a level place with a great throng of his disciples, and a large number of people from all over Judea and from Jerusalem and the seacoast district of Tyre and Sidon, who had come to hear him and to be cured of their diseases. And those who were troubled with foul spirits were cured. And all the people tried to touch him, because power went forth from him and cured them all. Then he fixed his eyes on his disciples, and said,

"Blessed are you who are poor, for the Kingdom of God is yours!

"Blessed are you who are hungry now, for you will be satisfied!

"Blessed are you who weep now, for you will laugh!

"Blessed are you when people hate you and exclude you and denounce you and spurn the name you bear as evil, on account of the Son of Man. Be glad when that happens, and leap for joy, for you will be richly rewarded in heaven, for that is the way their forefathers treated the prophets.

"But alas for you who are rich, for you have had your comfort!

"Alas for you who have plenty to eat now, for you will be hungry!

"Alas for you who laugh now, for you will mourn and weep!

"Alas for you when everyone speaks well of you, for that is the way their forefathers treated the false prophets!

"But I tell you who hear me, love your enemies, treat those who hate you well, bless those who curse you, pray for those who abuse you. To the man that strikes you on the cheek, offer the other also, and from the man who takes away your coat, do not keep back your shirt either. Give to everyone that asks of you, and if anyone takes away what is yours, do not demand it back. And treat men just as you wish them to treat you. If you love only those who love you, what merit is there in that? For even godless people love those who love them. And if you help only those who help you, what merit is there in that? Even godless people act in that way. And if you lend only to people from whom you expect to get something, what merit is there in that? Even godless people lend to godless people, meaning to get it back again in full. But love your enemies, and help them and lend to them, never despairing, and you will be richly rewarded, and you will be sons of the Most High, for he is kind even to the ungrateful and the wicked. You must be merciful, just as your Father is. Do not judge others, and they will not judge you. Do not condemn them, and they will not condemn you. Excuse others and they will excuse you. Give, and they will give to you;

good measure, pressed down, shaken together, and running over, they will pour into your lap. For the measure you use with others they in turn will use with you."

And he used a figure, saying,

"Can one blind man lead another? Will they not both fall into a hole? A pupil is not better than his teacher, but every pupil when he is fully trained will be like his teacher. Why do you keep looking at the speck in your brother's eye, and pay no attention to the beam that is in your own? How can you say to your brother, 'Brother, just let me get that speck out of your eye,' when you cannot see the beam in your own eye? You hypocrite! First get the beam out of your own eye, and then you can see to get out the speck in your brother's eye. For sound trees do not bear bad fruit, nor bad trees sound fruit. Every tree is known by its fruit. They do not pick figs off thorns, or gather grapes from brambles. A good man, out of the good he has accumulated in his heart, produces good, and a bad man, out of what he has accumulated that is bad, produces what is bad. For his mouth says only what his heart is full of. Why do you call me: 'Lord! Lord!' and not do what I tell you? If anyone comes to me and listens to this teaching of mine and acts upon it, I will show you whom he is like. He is like a man who was building a house, who dug deep and laid his foundation upon the rock, and when there was a flood the torrent burst upon that house and could not shake it, because it was well built. But the man who listens to it, and does not act upon it, is like a man who built a house on the ground without any foundation. The torrent burst upon it, and it collapsed at once, and the wreck of that house was complete.". . .

John's disciples told him of all this, and he called two of them to him, and sent them to the Master to ask him,

"Are you the one who was to come, or should we look for someone else?"

And the men went to him and said,

"John the Baptist sent us to you to ask, 'Are you the one who was to come, or should we look for someone else?' "

Just then he cured many of diseases and ailments and evil spirits, and he gave sight to many who were blind. And he answered them,

"Go and report to John what you have seen and heard. The blind are regaining their sight, the lame can walk, the lepers are being cured and the deaf can hear, the dead are being raised and good news is being preached to the poor. And blessed is the man who finds nothing that repels him in me."

When John's messengers were gone, he began to speak to the crowds about John.

"What was it that you went out into the desert to look at? A reed swaying in the wind? Then what did you go out there to see? A man luxuriously dressed? Men who wear fine clothes and live in luxury you find in palaces. Then what did you go out there to see? A prophet? Yes, I tell you, and far more than a prophet! This is the man of whom the Scripture says,

" 'Here I send my messenger on before you,

He will prepare the road ahead of you!'

"I tell you, among men born of women there is none greater than John; and yet those who are of little importance in the Kingdom of God are greater than he. And all the people, even the tax-collectors, when they heard him, acknowledged the justice of God's demands, by accepting baptism from John, but the Pharisees and experts in the Law thwarted God's purpose for themselves, by refusing to be baptized by him. So what is there to which I can compare the men of this age? What are they like? They are like children sitting about in the bazaar and calling out to one another,

" 'We have played the flute for you, and you would not dance!
We have wailed and you would not weep!'

"For when John the Baptist came, he did not eat any bread or drink any wine, and you said, 'He has a demon!' Now that the Son of Man has come, he does eat and drink, and you say, 'Look at him! A glutton and a drinker, the companion of tax-collectors and irreligious people!' So wisdom is vindicated by all who are really wise.". . .

Then he called the Twelve together, and gave them power and authority over all the demons, and to cure diseases, and he sent them out to proclaim the Kingdom of God and to cure the sick. He said to them,

"Do not take anything for your journey, no staff nor bag nor bread nor money, nor an extra shirt. Whatever house you go to stay in, remain there, and start on again from it. And where they will not welcome you, leave that town and shake off the very dust from your feet as a protest against them."

And they set forth and went from village to village, telling the good news and curing people everywhere.

Herod the governor heard of all that was happening, and he was perplexed because some people said that John had risen from the dead, and some that Elijah had appeared, and others that one of the ancient prophets had come back to life. But Herod said,

"John I have beheaded, but who can this be about whom I hear such reports?"

And he endeavored to see him. . . .

Once when he was praying by himself, with only the disciples near him, he asked them,

"Who do the people say that I am?"

They answered,

"John the Baptist, though others say, Elijah, and others that one of the old prophets has come back to life."

And he said to them,

"But who do you say that I am?"

Peter answered,

"The Christ [i.e. Messiah, or Anointed One] of God!"

But he warned them particularly not to tell this to anyone, and said,

"The Son of Man must endure great suffering and be refused by the elders, the high priests, and the scribes, and be killed, and be raised to life on the third day."

And he said to everyone,

"If anyone wants to go with me, he must disregard himself, and take his cross day after day and follow me. For whoever wants to preserve his life will lose it, and whoever loses his life for me will preserve it. What good does it do a man to gain the whole world and lose or forfeit himself? For if anyone is ashamed of me and my teaching the Son of Man will be ashamed of him, when he comes with all the glory of his Father and of the holy angels. I tell you, some of you who stand here will certainly live to see the Kingdom of God!". . .

Then an expert in the Law got up to test him and said,

"Master, what must I do to make sure of eternal life?"

Jesus said to him,

"What does the Law say? How does it read?"

He answered,

" 'You must love the Lord your God with your whole heart, your whole soul, your whole strength, and your whole mind,' and 'your neighbor as you do yourself.' "

Jesus said to him,

"You are right. Do that, and you will live."

But he, wishing to justify his question, said,

"And who is my neighbor?"

Jesus replied,

"A man was on his way down from Jerusalem to Jericho, when he fell into the hands of robbers, and they stripped him and beat him and went off leaving him half dead. Now a priest happened to be going that way, and when he saw him, he went by on the other side of the road. And a Levite also came to the place, and when he saw him, he went by on the other side. But a Samaritan who was traveling that way came upon him, and when he saw him he pitied him, and he went up to him and dressed his wounds with oil and wine and bound them up. And he put him on his own mule and brought him to an inn and took care of him. The next day he took out a dollar and gave it to the innkeeper and said, 'Take care of him, and whatever more you spend I will refund to you on my way back.' Which of these three do you think proved himself a neighbor to the man who fell into the robbers' hands?"

He said,

"The man who took pity on him."

Jesus said to him,

"Go and do so yourself!". . .

Once as he was praying in a certain place, when he stopped, one of his disciples said to him,

"Master, teach us to pray, as John taught his disciples."

He said to them,

"When you pray, say, 'Father, your name be revered! Your kingdom come! Give us each day our bread for the day, and forgive us our sins, for we ourselves forgive anyone who wrongs us; and do not subject us to temptation.' ". . .

A Pharisee asked him to lunch with him, and he went to his house and took his place at table. The Pharisee noticed that he did not wash before the meal, and he was surprised. But the Master said to him,

"You Pharisees clean the outside of cups and dishes, but inside you are full of greed and wickedness. You fools! Did not the Creator of the outside make the inside too? But give your inmost life as charity, and you will immediately find everything clean. But alas for you Pharisees! For you pay tithes on mint, rue, and every tiny herb, and disregard justice and the love of God. But you should have observed these, without neglecting the others. Alas for you Pharisees! For you love to have the front seat in the synagogues and to be saluted with respect in public places. Alas for you! For you are like unmarked graves which men tread upon without knowing it."

At this, one of the experts in the Law said to him,

"Master, when you say that, you affront us too."

But he said,

"Yes, alas for you experts in the Law too! For you load men with burdens they can hardly carry, and you will not touch them yourselves with a single finger. Alas for you! For you build monuments for the prophets, whom your forefathers killed. So you testify to what your fathers did and approve it, for they killed them and you build their monuments. This is why the Wisdom of God said, 'I will send prophets and apostles to them, and some of them they will kill and some they will persecute'—so that this age may be charged with the blood of all the prophets that has been shed since the creation of the world, from the blood of Abel to the blood of Zechariah, who perished between the altar and the sanctuary. Yes, I tell you! This age will be charged with it all! Alas for you experts in the Law! For you have taken the key to the door of knowledge, but you have not entered it yourselves, and you have kept out those who tried to enter."

After he left the house, the scribes and the Pharisees began to watch him closely and to try to draw him out on many subjects, plotting to entrap him in something he might say. . . .

And he said to his disciples,

"Therefore, I tell you, do not worry about life, wondering what you will have to eat, or about your body, wondering what you will have to wear. Life is more important than food, and the body than clothes. Think of the crows! They do not sow or reap, and they have no storehouses or barns, and God feeds them. How much more you are worth than the birds! Which of you with all his worry can add a single hour to his life? So if you cannot do the least good, why should you worry about the rest? See how the lilies grow. They do not toil or spin, but, I tell you, even Solomon in all his splendor was never dressed like one of them. But if God so dresses the wild grass, which is alive today, and is thrown into the furnace tomorrow, how much more surely will he clothe you, who have so little faith? So you must not ask what you are to have to eat or drink, and you must not be anxious about it. For these are all things the nations of the world are in pursuit of, and your Father knows well that you need them. But you must strive to find his kingdom, and you will have these other things besides. Do not be afraid, little flock, for your Father has chosen to give you the kingdom. Sell what belongs to you, and give away the money! Get yourselves purses that will never wear out, inexhaustible riches in heaven, where thieves cannot get near nor moths destroy. For wherever your treasure is, your heart will be too. You must be ready with your lamps burning, like men waiting for their master to come home from a wedding, so that when he comes and knocks, they can open the door for him at once. Blessed are the slaves whom their master will find on the watch when he comes. I tell you, he will gird up his robe and make them take their places at table, and go around and wait on them. Whether he comes late at night or early in the morning and finds them on the watch, they are blessed. But you may be sure of this, that if the master of the house had known what time the thief was coming, he would have been on the watch, and would not have let his house be broken into. You must be ready too, for the Son of Man is coming at a time when you do not expect him."

Peter said to him,

"Master, do you mean this figure for us, or is it for everybody?"

And the Master said,

"Who then will be the faithful, thoughtful manager, whom his master will put in charge of his household, to give the members of it their supplies at the proper time? Blessed is that slave if his master when he returns finds him doing it. I tell you, he will put him in charge of all his property. But if the slave says to himself, 'My master is not coming back for a long time,' and begins to beat the men and women slaves and to eat and drink and get drunk, that slave's master will come back some day when he does not expect him, and at some time of which he does not know, and will cut him in two, and put him with the unbelievers. The slave who knows his master's wishes, but does not get ready or act upon them, will be severely punished. But one who does wrong without knowing them will be lightly punished. From anyone who has been given much, much will be required, and of the man to whom people have intrusted much, they will demand even more. I have come to bring fire down to the earth, and how I wish it were kindled already! I have a baptism to undergo, and how distressed I am till it is over! Do you think I have come to bring peace to the earth? Not peace, I tell you, but discord! For from now on if there are five people in a house they will be divided three against two and two against three. Father will be against son, and son against father, mother against daughter and daughter against mother, mother-in-law against her daughter-in-law and daughter-in-law against her mother-in-law.". . .

One Sabbath he was teaching in one of the synagogues, and there was a woman there who for eighteen years had had a sickness caused by a spirit. She was bent double and could not straighten herself up at all. When Jesus saw her he called to her,

"You are freed from your sickness!"

And he laid his hands on her, and she instantly became erect, and praised God. But the leader of the synagogue, in his vexation because Jesus had cured her on the Sabbath, spoke out and said to the crowd,

"There are six days on which it is right to work. Come on them and be cured, but not on the Sabbath day."

But the Master answered,

"You hypocrites! Does not every one of you untie his ox or his donkey from the stall on the Sabbath and lead him away to water him? And did not this woman, who is a descendant of Abraham, whom Satan has kept bound for eighteen years, have to be released from those bonds on the Sabbath day?"

When he said this, all his opponents were humiliated, and all the people were delighted at all the splendid things that he did.

He said, therefore,

"What is the Kingdom of God like, and to what can I compare it? It is like a mustard seed that a man took and dropped in his garden, and it grew and became a tree, and the wild birds roosted on its branches."

And he went on,

"To what can I compare the Kingdom of God? It is like yeast that a woman took and hid in a bushel of flour, till it all rose."

So he went about among the towns and villages, teaching and making his way toward Jerusalem. And someone said to him,

"Are only a few to be saved, Master?"

He said to them,

"You must strain every nerve to get in through the narrow door, for I tell you many will try to get in, and will not succeed, when the master of the house gets up and shuts the door, and you begin to stand outside and to knock on the door, and say, 'Open it for us, sir!' Then he will answer you and say, 'I do not know where you come from.' Then you will go on to say, 'We have been entertained with you, and you have taught in our streets!' And he will say to you, 'I do not know where you come from. Get away from me, all you wrongdoers!' There you will weep and gnash your teeth when you see Abraham and Isaac and Jacob and all the prophets in the Kingdom of God, while you are put outside. People will come from the east and west and the north and south, and take their places in the Kingdom of God. There are those now last who will then be first, and there are those now first who will be last.". . .

There were great crowds accompanying him, and once he turned and said to them,

"If anyone comes to me without hating his own father and mother and wife and children and brothers and sisters, and his very life too, he cannot be a disciple of mine. For no one who does not take up his own cross and come after me can be a disciple of mine. What man among you if he wishes to build a tower does not first sit down and estimate the cost of it, to see whether he has enough to complete it? Or else when he has laid his foundation and cannot finish the building, everyone who sees it will begin to ridicule him, and say, 'This man started to erect a building, and could not finish it!' Or what king, if he is going to meet another king in battle, does not sit down first and consider whether he is able with ten thousand men to meet the other who is coming against him with twenty thousand? And if he cannot, while the other is still far away, he sends envoys to him and asks on what terms he will make peace. In just that way, no one of you who does not say goodbye to all he has can be a disciple of mine. Salt is good; but if salt loses its strength, what can it be seasoned with? It is fit neither for the ground nor the manure heap; people throw it away. Let him who has ears to hear with, listen!". . .

And he said,

"A man had two sons. The younger of them said to his father, 'Father, give me my share of the property.' So he divided his property between them. Not many days later, the younger son gathered up all he had, and went away to a distant country, and there he squandered his property by fast living. After he had spent it all, a severe famine arose in that country, and he began to be in want. And he went and hired himself out to a resident of the country, and he sent him into his fields to tend pigs. And he was ready to fill himself with the pods the pigs were eating, and no one would give him anything. When he came to himself he said, 'How many hired men my father has, who have more than enough to eat, and here I am, dying of hunger! I will get up, and go to my father, and say to him, "Father, I have sinned against heaven and in your eyes; I no longer deserve to be called your son; treat me like one of your hired men!" ' And he got up and went to his father. But while he was still a long way off, his father saw him, and pitied him, and ran and fell on his neck, and kissed him. His son said to him, 'Father, I have sinned against heaven, and in your eyes; I no longer deserve to be called your son; treat me like one of your hired men!' But his father said to his slave, 'Make haste and get out the best robe, and put it on him, and put a ring on his hand, and shoes on his feet; and get the calf we are fattening, and kill it, and let us feast and celebrate, for my son here was dead, and he has come to life; he was lost, and he is found!' So they began to celebrate. But his elder son was in the field. When he came in and approached the house, he heard music and dancing, and he called one of the servants to him and asked him what it meant. He said to him, 'Your brother has come, and your father has killed the calf he has been fattening, because he has gotten him back alive and well.' But he was angry, and would not go into the house. And his father came out and urged him. And he said to his father, 'Here I have served you all these years, and have never disobeyed an order of yours, and you have never given me a kid, so that I could entertain my friends. But when your son here came, who has eaten up your property with women of the streets, for him you killed the calf you have been fattening!' But he said to him, 'My child, you have been with me all the time, and everything I have is yours. But we had to celebrate and be glad, because your brother was dead, and has come to life, and was lost and is found!' ". . .

"So I tell you, make friends for yourselves with your ill-gotten wealth, so that when it fails, they may take you into the eternal dwellings. The man who can be trusted in a very small matter can be trusted in a large one, and the man who cannot be trusted in a very small matter cannot be trusted in a large one. So if you have proved untrustworthy in using your ill-gotten wealth, who will trust you with true riches? And if you have been untrustworthy about what belonged to someone else, who will give you what belongs to you? No servant can belong to two masters, for he will either hate one and love the other, or he will stand by one and make light of the other. You cannot serve God and money!"

The Pharisees, who were avaricious, heard all this, and they ridiculed him. And he said to them,

"You are the men who parade your uprightness before people, but God knows your hearts. For what men consider great is detestable in the sight of God. Until John came, it was the Law and the Prophets. From that time the Kingdom of God has been proclaimed, and everyone has been crowding into it. But it is easier for heaven and earth to pass away than for one dotting of an *i* in the Law to go unfulfilled. Anyone who divorces his wife and marries another woman commits adultery, and whoever marries a woman who has been divorced from her husband commits adultery.". . .

To some who were confident of their own uprightness, and thought nothing of others, he used this illustration:

"Two men went up to the Temple to pray; one was a Pharisee and the other a tax-collector. The Pharisee stood up and uttered this prayer to himself: 'O God, I thank you that I am not like other men, greedy, dishonest, or adulterous, like that tax-collector. I fast two days in the week; I pay tithes on everything I get.' But the tax-collector stood at a distance and would not even raise his eyes to heaven, but struck his breast, and said, 'O God, have mercy on a sinner like me!' I tell you, it was he who went back to his house with God's approval, and not the other. For everyone who exalts himself will be humbled, but the man who humbles himself will be exalted."

People brought babies to him to have him touch them, but the disciples, when they saw it, reproved them for it. But Jesus called them up to him and said,

"Let the children come to me and do not try to stop them, for the Kingdom of God belongs to such as they. I tell you whoever does not accept the Kingdom of God like a child will not enter it at all.". . .

When some spoke about the Temple and its decoration with costly stone and votive offerings, he said,

"As for all this that you are looking at, the time is coming when not one stone will be left here upon another that will not be torn down!"

Then they asked him,

"Master, when will this happen, and what will be the sign that it is going to take place?"

And he said,

"Take care not to be misled. For many will come under my name, and say, 'I am he,' and 'The time is at hand.' Do not follow them. But when you hear of wars and outbreaks, do not be alarmed. These have to come first, but the end does not follow immediately."

Then he said to them,

"Nation will rise in arms against nation, and kingdom against kingdom. There will be great earthquakes, and pestilence and famine here and there. There will be horrors and great signs in the sky. But before all this, men will arrest you and persecute you, and hand you over to synagogues and prisons and have you brought before kings and governors on my account. It will all lead to your testifying. So make up your minds not to prepare your defense, for I will give you such wisdom of utterance as none of your opponents will be able to resist or dispute. You will be betrayed even by your parents and brothers and kinsmen and friends and they will put some of you to death, and you will be hated by everyone because you bear my name. Yet not a hair of your head will perish! It is by your endurance that you will win your souls. But when you see Jerusalem being surrounded by armies, then you must understand that her devastation is at hand. Then those who are in Judea must fly to the hills, those who are in the city must get out of it, and those who are in the country must not go into it, for those are the days of vengeance, when all that is written in the Scriptures will be fulfilled. But alas for women who are with child at that time, or who have babies, for there will be great misery in the land and anger at this people. They will fall by the edge of the sword, and be carried off as prisoners among all nations, and Jerusalem will be trampled under foot by the heathen, until the time of the heathen comes. There will be signs too in sun, moon, and stars, and on earth dismay among the heathen, bewildered at the roar of the sea and the waves. Men will swoon with fear and foreboding of what is to happen to the world, for the forces in the sky will shake. Then they will see the Son of Man coming in a cloud with great power and glory. But when this begins to happen, look up and raise your heads, for your deliverance will be at hand."

And he gave them an illustration:

"See the fig tree and all the trees. As soon as they put out their leaves, you see them and you know without being told that summer is coming. So when you see these things happen, you must know that the Kingdom of God is at hand. I tell you, it will all happen before the present generation passes away. Earth and sky will pass away, but my words will not. But take care that your hearts are not loaded down with self-indulgence and drunkenness and worldly cares, and that day takes you by surprise, like a trap. For it will come on all who are living anywhere on the face of the earth. But you must be vigilant and always pray that you may succeed in escaping all this that is going to happen, and in standing in the presence of the Son of Man.". . .

The festival of Unleavened Bread, which is called the Passover, was approaching. And the high priests and the scribes were casting about for a way to put him to death, for they were afraid of the people.

But Satan entered into Judas, who was called Iscariot, a member of the Twelve. And he went off and discussed with the high priests and captains of the Temple how he could betray him to them. And they were delighted and agreed to pay him for it. And he accepted their offer, and watched for an opportunity to betray him to them without a disturbance.

When the day of Unleavened Bread came, on which the Passover lamb had to be sacrificed, Jesus sent Peter and John, saying to them,

"Go and make preparations for us to eat the Passover."

They said to him,

"Where do you want us to prepare it?"

He said to them,

"Just after you enter the city, you will meet a man carrying a pitcher of water. Follow him to the house to which he goes, and say to the man of the house, 'Our Master says to you, "Where is the room where I can eat the Passover supper with my disciples?" ' And he will show you a large room upstairs with the necessary furniture. Make your preparations there."

So they went and found everything just as he had told them, and they prepared the Passover supper.

When the time came, he took his place at the table, with the apostles about him. And he said to them,

"I have greatly desired to eat this Passover supper with you before I suffer. For I tell you, I will never eat one again until it reaches its fulfilment in the Kingdom of God."

And when he was handed a cup, he thanked God, and then said,

"Take this and share it among you, for I tell you, I will not drink the product of the vine again until the Kingdom of God comes."

And he took a loaf of bread and thanked God, and broke it in pieces, and gave it to them, saying,

"This is my body. Yet look! The hand of the man who is betraying me is beside me on the table! For the Son of Man is going his way, as it has been decreed, but alas for the man by whom the Son of Man is betrayed!"

And they began to discuss with one another which of them it was who was going to do this. A dispute also arose among them, as to which one of them ought to be considered the greatest. But he said to them,

"The kings of the heathen lord it over them, and their authorities are given the title of Benefactor. But you are not to do so, but whoever is greatest among you must be like the youngest, and the leader like a servant. For which is greater, the man at the table, or the servant who waits on him? Is not the man at the table? Yet I am like a servant among you. But it is you who have stood by me in my trials. So just as my Father has conferred a kingdom on me, I confer on you the right to eat and drink at my table in my kingdom, and to sit on thrones and judge the twelve tribes of Israel! O Simon, Simon! Satan has obtained permission to sift all of you like wheat, but I have prayed that your own faith may not fail. And afterward you yourself must turn and strengthen your brothers."

Peter said to him,

"Master, I am ready to go to prison and to death with you!"

But he said,

"I tell you, Peter, the cock will not crow today before you deny three times that you know me!"

And he said to them,

"When I sent you out without any purse or bag or shoes, was there anything you needed?"

They said,

"No, nothing."

He said to them,

"But now, if a man has a purse let him take it, and a bag too. And a man who has no sword must sell his coat and buy one. For I tell you that this saying of Scripture must find its fulfilment in me: 'He was rated an outlaw.' Yes, that saying about me is to be fulfilled!"

But they said,

"See, Master, here are two swords!"

And he said to them,

"Enough of this!"

And he went out of the city and up on the Mount of Olives as he was accustomed to do, and with his disciples following him. . . .

While he was speaking, a crowd of people came up, with the man called Judas, one of the Twelve, at their head, and he stepped up to Jesus to kiss him. Jesus said to him,

"Would you betray the Son of Man with a kiss?". . .

And Jesus said to the high priests, captains of the Temple, and elders who had come to take him,

"Have you come out with swords and clubs as though I were a robber? When I was among you day after day in the Temple you never laid a hand on me! But you choose this hour, and the cover of darkness!"

Then they arrested him and led him away and took him to the house of the high priest. And Peter followed at a distance. And they kindled a fire in the middle of the courtyard and sat about it, and Peter sat down among them. A maid saw him sitting by the fire and looked at him and said,

"This man was with him too."

But he denied it, and said,

"I do not know him."

Shortly after, a man saw him and said,

"You are one of them too!"

But Peter said,

"I am not!"

About an hour later, another man insisted,

"This man was certainly with him too, for he is a Galilean!"

But Peter said,

"I do not know what you mean."

And immediately, just as he spoke, a cock crowed. And the Master turned and looked at Peter, and Peter remembered the words the Master had said to him—"Before the cock crows today, you will disown me three times!" And he went outside and wept bitterly. . . .

As soon as it was day, the elders of the people and the high priests and scribes assembled, and brought him before their council, and said to him,

"If you are the Christ, tell us so."

But he said to them,

"If I tell you, you will not believe me, and if I ask you a question, you will not answer me. But from this time on, the Son of Man will be seated at the right hand of God Almighty!"

And they all said,

"Are you the Son of God then?"

And he said to them,

"I am, as you say!"

Then they said,

"What do we want of testimony now? We have heard it ourselves from his own mouth!"

Then they arose in a body and took him to Pilate, and they made this charge against him:

"Here is a man whom we have found misleading our nation, and forbidding the payment of taxes to the emperor, and claiming to be an anointed king himself."

And Pilate asked him,

"Are you the king of the Jews?"

He answered,

"Yes."

And Pilate said to the high priests and the crowd,

"I cannot find anything criminal about this man."

But they persisted and said,

"He is stirring up the people all over Judea by his teaching. He began in Galilee and he has come here."

When Pilate heard this, he asked if the man were a Galilean and learning that he belonged to Herod's jurisdiction, he turned him over to Herod, for Herod was in Jerusalem at that time. When Herod saw Jesus he was delighted, for he had wanted for a long time to see him, because he had heard about him and he hoped to see some wonder done by him. And he questioned him at some length, but he made him no answer. Meanwhile the high priests and the scribes stood by and vehemently accused him. And Herod and his guards made light of him and ridiculed him, and they put a gorgeous robe on him and sent him back to Pilate. And Herod and Pilate became friends that day, for they had been at enmity before.

Pilate summoned the high priests and the leading members of the council and the people, and said to them,

"You brought this man before me charged with misleading the people, and here I have examined him before you and not found him guilty of any of the things that you accuse him of. Neither has Herod, for he has sent him back to us. You see he has done nothing to call for his death. So I will teach him a lesson and let him go."

But they all shouted out,

"Kill him, and release Barabbas for us!"

(He was a man who had been put in prison for a riot that had taken place in the city and for murder.) But Pilate wanted to let Jesus go, and he called out to them again. But they kept on shouting,

"Crucify him! Crucify him!"

And he said to them a third time,

"Why, what has he done that is wrong? For I have found nothing about him to call for his death. So I will teach him a lesson and let him go."

But they persisted with loud outcries in demanding that he be crucified, and their shouting won. And Pilate pronounced sentence that what they asked for should be done. He released the man they asked for, who had been put in prison for riot and murder, and handed Jesus over to their will.

As they led Jesus away, they seized a man named Simon, from Cyrene, who was coming in from the country, and put the cross on his back, for him to carry behind Jesus. He was followed by a great crowd of people and of women who were beating their breasts and lamenting him. But Jesus turned to them and said,

"Women of Jerusalem, do not weep for me but weep for yourselves and for your children, for a time is coming when they will say, 'Happy are the childless women, and those who have never borne or nursed children!' Then people will begin to say to the mountains, 'Fall on us!' and to the hills, 'Cover us up!' For if this is what they do when the wood is green, what will happen when it is dry?"

Two criminals were also led out to execution with him.

When they reached the place called the Skull, they crucified him there, with the criminals one at his right and one at his left. And they divided up his clothes among them by drawing lots for them, while the people stood looking on. Even the leading councilors jeered at him, and said,

"He has saved others, let him save himself, if he is really God's Christ, his chosen One!"

The soldiers also made sport of him, coming up and offering him sour wine, saying,

"If you are the king of the Jews, save yourself!"

For there was a notice above his head, "This is the king of the Jews!"

One of the criminals who were hanging there, abused him, saying,

"Are you not the Christ? Save yourself and us too!"

But the other reproved him and said,

"Have you no fear even of God when you are suffering the same penalty? And we are suffering it justly, for we are only getting our deserts, but this man has done nothing wrong."

And he said,

"Jesus, remember me when you come into your kingdom!"

And he said to him,

"I tell you, you will be in Paradise with me today!"

It was now about noon, and darkness came over the whole country, and lasted until three in the afternoon, as the sun was in eclipse. And the curtain before the sanctuary was torn in two. Then Jesus gave a loud cry, and said,

"Father, I intrust my spirit to your hands!"

With these words he expired.

When the captain saw what had happened he praised God, and said,

"This man was really innocent!"

And all the crowds that had collected for the sight, when they saw what happened, returned to the city beating their breasts. And all his acquaintances and the women who had come with him from Galilee, stood at a distance looking on.

Now there was a man named Joseph, a member of the council, a good and upright man, who had not voted for the plan or action of the council. He came from the Jewish town of Arimathea and lived in expectation of the Kingdom of God. He went to Pilate and asked for Jesus' body. Then he took it down from the cross and wrapped it in linen and laid it in a tomb hewn in the rock, where no one had yet been laid. It was the Preparation Day, and the Sabbath was just beginning. The women who had followed Jesus from Galilee followed and saw the tomb and how his body was put there. Then they went home, and prepared spices and perfumes.

On the Sabbath they rested in obedience to the commandment, but on the first day of the week, at early dawn, they went to the tomb, taking spices they had prepared. But they found the stone rolled back from the tomb, and when they went inside they could not find the body. They were in great perplexity over this, when suddenly two men in dazzling clothing stood beside them. The women were frightened and bowed their faces to the ground, but the men said to them,

"Why do you look among the dead for him who is alive? Remember what he told you while he was still in Galilee, when he said that the Son of Man must be handed over to wicked men and be crucified and rise again on the third day."

Then they remembered his words, and they went back from the tomb and told all this to the eleven and all the rest. They were Mary of Magdala and Joanna and Mary,

James's mother; and the other women also told this to the apostles. But the story seemed to them to be nonsense and they would not believe them.

That same day two of them were going to a village called Emmaus, about seven miles from Jerusalem, and they were talking together about all these things that had happened. And as they were talking and discussing them, Jesus himself came up and went with them, but they were prevented from recognizing him. And he said to them,

"What is all this that you are discussing with each other on your way?"

They stopped sadly, and one of them named Cleopas said to him,

"Are you the only visitor to Jerusalem who does not know what has happened there lately?"

And he said,

"What is it?"

They said to him,

"About Jesus of Nazareth, who in the eyes of God and of all the people was a prophet mighty in deed and word, and how the high priests and our leading men gave him up to be sentenced to death, and had him crucified. But we were hoping that he was to be the deliverer of Israel. Why, besides all this, it is three days since it happened. But some women of our number have astounded us. They went to the tomb early this morning and could not find his body, but came back and said that they had actually seen a vision of angels who said that he was alive. Then some of our party went to the tomb and found things just as the women had said, but they did not see him."

Then he said to them,

"How foolish you are and how slow to believe all that the prophets have said! Did not the Christ have to suffer thus before entering upon his glory?"

And he began with Moses and all the prophets and explained to them the passages all through the Scriptures that referred to himself. When they reached the village to which they were going, he acted as though he were going on, but they urged him not to, and said,

"Stay with us, for it is getting toward evening, and the day is nearly over."

So he went in to stay with them. And when he took his place with them at table, he took the bread and blessed it and broke it in pieces and handed it to them. Then their eyes were opened and they knew him, and he vanished from them. And they said to each other,

"Did not our hearts glow when he was talking to us on the road, and was explaining the Scriptures to us?"

And they got up immediately and went back to Jerusalem, and found the eleven and their party all together, and learned from them that the Master had really risen and had been seen by Simon. And they told what had happened on the road, and how they had known him when he broke the bread in pieces.

While they were still talking of these things, he himself stood among them. They were startled and panic-stricken, and thought they saw a ghost. But he said to them,

"Why are you so disturbed, and why do doubts arise in your minds? Look at my hands and feet, for it is I myself! Feel of me and see, for a ghost has not flesh and bones, as you see I have."

But they could not yet believe it for sheer joy and they were amazed. And he said to them,

"Have you anything here to eat?"

And they gave him a piece of broiled fish, and he took it and ate it before their eyes.

Then he said to them,

"This is what I told you when I was still with you—that everything that is written about me in the Law of Moses and the Prophets and the Psalms must come true."

Then he opened their minds to the understanding of the Scriptures, and said to them,

"The Scriptures said that Christ should suffer as he has done, and rise from the dead on the third day, and that repentance leading to the forgiveness of sins should be preached to all the heathen in his name. You are to be witnesses to all this, beginning at Jerusalem. And I will send down upon you what my Father has promised. Wait here in the city until you are clothed with power from on high."

And he led them out as far as Bethany. Then he lifted up his hands and blessed them. And as he was blessing them, he parted from them. And they went back with great joy to Jerusalem, and were constantly in the Temple, blessing God.

◆§ EPISTLE TO THE ROMANS

Paul

Saul of Tarsus, called Paul after his conversion to Christianity, was a well-educated Jew and a student of the rabbinical academies. He was thoroughly imbued with the doctrines and spirit of the Pharisees of his day. In addition, his tense and introspective temperament led him to take spiritual matters very seriously. He consequently became an almost fanatical opponent of the disciples of Jesus, whom he must have seen as a seriously disruptive force. As a result of what he believed to have been divine intervention, combined with a fundamental affinity for their mysticism and apocalyptic message, he became an equally devoted leader of the Christians. As such he brought a remarkable evangelistic fervor, brilliant literary power, and astute organizational ability to the councils of the early apostles. It was primarily due to his influence that the decision was made to extend the new religion beyond the bounds of Judaism (see Acts of the Apostles, pages 369–371), and its consequent spread throughout the eastern Mediterranean area was largely his personal work.

The Bible has preserved many of the letters he wrote to the fledgling churches he established in various places. The letter to the Romans (that is, the Christians living in Rome) is a major statement of the role of Law (Torah, as represented in our selections from Deuteronomy and the

Mishnah) *in the lives of Christians as opposed to traditional Jews. When Paul refers to "Jews," he means Christians of Jewish origin; by "Greeks," Christians who were converted directly from paganism. The immediate question at hand, then, is the relationship between these two groups, especially with regard to the Law revealed only to the former. But the topic broadens to include a theological discussion of the relationship between observance of the Law and adherence to God's will through faith.*

. . . You have no excuse, whoever you are, if you pose as a judge, for when you pass judgment on someone else, you are condemning yourself, for you, who sit in judgment, do the very same things yourself. We know that God's judgment rightfully falls upon those who do such things as these. And do you suppose, when you sit in judgment upon those who do such things and yet do them yourself, that you will escape the judgment of God? Do you think so lightly of his wealth of kindness, forbearance, and patience, and fail to see that God's kindness ought to induce you to repent? But in your obstinacy and impenitence you are storing up wrath for yourself on the Day of Wrath, when the justice of God will burst forth. For he will pay every man for what he has done. Those who by persistently doing right strive for glory, honor, and immortality will have eternal life, but self-seeking people who are disloyal to the truth and responsive only to what is wrong will experience anger and fury, crushing distress and anguish, every human soul of them that actually does what is wrong—the Jew first, and the Greek also; but there will be glory, honor, and peace for everyone who does right, the Jew first, and the Greek also, for God shows no partiality.

All who sin without having the Law will perish without regard to the Law, and all who sin under the Law will be judged by the Law. For merely hearing the Law read does not make a man upright in the sight of God; men must obey the Law to be made upright. When heathen who have no Law instinctively obey what the Law demands, even though they have no law they are a law to themselves, for they show that what the Law demands is written on their hearts, and their consciences will testify for them, and with their thoughts they will either accuse or perhaps defend themselves, on that Day when, as the good news I preach teaches, God through Christ Jesus judges what men have kept secret.

Suppose you call yourself a Jew, and rely on law, and boast about God, and can understand his will, and from hearing the Law read can tell what is right, and you are sure that you can guide the blind, enlighten people who are in the dark, train the foolish, teach the young, since you have knowledge and truth formulated in the Law—why, then, will you teach others and refuse to teach yourself? Will you preach against stealing, and yet steal yourself? Will you warn men against adultery, and yet practice it yourself? Will you pretend to detest idols, and yet rob their temples? Will you boast of the Law and yet dishonor God by breaking it? For, as the Scripture says,

The Complete Bible: An American Translation **(Chicago: The University of Chicago Press, 1948); The New Testament, trans. E. J. Goodspeed, pp. 143–151.**

the very name of God is abused among the heathen, because of you! Circumcision will help you only if you observe the Law; but if you are a lawbreaker, you might as well be uncircumcised. So if people who are uncircumcised observe the requirements of the Law, will they not be treated as though they were circumcised? And if, although they are physically uncircumcised, they obey the Law, they will condemn you, who break the Law, although you have it in writing, and are circumcised. For the real Jew is not the man who is one outwardly, and the real circumcision is not something physical and external. The real Jew is the man who is one inwardly, and real circumcision is a matter of the heart, a spiritual, not a literal, thing. Such a man receives his praise not from men, but from God.

What advantage is there then in being a Jew, and what is the use of circumcision? A great deal, from every point of view. In the first place, the Jews were intrusted with the utterances of God. What if some of them have shown a lack of faith? Can their lack of it nullify the faithfulness of God? By no means! God must prove true, though every man be false; as the Scripture says,

"That you may be shown to be upright in what you say,
And win your case when you go into court."

But if our wrongdoing brings out the uprightness of God, what are we to say? Is it wrong in God (I am putting it in ordinary human terms) to inflict punishment? By no means, for then how could he judge the world? But, you say, if a falsehood of mine has brought great honor to God by bringing out his truthfulness, why am I tried for being a sinner? And why not say, as people abuse us for saying and charge us with saying, "Let us do evil that good may come out of it"? Such people will be condemned as they deserve!

What does this mean? Are we Jews at a disadvantage? Not at all. We have already charged Jews and Greeks all alike with being under the control of sin. As the Scripture says,

"There is not a single man who is upright,
No one understands, no one searches for God.
All have turned away, they are one and all worthless,
No one does right, not a single one!
Their throats are like open graves,
They use their tongues to deceive;
The venom of asps is behind their lips,
And their mouths are full of bitter curses.
Their feet are swift when it comes to shedding blood,
Ruin and wretchedness mark their paths,
They do not know the way of peace.
There is no reverence for God before their eyes!"

Now we know that everything the Law says is addressed to those under its authority, so that every mouth may be shut, and the whole world be made accountable to God. For no human being can be made upright in the sight of God by observing the Law. All that the Law can do is to make men conscious of sin. But now God's way of uprightness has been disclosed without any reference to law, though the Law and the Prophets bear witness to it. It is God's way of uprightness and comes through having faith in Jesus Christ, and it is for all who have faith, without distinction. For all men sin and come short of the glory of God, but by his mercy they are made upright for nothing, by the deliverance secured through Christ Jesus. For God showed him publicly dying as a sacrifice of reconciliation to be taken advantage of through faith. This was to vindicate his own justice (for in his forbearance, God passed over men's former sins) —to vindicate his justice at the present time, and show that he is upright himself, and that he makes those who have faith in Jesus upright also.

Then what becomes of our boasting? It is shut out. On what principle? What a man does? No, but whether a man has faith. For we hold that a man is made upright by faith; the observance of the Law has nothing to do with it. Does God belong to the Jews alone? Does he not belong to the heathen too? Of course he belongs to the heathen too; there is but one God, and he will make the circumcised upright on the ground of their faith and the uncircumcised upright because of theirs. Is this using faith to overthrow law? Far from it. This confirms the Law.

Then what are we to say about our ancestor Abraham? For if he was made upright by what he did, it is something to be proud of. But not to be proud of before God, for what does the Scripture say? "Abraham had faith in God, and it was credited to him as uprightness." Now paying a workman is not considered a favor, but an obligation, but a man who has no work to offer, but has faith in him who can make the ungodly upright, has his faith credited to him as uprightness. So David himself says of the happiness of those whom God merits uprightness without any reference to their actions,

> "Happy are they whose violations of the Law have been forgiven, whose sins are covered up!
> Happy is the man whose sin the Lord will take no account of!"

Does this happiness apply to those who are circumcised, or to those who are uncircumcised as well? What we say is, Abraham's faith was credited to him as uprightness. In what circumstances? Was it after he was circumcised or before? Not after he was circumcised, but before; and he was afterward given the mark of circumcision as the stamp of God's acknowledgment of the uprightness based on faith that was his before he was circumcised, so that he should be the forefather of all who, without being circumcised, have faith and so are credited with uprightness, and the forefather of those circumcised persons who not only share his circumcision but follow our forefather Abraham's example in the faith he had before he was circumcised.

For the promise made to Abraham and his descendants that the world should belong to him did not come to him or his descendants through the Law, but through the uprightness that resulted from his faith. For if it is the adherents of the Law who are to possess it, faith is nullified and the promise amounts to nothing! For the Law only brings down God's wrath; where there is no law, there is no violation of it. That is why it all turns upon faith; it is to make it a matter of God's favor, so that the promise may hold good for all Abraham's descendants, not only those who are adherents of the Law, but also those who share the faith of Abraham. For he is the father of all of us; as the Scripture says, "I have made you the father of many nations."

The promise is guaranteed in the very sight of God in whom he had faith, who can bring the dead to life and call into being what does not exist. Abraham, hoping against hope, had faith, and so became the father of many nations, in fulfilment of the Scripture, "So countless shall your descendants be." His faith did not weaken, although he realized that his own body was worn out, for he was about a hundred years old, and that Sarah was past bearing children. He did not incredulously question God's promise, but his faith gave him power and he praised God in the full assurance that God was able to do what he had promised. That was why it was credited to him as uprightness.

It was not on his account alone that these words, "it was credited to him," were written, but also on ours, for it is to be credited also to us who have faith in him who raised from the dead our Lord Jesus, who was given up to death to make up for our offenses, and raised to life to make us upright.

So as we have been made upright by faith, let us live in peace with God through our Lord Jesus Christ, by whom we have been introduced through faith to the favor of God that we now enjoy, and let us glory in our hope of sharing the glory of God. More than that, we ought to glory in our troubles, for we know that trouble produces endurance, and endurance, character, and character, hope, and hope will not disappoint us. For, through the holy Spirit that has been given us, God's love has flooded our hearts. For when we were still helpless, at the decisive moment Christ died for us godless men. Why, a man will hardly give his life for an upright person, though perhaps for a really good man some may be brave enough to die. But God proves his love for us by the fact that Christ died for us when we were still sinners. So if we have already been made upright by his death, it is far more certain that through him we shall be saved from God's anger! If, when we were God's enemies, we were reconciled to him through the death of his Son, it is far more certain that now that we are reconciled we shall be saved through sharing in his life! More than that, we actually glory in God through our Lord Jesus Christ, to whom we owe our reconciliation.

It is just like the way in which through one man sin came into the world, and death followed sin, and so death spread to all men, because all men sinned. It is true sin was in the world before the Law was given, and men are not charged with sin where there is no law. Still death reigned from Adam to Moses, even over those who had not sinned as Adam had, in the face of an express command. So Adam foreshadowed the one who was to come. But there is no comparison between God's gift and that offense. For if one man's offense made the mass of mankind die, God's mercy and his gift given through the favor of the one man Jesus Christ have far more powerfully affected mankind. Nor is there any comparison between the gift and the effects of that one man's sin. That sentence arose from the act of one man, and was for condemnation: but God's gift arose out of many offenses and results in acquittal. For if that one man's offense made death reign through that one man, all the more will those who receive God's overflowing mercy and his gift of uprightness live and reign through the one individual Jesus Christ.

So as one offense meant condemnation for all men, just so one righteous act means acquittal and life for all men. For just as that one man's disobedience made the mass of mankind sinners, so this one's obedience will make the mass of them upright. Then aw slipped in, and multiplied the offense. But greatly as sin multiplied, God's mercy 1as far surpassed it, so that just as sin had reigned through death, mercy might reign hrough uprightness and bring eternal life through Jesus Christ our Lord. . . .

So sin must not reign over your mortal bodies, and make you obey their cravings, nd you must not offer the parts of your bodies to sin as the instruments of wrong, but ffer yourselves to God as men brought back from death to life, and offer the parts of our bodies to him as instruments of uprightness. For sin must no longer control you, or you live not under law but under mercy.

What follows, then? Are we to sin, because we live not under law but under mercy? Certainly not! Do you not know that when you submit to being someone's slaves, and beying him, you are the slaves of the one whom you obey, whether your slavery is to in, and leads to death, or is to obedience, and leads to uprightness? But, thank God! hough you were once slaves of sin, you have become obedient from your hearts to the tandard of teaching that you received, and so you have been freed from sin, and nade slaves of uprightness. I use these familiar human terms because of the limitations of your nature. For just as you before gave up the parts of your bodies in slavery to vice and greater and greater license, you must now give them up in slavery to upright-ness, which leads to consecration. For when you were slaves of sin, you were free as ar as uprightness was concerned. What good did you get from doing the things you re now ashamed of? Why, they result in death! But now that you have been freed rom sin and have become slaves of God, the benefit you get is consecration, and the inal result is eternal life. For the wages sin pays is death, but the gift God gives is eternal life through union with Christ Jesus our Lord. . . .

Then what shall we conclude? That the Law is sin? Certainly not! Yet, if it had not een for the Law, I should never have learned what sin was; I should not have known what it was to covet if the Law had not said, "You must not covet." That command gave sin an opening, and it led me to all sorts of covetous ways, for sin is lifeless without law. I was once alive and without law, but when the command came, sin woke and then I died; and the command that should have meant life in my case roved to mean death. The command gave sin an opening and sin deceived me and illed me with it. So the Law itself is holy, and each command is holy, just, and good.

Did what was good, then, prove the death of me? Certainly not! It was sin that did o, so that it might be recognized as sin, because even through something that was good it effected my death, so that through the command it might appear how im-measurably sinful sin was. We know that the Law is spiritual, but I am physical, sold nto slavery to sin. I do not understand what I am doing, for I do not do what I want o do; I do things that I hate. But if I do what I do not want to do, I acknowledge hat the Law is right. In reality, it is not I that do these things; it is sin, which has ossession of me. For I know that nothing good resides in me, that is, in my physical elf; I can will, but I cannot do what is right. I do not do the good things that I want to do; I do the wrong things that I do not want to do. But if I do the things that I do not want to do, it is not I that am acting, it is sin, which has possession of me. I ind the law to be that I who want to do right am dogged by what is wrong. My inner nature agrees with the divine law, but all through my body I see another principle in onflict with the law of my reason, which makes me a prisoner to that law of sin that runs through my body. What a wretched man I am! Who can save me from the doomed body? Thank God! it is done through Jesus Christ our Lord! So mentally I am a slave to God's law, but physically to the law of sin. . . .

I am telling the truth as a Christian, it is no falsehood, for my conscience under the holy Spirit's influence bears me witness in it, when I say that I am greatly pained and my heart is constantly distressed, for I could wish myself accused and cut off from Christ for the sake of my brothers, my natural kindred. For they are Israelites, and to them belong the rights of sonship, God's glorious presence, the divine agreements and legislation, the Temple service, the promises, and the patriarchs, and from them physically Christ came—God who is over all be blessed forever! Amen. Not that God's message has failed. For not everybody who is descended from Israel really belongs to Israel, nor are they all children of Abraham because they are descended from him, but he was told, "The line of Isaac will be called your descendants." That is to say, it is not his physical descendants who are children of God, but his descendants born in fulfilment of the promise who are considered his true posterity. For this is what the promise said: "When I come back at this time next year, Sarah will have a son." And that is not all, for there was Rebecca too, when she was about to bear twin sons to our forefather Isaac. For before the children were born or had done anything either good or bad, in order to carry out God's purpose of selection, which depends not on what men do but on his calling them, she was told, "The elder will be the younger's slave." As the Scripture says, "I loved Jacob, but I hated Esau."

What do we conclude? That God is guilty of injustice? By no means. He said to Moses, "I will have mercy on the man on whom I choose to have mercy, and take pity on the man on whom I choose to take pity." So it depends not on human will or exertion, but on the mercy of God. The Scripture says to Pharaoh, "I have raised you to your position for the very purpose of displaying my power in dealing with you, and making my name known all over the world." So he has mercy on anyone he pleases, and hardens the heart of anyone he pleases.

"Why, then," you will ask, "does he still find fault? For who can resist his will?" On the contrary, who are you, my friend, to answer back to God? Can something a man shapes say to the man who shaped it, "Why did you make me like this?" Has not the potter with his clay the right to make from the same lump one thing for exalted uses and another for menial ones? Then what if God, though he wanted to display his anger and show his power, has shown great patience toward the objects of his anger, already ripe for destruction, so as to show all the wealth of his glory in dealing with the objects of his mercy, whom he has prepared from the beginning to share his glory, including us whom he has called not only from among the Jews but from among the heathen? Just as he says in Hosea,

"I will call a people that was not mine, my people,
And her who was not beloved, my beloved,
And in the very place where they were told, 'You are no people of mine,'
They shall be called sons of the living God."

And Isaiah cries out about Israel, "Although the sons of Israel are as numerous as the sand of the sea, only a remnant of them will be saved, for the Lord will execute his sentence rigorously and swiftly on the earth." As Isaiah foretold,

"If the Lord of Hosts had not left us children,
We would have been like Sodom, and have resembled Gomorrah!"

Then what do we conclude? That heathen who were not striving for uprightness attained it, that is, an uprightness which was produced by faith; while Israel, straining after a law that should bring uprightness, did not come up to it. And why? Because they did not seek it through faith, but through doing certain things. They stumbled over that stone that makes people stumble, as the Scripture says,

"See, I will put a stone on Zion to make people stumble, and a rock to trip over,
But no one who has faith in it will be disappointed."

Brothers, my heart is full of good will toward them; my prayer to God is that they may be saved. I can testify to their sincere devotion to God, but it is not an intelligent devotion. For in their ignorance of God's way of uprightness and in the attempt to set up one of their own, they refused to conform to God's way of uprightness. For Christ marks the termination of law, so that now anyone who has faith may attain uprightness. Moses said that anyone who carried out the uprightness the Law prescribed would find life through it. But this is what the uprightness that springs from faith says: "Do not say to yourself, 'Who will go up to heaven?' " that is, to bring Christ down; or " 'Who will go down into the depths?' " that is, to bring Christ up from the dead. No! This is what it says: "God's message is close to you, on your lips and in your mind"—that is, the message about faith that we preach. For if with your lips you acknowledge the message that Jesus is Lord, and with your mind you believe that God raised him from the dead, you will be saved. For with their minds men believe and are made upright, and with their lips they make the acknowledgment and are saved. For the Scripture says, "No one who has faith in him will be disappointed." There is no distinction between Jew and Greek, for they all have the same Lord, and he is generous to all who call upon him. For everyone who calls upon the name of the Lord will be saved. . . .

I ask then, has God repudiated his people? By no means. Why, I am an Israelite myself, I am descended from Abraham, and I belong to the tribe of Benjamin. God has not repudiated his people, which he had marked out from the first. Do you not know what the Scripture says in speaking of Elijah, how he appealed to God against Israel? "Lord, they have killed your prophets, they have demolished your altars, I am the only one left and they are trying to take my life." But what is God's reply? "I have left myself seven thousand men who have never knelt to Baal!" So too at the present time there is a remnant selected by God's mercy. But if it is by his mercy, it is not for anything they have done. Otherwise, his mercy would not be mercy at all. What follows? Israel failed to get what it sought, but those whom God selected got it. The rest became callous; as the Scripture says, "God has thrown them into a state of spiritual insensibility, with eyes that cannot see and ears that cannot hear, that has lasted down to this day." And David said,

"Let their feasting prove a snare and a trap to them,
Their ruin and their retribution.
Let their eyes be darkened, so that they cannot see;
Make their backs bend forever under their burden!"

I ask then, has their stumbling led to their absolute ruin? By no means. Through their false step salvation has gone to the heathen, so as to make the Israelites jealous But if their false step has so enriched the world, and their defeat has so enriched the heathen, how much more good the addition of their full number will do!

But it is to you who are of the heathen that I am speaking. So far then as I am an apostle to the heathen, I make the most of my ministry, in the hope of making my countrymen jealous, and thus saving some of them. For if their rejection has mean the reconciling of the world, what can the acceptance of them mean but life from the dead? If the first handful of dough is consecrated, the whole mass is, and if the roo of a tree is consecrated, so are its branches.

If some of the branches have been broken off, and you who were only a wild olive shoot have been grafted in, in place of them, and made to share the richness of the olive's root, you must not look down upon the branches. If you do, remember that you do not support the root; the root supports you.

"But," you will say, "branches were broken off so that I could be grafted in!"

That is true; but it was for their want of faith that they were broken off, and it i through your faith that you stand where you do. You ought not to feel proud; you ought to be afraid, for if God did not spare the natural branches, he will not spare you. Observe then the goodness and severity of God—severity to those who have fallen, but goodness to you, provided you abide by his goodness, for otherwise, you in your turn will be pruned away. Those others too, if they do not cling to their unbelief will be grafted in, for God has the power to graft them in again. For if you were cut from a wild olive and unnaturally grafted upon a cultivated one, how much easier i will be to graft them upon the olive to which they properly belong!

For to keep you from thinking too well of yourselves, brothers, I do not want you to miss this secret, that only partial insensibility has come upon Israel, to last until al the heathen have come in, and then all Israel will be saved, just as the Scripture says

> "The deliverer will come from Zion,
> He will drive all ungodliness away from Jacob,
> And this will be my agreement with them,
> When I take away their sins."

From the point of view of the good news they are treated as enemies of God on your account; but from the point of view of God's choice, they are dear to him because o their forefathers, for God does not change his mind about those to whom he gives hi blessings or sends his call. For just as you once disobeyed God, but now have had mercy shown you because they disobeyed, so they are now disobedient in order tha they in turn may experience the same mercy as you. For God has made all men pris oners of disobedience so as to have mercy upon them all. How inexhaustible God' resources, wisdom, and knowledge are! How unfathomable his decisions are, and how untraceable his ways!

"Who has ever known the Lord's thoughts, or advised him?

"Or who has advanced anything to him, for which he will have to be repaid?"

For from him everything comes; through him everything exists; and in him every thing ends! Glory to him forever! Amen. . . .

Formation of a Christian Church

In the generation after the death of Jesus, the decisions were made to establish out of a Jewish sect a new church and to derive its membership from all men, not only Jews. The decisions were not easily reached; witness the Acts of the Apostles, one of the books of the New Testament. Although Luke, the author, was a partisan of Paul (notice the occasional lapses into first-person narrative), and consequently in favor of the solution eventually reached, he provides a great deal of material in which we can discern the issues involved and watch them being resolved. As in the case of Luke's Gospel, the narrative skill is noteworthy, and the missionary voyages of Paul, which take up a large part of the volume, are described with almost epic fervor. The book ends with Paul in the capital city of the civilized world, Rome.

The young church needed an organization, and Paul was a skillful supervisor of the efforts to build one. The second selection is from his first letter to Timothy, which is a detailed set of instructions putting forth the responsibilities of a superintendent of the church. These principles of pastoral care have remained the basis of episcopal responsibility in all branches of Christianity.

THE ACTS OF THE APOSTLES

Luke

In my first volume, Theophilus, I dealt with all that Jesus did and taught from the beginning until the day when through the holy Spirit he gave the apostles he had chosen their instructions, and was taken up to heaven. . . . And while they were gazing after him into the sky, two men dressed in white suddenly stood beside them, and said to them,

"Men of Galilee, why do you stand looking up into the sky? This very Jesus who has been caught up from you into heaven will come in just the way that you have seen him go up to heaven."

The Complete Bible: An American Translation **(Chicago: The University of Chicago Press, 1948); The New Testament, trans. E. J. Goodspeed, pp. 197–200, 212–214, 217–218, 224–226, 228–230, 236–237, 249–250.**

Then they went back to Jerusalem from the hill called the Olive-orchard, which i
near Jerusalem, half a mile away.

When they entered the city they went to the upstairs room where they were staying
There were Peter, John, James and Andrew, Philip and Thomas, Bartholomew an
Matthew, James, the son of Alpheus, Simon the Zealot, and Judas, the son of James
They were all devoting themselves with one mind to prayer, with the women an
Mary, Jesus' mother, and his brothers.

It was at that time that Peter got up among the brothers—there were about a hun
dred and twenty persons present—and said,

"Brothers, the prediction of the Scriptures had to come true that the holy Spiri
uttered by the lips of David, about Judas, who acted as guide for the men that arreste
Jesus—for he was one of our number and a share in this ministry of ours fell to hi
lot. . . . For in the Book of Psalms it is written,

" 'Let his estate be desolate, with no one to live on it,'

and

" 'Let someone else take his position.'

"So one of the men who has been associated with us all the time that the Lor
Jesus moved about among us, from his baptism by John to the time when he wa
caught up from us, must join us as a witness to his resurrection."

Then they proposed two men, Joseph called Barsabbas, who was known as Justus
and Matthias. And they prayed, saying,

"Lord, you who know all hearts, show us which one of these two you have chose
to take this place of service as an apostle which Judas left to go where he belonged."

Then they drew lots between them, and the lot fell on Matthias, and he was adde
to the eleven apostles.

On the day of the Harvest Festival, they were all meeting together, when suddenl
there came from the sky a sound like a violent blast of wind, and it filled the whol
house where they were sitting. And they saw tongues like flames separating and set
tling one on the head of each of them, and they were all filled with the holy Spiri
and began to say in foreign languages whatever the Spirit prompted them to utter.

Now there were devout Jews from every part of the world living in Jerusalem. An
when this sound was heard, the crowd gathered in great excitement, because each on
heard them speaking in his own language. They were perfectly amazed and said i
their astonishment,

"Are not all these men who are speaking Galileans? Then how is it that each of u
hears his own native tongue? Parthians, Medes, Elamites, residents of Mesopotamia
of Judea and Cappadocia, of Pontus and Asia, of Phrygia and Pamphylia, of Egypt an
the district of Africa about Cyrene, visitors from Rome, Jews and proselytes, Cretan
and Arabs—we all hear them tell in our native tongues the mighty deeds of God."

And they were all amazed and bewildered and said to one another,

"What can this mean?"

But others said derisively,

"They have had too much new wine!"

Then Peter stood up with the eleven around him, and raising his voice addresse
them.

"Men of Judea," he said, "and all you residents of Jerusalem, let me explain this to ou, and pay attention to what I say. These men are not drunk as you suppose, for it is nly nine in the morning. But this is what was predicted by the prophet Joel,

" 'It will come about in the last days, God says,
That I will pour out my Spirit upon all mankind;
Your sons and daughters will become prophets,
Your young men will have visions,
And your old men will have dreams.
Even on my slaves, both men and women,
I will pour out my Spirit in those days,
And they will become prophets.
I will show wonders in the sky above,
And signs on the earth below,
Blood and fire and thick smoke.
The sun will turn to darkness,
And the moon to blood,
Before the coming of the great, splendid Day of the Lord.
Then everyone who calls on the name of the Lord will be saved.'

"Men of Israel, listen to what I say. Jesus of Nazareth, as you know, was a man vhom God commended to you by the wonders, portents, and signs that God did right mong you through him. But you, by the fixed purpose and intention of God, handed im over to wicked men, and had him crucified. But God set aside the pain of death nd raised him up, for death could not control him. For David says of him,

" 'I constantly regarded the Lord before me,
For he is at my right hand, so that I may not be displaced.
Therefore my heart is glad, and my tongue rejoices,
And my body will still live in hope.
For you will not desert my soul in death,
You will not let your Holy One be destroyed.
You have made the ways of life known to me,
And you will fill me with joy in your presence.'

"Brothers, one may say to you confidently of the patriarch David that he died and vas buried, and his grave is here among us to this very day. But as he was a prophet, nd knew that God had promised him with an oath that he would put one of his lescendants upon his throne, he foresaw the resurrection of the Christ and told of it, or he was not deserted in death and his body was not destroyed. He is Jesus, whom God raised from the dead, and to whose resurrection we are all witnesses. So he has een exalted to God's right hand, and has received from his Father and poured over ıs the holy Spirit that had been promised, as you see and hear.

"For David did not go up to heaven, but he said,

" 'The Lord said to my lord, Sit at my right hand,
Until I make your enemies your footstool.'

"Therefore the whole nation of Israel must understand that God has declared thi Jesus whom you crucified both Lord and Christ."

When they heard this, they were stung to the heart, and they said to Peter and th rest of the apostles,

"Brothers, what shall we do?"

Peter said to them,

"You must repent, and every one of you be baptized in the name of Jesus Christ, i order to have your sins forgiven; then you will receive the gift of the holy Spirit, fo the promise of it belongs to you and your children, as well as to all those far awa whom the Lord our God calls to him."

He said much more besides in giving his testimony, and urged them to save them selves from that crooked age. So they welcomed his message and were baptized, an about three thousand people joined them that day. And they devoted themselves to th teaching and the society of the apostles, the breaking of bread, and prayer.

Everyone felt a sense of awe, and many wonders and signs were done by the apostles The believers all shared everything they had with one another, and sold their propert and belongings, and divided the money with all the rest, according to their specia needs. Day after day they all went regularly to the Temple, they broke their brea together in their homes, and they ate their food with glad and simple hearts, con stantly praising God and respected by all the people. And every day the Lord adde people who were saved to their number. . . .

Now Saul, still breathing murderous threats against the Lord's disciples, went t the high priest and asked him for letters to the synagogues in Damascus, so that if h found any men or women there who belonged to the Way, he might bring them i chains to Jerusalem. But on his journey, as he was approaching Damascus, a sudde light flashed around him from heaven, and he fell to the ground. Then he heard voice saying to him,

"Saul! Saul! Why do you persecute me?"

"Who are you, sir?" he asked.

"I am Jesus, whom you are persecuting," said the voice. "But get up and go int the city, and there you will be told what you ought to do."

Saul's fellow-travelers stood speechless, for they heard the voice but could not se anyone. When he got up from the ground and opened his eyes he could see nothing They had to take him by the hand and lead him into Damascus, and for three days h could not see, and neither ate nor drank.

There was at Damascus a disciple named Ananias, and the Lord said to him in vision,

"Ananias!"

And he answered,

"Yes, Lord!"

The Lord said to him,

"Get up and go to the street called the Straight Street, and ask at the house o Judas for a man named Saul, from Tarsus, for he is there praying. He has had a visio and seen a man named Ananias come in and lay his hands on him, to restore his sight."

But Ananias answered,

"Lord, I have heard many people tell of this man, and the harm he has done to your eople in Jerusalem. He is here with authority to arrest everyone who calls upon your ame."

The Lord said to him,

"Go! This man is the means I have chosen for carrying my name among the heathen nd their kings, and among the descendants of Israel. For I am going to show him hat he will have to endure for my sake."

Ananias set out and went to the house, and there he laid his hands upon Saul, and aid to him,

"Saul, my brother, I have been sent by the Lord Jesus, who appeared to you on your ourney, so that you may regain your sight and be filled with the holy Spirit."

Something like scales immediately dropped from his eyes, and his sight was restored, nd he got up and was baptized, and, after taking some food, regained his strength.

Saul stayed for some time with the disciples at Damascus, and began at once to eclare in the synagogues that Jesus was the Son of God. Everyone was astonished, nd said,

"Is not he the man who made such havoc of the people in Jerusalem who call upon hat name, and who came here especially for the purpose of arresting such persons nd taking them before the high priests?"

But Saul grew more and more powerful, and bewildered the Jews who lived in amascus by his proofs that Jesus was the Christ.

After some time had passed, the Jews made a plot to kill him, but Saul found out bout the plot. They watched the city gates day and night, in order to kill him, but his isciples took him one night and let him down over the wall, lowering him in a asket.

When he reached Jerusalem he tried to join the disciples, and they were all afraid of im, for they could not believe that he was really a disciple. But Barnabas got hold of im and introduced him to the apostles, and he told them how on his journey he had een the Lord, and that he had spoken to him, and how boldly he had spoken for the ause of Jesus at Damascus. After that, he associated with them freely in Jerusalem, nd spoke boldly for the Lord's cause, talking and debating with the Greek-speaking ews. But they tried to kill him. When the brothers found this out, they took him down Caesarea, and sent him away to Tarsus.

So the church all over Judea, Galilee, and Samaria was at peace and became estab- shed. It lived in reverence for the Lord and, stimulated by the holy Spirit, it grew eadily in numbers. . . .

The apostles and brothers all over Judea heard that the heathen had also accepted od's message, and when Peter returned to Jerusalem, the advocates of circumcision ok him to task, charging him with having visited and eaten with men who were not ews. Then Peter explained the matter to them from beginning to end. He said,

"I was praying in the town of Joppa, and while in a trance I had a vision. Some- ing like a great sheet came down out of the sky, lowered by its four corners. It came ght down to me, and when I looked at it, I saw in it quadrupeds, wild animals, rep- les, and wild birds. And I heard a voice say to me, 'Get up, Peter! Kill something nd eat it!' But I said, 'Never, sir! For nothing that was not ceremonially cleansed has ever passed my lips.' Then the voice from heaven answered again, 'Do not call wha God has cleansed unclean!' This happened three times; then it was all drawn bac again into the sky. Just at that moment three men, who had been sent from Caesare to find me, reached the house where we were staying, and the Spirit told me not t hesitate to go with them. These six brothers here also went with me, and we went t the man's house. Then he told us how he had seen the angel stand in his house an say, 'Send to Joppa for a man named Simon who is also called Peter, and he will te you things that will save you and your whole household.' When I began to speak t them, the holy Spirit fell upon them just as it did upon us at the beginning, and remembered the saying of the Lord, 'John baptized in water, but you will be bap tized in the holy Spirit.' So if God had given them the same gift that we receive when we believed in the Lord Jesus Christ, who was I, to be able to interfere wit God?"

When they heard this, they made no further objection, but they gave honor to Go and said,

"Then God has given even the heathen repentance and the hope of life!"

The fugitives from the persecution that had broken out over Stephen went all th way to Phoenicia, Cyprus, and Antioch, but they told the message to none but Jew There were some men from Cyprus and Cyrene among them, however, who whe they reached Antioch spoke to the Greeks also, and told them the good news abou the Lord Jesus. The Lord's hand was with them, and there were a great many wh believed and turned to the Lord. The news about them came to the ears of the churc in Jerusalem, and they sent Barnabas all the way to Antioch. When he reached the and saw the favor God had shown them, he was delighted, and encouraged them all t be resolute and steadfast in their devotion to the Lord, for he was an excellent ma full of the holy Spirit and faith. So a considerable number of people came over to th Lord. Then Barnabas went over to Tarsus to seek out Saul, and found him an brought him to Antioch. The result was that for a whole year they met with th church, and taught large numbers of people, and it was at Antioch that the discipl first came to be known as Christians. . . .

Some people came down from Judea and began to teach the brothers that unle they were circumcised as Moses prescribed, they could not be saved. This created a di turbance and a serious discussion between Paul and Barnabas and them, and it w agreed that Paul and Barnabas and some others of their number should go up to Jer salem to confer with the apostles and elders about this question.

The church saw them off upon their journey, and as they traveled through Phoenic and Samaria they told of the conversion of the heathen, and caused great rejoicin among all the brothers. When they reached Jerusalem, they were welcomed by th church, the apostles, and the elders, and they reported how God had worked wit them. But some members of the Pharisees' party who had become believers got up an said that such converts ought to be circumcised and told to obey the Law of Moses.

The apostles and elders had a meeting to look into this matter. After a long di cussion, Peter got up and said to them,

"Brothers, you know that in the early days God chose that of you all I should the one from whose lips the heathen should hear the message of the good news a elieve it. And God who knows men's hearts testified for them by giving them the oly Spirit just as he had done to us, making no difference between us and them, but leansing their hearts by faith. Then why do you now try to test God, by putting on he necks of these disciples a yoke that neither our forefathers nor we have been able o bear? Why, we believe that it is by the mercy of the Lord Jesus that we are saved ust as they are."

This quieted the whole meeting, and they listened while Barnabas and Paul told of he signs and wonders which God had done among the heathen through them. When hey finished James made this response:

"Brothers, listen to me. Symeon has told how God first showed an interest in taking rom among the heathen a people to bear his name. And this agrees with the predic-ons of the prophets which say,

" 'Afterward I will return, and rebuild David's fallen dwelling.
I will rebuild its very ruins, and set it up again,
So that the rest of mankind may seek the Lord,
And all the heathen who are called by my name,
Says the Lord, who has been making this known from of old.'

n my opinion, therefore, we ought not to put obstacles in the way of those of the eathen who are turning to God, but we should write to them to avoid anything that as been contaminated by idols, immorality, the meat of strangled animals, and the asting of blood. For Moses for generations past has had his preachers in every town, nd has been read aloud in the synagogues every Sabbath."

Then the apostles and elders with the whole church resolved to select representa-ives and send them with Paul and Barnabas to Antioch. They were Judas who was alled Barsabbas, and Silas, both leading men among the brothers. They were the earers of this letter: "The apostles and the brothers who are elders send greeting to he brothers of heathen birth in Antioch, Syria, and Cilicia. As we have heard that ome of our number, without any instructions from us, have disturbed you by their eaching and unsettled your minds, we have unanimously resolved to select representa-ives and send them to you with our dear brothers Barnabas and Paul, who have risked heir lives for the sake of our Lord Jesus Christ. So we send Judas and Silas to you, o give you this same message by word of mouth. For the holy Spirit and we have ecided not to lay upon you any burden but this indispensable one, that you avoid hatever has been sacrificed to idols, the tasting of blood and of the meat of animals hat have been strangled, and immorality. Keep yourselves free from these things and ou will get on well. Goodbye."

So the delegates went down to Antioch and gathered the congregation together and elivered the letter; and when they read it they were delighed with the encouragement gave them. Judas and Silas were themselves prophets, and gave the brothers much ncouragement and strength by their words. After they had stayed some time, the rothers let them go, with a greeting to those who had sent them.

But Paul and Barnabas stayed on in Antioch and taught, and with many others reached the good news of the Lord's message.

Some time after, Paul said to Barnabas,

"Come, let us go back and revisit the brothers in each of the towns where we made the Lord's message known, to see how they are doing.

Now Barnabas wanted to take John who was called Mark with them. But Paul did not approve of taking with them a man who had deserted them in Pamphylia instead of going on with them to their work. They differed so sharply about it that they separated, and Barnabas took Mark and sailed for Cyprus. But Paul selected Silas and set out, the brothers commending him to the Lord's favor. He traveled through Syria and Cilicia and strengthened the churches. . . .

After passing through Amphipolis and Apollonia, they reached Thessalonica, where the Jews had a synagogue. Paul went to it as he was accustomed to do, and for three Sabbaths he discussed the Scriptures with them, explaining them and showing that the Christ had to suffer and rise from the dead.

"Jesus," he said, "of whom I am telling you, is the Christ!"

He convinced some of them, and they joined Paul and Silas, along with a great many devout Greeks and a number of the principal women. This offended the Jews and they gathered some unprincipled loafers, formed a mob and started a riot in the town. They attacked Jason's house, to find them and bring them out among the people. As they could not find them, they dragged Jason and some of the brothers before the town magistrates, shouting,

"The men who have made trouble all over the world have come here too, and Jason has taken them in. They all disobey the emperor's decrees, and claim that someone else called Jesus is king."

The crowd and the magistrates were very much excited at hearing this, and they put Jason and the others under bonds before they let them go.

The brothers sent Paul and Silas away immediately, in the course of the following night, to Berea. On arriving there they went to the Jewish synagogue. The Jews there were more high-minded than those at Thessalonica, and received the message with great eagerness and studied the Scriptures every day, to find out whether it was true. Many of them became believers and so did no small number of Greek women of position, and men too. But when the Jews at Thessalonica found out that God's message had been delivered at Berea by Paul, they came there too to excite and stir up the populace. Then the brothers immediately sent Paul off to the coast, while Silas and Timothy stayed behind. The men who went with Paul took him all the way to Athens, and came back with instructions for Silas and Timothy to rejoin them as soon as possible.

While Paul waited for them at Athens, he was exasperated to see how idolatrous the city was. He had discussions at the synagogue with the Jews and those who worshiped with them, and every day in the public square with any whom he happened to find. Some of the Epicurean and Stoic philosophers debated with him. Some of them said,

"What is this rag-picker trying to make out?"

Others said,

"He seems to be preaching some foreign deities."

This was because he was telling the good news of Jesus and the resurrection. So they took him and brought him to the council of the Areopagus and said,

"May we know just what this new teaching of yours is? Some of the things you tell us sound strange to us, and we want to know just what they mean."

For all Athenians and all visitors there from abroad used to spend all their time telling or listening to something new.

Then Paul stood up in the middle of the council and said,

"Men of Athens, from every point of view I see that you are extremely religious. For as I was going about and looking at the things you worship, I even found an altar with this inscription: 'To an Unknown God.' So it is what you already worship in ignorance that I am now telling you of. God who created the world and all that is in it, since he is Lord of heaven and earth, does not live in temples built by human hands, nor is he waited on by human hands as though he were in need of anything, for he himself gives all men life and breath and everything. From one forefather he has created every nation of mankind, and made them live all over the face of the earth, fixing their appointed times and the limits of their lands, so that they might search for God, and perhaps grope for him and find him, though he is never far from any of us. For it is through union with him that we live and move and exist, as some of your poets have said,

" 'For we are also his offspring.'

So if we are God's children we ought not to imagine that the divine nature is like gold or silver or stone, wrought by human art and thought. While God overlooked those times of ignorance, he now calls upon all men everywhere to repent, since he has fixed a day on which he will justly judge the world through a man whom he has appointed, and whom he has guaranteed to all men by raising him from the dead."

When they heard of the resurrection of the dead, some of them sneered, but others said,

"We should like to hear you again on this subject."

So Paul left the council. Some persons joined him, however, and became believers, among them Dionysius, a member of the council, and a woman named Damaris, and some others. . . .

After this we made our preparation and started for Jerusalem. Some of the disciples from Caesarea went with us and took us to the house of Mnason, a man from Cyprus, one of the early disciples, to spend the night. When we reached Jerusalem, the brothers there gave us a hearty welcome. On the next day we went with Paul to see James, and all the elders came in. Paul greeted them warmly and gave a detailed account of what God had done among the heathen through his efforts. They praised God when they heard it, and they said to him,

"You see, brother, how many thousand believers there are among the Jews, all of them zealous upholders of the Law. They have been told that you teach all Jews who live among the heathen to turn away from Moses, and that you tell them not to circumcise their children nor to observe the old customs. What then? They will be sure to hear that you have come. So do what we tell you. We have four men here who are under a vow. Join them, undergo the rites of purification with them, and pay their expenses so that they can have their heads shaved. Then everybody will understand that there is no truth in the stories about you, but that you yourself observe the Law. As for the heathen who have become believers, we have written them our decision that

they must avoid anything that has been contaminated by idols, the tasting of blood
the meat of strangled animals, and immorality."

Then Paul joined the men and went through the rites of purification with them an
the next day went to the Temple to give notice of the time when, upon the offerin
of the sacrifice for each one of them, their days of purification would be over. . . .

When we reached Rome, Paul was given permission to live by himself, with a sol
dier to guard him.

Three days later, he invited the leading Jews to come to see him, and when the
came he said to them,

"Brothers, I have done nothing against our people, or the customs of our fore
fathers, yet I was turned over to the Romans as a prisoner at Jerusalem. They examine
me and were ready to let me go, as I was innocent of any crime that deserved death
But the Jews objected, and I was obliged to appeal to the emperor—not that I ha
any charge to make against my own nation. That is why I asked to see you and spea
with you, for it is on account of Israel's hope that I have to wear this chain."

"We have had no letters about you from Judea," they answered, "and none of th
brothers who have come here has reported or said anything against you. But we wan
to hear you state your views, for as far as this sect is concerned, we understand tha
everywhere it is denounced."

So they fixed a day, and came in even larger numbers to the place where he wa
staying, and from morning till night he explained to them the Kingdom of God an
gave his testimony, trying to convince them about Jesus from the Law of Moses an
the Prophets. Some of them were convinced by what he said, but others would no
believe. As they could not agree among themselves, they started to leave, when Pau
added one last word.

"The holy Spirit put it finely," he said, "when it said to your forefathers throug
the prophet Isaiah,

" 'Go to this Nation and say to them,
"You will listen, and listen, and never understand,
And you will look, and look, and never see!
For this nation's mind has grown dull,
And they hear faintly with their ears,
And they have shut their eyes,
So as never to see with their eyes,
And hear with their ears,
And understand with their minds, and turn back,
And let me cure them!" '

"Understand then that this message of God's salvation has been sent to the heathen
They will listen to it!"

So they stayed for two full years in rented lodgings of his own, and welcome
everybody who came to see him, preaching the Kingdom of God to them and teach
ing about the Lord Jesus Christ openly and unhindered.

FIRST EPISTLE TO TIMOTHY

Paul

Paul, an apostle of Christ Jesus by order of God our Savior and of Jesus Christ our hope, to Timothy, my true child in faith; God the Father and Christ Jesus our Lord bless you and be merciful to you, and give you peace. . . .

These are the instructions that I intrust to you, my son Timothy, and they are in accordance with the predictions made long ago about you. Fight the good fight with their aid, keeping hold of faith and a good conscience. For some people have let that go and have had their faith ruined, like Hymenaeus and Alexander, whom I turned over to Satan, to be taught not to blaspheme.

First of all, then, I urge that entreaties, prayers, petitions, and thanksgivings be offered for all men, for emperors and all who are in authority, so that we may live tranquil, quiet lives, with perfect piety and probity. It is right to do this, and it pleases God our Savior, who wants all men to be saved and to come to know the truth.

For there is but one God, and one intermediary between God and men—the man Christ Jesus, who gave himself as a ransom for all men. This is what was testified to at the proper times, and I was appointed a herald and apostle of it—I am telling the truth, I am not lying—to teach the heathen faith and truth.

I want the men everywhere to offer prayer, lifting to heaven hands that are holy, without any angry disputes. Women for their part are to dress modestly and sensibly in proper clothes, not adorning themselves by braiding their hair or with gold or pearls or expensive clothing, but, as is appropriate for women who profess to be religious, with good actions.

Women must listen quietly in church and be perfectly submissive. I do not allow women to teach or to domineer over men; they must keep quiet. For Adam was formed first, and then Eve; and it was not Adam who was deceived, it was the woman who was deluded and fell into sin. But they will be saved through motherhood, if they continue to have faith and to be loving and holy, and sensible as well. This is a trustworthy saying.

Whoever aspires to the office of superintendent sets his heart on a fine work. A superintendent must be a man above reproach, only once married, temperate, sensible, a man of good behavior, hospitable, able to teach; not addicted to drink, or pugnacious, but a man of moderation and peace, not avaricious, managing his own house well, and keeping his children under control and perfectly respectful—for if a man does not know how to conduct his own household, how can he look after a church of God? He must not be a new convert, or he may grow conceited and incur criticism from slanderous people. He must also be a man of good standing with outsiders, or he may get into disgrace and be entrapped by the slanderers. Assistants, in turn, must be serious, straightforward men, not addicted to wine or dishonest gain, but holding the divine truth of the faith with a clear conscience. They should first be tested, and

The Complete Bible: An American Translation (Chicago: The University of Chicago Press, 1948); The New Testament, trans. E. J. Goodspeed, pp. 338–343.

afterward, if there is no fault to be found with them, they can serve as assistants. Their wives too must be serious, not gossips; they must be temperate, and perfectly trustworthy. The assistants must be only once married, and manage their children and their households well. For those who do good service as assistants gain a good standing for themselves and great confidence in their faith in Christ Jesus.

I hope to come to you soon, but I am writing you all this so that if I am delayed, you may know how we are to conduct ourselves in the household of God, for it is the church of the living God, the pillar and foundation of the truth. No one can deny the profundity of the divine truth of our religion! . . .

Let worldly fictions and old wives' tales alone. Train yourself for the religious life. Physical training is of some service, but religion is of service in every way, for it carries with it the promise of life here and hereafter. This is a trustworthy saying, entitled to the fullest acceptance. It is for this that we toil, and struggle, for we have fixed our hopes on the living God, the Savior of all men, especially those who believe.

This is what you must urge and teach. Let no one look down on you because you are young, but set those who believe an example in speech, conduct, love, faith, and purity. Until I come, devote yourself to the public reading of Scripture, preaching, and teaching. Do not neglect the gift you have, that was given you with predictions of your work, when the elders laid their hands upon you. Cultivate these things, devote yourself to them, so that everyone will see your progress. Look out for yourself and for your teaching. Persevere in your work, for if you do you will save both yourself and those who listen to you.

Never reprove an older man, but appeal to him as a father. Treat younger men like brothers, older women like mothers, younger ones like sisters, with absolute purity. Look after widows who are really dependent. If a widow has children or grandchildren, let them learn first to show piety in the treatment of their own families, and to return the care of those who brought them up, for that is what God approves. But a woman who is really a widow, and has no children, has fixed her hope on God, and devotes herself to prayers and entreaties night and day. A widow who gives herself up to pleasure is dead while she is still alive. Insist upon these points, so that people may be irreproachable. Whoever fails to provide for his own relatives, and particularly for members of his own family, has disowned the faith and is worse than an unbeliever. No one under sixty years of age should be put on the list of widows. A widow must have been married but once, and have a good reputation for Christian service, such as bringing up children, being hospitable to strangers, washing the feet of God's people, helping people in distress, or devoting herself to any form of doing good. Do not put young women on the list of widows, for when their youthful vigor comes between them and Christ, they want to marry, and become guilty of breaking their previous pledge. Besides, as they go about from house to house they learn to be idle, and not only idle but gossips and busybodies, and talk of things they ought not to mention. So I would have young women marry and have children and keep house and avoid giving our opponents any excuse for abusing us. For some widows have already turned aside to follow Satan. Any Christian woman who has widowed relatives should look after them, and relieve the church, so that it can look after widows who are really dependent.

Elders who do their duties well should be considered as deserving twice as much as they get, particularly those who work at preaching and teaching. For the Scripture says, "You must not muzzle an ox when it is treading out the grain," and the workman deserves his wages. Do not listen to an accusation made against an elder, unless it is supported by two or three witnesses. Those who are found guilty you must reprove publicly, as a warning to others. I charge you before God and Christ Jesus and the chosen angels to observe these rules without any discrimination, and to be perfectly impartial. Never ordain anyone hastily; do not make yourself responsible for the sins of others; keep your life pure. Stop drinking nothing but water; take a little wine for the good of your digestion and for your frequent attacks of illness. Some men's sins are perfectly evident, and lead them right on to judgment, but there are others whose sins only dog their steps. Good deeds too are evident enough, or when they are not, they cannot be wholly concealed.

All who are under the yoke of slavery must treat their masters with the greatest respect, so that the name of God and our teaching may not be abused. Those who have Christian masters must not think lightly of them because they are brothers; they must serve them all the more faithfully, because those who benefit by it are believers and hence dear to them.

These are the things you must teach and preach. Anyone who teaches different views and does not agree with the wholesome instruction which comes from our Lord Jesus Christ and with religious teaching is a conceited, ignorant person, with a morbid craving for speculations and arguments which result only in envy, quarreling, abuse, base suspicions, and mutual irritation between people of depraved minds, who are lost to the truth and think of religion only as a means of gain. . . . Love of money is the root of all the evils, and in their eagerness to get rich, some men wander away from the faith and pierce themselves to the heart with many a pang.

But you, man of God, must fly from these things. Strive for uprightness, godliness, faith, love, steadfastness, gentleness. Enter the great contest of faith! Take hold of eternal life, to which God called you, when before many witnesses you made the great profession of faith. Before God who maintains all life, and before Christ Jesus who in testifying before Pontius Pilate made his great profession, I charge you to keep his command stainless and irreproachable until the appearance of our Lord Jesus Christ, which will be brought about in his own time by the blessed, only Sovereign, the King of kings and Lord of lords, who alone possesses immortality and dwells in unapproachable light, whom no man has ever seen or can see. To him be honor and eternal dominion. Amen.

Charge the rich of this world not to be arrogant, nor to set their hopes on such an uncertain thing as riches, but on God who richly provides us with everything for our enjoyment. Charge them to do good, to be rich in good deeds, open-handed and generous, storing up a valuable treasure for themselves for the future, so as to grasp the life that is life indeed.

Timothy, guard what has been intrusted to you. Keep away from the worldly, empty phrases and contradictions of what they falsely call knowledge, through professing which some people have made a failure of the faith. God bless you all.

CONSTITUTIONS OF THE HOLY APOSTLES

As time went on, the ecclesiastical tendency in early Christianity develope rapidly. By the third century after Christ, liturgy and church structure had been thoroughly institutionalized, and the summary called the Constitutions of the Holy Apostles *had been produced somewhere in the East, perhaps Asia Minor. Although practices must still have differed widely at that time, our selections (from Book II, "Of Bishops, Presbyters, and Deacons") give an idea of what had become typical. Responsibilities of bishops, of priests, and of the laity are laid out, and the final selection actually takes us inside a church assembly. We are now very far removed from the days of John the Baptist, Jesus, and their followers.*

BOOK TWO

That a Bishop Must Not Be Given to Filthy Lucre, Nor Be a Surety Nor a Advocate

vi Let not a bishop be given to filthy lucre, especially before the Gentiles,* rathe suffering than offering injuries; not covetous, nor rapacious; no purloiner; no admire of the rich, nor hater of the poor; no evil-speaker, nor false witness; not given t anger; no brawler; not entangled with the affairs of this life; not a surety for any one nor an accuser in suits about money; not ambitious; not double-minded, nor double tongued; not ready to hearken to calumny or evil-speaking; not a dissembler; no addicted to the heathen festivals; not given to vain deceits; not eager after worldl things, nor a lover of money. For all these things are opposite to God, and pleasin to demons. Let the bishop earnestly give all these precepts in charge to the laity also persuading them to imitate his conduct. For, says He, "Do ye make the children o Israel pious." Let him be prudent, humble, apt to admonish with the instructions o the Lord, well-disposed, one who has renounced all the wicked projects of this world and all heathenish lusts; let him be orderly, sharp in observing the wicked, and tak ing heed of them, but yet a friend to all; just, discerning; and whatsoever qualitie are commendable among men, let the bishop possess them in himself. For if the pasto be unblameable as to any wickedness, he will compel his own disciples, and by his ver mode of life press them to become worthy imitators of his own actions. As the prophe somewhere says, "And it will be, as is the priest, so is the people;" for our Lord an Teacher Jesus Christ, the Son of God, began first to do, and then to teach, as Luk

***The Ante-Nicene Fathers*, ed. A. Roberts and J. Donaldson (Grand Rapids, Mich.: Wm. B Eerdmans Publishing Co., n.d.), Vol. VII, 397–398, 404–405, 410, 412–413, 421–422.**

* ["Gentiles": non-Christians. (*Ed.*)]

somewhere says: "which Jesus began to do and to teach." Wherefore he says: "Whosoever shall do and teach he shall be called great in the kingdom of God." For you bishops are to be guides and watchmen to the people, as you yourselves have Christ for your guide and watchman. Do you therefore become good guides and watchmen to the people of God. For the Lord says by Ezekiel, speaking to every one of you: "Son of man, I have given thee for a watchman to the house of Israel; and thou shalt hear the word from my mouth, and shalt observe, and shalt declare it from me. When I say unto the wicked, Thou shalt surely die; if thou dost not speak to warn the wicked from his wickedness, that wicked man shall die in his iniquity, and his blood will I require at thine hand. But if thou warn the wicked from his way, that he may turn from it, and he does not turn from it, he shall die in his iniquity, and thou hast delivered thy soul." "In the same manner, if the sword of war be approaching, and the people set a watchman to watch, and he see the same approach, and does not forewarn them, and the sword come and take one of them, he is taken away in his iniquity; but his blood shall be required at the watchman's hand, because he did not blow the trumpet. But if he blew the trumpet, and he who heard it would not take warning, and the sword come and take him away, his blood shall be upon him, because he heard the trumpet and took not warning. But he who took warning has delivered his soul; and the watchman, because he gave warning, shall surely live." The sword here is the judgment; the trumpet is the holy Gospel; the watchman is the bishop, who is set in the Church, who is obliged by his preaching to testify and vehemently to forewarn concerning that judgment. If ye do not declare and testify this to the people, the sins of those who are ignorant of it will be found upon you. Wherefore do you warn and reprove the uninstructed with boldness, teach the ignorant, confirm those that understand, bring back those that go astray. If we repeat the very same things on the same occasions, brethren, we shall not do amiss. For by frequent hearing it is to be hoped that some will be made ashamed, and at least do some good action, and avoid some wicked one. For says God by the prophet: "Testify those things to them; perhaps they will hear thy voice." And again: "If perhaps they will hear, if perhaps they will submit." Moses also says to the people: "If hearing thou wilt hear the Lord God, and do that which is good and right in His eyes." And again: "Hear, O Israel; the Lord our God is one Lord." And our Lord is often recorded in the Gospel to have said: "He that hath ears to hear, let him hear." And wise Solomon says: "My son, hear the instruction of thy father, and reject not the laws of thy mother." And, indeed, to this day men have not heard; for while they seem to have heard, they have not heard aright, as appears by their having left the one and only true God, and their being drawn into destructive and dangerous heresies, concerning which we shall speak again afterwards.

How the Governed Are to Obey the Bishops Who Are Set over Them

XX As to a good shepherd, let the lay person honour him, love him, reverence him, as his lord, as his master, as the high priest of God, as a teacher of piety. For he that heareth him, heareth Christ; and he that rejecteth him, rejecteth Christ; and he who does not receive Christ, does not receive His God and Father: for, says He, "He that heareth you, heareth me; and he that rejecteth you, rejecteth me; and he that rejecteth me, rejecteth Him that sent me." In like manner, let the bishop love the laity as his children, fostering and cherishing them with affectionate diligence; as eggs, in order to the hatching of young ones; or as young ones, taking them in his arms, to the rearing them into birds: admonishing all men; reproving all who stand in need of reproof; reproving, that is, but not striking; beating them down to make them ashamed, but not overthrowing them; warning them in order to their conversion; chiding them in order to their reformation and better course of life; watching the strong, that is, keeping him firm in the faith who is already strong; feeding the people peaceably; strengthening the weak, that is, confirming with exhortation that which is tempted; healing that which is sick, that is, curing by instruction that which is weak in the faith through doubtfulness of mind; binding up that which is broken, that is, binding up by comfortable admonitions that which is gone astray, or wounded, bruised, or broken by their sins, and put out of the way; easing it of its offences, and giving hope: by this means restore it in strength to the Church, bringing it back into the flock. Bring again that which is driven away, that is, do not permit that which is in its sins, and is cast out by way of punishment, to continue excluded; but receiving it, and bringing it back, restore it to the flock, that is, to the people of the undefiled Church. Seek for that which is lost, that is, do not suffer that which desponds of its salvation, by reason of the multitude of its offences, utterly to perish. Do thou search for that which is grown sleepy, drowsy, and sluggish, and that which is unmindful of its own life, through the depth of its sleep, and which is at a great distance from its own flock, so as to be in danger of falling among the wolves, and being devoured by them. Bring it back by admonition, exhort it to be watchful; and insinuate hope, not permitting it to say that which was said by some: "Our impieties are upon us, and we pine away in them; how shall we then live?" As far as possible, therefore, let the bishop make the offence his own, and say to the sinner, Do thou but return, and I will undertake to suffer death for thee, as our Lord suffered death for me, and for all men. For "the good shepherd lays down his life for the sheep; but he that is an hireling, and not the shepherd, whose own the sheep are not, seeth the wolf coming, that is, the devil, and he leaveth the sheep, and fleeth, and the wolf seizes upon them." We must know, therefore, that God is very merciful to those who have offended, and hath promised repentance with an oath. But he who has offended, and is unacquainted with this promise of God concerning repentance, and does not understand His long-suffering and forbearance, and besides is ignorant of the Holy Scriptures, which proclaim repentance, inasmuch as he has never learned them from you, perishes through his folly. But do thou, like a compassionate shepherd, and a diligent feeder of the flock, search out, and keep an account of thy flock. Seek that which is wanting; as the Lord God our gracious Father has sent His own Son, the good Shepherd and Saviour, our Master Jesus, and has commanded Him to "leave the ninety-nine upon the mountains, and to go in search after that which was lost, and when He had found it, to take it upon His shoulders, and to carry it into the flock, rejoicing that He had found that which was lost." In like manner, be obedient, O bishop, and do thou seek that which was lost, guide that which has wandered out of the right way, bring back that which is gone astray: for thou hast authority to bring them back, and to deliver those that are broken-hearted by remission. For by thee does our Saviour say to him who is discouraged under the sense of his sins, "Thy sins are forgiven thee: thy faith hath saved thee; go in peace." But this peace and haven of tranquillity is the Church of Christ, into which do thou, when thou hast loosed them from their sins, restore them, as being now sound and unblameable, of good hope, diligent, laborious in good works. As a skilful and compassionate physician, heal all such as have wandered in the ways of sin; for "they that are whole have no need of a physician, but they that are sick. For the Son of man came to save and to seek that which was lost." Since thou art therefore a physician of the Lord's Church, provide remedies suitable to every patient's case. Cure them, heal them by all means possible; restore them sound to the Church. Feed the flock, "not with insolence and contempt, as lording it over them," but as a gentle shepherd, "gathering the lambs into thy bosom, and gently leading those which are with young."

According to What Patterns and Dignity Every Order of the Clergy Is Appointed by God

xxvi The bishop, he is the minister of the word, the keeper of knowledge, the mediator between God and you in the several parts of your divine worship. He is the teacher of piety; and, next after God, he is your father, who has begotten you again to the adoption of sons by water and the Spirit. He is your ruler and governor; he is your king and potenate; he is, next after God, your earthly god, who has a right to be honoured by you. For concerning him, and such as he, it is that God pronounces, "I have said, Ye are gods; and ye are all children of the Most High." And, "Ye shall not speak evil of the gods." For let the bishop preside over you as one honoured with the authority of God, which he is to exercise over the clergy, and by which he is to govern all the people. But let the deacon minister to him, as Christ does to His Father; and let him serve him unblameably in all things, as Christ does nothing of Himself, but does always those things that please His Father. Let also the deaconess be honoured by you in the place of the Holy Ghost, and not do or say anything without the deacon; as neither does the Comforter say or do anything of Himself, but gives glory to Christ by waiting for His pleasure. And as we cannot believe on Christ without the teaching of the Spirit, so let not any woman address herself to the deacon or bishop without the deaconess. Let the presbyters be esteemed by you to represent us with the apostles, and let them be the teachers of divine knowledge; since our Lord, when He sent us, said, "Go ye, and make disciples of all nations, baptizing them in the name of the Father, and of the Son, and of the Holy Ghost: teaching them to observe all things whatsoever I have commanded you." Let the widows and orphans be esteemed as representing the altar of burnt-offering; and let the virgins be honoured as representing the altar of incense, and the incense itself.

That Priests Are to Be Preferred before Rulers and Kings

xxxiv Account these worthy to be esteemed your rulers and your kings, and bring them tribute as to kings; for by you they and their families ought to be maintained. As Samuel made constitutions for the people concerning a king, in the first book of Kings, and Moses did so concerning priests in Leviticus, so do we also make constitutions for you concerning bishops. For if there the multitude distributed the inferior services in proportion to so great a king, ought not therefore the bishop much more now to receive of you those things which are determined by God for the sustenance of himself and of the rest of the clergy belonging to him? But if we may add somewhat further, let the bishop receive more than the other received of old: for he only managed the affairs of the soldiery, being entrusted with war and peace for the preservation of men's bodies; but the other is entrusted with the exercise of the priestly office in relation to God, in order to preserve both body and soul from dangers. By how much, therefore, the soul is more valuable than the body, so much the priestly office is beyond the kingly. For it binds and looses those that are worthy of punishment or of remission. Wherefore you ought to love the bishop as your father, and fear him as your king, and honour him as your lord, bringing to him your fruits and the works of your hands, for a blessing upon you, giving to him your first-fruits, and your tithes, and your oblations, and your gifts, as to the priest of God; the first-fruits of your wheat, and wine, and oil, and autumnal fruits, and wool, and all things which the Lord God gives thee. And thy offering shall be accepted as a savour of a sweet smell to the Lord thy God; and the Lord will bless the work of thy hands, and will multiply the good things of the land. "For a blessing is upon the head of him that giveth."

An Exact Description of a Church and the Clergy, and What Things in Particular Every One Is to Do in the Solemn Assemblies of the Clergy and Laity for Religious Worship

lvii But be thou, O bishop, holy, unblameable, no striker, not soon angry, not cruel; but a builder up, a converter, apt to teach, forbearing of evil, of a gentle mind, meek, long-suffering, ready to exhort, ready to comfort, as a man of God.

When thou callest an assembly of the Church as one that is the commander of a great ship, appoint the assemblies to be made with all possible skill, charging the deacons as mariners to prepare places for the brethren as for passengers, with all due care and decency. And first, let the building be long, with its head to the east, with its vestries on both sides at the east end, and so it will be like a ship. In the middle let the bishop's throne be placed, and on each side of him let the presbytery sit down; and let the deacons stand near at hand, in close and small girt garments, for they are like the mariners and managers of the ship: with regard to these, let the laity sit on the other side, with all quietness and good order. And let the women sit by themselves, they also keeping silence. In the middle, let the reader stand upon some high place; let him read the books of Moses, of Joshua the son of Nun, of the Judges, and of the Kings and of the Chronicles, and those written after the return from the captivity; and besides these, the books of Job and of Solomon, and of the sixteen prophets. But when there have been two lessons severally read, let some other person sing the hymns of David, and let the people join at the conclusions of the verses. Afterwards let our Acts be read, and the Epistles of Paul our fellow-worker, which he sent to the churches under the conduct of the Holy Spirit; and afterwards let a deacon or a presbyter read the Gospels, both those which Matthew and John have delivered to you, and those which the fellow-workers of Paul received and left to you, Luke and Mark. And while the Gospel is read, let all the presbyters and deacons, and all the people, stand up in great silence; for it is written: "Be silent, and hear, O Israel." And again: "But do thou stand there, and hear." In the next place, let the presbyters one by one, not all together, exhort the people, and the bishop in the last place, as being the commander. Let the porters stand at the entries of the men, and observe them. Let the deaconesses also stand at those of the women, like shipmen. For the same description and pattern was both in the tabernacle of the testimony and in the temple of God. But if any one be found sitting out of his place, let him be rebuked by the deacon, as a manager of the foreship, and be removed into the place proper for him; for the Church is not only like a ship, but also like a sheepfold. For as the shepherds place all the brute creatures distinctly, I mean goats and sheep, according to their kind and age, and still every one runs together, like to his like; so is it to be in the Church. Let the young persons sit by themselves, if there be a place for them; if not, let them stand upright. But let those that are already stricken in years sit in order. For the children which stand, let their fathers and mothers take them to them. Let the younger women also sit by themselves, if there be a place for them; but if there be not, let them stand behind the women. Let those women which are married, and have children, be placed by themselves; but let the virgins, and the widows, and the elder women, stand or sit before all the rest; and let the deacon be the disposer of the places, that every one of those that comes in may go to his proper place, and may not sit at the entrance. In like manner, let the deacon oversee the people, that nobody may whisper, nor slumber, nor laugh, nor nod; for all ought in the church to stand wisely, and soberly, and attentively, having their attention fixed upon the word of the Lord. After this, let all rise up with one consent, and looking towards the east, after the catechumens and penitents are gone out, pray to God eastward, who ascended up to the heaven of heavens to the east; remembering also the ancient situation of paradise in the east, from whence the first man, when he had yielded to the persuasion of the serpent, and disobeyed the command of God, was expelled. As to the deacons, after the prayer is over, let some of them attend upon the oblation of the Eucharist, ministering to the Lord's body with fear. L[illegible]rs of them watch the multitude, and keep them silent. But let that deacon who is [illegible]he high priest's hand say to the people, Let no one have any quarrel against another; let no one come in hypocrisy. Then let the men give the men, and the women give the women, the Lord's kiss. But let no one do it with deceit, as Judas betrayed the Lord with a kiss. After this let the deacon pray for the whole Church, for the whole world, and the several parts of it, and the fruits of it; for the priests and the rulers, for the high priest and the king, and the peace of the universe. After this let the high priest pray for peace upon the people, and bless them, as Moses commanded the priests to bless the people, in these words: "The Lord bless thee, and keep thee: the Lord make His face to shine upon thee, and give thee peace." Let the bishop pray for the people, and say: "Save Thy people, O Lord, and bless Thine inheritance, which Thou hast obtained with the precious blood of Thy Christ, and hast called a royal priesthood, and an holy nation." After this let the sacrifice follow, the people standing, and praying silently; and when the oblation has been made, let every rank by itself partake of the Lord's body and precious blood in order, and approach with reverence and holy fear, as to the body of their king. Let the women approach with their heads covered, as is becoming the order of women; but let the door be watched, lest any unbeliever, or one not yet initiated, come in.

ECCLESIASTICAL HISTORY

Theodoret

The development of early Christian church structure and ritual was matched by the evolution of theological speculation. By the early fourth century after Christ there were a number of serious controversies which threatened to tear Christianity apart. The decision to attempt to reach doctrinal uniformity, that is, to produce a creed that would clearly separate believers from heretics, was made by the Emperor Constantine, and the technique chosen was the calling of a council of bishops from all Christendom. The first council, held in the summer of A.D. *325 at Nicaea near Constantinople, set the pattern for all subsequent councils, producing a creed (the "Nicene") which has remained amazingly stable for 1,600 years, clearly establishing the principle of uniformity as a spiritual necessity.*

Our selection is from the Ecclesiastical History *of Theodoret, a bishop of the early fifth century after Christ who had access to important documentary material and who is distinguished by a strikingly fair-minded approach in an area of great controversy. In our excerpt, he describes the Council and reproduces the resultant Creed; but more important, he gives an excellent idea of the intense political tensions revealed in the deliberations and even lets one of the bishops on the losing side have his say. This is a first-rate view of the early Church at work, resolving a theological controversy with many nontheological implications.*

The actual substance of the controversy is of relatively minor importance to us now. Arianism, declared a heresy at the Council, was a view of Christ as subordinate to God (and created by him), rather than identical to him in substance. For a fuller explanation of the victorious Athanasian (or Trinitarian) view, see the selection by Vincent of Lérins *(pages 392–398)*.

BOOK ONE

Chapter VI

General Council of Nicaea The emperor, who possessed the most profound wisdom, having heard of these things,* endeavoured, as a first step, to stop up their fountain-

A Select Library of Nicene and Post-Nicene Fathers of the Christian Church, ed. P. Schaff and H. Wace (second series; Grand Rapids, Mich.: Wm. B. Eerdmans Publishing Co., n.d.), Vol. III, 43–46, 49–51.

* ["These things": the doctrinal differences mentioned in the introduction. (*Ed.*)]

head. He therefore despatched a messenger renowned for his ready wit to Alexandria with letters, in the endeavour to extinguish the dispute, and expecting to reconcile the disputants. But his hopes having been frustrated, he proceeded to summon the celebrated council of Nicaea; and pledged his word that the bishops and their officials should be furnished with asses, mules, and horses for their journey at the public expense. When all those who were capable of enduring the fatigue of the journey had arrived at Nicaea, he went thither himself, with both the wish of seeing the multitude of bishops, and the yearning desire of maintaining unanimity amongst them. He at once arranged that all their wants should be liberally supplied. Three hundred and eighteen bishops were assembled. The bishop of Rome, on account of his very advanced age, was absent, but he sent two presbyters to the council, with authority to agree to what was done.

At this period many individuals were richly endowed with apostolical gifts; and many, like the holy apostle, bore in their bodies the marks of the Lord Jesus Christ. James, bishop of Antioch, a city of Mygdonia, which is called Nisibis by the Syrians and Assyrians, raised the dead and restored them to life, and performed many other wonders which it would be superfluous to mention again in detail in this history, as I have already given an account of them in my work, entitled "Philotheus." Paul, bishop of Neo-Caesarea, a fortress situated on the banks of the Euphrates, had suffered from the frantic rage of Licinius. He had been deprived of the use of both hands by the application of a red-hot iron, by which the nerves which give motion to the muscles had been contracted and rendered dead. Some had had the right eye dug out, others had lost the right arm. Among these was Paphnutius of Egypt. In short, the council looked like an assembled army of martyrs. Yet this holy and celebrated gathering was not entirely free from the element of opposition; for there were some, though so few as easily to be reckoned, of fair surface, like dangerous shallows, who really, though not openly, supported the blasphemy of Arius.

When they were all assembled, the emperor ordered a great hall to be prepared for their accommodation in the palace, in which a sufficient number of benches and seats were placed; and having thus arranged that they should be treated with becoming dignity, he desired the bishops to enter in, and discuss the subjects proposed. The emperor, with a few attendants, was the last to enter the room; remarkable for his lofty stature, and worthy of admiration for personal beauty, and for the still more marvellous modesty which dwelt on his countenance. A low stool was placed for him in the middle of the assembly, upon which, however, he did not seat himself until he had asked the permission of the bishops. Then all the sacred assembly sat down around him. Then forthwith rose first the great Eustathius, bishop of Antioch, who, upon the translation of Philogonius, already referred to, to a better life, had been compelled reluctantly to become his successor by the unanimous suffrages of the bishops, priests, aand of the Christ-loving laity. He crowned the emperor's head with the flowers of panegyric, and commended the diligent attention he had manifested in the regulation of ecclesiastical affairs.

The excellent emperor next exhorted the bishops to unanimity and concord; he recalled to their remembrance the cruelty of the late tyrants, and reminded them of the honourable peace which God had, in his reign and by his means, accorded them.

He pointed out how dreadful it was, aye, very dreadful, that at the very time when their enemies were destroyed, and when no one dared to oppose them, they should fall upon one another, and make their amused adversaries laugh, especially as they were debating about holy things, concerning which they had the written teaching of the Holy Spirit. "For the gospels" (continued he), "the apostolical writings, and the oracles of the ancient prophets, clearly teach us what we ought to believe concerning the divine nature. Let, then, all contentious disputation be discarded; and let us seek in the divinely-inspired word the solution of the questions at issue." These and similar exhortations he, like an affectionate son, addressed to the bishops as to fathers, labouring to bring about their unanimity in the apostolical doctrines. Most members of the synod, won over by his arguments, established concord among themselves, and embraced sound doctrine. There were, however, a few, of whom mention has been already made, who opposed these doctrines, and sided with Arius; and amongst them were Menophantus, bishop of Ephesus, Patrophilus, bishop of Scythopolis, Theognis, bishop of Nicaea, and Narcissus, bishop of Neronias, which is a town of the second Cilicia, and is now called Irenopolis; also Theonas, bishop of Marmarica, and Secundus, bishop of Ptolemais in Egypt. They drew up a formulary of their faith, and presented it to the council. As soon as it was read it was torn to pieces, and was declared to be spurious and false. So great was the uproar raised against them, and so many were the reproaches cast on them for having betrayed religion, that they all, with the exception of Secundus and Theonas, stood up and took the lead in publicly renouncing Arius. This impious man, having thus been expelled from the Church, a confession of faith which is received to this day was drawn up by unanimous consent; and, as soon as it was signed, the council was dissolved.

Chapter VII

Confutation of Arianism Deduced from the Writings of Eustathius and Athanasius The above-named bishops, however, did not consent to it in sincerity, but only in appearance. This was afterwards shewn by their plotting against those who were foremost in zeal for religion, as well as by what these latter have written about them. For instance, Eustathius, the famous bishop of Antioch, who has been already mentioned, when explaining the text in the Proverbs, *'The Lord created me in the beginning of His way, before His works of old,'* wrote against them, and refuted their blasphemy.

"I will now proceed to relate how these different events occurred. A general council was summoned at Nicaea, and about two hundred and seventy bishops were convened. There were, however, so many assembled that I cannot state their exact number, neither, indeed, have I taken any great trouble to ascertain this point. When they began to inquire into the nature of the faith, the formulary of Eusebius was brought forward, which contained undisguised evidence of his blasphemy. The reading of it before all occasioned great grief to the audience, on account of its departure from the faith, while it inflicted irremediable shame on the writer. After the Eusebian gang had been clearly convicted, and the impious writing had been torn up in the sight of all, some amongst them by concert, under the pretence of preserving peace, imposed silence on all the ablest speakers. The Ariomaniacs, fearing lest they should be ejected from the Church by so numerous a council of bishops, sprang forward to anathematize and condemn the doctrines condemned, and unanimously signed the confession of faith. Thus having retained possession of their episcopal seats through the most shameful deception, although they ought rather to have been degraded, they continue, sometimes secretly, and sometimes openly, to patronize the condemned doctrines, plotting against the truth by various arguments. Wholly bent upon establishing these plantations of tares, they shrink from the scrutiny of the intelligent, avoid the observant, and attack the preachers of godliness. But we do not believe that these atheists can ever thus overcome the Deity. For though they *'gird themselves'* they *'shall be broken in pieces,'* according to the solemn prophecy of Isaiah."

These are the words of the great Eustathius. Athanasius, his fellow combatant, the champion of the truth, who succeeded the celebrated Alexander in the episcopate, added the following, in a letter addressed to the Africans.

"The bishops convened in council being desirous of refuting the impious assertions invented by the Arians, that the Son was created out of that which was non-existent, that He is a creature and created being, that there was a period in which He was not, and that He is mutable by nature, and being all agreed in propounding the following declarations, which are in accordance with the holy Scriptures; namely, that the Son is by nature only-begotten of God, Word, Power, and sole Wisdom of the Father; that He is, as John said, 'the true God,' and, as Paul has written, 'the brightness of the glory, and the express image of the person of the Father,' the followers of Eusebius, drawn aside by their own vile doctrine, then began to say one to another, Let us agree, for we are also of God; *'There is but one God, by whom we are all things;'* *'Old things are passed away; behold, all things are become new, and all things are of God.'* They also dwelt particularly upon what is contained in 'The Shepherd:' 'Believe above all that there is one God, who created and fashioned all things, and making them to be out of that which is not.'

"But the bishops saw through their evil design and impious artifice, and gave a clearer elucidation of the words 'of God,' and wrote, that the Son is of the substance of God; in order that while the creatures, which do not in any way derive their existence of or from themselves, are said to be of God, the Son alone is said to be of the substance of the Father; this being peculiar to the only-begotten Son, the true Word of the Father. This is the reason why the bishops wrote, that He is of the substance of the Father.

"But when the Arians, who seemed few in number, were again interrogated by the bishops as to whether they admitted 'that the Son is not a creature, but Power, and sole Wisdom, and eternal unchangeable Image of the Father; and that He is very God,' the Eusebians were noticed making signs to one another to shew that these declarations were equally applicable to us. For it is said, that we are *'the image and glory of God;'* and *'for always we who live:'* there are, also, they said, many powers; for it is written—*All the power of God went out of the land of Egypt.'* The canker-worm and the locust are said to be *'a great power.'* And elsewhere it is written, *'The God of powers is with us, the God of Jacob is our helper.'* To which may be added that we are God's own not simply, but because the Son called us *'brethren.'* The declaration that Christ is 'the true God' does not distress us, for, having come into being, He is true.

"Such was the corrupt opinion of the Arians; but on this the bishops, having detected their deceitfulness in this matter, collected from Scripture those passages which say of Christ that He is the glory, the fountain, the stream, and the express image of the person; and they quoted the following words: *'In thy light we shall see light;'* and likewise, *'I and the Father are one.'* They then, with still greater clearness, briefly declared that the Son is of one substance with the Father; for this, indeed, is the signification of the passages which have been quoted. The complaint of the Arians, that these precise words are not to be found in Scripture, is proved groundless by their own practice, for their own impious assertions are not taken from Scripture; for it is not written that the Son is of the non-existent, and that there was a time when He was not: and yet they complain of having been condemned by expressions which, though not actually in Scripture, are in accordance with true religion. They themselves, on the other hand, as though they had found that their words on a dunghill, uttered things verily of earth. The bishops, on the contrary, did not find their expressions for themselves; but, received their testimony from the fathers, and wrote accordingly. Indeed, there were bishops of old time, nearly one hundred and thirty years ago, both of the great city of Rome and of our own city, who condemned those who asserted that the Son is a creature, and that He is not of one substance with the Father. Eusebius, the bishop of Caesarea, was acquainted with these facts; he, at one time, favoured the Arian heresy, but he afterwards signed the confession of faith of the council of Nicaea. He wrote to the people of his diocese, maintaining that the word 'consubstantial' was 'used by illustrious bishops and learned writers as a term for expressing the divinity of the Father and of the Son.' "

So these men concealed their unsoundness through fear of the majority, and gave their assent to the decisions of the council, thus drawing upon themselves the condemnation of the prophet, for the God of all cries unto them, *"This people honour Me with their lips, but in their hearts they are far from me."* Theonas and Secundus, however, did not like to take this course, and were excommunicated by common consent as men who esteemed the Arian blasphemy above evangelical doctrine. The bishops then returned to the council, and drew up twenty laws to regulate the discipline of the Church.

Chapter XI

I shall here insert the letter respecting the faith, written by Eusebius, bishop of Caesarea, as it describes the effrontery of the Arians, who not only despise our fathers, but reject their own: it contains a convincing proof of their madness. They certainly honour Eusebius, because he adopted their sentiments, but yet they openly contradict his writings. He wrote this epistle to some of the Arians, who were accusing him, it seems, of treachery. The letter itself explains the writer's object.

Epistle of Eusebius, Bishop of Caesarea, Which He Wrote from Nicaea When the Great Council Was Assembled "You will have probably learnt from other sources what was decided respecting the faith of the Church at the general council of Nicaea, for the fame of great transactions generally outruns the accurate account of them: but lest rumours not in strict accordance with the truth should reach you, I think it necessary to send to you, first, the formulary of faith originally proposed by us, and, next, the second, published with additions made to our terms. The following is our formulary, which was read in the presence of our most pious emperor, and declared to be couched in right and proper language.

The faith put forth by us. " 'As in our first catechetical instruction, and at the time of our baptism, we received from the bishops who were before us and as we have learnt as we have learnt from the Holy Scriptures, and, alike as presbyters, and as bishops, were wont to believe and teach; so we now believe and thus declare our faith. It is as follows:—

" 'We believe in one God, Father Almighty, the Maker of all things, visible and invisible; and in one Lord Jesus Christ, the Word of God, God of God, Light of Light, Life of Life, Only-begotten Son, First-born of every creature, begotten of the Father before all worlds; by Whom all things were made; Who for our salvation was incarnate, and lived among men. He suffered and rose again the third day, and ascended to the Father; and He will come again in glory to judge the quick and the dead. We also believe in one Holy Ghost.

" 'We believe in the being and continual existence of each of these; that the Father is in truth the Father; the Son in truth the Son; the Holy Ghost in truth the Holy Ghost; as our Lord, when sending out His disciples to preach the Gospel, said, '*Go forth and teach all nations, baptizing them into the name of the Father, and of the Son, and of the Holy Ghost.*' We positively affirm that we hold this faith, that we have always held it, and that we adhere to it even unto death, condemning all ungodly heresy. We testify, as before God the Almighty and our Lord Jesus Christ, that we have thought thus from the heart, and from the soul, ever since we have known ourselves; and we have the means of showing, and, indeed, of convincing you, that we have always during the past thus believed and preached.

"When this formulary had been set forth by us, there was no room to gainsay it; but our beloved emperor himself was the first to testify that it was most orthodox, and that he coincided in opinion with it; and he exhorted the others to sign it, and to receive all the doctrine it contained, with the single addition of the one word— consubstantial.' He explained that this term implied no bodily condition or change, for that the Son did not derive His existence from the Father either by means of division or of abscission, since an immaterial, intellectual, and incorporeal nature could not be subject to any bodily condition or change. These things must be understood as bearing a divine and mysterious signification. Thus reasoned our wisest and most religious emperor. The addition of the word consubstantial has given occasion for the composition of the following formulary:—

The creed published by the council. " 'We believe in one God, Father Almighty, Maker of all things visible and invisible. And in one Lord Jesus Christ, the Son of God, begotten of the Father; only-begotten, that is, of the substance of the Father, God of God, Light of Light, Very God of very God, begotten not made, being of one substance with the Father: by Whom all things were made both in heaven and on earth: Who for us men, and for our salvation, came down from heaven, and was incarnate, and was made man; He suffered, and rose again the third day; He ascended into heaven, and is coming to judge both quick and dead. And we believe in the Holy

Ghost. The holy Catholic and Apostolic Church anathematizes all who say that there was a time when the Son of God was not; that before He was begotten He was not; that He was made out of the non-existent; or that He is of a different essence and of a different substance from the Father; and that He is susceptible of variation or change.'

"When they had set forth this formulary, we did not leave without examination that passage in which it is said that the Son is of the substance of the Father, and consubstantial with the Father. Questions and arguments thence arose, and the meaning of the terms was exactly tested. Accordingly they were led to confess that the word consubstantial signifies that the Son is of the Father, but not as being a part of the Father. We deemed it right to receive this opinion; for that is sound doctrine which teaches that the Son is of the Father, but not part of His substance. From the love of peace, and lest we should fall from the true belief, we also accept this view, neither do we reject the term 'consubstantial.' For the same reason we admitted the expression, 'begotten, but not made;' for they alleged that the word 'made' applies generally to all things which were created by the Son, to which the Son is in no respect similar; and that consequently He is not a created thing, like the things made by Him, but is of a substance superior to all created objects. The Holy Scriptures teach Him to be begotten of the Father, by a mode of generation which is incomprehensible and inexplicable to all created beings. So also the term 'of one substance with the Father,' when investigated, was accepted not in accordance with bodily relations or similarity to mortal beings. For it was also shown that it does not either imply division of substance, nor abscission, nor any modification or change or diminution in the power of the Father, all of which are alien from the nature of the unbegotten Father. It was concluded that the expression *'being of one substance with the Father,'* implies that the Son of God does not resemble, in any one respect, the creatures which He has made; but that to the Father alone, who begat Him, He is in all points perfectly like: for He is of the essence and of the substance of none save of the Father. This interpretation having been given of the doctrine, it appeared right to us to assent to it, especially as we were aware that of the ancients some learned and celebrated bishops and writers have used the term 'consubstantial' with respect to the divinity of the Father and of the Son.

"These are the circumstances which I had to communicate respecting the published formulary of the faith. To it we all agreed, not without investigation, but, after having subjected the views submitted to us to thorough examination in the presence of our most beloved emperor, for the above reasons we all acquiesced in it. We also allowed that the anathema appended by them to their formulary of faith should be accepted, because it prohibits the use of words which are not scriptural; through which almost all the disorder and troubles of the Church have arisen. And since no passage of the inspired Scripture uses the terms 'out of the non-existent,' or that 'there was a time when He was not,' nor indeed any of the other phrases of the same class, it did not appear reasonable to assert or to teach such things. In this opinion, therefore, we judged it right to agree, since, indeed, we had never, at any former period, been accustomed to use such terms. Moreover, the condemnation of the assertion that before He was begotten He was not, did not appear to involve any incongruity, because all assent to the fact that He was the Son of God before He was begotten according to the flesh. And here our emperor, most beloved by God, began to reason concerning His divine origin, and His existence before all ages. He was virtually in the Father without generation, even before He was actually begotten, the Father having always been the Father, just as He has always been a King and a Saviour, and, virtually, all things, and has never known any change of being or action.

"We have thought it requisite, beloved brethren, to transmit you an account of these circumstances, in order to show you what examination and investigation we bestowed on all the questions which we had to decide; and also to prove how at one time we resisted firmly, even to the last hour, when doctrines improperly expressed offended us, and, at another time, we, without contention, accepted the articles which contained nothing objectionable, when after a thorough and candid investigation of their signification, they appeared perfectly comformable with what had been confessed by us in the formulary of faith which we had published."

COMMONITORY

Vincent of Lérins

By the middle of the fifth century after Christ, although a credal tradition had been established, the problem of theological disagreement had again become seriously disruptive. A number of heresies having to do with the Trinity forced an investigation into the criteria for distinguishing theological truth from heresy. Vincent, a monk of Gallic nationality who lived in the monastery of Lérins (in what is now France), undertook such a study and summed up his results in his Commonitory (A.D. *434*)*. Although allowing for theological development if it comes about in an orderly, gradualist way, he proclaims the danger of the heresies of his own day, and for good measure (and conveniently for us) sums up the doctrine of the Trinity as he saw it.*

*The Donatists (so called after Donatus, a fourth-century bishop of Carthage) believed that sanctity is essential for the administration of sacraments and church membership; their great strictness on this point led them to secede from the rest of the African Church because of its willingness to endure what they considered evil men in its midst. The Arians (named after Arius, a fourth-century Greek theologian) denied the co-eternity and consubstantiality of Christ and God, that is, the doctrine that the Son is of the same substance as the Father (**see Theodoret, pages 384–391**).*

Chapter II. A General Rule for Distinguishing the Truth of the Catholic Faith from the Falsehood of Heretical Pravity

I have often then inquired earnestly and attentively of very many men eminent for sanctity and learning, how and by what sure and so to speak universal rule I may be able to distinguish the truth of Catholic faith from the falsehood of heretical pravity; and I have always, and in almost every instance, received an answer to this effect: That whether I or any one else should wish to detect the frauds and avoid the snares of heretics as they rise, and to continue sound and complete in the Catholic faith, we must, the Lord helping, fortify our own belief in two ways; first, by the authority of the Divine Law, and then, by the Tradition of the Catholic Church.

But here some one perhaps will ask, Since the canon of Scripture is complete, and sufficient of itself for everything, and more than sufficient, what need is there to join with it the authority of the Church's interpretation? For this reason,—because, owing to the depth of Holy Scripture, all do not accept it in one and the same sense, but one understands its words in one way, another in another; so that it seems to be capable of as many interpretations as there are interpreters. For Novatian expounds it one way, Sabellius another, Donatus another, Arius, Eunomius, Macedonius, another, Photinus, Apollinaris, Priscillian, another, Iovinian, Pelagius, Celestius, another, lastly, Nestorius another. Therefore, it is very necessary, on account of so great intricacies of such various error, that the rule for the right understanding of the prophets and apostles should be framed in accordance with the standard of Ecclesiastical and Catholic interpretation.

Moreover, in the Catholic Church itself, all possible care must be taken, that we hold that faith which has been believed everywhere, always, by all. For that is truly and in the strictest sense "Catholic," which, as the name itself and the reason of the thing declare, comprehends all universally. This rule we shall observe if we follow universality, antiquity, consent. We shall follow universality if we confess that one faith to be true, which the whole Church throughout the world confesses; antiquity, if we in no wise depart from those interpretations which it is manifest were notoriously held by our holy ancestors and fathers; consent, in like manner, if in antiquity itself we adhere to the consentient definitions and determinations of all, or at the least of almost all priests and doctors.

Chapter III. What Is to Be Done if One or More Dissent from the Rest

What then will a Catholic Christian do, if a small portion of the Church have cut itself off from the communion of the universal faith? What, surely, but prefer the soundness of the whole body to the unsoundness of a pestilent and corrupt member? What, if some novel contagion seek to infect not merely an insignificant portion of the Church, but the whole? Then it will be his care to cleave to antiquity, which at this day cannot possibly be seduced by any fraud of novelty.

But what, if in antiquity itself there be found error on the part of two or three men, or at any rate of a city or even of a province? Then it will be his care by all means, to

A Select Library of Nicene and Post-Nicene Fathers of the Christian Church, ed. P. Schaff and H. Wace (second series; Grand Rapids, Mich.: Wm. Eerdmans Publishing Co., 1955), Vol. XI, 132–134, 140–142, 147–149.

prefer the decrees, if such there be, of an ancient General Council to the rashness and ignorance of a few. But what, if some error should spring up on which no such decree is found to bear? Then he must collate and consult and interrogate the opinions of the ancients, of those, namely, who, though living in divers times and places, yet continuing in the communion and faith of the one Catholic Church, stand forth acknowledged and approved authorities: and whatsoever he shall ascertain to have been held, written, taught, not by one or two of these only, but by all, equally, with one consent, openly, frequently, persistently, that he must understand that he himself also is to believe without any doubt or hesitation.

Chapter IV. The Evil Resulting from the Bringing in of Novel Doctrine Shown in the Instances of the Donatists and Arians

But that we may make what we say more intelligible, we must illustrate it by individual examples, and enlarge upon it somewhat more fully, lest by aiming at too great brevity important matters be hurried over and lost sight of.

In the time of Donatus, from whom his followers were called Donatists, when great numbers in Africa were rushing headlong into their own mad error, and unmindful of their name, their religion, their profession, were preferring the sacrilegious temerity of one man before the Church of Christ, then they alone throughout Africa were safe within the sacred precincts of the Catholic faith, who, detesting the profane schism, continued in communion with the universal Church, leaving to posterity an illustrious example, how, and how well in future the soundness of the whole body should be preferred before the madness of one, or at most of a few.

So also when the Arian poison had infected not an insignificant portion of the Church but almost the whole world, so that a sort of blindness had fallen upon almost all the bishops of the Latin tongue, circumvented partly by force partly by fraud, and was preventing them from seeing what was most expedient to be done in the midst of so much confusion, then whoever was a true lover and worshipper of Christ, preferring the ancient belief to the novel misbelief, escaped the pestilent infection.

By the peril of which time was abundantly shown how great a calamity the introduction of a novel doctrine causes. For then truly not only interests of small account, but others of the very gravest importance, were subverted. For not only affinities, relationships, friendships, families, but moreover, cities, peoples, provinces, nations, at last the whole Roman Empire, were shaken to their foundation and ruined.

For when this same profane Arian novelty, like a Bellona or a Fury, had first taken captive the Emperor, and had then subjected all the principal persons of the palace to new laws, from that time it never ceased to involve everything in confusion, disturbing all things, public and private, sacred and profane, paying no regard to what was good and true, but, as though holding a position of authority, smiting whomsoever it pleased. Then wives were violated, widows ravished, virgins profaned, monasteries demolished, clergymen ejected, the inferior clergy scourged, priests driven into exile, jails, prisons, mines, filled with saints, of whom the greater part, forbidden to enter into cities, thrust forth from their homes to wander in deserts and caves, among rocks and the haunts of wild beasts, exposed to nakedness, hunger, thirst, were worn out and consumed. Of all of which there was no other cause than that, while human superstitions are being brought in to supplant heavenly doctrine, while well established antiquity is being subverted by wicked novelty, while the institutions of former ages are being set at naught, while the decrees of our fathers are being rescinded, while the determinations of our ancestors are being torn in pieces, the lust of profane and novel curiosity refuses to restrict itself within the most chaste limits of hallowed and uncorrupt antiquity.

Chapter XIII. The Catholic Doctrine of the Trinity and the Incarnation Explained

In these ways then do these rabid dogs, Nestorius, Apollinaris, and Photinus, bark against the Catholic faith: Photinus, by denying the Trinity; Apollinaris, by teaching that the nature of the Word is mutable, and refusing to acknowledge that there are two substances in Christ, denying moreover either that Christ had a soul at all, or, at all events, that he had a rational soul, and asserting that the Word of God supplied the place of the rational soul; Nestorius, by affirming that there were always or at any rate that once there were two Christs. But the Catholic Church, holding the right faith both concerning God and concerning our Saviour, is guilty of blasphemy neither in the mystery of the Trinity, nor in that of the Incarnation of Christ. For she worships both one Godhead in the plenitude of the Trinity, and the equality of the Trinity in one and the same majesty, and she confesses one Christ Jesus, not two; the same both God and man, the one as truly as the other. One Person indeed she believes in Him, but two substances; two substances but one Person: Two substances, because the Word of God is not mutable, so as to be convertible into flesh; one Person, lest by acknowledging two sons she should seem to worship not a Trinity, but a Quaternity.

But it will be well to unfold this same doctrine more distinctly and explicitly again and again.

In God there is one substance, but three Persons; in Christ two substances, but one Person. In the Trinity, another and another Person, not another and another substance (distinct Persons, not distinct substances); in the Saviour another and another substance, not another and another Person, (distinct substances, not distinct Persons). How in the Trinity another and another Person (distinct Persons) not another and another substance (distinct substances)? Because there is one Person of the Father, another of the Son, another of the Holy Ghost; but yet there is not another and another nature (distinct natures) but one and the same nature. How in the Saviour another and another substance, not another and another Person (two distinct substances, not two distinct Persons)? Because there is one substance of the Godhead, another of the manhood. But yet the Godhead and the manhood are not another and another Person (two distinct Persons), but one and the same Christ, one and the same Son of God, and one and the same Person of one and the same Christ and Son of God, in like manner as in man the flesh is one thing and the soul another, but one and the same man, both soul and flesh. In Peter and Paul the soul is one thing, the flesh another; yet there are not two Peters,—one soul, the other flesh, or two Pauls, one soul, the other flesh,—but one and the same Peter, and one and the same Paul, consisting each of two diverse natures, soul and body. Thus, then, in one and the same Christ there are two substances, one divine, the other human; one of (ex) God the Father, the other of (ex) the Virgin Mother; one co-eternal with and co-equal with the Father, the other temporal and inferior to the Father; one consubstantial with his Father, the other consubstantial with his Mother, but one and the same Christ in both substances. There is not, therefore, one Christ God, the other man, not one uncreated, the other created; not one impassible, the other passible; not one equal to the Father, the other inferior to the Father; not one of his Father (ex), the other of his Mother (ex), but one and the same Christ, God and man, the same uncreated and created, the same unchangeable and incapable of suffering, the same acquainted by experience with both change and suffering, the same equal to the Father and inferior to the Father, the same begotten of the Father before time, ("before the world"), the same born of his mother in time ("in the world"), perfect God, perfect Man. In God supreme divinity, in man perfect humanity. Perfect humanity, I say, forasmuch as it hath both soul and flesh; the flesh, very flesh; our flesh, his mother's flesh the soul, intellectual, endowed with mind and reason. There is then in Christ the Word, the soul, the flesh; but the whole is one Christ, one Son of God, and one our Saviour and Redeemer: One, not by I know not what corruptible confusion of Godhead and manhood, but by a certain entire and singular unity of Person. For the conjunction hath not converted and changed the one nature into the other, (which is the characteristic error of the Arians), but rather hath in such wise compacted both into one that while there always remains in Christ the singularity of one and the self-same Person, there abides eternally withal the characteristic property of each nature; whence it follows, that neither doth God (i.e., the divine nature) even begin to be body, nor doth the body ever cease to be body. The which may be illustrated in human nature: for not only in the present life, but in the future also, each individual man will consist of soul and body; nor will his body ever be converted into soul, or his soul into body; but while each individual man will live for ever, the distinction between the two substances will continue in each individual man for ever. So likewise in Christ each substance will for ever retain its own characteristic property, yet without prejudice to the unity of Person.

Chapter XIV. Jesus Christ Man in Truth, Not in Semblance

But when we use the word "Person," and say that God became man by means of a Person, there is reason to fear that our meaning may be taken to be, that God the Word assumed our nature merely in imitation, and performed the actions of man, being man not in reality, but only in semblance, just as in a theatre, one man within a brief space represents several persons, not one of whom himself is. For when one undertakes to sustain the part of another, he performs the offices, or does the acts, of the person whose part he sustains, but he is not himself that person. So, to take an illustration from secular life and one in high favour with the Manichees, when a tragedian represents a priest or a king, he is not really a priest or a king. For, as soon as the play is over, the person or character whom he represented ceases to be. God forbid that we should have anything to do with such nefarious and wicked mockery. Be it the infatuation of the Manichees, those preachers of hallucination, who say that the Son of God, God, was not a human person really and truly, but that He counterfeited the person of a man in feigned conversation and manner of life.

But the Catholic Faith teaches that the Word of God became man in such wise, that He took upon Him our nature, not feignedly and in semblance, but in reality and truth, and performed human actions, not as though He were imitating the actions of another, but as performing His own, and as being in reality the person whose part He sustained. Just as we ourselves also, when we speak, reason, live, subsist, do not imitate men, but are men. Peter and John, for instance, were men, not by imitation, but by being men in reality. Paul did not counterfeit an apostle, or feign himself to be Paul, but was an apostle, was Paul. So, also, that which God the Word did, in His condescension, in assuming and having flesh, in speaking, acting, and suffering, through the instrumentality of flesh, yet without any marring of His own divine nature, came in one word to this:—He did not imitate or feign Himself to be perfect man, but He shewed Himself to be very man in reality and truth. Therefore, as the soul united to the flesh, but yet not changed into flesh, does not imitate man, but is man, and man not feignedly but substantially, so also God the Word, without any conversion of Himself, in uniting Himself to man, became man, not by confusion, not by imitation, but by actually being and subsisting. Away then, once and for all, with the notion of His Person as of an assumed fictitious character, where always what is is one thing, what is counterfeited another, where the man who acts never is the man whose part he acts. God forbid that we should believe God the Word to have taken upon Himself the person of a man in this illusory way. Rather let us acknowledge that while His own unchangeable substance remained, and while He took upon Himself the nature of perfect man, Himself actually was flesh, Himself actually was man, Himself actually was personally man; not feignedly, but in truth, not in imitation, but in substance; not, finally, so as to cease to be when the performance was over, but so as to be, and continue to be substantially and permanently.

Chapter XXIII. On Development in Religious Knowledge

But some one will say perhaps, Shall there, then, be no progress in Christ's Church? Certainly; all possible progress. For what being is there, so envious of men, so full of hatred to God, who would seek to forbid it? Yet on condition that it be real progress, not alteration of the faith. For progress requires that the subject be enlarged in itself, alteration that it be transformed into something else. The intelligence, then, the knowledge, the wisdom, as well of individuals as of all, as well of one man as of the whole Church, ought, in the course of ages and centuries, to increase and make much and vigorous progress; but yet only in its own kind; that is to say, in the same doctrine, in the same sense, and in the same meaning.

The growth of religion in the soul must be analogous to the growth of the body, which, though in process of years it is developed and attains its full size, yet remains still the same. There is a wide difference between the flower of youth and the maturity of age; yet they who were once young are still the same now that they have become old, insomuch that though the stature and outward form of the individual are changed, yet his nature is one and the same, his person is one and the same. An infant's limbs are small, a young man's large, yet the infant and the young man are the same. Men when full grown have the same number of joints that they had when children; and if there be any to which maturer age has given birth, these were already present in embryo, so that nothing new is produced in them when old which was not already latent in them when children. This, then, is undoubtedly the true and legitimate rule of progress, this the established and most beautiful order of growth, that mature age ever develops in the man those parts and forms which the wisdom of the Creator had already framed eforehand in the infant. Whereas, if the human form were changed into some shape elonging to another kind, or at any rate, if the number of its limbs were increased or liminished, the result would be that the whole body would become either a wreck or a nonster, or, at the least, would be impaired and enfeebled.

In like manner, it behoves Christian doctrine to follow the same laws of progress, o as to be consolidated by years, enlarged by time, refined by age, and yet, withal, to ontinue uncorrupt and unadulterate, complete and perfect in all the measurement of ts parts, and, so to speak, in all its proper members and senses, admitting no change, o waste of its distinctive property, no variation in its limits.

For example: Our forefathers in the old time sowed wheat in the Church's field. It vould be most unmeet and iniquitous if we, their descendants, instead of the genuine ruth of corn, should reap the counterfeit error of tares. This rather should be the esult,—there should be no discrepancy between the first and the last. From doctrine vhich was sown as wheat, we should reap, in the increase, doctrine of the same kind— vheat also; so that when in process of time any of the original seed is developed, and ow flourishes under cultivation, no change may ensue in the character of the plant. There may supervene shape, form, variation in outward appearance, but the nature of ach kind must remain the same. God forbid that those rose-beds of Catholic interpre- ation should be converted into thorns and thistles. God forbid that in that spiritual aradise from plants of cinnamon and balsam darnel and wolfsbane should of a sud- len shoot forth.

Therefore, whatever has been sown by the fidelity of the Fathers in this husbandry f God's Church, the same ought to be cultivated and taken care of by the industry of heir children, the same ought to flourish and ripen, the same ought to advance and o forward to perfection. For it is right that those ancient doctrines of heavenly philos- phy should, as time goes on, be cared for, smoothed, polished; but not that they hould be changed, not that they should be maimed, not that they should be mutilated. They may receive proof, illustration, definiteness; but they must retain withal their ompleteness, their integrity, their characteristic properties.

For if once this license of impious fraud be admitted, I dread to say in how great langer religion will be of being utterly destroyed and annihilated. For if any one art of Catholic truth be given up, another, and another, and another will thence- orward be given up as a matter of course, and the several individual portions having een rejected, what will follow in the end but the rejection of the whole? On the ther hand, if what is new begins to be mingled with what is old, foreign with domes- ic, profane with sacred, the custom will of necessity creep on universally, till at last he Church will have nothing left untampered with, nothing unadulterated, nothing ound, nothing pure; but where formerly there was a sanctuary of chaste and un- lefiled truth, thenceforward there will be a brothel of impious and base errors. May God's mercy avert this wickedness from the minds of his servants; be it rather the renzy of the ungodly.

But the Church of Christ, the careful and watchful guardian of the doctrines depos- ted in her charge, never changes anything in them, never diminishes, never adds, does ot cut off what is necessary, does not add what is superfluous, does not lose her own, loes not appropriate what is another's, but while dealing faithfully and judiciously with ancient doctrine, keeps this one object carefully in view,—if there be anything which antiquity has left shapeless and rudimentary, to fashion and polish it, if anything already reduced to shape and developed, to consolidate and strengthen it, if any already ratified and defined to keep and guard it. Finally, what other object have Councils ever aimed at in their decrees, than to provide that what was before believed in simplicity should in future be believed intelligently, that what was before preached coldly should in future be preached earnestly, that what was before practised negligently should thenceforward be practised with double solicitude? This, I say, is what the Catholic Church, roused by the novelties of heretics, has accomplished by the decrees of her Councils,—this, and nothing else,—she has thenceforward consigned to posterity in writing what she had received from those of olden times only by tradition, comprising a great amount of matter in a few words, and often, for the better understanding, designating an old article of the faith by the characteristic of a new name.

ENCHIRIDION

Augustine of Hippo

St. Augustine of Hippo (A.D. *354–430*) *was born near Carthage in North Africa. He tells us in his* Confessions *of his dissolute youth and of how he was educated at Carthage and Rome to be a rhetorician, thus preparing himself for an illustrious career in public life. But he was also a philosopher, at least in the sense of a seeker after truth; and he successively adopted and then abandoned the major systems of thought then current: Manichaeism, astrology, scepticism, and Neoplatonism. Finally, in* A.D. *386, he was converted to Christianity. He went on to become a bishop and one of the four great Fathers of the Latin Church.*

Within the Church Augustine found ample outlet for his skill and training in rhetoric. Again and again he was called on to write definitive refutations of heresies. Even while leading the busy life of an administrator in charge of an important North African bishopric, he found time to write over a hundred books and hundreds of letters and sermons.

Most of these writings fall into three broad categories, each directed against one of the major heresies of the age: Manichaeism, Donatism, and Pelagianism. Against the Manichees (*and Christians influenced by this Persian religion of the third century after Christ*), *he insisted that God had created the entire universe and was thus supreme over all of it, and not doomed to engage in an endless struggle with the forces of evil. He defended the unity of the international Church against the Donatist view that individual priests and bishops who yielded to Roman torture lost their sacramental powers. And against Pelagius he argued that through his own efforts alone man could never merit heaven, and that his only hope is to pray for God's grace to aid him. It is this last polemic that he had chiefly in mind in writing his* Enchiridion *("Manual"), from which the selections below were taken.*

Chap. 25. The Death of the Body Is Man's Peculiar Punishment

There is one form of punishment peculiar to man—the death of the body. God had threatened him with this punishment of death if he should sin, leaving him indeed to the freedom of his own will, but yet commanding his obedience under pain of death; and He placed him amid the happiness of Eden, as it were in a protected nook of life, with the intention that, if he preserved his righteousness, he should thence ascend to a better place.

Chap. 26. Through Adam's Sin His Whole Posterity Were Corrupted, and Were Born under the Penalty of Death, Which He Had Incurred

Thence, after his sin, he was driven into exile, and by his sin the whole race of which he was the root was corrupted in him, and thereby subjected to the penalty of death. And so it happens that all descended from him, and from the woman who had led him into sin, and was condemned at the same time with him,—being the offspring of carnal lust on which the same punishment of disobedience was visited,—were tainted with the original sin, and were by it drawn through divers errors and sufferings into that last and endless punishment which they suffer in common with the fallen angels, their corrupters and masters, and the partakers of their doom. And thus "by one man sin entered into the world, and death by sin; and so death passed upon all men, for that all have sinned." By "the world" the apostle, of course, means in this place the whole human race.

Chap. 27. The State of Misery to Which Adam's Sin Reduced Mankind, and the Restoration Effected through the Mercy of God

Thus, then, matters stood. The whole mass of the human race was under condemnation, was lying steeped and wallowing in misery, and was being tossed from one form of evil to another, and, having joined the faction of the fallen angels, was paying the well-merited penalty of that impious rebellion. For whatever the wicked freely do through blind and unbridled lust, and whatever they suffer against their will in the way of open punishment, this all evidently pertains to the just wrath of God. But the goodness of the Creator never fails either to supply life and vital power to the wicked angels (without which their existence would soon come to an end); or, in the case of

A Select Library of the Nicene and Post-Nicene Fathers of the Christian Church, ed. Philip Schaff (Grand Rapids, Mich.: Wm. B. Eerdmans Publishing Co., 1956), Vol. III, 246–249, 252–254, 263–264, 267–271.

mankind, who spring from a condemned and corrupt stock, to impart form and life to their seed, to fashion their members, and through the various seasons of their life, and in the different parts of the earth, to quicken their senses, and bestow upon them the nourishment they need. For He judged it better to bring good out of evil, than not to permit any evil to exist. And if He had determined that in the case of men, as in the case of the fallen angels, there should be no restoration to happiness, would it not have been quite just, that the being who rebelled against God, who in the abuse of his freedom spurned and transgressed the command of his Creator when he could so easily have kept it, who defaced in himself the image of his Creator by stubbornly turning away from His light, who by an evil use of his free-will broke away from his wholesome bondage to the Creator's laws,—would it not have been just that such a being should have been wholly and to all eternity deserted by God, and left to suffer the everlasting punishment he had so richly earned? Certainly so God would have done, had He been only just and not also merciful, and had He not designed that His unmerited mercy should shine forth the more brightly in contrast with the unworthiness of its objects.

Chap. 29. The Restored Part of Humanity Shall, in Accordance with the Promises of God, Succeed to the Place Which the Rebellious Angels Lost

And so it pleased God, the Creator and Governor of the universe, that, since the whole body of the angels had not fallen into rebellion, the part of them which had fallen should remain in perdition eternally, and that the other part, which had in the rebellion remained steadfastly loyal, should rejoice in the sure and certain knowledge of their eternal happiness; but that, on the other hand, mankind, who constituted the remainder of the intelligent creation, having perished without exception under sin, both original and actual, and the consequent punishment, should be in part restored, and should fill up the gap which the rebellion and fall of the devils had left in the company of the angels. For this is the promise to the saints, that at the resurrection they shall be equal to the angels of God. . . .

Chap. 30. Men Are Not Saved by Good Works, Nor by the Free Determination of Their Own Will, but by the Grace of God through Faith

But this part of the human race to which God has promised pardon and a share in His eternal kingdom, can they be restored through the merit of their own works? God forbid. For what good work can a lost man perform, except so far as he has been delivered from perdition? Can they do anything by the free determination of their own will? Again I say, God forbid. For it was by the evil use of his free-will that man destroyed both it and himself. For, as a man who kills himself must, of course, be alive when he kills himself, but after he has killed himself ceases to live, and cannot restore himself to life; so, when man by his own free-will sinned, then sin being victorious over him, the freedom of his will was lost. "For of whom a man is overcome, of the same is he brought in bondage." This is the judgment of the Apostle Peter. And as it is certainly true, what kind of liberty, I ask, can the bond-slave possess, except when it pleases him to sin? For he is freely in bondage who does with pleasure the will of his master. Accordingly, he who is the servant of sin is free to sin. And hence he will not be free to do right, until, being freed from sin, he shall begin to be the servant of righteousness. And this is true liberty, for he has pleasure in the righteous deed; and it is at the same time a holy bondage, for he is obedient to the will of God. But whence comes this liberty to do right to the man who is in bondage and sold under sin, except he be redeemed by Him who has said, "If the Son shall make you free, ye shall be free indeed"? And before this redemption is wrought in a man, whn he is not yet free to do what is right, how can he talk of the freedom of his will and his good works, except he be inflated by that foolish pride of boasting which the apostle restrains when he says, "By grace are ye saved, through faith."

Chap. 31. Faith Itself Is the Gift of God; and Good Works Will Not Be Wanting in Those Who Believe

And lest men should arrogate to themselves the merit of their own faith at least, not understanding that this too is the gift of God, this same apostle, who says in another place that he had "obtained mercy of the Lord to be faithful," here also adds: "and that not of yourselves; it is the gift of God: not of works, lest any man should boast." And lest it should be thought that good works will be wanting in those who believe, he adds further: "For we are His workmanship, created in Christ Jesus unto good works, which God hath before ordained that we should walk in them." We shall be made truly free, then, when God fashions us, that is, forms and creates us anew, not as men —for He has done that already—but as good men, which His grace is now doing, that we may be a new creation in Christ Jesus, according as it is said: "Create in me a clean heart, O God." For God has already created his heart, so far as the physical structure of the human heart is concerned; but the psalmist prays for the renewal of the life which was still lingering in his heart.

Chap. 32. The Freedom of the Will Is Also the Gift of God, for God Worketh in Us Both to Will and to Do

And further, should any one be inclined to boast, not indeed of his works, but of the freedom of his will, as if the first merit belonged to him, this very liberty of good action being given to him as a reward he had earned, let him listen to this same preacher of grace, when he says: "For it is God which worketh in you, both to will and to do of His own good pleasure;" and in another place: "So, then, it is not of him that willeth, nor of him that runneth, but of God that showeth mercy." Now as, undoubtedly, if a man is of the age to use his reason, he cannot believe, hope, love, unless he will to do so, nor obtain the prize of the high calling of God unless he voluntarily run for it; in what sense is it "not of him that willeth, nor of him that runneth, but of God that showeth mercy," except that, as it is written, "the preparation of the heart is from the Lord"? Otherwise, if it is said, "It is not of him that willeth, nor of him that runneth, but of God that showeth mercy," because it is of both, that is, both of the will of man and of the mercy of God, so that we are to understand the saying, "It is not of him that willeth, nor of him that runneth, but of God that showeth mercy," as if it meant the will of man alone is not sufficient, if the mercy of God go not with it,—then it will follow that the mercy of God alone is not sufficient, if the will of man go not with it; and therefore, if we may rightly say, "it is not of man that willeth, but of God that showeth mercy," because the will of man by itself is not enough, why may we not also rightly put it in the converse way: "It is not of God that showeth mercy, but of man that willeth," because the mercy of God by itself does not suffice? Surely, if no Christian will dare to say this, "It is not of God that showeth mercy, but of man that willeth," lest he should openly contradict the apostle, it follows that the true interpretation of the saying, "It is not of him that willeth, nor of him that runneth, but of God that showeth mercy," is that the whole work belongs to God, who both makes the will of man righteous, and thus prepares it for assistance, and assists it when it is prepared. For the man's righteousness of will precedes many of God's gifts, but not all; and it must itself be included among those which it does not precede. We read in Holy Scripture, both that God's mercy "shall meet me," and that His mercy "shall follow me." It goes before the unwilling to make him willing; it follows the willing to make his will effectual. Why are we taught to pray for our enemies, who are plainly unwilling to lead a holy life, unless that God may work willingness in them? And why are we ourselves taught to ask that we may receive, unless that He who has created in us the wish, may Himself satisfy the wish? We pray, then, for our enemies, that the mercy of God may prevent them, as it has prevented us: we pray for ourselves that His mercy may follow us.

Chap. 33. Men, Being by Nature the Children of Wrath, Needed a Mediator In What Sense God Is Said to Be Angry

And so the human race was lying under a just condemnation, and all men were the children of wrath. . . . Now as men were lying under this wrath by reason of thei original sin, and as the original sin was the more heavy and deadly in proportion tc the number and magnitude of the actual sins which were added to it, there was neec for a Mediator, that is, for a reconciler, who, by the offering of one sacrifice, of whic all the sacrifices of the law and the prophets were types, should take away this wrath Wherefore the apostle says: "For if, when we were enemies, we were reconciled t God by the death of His Son, much more, being reconciled, we shall be saved by Hi life.". . . But our being reconciled to God through a Mediator, and receiving th Holy Spirit, so that we who were enemies are made sons ("For as many as are led b the Spirit of God, they are the sons of God"): this is the grace of God through Jesu Christ our Lord.

Chap. 42. The Sacrament of Baptism Indicates Our Death with Christ to Sin and Our Resurrection with Him to Newness of Life

And this is the meaning of the great sacrament of baptism which is solemnized amon us, that all who attain to this grace should die to sin, as He is said to have died to sin because He died in the flesh, which is the likeness of sin; and rising from the fon regenerate, as He arose alive from the grave, should begin a new life in the Spirit whatever may be the age of the body.

Chap. 43. Baptism and the Grace Which It Typifies Are Open to All, Bot Infants and Adults

For from the infant newly born to the old man bent with age, as there is none shu out from baptism, so there is none who in baptism does not die to sin. But infants di only to original sin; those who are older die also to all the sins which their evil live have added to the sin which they brought with them.

Chap. 44. In Speaking of Sin, the Singular Number Is Often Put for the Plural, and the Plural for the Singular

But even these latter are frequently said to die to sin, though undoubtedly they die not to one sin, but to all the numerous actual sins they have committed in thought, word, or deed: for the singular number is often put for the plural. . . .

Chap. 45. In Adam's First Sin, Many Kinds of Sin Were Involved

However, even in that one sin which "by one man entered into the world, and so passed upon all men," and on account of which infants are baptized, a number of distinct sins may be observed, if it be analyzed as it were into its separate elements. For there is in it pride, because man chose to be under his own dominion, rather than under the dominion of God; and blasphemy, because he did not believe God; and murder, for he brought death upon himself; and spiritual fornication, for the purity of the human soul was corrupted by the seducing blandishments of the serpent; and theft, for man turned to his own use the food he had been forbidden to touch; and avarice, for he had a craving for more than should have been sufficient for him; and whatever other sin can be discovered on careful reflection to be involved in this one admitted sin.

Chap. 46. It Is Probable That Children Are Involved in the Guilt Not Only of the First Pair, but of Their Own Immediate Parents

And it is said, with much appearance of probabilty, that infants are involved in the guilt of the sins not only of the first pair, but of their own immediate parents. For that divine judgment, "I shall visit the iniquities of the fathers upon the children," certainly applies to them before they come under the new covenant by regeneration. And it was this new covenant that was prophesied or, which it was said by Ezekiel, that the sons should not bear the iniquity of the fathers, and that it should no longer be a proverb in Israel, "The fathers have eaten sour grapes, and the children's teeth are set on edge." Here lies the necessity that each man should be born again, that he might be freed from the sin in which he was born. For the sins committed afterwards can be cured by penitence, as we see is the case after baptism. And therefore the new birth would not have been appointed only that the first birth was sinful, so sinful that even one who was legitimately born in wedlock says: "I was shapen in iniquities, and in sins did my mother conceive me." He did not say in *iniquity,* or in *sin,* though he migh have said so correctly; but he preferred to say "iniquities" and "sins," because in that one sin which passed upon all men, and which was so great that human nature was by it made subject to inevitable death, many sins, as I showed above, may be discriminated; and further, because there are other sins of the immediate parents, which, though they have not the same effect in producing a change of nature, yet subject the children to guilt unless the divine grace and mercy interpose to rescue them.

Chap. 47. It Is Difficult to Decide Whether the Sins of a Man's Other Progenitors Are Imputed to Him

But about the sins of the other progenitors who intervene between Adam and a man's own parents, a question may very well be raised. Whether every one who is born is involved in all their accumulated evil acts, in all their multiplied original guilt, so tha the later he is born, so much the worse is his condition; or whether God threatens t visit the iniquity of the fathers upon the children unto the third and fourth generations because in His mercy He does not extend His wrath against the sins of the progenitor further than that, lest those who do not obtain the grace of regeneration might b crushed down under too heavy a burden if they were compelled to bear as origina guilt all the sins of all their progenitors from the very beginning of the human race and to pay the penalty due to them; or whether any other solution of this great ques tion may or may not be found in Scripture by a more diligent search and a more care ful interpretation, I dare not rashly affirm.

Chap. 48. The Guilt of the First Sin Is So Great That It Can Be Washed Awa Only in the Blood of the Mediator, Jesus Christ

Nevertheless, that one sin, admitted into a place where such perfect happiness reigned was of so heinous a character, that in one man the whole human race was originally and as one may say, radically, condemned; and it cannot be pardoned and blotted ou except through the one Mediator between God and men, the man Christ Jesus, wh only has had power to be so born as not to need a second birth.

Chap. 50. Christ Took Away Not Only the One Original Sin, but All the Othe Sins That Have Been Added to It

The first man brought one sin into the world, but this man took away not only tha one sin, but all that He found added to it. Hence the apostle says: "And not as it wa by one that sinned, so is the gift: for the judgment was by one to condemnation, bu the free gift is of many offenses unto justification." For it is evident that the one si which we bring with us by nature would, even if it stood alone, bring us under con demnation; but the free gift justifies man from many offenses: for each man, in addi tion to the one sin which, in common with all his kind, he brings with him by natur has committed many sins that are strictly his own.

Chap. 51. All Men Born of Adam Are under Condemnation, and Only If Ne Born in Christ Are Freed from Condemnation

But what he say a little after, "Therefore, as by the offense of one judgment cam upon all men to condemnation; even so by the righteousness of one the free gif came upon all men unto justification of life," shows clearly enough that there is n one born of Adam but is subject to condemnation, and that no one, unless he be ne born in Christ, is freed from condemnation.

Chap. 52. In Baptism, Which Is the Similitude of the Death and Resurrection o Christ, All, Both Infants and Adults, Die to Sin That They May Walk in Ne ness of Life

And after he has said as much about the condemnation through one man, and the fr gift through one man, as he deemed sufficient for that part of his epistle, the apost goes on to speak of the great mystery of holy baptism in the cross of Christ, and t clearly explain to us that baptism in Christ is nothing else than a similitude of the death of Christ, and that the death of Christ on the cross is nothing but a similitude of the pardon of sin: so that just as real as is His death, so real is the remission of our sins; and just as real as is His resurrection, so real is our justification. He says: "What shall we say, then? Shall we continue in sin, that grace may abound?" For he had said previously, "But where sin abounded, grace did much more abound." And therefore he proposes to himself the question, whether it would be right to continue in sin for the sake of the consequent abounding grace. But he answers, "God forbid;" and adds, "How shall we, that are dead to sin, live any longer therein?" Then, to show that we are dead to sin, "Know ye not," he says, "that so many of us as were baptized into Jesus Christ, were baptized into His death?" If, then, the fact that we were baptized into the death of Christ proves that we are dead to sin, it follows that even infants who are baptized into Christ die to sin, being baptized into His death. For there is no exception made: "So many of us as were baptized into Jesus Christ, were baptized into His death." And this is said to prove that we are dead to sin. Now, to what sin do infants die in their regeneration but that sin which they bring with them at birth? And therefore to these also applies what follows: "Therefore we are buried with Him by baptism into death; that, like as Christ was raised up from the dead by the glory of the Father, even so we also should walk in newness of life. For if we have been planted together in the likeness of His death, we shall be also in the likeness of His resurrection: knowing this, that our old man is crucified with Him, that the body of sin might be destroyed, that henceforth we should not serve sin. For he that is dead is freed from sin. Now if we be dead with Christ, we believe that we shall also live with Him: knowing that Christ, being raised from the dead, dieth no more; death hath no more dominion over Him. For in that He died, He died unto sin once; but in that He liveth, He liveth unto God. Likewise reckon ye also yourselves to be dead indeed unto sin, but alive unto God through Jesus Christ our Lord." Now he had commenced with proving that we must not continue in sin that grace may abound, and had said: "How shall we that are dead to sin live any longer therein?" And to show that we are dead to sin, he added: "Know ye not, that so many of us as were baptized into Jesus Christ, were baptized into His death?" And so he concludes this whole passage just as he began it. For he has brought in the death of Christ in such a way as to imply that Christ Himself also died to sin. To what sin did He die if not to the flesh, in which there was not sin, but the likeness of sin, and which was therefore called by the name of sin? To those who are baptized into the death of Christ, then,—and this class includes not adults only, but infants as well,—he says: "Likewise reckon ye also yourselves to be dead indeed unto sin, but alive unto God through Jesus Christ our Lord."

Chap. 80. Sins, However Great and Detestable, Seem Trivial When We Are Accustomed to Them

Sins, however great and destestable they may be, are looked upon as trivial, or as not sins at all, when men get accustomed to them; and so far does this go, that such sins are not only not concealed, but are boasted of, and published far and wide; and thus, as it is written, "The wicked boasteth of his heart's desire, and blesseth the covetous, whom the Lord abhorreth." Iniquity of this kind is in Scripture called a *cry.* You have an instance in the prophet Isaiah, in the case of the evil vineyard: "He looked for judgment, but behold oppression; for righteousness, but behold a cry." Whence also the expression in Genesis: "The cry of Sodom and Gomorrah is great," because in these cities crimes were not only not punished, but were openly committed, as if under the protection of the law. And so in our own times: many forms of sin, though not just the same as those of Sodom and Gomorrah, are now so openly and habitually practised, that not only dare we not excommunicate a layman, we dare not even degrade a clergyman, for the commission of them. So that when, a few years ago, I was expounding the Epistle to the Galatians, in commenting on that very place where the apostle says, "I am afraid of you, lest I have bestowed labor upon you in vain," I was compelled to exclaim, "Woe to the sins of men! for it is only when we are not accustomed to them that we shrink from them: when once we are accustomed to them, though the blood of the Son of God was poured out to wash them away, though they are so great that the kingdom of God is wholly shut against them, constant familiarity leads to the toleration of them all, and habitual toleration leads to the practice of many of them. And grant, O Lord, that we may not come to practise all that we have not the power to hinder." But I shall see whether the extravagance of grief did not betray me into rashness of speech.

Chap. 81. There Are Two Causes of Sin, Ignorance and Weakness; and We Need Divine Help to Overcome Both

I shall now say this, which I have often said before in other places of my works. There are two causes that lead to sin: either we do not yet know our duty, or we do not perform the duty that we know. The former is the sin of ignorance, the latter of weakness. Now against these it is our duty to struggle; but we shall certainly be beaten in the fight, unless we are helped by God, not only to see our duty, but also, when we clearly see it, to make the love of righteousness stronger in us than the love of earthly things, the eager longing after which, or the fear of losing which, leads us with our eyes open into known sin. In the latter case we are not only sinners, for we are so even when we err through ignorance, but we are also transgressors of the law; for we leave undone what we know we ought to do, and we do what we know we ought not to do. Wherefore not only ought we to pray for pardon when we have sinned, saying, "Forgive us our debts, as we forgive our debtors;" but we ought to pray for guidance that we may be kept from sinning, saying, "and lead us not into temptation." And we are to pray to Him of whom the Psalmist says, "The Lord is my light and my salvation:" my light, for He removes my ignorance; my salvation, for He takes away my infirmity.

Chap. 82. The Mercy of God Is Necessary to True Repentance

Now even penance itself, when by the law of the Church there is sufficient reason for its being gone through, is frequently evaded through infirmity; for shame is the fear of losing pleasure when the good opinion of men gives more pleasure than the righteousness which leads a man to humble himself in penitence. Wherefore the mercy of God is necessary not only when a man repents, but even to lead him to repent. How else explain what the apostle says of certain persons: "if God peradventure will give them repentance"? And before Peter wept bitterly, we are told by the evangelist, "The Lord turned, and looked upon him."

Chap. 83. The Man Who Despises the Mercy of God Is Guilty of the Sin against the Holy Ghost

Now the man who, not believing that sins are remitted in the Church, despises this great gift of God's mercy, and persists to the last day of his life in his obstinacy of heart, is guilty of the unpardonable sin against the Holy Ghost, in whom Christ forgives sins. But this difficult question I have discussed as clearly as I could in a book devoted exclusively to this one point.

Chap. 97. In What Sense Does the Apostle Say That "God Will Have All Men to Be Saved," When, as a Matter of Fact, All Are Not Saved?

We must inquire in what sense is said of God what the apostle has mostly truly said: "Who will have all men to be saved." For, as a matter of fact, not all, nor even a majority, are saved: so that it would seem that what God wills is not done, man's will interfering with, and hindering the will of God. When we ask the reason why all men are not saved, the ordinary answer is: "Because men themselves are not willing." This, indeed, cannot be said of infants, for it is not in their power either to will or not to will. But if we could attribute to their will the childish movements they make at baptism, when they make all the resistance they can, we should say that even they are not willing to be saved. Our Lord says plainly, however, in the Gospel, when upbraiding the impious city: "How often would I have gathered thy children together, even as a hen gathereth her chickens under her wings, and ye would not!" as if the will of God had been overcome by the will of men, and when the weakest stood in the way with their want of will, the will of the strongest could not be carried out. And where is that omnipotence which hath done all that it pleased on earth and in heaven, if God willed to gather the children of Jerusalem, and did not accomplish it? or rather, Jerusalem was not willing that her children should be gathered together? But even though she was unwilling, He gathered together as many of her children as He wished: for He does not will some things and do them, and will others and do them not; but "He hath done all that He pleased in heaven and in earth."

Chap. 98. Predestination to Eternal Life Is Wholly of God's Free Grace

And, moreover, who will be so foolish and blasphemous as to say that God cannot change the evil wills of men, whichever, whenever, and wheresoever He chooses, and direct them to what is good? But when He does this, He does it of mercy; when He does it not, it is of justice that He does it not; for "He hath mercy on whom He will have mercy, and whom He will He hardeneth." And when the apostle said this, he was illustrating the grace of God, in connection with which he had just spoken of the twins in the womb of Rebecca, "who being not yet born, neither having done any good or evil, that the purpose of God according to election might stand, not of work, but of Him that calleth, it was said unto her, The elder shall serve the younger." And in reference to this matter he quotes another prophetic testimony: "Jacob have I loved, but Esau have I hated." But perceiving how what he had said might affect those who could not penetrate by their understanding the depth of this grace: "What shall we say then?" he says: "Is there unrighteousness with God? God forbid." For it seems unjust that, in the absence of any merit or demerit, from good or evil works, God should love the one and hate the other. Now, if the apostle had wished us to understand that there were future good works of the one, and evil works of the other, which of course God foreknew, he would never have said, "not of works," but, "of future works," and in that way would have solved the difficulty, or rather there would then have been no difficulty to solve. As it is, however, after answering, "God forbid;" that is, God forbid that there should be unrighteousness with God; he goes on to prove that there is no unrighteousness in God's doing this, and says: "For He saith to Moses, I will have mercy on whom I will have mercy, and I will have compassion on whom I will have compassion." Now, who but a fool would think that God was unrighteous, either in inflicting penal justice on those who had earned it, or in extending mercy to the unworthy? Then he draws his conclusion: "So then it is not of him that willeth, nor of him that runneth, but of God that showeth mercy." Thus both the twins were born children of wrath, not on account of any works of their own, but because they were bound in the fetters of that original condemnation which came through Adam. But He who said, "I will have mercy on whom I will have mercy," loved Jacob of His undeserved grace, and hated Esau of His deserved judgment. And as this judgment was due to both, the former learnt from the case of the latter that the fact of the same punishment not falling upon himself gave him no room to glory in any merit of his own, but only in the riches of the divine grace; because "it is not of him that willeth, nor of him that runneth, but of God that showeth mercy." And indeed the whole face, and, if I may use the expression, every lineament of the countenance of Scripture conveys by a very profound analogy this wholesome warning to every one who looks carefully into it, that he who glories should glory in the Lord.

Chap. 99. As God's Mercy Is Free, So His Judgments Are Just, and Cannot Be Gainsaid

Now after commending the mercy of God, saying, "So it is not of him that willeth, nor of him that runneth, but of God that showeth mercy," that he might commend His justice also (for the man who does not obtain mercy finds, not iniquity, but justice, there being no iniquity with God), he immediately adds: "For the Scripture saith unto Pharoah, Even for this same purpose have I raised thee up, that I might show my power in thee, and that my name might be declared throughout all the earth." And then he draws a conclusion that applies to both, that is, both to His mercy and His justice: "Therefore hath He mercy on whom He will have mercy, and whom He will He hardeneth." "He hath mercy" of His great goodness, "He hardeneth" without any injustice; so that neither can he that is pardoned glory in any merit of his own, nor he that is condemned complain of anything but his own demerit. For it is grace alone that separates the redeemed from the lost, all having been involved in one common perdition through their common origin. Now if any one, on hearing this should say, "Why doth He yet find fault? for who hath resisted His will?" as if a man ought not to be blamed for being bad, because God hath mercy on whom He will have mercy, and whom He will He hardeneth, God forbid that we should be ashamed

o answer as we see the apostle answered: "Nay, but, O man, who art thou that repli-
st against God? Shall the thing formed say to Him that formed it, Why hast Thou
nade me thus? Hath not the potter power over the clay, of the same lump to make
ne vessel unto honor, and another unto dishonor?" Now some foolish people think
hat in this place the apostle had no answer to give; and for want of a reason to
ender, rebuked the presumption of his interrogator. But there is great weight in this
aying: "Nay, but, O man, who art thou?" and in such a matter as this it suggests to
man in a single word the limits of his capacity, and at the same time does in reality
onvey an important reason. For if a man does not understand these matters, who is
e that he should reply against God? And if he does understand them, he finds no
urther room for reply. For then he perceives that the whole human race was con-
lemned in its rebellious head by a divine judgment so just, that if not a single mem-
er of the race had been redeemed, no one could justly have questioned the justice of
God; and that it was right that those who are redeemed should be redeemed in such
way as to show, by the greater number who are unredeemed and left in their just
ondemnation, what the whole race deserved, and whither the deserved judgment of
God would lead even the redeemed, did not His undeserved mercy interpose, so that
very mouth might be stopped of those who wish to glory in their own merits, and
hat he that glorieth might glory in the Lord.

Chap. 100. The Will of God Is Never Defeated, though Much Is Done That Is Contrary to His Will

These are the great works of the Lord, sought out according to all His pleasure, and
o wisely sought out, that when the intelligent creation, both angelic and human,
inned, doing not His will but their own, He used the very will of the creature which
vas working in opposition to the Creator's will as an instrument for carrying out His
vill, the supremely Good thus turning to good account even what is evil, to the con-
lemnation of those whom in His justice He has predestined to punishment, and to the
alvation of those whom in His mercy He has predestined to grace. For, as far as
elates to their own consciousness, these creatures did what God wished not to be
lone: but in view of God's omnipotence, they could in no wise effect their purpose.
For in the very fact that they acted in opposition to His will, His will concerning
hem was fulfilled. And hence it is that "the works of the Lord are great, sought out
ccording to all His pleasure," because in a way unspeakably strange and wonderful,
ven what is done in opposition to His will does not defeat His will. For it would not
e done did He not permit it (and of course His permission is not unwilling, but will-
ng); nor would a Good Being permit evil to be done only that in His omnipotence
He can turn evil into good.

Chap. 101. The Will of God, Which Is Always Good, Is Sometimes Fulfilled through the Evil Will of Man

Sometimes, however, a man in the goodness of his will desires something that God
loes not desire, even though God's will is also good, nay, much more fully and more
urely good (for His will never can be evil): for example, if a good son is anxious
hat his father should live, when it is God's good will that he should die. Again, it is

possible for a man with evil will to desire what God wills in His goodness: for example, if a bad son wishes his father to die, when this is also the will of God. It is plain that the former wishes what God does not wish, and that the latter wishes what God does wish; and yet the filial love of the former is more in harmony with the good will of God, though its desire is different from God's, than the want of filial affection of the latter, though its desire is the same as God's. So necessary is it, in determining whether a man's desire is one to be approved or disapproved, to consider what it is proper for man, and what it is proper for God, to desire, and what is in each case the real motive of the will. For God accomplishes some of His purposes, which of course are all good, through the evil desires of wicked men: for example, it was through the wicked designs of the Jews, working out the good purpose of the Father, that Christ was slain; and this event was so truly good, that when the Apostle Peter expressed his unwillingness that it should take place, he was designated Satan by Him who had come to be slain. How good seemed the intentions of the pious believers who were unwilling that Paul should go up to Jerusalem lest the evils which Agabus had foretold should there befall him! And yet it was God's purpose that he should suffer these evils for preaching the faith of Christ, and thereby become a witness for Christ. And this purpose of His, which was good, God did not fulfill through the good counsels of the Christians, but through the evil counsels of the Jews; so that those who opposed His purpose were more truly His servants than those who were the willing instruments of its accomplishment.

Chap. 102. The Will of the Omnipotent God Is Never Defeated, and Is Never Evil

But however strong may be the purposes either of angels or of men, whether of good or bad, whether these purposes fall in with the will of God or run counter to it, the will of the Omnipotent is never defeated; and His will never can be evil; because even when it inflicts evil it is just, and what is just is certainly not evil. The omnipotent God, then, whether in mercy He pitieth whom He will, or in judgment hardeneth whom He will, is never unjust in what He does, never does anything except of His own free-will, and never wills anything that He does not perform.

Chap. 103. Interpretation of the Expression in I Tim. II. 4: "Who Will Have All Men to Be Saved"

Accordingly, when we hear and read in Scripture that He "will have all men to be saved," although we know well that all men are not saved, we are not on that account to restrict the omnipotence of God, but are rather to understand the Scripture, "Who will have all men to be saved," as meaning that no man is saved unless God wills his salvation: not that there is no man whose salvation He does not will, but that no man is saved apart from His will; and that, therefore, we should pray Him to will our salvation, because if He will it, it must necessarily be accomplished. And it was of prayer to God that the apostle was speaking when he used this expression. And on the same principle we interpret the expression in the Gospel: "The true light which ighteth every man that cometh into the world:" not that there is no man who is not ·nlightened, but that no man is enlightened except by Him. Or, it is said, "Who will ıave all men to be saved;" not that there is no man whose salvation He does not will for how, then, explain the fact that He was unwilling to work miracles in the pres- nce of some who, He said, would have repented if He had worked them?), but that ve are to understand by "all men," the human race in all its varieties of rank and ircumstances,—kings, subjects; noble, plebeian, high, low, learned, and unlearned; he sound in body, the feeble, the clever, the dull, the foolish, the rich, the poor, and hose of middling circumstances; males, females, infants, boys, youths; young, middle- ged, and old men; of every tongue, of every fashion, of all arts, of all professions, vith all the innumerable differences of will and conscience, and whatever else there is hat makes a distinction among men. For which of all these classes is there out of vhich God does not will that men should be saved in all nations through His only- egotten Son, our Lord, and therefore does save them; for the Omnipotent cannot will n vain, whatsoever He may will? Now the apostle had enjoined that prayers should be nade for all men, and had especially added, "For kings, and for all that are in uthority," who might be supposed, in the pride and pomp of worldly station, to hrink from the humility of the Christian faith. Then saying, "For this is good and cceptable in the sight of God our Saviour," that is, that prayers should be made for uch as these, he immediately adds, as if to remove any ground of despair, "Who will ave all men to be saved, and to come unto the knowledge of the truth." God, then, n His great condescension has judged it good to grant to the prayers of the humble he salvation of the exalted; and assuredly we have many examples of this. Our Lord, oo, makes use of the same mode of speech in the Gospel, when He says to the Phari- ees: "Ye tithe mint, and rue, and every herb." For, the Pharisees did not tithe what elonged to others, nor all the herbs of all the inhabitants of other lands. As, then, in his place we must understand by "every herb," every kind of herbs, so in the former assage we may understand by "all men," every sort of men. And we may interpret it n any other way we please, so long as we are not compelled to believe that the omnip- tent God has willed anything to be done which was not done: for, setting aside all mbiguities, if "He hath done all that He pleased in heaven and in earth," as the salmist sings of Him, He certainly did not will to do anything that He hath not done.

Chap. 104. God, Foreknowing the Sin of the First Man, Ordered His Own 'urposes Accordingly

Vherefore, God would have been willing to preserve even the first man in that state of alvation in which he was created, and after he had begotten sons to remove him at a t time, without the intervention of death, to a better place, where he should have een not only free from sin, but free even from the desire of sinning, if He had fore- een that man would have the steadfast will to persist in the state of innocence in hich he was created. But as He foresaw that man would make a bad use of his free- ill, that is, would sin, God arranged His own designs rather with a view to do good man even in his sinfulness, that thus the good will of the Omnipotent might not be nade void by the evil will of man, but might be fulfilled in spite of it.

Chap. 105. Man Was So Created As to Be Able to Choose Either Good or Evil in the Future Life, the Choice of Evil Will Be Impossible

Now it was expedient that man should be at first so created, as to have it in his power both to will what was right and to will what was wrong; not without reward if he willed the former, and not without punishment if he willed the latter. But in the future life it shall not be in his power to will evil; and yet this will constitute no restriction on the freedom of his will. On the contrary, his will shall be much freer when it shall be wholly impossible for him to be the slave of sin. We should never think of blaming the will, or saying that it was no will, or that it was not to be called free, when we so desire happiness, that not only do we shrink from misery, but find it utterly impossible to do otherwise. As, then, the soul even now finds it impossible to desire unhappiness so in future it shall be wholly impossible for it to desire sin. But God's arrangement was not to be broken, according to which He willed to show how good is a rational being who is able even to refrain from sin, and yet how much better is one who cannot sin at all; just as that was an inferior sort of immortality, and yet it was immortality, when it was possible for man to avoid death, although there is reserved for the future a more perfect immortality, when it shall be impossible for man to die.

AGAINST CELSUS

Origen

How did the cultured men of the classical world, the intellectual heirs of Plato, Aristotle, and Cicero, respond to the development of Christianity? Origen, a Church Father of the early third century after Christ, provides some answers in his long and detailed refutation of the True Discourse, *written by Celsus, a Roman Epicurean, in the last half of the second century. There are numerous quotations from Celsus in Origen's work, and the tone as well as the content of Celsus' wide-ranging attack are clear.*

Origen (A.D. ca. *185*-ca. *254*), *a native of Alexandria in Egypt, had a wide background in Roman as well as Greek literature and history. He was an extremely influential teacher, the head of important philosophical and theological studies in schools in Alexandria and Caesarea. His influence was all the greater because he stood firm in the face of the intense anti-Christian agitation of the day, and because Christianity in his day was in need of the systematic pruning and clarification that his theology helped to provide.*

OOK ONE

Chap. I

'he first point which Celsus brings forward, in his desire to throw discredit upon Christianity, is, that the Christians entered into secret associations with each other con-rary to law, saying, that "of associations some are public, and that these are in accord-nce with the laws; others, again, secret, and maintained in violation of the laws." And his wish is to bring into disrepute what are termed the "love-feasts" of the Christians, as if they had their origin in the common danger, and were more binding han any oaths. Since, then, he babbles about the public law, alleging that the associa-ions of the Christians are in violation of it, we have to reply, that if a man were laced among Scythians, whose laws were unholy, and having no opportunity of scape, were compelled to live among them, such an one would with good reason, for he sake of the law of truth, which the Scythians would regard as wickedness, enter into ssociations contrary to their laws, with those likeminded with himself; so, if truth is o decide, the laws of the heathens which relate to images, and an atheistical polythe-sm, are "Scythian" laws, or more impious even than these, if there be any such. It is ot irrational, then, to form associations in opposition to existing laws, if done for the ake of the truth. For as those persons would do well who should enter into a secret ssociation in order to put to death a tyrant who had seized upon the liberties of a tate, so Christians also, when tyrannized over by him who is called the devil, and by alsehood, form leagues contrary to the laws of the devil, against his power, and for he safety of those others whom they may succeed in persuading to revolt from a gov-rnment which is, as it were, "Scythian," and despotic.

Chap. IX

Ie next proceeds to recommend, that in adopting opinions we should follow reason nd a rational guide, since he who assents to opinions without following this course is ery liable to be deceived. And he compares inconsiderate believers to Metragyrtae, nd soothsayers, and Mithrae, and Sabbadians, and to anything else that one may fall n with, and to the phantoms of Hecate, or any other demon or demons. For as mongst such persons are frequently to be found wicked men, who, taking advan-age of the ignorance of those who are easily deceived, lead them away whither they vill, so also, he says, is the case among Christians. And he asserts that certain persons vho do not wish either to give or receive a reason for their belief, keep repeating, Do not examine, but believe!" and, "Your faith will save you!" And he alleges that uch also say, "The wisdom of this life is bad, but that foolishness is a good thing!" 'o which we have to answer, that if it were possible for all to leave the business of ife, and devote themselves to philosophy, no other method ought to be adopted by ny one, but this alone. For in the Christian system also it will be found that there is,

'he Ante-Nicene Fathers, ed. A. Roberts and J. Donaldson (Grand Rapids, Mich.: Wm. B. erdmans Publishing Co., 1956), Vol. IV, 397, 399–401, 410, 455–501, 513–514, 632–633, 40–641, 660–661, 666.

not to speak at all arrogantly, at least as much of investigation into articles of belief and of explanation of dark sayings, occurring in the prophetical writings, and of the parables in the Gospels, and of countless other things, which either were narrated or enacted with a symbolical ssignification, (as is the case with other systems). But since the course alluded to is impossible, partly on account of the necessities of life, partly on account of the weakness of men, as only a very few individuals devote themselves earnestly to study, what better method could be devised with a view of assisting the multitude, than that which was delievered by Jesus to the heathen? And let us inquire with respect to the great multitude of believers, who have washed away the mire of wickedness in which they formerly wallowed, whether it were better for them to believe without a reason, and (so) to have become reformed and improved in their habits, through the belief that men are chastised for sins, and honoured for good works; or not to have allowed themselves to be converted on the strength of mere faith, but (to have waited) until they could give themselves to a thorough examination of the (necessary) reasons. For it is manifest that, (on such a plan), all men with very few exception, would not obtain this (amelioration of conduct) which they have obtained through a simple faith, but would continue to remain in the practice of a wicked life. Now, whatever other evidence can be furnished of the fact, that it was not without divine intervention that the philanthropic scheme of Christianity was introduced among men, this also must be added. For a pious man will not believe that even a physician of the body, who restores the sick to better health, could take up his abode in any city or country without divine permission, since no good happens to men without the help of God. And if he who has cured the *bodies* of many, or restored them to better health, does not effect his cures without the help of God, how much more He who has healed the *souls* of many, and has turned them (to virtue), and improved their nature, and attached them to God who is over all things, and taught them to refer every action to His good pleasure, and to shun all that is displeasing to Him, even to the least of their words or deeds, or even of the thoughts of their hearts

Chap. X

In the next place, since our opponents keep repeating those statements about faith, we must say that, considering it as a useful thing for the multitude, we admit that we teach those men to believe without reasons, who are unable to abandon all other employments, and give themselves to an examination of arguments; and our opponents although they do not acknowledge it, yet practically do the same. For who is there that on betaking himself to the study of philosophy, and throwing himself into the ranks of some sect, either by chance, or because he is provided with a teacher of that school adopts such a course for any other reason, except that he *believes* his particular sect to be superior to any other? For, not waiting to hear the arguments of all the other philosophers, and of all the different sects, and the reasons for condemning one system and for supporting another, he in this way elects to become a Stoic, e.g., or a Platonist, or a Peripatetic, or an Epicurean, or a follower of some other school, and is thus borne, although they will not admit it, by a kind of irrational impulse to the practice, say of Stoicism, to the disregard of the others; despising either Platonism, as being marked by greater humility than the others; or Peripateticism, as more human and as admitting with more fairness than other systems the blessings of human life. And some also, alarmed at first sight about the doctrine of providence, from seeing what happens in the world to the vicious and to the virtuous, have rashly concluded that there is no divine providence at all, and have adopted the views of Epicurus and Celsus.

Chap. XI

Since, then, as reason teaches, we must repose faith in some one of those who have been the introducers of sects among the Greeks or Barbarians, why should we not rather believe in God who is over all things, and in Him who teaches that worship is due to God alone, and that other things are to be passed by, either as non-existent, or as existing indeed, and worthy of honour, but not of worship and reverence? And respecting these things, he who not only believes, but who contemplates things with the eye of reason, will state the demonstrations that occur to him, and which are the result of careful investigation. And why should it not be more reasonable, seeing all human things are dependent upon faith, to believe God rather than them? For who enters on a voyage, or contracts a marriage, or becomes the father of children, or casts seed into the ground, without believing that better things will result from so doing, although the contrary might and sometimes does happen? And yet the belief that better things, even agreeably to their wishes, will follow, makes all men venture upon uncertain enterprises, which may turn out diflerently from what they expect. And if the hope and belief of a better future be the support of life in every uncertain enterprise, why shall not this faith rather be rationally accepted by him who believes on better grounds than he who sails the sea, or tills the ground, or marries a wife, or engages in any other human pursuit, in the existence of a God who was the Creator of all these things, and in Him who with surpassing wisdom and divine greatness of mind dared to make known this doctrine to men in every part of the world, at the cost of great danger, and of a death considered infamous, which He underwent for the sake of the human race; having also taught those who were persuaded to embrace His doctrine at the first, to proceed, under the peril of every danger, and of ever impending death, to all quarters of the world to ensure the salvation of men?

Chap. XXXII

But let us now return to where the Jew is introduced, speaking of the mother of Jesus, and saying that "when she was pregnant she was turned out of doors by the carpenter to whom she had been betrothed, as having been guilty of adultery, and that she bore a child to a certain soldier named Panthera;" and let us see whether those who have blindly concocted these fables about the adultery of the Virgin with Panthera, and her rejection by the carpenter, did not invent these stories to overturn His miraculous conception by the Holy Ghost: for they could have falsified the history in a different manner, on account of its extremely miraculous character, and not have admitted, as it were against their will, that Jesus was born of no ordinary human marriage. It was to be expected, indeed, that those who would not believe the miraculous birth of Jesus would invent some falsehood. And their not doing this in a credible manner, but (their) preserving the fact that it was not by Joseph that the Virgin conceived Jesus, rendered the falsehood very palpable to those who can understand and detect such inventions. Is it at all agreeable to reason, that he who dared to do so much for the human race, in order that, as far as in him lay, all the Greeks and Barbarians, who were looking for divine condemnation, might depart from evil, and regulate their entire conduct in a manner pleasing to the Creator of the world, should not have had a miraculous birth, but one the vilest and most disgraceful of all? And I will ask of them as Greeks, and particularly of Celsus, who either holds or not the sentiments of Plato, and at any rate quotes them, whether He who sends souls down into the bodies of men, degraded Him who was to dare such mighty acts, and to teach so many men, and to reform so many from the mass of wickedness in the world, to a birth more disgraceful than any other, and did not rather introduce Him into the world through a lawful marriage? Or is it not more in conformity with reason, that every soul, for certain mysterious reasons (I speak now according to the opinion of Pythagoras, and Plato, and Empedocles, whom Celsus frequently names), is introduced into a body, and introduced according to its deserts and former actions? It is probable, therefore, that this soul also, which conferred more benefit by its residence in the flesh than that of many men (to avoid prejudice, I do not say "all"), stood in need of a body not only superior to others, but invested with all excellent qualities.

BOOK TWO

Chap. LX

In the next place, as if this were possible, viz., that the image of a man who was dead could appear to another as if he were still living, he adopts this opinion as an Epicurean, and says, "That some one having so dreamed owing to a peculiar state of mind, or having, under the influence of a perverted imagination, formed such an appearance as he himself desired, reported that such had been seen; and this," he continues, "has been the case with numberless individuals." But even if this statement of his seems to have a considerable degree of force, it is nevertheless only fitted to confirm a necessary doctrine, that the soul of the dead exists in a separate state (from the body); and he who adopts such an opinion does not believe without good reason in the immortality, or at least continued existence, of the soul, as even Plato says in his treatise on the Soul that shadowy phantoms of persons already dead have appeared to some around their sepulchres. Now the phantoms which exist about the soul of the dead are produced by some substance, and this substance is in the soul, which exists apart in a body said to be of splendid appearance. But Celsus, unwilling to admit any such view, will have it that some dreamed a waking dream, and, under the influence of a perverted imagination, formed to themselves such an image as they desired. Now it is not irrational to believe that a dream may take place while one is asleep; but to suppose a waking vision in the case of those who are not altogether out of their senses and under the influence of delirium or hypochondria, is incredible. And Celsus, seeing this, called the woman "half-mad,"—a statement which is not made by the history recording the fact, but from which he took occasion to charge the occurrences with being untrue.

BOOK FOUR

Chap. X

In the next place, Celsus, as is his custom, having neither proved nor established anything, proceeds to say, as if we talked of God in a manner that was neither holy nor pious, that "it is perfectly manifest that they babble about God in a way that is neither holy nor reverential;" and he imagines that we do these things to excite the astonishment of the ignorant, and that we do not speak the truth regarding the necessity of punishments for those who have sinned. And accordingly he likens us to those who "in the Bacchic mysteries introduce phantoms and objects of terror." With respect to the mysteries of Bacchus, whether there is any trustworthy account of them, or none that is such, let the Greeks tell, and let Celsus and his boon-companions listen. But we defend our own procedure, when we say that our object is to reform the human race, either by the threats of punishments which we are persuaded are necessary for the whole world, and which perhaps are not without use to those who are to endure them; or by the promises made to those who have lived virtuous lives, and in which are contained the statements regarding the blessed termination which is to be found in the kingdom of God, reserved for those who are worthy of becoming His subjects.

Chap. XXXVI

Celsus in the next place, producing from history other than that of the divine record, those passages which bear upon the claims to great antiquity put forth by many nations, as the Athenians, and Egyptians, and Arcadians, and Phrygians, who assert that certain individuals have existed among them who sprang from the earth, and who each adduce proofs of these assertions, says: "The Jews, then, leading a grovelling life in some corner of Palestine, and being a wholly uneducated people, who had not heard that these matters had been committed to verse long ago by Hesiod and innumerable other inspired men, wove together some most incredible and insipid stories, viz., that a certain man was formed by the hands of God, and had breathed into him the breath of life, and that a woman was taken from his side, and that God issued certain commands, and that a serpent opposed these, and gained a victory over the commandments of God; thus relating certain old wives' fables, and most impiously representing God as weak at the very beginning (of things), and unable to convince even a single human being whom He Himself had formed." By these instances, indeed, this deeply read and learned Celsus, who accuses Jews and Christians of ignorance and want of instruction, clearly evinces the accuracy of his knowledge of the chronology of the respective historians, whether Greek or Barbarian, since he imagines that Hesiod and the "innumerable" others, whom he styles "inspired" men, are older than Moses and his writings—that very Moses who is shown to be much older than the time of the Trojan war! It is not the Jews, then, who have composed incredible and insipid stories regarding the birth of man from the earth, but these "inspired" men of Celsus, Hesiod and his other "innumerable" companions, who, having neither learned nor heard of the far older and most venerable accounts existing in Palestine, have written such histories as their Theogonies, attributing, so far as in their power, "generation" to their deities, and innumerable other absurdities. And these are the writers whom Plato expels from his "State" as being corrupters of the youth,—Homer, viz., and those who have composed poems of a similar description! Now it is evident that Plato did not regard as "inspired" those men who had left behind them such works. But perhaps it was from a desire to cast reproach upon us, that this Epicurean Celsus, who is better able to judge than Plato (if it be the same Celsus who composed two other books against the Christians), called those individuals "inspired" whom he did not in reality regard as such.

Chap. XXXVIII

In the next place, as it is his object to slander our Scriptures, he ridicules the following statement: "And God caused a deep sleep to fall upon Adam, and he slept: and He took one of his ribs, and closed up the flesh instead thereof. And the rib, which He had taken from the man, made He a woman," and so on; without quoting the words, which would give the hearer the impression that they are spoken with a figurative meaning. He would not even have it appear that the words were used allegorically, although he says afterwards, that "the more modest among Jews and Christians are ashamed of these things, and endeavour to give them somehow an allegorical signification." Now we might say to him, Are the statements of your "inspired" Hesiod, which he makes regarding the woman in the form of a myth, to be explained allegorically, in the sense that she was given by Jove to men as an evil thing, and as a retribution for the theft of "the fire;" while that regarding the woman who was taken from the side of the man (after he had been buried in deep slumber), and was formed by God, appears to you to be related without any rational meaning and secret signification? But is it not uncandid, not to ridicule the former as myths, but to admire them as philosophical ideas in a mythical dress, and to treat with contempt the latter, as offending the understanding, and to declare that they are of no account? For if, because of the mere phraseology, we are to find fault with what is intended to have a secret meaning, see whether the following lines of Hesiod, a man, as you say, "inspired," are not better fitted to excite laughter:—

" 'Son of Iapetus!' * with wrathful heart
Spake the cloud-gatherer: 'Oh, unmatched in art!
Exultest thou in this the flame retrieved,
And dost thou triumph in the god deceived?
But thou, with the posterity of man,
Shalt rue the fraud whence mightier ills began;
I will send evil for thy stealthy fire,
While all embrace it, and their bane desire.'
The sire, who rules the earth, and sways the pole,
Had said, and laughter fill'd his secret soul.
He bade the artist-god his hest obey,
And mould with tempering waters ductile clay:
Infuse, as breathing life and form began,

* [Prometheus. (*Ed.*)]

The supple vigour, and the voice of man:
Her aspect fair as goddesses above,
A virgin's likeness, with the brows of love.
He bade Minerva teach the skill that dyes
The web with colours, as the shuttle flies;
He called the magic of Love's Queen to shed
A nameless grace around her courteous head;
Instil the wish that longs with restless aim,
And cares of dress that feed upon the frame:
Bade Hermes last implant the craft refined
Of artful manners, and a shameless mind.
He said; their king th' inferior powers obeyed:
The fictile likeness of a bashful maid
Rose from the temper'd earth, by Jove's behest,
Under the forming god; the zone and vest
Were clasp'd and folded by Minerva's hand:
The heaven-born graces, and persuasion bland
Deck'd her round limbs with chains of gold: the hours
Of loose locks twined her temples with spring flowers.
The whole attire Minerva's curious care
Form'd to her shape, and fitted to her air.
But in her breast the herald from above,
Full of the counsels of deep thundering Jove,
Wrought artful manners, wrought perfidious lies,
And speech that thrills the blood, and lulls the wise.
Her did th' interpreter of gods proclaim,
And named the woman with Pandora's name;
Since all the gods conferr'd their gifts, to charm,
For man's inventive race, this beauteous harm."

Moreover, what is said also about the casket is fitted of itself to excite laughter; for example:—

"Whilome on earth the sons of men abode
From ills apart, and labour's irksome load,
And sore diseases, bringing age to man;
Now the sad life of mortals is a span.
The woman's hands a mighty casket bear;
She lifts the lid; she scatters griefs in air:
Alone, beneath the vessel's rims detained,
Hope still within th' unbroken cell remained,
Nor fled abroad; so will'd cloud-gatherer Jove:
The woman's hand had dropp'd the lid above."

Now, to him who would give to these lines a grave allegorical meaning (whether any such meaning be contained in them or not), we would say: Are the Greeks alone at liberty to convey a philosophic meaning in a secret covering? or perhaps also the

Egyptians, and those of the Barbarians who pride themselves upon their mysteries and the truth (which is concealed within them); while the Jews alone, with their lawgiver and historians, appear to you the most unintelligent of men? And is this the only nation which has not received a share of divine power, and which yet was so grandly instructed how to rise upwards to the uncreated nature of God, and to gaze on Him alone, and to expect from Him alone (the fulfilment of) their hopes?

BOOK SEVEN

Chap. LIII

After these remarks of Celsus, which we have done our best to refute, he goes on to address us thus: "Seeing you are so eager for some novelty, how much better it would have been if you had chosen as the object of your zealous homage some one of those who died a glorious death, and whose divinity might have received the support or some myth to perpetuate his memory! Why, if you were not satisfied with Hercules or Aesculapius, and other heroes of antiquity, you had Orpheus, who was confessedly a divinely inspired man, who died a violent death. But perhaps some others have taken him up before you. You may then take Anaxarchus, who, when cast into a mortar, and beaten most barbarously, showed a noble contempt for his suffering, and said, 'Beat, beat the shell of Anaxarchus, for himself you do not beat,'—a speech surely of a spirit truly divine. But others were before you in following his interpretation of the laws of nature. Might you not, then, take Epictetus, who, when his master was twisting his leg, said, smiling and unmoved, 'You will break my leg;' and when it was broken, he added, 'Did I not tell you that you would break it?' What saying equal to these did your god utter under suffering? If you had said even of the Sibyl, whose authority some of you acknowledge, that she was a child of God, you would have said something more reasonable. But you have had the presumption to include in her writings many impious things, and set up as a god one who ended a most infamous life by a most miserable death. How much more suitable than he would have been Jonah in the whale's belly, or Daniel delivered from the wild beasts, or any of a still more portentous kind!"

Chap. LIV

But since he sends us to Hercules, let him repeat to us any of his sayings, and let him justify his shameful subjection to Omphale. Let him show that divine honours should be paid to one who, like a highway robber, carries off a farmer's ox by force, and afterwards devours it, amusing himself meanwhile with the curses of the owner; in memory of which even to this day sacrifices offered to the demon of Hercules are accompanied with curses. Again he proposes Aesculapius to us, as if to oblige us to repeat what we have said already; but we forbear. In regard to Orpheus, what does he admire in him to make him assert that, by common consent, he was regarded as a divinely inspired man, and lived a noble life? I am greatly deceived if it is not the desire which Celsus has to oppose us and put down Jesus that leads him to sound forth the praises of Orpheus; and whether, when he made himself acquainted with his impious fables about the gods, he did not cast them aside as deserving, even more than the poems of Homer, to be excluded from a well-ordered state. For, indeed, Orpheus says much worse things than Homer of those whom they call gods. Noble, indeed, it was in Anaxarchus to say to Aristocreon, tyrant of Cyprus, "Beat on, beat the shell of Anaxarchus," but it is the one admirable incident in the life of Anaxarchus known to the Greeks; and although, on the strength of that, some like Celsus might deservedly honour the man for his courage, yet to look up to Anaxarchus as a god is not consistent with reason. He also directs us to Epictetus, whose firmness is justly admired, although his saying when his leg was broken by his master is not to be compared with the marvellous acts and words of Jesus which Celsus refuses to believe; and these words were accompanied by such a divine power, that even to this day they convert not only some of the more ignorant and simple, but many also of the most enlightened of men.

Chap. LV

When, to his enumeration of those to whom he would send us, he adds, "What saying equal to these did your god utter under sufferings?" we would reply, that the silence of Jesus under scourgings, and amidst all His sufferings, spoke more for His firmness and submission than all that was said by the Greeks when beset by calamity. Perhaps Celsus may believe what was recorded with all sincerity by trustworthy men, who, while giving a truthful account of all the wonders performed by Jesus, specify among these the silence which He preserved when subjected to scourgings; showing the same singular meekness under the insults which were heaped upon Him, when they put upon Him the purple robe, and set the crown of thorns upon His head, and when they put in His hand a reed in place of a sceptre: no unworthy or angry word escaped Him against those who subjected Him to such outrages. Since, then, He received the scourgings with silent firmness, and bore with meekness all the insults of those who outraged Him, it cannot be said, as is said by some, that it was in cowardly weakness that He uttered the words: "Father, if it be possible, let this cup pass from Me: nevertheless, not as I will, but as Thou wilt." The prayer which seems to be contained in these words for the removal of what He calls "the cup" bears a sense which we have elsewhere examined and set forth at large. But taking it in its more obvious sense, consider if it be not a prayer offered to God with all piety. For no man naturally regards anything which may befall him as necessary and inevitable; though he may submit to what is not inevitable, if occasion requires. Besides, these words, "nevertheless, not as I will, but as Thou wilt," are not the language of one who yielded to necessity, but of one who was contented with what was befalling Him, and who submitted with reverence to the arrangements of Providence.

BOOK EIGHT

Chap. II

In a passage previously quoted Celsus asks us why we do not worship demons, and to his remarks on demons we gave such an answer as seemed to us in accordance with the divine word. After having put this question for the purpose of leading us to the worship of demons, he represents us as answering that it is impossible to serve many masters. "This," he goes on to say, "is the language of sedition, and is only used by those who separate themselves and stand aloof from all human society. Those who speak in this way ascribe," as he supposes, "their own feelings and passions to God. It does hold true among men, that he who is in the service of one master cannot well serve another, because the service which he renders to the one interferes with that which he owes to the other; and no one, therefore, who has already engaged himself to the service of one, must accept that of another. And, in like manner, it is impossible to serve at the same time heroes or demons of different natures. But in regard to God, who is subject to no suffering or loss, it is," he thinks, "absurd to be on our guard against serving more gods, as though we had to do with demi-gods, or other spirits of that sort." He says also, "He who serves many gods does that which is pleasing to the Most High, because he honours that which belongs to Him." And he adds, "It is indeed wrong to give honour to any to whom God has not given honour." "Wherefore," he says, "in honouring and worshipping all belonging to God, we will not displease Him to whom they all belong."

Chap. V

Whilst there are thus many gods and lords, whereof some are such in reality, and others are such only in name, we strive to rise not only above those whom the nations of the earth worship as gods, but also beyond those spoke of as gods in Scripture, of whom they are wholly ignorant who are strangers to the covenants of God given by Moses and by our Saviour Jesus, and who have no part in the promises which He has made to us through them. . . . And he who considers that "the earnest expectation of the creature waiteth for the manifestation of the sons of God, not willingly, but by reason of him who subjected the same in hope," whilst he praises the creature, and sees how "it shall be freed altogether from the bondage of corruption, and restored to the glorious liberty of the children of God," —such a one cannot be induced to combine with the service of God the service of any other, or to serve two masters. There is therefore nothing seditious or factious in the language of those who hold these views, and who refuse to serve more masters than one. To them Jesus Christ is an all-sufficient Lord, who Himself instructs them, in order that when fully instructed He may form them into a kingdom worthy of God, and present them to God the Father. But indeed they do in a sense separate themselves and stand aloof from those who are aliens from the commonwealth of God and strangers to His covenants, in order that they may live as citizens of heaven, "coming to the living God, and to the city of God, the heavenly Jerusalem, and to an innumerable company of angels, to the general assembly and Church of the first-born, which are written in heaven."

Chap. LV

Celsus goes on to say: "They must make their choice between two alternatives. If they refuse to render due service to the gods, and to respect those who are set over this service, let them not come to manhood, or marry wives, or have children, or indeed take any share in the affairs of life; but let them depart hence with all speed, and leave no posterity behind them, that such a race may become extinct from the face of the earth. Or, on the other hand, if they will take wives, and bring up children, and taste of the fruits of the earth, and partake of all the blessings of life, and bear its appointed sorrows (for nature herself hath allotted sorrows to all men; for sorrows must exist, and earth is the only place for them), then must they discharge the duties of life until they are released from its bonds, and render due honour to those beings who control the affairs of this life, if they would not show themselves ungrateful to them. For it would be unjust in them, after receiving the good things which they dispense, to pay them no tribute in return." To this we reply, that there appears to us to be no good reason for our leaving this world, except when piety and virtue require it; as when, for example, those who are set as judges, and think that they have power over our lives, place before us the alternative either to live in violation of the commands of Jesus, or to die if we continue obedient to them. But God has allowed us to marry, because all are not fit for the higher, that is, the perfectly pure life; and God would have us to bring us all our children, and not to destroy any of the offspring given us by His providence. And this does not conflict with our purpose not to obey the demons that are on the earth; for, "being armed with the whole armour of God, we stand" as athletes of piety against the race of demons that plot against us.

Chap. LVI

Although, therefore, Celsus would, in his own words, "drive us with all haste out of life," so that "such a race may become extinct from the earth;" yet we, along with those who worship the Creator, will live according to the laws of God, never consenting to obey the laws of sin. We will marry if we wish, and bring up the children given to us in marriage; and if need be, we will not only partake of the blessings of life, but bear its appointed sorrows as a trial to our souls. For in this way is divine Scripture accustomed to speak of human afflictions, by which, as gold is tried in the fire, so the spirit of man is tried, and is found to be worthy either of condemnation or of praise. For those things which Celsus calls evils we are therefore prepared, and are ready to say, "Try me, O LORD, and prove me; purge my reins and my heart." For "no one will be crowned," unless here upon earth, with this body of humiliation, "he strive lawfully." Further, we do not pay honours supposed to be due to those whom Celsus speaks of as being set over the affairs of the world. For we worship the Lord our God, and Him only do we serve, and desire to be followers of Christ, who, when the devil said to Him, "All these things will I give thee if thou wilt fall down and worship me," answered him by the words, "Thou shalt worship the LORD thy God, and Him only shalt thou serve." Wherefore we do not render the honour supposed to be due to those who, according to Celsus, are set over the affairs of this world; for "no man can serve two masters," and we "cannot serve God and mammon," whether this name be applied to one or more. Moreover, if any one "by transgressing the law dishonours the lawgiver," it seems clear to us that if the two laws, the law of God and the law of mammon, are completely opposed to each other, it is better for us by transgressing the law of mammon to dishonour mammon, that we may honour God by keeping His law, than by transgressing the law of God to dishonour God, that by obeying the law of mammon we may honour mammon.

Chap. LVII

Celsus supposes that men "discharge the duties of life until they are loosened from its bonds," when, in accordance with commonly received customs, they offer sacrifies to each of the gods recognised in the state; and he fails to perceive the true duty which is fulfilled by an earnest piety. For we say that he truly discharges the duties of life who is ever mindful who is his Creator, and what things are agreeable to Him, and who acts in all things so that he may please God. Again, Celsus wishes us to be thankful to these demons, imagining that we owe them thank-offerings. But we, while recognising the duty of thankfulness, maintain that we show no ingratitude by refusing to give thanks to beings who do us no good, but who rather set themselves against us when we neither sacrifice to them nor worship them. We are much more concerned lest we should be ungrateful to God, who has loaded us with His benefits, whose workmanship we are, who cares for us in whatever condition we may be, and who has given us hopes of things beyond this present life. And we have a symbol of gratitude to God in the bread which we call the Eucharist. Besides, as we have shown before, the demons have not the control of those things which have been created for our use; we commit no wrong, therefore, when we partake of created things, and yet refuse to offer sacrifices to beings who have no concern with them. Moreover, as we know that it is not demons, but angels, who have been set over the fruits of the earth, and over the birth of animals, it is the latter that we praise and bless, as having been appointed by God over the things needful for our race; yet even to them we will not give the honour which is due to God. For this would not be pleasing to God, nor would it be any pleasure to the angels committed. Indeed, they are much more pleased if we refrain from offering sacrifices to them than if we offer them; for they have no desire for the sacrificial odours which rise from the earth.

Chap. LXIX

Celsus, then, as if not observing that he was saying anything inconsistent with the words he had just used, "if all were to do the same as you," adds: "You surely do not say that if the Romans were, in compliance with your wish, to neglect their customary duties to gods and men, and were to worship the Most High, or whatever you please to call him, that he will come down and fight for them, so that they shall need no other help than his. For this same God, as yourselves say, promised of old this and much more to those who served him, and see in what way he has helped them and you! They, in place of being masters of the whole world, are left with not so much as a patch of ground or a home; and as for you, if any of you transgresses even in secret, he is sought out and punished with death." As the question started is, "What would happen if the Romans were persuaded to adopt the principles of the Christians, to despise the duties paid to the recognised gods and to men, and to worship the Most High?" this is my answer to the question. We say that "if two" of us "shall agree on earth as touching anything that they shall ask, it shall be done for them of the Father" of the just, "which is in heaven;" for God rejoices in the agreement of rational beings, and turns away from discord. And what are we to expect, if not only

very few agree, as at present, but the whole of the empire of Rome? For they will
ray to the Word, who of old said to the Hebrews, when they were pursued by the
gyptians, "The LORD shall fight for you, and ye shall hold your peace;" and if they
ll unite in prayer with one accord, they will be able to put to flight far more enemies
han those who were discomfited by the prayer of Moses when he cried to the Lord,
nd of those who prayed with him. Now, if what God promised to those who keep
Iis law has not come to pass, the reason of its nonfulfilment is not to be ascribed to
he unfaithfulness of God. But He had made the fulfilment of His promises to depend
n certain conditions,—namely, that they should observe and live according to His
aw; and if the Jews have not a plot of ground nor a habitation left to them, although
hey had received these conditional promises, the entire blame is to be laid upon
heir crimes, and especially upon their guilt in the treatment of Jesus.

Chap. LXX

But if all the Romans, according to the supposition of Celsus, embrace the Christian
aith, they will, when they pray, overcome their enemies; or rather, they will not
var at all, being guarded by that divine power which promised to save five entire
ities for the sake of fifty just persons. For men of God are assuredly the salt of the
arth: they preserve the order of the world; and society is held together as long as
he salt is uncorrupted: for "if the salt have lost its savour, it is neither fit for the
and nor for the dunghill; but it shall be cast out, and trodden under foot of men.
Ie that hath ears let him hear" the meaning of these words. When God gives to the
empter permission to persecute us, then we suffer persecution; and when God wishes
is to be free from suffering, even in the midst of a world that hates us, we enjoy a
vonderful peace, trusting in the protection of Him who said, "Be of good cheer, I
iave overcome the world." And truly He has overcome the world. Wherefore the
vorld prevails only so long as it is the pleasure of Him who received from the Father
ower to overcome the world; and from His victory we take courage. Should He even
vish us again to contend and struggle for our religion, let the enemy come against
is, and we will say to them, "I can do all things, through Christ Jesus our Lord, which
strengtheneth me." For of "two sparrows which are sold for a farthing," as the
Scripture says, "not one of them falls on the ground without our Father in heaven."
And so completely does the Divine Providence embrace all things, that not even the
iairs of our head fail to be numbered by Him.

THE CITY OF GOD

Augustine of Hippo

St. Augustine's City of God *is the longest and probably the greatest of hi many writings (see pages 398–399). It was written over a period of thirtee years, from* A.D. *413 to 426, and represents a vast compilation of Christian theology brought to bear on a single problem: the significance of the decline of Roman civilization. In* A.D. *410 the Goths under Alaric had sacked Rome, and it was becoming obvious to everyone that in the western Mediterranean, at least, the civilization that had dominated the known world for over 600 years was doomed.*

It is hard to appreciate what this must have meant to the educated classes of that time. For a parallel we would have to imagine an invasion of creatures from outer space, less intelligent than man, but clearly capable of taking over the earth within a short time. If such a thing were to happen, many voices would be heard attributing the disaster to our own failures; the rapid spread of Communism in recent years, in particular, would surel be denounced as both a symptom and a cause of the moral decay that had permitted such an "unnatural" course of events. Precisely such a charge was made about Christianity, which had been spreading rapidly since the conversion of Constantine in A.D. *325, when the incursions of barbarians (many of whom had already been converted to Christianity) increased in number and effectiveness.*

In his City of God, *St. Augustine took up the challenge of this charge against Christianity and attempted to refute it as decisively as he had dealt with variations of doctrine within the Church. Part I (Books I–X) is an exhaustive treatise on Roman culture and civilization, attempting to show that even at its best it bore the fatal marks of all merely human striving, and that its passing was inevitable and no more to be lamented than that of its predecessors: Egypt, Babylonia, Assyria, Persia, etc. Such breadth of perspective was possible only to one who was essentially an outsider in the world of Rome; and in Part II (Books XI–XXII), fro which the following selections are taken, Augustine develops the concept of a more durable "city" to which the Christian owes his real allegiance.*

OOK ELEVEN

hap. 1. Of This Part of the Work, Wherein We Begin to Explain the Origin nd End of the Two Cities

'he city of God we speak of is the same to which testimony is borne by that Scripture, 'hich excels all the writings of all nations by its divine authority, and has brought nder its influence all kinds of minds, and this not by a casual intellectual movement, ut obviously by an express providential arrangement. . . . We have learned that there a city of God, and its Founder has inspired us with a love which makes us covet s citizenship. To this Founder of the holy city the citizens of the earthly city prefer reir own gods, not knowing that He is the God of gods, not of false, *i.e.,* of impious nd proud gods, who, being deprived of His unchangeable and freely communicated ght, and so reduced to a kind of poverty-stricken power, eagerly grasp at their own rivate privileges, and seek divine honors from their deluded subjects; but of the pious nd holy gods, who are better pleased to submit themselves to one, than to subject nany to themselves, and who would rather worship God than be worshipped as God. 3ut to the enemies of this city we have replied in the ten preceding books, according ɔ our ability and the help afforded by our Lord and King. Now, recognizing what ; expected of me, and not unmindful of my promise, and relying, too, on the same uccor, I will endeavor to treat of the origin, and progress, and deserved destinies of he two cities (the earthly and the heavenly, to wit), which, as we said, are in this resent world commingled, and as it were entangled together. And, first, I will explain ow the foundations of these two cities were originally laid, in the difference that rose among the angels.

OOK FOURTEEN

hap. 1. That the Disobedience of the First Man Would Have Plunged All Men nto the Endless Misery of the Second Death, Had Not the Grace of God Rescued Many

We have already stated in the preceding books that God, desiring not only that the uman race might be able by their similarity of nature to associate with one another, ut also that they might be bound together in harmony and peace by the ties of elationship, was pleased to derive all men from one individual, and created man with uch a nature that the members of the race should not have died, had not the two first of whom the one was created out of nothing, and the other out of him) merited his by their disobedience; for by them so great a sin was committed, that by it the uman nature was altered for the worse, and was transmitted also to their posterity, iable to sin and subject to death. And the kingdom of death so reigned over men, hat the deserved penalty of sin would have hurled all headlong even into the second

A *Select Library of the Nicene and Post-Nicene Fathers of the Christian Church,* ed. Philip Schaff (Grand Rapids, Mich.: Wm. B. Eerdmans Publishing Co., 1953), Vol. II, 205, 262–265, 272–274, 282–283, 407–413 *passim.*

death, of which there is no end, had not the undeserved grace of God saved som therefrom. And thus it has come to pass, that though there are very many and grea nations all over the earth, whose rites and customs, speech, arms, and dress, ar distinguished by marked differences, yet there are no more than two kinds of huma society, which we may justly call two cities, according to the language of our Scriptures The one consists of those who wish to live after the flesh, the other of those wh wish to live after the spirit; and when they severally achieve what they wish, they liv in peace, each after their kind.

Chap. 2. Of Carnal Life, Which Is to Be Understood Not Only of Living i Bodily Indulgence, But Also of Living in the Vices of the Inner Man

First, we must see what it is to live after the flesh, and what to live after the spirit For any one who either does not recollect, or does not sufficiently weigh, the languag of sacred Scripture, may, on first hearing what we have said, suppose that the Epi curean philosophers live after the flesh, because they place man's highest good i bodily pleasure; and that those others do so who have been of opinion that in som form or other bodily good is man's supreme good; and that the mass of men do s who, without dogmatizing or philosophizing on the subject, are so prone to lust tha they cannot delight in any pleasure save such as they receive from bodily sensations and he may suppose that the Stoics, who place the supreme good of men in th soul, live after the spirit; for what is man's soul, if not spirit? But in the sense of th divine Scripture both are proved to live after the flesh. For by flesh it means not onl the body of a terrestrial and mortal animal, as when it says, "All flesh is not the sam flesh, but there is one kind of flesh of men, another flesh of beasts, another of fishes another of birds," but it uses this word in many other significations; and among thes various usages, a frequent one is to use flesh for man himself, the nature of ma taking the part for the whole, as in the words, "By the deeds of the law there shall n flesh be justified;" for what does he mean here by "no flesh" but "no man?" And this indeed, he shortly after says more plainly: "No man shall be justified by the law;' and in the Epistle to the Galatians, "Knowing that man is not justified by the work of the law." And so we understand the words, "And the Word was made flesh,"— that is, man, which some not accepting in its right sense, have supposed that Chris had not a human soul. For as the whole is used for the part in the words of Mar Magdalene in the Gospel, "They have taken away my Lord, and I know not wher they have laid Him," by which she meant only the flesh of Christ, which she supposed had been taken from the tomb where it had been buried, so the part is used for the whole, flesh being named, while man is referred to, as in the quotations above cited.

Since, then, Scripture uses the word flesh in many ways, which there is not time to collect and investigate, if we are to ascertain what it is to live after the flesh (which is certainly evil, though the nature of flesh is not itself evil), we must carefully examin that passage of the epistle which the Apostle Paul wrote to the Galatians, in which he says, "Now the works of the flesh are manifest, which are these: adultery, forni- cation, uncleanness, lasciviousness, idolatry, witchcraft, hatred, variance, emulations, wrath, strife, seditions, heresies, envyings, murders, drunkenness, revellings, and such like: of the which I tell you before, as I have also told you in time past, that they which do such things shall not inherit the kingdom of God." This whole passage of the postolic epistle being considered, so far as it bears on the matter in hand, will be ufficient to answer the question, what it is to live after the flesh. For among the works f the flesh which he said were manifest, and which he cited for condemnation, we nd not only those which concern the pleasure of the flesh, as fornications, unclean-ess, lasciviousness, drunkenness, revellings, but also those which, though they be emote from fleshly pleasure, reveal the vices of the soul. For who does not see that dolatries, witchcrafts, hatreds, variance, emulations, wrath, strife, heresies, envyings, re vices rather of the soul than of the flesh? For it is quite possible for a man to bstain from fleshly pleasures for the sake of idolatry or some heretical error; and yet, ven when he does so, he is proved by this apostolic authority to be living after the esh; and in abstaining from fleshly pleasure, he is proved to be practising damnable orks of the flesh. Who that has enmity has it not in his soul? or who would say to is enemy, or to the man he thinks his enemy, You have a bad flesh towards me, and ot rather, You have a bad spirit towards me? In fine, if any one heard of what I may all "carnalities," he would not fail to attribute them to the carnal part of man; so o one doubts that "animosities" belong to the soul of man. Why then does the octor of the Gentiles in faith and verity call all these and similar things works of the esh, unless because, by that mode of speech whereby the part is used for the whole, e means us to understand by the word flesh the man himself?

Chap. 3. That the Sin Is Caused Not by the Flesh, But by the Soul, and That the Corruption Contracted from Sin Is Not Sin But Sin's Punishment

But if any one says that the flesh is the cause of all vices and ill conduct, inasmuch s the soul lives wickedly only because it is moved by the flesh, it is certain he has ot carefully considered the whole nature of man. For "the corruptible body, indeed, veigheth down the soul." . . . We are burdened with this corruptible body; but nowing that the cause of this burdensomeness is not the nature and substance of the ody, but its corruption, we do not desire to be deprived of the body, but to be lothed with its immortality. For then, also, there will be a body, but it shall no onger be a burden, being no longer corruptible. . . .

Virgil, indeed, seems to express the sentiments of Plato in the beautiful lines, where e says,—

> "A fiery strength inspires their lives,
> An essence that from heaven derives,
> Though clogged in part by limbs of clay
> And the dull 'vesture of decay:' "

ut though he goes on to mention the four most common mental emotions,—desire, ear, joy, sorrow,—with the intention of showing that the body is the origin of all sins nd vices, saying,—

> "Hence wild desires and grovelling fears,
> And human laughter, human tears,
> Immured in dungeon-seeming night,
> They look abroad, yet see no light,"

et we believe quite otherwise. For the corruption of the body, which weighs down the soul, is not the cause but the punishment of the first sin; and it was not th corruptible flesh that made the soul sinful, but the sinful soul that made the fles corruptible. And though from this corruption of the flesh there arise certain incitement to vice, and indeed vicious desires, yet we must not attribute to the flesh all the vice of a wicked life, in case we thereby clear the devil of all these. . . .

Chap. 4. What It Is to Live According to Man, and What to Live According t God

When, therefore, man lives according to man, not according to God, he is like th devil. . . . When a man lives according to the truth, he lives not according to himsel but according to God; for He was God who said, "I am the truth." When, therefor man lives according to himself,—that is, according to man, not according to God,— assuredly he lives according to a lie; not that man himself is a lie, for God is hi author and creator, who is certainly not the author and creator of a lie, but becaus man was made upright, that he might not live according to himself, but according t Him that made him,—in other words, that he might do His will and not his own and not to live as he was made to live, that is a lie. . . .

In enunciating this proposition of ours, then, that because some live according t the flesh and others according to the spirit, there have arisen two diverse and conflictin cities, we might equally well have said, "because some live according to man, other according to God." For Paul says very plainly to the Corinthians, "For whereas ther is among you envying and strife, are ye not carnal, and walk according to man?" S that to walk according to man and to be carnal are the same; for by *flesh,* that is, b a part of man, man is meant. . . . For both the soul and the flesh, the componen parts of man, can be used to signify the whole man; and so the animal man and th carnal man are not two different things, but one and the same thing, viz., man livin according to man. In the same way it is nothing else than men that are meant eithe in the words, "By the deeds of the law there shall no *flesh* be justified;" or in th words, "Seventy-five *souls* went down into Egypt with Jacob." In the one passage "no flesh" signifies "no man;" and in the other, by "seventy-five souls" seventy-fiv men are meant. . . . And this is still more apparent in the words which followed "For while one saith, I am of Paul, and another, I am of Apollos, are ye not men?" The same thing which he had before expressed by "ye are animal," "ye are carnal," he now expresses by "ye are men;" that is, ye live according to man, not accordin to God, for if you lived according to Him, you should be gods.

Chap. 12. Of the Nature of Man's First Sin

If any one finds a difficulty in understanding why other sins do not alter huma nature as it was altered by the transgression of those first human beings, so that o account of it this nature is subject to the great corruption we feel and see, and t death, and is distracted and tossed with so many furious and contending emotions and is certainly far different from what it was before sin, even though it were the lodged in an animal body,—if, I say, any one is moved by this, he ought not t think that that sin was a small and light one because it was committed about food, an that not bad nor noxious, except because it was forbidden; for in that spot of singula felicity God could not have created and planted any evil thing. But by the precep

Ie gave, God commended obedience, which is, in a sort, the mother and guardian f all the virtues in the reasonable creature, which was so created that submission is dvantageous to it, while the fulfillment of its own will in preference to the Creator's destruction. And as this commandment enjoining abstinence from one kind of ood in the midst of great abundance of other kinds was so easy to keep,—so light burden to the memory,—and, above all, found no resistance to its observance in lust, hich only afterwards sprung up as the penal consequence of sin, the iniquity of iolating it was all the greater in proportion to the ease with which it might have been ept.

hap. 15. Of the Justice of the Punishment with Which Our First Parents Were 'isited for Their Disobedience

herefore, because the sin was a despising of the authority of God,—who had created ian; who had made him in His own image; who had set him above the other nimals; who had placed him in Paradise; who had enriched him with abundance f every kind and of safety; who had laid upon him neither many, nor great, nor ifficult commandments, but, in order to make a wholesome obedience easy to him, ad given him a single very brief and very light precept by which He reminded that reature whose service was to be free that He was Lord,—it was just that condemnation ollowed, and condemnation such that man, who by keeping the commandments should ave been spiritual even in his flesh, became fleshly even in his spirit; and as in is pride he had sought to be his own satisfaction, God in His justice abandoned him o himself, not to live in the absolute independence he affected, but instead of the iberty he desired, to live dissatisfied with himself in a hard and miserable bondage o him to whom by sinning he had yielded himself, doomed in spite of himself to die n body as he had willingly become dead in spirit, condemned even to eternal death had not the grace of God delivered him) because he had forsaken eternal life. Whoever thinks such punishment either excessive or unjust shows his inability to neasure the great iniquity of sinning where sin might so easily have been avoided. . . .

hap. 28. Of the Nature of the Two Cities, the Earthly and the Heavenly

Accordingly, two cities have been formed by two loves: the earthly by the love of self, ven to the contempt of God; the heavenly by the love of God, even to the contempt of self. The former, in a word, glories in itself, the latter in the Lord. For the one eeks glory from men; but the greatest glory of the other is God, the witness of onscience. The one lifts up its head in its own glory; the other says to its God, "Thou rt my glory, and the lifter up of mine head." In the one, the princes and the nations t subdues are ruled by the love of ruling; in the other, the princes and the subjects erve one another in love, the latter obeying, while the former take thought for all. The one delights in its own strength, represented in the persons of its rulers; the ther says to its God, "I will love Thee, O Lord, my strength." And therefore the vise men of the one city, living according to man, have sought for profit to their own odies or souls, or both, and those who have known God "glorified Him not as God, neither were thankful, but became vain in their imaginations, and their foolish heart vas darkened; professing themselves to be wise,"—that is, glorying in their own visdom, and being possessed by pride,—"they became fools, and changed the glory

of the incorruptible God into an image made like to corruptible man, and to bird
and four-footed beasts, and creeping things." For they were either leaders or followe
of the people in adoring images, "and worshipped and served the creature more tha
the Creator, who is blessed for ever." But in the other city there is no human wisdom
but only godliness, which offers due worship to the true God, and looks for its rewar
in the society of the saints, of holy angels as well as holy men, "that God may be a
in all."

BOOK NINETEEN

Chap. 12. That Even the Fierceness of War and All the Disquietude of Me Make towards This One End of Peace, Which Every Nature Desires

Whoever gives even moderate attention to human affairs and to our common natur
will recognize that if there is no man who does not wish to be joyful, neither is ther
any one who does not wish to have peace. For even they who make war desire nothin
but victory,—desire, that is to say, to attain to peace with glory. For what else i
victory than the conquest of those who resist us? and when this is done there is peace
It is therefore with the desire for peace that wars are waged, even by those who tak
pleasure in exercising their warlike nature in command and battle. And hence it i
obvious that peace is the end sought for by war. For every man seeks peace by wagin
war, but no man seeks war by making peace. For even they who intentionally interrup
the peace in which they are living have no hatred of peace, but only wish it change
into a peace that suits them better. They do not, therefore, wish to have no peace
but only one more to their mind. And in the case of sedition, when men have separate
themselves from the community, they yet do not effect what they wish, unless the
maintain some kind of peace with their fellow-conspirators. And therefore eve
robbers take care to maintain peace with their comrades, that they may with greate
effect and greater safety invade the peace of other men. And if an individual happe
to be of such unrivalled strength, and to be so jealous of partnership, that he trust
himself with no comrades, but makes his own plots, and commits depredations an
murders on his own account, yet he maintains some shadow of peace with such
persons as he is unable to kill, and from whom he wishes to conceal his deeds. In
his own home, too, he makes it his aim to be at peace with his wife and children
and any other members of his household; for unquestionably their prompt obedienc
to his every look is a source of pleasure to him. And if this be not rendered, he i
angry, he chides and punishes; and even by this storm he secures the calm peace o
his own home, as occasion demands. For he sees that peace cannot be maintained unles
all the members of the same domestic circle be subject to one head, such as he himsel
is in his own house. And therefore if a city or nation offered to submit itself to him
to serve him in the same style as he had made his household serve him, he would no
longer lurk in a brigand's hiding-places, but lift his head in open day as a king, though
the same covetousness and wickedness should remain in him. And thus all men
desire to have peace with their own circle whom they wish to govern as suits them
selves. For even those whom they make war against they wish to make their own
and impose on them the laws of their own peace. . . .

Chap. 13. Of the Universal Peace Which the Law of Nature Preserves through All Disturbances, and by Which Everyone Reaches His Desert in a Way Regulated by the Just Judge

The peace of the body then consists in the duly proportioned arrangement of its parts. The peace of the irrational soul is the harmonious repose of the appetites, and that of the rational soul the harmony of knowledge and action. The peace of body and soul is the well-ordered and harmonious life and health of the living creature. Peace between man and God is the well-ordered obedience of faith to eternal law. Peace between man and man is well-ordered concord. Domestic peace is the well-ordered concord between those of the family who rule and those who obey. Civil peace is a similar concord among the citizens. The peace of the celestial city is the perfectly ordered and harmonious enjoyment of God, and of one another in God. The peace of all things is the tranquility of order. Order is the distribution which allots things equal and unequal, each to its own place. And hence, though the miserable, in so far as they are such, do certainly not enjoy peace, but are severed from that tranquillity of order in which there is no disturbance, nevertheless, inasmuch as they are deservedly and justly miserable, they are by their very misery connected with order. They are not, indeed, conjoined with the blessed, but they are disjoined from them by the law of order. And though they are disquieted, their circumstances are notwithstanding adjusted to them, and consequently they have some tranquillity of order, and therefore some peace. But they are wretched because, although not wholly miserable, they are not in that place where any mixture of misery is impossible. They would, however, be more wretched if they had not that peace which arises from being in harmony with the natural order of things. When they suffer, their peace is in so far disturbed; but their peace continues in so far as they do not suffer, and in so far as their nature continues to exist. . . .

God, then, the most wise Creator and most just Ordainer of all natures, who placed the human race upon earth as its greatest ornament, imparted to men some good things adapted to this life, to wit, temporal peace, such as we can enjoy in this life from health and safety and human fellowship, and all things needful for the preservation and recovery of this peace, such as the objects which are accommodated to our outward senses, light, night, the air, and waters suitable for us, and everything the body requires to sustain, shelter, heal, or beautify it: and all under this most equitable condition, that every man who made a good use of these advantages suited to the peace of this mortal condition, should receive ampler and better blessings, namely, the peace of immortality, accompanied by glory and honor in an endless life made fit for the enjoyment of God and of one another in God; but that he who used the present blessings badly should both lose them and should not receive the others.

Chap. 14. Of the Order and Law Which Obtain in Heaven and Earth, Whereby It Comes to Pass That Human Society Is Served by Those Who Rule It

The whole use, then, of things temporal has a reference to this result of earthly peace in the earthly community, while in the city of God it is connected with eternal peace. And therefore, if we were irrational animals, we should desire nothing beyond the proper arrangement of the parts of the body and the satisfaction of the appetites,—nothing, therefore, but bodily comfort and abundance of pleasures, that the peace of the body might contribute to the peace of the soul. . . . But, as man has a rationa soul, he subordinates all this which he has in common with the beasts to the peace c his rational soul, that his intellect may have free play and may regulate his actions, an that he may thus enjoy the well-ordered harmony of knowledge and action which con stitutes, as we have said, the peace of the rational soul. . . . And this is the order o this concord, that a man, in the first place, injure no one, and, in the second, do goo to every one he can reach. Primarily, therefore, his own household are his care, for th law of nature and of society gives him readier access to them and greater opportunit of serving them. And hence the apostle says, "Now, if any provide not for his own and specially for those of his own house, he hath denied the faith, and is worse tha an infidel." This is the origin of domestic peace, or the well-ordered concord of thos in the family who rule and those who obey. For they who care for the rest rule,—th husband the wife, the parents the children, the masters the servants; and they wh are cared for obey,—the women their husbands, the children their parents, the serv ants their masters. But in the family of the just man who lives by faith and is as ye a pilgrim journeying on to the celestial city, even those who rule serve those whon they seem to command; for they rule not from a love of power, but from a sense o the duty they owe to others—not because they are proud of authority, but becaus they love mercy.

Chap. 15. Of the Liberty Proper to Man's Nature, and the Servitude Introduce by Sin,—a Servitude in Which the Man Whose Will Is Wicked Is the Slave o His Own Lust, though He Is Free So Far As Regards Other Men

This is prescribed by the order of nature: it is thus that God has created man. Fo "let them," He says, "have dominion over the fish of the sea, and over the fowl of th air, and over every creeping thing which creepeth on the earth." He did not inten that His rational creature, who was made in His image, should have dominion ove anything but the irrational creation,—not man over man, but man over the beasts And hence the righteous men in primitive times were made shepherds of cattle rathe than kings of men, God intending thus to teach us what the relative position of th creatures is, and what the desert of sin; for it is with justice, we believe, that the con dition of slavery is the result of sin. And this is why we do not find the word "slave" in any part of Scripture until righteous Noah branded the sin of his son with thi name. It is a name, therefore, introduced by sin and not by nature. The origin of th Latin word for slave is supposed to be found in the circumstance that those who b the law of war were liable to be killed were sometimes preserved by their victors, an were hence called servants. And these circumstances could never have arisen sav through sin. For even when we wage a just war, our adversaries must be sinning; an every victory, even though gained by wicked men, is a result of the first judgment o God, who humbles the vanquished either for the sake of removing or of punishin their sins. . . . The prime cause, then, of slavery is sin, which brings man under th dominion of his fellow,—that which does not happen save by the judgment of God with whom is no unrighteousness, and who knows how to award fit punishments t every variety of offence. But our Master in heaven says, "Every one who doeth sin i the servant of sin." And thus there are many wicked masters who have religious mer

s their slaves, and who are yet themselves in bondage; "for of whom a man is over-
ome, of the same is he brought in bondage." And beyond question it is a happier
hing to be the slave of a man than of a lust; for even this very lust of ruling, to men-
ion no others, lays waste men's hearts with the most ruthless dominion. Moreover,
vhen men are subjected to one another in a peaceful order, the lowly position does as
nuch good to the servant as the proud position does harm to the master. But by nature,
s God first created us, no one is the slave either of man or of sin. This servitude is,
owever, penal, and is appointed by that law which enjoins the preservation of the
atural order and forbids its disturbance; for if nothing had been done in violation of
hat law, there would have been nothing to restrain by penal servitude. And therefore
he apostle admonishes slaves to be subject to their masters, and to serve them heartily
nd with good-will, so that, if they cannot be freed by their masters, they may them-
elves make their slavery in some sort free, by serving not in crafty fear, but in faithful
ove, until all unrighteousness pass away, and all principality and every human power
e brought to nothing, and God be all in all.

hap. 16. Of Equitable Rule

nd therefore, although our righteous fathers had slaves, and administered their
lomestic affairs so as to distinguish between the condition of slaves and the heirship
f sons in regard to the blessings of this life, yet in regard to the worship of God, in
vhom we hope for eternal blessings, they took an equally loving oversight of all the
nembers of their household. And this is so much in accordance with the natural order,
hat the head of the household was called *paterfamilias;* and this name has been so
enerally accepted, that even those whose rule is unrighteous are glad to apply it to
hemselves. . . .

*hap. 17. What Produces Peace, and What Discord, between the Heavenly and
arthly Cities*

ut the families which do not live by faith seek their peace in the earthly advantages of
his life; while the families which live by faith look for those eternal blessings which
re promised, and use as pilgrims such advantages of time and of earth as do not fas-
inate and divert them from God, but rather aid them to endure with greater ease, and
o keep down the number of those burdens of the corruptible body which weigh upon
he soul. Thus the things necessary for this mortal life are used by both kinds of men and
amilies alike, but each has its own peculiar and widely different aim in using them.
The earthly city, which does not live by faith, seeks an earthly peace, and the end it
roposes, in the well-ordered concord of civic obedience and rule, is the combination
f men's wills to attain the things which are helpful to this life. The heavenly city, or
ather the part of it which sojourns on earth and lives by faith, makes use of this
eace only because it must, until this mortal condition which necessitates it shall pass
way. Consequently, so long as it lives like a captive and a stranger in the earthly city,
hough it has already received the promise of redemption, and the gift of the Spirit as
he earnest of it, it makes no scruple to obey the laws of the earthly city, whereby the
hings necessary for the maintenance of this mortal life are administered; and thus, as
his life is common to both cities, so there is a harmony between them in regard to

what belongs to it. But, as the earthly city has had some philosophers whose doctrin
is condemned by the divine teaching, and who, being deceived either by their ow
conjectures or by demons, supposed that many gods must be invited to take an interes
in human affairs, and assigned to each a separate function and a separate department
—to one the body, to another the soul; and in the body itself, to one the head, to an
other the neck, and each of the other members to one of the gods; and in like manner
in the soul, to one god the natural capacity was assigned, to another education, to an
other anger, to another lust; and so the various affairs of life were assigned,—cattl
to one, corn to another, wine to another, oil to another, the woods to another, mone
to another, navigation to another, wars and victories to another, marriages to another
births and fecundity to another, and other things to other gods: and as the celestia
city, on the other hand, knew that one God only was to be worshipped, and that t
Him alone was due that service which the Greeks call *latreia,* and which can be giver
only to a god, it has come to pass that the two cities could not have common laws o
religion, and that the heavenly city has been compelled in this matter to dissent, and t
become obnoxious to those who think differently, and to stand the brunt of their ange
and hatred and persecutions, except in so far as the minds of their enemies have beer
alarmed by the multitude of the Christians and quelled by the manifest protection o
God accorded to them. This heavenly city, then, while it sojourns on earth, calls citizens out of all nations, and gathers together a society of pilgrims of all languages, no
scrupling about diversities in the manners, laws, and institutions whereby earthly peac
is secured and maintained, but recognizing that, however various these are, they al
tend to one and the same end of earthly peace. It therefore is so far from rescinding
and abolishing these diversities, that it even preserves and adopts them, so long only
as no hindrance to the worship of the one supreme and true God is thus introduced
Even the heavenly city, therefore, while in its state of pilgrimage, avails itself of th
peace of earth, and, so far as it can without injuring faith and godliness, desires anc
maintains a common agreement among men regarding the acquisition of the necessarie
of life, and makes this earthly peace bear upon the peace of heaven; for this alone car
be truly called and esteemed the peace of the reasonable creatures, consisting as it doe
in the perfectly ordered and harmonious enjoyment of God and of one another ir
God. When we shall have reached that peace, this mortal life shall give place to on
that is eternal, and our body shall be no more this animal body which by its corruptior
weighs down the soul, but a spiritual body feeling no want, and in all its member
subjected to the will. In its pilgrim state the heavenly city possesses this peace by faith
and by this faith it lives righteously when it refers to the attainment of that peac
every good action towards God and man; for the life of the city is a social life.

THE RULE OF ST. BENEDICT

*Even before the time of Christ, there existed in the Near East a tradition of ascetic withdrawal from the world for the purpose of living a life of religious devotion. Christianity's stress on personal salvation increased the numbers of those who became hermits (ascetics who choose a solitary life) or monks (who live in groups). By the fourth century after Christ, it had become evident that asceticism was a major Christian institution, and a Greek bishop whom we usually call St. Basil the Great (*A.D. ca. *330–379) provided a rule by which small clusters of hermits could live together without disturbing each other's prayers. By the sixth century after Christ, the movement had expanded to the West and had embraced much larger numbers. St. Benedict of Nursia (*A.D. ca. *480–547) gave monasticism the form through which it was to dominate Western Europe in the Middle Ages and exercise a continuing influence on Christian ideas of community. His monastery at Monte Cassino, halfway between Rome and Naples, became the model for hundreds of similar communities throughout Europe; and his rule (the monks were later called regular clergy, from the Latin* regula, *"rule") was the constitution under which these communities operated; like any good constitution, it was flexible enough to allow for wide variations in practice.*

It was probably this organizational stability that enabled the monasteries to survive the early medieval invasions and cultural collapse; their survival in turn meant the preservation for posterity of many precious ancient manuscripts. In many cases the monks superimposed devotional works on the parchments containing copies of writings by Plato and Sophocles; salvation, after all, and not scholarship, was the monks' chief aim. But often manuscripts were treated more kindly and it may well be that without the monks the medieval and Renaissance revivals of ancient learning and literature would have been seriously retarded.

THE PROLOGUE

Listen, my son, and turn the ear of thine heart to the precepts of thy Master. Receive readily, and faithfully carry out the advice of a loving Father, so that by the work of

The Rule of St. Benedict*, trans. Abbot Gasquet (London: Chatto and Windus, 1909), pp. 1–2, 6–16, 26–35, 64–65, 84–87, 99–102, 108–114, 122–123.

obedience you may return to Him, whom you have left by the sloth of disobedience For thee, therefore, whosoever thou be, my words are intended, who, giving up th own will, dost take the all-powerful and excellent arms of obedience to fight unde the Lord Christ, the true King.

First, beg of Him with most earnest prayer to finish the good work begun; tha He who now hath deigned to count us among His children may never be grieved b our evil deeds. For at all times we must so serve Him with the good things He ha given us, that He may not, as an angry Father, disinherit His children, nor as a drea Lord, provoked by our evil deeds, deliver us to everlasting punishment as wicke servants who refuse to follow Him to glory. . . .

We are therefore now about to institute a school for the service of God, in whicl we hope nothing harsh nor burdensome will be ordained. But if we proceed in certai things with some little severity, sound reason so advising for the amendment of vice or the preserving of charity, do not for fear of this forthwith flee from the way o salvation, which is always narrow in the beginning. In living our life, however, an by the growth of faith, when the heart has been enlarged, the path of God's com mandments is run with unspeakable loving sweetness; so that never leaving Hi school, but persevering in the monastery until death in His teaching, we share by ou patience in the sufferings of Christ, and so merit to be partakers of His kingdom.

CHAPTER I: OF THE SEVERAL KINDS OF MONKS AND THEIR LIVES

It is recognized that there are four kinds of monks. The first are the Cenobites: that is those who live in a monastery under a Rule or an abbot. The second kind is that o Anchorites, or Hermits, who not in the first fervour of conversion, but after long tria in the monastery, and already taught by the example of many others, have learnt t fight against the devil, are well prepared to go forth from the ranks of the brotherhoo to the single combat of the desert. They can now, by God's help, safely fight agains the vices of their flesh and against evil thoughts singly, with their own hand and arn and without the encouragement of a companion. The third and worst kind of monks is that of the Sarabites, who have not been tried under any Rule nor schooled by ar experienced master, as gold is proved in the furnace, but soft as is lead and still ir their works cleaving to the world, are known to lie to God by their tonsure.

These in twos or threes, or more frequently singly, are shut up, without a shepherd; not in our Lord's fold, but in their own. The pleasure of carrying out their particular desires is their law, and whatever they dream of or choose this they call holy; but what they like not, that they account unlawful.

The fourth class of monks is called Gyrovagi (or Wanderers). These move about all their lives through various countries, staying as guests for three or four days at differ ent monasteries. They are always on the move and never settle down, and are slaves tc their own wills and to the enticements of gluttony. In every way they are worse than the Sarabites, and of their wretched way of life it is better to be silent than to speak.

Leaving these therefore aside, let us by God's help set down a Rule for Cenobites, who are the best kind of monks.

CHAPTER II: WHAT THE ABBOT SHOULD BE

An abbot to be fit to rule a monastery should ever remember what he is called, and in his acts illustrate his high calling. For in a monastery he is considered to take the place of Christ, since he is called by His name as the apostle saith, *Ye have received the spirit of the adoption of sons, whereby we cry, Abba, Father.** Therefore the abbot should neither teach, ordain, nor require anything against the command of our Lord (God forbid!), but in the minds of his disciples let his orders and teaching be mingled with the leaven of divine justice.

The abbot should ever be mindful that at the dread judgment of God there will be enquiry both as to his teaching and as to the obedience of his disciples. Let the abbot know that any lack of goodness, which the master of the family shall find in his flock, will be accounted the shepherd's fault. On the other hand, he shall be acquitted in so far as he shall have shown all the watchfulness of a shepherd over a restless and disobedient flock: and if as their pastor he shall have employed every care to cure their corrupt manners, he shall be declared guiltless in the Lord's judgment, and he may say with the prophet, *I have not hidden Thy justice in my heart; I have told Thy truth and Thy salvation; but they contemned and despised me.* And then in the end shall death be inflicted as a meet punishment upon the sheep which have not responded to his care. When, therefore, any one shall receive the name of abbot, he ought to rule his disciples with a twofold teaching: that is he should first show them in deeds rather than words all that is good and holy. To such as are understanding, indeed, he may expound the Lord's behests by words; but to the hard-hearted and to the simple-minded he must manifest the divine precepts in his life. Thus, what he has taught his disciples to be contrary to God's law, let him show in his own deeds that such things are not to be done, lest preaching to others *he himself become a castaway,* and God say unto him thus sinning, *Why dost thou declare My justices, and take My testament in thy mouth? Thou hast hated discipline, and cast My speeches behind thee.* And *Thou, who didst see the mote in thy brother's eye, hast thou not seen the beam that is in thine own?*

Let him make no distinction of persons in the monastery. Let not one be loved more than another, save such as be found to excel in obedience or good works. Let not the free-born be put before the serf-born in religion, unless there be other reasonable cause for it. If upon due consideration the abbot shall see such cause he may place him where he pleases; otherwise let all keep their own places, because *whether bond or free we are all one in Christ,* and bear an equal burden of service under one Lord: *for with God there is no accepting of persons.* For one thing only are we preferred by Him, if we are found better than others in good works and more humble. Let the abbot therefore have equal love for all, and let all, according to their deserts, be under the same discipline.

The abbot in his teaching should always observe that apostolic rule which saith,

* [This and all subsequent sentences in italics are quotations from Holy Scripture. Their frequency and relevance indicate St. Benedict's remarkable command of the Bible. (*Ed.*)]

Reprove, entreat, rebuke. That is to say, as occasions require he ought to mingle encouragement with reproofs. Let him manifest the sternness of a master and the loving affection of a father. He must reprove the undisciplined and restless severely, but he should exhort such as are obedient, quiet and patient, for their better profit. We charge him, however, to reprove and punish the stubborn and negligent. Let him not shut his eyes to the sins of offenders; but, directly they begin to show themselves and to grow, he must use every means to root them up utterly, remembering the fate of Heli, the priest of Silo. To the more virtuous and apprehensive, indeed, he may for the first or second time use words of warning; but in dealing with the stubborn, the hard-hearted, the proud and the disobedient, even at the very beginning of their sin, let him chastise them with stripes and with bodily punishment, knowing that it is written, *The fool is not corrected with words.* And again, *Strike thy son with a rod and thou shalt deliver his soul from death.*

The abbot ought ever to bear in mind what he is and what he is called; he ought to know that to whom more is entrusted, from him more is exacted. Let him recognize how difficult and how hard a task he has undertaken, to rule souls and to make himself a servant to the humours of many. One, forsooth, must be led by gentle words, another by sharp reprehension, another by persuasion; and thus shall he so shape and adapt himself to the character and intelligence of each, that he not only suffer no loss in the flock entrusted to his care, but may even rejoice in its good growth. Above all things let him not slight nor make little of the souls committed to his care, heeding more fleeting, worldly and frivolous things; but let him remember always that he has undertaken the government of souls, of which he shall also have to give an account. And that he may not complain of the want of temporal means, let him remember that it is written, *Seek first the kingdom of God, and His justice, and all things shall be given to you.* And again, *Nothing is wanting to such as fear Him.*

He should know that whoever undertakes the government of souls must prepare himself to account for them. And however great the number of the brethren under him may be, let him understand for certain that at the Day of Judgment he will have to give to our Lord an account of all their souls as well as of his own. In this way, by fearing the inquiry concerning his flock which the Shepherd will hold, he is solicitous on account of others' souls as well as of his own, and thus whilst reclaiming other men by his corrections, he frees himself also from all vice.

CHAPTER III: ON TAKING COUNSEL OF THE BRETHREN

Whenever any weighty matters have to be transacted in the monastery let the abbot call together all the community and himself propose the matter for discussion. After hearing the advice of the brethren let him consider it in his own mind, and then do what he shall judge most expedient. We ordain that all must be called to council, because the Lord often reveals to a younger member what is best. And let the brethren give their advice with all humble subjection, and presume not stiffly to defend their own opinion. Let them rather leave the matter to the abbot's discretion, so that all submit to what he shall deem best. As it becometh disciples to obey their master, so doth it behove the master to dispose of all things with forethought and justice.

In all things, therefore, every one shall follow the Rule as their master, and let no one rashly depart from it. In the monastery no one is to be led by the desires of his own heart, neither shall any one within or without the monastery presume to argue wantonly with his abbot. If he presume to do so let him be subjected to punishment according to the Rule.

The abbot, however, must himself do all things in the fear of God and according to the Rule, knowing that he shall undoubtedly have to give an account of his whole government to God, the most just Judge.

If anything of less moment has to be done in the monastery let the abbot take advice of the seniors only, as it is written, *Do all things with counsel, and thou shalt not afterwards repent of it.*

CHAPTER VII: ON HUMILITY

Brethren, Holy Scripture cries out to us, saying, *Every one who exalteth himself shall be humbled, and he who humbleth himself shall be exalted.* In this it tells us every form of self-exaltation is a kind of pride, which the prophet declares he carefully avoided, where he says, *Lord, my heart is not exalted, neither are my eyes lifted up; neither have I walked in great things, nor in wonders above myself.* And why? *If I did not think humbly, but exalted my soul: as a child weaned from his mother, so wilt Thou reward my soul.*

Wherefore, brethren, if we would scale the summit of humility, and swiftly gain the heavenly height which is reached by our lowliness in this present life, we must set up a ladder of climbing deeds like that which Jacob saw in his dream, whereon angels were descending and ascending. Without doubt that descending and ascending is to be understood by us as signifying that we descend by exalting ourselves and ascend by humbling ourselves. But the ladder itself thus set up is our life in this world, which by humility of heart is lifted by our Lord to heaven. Our body and soul we may indeed call the sides of the ladder in which our divine vocation has set the divers steps of humility and discipline we have to ascend.

The first step of humility, then, is reached when a man, with the fear of God always before his eyes, does not allow himself to forget, but is ever mindful of all God's commandments. He remembers, moreover, that such as contemn God fall into hell for their sins, and that life eternal awaits such as fear Him. And warding off at each moment all sin and defect in thought and word, of eye, hand or foot, of self-will, let such a one bestir himself to prune away the lusts of the flesh.

Let him think that he is seen at all times by God from heaven; and that wheresoever he may be, all his actions are visible to the eye of God and at all times are reported by the angels. The prophet shows us this when he says that God is ever present to our thoughts: *God searcheth the hearts and reins.* And again, *The Lord knoweth the thoughts of men that they are vain.* He also saith, *Thou hast understood my thoughts afar off;* and again, *The thought of man shall confess Thee.* In order then, that the humble brother may be careful to avoid wrong thoughts let him alway say in his heart, *Then shall I be without spot before Him, if I shall keep me from m iniquity.*

We are forbidden to do our own will, since Scripture tells us, *Leave thy own wil and desire.* And again, *We beg of God in prayer that His will may be done in us.*

Rightly are we taught, therefore, not to do our own will, if we take heed of what th Scripture teaches: *There are ways which to men seem right, the end whereof plunget even into the deep pit of hell.* And again, when we fear what is said about the negli gent, *They are corrupted, and made abominable in their pleasures.* But in regard o the desires of the flesh we ought to believe that God is present with us; as the prophe says, speaking to the Lord, *O Lord, all my desire is before Thee.*

We have therefore to beware of evil desires, since death stands close at the door o pleasure. It is for this reason that Scripture bids us, *Follow not thy concupiscences.* If therefore, the eyes of the Lord behold both the good and the bad; if He be ever look ing down from heaven upon the sons of men to find one who thinks of God or seek Him; and if day and night what we do is made known to Him—for these reasons, b the angels appointed to watch over us, we should always take heed, brethren, lest Go may sometime or other see us, as the prophet says in the Psalm, *inclined to evil an become unprofitable servants.* Even though He spare us for a time, because He i loving and waits for our conversion to better ways, let us fear that He may say to u hereafter, *These things thou hast done and I held my peace.*

The second step of humility is reached when any one not loving self-will takes n heed to satisfy his own desires, but copies in his life what our Lord said, *I came no to do My own will, but the will of Him Who sent Me.* Scripture likewise proclaim that self-will engendereth punishment, and necessity purchaseth a crown.

The third step of humility is reached when a man, for the love of God, submits him self with all obedience to a superior, imitating our Lord, of whom the apostle saith, *H was made obedient even unto death.*

The fourth step of humility is reached when any one in the exercise of his obedi ence patiently and with a quiet mind bears all that is inflicted on him, things con trary to nature, and even at times unjust, and in suffering all these he neither wearie nor gives over the work, since the Scripture says, *He only that persevereth to the en shall be saved;* also *Let thy heart be comforted, and expect the Lord.* And in order t show that for our Lord's sake the faithful man ought to bear all things, no matter ho contrary to nature they may be (the psalmist), in the person of the sufferers, says *For thee we suffer death all the day long; we are esteemed as sheep for the slaughte* Secure in the hope of divine reward they rejoice, saying, *But in all things we ove come by the help of Him Who hath loved us.*

Elsewhere also Scripture says, *Thou hast proved us, O Lord; Thou hast tried us, a silver is tried, with fire. Thou hast brought us into the snare; Thou hast laid tribul tion upon our backs.* And to show that we ought to be subject to a prior (or superior it goes on, *Thou hast placed men over our heads.* And, moreover, they fulfil th Lord's command by patience in adversity and injury, who, *when struck on one chee offer the other;* when one *taketh away their coat leave go their cloak also,* and wh being compelled to carry a burden one mile, go two; who, with Paul the apostle, suffer false brethren, and bless those who speak ill of them.

The fifth step of humility is reached when a monk manifests to his abbot, by humble confession, all the evil thoughts of his heart and his secret faults. The Scripture urges us to do this where it says, *Reveal thy way to the Lord and hope in Him.* It also says, *Confess to the Lord, because He is good, because His mercy endureth for ever.* And the prophet also says, *I have made known unto Thee mine offence, and mine injustices I have not hidden. I have said, I will declare openly against myself mine injustices to the Lord; and Thou hast pardoned the wickedness of my heart.*

The sixth step of humility is reached when a monk is content with all that is mean and vile; and in regard to everything enjoined him accounts himself a poor and worthless workman, saying with the prophet, *I have been brought to nothing, and knew it not. I have become as a beast before Thee, and I am always with Thee.*

The seventh step of humility is reached when a man not only confesses with his tongue that he is most lowly and inferior to others, but in his inmost heart believes so. Such a one, humbling himself, exclaims with the prophet, *I am a worm and no man, the reproach of men and the outcast of the people. I have been exalted and am humbled and confounded.* And again, *It is good for me that Thou hast humbled me, that I may learn Thy commandments.*

The eighth step of humility is reached when a monk does nothing but what the common rule of the monastery, or the example of his seniors, enforces.

The ninth step of humility is reached when a monk restrains his tongue from talking, and, practising silence, speaks not till a question be asked him, since Scripture says, *In many words thou shalt not avoid sin,* and *a talkative man shall not be directed upon the earth.*

The tenth step of humility is attained to when one is not easily and quickly moved to laughter, for it is written, *The fool lifteth his voice in laughter.*

The eleventh step of humility is reached when a monk, in speaking, does so quietly and without laughter, humbly, gravely and in a few words and not with a loud voice, for it is written, *A wise man is known by a few words.*

The twelfth step of humility is reached when a monk not only has humility in his heart, but even shows it also exteriorly to all who behold him. Thus, whether he be in the oratory at the "Work of God," in the monastery, or in the garden, on a journey, or in the fields, or wheresoever he be, sitting, standing or walking, always let him, with head bent and eyes fixed on the ground, bethink himself of his sins and imagine that he is arraigned before the dread judgment of God. Let him be ever saying to himself, with the publican in the Gospel, *Lord, I a sinner am not worthy to lift mine eyes to heaven;* and with the prophet, *I am bowed down and humbled on every side.*

When all these steps of humility have been mounted the monk will presently attain to that love of God which is perfect and casteth out fear. By means of this love everything which before he had observed not without fear, he shall now begin to do by habit, without any trouble and, as it were, naturally. He acts now not through fear of hell, but for the love of Christ, out of a good habit and a delight in virtue. All this our Lord will vouchsafe to work by the Holy Ghost in His servant, now cleansed from vice and sin.

CHAPTER XXXIII: OUGHT MONKS TO HAVE ANYTHING OF THEIR OWN?

Above all others, let this vice be extirpated in the monastery. No one, without leav of the abbot, shall presume to give, or receive, or keep as his own, anything whatever neither book, nor tablets, nor pen: nothing at all. For monks are men who can clair no dominion even over their own bodies or wills. All that is necessary, however, the may hope from the Father of the monastery; but they shall keep nothing which th abbot has not given or allowed. All things are to be common to all, as it is writter *Neither did any one say or think that aught was his own.* Hence if any one shall b found given to this most wicked vice let him be admonished once or twice, and if h do not amend let him be subjected to correction.

CHAPTER XLVIII: OF DAILY MANUAL LABOUR

Idleness is an enemy of the soul. Because this is so the brethren ought to be occupie at specified times in manual labour, and at other fixed hours in holy reading. W therefore think that both these may be arranged for as follows: from Easter to th first of October, on coming out from Prime [the prayer said at about 6 A.M.], let th brethren labour till about the fourth hour [10 A.M.] From the fourth till close upo the sixth hour [noon] let them employ themselves in reading. On rising from tab after the sixth hour let them rest on their beds in strict silence; but if any one sha wish to read, let him do so in such a way as not to disturb any one else.

Let None [the prayer said at about 3 P.M.] be said somewhat before the tim about the middle of the eighth hour [2:30 P.M.], and after this all shall work at wh they have to do till evening. If, however, the nature of the place or poverty requi them to labour at gathering in the harvest, let them not grieve at that, for then a they truly monks when they live by the labour of their hands, as our Fathers and th Apostles did. Let everything, however, be done with moderation for the sake of th faint-hearted.

From the first of October till the beginning of Lent let the brethren be occupied i reading till the end of the second hour [8 A.M.]. At that time Tierce [the prayer us ally said at about 9 A.M.] shall be said, after which they shall labour at the work e joined them till None. At the first signal for the Hour of None all shall cease to wor so as to be ready when the second signal is given. After their meal they shall be en ployed in reading or on the psalms.

On the days of Lent, from the morning till the end of the third [9 A.M.] hour, th brethren are to have time for reading, after which let them work at what is set the to do till the close of the tenth hour [4 P.M.]. During these Lenten days let each on have some book from the library which he shall read through carefully. These boo are to be given out at the beginning of Lent.

It is of much import that one or two seniors be appointed to go about the monaste at such times as the brethren are free to read, in order to see that no one is slothfu given to idleness or foolish talking instead of reading, and so not only makes n rofit himself but also distracts others. If any such be found (which God forbid) let im be corrected once or twice, and if he amend not let him be subjected to regular iscipline of such a character that the rest may take warning. Moreover one brother hall not associate with another at unsuitable hours.

On Sunday also, all, save those who are assigned to various offices, shall have time or reading. If, however, any one be so negligent and slothful as to be unwilling or nable to read or meditate, he must have some work given him, so as not to be idle. 'or weak brethren, or those of delicate constitutions, some work or craft shall be ound to keep them from idleness, and yet not such as to crush them by the heavy abour or to drive them away. The weakness of such brethren must be taken into onsideration by the abbot.

HAPTER LVIII: THE MANNER OF RECEIVING THE BRETHREN TO RELIGION

ny one on first coming to the religious life should not find the entrance made easy, ut as the apostle saith, *Try the spirits, if they be of God.* If, however, the newcomer ontinues to knock, and for four or five days shows a patient bearing, both of the arshness shown him and of the difficulty made about admitting him, and persist in is petition he shall then be allowed to enter the guest-place for a few days. After that t him be in the noviciate, where he shall meditate and eat and sleep.

And let a senior, such as has the skill of winning souls, be appointed to watch carelly over him, to discover whether he truly seeks God and is eager for the Divine Office, for obedience and humiliations. Let all the rigour and austerity of our journey God be put clearly before him. If he promise to continue in a steadfast perseverance, t the end of two months the entire Rule shall be read to him, and let him be told, See the law under which you wish to fight if you can observe it enter upon the life; you cannot you are free to depart."

If he still persevere let him be brought back to the noviciate and again tried in all atience. And after the lapse of six months let the Rule be read to him again, that he ay fully know the kind of life he is entering upon. If he yet persevere, after four onths the Rule shall be read to him once more. If after due deliberation he shall ien promise to keep all the law and to do whatever is commanded of him, let him e received into the community, knowing that he is now under the law of the Rule, that he can henceforth neither leave the monastery nor withdraw his neck from the oke of the Rule which after so long a deliberation he was free to have taken or efused.

When he is to be admitted into the community let him in the oratory, and in the resence of all, promise before God and His saints stability, amendment of manners id obedience, in order that if at any time he shall act otherwise he may know that he iall be condemned by Him Whom he mocketh. He shall draw up the form of his romise in the name of the saints, whose relics are reposing there, and of the abbot iere present. Let him write out this form himself, or at least, if he is uneducated an-her at his request must write it for him, and to this the novice himself shall set his ark and with his own hand lay it upon the altar.

After he has placed it there let the novice immediately begin the verse, *Uphold me, O Lord, according to Thy word, and I shall live, and let me not be confounded in my expectation.* This verse the community shall repeat three times, adding at the end *Glory be to the Father,* etc. Then the brother novice shall cast himself at the feet of all, asking their prayers, and from that time he shall be counted as one of the community. If he has any property he must first either give it to the poor, or by formal gift make it over to the monastery without any reservation for himself since he must know that he has henceforth no power even over his own body. Let him, therefore, forthwith be divested in the oratory of his own garments and be clothed in those of the monastery. The clothes he has taken off, however, are to be kept in the wardrobe, so that if (which God forbid) he should by the persuasion of the devil, resolve to leave the monastery he may be stripped of his monastic dress and expelled. The form of profession which the abbot took from him at the altar he shall not receive back, but it shall be kept in the monastery.

CHAPTER LXIII: THE ORDER OF THE COMMUNITY

The brethren shall take their places according to the date of their conversion, the merit of their lives, or the appointment of their abbot. And the abbot must not disturb the flock committed to him, nor, as it were, by any arbitrary use of his power ordain anything unjustly. But let him always remember that he will have to render an account to God of all his judgments and of all his works.

Wherefore in the order he shall appoint, or in that which they hold amongst themselves, let the brethren receive the Pax, approach Communion, intone a psalm and stand in choir. In all places, without exception, order shall not be decided by age, for this shall not be a prejudice to any one, since Samuel and Daniel, though children, were judges of the priests. With the exception therefore of those who, as we have said, for some weighty reason, the abbot shall advance, or for certain causes shall put in a lower place, let all the rest remain in the order of their conversion. For example one who shall come to the monastery at the second hour of the day shall know that he is junior to him who has come at the first hour, no matter what his age or dignity may be. In regard to children, let them be kept by all under discipline in every way.

Let the juniors, therefore, honour their seniors, and the seniors love the juniors. In addressing each other in person no one shall call another by his mere name, but let the senior call the junior, *Brother,* and the junior call the senior, *Father.* But, because the abbot is held to take the place of Christ, he shall be called *Sir* and *Abbot,* not out of consideration for himself, but for the honour and love of Christ. He, however, should remember and so conduct himself as to be worthy of such an honour.

Wherever the brethren meet each other the junior shall ask a blessing from the senior. When a senior passes by let the junior rise and make place for him to sit down, neither shall the junior presume to sit unless the senior bid him so to do, in order to fulfil what is written, *In honour preventing one another.*

Little children or youths shall keep their respective places in the oratory and at able, under discipline. Outside watch shall be kept over them, everywhere indeed, till hey come to an age of understanding.

:HAPTER LXIV: THE ELECTION OF THE ABBOT

n the election of an abbot let the following points be always borne in mind: that he e made abbot whom the whole community, in the fear of God, make choice of, or a art of it, however small, acting with greater wisdom. Let him who is created abbot e chosen because of his virtuous life and his wisdom, even if he be the last in the ommunity. And although the whole community (which God forbid) shall unani- ously choose one who supports them in their evil practices, and their vicious lives ecome known to the bishop (to whose diocese the monastery belongs), or to the bbots or Christians of the neighbourhood, they shall annul the choice of these bad nen and appoint a worthy steward of God's House, knowing that for this they shall eceive a good reward provided they do it with pure intention and through zeal of iod, just as, on the other hand, they sin if they neglect to do it.

Let him who has been created abbot ever reflect upon the weighty burden he has aken up and remember unto Whom he shall give an account of his stewardship. Let im know also that it is better for him to profit others than to rule over them. He nust therefore be learned in the Divine Law that he may know when to *bring forth ew things and old.* He must be chaste, sober, merciful, and always exalt mercy above istice, that he may obtain mercy. He shall hate vice and love the brethren. Even in his orrection he shall act with prudence and not try too much, lest whilst too violently couring off the rust the vessel itself be broken. Let him always bear in mind his own railty, and remember that *the bruised reed must not be broken.*

In saying this we do not propose that he should allow vices to spring up, but, as e have declared before, seek to root them up and with charity, in the way he shall nink proper in each case. Let him aim at being loved rather than feared. He must not e worried nor anxious, neither should he be too exacting or obstinate, or jealous, or ver-suspicious, for then he will never be at rest. Even in what he orders, whether it elates to God or to worldly matters, let him be prudent and considerate. In all that e enjoins he should be discreet and moderate, meditating on the prudence of holy acob, who says, *If I shall cause my flocks to be over-driven, they will all die in one ay.* Wherefore adopting these and like principles of discretion, the mother of virtues, t him so temper all things that the strong may have their scope and the weak be not ared. And especially let him keep the present Rule in all things, so that when he nall have well administered it he may hear from our Lord what the good servant eard who gave corn to his fellow-servants in due season: *And I say to you, over all is goods will he place him.*

HAPTER LXXII: OF THE GOOD ZEAL MONKS SHOULD HAVE

s there is an evil and bitter emulation which separates from God and leads to hell, there is a good spirit of emulation which frees from vices and leads to God and life everlasting. Let monks therefore practise this emulation with most fervent love that is to say, let them *in honour prevent one another,* let them bear most patientl with each other's infirmities, whether of body or of manner. Let them contend with on another in their obedience. Let no one follow what he thinks most profitable to him self, but rather what is best for another. Let them show brotherly charity with a chast love. Let them fear God and love their abbot with sincere and humble affection, an set nothing whatever before Christ, Who can bring us unto eternal life.

Part Four

The Early Germans

ON GERMANY

Tacitus

At the time that Tacitus wrote On Germany, *in* A.D. *98, Rome had reached its peak of expansion. Spain and Britain on the west, the Rhine and the Danube on the north, Babylon and Egypt on the east and south, rang with Roman arms and yielded grain, metals, slaves, and silver to the conquerors.*

Internally the capital had recently experienced Nero, the struggle for power of the praetorian guard, murders and civil wars; but now Rome was about to enter more glorious and stable times. In A.D. *98, the emperor Trajan came to the purple. The forty-three-year-old Cornelius Tacitus, like so many of aristocratic and refined lineage, heralded the event as a time for a renewal of Roman virtue and for a thrust of new activity along the sagging frontiers.*

A year earlier he had started his Agricola, *the military biography of his resplendent father-in-law, and now he was writing about the Germans, perhaps intending to interest Romans again in martial glory, but also to warn of the hungry hordes north of the Rhine ("The liberty of the Germans is a deadlier foe than the tyranny of the kings of Parthia"). Though* On Germany *may have been offered as a political pamphlet, in it Tacitus has also left us one of the finest specimens—despite its shortness—of classical social analysis.*

On Germany *is an early work, for Tacitus was yet to tell the story of Rome's glory in his* Histories *and* Annals. *Thus one can observe the craftsman polishing his narrative art.* On Germany *reads easily, even for modern readers, because, like most of the histories of its day, it was meant to be read aloud. A sound of authenticity holds the reader even though Tacitus never, in fact, saw the Rhine. Yet in his posts of senator and consul he must have spoken with legates, generals, and merchants, savoring their far-off images of distant tribes and adopting them as his own.*

This sharply drawn portrait is one of our most complete early accounts. The following selection omits very little of the original.

Germany proper is separated from Gaul, Raetia, and Pannonia by the rivers Rhine and Danube; from Sarmatia and Dacia by mountains and mutual suspicion. The ocean

Tacitus, *Dialogus Agricola and Germania*, trans. W. Hamilton Frye (London: Oxford University Press, 1908), pp. 89–110, 112–119.

washes its other sides, embracing broad peninsulas and islands of vast size, where latel the disclosures of war have brought to our knowledge new peoples and their kings The Rhine, rising on an inaccessible peak of the Raetian Alps, takes a slight ben towards the west and mingles its waters in the North Sea. The Danube flows fron the gentle slopes of Mount Adnoba, reaching many peoples in its course, until i forces its way by six mouths into the Pontic Sea. The seventh mouth is drained b marshes.

The Germans themselves are, I am inclined to believe, an indigenous people, ver little affected by admixture with other races through immigration or intercourse. Fo in old days emigrants travelled not by land but in ships; and owing to the limitles extent of the sea beyond our ken, and what I may call its inhospitality, Germany wa seldom visited by ships from our clime. Besides, to say nothing of the dangers of th rough and unknown sea, who would leave Asia or Africa or Italy and sail for Germany with its grim scenery and severe climate, ill to visit and ill to live in—unless of cours it were his fatherland?

The ancient songs, which are their sole form of history and tradition, tell the praise of the earth-born god Tuisto, and his son Mannus. These are the fathers and founder of the race. To Mannus they assign three sons, after whom the tribes nearest the se are called Ingaevones, those in the interior Herminones, and the rest Istaevones. Som people maintain—antiquity invites conjecture—that there are more tribes of divin descent, and more group-names, such as Marsi, Gambrivii, Suebi, Vandilii, which the take to be real ancient names. However that may be, the origin and application of th word Germania are both recent. The tribe, now called Tungri, which first crossed th Rhine and drove out the Gauls, were then called Germani. Thus the name not of people but of a tribe gradually gained currency. It was first given to the whole rac by the conquerors to inspire fear: later, when the name had thus arisen, they all cam to call themselves Germans.

They tell stories of Hercules having lived amongst them, and when marching t battle they sing his praises as the prince of heroes. They have other songs of this kin which they intone. This they call 'shield-song'. It serves to raise their spirits, and fror the singing they take omens for the coming battle. For as they march and sing, the inspire fear or feel it according to the noise they make, which sounds more like unison of hearts than of voices. For their chief aim is to produce a rough and broke roar by putting their shields to their mouths, so that the reverberation may swell thei voices to a fuller and a deeper tone. Some people believe that Ulysses in his lon legendary wandering was carried into these seas and visited Germany, and tha Asciburgium, a town on the banks of the Rhine, which is still inhabited to-day, wa founded and named by him. . . .[1] They go on to say that an altar dedicated to Ulysses and bearing also the name of his father, Laertes, was once discovered on this sam spot, and that several barrows with memorial inscriptions in Greek are still to be foun on the frontier of Germany. It is not my intention either to argue in support of thes statements or to refute them. My readers must believe or disbelieve them each as h feels inclined.

Personally I incline to the opinion of those who hold that the peoples of German

[1] Some words are lost here.

e not contaminated by intermarriage with other tribes, but have remained a race eculiar, pure-bred, and unique. This accounts for their physical type, which, in spite their numbers, is universally the same. They have fierce blue eyes, red hair, and rge frames, only capable of sudden effort. They endure labour and service less atiently than we, and cannot support thirst and heat. But their climate and soil have customed them to cold and hunger.

The country, although very varied in appearance, generally consists of rough forests foul swamps. It is wetter where it faces Gaul, and windier on the side of Noricum ad Pannonia. Though fertile in crops, it bears no fruit-trees: it is rich in flocks, but ey are generally stunted. Even their cattle do not attain their natural beauty or the ll growth of their horns. They take pleasure in the size of their herds: these are eir sole form of wealth, and they are very proud of them. Whether it is in mercy anger that the gods have denied them silver and gold I do not know: nor could definitely assert that Germany produces no vein of gold or silver: for no one has xplored. But they are not affected in the same way that we are by its possession and se. You may see there silver vases which have been given as presents to their am- assadors and chiefs: but they hold them as cheap as earthenware pots. However, the ibes nearest to us have learnt through familiarity with trade to value gold and lver: they can recognize and pick out certain pieces of our money. The people of the terior use the more simple and ancient method of barter. They like best the old oinage with which they are familiar, with milled edges and with a two-horsed chariot amped on it. They also prefer silver to gold. This is not a matter of taste; but a umber of small silver coins is more useful for men who only buy cheap and common rticles.

Even iron is not plentiful, as one may gather from the nature of their weapons. words and long lances are rarely used: they carry spears, or, as they name them, 'rams,' which have a short, narrow head, but are so sharp and handy that they use e same weapon, as circumstances demand, for close and open fighting. The cavalry re content with shield and spear: the infantry also shower javelins: each man carries everal, and they can throw them a very long way. They fight naked or in a light plaid. hey have no elaborate apparel, and merely paint their shields with distinctive colours, f the brightest hue. Few wear cuirasses, hardly any helmets or caps. Their horses are istinguished neither for build nor for speed. They are not taught like our cavalry to escribe figures of eight, but they ride straight forward or make simple flank move- ents [to the right], keeping line so closely that none fall behind. All things con- dered, their infantry seem the stronger. They therefore fight in mixed order. A picked ody of infantry, chosen from the whole fighting strength, is stationed before the ain body, and these men are so swift of foot as to be fit for a cavalry engagement. heir number too is fixed: a hundred come from each village, and they are known to eir own people as 'the hundred'. Thus what was at first a mere number has come be an honourable name. The line is drawn up in wedge-battalions. To retire from our post, provided you charge again, is thought to show prudence, not fear. They arry away their dead, even after a doubtful battle. To lose your shield is the worst ishonour of all: one thus disgraced may not be present at a sacrifice or enter a council. fter a defeat many survivors have been known to hang themselves to end their infamy.

Kings they choose by family, generals by merit. But the kings have not an unfettere
power; and the generals lead less by authority than by force of example, accordin
as they win praise for energy, conspicuous bravery and daring. Powers of execution o
imprisonment and even of flogging are granted to none but the priests, nor are the
exercised as a penalty or at the general's command, but at the bidding—so they imagin
—of the tribal god whom they believe to be present in the ranks. Statues and certai
symbols are taken down from the trees of the grove and carried into battle. Th
troops of horse and the 'wedge-battalions' of infantry are formed not merely at hap
hazard but by families and clans. In this lies their chief incentive to bravery. Thei
dearest too are close at hand: the women's cries and the wailing of the babies reac
their ears. It is their testimony that each man respects, their praise he values most
They carry their wounds to show to mother and to wife: nor are the women frightene
to number and examine the blows: during battle they bring them food and encourage
ment.

There is a tradition that in some battles troops already wavering and beginning t
run have been rallied by the women, who offer unceasing prayers, bare their breasts
and point out that captivity lies waiting close at hand. This the Germans fear far mor
anxiously for the women's sake than for their own, and the strongest hold upon th
loyalty of these tribes is got by demanding as hostages girls of noble family. Indee
they believe that there is in women some divine spark of foreknowledge, and the
do not despise their advice or neglect their answers. We saw for ourselves in th
reign of the sainted Vespasian a woman named Velaeda, who was long credited b
many people with supernatural powers. In earlier days too they paid great respect t
Albruna and many other prophetesses, but not in a spirit of flattery nor as though the
wanted to make goddesses of them.

They worship Mercury more than any other of the gods. They do not think it wron
to propitiate him on certain days with human victims. Hercules and Mars they appeas
with more venial sacrifices. A portion of the Suebi also sacrifice to Isis. The origi
of this foreign rite is quite uncertain: but the symbol itself is made in the shape of
galley, which shows that the worship is imported. However, they consider that it il
accords with the majesty of heavenly beings to coop them within walls or to depic
them in any human shape. They consecrate groves and woods and give divine name
to that mysterious abstraction which they see by the eye of awe alone.

No people attach more importance to auspices and the decision of the lot. Thei
method of drawing lots is always the same. They lop off a branch of a fruit-tree an
cut it up into small wands. These they distinguish by certain marks and scatter then
at random over a white cloth. Next, if the deliberations be public, the tribal priest, or
if private, the head of the family himself, offers a prayer, and raising his eyes t
heaven picks up three wands, one at a time, and then interprets them according t
the marks already made on each. If the auspices are unfavourable, they do not consul
them again that day on the same matter. If assent is indicated, they still demand
further confirmation of their truth. For they have learnt to question, as we do, th
flight and cries of birds. They have also a method peculiar to themselves of obtainin
prophetic warning from horses, which are kept at public expense in the groves an
woods mentioned before. These horses are white and undefiled by human labour

'hey are yoked to a sacred car, and the priest, together with the king or chief man f the tribe, accompanies them and takes note of their neighing and whinnying. No ıethod of taking auspices is more completely trusted, not only by the common people, ut by the nobles also, and by the priests, who think themselves the gods' servants and he horses their confidants. They have also another method of taking auspices, by vhich they seek to discover the issue of important battles. They capture a prisoner, as est they can, from the tribe with whom they are at war, and pit him against a chosen varrior of their own, each with his native weapons. The victory of the one or the ther is taken as an omen.

On minor matters the chief men consult alone: on more important business they all ıeet. They provide, however, that all questions, the decision of which lies with the eople, may be previously discussed by the chiefs. Their meetings are, except in case f chance emergencies, on fixed days, either at new moon or full moon: such seasons hey believe to be the most auspicious for beginning business. They reckon the number, ot of the days as we do, but of the nights. It is thus that they make their appointments nd contracts. To them day seems to follow night. Their love of liberty makes them ndependent to a fault: they do not assemble all at once or as though they were under rders: but two or three days are wasted by their delay in arriving. They take their eats as they come, all in full armour. Silence is demanded by the priests, to whom are ranted special powers of coercion. Next, the king, or one of the chief men, according o claims of age, lineage, or military glory, receives a hearing, which he obtains more y power of persuasion than by any right of command. If the opinion expressed displeases them, their murmurs reject it: if they approve, they clash their spears. Such pplause is considered the most honourable form of assent.

At the meeting charges involving risk of capital punishment may be brought. The unishment fits the crime. They hang traitors and deserters on trees: cowards and ravens and evil-livers they plunge into a muddy swamp and put a hurdle on the top. These different penalties imply the distinction that crimes in being punished ought to e made public, while shameful offences ought to be concealed. They have also for ighter offences proportionate penalties: if convicted, they are fined a certain number f horses or cattle. Part of the fine is paid to the king or community, part to the injured nan or his kinsmen. In these same meetings they choose chiefs who administer justice n the shires and villages. Each of these is accompanied by a hundred companions of he common people, who give him both advice and authority.

They do no business public or private except in arms. But their custom is that no ne may carry arms until the community has approved his ability. Then before the vhole assembly either one of the chief men or the father or some kinsman adorns the oung warrior with shield and spear. This panoply is their 'toga', youth's first honour. Before this he is a member of the household, now a member of the state. Distinguished ineage or great services done by ancestors sometimes win for mere boys the rank f a chief: but these take their place among the other tougher warriors whom time as tried, and do not blush to be seen in the ranks. Within the train itself too there re degrees of honour, determined at the leader's discretion. And great rivalry prevails —the followers each striving to be first with their chief, the chiefs to have the largest nd most spirited following. Real distinction and strength belong to the chief who has

around him always a band of chosen warriors, to be a glory in peace and a protectio
in war. To have a following distinguished for its size and bravery brings fame an
glory not only among your own people, but among neighbouring tribes as well. Suc
trains are courted by legates, and honoured with gifts, and often decide the fortune o
a battle by the mere rumour of their presence.

When the fighting begins, it is shameful for a chief to be outdone in bravery, an
equally shameful for the followers not to match the bravery of their chief: to surviv
one's chief and to return from battle is a foul disgrace which lasts as long as life
To defend him, to support him, to turn one's own brave deeds to his glory, this i
their chief oath of allegiance. The chiefs fight for victory, the followers for thei
chief. Often youths of noble family, if the community in which they were born i
suffering the torpor of prolonged peace, go and seek out some tribe which happen
to be at war. They hate peace; and fame too comes more easily in times of danger
Nor can you support a large following save by war and violence: for they exact fron
their chief's liberality their charger and their murderous invincible spear. Feasts toc
rough though plentiful, are given for pay. The means of this liberality is won by wa
and plunder. It would be far harder to persuade them to plough the fields and wai
for the year's yield than to challenge the enemy and earn a wage of wounds. Indeed
they think it dull and lazy to get by the sweat of your own brow what may be wo
by shedding some one else's blood.

When they are not fighting, they spend little time in hunting, much more in doin
nothing. They devote themselves to sleeping and eating. Even the bravest and mos
warlike are quite idle, for they give over the care of house and fields to the wome
and the old men, and to all the weaklings of the household. They themselves merel
lounge, for from a strange contradiction of character they love idleness yet hate peace
It is usual for the tribe, man by man, to contribute a voluntary gift of cattle or cor
for the chiefs. They accept this as an honour, and it meets their needs. They tak
particular pleasure in gifts from neighbouring tribes. These are sent not only by indi
viduals but often by the community, and consist of picked horses, massive armour
bosses and collars. In these days we have also taught them to take money.

It is well known that none of the German tribes live in cities. They cannot endur
undetached houses. Their homes are separate and scattered, pitched at the call of river
plain, or wood. They build villages, but not as we do with the buildings all adjoinin
and connected. Each man has an open space round his homestead, either as a protec
tion against risk of fire, or because they do not know how to build otherwise. The
make no use even of quarry-stones or tiles. For all purposes they use timber roughl
hewn with no attempt at beauty or comfort. Some parts they carefully smear with ar
earth so pure and bright that it gives the effect of painting and coloured designs. The
often dig caverns under the earth and load heaps of mud above them: these make
refuge for them in winter and a storehouse for fruits. In such places as these the
temper the extreme cold: and if an enemy comes he carries off what he finds in th
open, while he knows nothing of all that is hidden and buried; or else it escapes jus
because there is no time to search for it.

They all wear for covering a plaid fastened with a brooch, or, in default of that,
thorn. Without any other clothing they spend whole days lying on the hearth befor

ıe fire. The wealthy are distinguished by a garment, which does not flow loose, as ith the Sarmatae and Parthians, but fits close and shows the shape of each limb. hey also use the skins of wild beasts. Those nearest the Rhine look comfortable in ıem, but the people of the interior wear them with elaborate care, since they are not et civilized by commerce. They choose their animal, skin it, and star the hide with ıe speckled fur of the beasts found in the further ocean and the unknown sea. The omen have the same clothing as the men, except that they more frequently wear nen garments which they ornament with purple stripes. The bodice has no sleeves, nd they leave the arm and forearm uncovered; the adjoining part of the breast is lso left bare. Nevertheless, their observance of the marriage-tie is very strict, and ıere is no point in their manners which deserves greater praise. Almost alone among arbarians they are content with one wife, with the exception of a very few. These re not lewd, but by reason of their lineage their hands are sought in several marriages.

The husband brings a dowry to the wife, not the wife to the husband. The parents ome to the wedding and inspect the presents. These are not designed to please a oman's taste, nor can a young bride wear them in her hair: they are oxen, and a ridled horse or a shield with spear and sword. This is the dowry which wins a wife, nd she in her turn brings her husband some gift of arms. This represents to them ur marriage bond, the mystic celebrations, and all the gods of matrimony. A woman ıust not think herself exempt from thoughts of bravery or the chances of war. By ıe ceremony which begins her married life she is warned that she comes to be her usband's partner in toil and in danger, to suffer and to dare with him alike in peace nd war. This is plainly shown by the yoked oxen, the bridled horse, and the gift of rms. Thus she must live, and thus she must die. She is receiving a trust which she ıust keep worthily and hand on to her children, a trust which her sons' wives may eceive in turn and pass on to their children.

So chastity is well cloistered in their lives. They are not corrupted by the allurements f the theatre or the subtle temptations of banquets. Neither men nor women know nything of clandestine correspondence. In proportion to their numbers adultery is ery rare: the husband is allowed to take immediate reprisal. He cuts off his wife's hair, rips her naked in the presence of her family, and flogs her all up the village street. or a woman who sells her chastity there is no pardon; neither beauty, nor youth, or wealth can find her a husband. For in Germany no one laughs at vice, nor calls ıutual corruption 'the spirit of the age'. Better still is the life of those tribes where nly virgins are married: their hopes and aspirations are settled once for all. Thus to ıe wife her husband is one body and one life with her: she has no thoughts beyond im, no further desires: it seems as though her love was not so much for her husband s for the married state. To limit the number of their offspring or to kill one of the ter-born children they consider a crime; and their good morals are of more avail ıan good laws in other places.

In every home you see the children dirty and naked, yet they grow to that strength f body and limb which we so much admire. Each mother feeds her children at her wn breast: they do not leave this duty to serving-maids and nurses. No delicacy in ıeir upbringing distinguishes masters from slaves. They grow up among the same attle on the same ground until maturity sets the free apart and valour claims them as her own. The boys develop late and grow to a lusty manhood. Nor are the girls hurrie into marriage. They have the same youthful vigour, the same tall stature as the youn men. In marriage husband and wife are matched in age and strength, and the childre prove their parents' powers. Sisters' sons have the same position with their uncle a with their father. Some people even consider this the stronger tie of blood, and i taking hostages insist on it more, thinking thus to get a firmer hold on the affection and a wider hold on the family. However, a man's heirs and successors are always hi own sons. They make no will. In default of sons the property goes to the next of kir brothers or uncles on either side. The greater the number of his kinsmen and co nexions, the greater an old man's honour. In Germany it does not pay to be childles

The family are bound to share the feuds as well as the friendships of father c kinsman. But these feuds are not irreconcilable. Even homicide has its price in a fixe tale of cattle or sheep: the whole family receives the recompense. This is good polic for the community, since feuds and freedom are dangerous side by side. In entertair ment and hospitality no people are more profuse and generous. It is thought wron to refuse shelter to any living man. Each according to his means receives his guest with a liberal spread. When his store fails, the former host sets out with his gue and guides him to another lodging. They proceed to the next house without an invitation. Nor does this make any difference: their welcome is no less warm. As fa as the right of hospitality is concerned no one makes any distinction between frien and stranger. On a guest's departure, should he ask for anything, their custom is t grant it; and the guest on his part feels just as free to ask. They like presents, but d not reckon them as a favour, nor feel under any obligation in accepting them.

Immediately they rise from sleep, which they frequently prolong into the day, the take a bath, usually of warm water, as is natural where winter takes the lion's shar of the year. After the bath they take a meal. They have separate seats and each hi own table. Then they proceed to business and often to feasts in full armour. No on is ashamed to drink from dawn to dawn. As is natural among drunkards, quarrels ar frequent, and their brawls are rarely settled without wounds and bloodshed. But the also frequently consult at their feasts about the reconciliation of feuds, the forming o family connexions, and the adoption of chiefs, and also upon peace and war. At n other time, they feel, is the heart so open to frank thoughts or so well warmed t great ones. Being as a race without much cunning or experience, they still open th secrets of their hearts in the freedom of jest. Thus the mind of each is laid bare. O the morrow they discuss the question again, thus preserving the advantages of eithe state. They debate, while incapable of deceit, and decide when they cannot be misled

Their drink is a liquid made from barley or wheat fermented into a faint resem blance of wine. Their food is simple, wild fruits, fresh game, or curdled milk. The simply satisfy their hunger without any refinement or preparation. In drinking they ar less temperate. If you pander to their intemperance by supplying as much as the want, their vices will conquer them as effectively as any troops.

They have but one kind of public show: in every gathering it is the same. Nake youths, who profess this sport, fling themselves in dance among swords and levelle lances. Practice has perfected their skill, and skill their grace; yet they do not do i to make money or a living. Daring as the game is, its sole reward is the spectators leasure. Gambling, with dice, it is strange to find, they reckon as a serious occupation. 'hey play while sober, and show such recklessness in winning and losing, that, when ll else fails, on the last throw of all they stake their liberty and person. The loser oes into voluntary slavery. Though he may be the younger and the stronger, he suffers imself to be bound and sold. This shows their wrong-headed obstinancy: they call it iemselves a sense of honour. Slaves thus obtained they usually sell in the market, to d themselves from the shame of such a victory.

Their ordinary slaves are not employed, as ours are, on distinct duties in the estab-shment. Each has his own hearth and home. The master fixes a certain measure of rain or number of cattle to be paid as a sort of rent: this forms the only obligation. ll the household duties are performed by the master's wife and children. Slaves are ery rarely beaten or condemned to imprisonment or taskwork. They are sometimes illed by their master, not, however, as a severe act of discipline, but simply in a fit f passion, just as one might kill a private enemy, except that it is legal to kill a slave. 'he position of freedmen is not much higher than that of slaves. In the household ey rarely have any influence, in the state never, except in those tribes which are ruled y kings. There they rise even above the free-born and above the nobles. In the other ibes the inferiority of freedmen is a proof of freedom.

The lending of money and its multiplication by interest is unknown to them. gnorance proves a better preventive than prohibition. The fields are held by village-ommunities in proportion to their numbers, and are allotted to individuals according o rank. The extent of the land makes the division easy. They never till the same field wo years in succession, yet there is always land to spare. They do not labour to improve ne richness or extent of the soil by planting orchards, enclosing meadows, and irrigat-ng gardens: their sole demand upon the land is corn. Thus they do not divide the ear into as many seasons as we do. They distinguish winter, spring, and summer, and ive them names; but they know neither the name nor the blessings of autumn.

Their funerals are not ostentatious. The only custom they observe is that of using ertain kinds of wood for the cremation of famous men. They do not load the pyre vith garments or perfumes. The dead man's armour goes into the flames, and in some ases his horse as well. The tomb is built of turf. They dislike a tall and elaborate nonument: it seems an honour that weighs heavy on the dead. They soon cease from ears and mourning, but are slow to forget their grief. 'Women must weep', they say, and men remember'.

Such is the general information that has reached us concerning the origin and nanners of all the German tribes. I shall now describe the customs and observances f particular peoples, wherever they differ, and state which of the tribes have migrated rom Germany into Gaul.

We have the very high authority of the sainted Julius for the statement that the Gauls were once more powerful than the Germans. This makes it probable that the Gauls migrated across the Rhine into Germany. As each tribe grew in strength and umbers, the river would be no obstacle to their migrating to the opposite bank and eizing there lands, which had hitherto been unappropriated and not included in the ealm of any powerful kingdom. Thus in the country between the Hercynian Forest

and the rivers Rhine and Main, the Helvetii have seized territory, and beyond ther
the Boii. The name Boiohaemi still exists, and, although the inhabitants are change
it bears out the old traditions of the country. But whether the Aravisci migrated int
Pannonia from the Osi or the Osi from the Aravisci into Germany it is impossible t
decide. Both have still the same language and the same manners and customs: nc
was there much to choose between the two banks of the Danube. The advantages an
disadvantages were much the same. On either side they would be free and poor. Th
Treveri and the Nervii openly boast of their claim to German blood. They seem to fee
that the glory of their descent marks them off from the inactive Gauls. On the we
bank of the Rhine live the Vangiones, Triboci, and Nemetes, whose German origin i
undoubted. Even the Ubii, although they have earned the status of a Roman colon
and prefer to be called Agrippinenses after their founder Agrippina, are yet n
ashamed of their German origin. At some past date they crossed the Rhine, an
having given proof of their loyalty to Rome, were settled on the west bank, not becaus
they needed watching, but in order that they might hold the frontier.

The Batavi, who are the bravest of all these peoples, live partly on the bank of th
Rhine, but chiefly on the island in the river. Once a tribe of the Chatti, a faction a
home drove them across to their present homes, where they were destined to becom
a portion of the Roman Empire. They still retain an honourable status which bea
witness to their old alliance with Rome: for they do not suffer the indignity of havin
to pay tribute, nor are they ground down by the tax-farmer. They are exempt fror
all burdens and contributions, and are reserved simply for fighting, like spears an
shields which are kept for use in battle. The Mattiaci enjoy a similar status. For th
Roman people have spread the fear of their great name beyond the Rhine and the ol
boundaries of the empire. Thus, although they live on the German bank of the rive
in sentiment and in spirit they are Roman. In other respects they resemble the Batav
except that the soil and climate of their native country make them more vigorous an
brave.

I should not reckon among the peoples of Germany those who cultivate the 'Tithe
lands', although they have made their homes on the far side of the Rhine and Danube
They are the dregs of the Gauls, who, made desperate by poverty have squatted on thi
land and been content with a doubtful tenure. Now that the frontier has been draw
and the line of fortresses moved forward, they count as a part of the province and
nook of the empire.

Beyond these peoples, at the edge of the Hercynian Forest, begins the territory o
the Chatti, which is much less flat and marshy than the country of the other tribe
who live in the open plains of Germany. The hills, which gradually open out into th
plain, continue all through their country. The Hercynian Forest is like their hire
servant: it escorts them all the way to their frontier and takes leave of them there
The Chatti have close-knit limbs, a menacing expression, and tougher frames and greate
vigour of mind than the other tribes. For Germans, they show a good deal of metho
and ingenuity. They elect their own leaders, and obey commands; they understan
military drill and strategy; they have learnt to reserve their attack, to portion out th
day, and to entrench themselves for the night; they realize that fortune is fickle, whil
bravery can be depended on; and, what is rarest of all and seldom found except i

ained Roman troops, they put more faith in the general than in the army. All their :rength is in their infantry: these carry heavy burdens of tools and provisions besides ieir arms. You may see other tribes going out to fight, but the Chatti conduct a real ampaign. With them sudden raids and casual engagements are rare. This is because iey fight on foot. It is the function of cavalry to win a quick victory or beat a quick etreat: speed and timidity go together; but deliberate movement breeds steadiness.

The Chatti have adopted as a universal custom a practice which among the other ;erman tribes is rare and left to individual enterprise. As soon as they reach manhood iey let the hair and beard grow long. Its growth they regard as a symbol of their olemn devotion to war, and each vows not to shave until he has killed his man. Jot until they are standing over the spoil of the bleeding enemy do they clear the iat of hair from their faces: not until then do they consider that they have paid for heir upbringing and proved themselves worthy sons of their parents and their father- ind. Cowards and cravens never shave. All the bravest warriors wear also an iron ring ike a manacle upon their arms, which they regard as a mark of disgrace, until they iave set themselves free by killing an enemy. Many of the Chatti, however, are proud f their long hair, and wear it until they are grey-headed. They are thus very con- picuous and easily recognized by their own side and by the enemy. It always rests vith these to begin a battle: they always form the front rank, and a strange spectacle hey make. Even in time of peace they preserve a no less fierce and wild appearance. None of them have homes or fields or any occupation. Prodigal of other peoples' roperty and careless of their own, they find their food wherever they go; and thus hey live until the pale decay of age unfits them for this hardy life of daring.

Next to the Chatti, where the channel of the Rhine is well enough defined to form frontier, live the Usipi and Tencteri. The Tencteri, like all Germans, are famous ighters, but they also excel in the art of riding. Indeed, the Chatti are not more amous for their infantry than the Tencteri for their cavalry. Riding is with them an old ustom in which they imitate their ancestors. It is the baby's one game, the boy's one mbition: even the old men do not give it up. Horses are bequeathed with the home nd the household goods as part of a man's property. However it is not the eldest on who inherits them, as in the case of other property, but the son who shows himself he best soldier.

The Bructeri once lived next to the Tencteri. Now, we are told, the Chamavi and Angrivarii have migrated thither, for the Bructeri were conquered and utterly anni- iilated by a coalition of the neighbouring tribes. Perhaps they hated the pride of the Bructeri: perhaps they were tempted by the prospect of loot: or it may have happened y a special intervention of Providence in our favour. For we were even permitted o enjoy the spectacle of the battle. Over 60,000 of them fell, not under the swords f Rome, but, what was far more magnificent, simply as a show for our gratification. f the natives will not love us, long let them hate each other. May that spirit never die mong them. The destiny of empire is a heavy burden. No gift of heaven could be nore welcome in these days than disunion among our enemies.

Behind the Angrivarii and Chamavi live the Dulgubnii and Chasuarii and other ribes which are less well known. Next to them in front come the Frisii. They are livided, according to their strength, into the great and the lesser Frisii. Both tribes live along the borders of the Rhine right up to the mouth, and their country include also huge lakes on which Roman ships have sailed. Indeed we have even venture on the sea off their coast; and a rumour was current that the Columns of Hercule could be discovered there. Perhaps Hercules visited this country: or is it rather tha anything magnificent in any part of the world is by general consent associated with hi name? At any rate the mystery was never solved. It was not that Drusus Germanicu lacked enterprise, but the sea rudely resisted any inquiries either into its own secret or those of Hercules. No one has had the enterprise to try again. It was evidentl thought that, where a god is concerned, faith is more reverent than knowledge. . .

I must now give some account of the Suebi. They do not form a single tribe like th Chatti or Tencteri, but spread over a great part of Germany, and are still divide into separate tribes each with a name of its own, while the name Suebi is given to then all in common. A peculiarity of these people is the way in which they turn thei hair back and tie it in a knot behind. This distinguishes the Suebi from the othe German tribes, and the free-born Suebians from their slaves. In other parts of German this custom is found, and seems due either to kinship with the Suebi, or, as ofte happens, to imitation; but it is rare and confined to the young. The Suebi twist bac their stiff hair until it is grey with age, and often tie it in a knot on the top of th head. The chiefs dress their hair even more elaborately. Such is their care for persona appearance; but it is quite innocent. Their object is not lovemaking, like ours. The adopt this ornate arrangement for the eyes of the enemy—to make them look talle and to inspire terror when they go to battle.

The Semnones believe themselves to be the oldest and noblest of the Suebi; and on of their religious ceremonies confirms this claim. On a fixed date all the tribes wh own a common origin send representatives to a meeting held in a wood made sacre by 'ancestral rites and immemorial awe'. There they initiate their savage worship b a public human sacrifice. There is another superstition connected with this grove. Ever one who enters it is fettered with a chain, as a token of his own inferiority and of th divine power. If any one happens to fall, he is not allowed to get up. They roll ou along the ground. All this superstitious ritual seems meant to imply that the natio derived its origin from this grove; that the god there reigns supreme and claims obedi-ence and homage from all other beings. The success of the Semnones lends weight t their claims. They inhabit a thousand villages, and it is on the size of their communit that they base their claim to be the chief tribe of the Suebi. . . .

Nearer to us, following now the Danube, just as above we followed the line o the Rhine, comes the tribe of the Hermunduri, faithful subjects of Rome. Their com-merce is not confined to the bank of the Danube, but, unlike the other Germans, the carry on their trade far from the frontier in the wealthiest colony of the province o Raetia. No garrison is set over them, and they are allowed to cross the frontie wherever they like. We let the other tribes see nothing but camps and armies, but we have opened our towns and our houses to the Hermunduri, since they showed no desire to plunder them. In their country rises the famous river Elbe, once well know to Roman eyes. Now we only hear tales about it.

Besides the Hermunduri live the Naristi, and next to them the Marcomani and the Quadi. The Marcomani are famous for their strength, and by their prowess in old days they even won their home by driving out the Boii. Nor are the Naristi or Quadi degenerate. These four tribes form, as it were, the face and front of Germany, where it is girdled by the Danube. The Marcomani and the Quadi within living memory have still been governed by kings of their own blood, members of the noble family of Maroboduus and Tudrus. Now they endure a foreign rule. But the power and authority of their kings is derived from Roman support. They are rarely helped by our army, far more often by our gold. It proves equally effective. . . .

For the rest, the Harii are a stronger tribe than any of those I have just mentioned. But besides their military strength they are singularly savage, and add to the effect of their natural ferocity by the aid of art and opportunity. They colour their limbs and carry black shields. They choose dark nights for battle, and their terrible and shadowy aspect, as of an army of ghosts, creates such a panic that no enemy can endure their strange and almost hellish appearance. For in battle it is always the eye that first surrenders.

Beyond the border of the Lygii live the Gotones who are governed by kings. Their rule is rather more strict than in the other tribes of Germany, yet not inconsistent with freedom. Next in order come the Rugii and Lemovii, whose country stretches to the sea. All these tribes are distinguished by round shields, short swords, and submission to kings.

Next come the Suionese communities, living on islands in the sea. Their strength lies not only in military forces but also in their fleet. Their ships differ in build from ours, having bows at either end, so that they can always put to land without turning. They do not use sails, nor regular banks of oars fixed to the sides, but the oars are loose, as you sometimes see in river boats, and can be shifted, as occasion demands, from one side to the other. These people also pay respect to wealth, and the richest man among them is their king. Here there are no restrictions to the power of the monarch. He rules not on sufferance but by right. Weapons are not in general use here, as in other parts of Germany, but are kept shut up, and moreover in the keeping of a slave. The reason for this is that the sea protects them from sudden invasion, and in peace men with arms in their hands are likely to grow insubordinate; and, further, it is to the king's interest that the weapons should be in the keeping of a slave, not of a noble or a free citizen, or even of a freedman.

Beyond the Suiones lies another sea, which is sluggish and almost always calm. It is believed to form a girdle round the edge of the earth, on the ground that the last rays of the setting sun last there until dawn, and the twilight is bright enough to dim the stars. Popular superstition adds that you can hear the sea hiss as the sun rises out of it, and see plainly the shapes of the god's horses and the halo round his head. This region, they say, is the end of the world, and I can well believe it.

Passing then to the east along the shore of the Suebic sea, we find the tribes of the Aestii, who have the same observances and general appearance as the Suebi, while their language is more like the British tongue. They worship the Mother of the Gods. As the symbol of their religion they carry figures of boars. They believe that, without weapons or protection of any other kind, this charm preserves a devotee of the goddess from harm even among his enemies. They rarely use iron weapons, far more frequently clubs. They labour at the cultivation of crops and fruit-trees with a perseverance which is in contrast with the usual indolence of the Germans. They also scour the sea, and are the only people who gather amber. They themselves call it 'glaess', and they find it in the shallow water or actually on the shore. Like barbarians they have never discovered or inquired by what natural process it is produced. For long it lay among the jetsam of the tide until Roman luxury called attention to it. They make no use of it themselves. They gather it in a rough state, sell it in shapeless lumps, and are surprised at being paid for it. You can tell, however, that it is the gum of a tree from the fact that land insects and sometimes even winged creatures are preserved in it, having got stuck in the liquid which subsequently hardened. My belief is that, as in the far East there are woods and forests more luxuriant than with us, the trees of which exude frankincense and balm, so too in the continents and islands of the West there are to be found substances drawn from the trees by the heat of the sun (which rises there close to the earth) and carried in a liquid state to the nearest sea, whence storms fling them up on the opposite coasts. If you test the amber by applying a light, it burns like a pine-torch and gives off a thick and strongly-scented flame, finally dissolving into a sort of pitch or resin.

Next to the Suiones come the tribes of the Sitones, who differ from them only in one particular. They have not only lost their liberty, but have even sunk below the condition of slaves: for they are ruled by a woman.

At this point Suebia ends. I am uncertain whether to assign to Germany or to Sarmatia the tribes of the Peucini, Venedi, and Fenni, though the Peucini, whom some call the Bastarnae, are German in their language, their mode of life, and their custom of living in fixed settlements. Dirt and laziness characterize them all. Their physical type has degenerated through mixed marriages, and their chiefs have faces of a Sarmatian cast. The Venedi have also derived their manners largely from the Sarmatae, for their raids have led them all over the wooded ridge of country which rises between the Peucini and the Fenni. However, it is perhaps better to class them as Germans, for they have fixed homes, and carry shields, and pride themselves on their fleetness of foot; and in all these points they differ from the Sarmatae, who live in wagons or on horseback. The Fenni are wonderfully fierce and wretchedly poor. They have neither arms, nor horses, nor homes. Their food is grass, their clothing skins, their bed the ground. They put their faith in arrows, which they point with stone heads, in default of iron. Men and women alike live by hunting. The women accompany the men wherever they go, and expect to share the spoils of the chase. The children have no other protection against the wild beasts and the weather except a shelter of woven boughs. To this the young men come home from hunting, and it is the old men's day-long refuge. Still they think this a happier life than toiling dolefully at agriculture, labouring at household work, and speculating between hope and fear with your own and other people's money. They care neither for man nor for god, and indeed have nothing to pray for—a consummation very hard to reach. Beyond this point lies the region of fable. The Hellusii and Oxiones, we are told, have the heads and faces of men, the bodies and limbs of beasts. Of this we need more evidence. I will leave it an open question.

◆§ THE LAW OF THE SALIAN FRANKS

As Tacitus observed, the Germans kept no written records of their laws, handing them down through verbal tradition. But in the fifth century after Christ, with Goth and Frank settled on land which once had belonged to Rome, it became fashionable to emulate the features of Roman government. The Church, too, prompted newly converted kings to set examples to their subjects—above all, to set models before them of their laws.

The Law of the Salian Franks, issued by Clovis about A.D. *496, is the most renowned of the early laws for a number of reasons. It was reissued many times, later becoming the basis for Charlemagne's codification. It is typical, too, of all the laws that were being issued by kings and chieftains from Britain to the mouth of the Danube. Finally, one clause was singled out by a French king in the fourteenth century as the basis for his rejection of an English claim to France through maternal succession. The Salic Law, he said, forbade inheritance through the female line, though the law itself said nothing about royal succession.*

The reading of laws, especially when we have little else to go on, can tell us much about early societies. What was loved; what was feared; what things were prized? Above all, what kinds of social problems seemed important enough to be framed in law by the king? Certain terms require explanation: the "thing" was a local court which met every six weeks; wergeld, *or "man-money," was the amount of a person's worth under law, frequently used as the monetary measure of compensation in the crime of murder; the* fisc *was the king's treasury.*

Title I. Concerning Summonses

1 If any one be summoned before the "Thing" by the king's law, and do not come, he shall be sentenced to 600 denars, which make 15 shillings (solidi).

2 But he who summons another, and does not come himself, shall, if a lawful impediment have not delayed him, be sentenced to 15 shillings, to be paid to him whom he summoned.

3 And he who summons another shall walk with witnesses to the home of that man, and, if he be not at home, shall bid the wife or any one of the family to make known to him that he has been summoned to court.

Ernest F. Henderson, *Select Historical Documents of the Middle Ages* (London, 1912), pp. 176–189.

4 But if he be occupied in the king's service he can not summon him.

5 But if he shall be inside the hundred seeing about his own affairs, he can summon him in the manner explained above.

Title II. Concerning Thefts of Pigs, Etc.

1 If any one steal a sucking pig, and it be proved against him, he shall be sentenced to 120 denars, which make three shillings.

2 If any one steal a pig that can live without its mother, and it be proved on him he shall be sentenced to 40 denars—that is, 1 shilling.

14 If any one steal 25 sheep where there were no more in that flock, and it be proved on him, he shall be sentenced to 2500 denars—that is, 62 shillings.

Title III. Concerning Thefts of Cattle

4 If any one steal that bull which rules the herd and never has been yoked, he shall be sentenced to 1800 denars, which make 45 shillings.

5 But if that bull is used for the cows of three villages in common, he who stole him shall be sentenced to three times 45 shillings.

6 If any one steal a bull belonging to the king he shall be sentenced to 3600 denars, which make 90 shillings.

Title IV. Concerning Damage Done among Crops or in Any Enclosure

1 If any one finds cattle, or a horse, or flocks of any kind in his crops, he shall not at all mutilate them.

2 If he do this and confess it, he shall restore the worth of the animal in place of it, and shall himself keep the mutilated one.

3 But if he have not confessed it, and it have been proved on him, he shall be sentenced, besides the value of the animal and the fines for delay, to 600 denars, which make 15 shillings.

Title XI. Concerning Thefts or Housebreakings of Freemen

1 If any freeman steal, outside of the house, something worth 2 denars, he shall be sentenced to 600 denars, which make 15 shillings.

2 But if he steal, outside of the house, something worth 40 denars, and it be proved on him, he shall be sentenced, besides the amount and the fines for delay, to 1400 denars, which make 35 shillings.

3 If a freeman break into a house and steal something worth 2 denars, and it be proved on him, he shall be sentenced to 15 shillings.

4 But if he shall have stolen something worth more than 5 denars, and it have been proved on him, he shall be sentenced, besides the worth of the object and the fines for delay, to 1400 denars, which make 35 shillings.

5 But if he have broken, or tampered with, the lock, and thus have entered the house and stolen anything from it, he shall be sentenced, besides the worth of the object and the fines for delay, to 1800 denars, which make 45 shillings.

6 And if he have taken nothing, or have escaped by flight, he shall, for the ousebreaking alone, be sentenced to 1200 denars, which make 30 shillings.

itle XII. Concerning Thefts or Housebreakings on the Part of Slaves

If a slave steal, outside of the house, something worth two denars, he shall, besides aying the worth of the object and the fines for delay, be stretched out and receive 20 blows.

2 But if he steal something worth 40 denars, he shall either be castrated or pay shillings. But the lord of the slave who committed the theft shall restore to the laintiff the worth of the object and the fines for delay.

itle XIII. Concerning Rape Committed by Freemen

If three men carry off a free born girl, they shall be compelled to pay 30 shillings.

2 If there are more than three, each one shall pay 5 shillings.

3 Those who shall have been present with boats shall be sentenced to three shillings.

4 But those who commit rape shall be compelled to pay 2500 denars, which make 3 shillings.

5 But if they have carried off that girl from behind lock and key, or from the pinning room, they shall be sentenced to the above price and penalty.

6 But if the girl who is carried off be under the king's protection, then the "frith" peace-money) shall be 2500 denars, which make 63 shillings.

7 But if a bondsman of the king, or a leet, should carry off a free woman he hall be sentenced to death.

8 But if a free woman have followed a slave of her own will, she shall lose her reedom.

9 If a freeborn man shall have taken an alien bondswoman, he shall suffer imilarly.

10 If any body take an alien spouse and join her to himself in matrimony, he hall be sentenced to 2500 denars, which make 63 shillings.

itle XIV. Concerning Assault and Robbery

If any one have assaulted and plundered a free man, and it be proved on him, he hall be sentenced to 2500 denars, which make 63 shillings.

2 If a Roman have plundered a Salian Frank, the above law shall be observed.

3 But if a Frank have plundered a Roman, he shall be sentenced to 35 shillings.

4 If any man should wish to migrate, and has permission from the king, and hall have shown this in the public "Thing:" whoever, contrary to the decree of the ing, shall presume to oppose him, shall be sentenced to 8000 denars, which make 00 shillings.

itle XV. Concerning Arson

If any one shall set fire to a house in which men were sleeping, as many freemen s were in it can make complaint before the "Thing;" and if any one shall have been urned in it, the incendiary shall be sentenced to 2500 denars, which make 63 shillings.

Title XVII. Concerning Wounds

1 If any one have wished to kill another person, and the blow have missed, he on whom it was proved shall be sentenced to 2500 denars, which make 63 shillings.

2 If any person have wished to strike another with a poisoned arrow, and the arrow have glanced aside, and it shall be proved on him: he shall be sentenced to 2500 denars, which make 63 shillings.

3 If any person strike another on the head so that the brain appears, and the three bones which lie above the brain shall project, he shall be sentenced to 1200 denars, which make 30 shillings.

4 But if it shall have been between the ribs or in the stomach, so that the wound appears and reaches to the entrails, he shall be sentenced to 1200 denars—which make 30 shillings—besides five shillings for the physician's pay.

5 If any one shall have struck a man so that blood falls to the floor, and it be proved on him, he shall be sentenced to 600 denars, which make 15 shillings.

6 But if a freeman strike a freeman with his fist so that blood does not flow, he shall be sentenced for each blow—up to 3 blows—to 120 denars, which make 3 shillings.

Title XVIII. Concerning Him Who, before the King, Accuses an Innocent Man

If any one, before the king, accuse an innocent man who is absent, he shall be sentenced to 2500 denars, which make 63 shillings.

Title XIX. Concerning Magicians

1 If any one have given herbs to another so that he die, he shall be sentenced to 200 shillings (or shall surely be given over to fire).

2 If any person have bewitched another, and he who was thus treated shall escape, the author of the crime, who is proved to have committed it, shall be sentenced to 2500 denars, which make 63 shillings.

Title XXIV. Concerning the Killing of Little Children and Women

1 If any one have slain a boy under 10 years—up to the end of the tenth—and it shall have been proved on him, he shall be sentenced to 24000 denars, which make 600 shillings.

3 If any one have hit a free woman who is pregnant, and she dies, he shall be sentenced to 28000 denars, which make 700 shillings.

6 If any one have killed a free woman after she has begun bearing children, he shall be sentenced to 24000 denars, which make 600 shillings.

7 After she can have no more children, he who kills her shall be sentenced to 8000 denars, which make 200 shillings.

Title XXX. Concerning Insults

3 If any one, man or woman, shall have called a woman harlot, and shall not have been able to prove it, he shall be sentenced to 1800 denars, which make 45 shillings.

4 If any person shall have called another "fox," he shall be sentenced to 3 shillings.

5 If any man shall have called another "hare," he shall be sentenced to 3 shillings.

6 If any man shall have brought it up against another that he have thrown away his shield, and shall not have been able to prove it, he shall be sentenced to 120 denars, which make 3 shillings.

7 If any man shall have called another "spy" or "perjurer," and shall not have been able to prove it, he shall be sentenced to 600 denars, which make 15 shillings.

Title XXXIII. Concerning the Theft of Hunting Animals

2 If any one have stolen a tame marked stag (-hound?), trained to hunting, and it shall have been proved through witnesses that this master had him for hunting, or had killed with him two or three beasts, he shall be sentenced to 1800 denars, which make 45 shillings.

Title XXXIV. Concerning the Stealing of Fences

1 If any man shall have cut 3 staves by which a fence is bound or held together, or have stolen or cut the heads of 3 stakes, he shall be sentenced to 600 denars, which make 15 shillings.

2 If any one shall have drawn a harrow through another's harvest after it has sprouted, or shall have gone through it with a waggon where there was no road, he shall be sentenced to 120 denars, which make 3 shillings.

3 If any one shall have gone, where there is no way or path, through another's harvest which has already become thick, he shall be sentenced to 600 denars, which make 15 shillings.

Title XLI. Concerning the Murder of Free Men

1 If any one shall have killed a free Frank, or a barbarian living under the Salic law, and it have been proved on him, he shall be sentenced to 8000 denars.

2 But if he shall have thrown him into a well or into the water, or shall have covered him with branches or anything else, to conceal him, he shall be sentenced to 24000 denars, which make 600 shillings.

3 But if any one has slain a man who is in the service of the king, he shall be sentenced to 24000 denars, which make 600 shillings.

4 But if he have put him in the water or in a well, and covered him with anything to conceal him, he shall be sentenced to 72000 denars, which make 1800 shillings.

5 If any one have slain a Roman who eats in the king's palace, and it have been proved on him, he shall be sentenced to 12000 denars, which make 300 shillings.

6 But if the Roman shall not have been a landed proprietor and table companion of the king, he who killed him shall be sentenced to 4000 denars, which make 100 shillings.

7 But if he shall have killed a Roman who was obliged to pay tribute, he shall be sentenced to 63 shillings.

9 If any one have thrown a free man into a well, and he have escaped alive, he (the criminal) shall be sentenced to 4000 denars, which make 100 shillings.

Title XLV. Concerning Migrators

1 If any one wish to migrate to another village and if one or more who live in tha village do not wish to receive him,—if there be only one who objects, he shall no have leave to move there.

2 But if he shall have presumed to settle in that village in spite of his rejectio by one or two men, then some one shall give him warning. And if he be unwillin to go away, he who gives him warning shall give him warning, with witnesses, a follows: I warn thee that thou may'st remain here this next night as the Salic la demands, and I warn thee that within 10 nights thou shalt go forth from this village After another 10 nights he shall again come to him and warn him again within 1 nights to go away. If he still refuse to go, again 10 nights shall be added to th command, that the number of 30 nights may be full. If he will not go away eve then, then he shall summon him to the "Thing," and present his witnesses as to th separate commands to leave. If he who has been warned will not then move away, an no valid reason detains him, and all the above warnings which we have mentione have been given according to law: then he who gave him warning shall take the matte into his own hands and request the "comes" to go to that place and expel him. An because he would not listen to the law, that man shall relinquish all that he ha earned there, and, besides, shall be sentenced to 1200 denars, which make 30 shillings

3 But if anyone have moved there, and within 12 months no one have given hin warning, he shall remain as secure as the other neighbours.

Title XLVI. Concerning Transfers of Property

1 The observance shall be that the Thunginus or Centenarius shall call together "Thing," and shall have his shield in the "Thing," and shall demand three men a witnesses for each of the three transactions. He (the owner of the land to be trans ferred) shall seek a man who has no connection with himself, and shall throw a stal into his lap. And to him into whose lap he has thrown the stalk he shall tell, con cerning his property, how much of it—or whether the whole or a half—he wishes t give. He in whose lap he threw the stalk shall remain in his (the owner's) house and shall collect three or more guests, and shall have the property—as much as i given him—in his power. And, afterwards, he to whom that property is entruste shall discuss all these things with the witnesses collected afterwards, either befor the king or in the regular "Thing," he shall give the property up to him for whom i was intended. He shall take the stalk in the "Thing," and, before 12 months are over shall throw it into the lap of him whom the owner has named heir; and he sha restore not more nor less, but exactly as much as was entrusted to him.

2 And if any one shall wish to say anything against this, three sworn witnesse shall say that they were in the "Thing" which the "Thunginus" or "Centenarius" called together, and that they saw that man who wished to give his property thro a stalk into the lap of him whom he had selected. They shall name by name him wh threw his property into the lap of the other, and, likewise, shall name him whom h named his heir. And three other sworn witnesses shall say that he in whose lap th stalk was thrown had remained in the house of him who gave his property, and ha here collected three or more guests, and that they had eaten porridge at table, and that e had collected those who were bearing witness, and that those guests had thanked im for their entertainment. All this those other sworn witnesses shall say, and that he vho received that property in his lap in the "Thing" held before the king, or in the egular public "Thing," did publicly, before the people, either in the presence of the ing or in public "Thing". . . throw the stalk into the lap of him whom the owner ad named as heir. And thus 9 witnesses shall confirm all this.

Title L. Concerning Promises to Pay

1 If any freeman or leet have made to another a promise to pay, then he to whom he promise was made shall, within 40 days or within such term as was agreed when e made the promise, go to the house of that man with witnesses, or with appraisers. And if he (the debtor) be unwilling to make the promised payment, he shall be entenced to 15 shillings above the debt which he had promised.

2 If he then be unwilling to pay, he (the creditor) shall summon him before he "Thing" and thus accuse him: "I ask thee, 'Thunginus,' to bann my opponent who made me a promise to pay and owes me a debt." And he shall state how much e owes and promised to pay. Then the "Thunginus" shall say: "I bann thy opponent o what the Salic law decrees." Then he to whom the promise was made shall warn im (the debtor) to make no payment or pledge of payment to any body else until e have fulfilled his promise to him (the creditor). And straightway on that same day, before the sun sets, he shall go to the house of that man with witnesses, and shall ask if he will pay that debt. If he will not, he (the creditor) shall wait until after sunset; then, if he have waited until after sunset, 120 denars, which make 3 shillings shall be added on to the debt. And this shall be done up to 3 times in 3 weeks. And if at the third time he will not pay all this, it (the sum) shall increase to 360 denars, or 9 shillings: so, namely, that, after each admonition or waiting until after sunset, 3 shillings shall be added to the debt.

3 If any one be unwilling to fulfil his promise in the regular assembly,—then he o whom the promise was made shall go the count of that place, in whose district he ives, and shall take the stalk and shall say: oh count, that man made me a promise o pay, and I have lawfully summoned him before the court according to the Salic aw on this matter; I pledge thee myself and my fortune that thou may'st safely seize his property. And he shall state the case to him, and shall tell how much he (the debtor) had agreed to pay. Then the count shall collect 7 suitable bailiffs, and shall go with them to the house of him who made the promise and shall say: thou who art here present pay voluntarily to that man what thou didst promise, and choose any two of those bailiffs who shall appraise that from which thou shalt pay; and make good what thou dost owe, according to a just appraisal. But if he will not hear, or be absent, then the bailiffs shall take from his property the value of the debt which he owes. And, according to the law, the accuser shall take two thirds of that which the debtor owes, and the count shall collect for himself the other third as peace money; unless the peace money shall have been paid to him before in this same matter.

4 If the count have been appealed to, and no sufficient reason, and no duty of the king, have detained him—and if he have put off going, and have sent no substitute

to demand law and justice: he shall answer for it with his life, or shall redeem himself with his "wergeld."

Title LIV. Concerning the Slaying of a Count

1 If any one slay a count, he shall be sentenced to 24000 denars, which make 600 shillings.

Title LV. Concerning the Plundering of Corpses

2 If any one shall have dug up and plundered a corpse already buried, and it shall have been proved on him, he shall be outlawed until the day when he comes to an agreement with the relatives of the dead man, and they ask for him that he be allowed to come among men. And whoever, before he come to an arrangement with the relative, shall give him bread or shelter—even if they are his relations or his own wife—shall be sentenced to 600 denars which make 15 shillings.

3 But he who is proved to have committed the crime shall be sentenced to 8000 denars, which make 200 shillings.

Title LVI. Concerning Him Who Shall Have Scorned to Come to Court

1 If any man shall have scorned to come to court, and shall have put off fulfilling the injunction of the bailiffs, and shall not have been willing to consent to undergo the fine, or the kettle ordeal, or anything prescribed by law: then he (the plaintiff) shall summon him to the presence of the king. And there shall be 12 witnesses who—3 at a time being sworn—shall testify that they were present when the bailiff enjoined him (the accused) either to go to the kettle ordeal, or to agree concerning the fine; and that he had scorned the injunction. Then 3 others shall swear that they were there on the day when the bailiffs enjoined that he should free himself by the kettle ordeal or by composition; and that 40 days after, . . . he (the accuser) had again waited until after sunset, and that he (the accused) would not obey the law. Then he (the accuser) shall summon him before the king for a fortnight thence; and three witnesses shall swear that they were there when he summoned him and when he waited for sunset. If he does not then come, those 9, being sworn, shall give testimony as we have above explained. On that day likewise, if he do not come, he (the accuser) shall let the sun go down on him, and shall have 3 witnesses who shall be there when he waits till sunset. But if the accuser shall have fulfilled all this, and the accused shall not have been willing to come to any court, then the king, before whom he has been summoned, shall withdraw his protection from him. Then he shall be guilty, and all his goods shall belong to the fisc, or to him to whom the fisc may wish to give them. And whoever shall have fed or housed him—even if it were his own wife—shall be sentenced to 600 denars, which make 15 shillings; until he (the debtor) shall have made good all that has been laid to his charge.

Title LVII. Concerning the "Chrenecruda"

1 If any one have killed a man, and, having given up all his property, has not enough to comply with the full terms of the law, he shall present 12 sworn witnesses to the effect that, neither above the earth nor under it, has he any more property

an he has already given. And he shall afterwards go into his house, and shall collect his hand dust from the four corners of it, and shall afterwards stand upon the reshold, looking inwards into the house. And then, with his left hand, he shall row over his shoulder some of that dust on the nearest relative that he has. But his father and (his father's) brothers have already paid, he shall then throw that ust on their (the brothers') children—that is, over three (relatives) who are nearest n the father's and three on the mother's side. And after that, in his shirt, without irdle and without shoes, a staff in his hand, he shall spring over the hedge. And ıen those three shall pay half of what is lacking of the compounding money or the gal fine; that is, those others who are descended in the paternal line shall do this.

2 But if there be one of those relatives who has not enough to pay his whole ıdebtedness, he, the poorer one, shall in turn throw the "chrenecruda" on him of ıem who has the most, so that he shall pay the whole fine.

3 But if he also have not enough to pay the whole, then he who has charge of ıe murderer shall bring him before the "Thing," and afterwards to 4 Things, in rder that they (his friends) may take him under their protection. And if no one ave taken him under his protection—that is, so as to redeem him for what he can ot pay—then he shall have to atone with his life.

itle LIX. Concerning Private Property

If any man die and leave no sons, if the father and mother survive, they shall herit.

3 If the father and mother do not survive, and he leave brothers or sisters, they hall inherit.

3 But if there are none, the sisters of the father shall inherit.

4 But if there are no sisters of the father, the sisters of the mother shall claim that ıheritance.

5 If there are none of these, the nearest relatives on the father's side shall succeed) that inheritance.

6 But of Salic land no portion of the inheritance shall come to a woman; but the hole inheritance of the land shall come to the male sex.

itle LXII. Concerning Wergeld

If any one's father have been killed, the sons shall have half the compounding ıoney (wergeld); and the other half the nearest relatives, as well as on the mother's s on the father's side, shall divide among themselves.

2 But if there are no relatives, paternal or maternal, that portion shall go to the fisc.

German Culture after the Fall of Rome: Early Saxon Poetry

Of all the sources that we possess describing the ancient "Germans" (th term here is used to designate all those peoples who originally inhabited the area north of the Rhine: Franks, Saxons, Angles, Goths, etc.), the best and the rarest are those written by the Germans themselves. Though we learn much from Tacitus, he was, after all, describing his subject on the basis of secondhand information; and later accounts drawn from Bed or Gregory of Tours are written by self-conscious latinists concerned with eradicating their barbaric antecedents. The three poems that appear belo come as close to a direct confrontation as is possible with those mighty warriors who exhausted and supplanted the proud Romans, finally demolishing their empire.

"The Ruined City" (the only existing fragment is given here) is one of the earliest extant Saxon poems. Its description of a ruined Roman center —perhaps Bath, England, which fell to the Saxons in A.D. 577—may well date from the early seventh century after Christ. Ancient Germanic verse is noted for its rich description, colorful action, and occasional gloomy, morose reflection. The last characteristic is particularly well displayed by this anonymous poet.

Saxon records of historical actions were invariably set down in epic verse "The Battle of Brunanburh" is this form of historical account and is entered in the Anglo-Saxon Chronicle under the date A.D. 937. Of the battle itself little is known except that it was fought between Athelstan grandson of Alfred the Great, and the joint armies of Danes and Scots under Olaf (Anlaf) and Constantine II of Scotland. The account could be a description of the clash and color of any battle, as tactical exactitude is sacrificed for valor and dash. Yet the event was a forward step for the West Saxons, towards hegemony over all England.

"The Exodus" is a typical Germanic rendering of the Old Testament, transforming Judaic and Roman idioms into terms more meaningful to th German mind: Moses and the Hebrews appear in this retelling as a Saxon chieftan and his band of warriors. A comparison of this poem with "The Battle of Brunanburh" can go far to explain how Christianity was reshaped by the Germans and, perhaps, why the knights of medieval Europe saw no contradiction between their warlike ways and Christian ethics.

§ THE RUINED CITY

Wondrously wrought and fair its wall of stone,
Shattered by Fate! The castles rend asunder,
The work of giants moldereth away,
Its roofs are breaking and falling; its towers crumble
In ruin. Plundered those walls with grated doors—
Their mortar white with frost. Its battered ramparts
Are shorn away and ruined, all undermined
By eating age. The mighty men that built it,
Departed hence, undone by death, are held
Fast in the earth's embrace. Tight is the clutch
Of the grave, while overhead for living men
A hundred generations pass away.
   Long this red wall, now mossy gray, withstood,
While kingdom followed kingdom in the land,
Unshaken 'neath the storms of heaven—yet now
Its towering gate hath fallen. . . .
   Radiant the mead-halls in that city bright,
Yea, many were its baths. High rose its wealth
Of hornèd pinnacles, while loud within
Was heard the joyous revelry of men—
Till mighty Fate came with her sudden change!
   Wide-wasting was the battle where they fell.
Plague-laden days upon the city came;
Death snatched away that mighty host of men.

. . .

There in the olden time full many a thane,
Shining with gold, all gloriously adorned,
Haughty in heart, rejoiced when hot with wine;
Upon him gleamed his armor, and he gazed
On gold and silver and all precious gems;
On riches and on wealth and treasured jewels,
A radiant city in a kingdom wide.
   There stood the courts of stone. Hotly within,
The stream flowed with its mighty surge. The wall
Surrounded all with its bright bosom; there
The baths stood, hot within its heart.

. . .

[S]elections from Old English Poetry, eds. Albert S. Cook and Chauncey B. Tinker (Boston: [G]inn and Company, 1902), pp. 56–57.

THE BATTLE OF BRUNANBURH

I

Athelstan King,
Lord among Earls,
Bracelet-bestower and
Baron of Barons,
He with his brother,
Edmund Atheling,
Gaining a lifelong
Glory in battle,
Slew with the sword-edge
There by Brunanburh,
Brake the shield-wall,
Hewed the [shields of] linden-wood,
Hacked the battle-shield,
Sons of Edward with hammered brands.

II

Theirs was a greatness
Got from their grandsires—
Theirs that so often in
Strife with their enemies
Struck for their hoards and their hearths and their homes.

III

Bowed the spoiler,
Bent the Scotsman,
Fell the ship-crews
Doomed to the death.
All the field with blood of the fighters
Flowed, from when first the great
Sun-star of morning-tide,
Lamp of the Lord God
Lord everlasting,
Glode over earth till the glorious creature
Sank to his setting.

***Selections from Old English Poetry*, eds. Albert S. Cook and Chauncey B. Tinker (Boston Ginn and Company, 1902), pp. 26–30.**

IV

There lay many a man
Marred by the javelin,
Men of the Northland
Shot over shield.
There was the Scotsman
Weary of war.

V

We the West-Saxons,
Long as the daylight
Lasted, in companies
Troubled the track of the host that we hated.
Grimly with swords that were sharp from the grindstone,
Fiercely we hacked at the flyers before us.

VI

Mighty the Mercian,
Hard was his hand-play,
Sparing not any of
Those that with Anlaf,
Warriors over the
Weltering waters
Borne in the bark's-bosom,
Drew to this island—
Doomed to the death.

VII

Five young kings put asleep by the sword-stroke,
Seven strong Earls of the army of Anlaf
Fell on the war-field, numberless numbers,
Shipmen and Scotsmen.

VIII

Then the Norse leader,
Dire was his need of it,

Few were his following,
Fled to his war-ship;
Fleeted his vessel to sea with the king in it,
Saving his life on the fallow flood.

IX

Also the crafty one,
Constantinus,
Crept to his North again,
Hoar-headed hero!

X

Slender warrant had
He to be proud of
The welcome of war-knives—
He that was reft of his
Folk and his friends that had
Fallen in conflict,
Leaving his son too
Lost in the carnage,
Mangled to morsels,
A youngster in war!

XI

Slender reason had
He to be glad of
The clash of the war-glaive—
Traitor and trickster
And spurner of treaties—
He nor had Anlaf
With armies so broken
A reason for bragging
That they had the better
In perils of battle
On places of slaughter—
The struggle of standards,
The rush of the javelins,
The crash of the charges,

The wielding of weapons—
The play that they played with
The children of Edward.

XII

Then with their nailed prows
Parted the Norsemen, a
Blood-reddened relic of
Javelins over
The jarring breaker, the deep-sea billow,
Shaping their way toward Dyflen [Dublin] again,
Shamed in their souls.

XIII

Also the brethren,
King and Atheling,
Each in his glory,
Went to his own in his own West-Saxonland,
Glad of the war.

XIV

Many a carcase they left to be carrion,
Many a livid one, many a sallow-skin—
Left for the white-tailed eagle to tear it, and
Left for the horny-nibbed raven to rend it, and
Gave to the garbaging war-hawk to gorge it, and
That gray beast, the wolf of the weald.

XV

Never had huger
Slaughter of heroes
Slain by the sword-edge—
Such as old writers
Have writ of in histories—
Hapt in this isle, since
Up from the East hither
Saxon and Angle from

Over the broad billow
Broke into Britain with
Haughty war-workers who
Harried the Welshman, when
Earls that were lured by the
Hunger of glory gat
Hold of the land.

SELECTIONS FROM THE EXODUS

I. THE PILLAR OF FIRE

Then I have heard that the brave of heart
Blew in the morn a glorious blast
With the blare of trumpets. The troop arose,
The force of the brave, the folk of the Lord,
The eager army, as Moses commanded,
The famous captain of kindred hosts.
Ahead they beheld the leader of life
Measure the way of the air; the cloud
Guided their journey as soon as the seamen [the Israelites]
Fared on their way to the sea. The folk
Were joyful, loud was the cry of the host.
Arose at evening a heavenly beacon,
A second wonder; after the sunset
They saw the marvel above the people
Shining with flame, a burning pillar.
Above the bowmen the white rays glittered,
The shield-walls shone, the shades departed,
The sloping night-shadows could not cover
Their place of concealment. The candle of heaven
Burned; a new warden by night was appointed
O'er the army to dwell, lest by fear of the desert,
By sudden seizure, by ocean-like tempests,
The hoary heath should distract their hearts.
Had the foregoer locks of fire,
Radiant beams; with terror of burning,
With heat of flame he threatened the throng
That he should destroy in the desert the host,

Selections from Old English Poetry, eds. Albert S. Cook and Chauncey B. Tinker (Bost
Ginn and Company, 1902), pp. 117–120.

Unless they listened, the swift of spirit,
To Moses' voice. The host shone bright,
Glistened the shields; the warriors saw,
Ready to guide them forth on their way,
The ensign pointing the path direct,
Until, at the edge of the land, the sea
Like a bulwark barred the way of the host.

THE MARCHING OF PHARAOH'S HOST

Then the heroes' hearts every one grew hopeless,
For afar they saw, on the southern ways,
The war-array of Pharaoh forward faring.
Sparkled his battle-line, bucklers they were bearing;
Already whirred the arrows, onward moved the war,
Shields were brightly shining, and the trumpets sang;
There the banners waved, where the war-troop trod.
In circles soared above them the vultures, slaughter-seekers,
Hungry for the fighting; [above them flew the raven,]
Dusky carrion-lover, on his dewy wing,
Over those dead warriors. There the wolves howled
A direful even-song, deeming their food was nigh.

THE DESTRUCTION OF THE EGYPTIANS

Then with blood-clots was the blue sky blotted;
Then the resounding ocean, that road of seamen,
Threatened bloody horror, till by Moses' hand
The great lord of fate freed the mad waters.
Wide the sea drove, swept with its death-grip,
Foamed all the deluge, the doomed ones yielded,
Seas fell on that track, all the sky was troubled,
Fell those steadfast ramparts, down crashed the floods.
Melted were those sea-towers, when the mighty One,
Lord of heaven's realm, smote with holy hand
Those heroes strong as pines, that people proud. . . .
The yawning sea was mad,
Up it drew, down swirled; dread stood about them,
Forth welled the sea-wounds. On those war-troops fell,
As from the heaven high, that handiwork of God.
Thus swept He down the sea-wall, foamy-billowed,
The sea that never shelters, struck by His ancient sword,
Till, by its dint of death, slept the doughty ones;

An army of sinners, fast surrounded there,
The sea-pale, sodden warriors their souls up yielded.
Then the dark upweltering, of haughty waves the greatest,
Over them spread; all the host sank deep.
And thus were drowned the doughtiest of Egypt,
Pharaoh with his folk. That foe to God,
Full soon he saw, yea, e'en as he sank,
That mightier than he was the Master of the waters,
With His death-grip, determined to end the battle,
Angered and awful.

The Coming of Christianity to the North

Throughout his life, Gregory of Tours (A.D. 538–594) moved in the circle of the ecclesiastical barons of central France. His family was of that small group which maintained whatever there was of Christianity in central Gaul after the collapse of Roman authority. Bishop Gregory w[a]s always on the move, settling disputes between clerics, nobles, and kings, battling the Arian heresy; it was believed that he even performed miracles when the occasion required.

The History of the Franks *begins with a full chapter on Biblical history, retelling and relating the story of Christianity for a Gallic audience. Implicit is Gregory's belief that the major event in Gallic history is the relationship between the life of St. Martin and the rise of King Clovis. Between the battle of Poitiers in* A.D. *507 and his death in* A.D. *511, Clovis defeated the Goths and the Gauls in a swift series of engagements and annexed most of Gaul to his Frankish kingdom. St. Martin, the most influential of Gallic missionaries, had been perhaps the central force in the spread of the new religion. By the time he died in* A.D. *397, Christianity was becoming the major faith of those whom Clovis would conquer a century later. No doubt Clovis' successes would have been little regarded by the Church had he not adopted Christianity as the official religion of his court and army during the process of centralization. Gregory regarded Clovis as a monstrous, butchering heathen before his conversion; but afterwards, though the butchery continued, in his typically unsophisticated manner he celebrated Clovis as an agent of God's will, protector of the Church, and inheritor of the Roman unity of state and church.*

Yet the History of the Franks *is regarded as one of the most revealing social documents of those bleak years after Rome's fall, for it does, despite Gregory's oddities, deal in historical fact. The following selections, including a section from the* Eight Books of Miracles, *yield lively impressions of Gaul's kings, nobles, and priests, and the raw ingredients of feudal codes and religious piety which were to undergo great sophistication and elaboration in coming centuries.*

HISTORY OF THE FRANKS

Gregory of Tours

ter these events Childeric died and Clovis his son reigned in his stead. In the fifth ır of his reign Siagrius, king of the Romans, son of Egidius, had his seat in the y of Soissons which Egidius, who has been mentioned before, once held. And Clovis ne against him with Ragnachar, his kinsman, because he used to possess the kingm, and demanded that they make ready a battle-field. And Siagrius did not delay r was he afraid to resist. And so they fought against each other and Siagrius, seeing army crushed, turned his back and fled swiftly to king Alaric at Toulouse. And ovis sent to Alaric to send him back, otherwise he was to know that Clovis would ke war on him for his refusal. And Alaric was afraid that he would incur the ger of the Franks on account of Siagrius, seeing it is the fashion of the Goths to be rified, and he surrendered him in chains to Clovis' envoys. And Clovis took him d gave orders to put him under guard, and when he had got his kingdom he directed ıt he be executed secretly. At that time many churches were despoiled by Clovis' ny, since he was as yet involved in heathen error. Now the army had taken from a tain church a vase of wonderful size and beauty, along with the remainder of the ensils for the service of the church. And the bishop of the church sent messengers the king asking that the vase at least be returned, if he could not get back any re of the sacred dishes. On hearing this the king said to the messenger: "Follow as far as Soissons, because all that has been taken is to be divided there and when e lot assigns me that dish I will do what the [bishop] asks." Then when he came to issons and all the booty was set in their midst, the king said: "I ask of you, brave warrs, not to refuse to grant me in addition to my share, yonder dish," that is, he was eaking of the vase just mentioned. In answer to the speech of the king those of ore sense replied: "Glorious king, all that we see is yours, and we ourselves are

egory of Tours, *History of the Franks*, trans. Ernest Brehaut (New York: Columbia University Press, 1916), pp. 36–41, 235–239, 249–255.

subject to your rule. Now do what seems well-pleasing to you; for no one is able resist your power." When they said this a foolish, envious and excitable fellow lift his battle-ax and struck the vase, and cried in a loud voice: "You shall get nothi here except what the lot fairly bestows on you." At this all were stupefied, but t king endured the insult with the gentleness of patience, and taking the vase handed it over to the messenger of the church, nursing the wound deep in his hea And at the end of the year he ordered the whole army to come with their equipme of armor, to show the brightness of their arms on the field of March. And when was reviewing them all carefully, he came to the man who struck the vase, and sa to him: "No one has brought armor so carelessly kept as you; for neither your spe nor sword nor ax is in serviceable condtion." And seizing his ax he cast it to the ear and when the other had bent over somewhat to pick it up, the king raised his han and drove his own ax into the man's head. "This," said he, "is what you did at So sons to the vase." Upon the death of this man, he ordered the rest to depart, raisi great dread of himself by this action. He made many wars and gained many victori In the tenth year of his reign he made war on the Thuringi and brought them unc his dominion.

Now the king of the Burgundians was Gundevech, of the family of king Athana the persecutor. . . . He had four sons; Gundobad, Godegisel, Chilperic and Goc mar. Gundobad killed his brother Chilperic with the sword, and sank his wife water with a stone tied to her neck. His two daughters he condemned to exile; t older of these, who became a nun, was called Chrona, and the younger Clotilda. A as Clovis often sent embassies to Burgundy, the maiden Clotilda was found by envoys. And when they saw that she was of good bearing and wise, and learned th she was of the family of the king, they reported this to King Clovis, and he sent embassy to Gundobad without delay asking her in marriage. And Gundobad was afra to refuse, and surrendered her to the men, and they took the girl and brought h swiftly to the king. The king was very glad when he saw her, and married her, havi already by a concubine a son named Theodoric.

He had a first-born son by queen Clotilda, and as his wife wished to consecra him in baptism, she tried unceasingly to persuade her husband, saying: "The go you worship are nothing, and they will be unable to help themselves or any one el For they are graven out of stone or wood or some metal. And the names you ha given them are names of men and not of gods, as Saturn, who is declared to have fl in fear of being banished from his kingdom by his son; as Jove himself, the fo perpetrator of all shameful crimes, committing incest with men, mocking at his kin women, not able to refrain from intercourse with his own sister as she herself say *Jovisque et soror et conjunx.* What could Mars or Mercury do? They are endow rather with the magic arts than with the power of the divine name. But he oug rather to be worshipped who created by his word heaven and earth, the sea and that in them is out of a state of nothingness, who made the sun shine, and adorn the heavens with stars, who filled the waters with creeping things, the earth with l ing things and the air with creatures that fly, at whose nod the earth is decked wi growing crops, the trees with fruit, the vines with grapes, by whose hand manki was created, by whose generosity all that creation serves and helps man whom

ated as his own." But though the queen said this the spirit of the king was by no means
oved to belief, and he said: "It was at the command of our gods that all things
re created and came forth, and it is plain that your God has no power and, what
more, he is proven not to belong to the family of the gods." Meantime the faithful
een made her son ready for baptism; she gave command to adorn the church with
ngings and curtains, in order that he who could not be moved by persuasion might
urged to belief by this mystery. The boy, whom they named Ingomer, died after
ing baptized, still wearing the white garments in which he became regenerate. At
s the king was violently angry, and reproached the queen harshly, saying: "If the
y had been dedicated in the name of my gods he would certainly have lived; but
it is, since he was baptized in the name of your God, he could not live at all."
this the queen said: "I give thanks to the omnipotent God, creator of all, who
s judged me not wholly unworthy, that he should deign to take to his kingdom
e born from my womb. My soul is not stricken with grief for his sake, because I
ow that, summoned from this world as he was in his baptismal garments, he will
fed by the vision of God."

After this she bore another son, whom she named Chlodomer at baptism; and
en he fell sick, the king said: "It is impossible that anything else should happen to
m than happened to his brother, namely, that being baptized in the name of your
rist, he should die at once." But through the prayers of his mother, and the Lord's
mmand, he became well.

The queen did not cease to urge him to recognize the true God and cease worshiping
ols. But he could not be influenced in any way to this belief, until at last a war
ose with the Alamanni, in which he was driven by necessity to confess what before
had of his free will denied. It came about that as the two armies were fighting
rcely, there was much slaughter, and Clovis's army began to be in danger of destruc-
on. He saw it and raised his eyes to heaven, and with remorse in his heart he burst
to tears and cried: "Jesus Christ, whom Clotilda asserts to be the son of the living
od, who art said to give aid to those in distress, and to bestow victory on those who
pe in thee, I beseech the glory of thy aid, with the vow that if thou wilt grant me
ctory over these enemies, and I shall know that power which she says that people
dicated in thy name have had from thee, I will believe in thee and be baptized in
y name. For I have invoked my own gods, but, as I find, they had withdrawn from
ding me; and therefore I believe that they possess no power, since they do not help
ose who obey them. I now call upon thee, I desire to believe thee, only let me be
scued from my adversaries." And when he said this, the Alamanni turned their backs,
d began to disperse in flight. And when they saw that their king was killed, they
bmitted to the dominion of Clovis, saying: "Let not the people perish further, we
ay; we are yours now." And he stopped the fighting, and after encouraging his
en, retired in peace and told the queen how he had had merit to win the victory by
lling on the name of Christ. This happened in the fifteenth year of his reign.

Then the queen asked saint Remi, bishop of Rheims, to summon Clovis secretly,
ging him to introduce the king to the word of salvation. And the bishop sent for
m secretly and began to urge him to believe in the true God, maker of heaven and
rth, and to cease worshiping idols, which could help neither themselves nor any

one else. But the king said: "I gladly hear you, most holy father; but there rema
one thing: the people who follow me cannot endure to abandon their gods; bu
shall go and speak to them according to your words." He met with his followers, l
before he could speak the power of God anticipated him, and all the people cried
together: "O pious king, we reject our mortal gods, and we are ready to follow
immortal God whom Remi preaches." This was reported to the bishop, who w
greatly rejoiced, and bade them get ready the baptismal font. The squares were shad
with tapestried canopies, the churches adorned with white curtains, the baptistery
in order, the aroma of incense spread, candles of fragrant odor burned brightly, a
the whole shrine of the baptistery was filled with a divine fragrance: and the Lo
gave such grace to those who stood by that they thought they were placed amid t
odors of paradise. And the king was the first to ask to be baptized by the bisho
Another Constantine advanced to the baptismal font, to terminate the disease
ancient leprosy and wash away with fresh water the foul spots that had long be
borne. And when he entered to be baptized, the saint of God began with ready speec
"Gently bend your neck, Sigamber; worship what you burned; burn what you wo
shipped." The holy bishop Remi was a man of excellent wisdom and especially train
in rhetorical studies, and of such surpassing holiness that he equalled the miracles
Silvester. For there is extant a book of his life which tells that he raised a dead ma
And so the king confessed all-powerful God in the Trinity, and was baptized
the name of the Father, Son and holy Spirit, and was anointed with the holy ointme
with the sign of the cross of Christ. And of his army more than 3000 were baptize
His sister also, Albofled, was baptized, who not long after passed to the Lord. A
when the king was in mourning for her, the holy Remi sent a letter of consolati
which began in this way: "The reason of your mourning pains me, and pains
greatly, that Albofled your sister, of good memory, has passed away. But I can gi
you this comfort, that her departure from the world was such that she ought to
envied rather than mourned." Another sister also was converted, Lanthechild by nan
who had fallen into the heresy of the Arians, and she confessed that the Son and t
holy Spirit were equal to the Father, and was anointed. . . .

In the fifteenth year of king Childebert which is the twenty-ninth of Gunthra
while king Gunthram was hunting in the Vosges forest he found traces of the killi
of a buffalo. And when he harshly demanded of the keeper of the forest who had dar
to do this in the king's forest, the keeper named Chundo the king's chamberlain. Up
this he ordered Chundo to be arrested and taken to Chalon loaded with chains. A
when the two were confronted with each other in the king's presence and Chun
said that he had never presumed to do what he was charged with, the king order
a trial by battle. Then the chamberlain offered his nephew to engage in the fight
his place and both appeared on the field; the youth hurled his lance at the keeper
the forest and pierced his foot; and he presently fell on his back. The youth th
drew the sword which hung from his belt but while he sought to cut his fallen adve
sary's throat he himself received a dagger thrust in the belly. Both fell dead. Seei
this Chundo started to run to Saint Marcellus's church. But the king shouted to sei
him before he touched the sacred threshold and he was caught and tied to a sta
and stoned. After this the king was very penitent at having shown himself so headlo

anger as to kill hastily for a trifling guilt a man who was faithful and useful to n. . . .

The scandal which by the help of the devil had arisen in the monastery at Poitiers s growing worse every day and Chrodield [1] was sitting all prepared for strife, having thered to herself . . . murderers, sorcerers, adulterers, run-away slaves and men ilty of all other crimes. And so she gave orders to them to break into the monastery night and drag the abbess from it. But the latter heard the uproar coming and asked be carried to the chest containing the relics of the holy cross—for she was painfully ubled with gout—thinking tht she would be kept safe by their aid. Accordingly ien the men had entered and lit the candles and were hurrying with weapons ready re and there through the monastery looking for her, they went into the oratory and und her lying on the ground before the chest of the holy cross. Thereupon one who s fiercer than the rest, having come on purpose to commit this crime, namely, to ave the abbess in two with the sword, was given a knife stab by another, the divine ovidence aiding in this, I suppose. The blood gushed out and he fell to the ground thout fulfilling the vow he had foolishly made. Meantime Justina, the prioress, and e other sisters had taken the cloth of the altar which was before the Lord's cross d covered the abbess with it, putting the lights out at the same time. But the men ne with drawn swords and spears and tore the nuns' clothes and almost crushed eir hands and seized the prioress instead of the abbess, since it was dark, and pulled r robes off and tore her hair down and dragged her out and carried her off to place r under guard at St. Hilary's Church; but, as the dawn was coming on, they perived when near the church that it was not the abbess, and presently they told the oman to return to the monastery. They returned, too, and seized the abbess and agged her away and confined her near St. Hilary's Church . . . setting guards at e door so that no one should give aid to the captive. At the next twilight they entered e monastery and when they found no candles to light they took a cask from the orehouse which had been pitched and left to dry and set fire to it, and there was a eat light while it burned, and they made plunder of all the furniture of the monasy, leaving only what they were unable to carry off. This happened seven days before ster. And as the bishop was distressed at all this and could not calm this strife the devil, he sent to Chrodield, saying: "Let the abbess go, so that she shall not kept in prison during these days; otherwise I will not celebrate the Lord's Easter stival nor shall any catechumen receive baptism in this city unless you order the bess to be set free from the confinement in which she is held. And if you refuse let her go, I will call the citizens together and rescue her." When he said this, rodield appointed assassins, saying: "If any one tries to carry her off by violence, ve her a thrust with the sword at once." Now Flavian came in those days; he had ely been appointed *domesticus,* and by his aid the abbess entered St. Hilary's Church d was free. Meantime murders were being committed at the holy Radegunda's tomb, d certain persons were hacked to death in a disturbance before the very chest that ntained the relics of the holy cross. And since this madness increased daily because Chrodield's pride, and continual murders and other deeds of violence, such as I

[1] *Daughter of king Charibert; she had seceded from the monastery with a large following of ns and was at this time at St. Hilary's church in Poitiers.*

have mentioned above, were being done by her faction, and she had become so swoll up with boastfulness that she looked down with lofty contempt upon her own cous Basina, the latter began to repent and say: "I have done wrong in supporting haugh Chrodield. Behold I am an object of contempt to her and am made to appear a reb against my abbess." She changed her course and humbled herself before the abbe and asked for peace with her; and they were equally of one thought and purpose. Th when the outrages broke out again, the men who were with the abbess, while resisti an attack which Chrodield's followers had made, wounded one of Basina's men w fell dead. But the abbess' men took refuge behind the abbess in the church of t confessor, and on this account Basina left the abbess and departed. But the men fl a second time, and the abbess and Basina entered again into friendly relations before. Afterward many feuds arose between these factions; and who could ever s forth in words such wounds, such killings, and such wrong-doings, where scarce a day passed without a murder, or an hour without a quarrel, or a moment witho tears. King Childebert heard of this, and sent an embassy to king Gunthram propose that bishops of both kingdoms should meet and punish these actions in accor ance with the canons. And king Childebert ordered my humble self to sit on this cas together with Eberegisel of Cologne and Maroveus himself, bishop of Poitiers; ar king Gunthram sent Gundigisil of Bordeaux with his provincials, since he was t metropolitan of this city. But I began to object, saying: "I will not go to this pla unless the rebellion which has arisen because of Chrodield, is forcibly put down the [count]." For this reason a command was sent to Macco, who was then count, which he was ordered to put the rebellion down by force if they should resi Chrodield heard of this and ordered her assassins to stand armed before the door the oratory, thinking they would fight against the [count], and if he wished to u force, they would resist with equal force. So it was necessary for this count to go the with armed men and to beat some with clubs and pierce others with spears, and wh they resisted fiercely he had to attack and overwhelm them with the sword. Wh Chrodield saw this, she took the Lord's cross, the miraculous power of which she h before despised, and came out to meet them saying: "Do no violence to me, I beg you, for I am a queen, daughter of one king and cousin of another; don't do it, le a time may come for me to take vengeance on you." But the throng paid little heed what she said but rushed, as I have said, upon those who were resisting and bour them and dragged them from the monastery and tied them to stakes and beat the fiercely and cut off the hair of some, the hands of others, and in a good many cas the ears and nose, and the rebellion was crushed and there was peace. Then the bisho who were present sat on the tribunal of the church, and Chrodield appeared and ga vent to much abuse of the abbess and many charges, asserting that she had a m in the monastery who wore woman's clothes and was treated as a woman although had been very clearly shown to be a man, and that he was in constant attendance the abbess herself, and she pointed her finger at him and said: "There he is himself And when this man had taken the stand before all in woman's clothes, as I ha stated, he said that he was impotent and therefore had put these clothes on; b he did not know the abbess except by name and he asserted that he had never se her or spoken with her, as he lived more than forty miles from the city of Poitie ıen as she had not proved the abbess guilty of this crime, she added: "What holiness there in this abbess who makes men eunuchs and orders them to live with her as she were an empress." The abbess, being questioned, replied that she knew nothing this matter. Meantime when Chrodield had given the name of the man who was a nuch, Reoval, the chief physician, appeared and said: "This man when he was a ild was diseased in the thigh and was so ill that his life was despaired of; his other went to the holy Radegunda to request that he should have some attention. ıt she called me and bade me give what assistance I could. Then I castrated him in e way I had once seen physicians do in Constantinople, and restored the boy in od health to his sorrowing mother; I am sure the abbess knows nothing of this atter." Now when Chrodield had failed to prove the abbess guilty on this charge so, she began fiercely to make others. . . .

EIGHT BOOKS OF MIRACLES

Gregory of Tours

the territory of this city [Tours] at Lingeais, a woman who lived there moistened our on the Lord's day and shaped a loaf, and drawing the coals aside she covered it er with hot ashes to bake. When she did this her right hand was miraculously set fire and began to burn. She screamed and wept and hastened to the village church which relics of the blessed John are kept. And she prayed and made a vow that on is day sacred to the divine name she would do no work, but only pray. The next ght she made a candle as tall as herself. Then she spent the whole night in prayer, olding the candle in her hand all the time, and the flame went out and she returned ome safe and sound.

I shall now describe what was brought to pass through the relics which my father rried with him in former times. When [King] Theodobert gave orders that sons men in Auvergne should be taken as hostages, my father, at that time lately married, ished to be protected by relics of the saints, and he asked a certain bishop kindly give him some, thinking he would be kept safe by such protection when absent on is distant journey. Then he enclosed the holy ashes in a gold case the shape of a ea-pod and placed them around his neck; but the man did not know the blessed ames. He was accustomed to relate that he was saved by them from many dangers; r he bore witness that by their miraculous power he had often escaped attacks of ighwaymen and dangers on rivers and the furies of civil war and thrusts of the sword. nd I shall not fail to tell what I saw of these with my own eyes. After my father's eath my mother always wore these precious things on her person. Now the grain arvest had come and great grain stacks were gathered at the threshing places. And those days when the threshing was going on, a cold spell came on, and seeing at Limagne has no forests, being all covered with crops, the threshers made them-

selves fires of straw, since there was nothing else to make a fire of. Meantime all w
away to eat. And behold, the fire gradually increased and began to spread slowly str
by straw. Then the piles suddenly caught, with the south wind blowing; it was
great conflagration and there began a shouting of men and shrieking of women a
crying of children. Now this was happening on our own land. My mother, w
wore these relics hanging on her neck, learned this, and sprang from the table a
lifted up the holy relics against the masses of flame, and all the fire went out ir
moment so that scarcely a spark of fire could be found among the burnt piles
straw and it did no harm to the grain which it had just caught.

Many years later I received these relics from my mother; and when we w
going from Burgundy to Auvergne, a great storm came upon us and the sky flash
with many lightnings and roared with heavy crashes of thunder. Then I drew
blessed relics from my bosom and raised my hand against the cloud; it immediat
divided into two parts and passed on the right and left and did no harm to us
any one else thereafter. But being a young man of an ardent temperament I beg
to be pufled up with vain glory and to think silently that this had been granted not
much to the merits of the saints as to me personally, and I openly boasted to
comrades on the journey that I had merited by my blamelessness what God h
bestowed. At once my horse suddenly shied beneath me and dashed me to the groun
and I was so severely shaken up by the fall that I could hardly get up. I perceiv
that this had come of vanity, and it was enough to put me on guard thenceforth agai
being moved by the spur of vain glory. For whenever it happened after that tha
had the merit to behold any of the miracles of the saints, I loudly proclaimed t
they were wrought by God's gift through faith in the saints.

. . . On this matter I recall what I heard told in my youth. It was the day of t
suffering of the great martyr Polycarp, and his festival was being observed at Riom
village of Auvergne. The reading of the martyrdom had been finished and the otl
readings which the priestly canon requires, and the time came for offering the sacrifi
The deacon, having received the [vessel] in which the mystery of the Lord's body v
contained, started with it to the door, and when he entered the church to place it
the altar, it slipped from his hand and floated along in the air and thus came to t
altar, and the deacon was never able to lay hands on it; and I believe this happen
for no other reason than that he was defiled in his conscience. For it was often to
that he had committed adultery. It was granted only to one priest and three wom
of whom my mother was one, to see this; the rest did not see it. I was present
confess, at this festival at the time, but I had not the merit to see this miracle.

Pannichius, a priest of Poitou, when sitting at dinner with some friends he h
invited, asked for a drink. When it was served, a very troublesome fly kept flying ab
the cup and trying to soil it. The priest waved it off with his hand a number of tim
but it would go off a little and then try to get back, and he perceived that it was
crafty device of the [devil]. He changed the cup to his left hand and made a cross w
his right; then he divided the liquor in the cup into four parts and lifted it up hi
and poured it on the ground. For it was very plain that it was a device of the enen

At that time my father's brother Gallus was bishop of Auvergne, and I do not thi
I should fail to tell how he was aided in his youth by a miracle of the saint. N

ıave often described the ruin king Theodoric brought upon Auvergne, when none their property was left to either old or young except the bare land which the rbarians were unable to carry off. In those days, then, my uncle of glorious memory 10 afterwards, as I have told, governed the church of Auvergne in the high office bishop, was a ward; and his property was so plundered by the soldiers that there is nothing at all left that was available; and he himself used often to go on foot th only one attendant to the village of Brioude. It happened once when he was idging along on this journey, that he took his shoes off on account of the heat, and he walked in his bare feet he stepped on a sharp thorn. This by chance had been t, but was still lying on the ground and was concealed point upward in the green ass. It entered his foot and went clear through and then broke off and could not drawn out. The blood ran in streams and as he could not walk he begged the essed martyr's aid and after the pain had grown a little less he went on his way nping. But the third night the wound began to gather and there was great pain. hen he turned to the source from which he had already obtained help and threw mself down before the glorious tomb; when the watch was finished he returned to :d and was overcome by sleep while awaiting the miraculous help of the martyr. On ising later he felt no pain and examining his foot he could not see the thorn which ad entered it; and he perceived it had been drawn from his foot. He looked carefully r it and found it in his bed and saw with wonder how it had come out. When bishop e used to exhibit the place, where a great hollow was still to be seen, and to testify aat this had been a miracle of the blessed martyr.

A long time after, when the festival of the blessed martyr came, my father with l his household made haste to attend the joyful celebration. As we were on the ay, my older brother Peter was seized by a fever and became so ill that he could ot move about or take food. We journeyed on in great grief and it was doubtful hether he would recover or die. In this state of distress we at length arrived; we ntered the church and worshipped at the holy martyr's tomb. The sick boy cast himself own on the pavement, praying for a cure by the glorious martyr. Finishing his prayer e returned to his lodging and the fever went down a little. When night came we astened to keep watch and he asked to be carried along, and lying before the tomb e begged the martyr's favor all night long. When the watch was over he asked them gather dust from the blessed tomb and give it to him in a drink, and hang it about is neck. This was done, and the heat of the fever went down so that on the very ame day he took food without suffering and walked about wherever his fancy took im.

The miracles which the Lord our God deigned to work through the blessed Martin, is bishop, when living in the body, He still deigns to confirm daily in order to trengthen the faith of believers. He who worked miracles through him when he was n the world, now honors his tomb with miracles, and He who at that time sent him o save the perishing heathen, [now] bestows through him blessings on the Christians. Therefore let no one have doubt about the miracles worked in former time when he ees the bounty of the present wonders bestowed, when he looks upon the lame being aised up, the blind receiving sight, demons being driven out and every other kind of lisease being cured through his healing power. As for me I will establish belief in the book written about his life by earlier writers, by relating for posterity at God's cor mand his present-day miracles as far as I can recall them. This I would not presun to do if I had not been warned twice or thrice in a vision. I call all-powerful G to witness that I once saw in a dream at mid-day many who were crippled a overwhelmed by various diseases being cured in St. Martin's church, and I saw th in the presence of my mother who said to me: "Why are you so sluggish about writi of these things that you see?" I replied: "You know well enough that I am unskill in letters, and that, simple and untrained as I am, I would not dare to describe su wonderful miracles. I wish Severus or Paulinus were alive or that Fortunatus at t least were here to describe them. I have no skill for such a task and I should blamed if I undertook it." But she said: "Don't you know that now-a-days on accou of the people's ignorance one who speaks as you can is more clearly understoo Therefore do not hesitate or delay, for you will be guilty if you pass this over silence." So I wished to follow her advice and was doubly tortured with grief and fea grief that miracles as great as were done under our predecessors should not be r corded; fear of undertaking so noble a task, ignorant as I am. However, led on the hope of divine mercy, I am going to attempt the task thus urged upon me. Fo As I suppose, He who produced water in the desert from a dry rock and cooled t thirsty people, is able to set these matters forth in my words; and it will be sure proved that he has again opened the ass's mouth if he deigns to open my lips a make known these miracles through an untaught person like me. But why should fear my ignorance when the Lord our God and Redeemer chose not orators, b fishermen, not philosophers, but [peasants], to destroy the vanity of worldly wisdo I have confidence, then, thanks to your prayers, that even if my rude speech cann adorn the page, the great bishop will give it fame by his glorious miracles.

LIFE OF THE EMPEROR CHARLEMAGNE

Eginhard

Eginhard (A.D. ca. 775–ca. 840) *was a churchman who had held min court offices during the lifetime of Charlemagne before becoming private secretary to Charlemagne's successor. Eginhard's* Life *is therefore based on both personal acquaintance with his hero and the records available to a high government official in the years following Charles's death. Th biography seems to have been written soon after* A.D. *817. It appears have been widely read by the standards of the time: in any case, a larg number of manuscripts, some of them dating from the ninth and tenth centuries after Christ, have come down to us.*

Quite clearly Eginhard's biography was meant as a momument to a ruler whose greatness was recognized in his own time; this greatness became legendary in succeeding centuries. It is not surprising, therefore, that embarrassing or unfavorable aspects of Charlemagne's career should be passed over lightly. Even so, Eginhard's bias is offset by his unawareness of the incredible handicaps under which his ruler labored in administering the largest state to exist since the fifth century after Christ, when Roman rule had disintegrated in the West. Eginhard takes for granted a society in which urban life, trade, and money have all but disappeared and in which literacy is confined to a handful of courtiers, most of them churchmen. Even this modest cultural achievement must be credited to Charles's determined efforts to encourage the revival of Latin learning. Eginhard's biography, modeled as it is on the Life of Augustus *by Suetonius (second century after Christ), is itself one product of this "Carolingian Renaissance," which soon crumbled when lesser rulers were faced with waves of barbarian raiders and invaders. Charlemagne's reign represents a kind of synthesis of Germanic, Christian, and Roman traditions, but the synthesis proved so fragile that it was not reconstituted until 300 years later.*

REFACE

'hen I had made up my mind to describe the public and private life, and to some onsiderable extent the exploits, of my master who nurtured me, Karl [Charlemagne], e most noble and justly famous King, I comprised the subjejct within the smallest mpass within my power; taking care not to neglect what might come to my knowlge thereon, and also not to offend, by a too lengthy narration of each new particular, e taste of the most fastidious, if indeed it can in any way be avoided that they e not offended by modern-day writings, who view with disdain the chronicles of cient date compiled by the most learned and accomplished men.

And although I cannot doubt there are very many, possessed of leisure and addicted letters, who consider that the state of the present age ought not to be so neglected, at everything which is now taking place should pass into silence and oblivion, as ough it were unworthy of any remembrance, and, seduced by the desire of postumous fame, wish to record the noble deeds of others in any description of writing, ther than they should, by writing nothing, withhold the fame of their own name om the cognizance of posterity; still, I did not think that I ought to restrain myself om composition even of this kind, since I was conscious that no one could describe ore accurately than I could matters in which I was myself concerned, and which, ewitnessed, as they say, I faithfully took note of at the time, and whether they ould be recorded by another hand I could not clearly know.

ginhard, *Life of the Emperior Karl the Great*, trans. W. Glaister (London: G. Bell & Sons, td., 1877), pp. 23–91.

I therefore judged it better to hand down to posterity the same records, as it we in common with other writings, rather than that the brilliant life of the noblest Kin the greatest of all in his age, and that actions the most distinguished, and by men modern times little likely to be imitated, should be allowed by me to perish in t shades of oblivion.

There was in the background yet another cause, and one, in my opinion, not u reasonable, which, standing by itself, might even be sufficient to induce me to wri this history, viz., the nurture bestowed upon me and the friendship with himself a his children, which, from the time when I first began to frequent his palace, w never interrupted; by these ties he so bound me and made me his debtor in life a death that I should with justice seem to be, and be judged to be, most ungratef if, unmindful of so many kindnesses bestowed upon me, I were to pass over in silen the brilliant deeds of one who deserved so well of me, and were to allow his li as though he had never lived, to remain without a written remembrance and t praise which is its due.

But to describe and duly to unfold this subject, not my small talent, meagre a poor as it is—nay, rather I had said which hardly exists at all—but the unflaggi rhetoric of a Tully [Cicero] had sufficed.

Here, however, reader, is the book which contains the memorial of this great a most famous man, in which there is nothing, save only his noble deeds, to wonder unless haply you wonder that I, a barbarian, too little versed in the Roman tongu should have thought that I could write with any degree of elegance or propriety Latin, and should so far have transgressed the bounds of modesty as to imagine th I might despise the saying of Cicero, who, speaking of the Roman historians, as read in the first book of his "Tusculans," says, "For any one to commit his though to writing, who can neither arrange nor illustrate his ideas, nor by any pleasing a attract the reader, is the work of a man who recklessly misuses both leisure and books

This dictum of the consummate orator had, indeed, deterred me from writing, on that I held a preconceived opinion that it would be better for me by writing to expe ence the criticism of men, and make venture of my own small ability, rather than sparing myself to pass over the memory of so great a man.

THE LIFE OF KARL

The Franks in olden times used to choose their Kings from the family of the Merwing which royal line is considered to have come to an end in the person of Hilderic II who was deposed from the throne by command of Stephen, the Roman Pontiff, wh his long hair was cut off and he was placed in a monastery.[1]

Although the line of the Merwings actually ended with Hilderic, it had neverthele for some time previously been so utterly wanting in power that it had been able show no mark of royalty except the empty kingly title. All the resources and pow

[1] *The process of deposition took place at the annual assembly of the people at Soissons, in Marc 752, when Pippin was proclaimed King, and was consecreated by S. Boniface, Archbishop Mainz.*

the Kingdom had passed into the hands of the Prefects of the palace, who were lled the "Mayors of the palace," and by them the supreme government was admin-ered. Nothing was left to the King. He had to content himself with his royal title, ng hair, and hanging beard.[2] Seated in a chair of state, he used to display an appear-ce of power by receiving foreign ambassadors on their arrival, and by giving them their departure, as if on his own authority, those answers which he had been ight or commanded to give.

Thus, except his useless title, and an uncertain allowance for his subsistence, which e Prefect of the palace used to furnish at his pleasure, there was nothing that the ng could call his own, unless it were the profits of a single farm, and that a very all one, where was his home, and where he had such servants as were needful to it on him, and who paid him the scanty deference of a most meagre court.

Whenever he went anywhere he used to travel in a waggon drawn by a yoke of en, with a rustic oxherd for charioteer. In this manner he proceeded to the palace, d to the public assemblies of the people held every year for the despatch of the siness of the Kingdom,[3] and he returned home again in the same sort of state. e administration of the Kingdom, and every matter which had to be undertaken d carried through, at home and abroad, was managed by the Mayor of the palace.

At the time of the deposition of Hilderic the office of Mayor was filled by Pippin, e father of King Karl. The office seemed now to be almost hereditary; for Pippin's ther, Karl, had also held it, and with great renown, since he had quelled throughout Frank-land those usurpers who had tried to assume independent authority. He had so utterly defeated the Saracens, who were at that time attempting to establish them-lves in Gaul, in two great battles, the first in Aquitain, near the city of Poitiers, and e second near Narbonne on the river Birra, and had compelled them to retire into ain.

Karl had himself also been preceded in the Mayorship by his father, Pippin, an honour hich was conferred by the people only on those who were distinguished from the mmonalty by their noble birth and great wealth.

When Pippin had held for some years this office (nominally as the lieutenant of ing Hilderic), which had descended from father and grandfather to himself and his other Karloman, and had been by them jointly administered with the greatest good-ill, Karloman, we know not why, but probably because he desired a more secluded e, relinquished the arduous government of a temporal Kingdom and betook himself a private life at Rome. While he was there he became a monk, and put on the ess of the order. Having built a monastery on Mount Soracte, adjoining the Church S. Sylvester, he there enjoyed for several years the repose he sought for, in company ith the brothers of the order who had gone with him. He was, however, obliged to ange his place of residence, because many of the Frankish nobility, when making lgrimages to Rome to fulfil their vows, broke, by their frequent visits to him, that iet which he most of all desired, since they were unwilling to pass by unnoticed one

The long hair, hanging down the back and shoulders, was the distinctive mark of royalty among e Franks; the rest of the nation were obliged to cut their hair short.

These were the primitive popular assemblies of the Franks, the Placita or Plaids, held every year the month of March, in the open air; hence the March-field, the Champ de Mars.

who had formerly been their King. As constant interruptions of this sort hindered t
object of his retirement, he withdrew to the Monastery of S. Benedict on Mount Casin
in the province of Samnium, and there passed the remainder of his life in religio
exercises.

Pippin, however, who by the authority of the Roman Pontiff, from being the May
of the palace, had risen to be the King, governed the Franks solely in his own pers
for fully fifteen years. He died of dropsy at Paris towards the close of the Aquitani
war, which he had begun against Waifar, the Duke of that country, and which w
carried on continuously during nine years. He left two sons, Karl and Karloman, w
by God's will succeeded to the Kingdom.

The Franks, in a general assembly convened with much solemnity, appointed the
both Kings, as soon as they had agreed to the following conditions:—For the purpos
of government the whole realm was to be equally divided; Karl was to reign over th
part which had belonged to their father Pippin, and Karloman over that portic
which had belonged to their uncle Karloman.

When they had both agreed to these terms, each received that portion of the kin
dom which had been assigned him. Agreement between the brothers was thus esta
lished, though it was only preserved with the greatest difficulty, since many of t
friends of Karloman set themselves to work to break the friendship, some even goi
so far as to have thoughts of plunging the brothers into civil war. But there was mo
distrust than real danger, as in the end proved to be the case. For when Karlom
died, his wife, with his sons and some of his chief nobility, slighted her husband
brother and fled into Italy, and for no reason whatever placed herself and childr
under the protection of Dedier, King of the Lombards. Karloman died after two yea
years of joint sovereignty, when his brother Karl, with the consent of all the Frank
was made (sole) King.

I pass by the birth, infancy, and childhood of Karl, because there is no writt
record concerning them, nor is any one now known to survive who can speak fro
personal knowledge. I have therefore thought it foolish to write about them, and ha
given my attention to relating and explaining those actions, habits, and other portio
of his life which are not matters of uncertainty; first narrating his military exploits
home and abroad, then his domestic habits and occupations, then his administratic
of the kingdom, and lastly, about this death, omitting nothing that is worthy an
necessary to be narrated.

Karl was engaged in many wars. The first he undertook was the Aquitanian,[4] becau
there seemed to be good hope of quickly bringing it to an end. It had been begun
his father, but not finished.

His brother at this time was still living, and his aid was asked. Though King Ka
was disappointed of his brother's assistance, he nevertheless pursued the campaig

[4] *The Franks had not settled south of the Loire. The conquest of Aquitania had only been political conquest. The inhabitants were a mixture of Basque, Gaul, and Goth. The Kings Dukes were nominally subject to the Austrasian king, and were a younger branch of the Merwing Waifar was the last, and naturally a bitter enemy of the Karlings.*

had undertaken with the greatest vigour; he would not withdraw from what he had [be]gun, nor at all desist from the labour of the work, until by great and long-continued [pe]rseverance the most complete termination had been achieved. He obliged Hunold, [w]ho, after the death of Waifar, had attempted to seize Aquitain and renew the war [w]hich was almost ended, to flee from the country and seek refuge in Gascony. Karl, not [be]ing satisfied that he should remain there, crossed the river Garonne, and by his [am]bassadors ordered Loup, the King of the Gascons, to give up the fugitive, adding [th]at if he did not quickly do so, he would proceed to recover him by force of arms. [L]oup wisely surrendered Hunold. He also placed himself and the province over which [h]e ruled under the sovereignty of Karl.

When the war was finished and affairs settled in Aquitain—his partner in the gov[e]rnment being now dead—Karl was induced by the prayer and entreaty of Adrian, [B]ishop of the city of Rome, to undertake a war against the Lombards.

His father had undertaken such a war before, at the request of Pope Stephen, and [h]ad met with much difficulty in the matter, because some of the chief men of the [F]ranks, his councillors, had been much opposed to his wishes, and had gone so far [a]s to declare they would desert the King and return home. War had, however, been [m]ade against King Aistulf, and had been quickly finished.

There seemed to be a very similar, or rather the same, cause for war to King Karl [a]s there had been to his father. There was not, however, the same difficulty in carrying [i]t out, nor the same result at its conclusion.

Pippin, for his part, after a few days' siege of Pavia, had compelled Aistulf to give [h]ostages, and to restore the fortified towns and castles which he had taken from the [R]omans, and also to make oath that he would not attempt the recovery of what he [r]estored. Karl, on the other hand, when he had once begun hostilities, did not hold [h]is hand until Dedier, the King, worn out by a long siege, had surrendered at dis[c]retion. Adalgis, his son, on whom were fixed the hopes of the nation, was compelled [t]o quit the kingdom and leave Italy altogether. Karl restored to the Romans all that [h]ad been forcibly taken from them, and also crushed Hrudogast, Prefect of the parts [a]bout Friuli, who was attempting disturbances; and having brought all Italy under [h]is rule, he made his son Pippin King of the conquered territory.

The passage of the Alps into Italy was extremely difficult, and I would have here related how great was the toil of the Franks in overcoming the trackless chain of mountains, with peaks towering to the skies, and sharp and perilous rocks, had it not seemed to me to be my present task to record the charatcer of the King's life rather than the incidents of the wars which he waged.

Suffice it, then, to say that the end of this war was that Italy was conquered, King Dedier carried away into perpetual exile, Adalgis, his son, driven from Italy, and all that had been seized by the Lombard Kings was restored to Adrian, the rector of the Roman Church.

The Lombard war being thus finished, the Saxon war, which seemed for the time to have been neglected, was again renewed. No war undertaken by the Franks was so protracted or so fierce, or so full of toil and hardship, since the Saxons, like most of the nations inhabiting Germany, were naturally brave, and, being addicted to

heathenism, were hostile to our religion, and thought it no disgrace to dishonou
divine laws or violate human ones.

Causes, too, daily arose which contributed to disturb the peace. The boundaries c
their country and ours were in the open almost everywhere contiguous. It was only in
few places that large forests, or ranges of mountains coming between, formed a wel
defined and natural boundary line to both countries. On the borders therefore, plunde
ing, burning, and bloodshed never ceased.

The Franks were so enraged at this that they judged it now to be no longer
matter of making reprisals, but so important that it warranted them in undertaking a
avowed war against them. War therefore was declared, and was carried on continu
ously during thirty-three years, with much bitterness on both sides, but with greate
loss to the Saxons than to the Franks. It was the bad faith of the Saxons whic
prevented a more speedy termination. It is hard to say how often they were beaten
and humbly surrendered to the King, promising to obey his orders, giving up a
once the hostages he asked, and acknowledging the ambassadors sent to them; how
sometimes they were so tamed and compliant as even to promise to give up thei
idolatry, declaring they wished to embrace Christianity. But ready as they were a
times to undertake all these things, they were always far readier to renounce them. It i
difficult to state correctly to which failing they were more prone, since it is certainly
the fact that, after the war was begun, scarcely a single year passed in which they did
not pursue this shifty course.

But the magnanimity of the King, and the unwavering firmness of his disposition,
alike in adversity and prosperity, could not be shaken by any faithlessness on their
part, nor could they divert him from his purpose by tiring him out.

He never allowed any act of insincerity to be done with impunity; either taking the
command in person, or despatching an army under his counts, he took vengeance on
their perfidy and exacted from them a commensurate penalty.

He pursued this course until all who continued to resist him were overcome and
brought into submission. He then transported ten thousand men, taken from both
banks of the Elbe, together with their wives and children, and distributed them here
and there, in very small groups, in Gaul and Germany.

It was on the following terms, offered by the King and accepted by the Saxons, that
this war, which had lasted so many years, was brought to a close. The Saxons were to
put away their heathen worship and the religious ceremonies of their fathers; were to
accept the articles of the Christian faith and practice; and, being united to the Franks,
were to form with them one people.

Although the war lasted so long, the King himself did not fight more than two
pitched battles against the enemy, one near a hill called Osneng, near Theotmel, and
the other on the river Hasa, both in the same month and at a few days' interval.

In these two battles the enemy were so thoroughly broken in spirit, and beaten, that
they no more dared to challenge the King, or to oppose him on his march, except in
places where they were protected by fortifications. There fell in this war more of the
Frankish nobility, and of those who enjoyed the highest honours, than of their com-
peers among the Saxons, and it was in its thirty-third year before it was finished.

During those years many great wars sprang up against the Franks in different parts, hich were, by the skill of the King, so well managed that it was not without reason at men were perplexed whether to admire more the patience with which the King ursued his undertakings, or the good fortune which attended them.

This war was begun two years before the Italian war, and although it was carried n at the same time without any intermission there was no relaxation anywhere. In oth places the campaign was equally carried on without diminution of effort, for, f all contemporary sovereigns, King Karl took the highest rank for his good admin-tration, and was most distinguished for his ability. In all his undertakings and nterprises there was nothing he shrank from because of the toil, and nothing he eared because of the danger; but, skilful in weighing everything at its true value, e was neither yielding in adversity nor deceived by the smiles of fortune in prosperity.

It was during the time that the Saxon war was being vigorously and incessantly arried on, garrisons having been placed in all the most suitable places on the borders, nat Karl marched into Spain with the best-appointed army possible. Having crossed ne Pyrenean mountains, he reduced all the fortified towns and castles he came to, nd was on his march home with his army safe and sound, when, in the very pass f the Pyrenees on his way back, he had a slight experience of Gascon treachery.

The army was moving in column, and its formation was much extended, as the arrowness of the pass required, when the Gascons, who had placed ambuscades on he highest ledges of the mountains—the abundant thick cover of wood making the lace most suitable for the disposal of an ambush rushed down from their vantage round into the valley below, and threw themselves upon the extreme section of the aggage, and on those who were marching with it for its protection. The Gascons ttacked them in a hand-to-hand fight, killed them all to a man, and destroyed the aggage; and being protected by the darkness of the night, which was then coming on, hey quickly dispersed in all directions.

In this exploit the Gascons were much favoured by the lightness of their weapons nd the nature of the place where the attack was made, while the Franks, impeded y their heavy arms and the unevenness of the ground, were at a great disadvantage.

There were killed in this fight, Eggihard, the King's Sewer; Anselm, the Pfalsgraf; Roland,[5] Count of the Breton March, and many others. No revenge could be taken at he time for this defeat, for the enemy immediately dispersed, and so secretly that o trace was left by which they could be followed.

Karl also brought the Bretons into subjection. They dwelt on the coast in the xtreme west of Gaul. They were not obeying the King's orders, so an expedition vas sent against them, and they were compelled to give hostages that they would do s they were commanded.

After this the King led his army in person into Italy, and, passing through Rome, narched on to Capua, a city of Campania, and, pitching his camp there, he threatened o make war upon the Beneventines unless they submitted to him. Aragis, the Duke, voided this by sending his sons, Rumold and Grimold, with a large sum of money,

[5] *This is the only historical record of the defeat of Ronceavaux, which grew into such marvellous proportions in the romances of the thirteenth and following centuries, the "Chansons de Roland," etc.*

to meet the King. Aragis asked that his sons might be accepted as hostages, a promised that he and his people would obey the King, but prayed that he hims might be excused from personal attendance.

The King, having more regard for what was for the welfare of the people th for the man's obstinancy, granted his request, accepted the hostages he had sent, ar for a large sum of money excused him from personal attendance. Only the young son of Aragis was detained as a hostage; the elder was sent back to his father. Wh the ambassadors who had come to deliberate upon, and agree to, the engagemen of fidelity to be entered into by Aragis, on behalf of the Beneventines, had bee dismissed, the King returned to Rome.

Having passed some days there in reverend visitation of the sacred places of t city, he went back again into Gaul.

The next war was one which sprang up unexpectedly with the Bavarians. It on lasted for a short time. It was caused by the arrogance and senselessness of Duk Tassilo. He had married a daughter of King Dedier, who thought through her husban to avenge the exile of her father. Tassilo, being thus urged on by his wife, made a alliance with the Huns, whose territories joined those of the Bavarians on the East, an aimed not only at independence, but even challenged the King to war. Karl, unab to brook such immoderate insolence, moved forward a large army, composed of force gathered from all sides and commanded by himself, to the river Lech, determined t obtain satisfaction from the Bavarians. Having pitched his camp on the banks of tha river, which divides the Bavarians from the Alemanni, he resolved to send ambassador to sound the mind of the Duke before he entered their country.

It then seemed that Tassilo did not think that it would be for the advantage of eithe himself or his people to persist in his course of action; he therefore surrendered him self to the King's clemency, and gave the hostages demanded—among them his so Theodon. In addition to this, he pledged his faith with an oath that he would giv no heed to any one who might attempt to persuade him to revolt from the King' authority. It was thus that a war which had seemed likely to be a great one was brough to a speedy termination.

Tassilo, however, being soon after summoned to appear before the King was no permitted to return; and the province over which he ruled was no longer governed by a Duke, but was entrusted to the charge of Counts.

When these affairs had been thus settled, a war was begun against those Slavs whom we are accustomed to call Wiltzi, but who, according to their own pronunciation, are more properly called Welatabi. In this war the Saxons fought as our allies, but their allegiance was rather feigned than real. The cause of the war was this—the Welatabi could be restrained by no commands from harassing with constant invasions the Abodriti, who had long belonged to the Frankish league.

There is a gulf running in from the Western Ocean, stretching toward the East; its length has not been ascertained, but its breadth nowhere exceeds one hundred miles, and in many places it is much narrower. Several nations dwell around this gulf, such as the Danes and Swedes, whom we call Northmen, who occupy the northern shores and all the islands. The southern coasts are held by the Slavs and Aisti and other tions; chief among these were the Welatabi, against whom the King was now .ging war.

In one expedition under his own command he so crushed and tamed them, that they ,olved to submit to the uttermost and to refuse nothing.

The greatest of all the wars waged by the King, except the Saxon, was that which .w followed, against the Avars or Huns. He set about it with far more ardour and eparation than was bestowed upon any of the others. The King himself only made .e expedition into Pannonia—it was that province which the Avar race then inbited; the others he entrusted to the direction of his son Pippin, and to the prefects the provinces, and to the counts and lieutenants. Although these commanders used e greatest exertions, it was not until the eighth year that the war was finished.

How many battles were fought, and how much blood shed, is fully attested by the mplete depopulation of Pannonia; even the situation of the royal palace of the agan [6] is so obliterated that no trace remains of a human habitation.

In this war the whole nobility of the Avars perished, and the glory of their nation as destroyed. All their riches and treasures, which they had long been accumulating, ere carried away, nor can memory recall any war of the Franks in which they have .ined greater booty or by which they have been more enriched. Indeed, we may nfess that, up to this time, the Franks appeared to be a poor nation; but so much ld and silver was found in the palace, and such a quantity of valuable spoil was ken in the battles, as can scarcely be believed.

The Franks justly spoiled the Huns (Avars) of this booty, for the Huns themselves d no right to it, it being the plunder they had carried off from other nations.

Only two of the chief nobility among the Franks fell in this war—Eric, Duke of iuli, killed in Liburnia, near Tharsatica, a maritime state,[7] having been cut off by an nbush of the inhabitants; and Gerold, Prefect of the Bavarians, who was killed in nnonia, while drawing up his men in line of battle just before engaging the Huns. y whom he was killed is uncertain, since he was slain, with two others who accomnied him, while riding up and down the ranks, and encouraging each man indidually.

With these exceptions, the war was almost a bloodless one for the Franks, and though it lasted longer than its magnitude seemed to warrant, its result was most ccessful.

When this and the Saxon war had been brought to an end which their tediousness ade acceptable, the two wars which afterwards occurred, one against the Bohemians,[8] d the other against the Linonians,[9] were only of short duration, being quickly nished under the direction of Karl the younger.

The last war undertaken was against the Northmen who are called Danes, who, first as pirates, and afterwards with a larger fleet, were ravaging the coasts of Gaul

The Avar chieftain, or king, was so called.
On the Adriatic.
The Bohemians were a Slavic people. Though not Teutons, they were fully admitted into the erman confederation, and their King became one of the seven Electors of the Empire
Linonia, now Luneburg.

and Germany. Their King, Godfrey, was puffed up with the delusive hope of makin himself master of all Germany, and persisted in regarding Frisia and Saxony as h own provinces. He had already brought the Abodriti under his power and had mac them tributary to him.

He even used to boast that he would shortly appear with all his forces at Aache where the King's court was held. Foolish as his talk was, there were some who di not altogether discredit him. It was rather thought that he would have attempte something of the kind had not his sudden death prevented him. He was slain by on of his own servants, and thus his own life and the war he had begun were brough to an abrupt conclusion.

Such were the wars waged by the most potent prince with the greatest skill an success in different countries during the forty-seven years of his reign. Great an powerful as was the realm of the Franks, which Karl had received from his fathe Pippin, he nevertheless so splendidly enlarged it by these wars that he almost doubled it

For previously the Eastern Franks had only inhabited that part of Gaul which lie between the Rhine and the Loire, the ocean and Balearic Sea, and that part o Germany situated between Saxony and the Danube, the Rhine and the Saal, whic latter river divides the Thuringi from the Sorabi. The Alemanni and Bavarians als belonged to the Frankish confederation. But Karl, by the wars which have been men tioned, conquered and made tributary, first, Aquitania and Gascony, and the whol range of the Pyrenean mountains, as far as the river Ebro, which, rising in Navarr and flowing through the most fertile lands of Spain, mingles its waters with th Balearic Sea beneath the walls of Tortosa; then the whole of Italy, from Aosta t Lower Calabria, where are the boundaries of the Greeks and Beneventines, an exten of more than a thousand miles in length; then Saxony, which is indeed no smal portion of Germany, and is thought to be twice as wide as the part where the Frank dwell, and equal to it in length; then both Pannonias, and Dacia which lies on the other bank of the Danube; also Istria, Liburnia, and Dalmatia, with the exception o the maritime towns, which for friendship's sake, and on account of a treaty, he allowed the Constantinopolitan Emperor to hold; lastly, all the wild and barbarous nations which inhabit Germany between the Rhine and the Vistula, the ocean and the Danube, who speak a very similar language, but are widely different in manners and dress. Chief among these were the Welatabi, Sorabi, Abodriti, and Baemanni, for with these there was fighting; but the rest, who were more numerous, quietly surrendered.[10]

The renown of his Kingdom was also much increased by the friendly alliances he cultivated with different kings and nations. Alfonso, King of Gallicia and Asturias [in northern Spain], was so bound to him by the ties of friendship that, when he sent him letters or messengers, he used to command that he should be spoken of as being Karl's man. The Kings of the Scots, too, were by his munificence so devoted to his will, that they ever spoke of him as their Lord, and of themselves as his lieges and servants. Letters are still extant from them to him which show that this sort of relationship existed between them.

[10] *Slav nations. Baemanni,* i.e. *Bohemians.*

Haroun, king of the Persians, who, with the exception of India, ruled over nearly all e East, was held by the King in such hearty friendship, that he valued Karl's esteem ove that of all other Kings and princes of the world, and thought that he alone was orthy to be honoured by his regard and munificence. When the officers sent by King arl with offerings to the most sacred sepulchre and place of the resurrection of our ord and Saviour came to Haroun and announced the pleasure of their master, he not nly gave them permission to do as they desired, but granted that that revered and cred spot should be considered as belonging to King Karl. When the ambassadors t out on their return, he sent with them his own envoys, who conveyed to the King range and curious gifts, with garments and spices and other rich products of the East, st as he had sent him a few years before, upon his request, the only elephant he then ossessed.

The Constantinopolitan Emperors, Nicephorus, Michael, and Leo, of their own ccord, also sought his friendship and alliance, and sent to him several embassies; and ince by assuming the Imperial title he had laid himself open to the grave suspicion of ishing to deprive them of Empire, he made with them the most binding treaty possible, that there might be no occasion of offence between them. But the Romans and reeks always viewed with distrust the power of the Franks; hence arose the Greek roverb, "Have a Frank for a friend but not for a neighbour."

Illustrious as the King was in the work of enlarging his Kingdom and in conquerng foreign nations, and though so constantly occupied with such affairs, he neverthess began in several places very many works for the advantage and beautifying of his ingdom. Some of these he was able to finish. Chief among them may be mentioned, s deserving of notice, the Basilica of the Holy Mother of God, built at Aachen, a narvel of workmanship; and the bridge over the Rhine at Mainz, five hundred paces n length, so broad is the river at that place. This bridge, however, was destroyed by re the year before the King died, nor could it be restored on account of his approachng death, although it was in the King's mind to replace the wooden structure by a ridge of stone.

He also began some magnificent palaces, one not far from Mainz, near the village of ngelheim, and another at Nymeguen, on the river Waal, which flows past the island f the Batavians on the southern side. He was more especially particular in giving rders to the priests and fathers to see to the restoration of those churches under heir care, which in any part of his Kingdom he found had fallen into decay, taking are by his officers that his commands were obeyed. He also constructed a fleet for the var against the Northmen. For this purpose ships were built on the rivers of Gaul nd Germany which flow into the North Sea. As the Northmen were making a pracice of ravaging the coasts of Gaul and Germany with constant harryings, he posted owers and outlooks in all the harbours, and at the mouths of those rivers which ships ould navigate. By these defences he prevented any enemy from being able to pass. He lid the same thing in the south, on the coast of the provinces of Narbonne and Septinania, and all along the coast of Italy as far as Rome, for in those parts the Moors nad lately taken to piracy. Thus Italy suffered no great damage from the Moors, nor Gaul or Germany from the Northmen, during the reign of Karl, except that Civita Vecchia, a city of Etruria, was betrayed to the Moors, who took it and destroyed it, and in Frisia some islands off the German coast were plundered by t Northmen.

Such does it appear was the character of the King, in defending, enlarging, a beautifying his Kingdom, and one must be permitted to admire his mental gifts a his great firmness of purpose in all circumstances, whether of prosperity or adversit

I will now begin to speak of other matters relating to his private and domestic lif On the death of his father he bore all the jealousy and ill-will of his brother, in t division of the Kingdom, with so much patience and forbearance that he astonishe everybody, for he would not allow himself even to be provoked to anger by him.

It was by the desire of his mother that he took for his wife a daughter of Dedie King of the Lombards; but at the end of a year he divorced her, for what reason uncertain. He then married Hildegard, a Swabian lady of noble birth, by whom he ha three sons, Karl, Pippin, and Ludwig, and three daughters, Hruodrud, Berthrad, an Gisla. He had also three other daughters, Theoderada and Hiltrud by his wife Fa trada, a German of the Eastern Franks, and Ruodhaid by a concubine whose name do not remember. On the death of Fastrada he married Liudgard, of the Aleman nation. She bore him no children. After her death he had three concubines, Ge suinda, of the Saxon nation, by whom he had a daughter named Adaltrud; Regin who bore him Drogo and Hugh; and Adalinda, who had a son named Theoderic His mother Berthrad lived with him to old age, in great honour, being looked up t by her son with the greatest respect, so that no difference ever arose between then except with regard to the divorce of the daughter of King Dedier, whom she ha persuaded him to marry. She did not die until after the death of Hildegard, havin lived to see three grandsons and as many grand-daughters in the house of her son She was buried by the King with much honour in the church of S. Dionysius,[11] wher his father had been laid. He had one sister, Gisla, who was dedicated to a religiou life from her earliest years. Like his mother, she was regarded by the King with th greatest affection. She died a few years before him, and was buried in the convent t which she had retired.

The King thought so much about the education of his children that he caused bot sons and daughters to be early instructed in those liberal studies which attracted hi own attention. As soon as his sons were old enough he caused them to ride on horse back, as was the Frankish custom, and to practise themselves in arms and hunting. H bade his daughters should learn wool-spinning and the use of the distaff and spindle and be taught to employ themselves industriously in every virtuous occupation, tha they might not be enervated by idleness.

Of this large family, two sons and one daughter died before him—Karl, the eldest and Pippin, whom he had made King of Italy, and Hruodrud, his eldest girl, wh had been betrothed to Constantine VI., the Emperor of the Greeks. Pippin left surviv ing one son, Bernhard, and five daughters, Adalhaid, Atula, Guntrada, Berthaid, and Theoderada. The King showed marked tokens of his affection toward them, allowing his grandson to succeed to his father's Kingdom, and bringing up his grand-daughters with his own daughters. He bore the deaths of his sons and daughters with that great-

[11] *S. Denis, near Paris.*

ss of soul for which he was distinguished; but his resignation was not greater than his ection, for he mourned for them with tears. So also, when the death of Adrian, the man Pontiff, was announced to him, regarding him as his chief friend, he wept for m as if he had lost the son or brother that was dearest to him. For he was most sin- re in his friendships, being readily open to form them and most constant in retain- g them, cherishing with the most sacred regard those whom he had united to himself ties of affection.

He was so careful in the bringing up of his sons and daughters that when at home never dined without them, and they always accompanied him on his journeys, his ns riding by his side, and his daughters following close behind, attended by a train servants appointed for that purpose. His daughters were very fair, and he loved em passionately. Strange to say, he would never consent to give them in marriage, ther to any of his own nation or to foreigners; but he kept them all at home and ar his person at all times until his death, for he used to say that he could not deprive mself of their society. On account of this, although happy in all else, he here expe- enced the malignity of fortune; but he concealed his vexation, and conducted himself if they had never given rise to injurious suspicions, and as if no reports had ever ne abroad concerning them.

He had also by one of his concubines another son, Pippin, whom I have omitted to ention among others; he had a good countenance, but was deformed by a hunch ck. When his father was wintering in Bavaria, being detained there by the war ainst the Huns, this son Pippin pretended sickness, and formed a conspiracy against e King, together with some of the chief men of the Franks, who had seduced him ith the foolish hope of making him King. The plot being discovered and his fellow nspirators punished, Pippin's hair was shorn off, and he was allowed to pass his me in religious exercises in the abbey at Pruhm. To this he readily consented. An- her dangerous conspiracy against the King had been set on foot before in Germany. me of its authors were condemned to the loss of their eyes, others saved their limbs, it all were exiled. None, however, were put to death, except three, who drew their vords in defence against those sent to take them, and went so far as to kill some of em. These were slain because there was no other way of dealing with them.

It is thought that in both instances the cruelty of Queen Fastrada was the original use of these conspiracies against the King, and he seems to have departed very far om the usual gentleness and clemency of his natural disposition in permitting the ueen's inhumanity. The King himself during all his life was regarded by all men, oth at home and abroad, with such love and affection that he, at least, was never iarged by any one with wanton cruelty.

He had a great fondness for foreigners, and was so anxious to entertain them that ieir great numbers became an improper burden, not merely to the palace, but even the Kingdom. The King, however, in keeping with his generosity, was very little ppressed by any such thoughts, since a reputation for liberality and the reward of enown well compensated such inconveniences.

The person of Karl was large and robust, and of commanding stature, though not xceeding good proportions, for it appears that he measured seven feet in height. The

top of his head was round, his eyes large and animated, his nose somewhat long, h
hair white, and his face bright and pleasant; so that, whether standing or sitting,
showed very great presence and dignity. Although his neck was thick and rather sho
and his belly too prominent, still the fair proportions of his limbs concealed the
defects. His walk was firm, and the whole carriage of his body was manly. His voi
was clear, but not so strong as his frame would have led one to expect. His heal
was good until the last four years of his life, when he was attacked with freque
fevers, and latterly walked lame on one foot. Even in illness he leaned more on h
own judgment than on the advice of physicians, whom he greatly disliked, becau
they used to recommend him to leave off roasted meats, which he preferred, and
accustom himself to boiled.

He took constant exercise in riding and hunting, which was natural for a Fran
since scarcely any nation can be found to equal them in these pursuits. He also d
lighted in the natural warm baths, frequently exercising himself by swimming,
which he was very skilful, no one being able to outstrip him. It was on account of th
warm baths there that he built the palace at Aachen, living there constantly during th
last years of his life and until his death. He not only invited his sons to bathe wit
him, but also his chief men and friends, and occasionally even a crowd of his atten
ants and guards, so that at times one hundred men or more would be bathing togethe

He wore the dress of his native country—that is, the Frankish; on his body a line
shirt and linen drawers; then a tunic with a silver border, and stockings. He boun
his legs with garters and wore shoes on his feet. In the winter he protected his shou
ders and chest with a vest made of the skins of otters and sable. He wore a blue cloa
and was always girt with his sword, the hilt and belt being of gold and silver. Som
times he wore a jewelled sword, but only on great festivals, or when receiving foreig
ambassadors. He thoroughly disliked the dress of foreigners, however fine, and h
never put it on except at Rome—once at the request of Pope Adrian, and again a se
ond time, to please his successor, Pope Leo. He then wore a long tunic, chlamys, an
shoes made after the Roman fashion. On festivals he used to walk in processions cla
in a garment woven with gold, and shoes studded with jewels, his cloak fastene
with a golden clasp, and wearing a crown of gold set with precious stones. At oth
times his dress differed little from that of a private person.

In his eating and drinking he was temperate; more particularly so in his drinkin
since he had the greatest abhorrence of drunkenness in anybody, but more especial
in himself and his companions. He was unable to abstain from food for any length o
time, and often complained that fasting was injurious to him. He very rarely feaste
only on great festive occasions, when there were very large gatherings. The daily ser
ice of his table was only furnished with four dishes, in addition to the roast mea
which the hunters used to bring in on spits, and of which he partook more freely tha
of any other food.

When he was dining he listened to music or reading. History and the deeds of me
of old used to be read. He derived much pleasure from the works of St. Augustin
especially from his book called "Civitas Dei." He took very sparingly of wine an
other drinks, rarely taking at meals more than two or three draughts. In summer, afte

e mid-day repast, he would take some fruit and one draught, and then, throwing ide his clothes and shoes as at night, he would repose for two or three hours. He pt at night so lightly that he would break his rest four or five times, not merely by aking, but even getting up.

While he was dressing and binding on his sandals, he would receive his friends; d also, if the Count of the palace announced that there was any cause which could ly be settled by his decree, the suitors were immediately ordered into his presence, d, as if sitting in court, he heard the case and gave judgment. And this was not the ly business that used to be arranged at that time, for orders were then given for hatever had to be done on that day by any officer or servant.

He was ready and fluent in speaking, and able to express himself with great clear- ss. He did not confine himself to his native tongue,[12] but took pains to learn for- gn languages, acquiring such knowledge of Latin that he used to repeat his prayers that language as well as in his own. Greek he could better understand than pro- unce. In speaking he was so voluble that he almost gave one the impression of a atterer. He was an ardent admirer of the liberal arts, and greatly revered their pro- ssors, whom he promoted to high honours. In order to learn grammar, he attended e lectures of the aged Peter of Pisa, a deacon; and for other instruction he chose as s preceptor Albinus, otherwise called Alcuin, also a deacon—a Saxon by race, from itain, the most learned man of the day, with whom the King spent much time in arning rhetoric and logic, and more especially astronomy. He learned the art of mputation, and with deep thought and skill very carefully calculated the courses of e planets.

Karl also tried to write, and used to keep his tablets and writing-book under the llow of his couch, that when he had leisure he might practise his hand in forming tters; but he made little progress in a task too long deferred, and begun too late in fe.

The Christian religion, in which he had been brought up from infancy, was held Karl as most sacred, and he worshipped in it with the greatest piety. For this reason e built at Aachen a most beautiful church, which he enriched with gold and silver, d candlesticks, and also with lattices and doors of solid brass. When columns and arbles for the building could not be obtained from elsewhere, he had them brought om Rome and Ravenna.

As long as his health permitted, he was most regular in attending the church at atins and evensong, and also during the night, and at the time of the Sacrifice; and e took especial care that all the services of the church should be performed in the ost fitting manner possible, frequently cautioning the sacristans not to allow any- ing improper or unseemly to be brought into, or left in, the building.

He provided for the church an abundance of sacred vessels of gold and silver, and riestly vestments, so that when service was celebrated it was not necessary even for e doorkeepers, who are the lowest order of ecclesiastics, to perform their duties in rivate dress. He carefully revised the order of reading and singing, being well skilled

[12] *His native tongue was Low German.*

in both, though he did not read in public, nor sing, except in a low voice and on in the chorus.

He was most devoted in providing for the poor, and in charitable gifts, which t Greeks call almsgiving. In this matter he took thought not only for those of his ov country and kingdom, but also for those whom he heard were living in poverty b yond the seas, in Africa, Egypt, and Syria, at Carthage, Alexandria, and Jerusalem, whom he used to send money in compassion for their wants. It was on this accou especially that he courted the friendship of foreign princes, that he might be able become a solace and comfort to those Christians who were living under their rule.

He held the church of the blessed Peter the Apostle, at Rome, in far higher rega than any other place of sanctity and veneration, and he enriched its treasury with great quantity of gold, silver, and precious stones.

To the Pope he made many and rich presents; and nothing lay nearer his heart du ing his whole reign than that the city of Rome should attain to its ancient importan by his zeal and patronage, and that the church of S. Peter should, through him, n only be in safe keeping and protection, but should also by his wealth be ennobled an enriched beyond all other churches. Although he thought so much of this, it was on four times, during the forty-seven years of his reign, that he had leisure to go to Ron for prayer and supplication.

The last visit he paid to Rome was not only for the above reasons, but also becau the Romans had driven Pope Leo to ask his assistance—for they had grievously il treated him; indeed, his eyes had been plucked out and his tongue cut off.

Karl therefore went to Rome, and stayed there the whole winter in order to refor and quiet the Church, which was in a most disturbed state. It was at this time that l received the title of Emperor and Augustus, to which at first he was so averse that l remarked that had he known the intention of the Pope, he would not have entered th church on that day, great festival though it was.

He bore very quietly the displeasure of the Roman Emperors, who were exceed ingly indignant at his assumption of the Imperial title, and overcame their sullenne by his great magnanimity, in which, without doubt, he greatly excelled them, sendin them frequent embassies, and styling them his brothers in his letters to them.

After he had taken the Imperial title, he turned his attention to the laws of h people, which seemed greatly to need it, since the Franks have two laws,[13] which diff much in many places.

Karl's intention was to add what was wanting in each, to assimilate discrepancie and to correct what was mischievous and wrongly expressed. In the end, however, h did nothing more than add a few capitularies, and those imperfect ones.

He, however, caused the unwritten laws, of all the nations under his rule, to b tabulated and reduced to writing. He also wrote out and committed to memory th rude and very ancient songs which told of the exploits and wars of the kings of ol He also began a grammar of the speech of his country. He also gave names in th national tongue to the months of the year, for up to this time the Franks had disti

[13] *That is, the laws of the Salian Franks and the laws of the Ripuarian Franks.*

ished them partly by Latin and partly by barbarian names. He likewise gave the
oper names to the twelve winds, for previously names were known for hardly four.
The month January he called Wintarmanoth; February, Hornung; March, Lentrin-
noth; April, Ostarmanoth; May, Winnemanoth; June, Brachmanoth; July, Heuvi-
noth; August, Aranmanoth; September, Witumanoth; October, Windumemanoth;
ovember, Herbistmanoth; December, Heilagmanoth. And the winds thus: that
lled in Latin Subsolanus, he named Ostroniwint; Eurus, Ostsunderen; Euroauster,
ndostren; Auster, Sundren; Austroafricus, Sundwestren; Africus, Westsundren;
phyrus, Westren; Chorus, Westnordren; Circius, Nordwestren; Septentrio, Nord-
; Aquilo, Nordostren; Vulturnus, Ostnorden.

Towards the close of his life, when bowed down by disease and old age, he sum-
oned to him his son Ludwig, the King of Aquitain, who alone survived of the sons
Hildegard, and in a solemn assembly of the chief men of the whole realm of the
anks, and with their unanimous consent, appointed Ludwig his partner in the whole
ngdom and heir of the Imperial Title. He then placed the royal crown on his head
d bade that he be saluted as Emperor and Augustus.
This proposal was received by all who were present with great approbation. It
emed to them as if Heaven inspired the King in advancing the prosperity of the
ngdom, for this arrangement increased his own dignity and struck foreign nations
th no slight awe.
The King then dismissed his son into Aquitain, and, although weakened by age,
nt on his usual hunting expedition in the neighbourhood of the palace at Aachen.
this pursuit he passed the remainder of the autumn, and returned to Aachen early
November. During the winter, in the month of January, he was confined to his bed
a sharp attack of fever. He at once prescribed for himself a lowering diet, which
s his usual treatment of fever, thinking that by this means he could throw off the
sease, or at least control it; but inflammation of the side, which the Greeks call
urisy, supervened. He still continued to starve himself, only keeping himself up by
casionally taking liquids; and on the seventh day after he had been confined to his
d he received the Holy Communion, and died soon after, at nine o'clock, on the 28th
nuary, in the seventy-third year of his age and forty-seventh of his reign.

His body was reverently washed and tended, and then carried into the church and
ried, to the great grief of all his people. There was some doubt at first where was
e most proper place for his burial, for during his life he had given no orders on this
tter. At last it was agreed by all that he could be buried in no more fitting place
an in the church which he had built at his own cost at Aachen, out of love to God
d our Lord Christ, and to the honour of the ever blessed Virgin, His Mother. So
was buried there on the same day that he died. Above his tomb was erected a gilded
onument, with his effigy and title upon it. His dignity was thus described—

UNDER THIS TOMB IS PLACED THE BODY OF KARL, THE GREAT AND ORTHODOX EM-
ROR, WHO GLORIOUSLY ENLARGED THE REALM OF THE FRANKS, AND SUCCESSFULLY
IGNED DURING FORTY-SEVEN YEARS. HE DIED IN THE SEVENTY-THIRD YEAR OF HIS
E,

JANUARY XXVIII, ANNO DOMINI DCCCXIIII

Warnings of the approaching death of the King were very numerous, and we noticed by the King himself, as well as by others. For three years before his death the were frequent eclipses of the sun and moon, and black spots were noticed on t sun during seven successive days. The portico, which had been built with gre labour between the church and palace, suddenly fell down to the very foundation on t day of the Ascension of our Lord. Also the wooden bridge over the Rhine at Mainz, which a wondrous amount of toil and pains had been expended during ten years, that it seemed a thoroughly durable and permanent structure, was accidentally bur down in three hours. The destruction was so complete that there did not remain abo water-mark sufficient wood for the making of a lance shaft. Again, while the Ki was in Saxony, carrying on his last expedition against Godofrid, King of the Dan one day when the march had already begun, the King, having left the camp befo sunrise, saw fall suddenly from heaven, with a great light, a blazing torch passi through the clear sky from right to left. While all were wondering what this mig portend, the horse on which the King was riding fell down suddenly on its head, and was thrown to the ground with such violence that the clasp of his cloak was brok and his sword-belt burst.

He was ungirt by his attendants, who hastened to his assistance, and with so difficulty lifted up again. The javelin which he happened to be holding in his hand the time was thrown from his grasp a distance of more than twenty feet.

There occurred, too, frequent shakings of the palace at Aachen, and constant crac ings of the ceilings of the houses in which he dwelt. The church in which he w afterwards buried was struck by lightning, and the golden apple which adorned t summit of the roof was displaced and thrown on to the adjoining house of the prie There was in the same church, on the ring of the cornice, which ran round the interi of the building between the upper and lower arches, an inscription in red letters, whi related who was the founder of the church; the last line ended with the words KAR LUS PRINCEPS. It was noticed by some people that in the year in which he died, and few months before his death, the letters which formed the words PRINCEPS were faded as scarcely to appear at all. The King either pretended not to notice all the warnings from on high, or he despised them and treated them as if they in no w related to himself.